ATLANTIC STUDIES ON SOCIETY IN CHANGE

NO. 132

HUNGARY IN THE DUAL MONARCHY

1867–1914

László Katus

Translated by Paul Bődy and Andrew T. Gane
Copyedited by Matthew Suff
Typeset by Andrea T. Kulcsár

Social Science Monographs, Boulder, Colorado
Atlantic Research and Publications, Inc.
Highland Lakes, New Jersey

Distributed by Columbia University Press, New York
2008

EAST EUROPEAN MONOGRAPHS, NO DCCXXXVIII

The publication of this volume was made possible by grants from the
National Cultural Found
and the Hungarian Institute of International Affairs

Nemzeti Kulturális Alap

Magyar Külügyi Intézet
Hungarian Institute of International Affairs

ISBN 978-0-88033-636-9
Library of Congress Catalog Card Number 2008936734

Printed in Hungary

Table of Contents

Preface to the Series

The present volume is a component of a series that is intended to present a comprehensive survey of the history of East Central Europe.

The books in this series deal with peoples whose homelands lie between the Germans to the west, the Russians, Ukrainians and Belorussians to the east, the Baltic See to the north and the Mediterranean and Adriatic seas to the south. They constitute a particular civilization, one that is at once an integral part of Europe, yet substantially different from the West. The area is characterized by a rich diversity of languages, religions and governments. The study of this complex area demands a multidisciplinary approach, and, accordingly, our contributors to the series represent several academic disciplines. They have been drawn from universities and other scholarly institutions in the United States and Western Europe, as well as East and Central Central Europe.

The editor-in-chief is responsible for ensuring the comprehensiveness, cohesion, internal balance, and scholarly quality of the series he has launched. He cheerfully accepts these responsibilities and intends this work to be neither justification nor condemnation of the policies, attitudes, and activities of any person involved. At the same time, because the contributors represent so many different disciplines, interpretations, and schools of thought, our policy in this, as in the past and future volumes, is to present their contributions without major modifications.

The author of this volume is a distinguished historian, Professor Emeritus at the University of Pécs and the Péter Pázmány Catholic University. His primary research area is the 19th century history of Hungary and the Austro-Hungarian Monarchy.

Budapest, December 24, 2008

Ignác Romsics
Editor-in-Chief

1. THE ROAD TO THE "COMPROMISE" OF 1867

The Austro-Hungarian Compromise of 1867 created a dual state structure that was unique in contemporary Europe: the Austro-Hungarian Monarchy. It consisted of two independent and equal states with a common ruler, a common foreign policy, and a common army and navy. In addition, the two countries formed a common customs union, in modern terms a "common market," and used a common currency. Although each country had its own citizenship, the border between them had no practical significance, since there was free movement of persons and products from one country to the other.

The relationship between the two countries—the Lands of the Hungarian Crown and the hereditary provinces of the Habsburg dynasty—was not of recent origin. They had been closely related since the early sixteenth century. The Hungarian political leadership accepted, and even considered necessary, the integration of Hungary with the Habsburg Empire. In the period from the sixteenth to the eighteenth century this was justified by the threat of the Ottoman Empire, while in the nineteenth century the "northern colossus," the expansion of Tsarist Russia, was the predominant danger. The latter was aggravated by the increasing movements for national autonomy of several nationalities settled in Hungary, threatening to break up historical Hungary. The acceptance of integration into the Empire was contingent on the assurance of legislative and governmental autonomy, involving a separate status for Hungary. This principle was stated in Article 10 of the Act of 1791: "Hungary, including its adjoining territories, is a free and independent country with regard to its governmental and legal system. It is not subject to any other country, but has its own state and constitutional system. Therefore it must be governed and administered according to its own laws and customs and not according to those of other territories." This principle, however, was implemented very deficiently. It was the major objective of Hungarian politics in the eighteenth and nineteenth centuries to preserve, uphold and expand this limited autonomy. The act of 1867 involved a major qualitative change in the history of three and a half centuries of relationships; it meant the start of a new age. In 1867 the Habsburg Empire was reorganized according to Hungarian conceptions, on the basis of Dualism based on equality. In 1918, after half a century of this system, the common history of the two countries, Austria and Hungary, came to an end, and their future followed different roads.

In order to understand how this major change of 1867 was possible, we must trace events since the Revolutions of 1848.

Attempts to Reorganize the Habsburg Empire between 1848 and 1867

The Habsburg Empire, consisting of the Austrian Emperorship and the Lands of the Hungarian Crown until 1849, was a multiethnic, multinational state. Closely related to ethnic diversity was religious diversity. At the time of the Compromise there were nine ethnic communities with a million or more persons each—Germans, Hungarians, Czechs, Slovaks, Poles, Ruthenians, Croats, Serbs and Romanians—and six religious communities with a million or more members each—Roman and Greek Catholics, Orthodox, Lutherans, Calvinists and Jews.[1] It is important to note that the Slavic peoples as a whole constituted almost one half of the population, 47 percent, and they outnumbered the Germans and Hungarians combined. The Slav majority was especially significant in Austria, with 57.2 percent, outnumbering the Germans more than two to one. It is understandable, therefore, that in 1848 Czech politicians propagated the program of "Austro-Slavism," stating that modern Austria had to be transformed into a federal state with Slavic leadership. But it is equally understandable that in 1867 the German politician

Minister of Foreign Affairs Friedrich Ferdinand Beust wanted to base the future of the Monarchy against the Slavic majority on the cooperation of Germans and Hungarians.

According to the census taken in 1850–1851, the distribution of the population in nationalities is shown in the next table.

Table 1. The Distribution of the Civilian Population of the Empire According to Nationality in 1850 (%)

Nationality	Austria	Lands of the Hungarian Crown	Austro-Hungarian Monarchy (lands after 1867)	Italian Provinces (Lombardy and Venice)	Habsburg Monarchy (lands in 1850)
German	36.12	10.28	25.03	0.24	21.54
Magyar	0.03	36.52	15.70		13.49
Czech, Moravian, Slovak	22.74	13.19	18.64		16.02
Polish	11.44		6.53		5.61
Ruthenian	13.84	3.39	9.35		8.04
Slovenian	6.11	0.34	3.63	0.53	3.19
Croat	0.65	8.95	4.21		3.62
Serb	2.41	7.43	4.57		3.92
Bulgarian		0.17	0.07		0.06
Romanian	1.07	16.98	7.90		6.79
Italian, Ladin, Friuli	3.02	0.03	1.74	99.07	15.42
Armenian	0.03	0.08	0.05		0.04
Greek, Macedonian, Cincar		0.07	0.03		0.03
Albanian	0.01	0.01	0.01		0.01
Roma		0.63	0.27		0.23
Jewish	2.54	1.92	2.27	0.16	1.98
Slavic nations altogether	57.18	33.47	47.00	0.53	40.47
Neo-Roman nations altogether	4.09	17.01	9.64	99.07	22.21

In six Austrian provinces, Lower and Upper Austria, Salzburg, Styria, Carinthia, Tyrol and Vorarlberg, Germans formed an absolute majority, but in Styria and Carinthia there was a significant Slovenian minority (about one third) and in Tyrol there was an Italian minority. Carniola was almost completely Slovenian. On the Adriatic coast the majority of inhabitants were Slovenian or Croatian, with a significant Italian and Friuli-speaking minority. In the Dalmatian cities Italians formed a majority, but in rural areas there were only Serbs and Croats. In the three Czech provinces (Bohemia, Moravia and Silesia) the Czechs were in the absolute majority, but the proportion of the Germans exceeded one third. In the western part of Galicia Poles were in the majority, in the east the Ruthenians. But a substantial Jewish population was also present here. In Bukovina the Ruthenians and Romanians each formed 50 percent of the population. The Hungarian population was merely in a relative majority (45 percent) even in Hungary proper (without Transylvania and Croatia). In Transylvania the Romanians were in the absolute majority, while the proportion of Hungarians was 28 percent. In Croatia the Catholic Croats were in the majority, but one quarter of the population was Greek Orthodox Serb. In the Military Frontier the majority was Croat and Serb, but in the east, in the regiments of the Banat, there were many Romanian and German border guard families.

In 1848 the "old regime" collapsed throughout the Habsburg Empire, and the legal-institutional principles of a modernized economic and social system were enacted. Imperial edicts accepted and confirmed basic social reforms such as emancipation of the serfs, taxation of all classes, and abolition of noble privileges and entitlements, as well as the legal equality and personal liberties of all citizens. The March 1849 Olmütz Constitution, issued by the Emperor, also confirmed these reforms. But the basic question of the political structure of the Empire remained unresolved: how could the multinational Habsburg Empire be reorganized and modernized, thus enabling it to preserve its international status as a Great Power and to guarantee individual freedoms for its citizens and national rights for its nationalities?

In the two decades following the Revolution, three, or rather five, distinct proposals attempted to address this issue. Two of them gave high priority to the guarantee of Imperial unity and advocated a centralized form of government as the basic condition of ensuring political unity for the Empire with a great number of nationalities. Two other conceptions, on the other hand, regarded historical traditions and national rights as the most important considerations, and proposed some form of federation for the Empire. The centralist school included two distinct proposals: one advocated centralized absolutism, while the other favored a constitutional system. The first proposal was supported by the Imperial bureaucracy and military leaders as well as the dynasty, while the second received support from the German bourgeoisie of the hereditary provinces. There were also two types of federal proposals: conservative and ethnic. The first proposed a broad autonomy for the historical lands and provinces of the Empire, while the other wanted to establish a federal system based on ethnic boundaries. The latter received support from Slavic and Romanian political leaders, while the former was proposed by conservative aristocrats. Finally the Hungarian political elite advocated Dualism—the federation of two states with equal rights.

In 1848 the Hungarian Batthyány government represented Dualism based on personal union. It accepted the common ruler, but pursued an independent foreign policy, and initiated a separate Hungarian defense force and a separate issue of banknotes. In Austria, on the other hand, constitutional centralism was the guiding principle, advocating a central government for directing foreign policy, military command, central finances and commerce. This was also the underlying conception of the Olmütz Constitution, which established a unitary Austrian Empire as a constitutional state, at least on paper. The Lands of the Hungarian Crown lost their autonomy and were integrated as separate crown lands into the unified Austrian Empire.

The Schwarzenberg government, however, gradually rejected constitutionalism and introduced a modernized form of absolutism. On December 31, 1851, the "Sylvester Patent" cancelled the Olmütz Constitution and declared that the Emperor assumed full legislative and executive authority. This meant that absolutistic centralism became the predominant governmental system. Historians refer to this decade as neo-absolutism. In 1859 this system collapsed and conservative federalism emerged as a short-term solution to the reconstruction of the Monarchy. It found expression in the October Diploma of 1860, proposed by Hungarian conservative aristocrats, providing for territorial autonomy in local administration, judicial, religious and educational affairs.

This experiment, combining federal elements with centralization and preserving a substantial measure of absolutism, was rejected by practically all groups in the Empire. In early February 1861 the Emperor appointed Anton Schmerling, a prominent political leader of the Austro-German liberals, as state minister. The latter prepared the February Constitution, combining centralization with a semi-liberal constitutionalism acceptable to German liberals. It called for the creation of a central legislative assembly, the Imperial Council (*Reichsrat*), composed of representatives elected by territorial assemblies.

Convoked in the spring of 1861, the Hungarian Parliament expressed its position in parliamentary addresses prepared by Ferenc Deák, the unquestioned leader of the Hungarian liberals. The Hungarian Parliament rejected both the October Diploma and the February Constitution as incompatible with the Hungarian Constitution. It refused to send delegates to the *Reichsrat,* and demanded the restoration of the legal continuity of the 1848 April laws. The Parliament proposed to address the relationship with the Empire on the basis of personal union. Hungary was prepared to negotiate with the Empire "as an independent country" and decisively rejected "any subordination or fusion in legislative or governmental areas, since that would sacrifice our autonomy, which we cannot accept." The Parliament demanded the right to approve taxation, a government based on parliamentary authority, a responsible ministry, and freedom of the press, along with trial by jury, since these "are the strongest guarantees of constitutional liberty."[2]

As a result of the repudiation by the Hungarian and Croatian Parliaments, the *Reichsrat* failed to materialize as the legislative assembly of the whole Empire. It existed in a restricted form from

1861 to 1865 with the participation of the hereditary provinces, and from 1863 onwards representatives of Transylvanian Romanians and Saxons also participated.

The Process Leading to the "Compromise"

While in Austria a Parliament with limited authority functioned, in Hungary the absolutist system was provisionally restored in November 1861 in response to the refusal of Parliament and the resistance of the counties. Nevertheless, the desire for compromise with the Emperor and Austria increased significantly in this period. Natural disasters, economic difficulties and the movements of nationalities for autonomy convinced significant groups of the Hungarian political elite of the need for compromise. Many thought that "the price of compromise with the dynasty was less than that demanded by the nationalities."[3] Nor did international developments favor Hungarian independence. It was evident that the European powers were committed to the unimpaired preservation of the Habsburg Empire.

On the other hand, more and more members of the Parliament in Vienna, the *Reichsrat*, and the Austrian press called for the restoration of the Hungarian Constitution and the initiation of negotiations for compromise. At the end of 1862 Chief Justice Count György Apponyi prepared a compromise proposal at the request of the Emperor, providing for the principle of "dualism based on equal rights" and the parliamentary control of common affairs by the institution known subsequently as the "delegation." But this proposal was rejected in Vienna. At that point the Emperor took the initiative: at the end of December 1864 he sent his personal representative secretly to confer with Ferenc Deák, the recognized leader of the Hungarian liberals. Two further discussions followed. Several days after the last meeting Deák published his memorable "Easter article" in the April 16, 1865, issue of *Pesti Napló*, outlining the principles of the future Compromise.

Deák's conception was based on the Pragmatic Sanction, Acts 1–3 of 1723, which in his view "had in fact established the Monarchy, it forms the firm basis of the throne and it is the most important guarantee of Hungarian state law."[4] These laws accepted the legitimacy of the female line of succession of the dynasty; they declared that the Lands of the Hungarian Crown and all other territories of the Habsburg dynasty had to be governed "indivisibly and inseparably, reciprocally and jointly" and that all these territories should form a union "against external aggression." At the same time they confirmed the legislative and governmental autonomy of Hungary within the Empire. Deák also acknowledged that there were "common affairs" between Hungary and Austria. These included, in addition to the common ruler, foreign policy and military policy, derived from "the obligation of reciprocal defense" as stated in the Pragmatic Sanction.

Although Francis Joseph considered the views of Deák as a basis of negotiation, this did not mean that he accepted them fully. But he considered it to be necessary to continue the initiated political process. Therefore he dismissed Schmerling in July 1865, convoked the Hungarian and Transylvanian Parliaments as well as the Croatian *Sabor*, and in September suspended the February Constitution.

The Hungarian Parliament, including the representatives of Transylvania, who had taken a stance favoring the union of Transylvania and Hungary, prepared the bill on the settlement with Austria in the spring of 1866. But the legislative review had to be postponed due to the recent outbreak of military hostilities between Austria on the one hand and Prussia and Italy on the other. The Austrians defeated the Italians on land and sea, but on July 3 they suffered a major defeat in Königgrätz (Sadowa) at the hands of the Prussians. As a result, they had to surrender Venice, withdraw from the German Confederation and accept the leading role of Prussia in German affairs.

After the war the settlement was delayed, since the advocates of centralization and federalism exerted significant influence in Vienna. Nor did the head of the government, Count Richard Belcredi, support the dualist solution. The issue reached a turning point when the Emperor appointed Friedrich Ferdinand Beust, the former prime minister of Saxony, as minister of foreign affairs. He declared at his first personal appearance that "the first task of the government was the resolution of the Hungarian issue." Several weeks later he stated the following: "Today it is the consensus of Europe that the resolution of the Hungarian question is the most important issue of Austrian internal politics."[5] In his view, the Monarchy needed to be constructed on a firm foundation: "At the present time, this firm foundation is the alliance of Germans and Hungarians against Pan-Slavism. It is impossible for the government to seek support in the Slavic population while it is surrounded by an alienated German population."[6] Therefore the primary task was to address the needs of Germans and Hungarians at the expense of Slavic federalism.

In November 1866 the Hungarian Parliament was again called into session. In January 1867 Count Gyula Andrássy, Baron József Eötvös and Menyhért Lónyay negotiated in Vienna on the controversial issues. The major compromise accepted by the Hungarian leaders concerned the army: they accepted the traditional supreme military command of the Emperor. The Emperor, on his part, withdrew the majority of his earlier demands for the modification of the 1848 April Laws and accepted as a basis of discussion the bill of the Hungarian Parliament. The Council of Ministers of the Austrian government accepted the proposal of Beust in support of the settlement with Hungary on February 1, 1867, which represented the breakthrough of the negotiations. Beust argued thus: "The government can never favor all nations at the same time. At this moment, the aspirations of the nationalities are too divergent for a common government policy, and therefore our task is to seek the support of those with the highest level of viability, with common cultural traditions and common interests, the Germans and Hungarians."[7]

Belcredi resigned, and the Emperor appointed Beust as head of the government. On February 17, 1867, the Emperor appointed Gyula Andrássy as Hungarian prime minister. The Hungarian Parliament debated the bill establishing the Compromise from

March to May 1867 and approved it with a large majority vote. On June 8 Francis Joseph was crowned as King of Hungary and its associated territories. Then the Emperor signed the bill on "the common relationships and their government between the Lands of the Hungarian Crown and other countries under the reign of His Majesty," which was identical with Act 12 of 1867 on the Austro-Hungarian Compromise. Following the completion of these legal procedures, several important issues had to be addressed. Negotiations on the economic and financial relationships between the two countries were concluded at the end of 1867.

In summary, then, the Habsburg Monarchy was reconstructed according to the conception of the Hungarian political elite, the principle of Dualism, after a 19-year period of experimentation following the Revolution of 1848.

The Compromise was a commonsense settlement in which each party sacrificed a part of its previous position in the interests of agreement. Francis Joseph and the Austro-German politicians gave up the principle of a unitary Monarchy, a centralized Austrian Empire, even a central Parliament and government, to direct the common affairs of the Monarchy transcending the jurisdiction of the two countries. Francis Joseph considered himself to be ruler by the grace of God as a result of his education and the traditions of the dynasty. He would have preferred to rule in an absolute manner. But he acknowledged in this settlement that henceforth he would have to respect the constitution of his states. The majority of the Hungarian political elite for its part gave up dreams of full independence and also the principle of personal union as the only bond with the rest of the Empire, a principle asserted by the Parliament of 1861. It accepted the common affairs of the Monarchy and their government in cooperation with Austria.

The *Reichsrat* Accepts the Compromise

The question arises as to who the parties negotiating and giving birth to the dualist reconstruction of the Monarchy were. The Austrian legislature did not participate in the negotiations. The *Reichsrat* was dissolved in 1865 and it was called into session again in May 1867 after the completion of the Compromise. The representatives received the completed document as a *fait accompli* and their only role was to approve it. An elected committee of the Hungarian Parliament prepared the bill incorporating the Compromise proposal, based largely on the draft of Ferenc Deák, and this served as the basis of further negotiations. Several controversial issues were resolved in the course of these negotiations in Vienna, in which Andrássy, Eötvös and Lónyay represented Hungary, while Belcredi and Beust represented the Imperial government, and Count György Mailáth and Baron Pál Sennyey represented Imperial offices concerned with Hungarian affairs, the institutions of the Hungarian central government (the Hungarian Court Chancellery and the Consilium Locumtenentiale). The modifications proposed became legal with the approval of the Hungarian Parliament. Therefore the Compromise was an agreement negotiated and concluded by the Emperor, the Imperial government and the Hungarian Parliament, but without the involvement of the Austrian legislature.

In Austria the Compromise was unacceptable primarily for Slavic political leaders. They supported the federal reconstruction of the Empire. Slavs represented the absolute majority of the population in Austria, but Germans held the absolute majority in the *Reichsrat*, even though they made up only 36 percent of the population. This was brought about by the complicated electoral system of the 1861 Constitution. The Austro-Germans were willing to accept the settlement and cooperation with the Hungarians. The Austro-German liberals were primarily concerned with the Slav threat to the Empire, and "one of their basic political programs was Hungarian–German solidarity."[8] Since the 1840s Hungarian leaders had entertained similar ideas. Another of their basic programs was centralization. Given the new situation, however, they had to give up the latter in relation to the Empire as a whole, but they attempted to realize it in the Austrian half of the Empire. They wanted to establish an Austria under firm, unified German leadership. Although they were unhappy about being left out of the agreement with the Hungarians, they agreed to support the settlement. They disagreed with some of its provisions, such as the delegation, but they believed that there was no other solution that would ensure the preservation of the Empire. They chose the dualist system as the lesser evil.

The February 1861 Constitution, suspended since September 1865, was restored in Austria in 1867 following the completion of the Compromise negotiations. Accordingly the 17 provincial assemblies (*Landtage*) were convoked for the purpose of electing representatives to the *Reichsrat*. It should be noted that the *Reichsrat* was not directly elected by citizens, but was composed of delegates of the *Landtage*.

The *Reichsrat* held its first session on May 22. Out of 203 members 186 were present; the Czech delegates refused to participate. Beust persuaded the Poles to participate by expanding the autonomy of Galicia. The liberals had the absolute majority, and except for a few Italians they were all Germans. The majority supporting the Compromise comprised two previously formed liberal groups: the German "unionists" of Bohemia led by Eduard Herbst, professor of the University of Prague, and the "autonomists" of Styria and Upper Austria led by Count Moritz von Kaiserfeld of Graz. This combined group numbered close to 100 members. They argued that the *fait accompli*, the Compromise, had to be accepted, but close attention should be directed to negotiations of financial and economic terms with Hungary and thus the interests of Austria should be protected.

The liberals included a 20–25-member centralist group, some of whose leaders did not directly oppose the Compromise. The most significant opponents of the Compromise were Slav (Polish and Slovenian) federalists, supported by the 11-member group of Tyrol clerics.

The Austro-German liberals acknowledged the *fait accompli*, accepted the Compromise without modifications, and devoted primary attention to the liberal expansion of the Constitution. They considered the two procedures to be closely related. They argued that the Constitution was compensation for giving up the centralist state. In fact, the Compromise and constitutionalism in both parts of the Monarchy were closely related. The Hungarian view was that a basic condition of the Compromise was "that full constitutionalism be established in all other countries and territories of His Majesty."

In the autumn of 1867 the *Reichsrat* reviewed the bill on the common affairs and the Austro-Hungarian commercial and customs union recently negotiated. Although the 36-member parliamentary committee criticized the delegation as being ineffective and inappropriate, the majority of the representatives voted for the bill. The Austrian text deviated from the Hungarian in several places, which gave rise to subsequent debates concerning the manner of managing the common affairs.

In the second half of 1867 the *Reichsrat* enacted a series of important laws expanding and guaranteeing constitutional government in Austria. Several of these constitutional guarantees had been enacted in Hungary by the April 1848 laws. Acts of the *Reichsrat* affirmed ministerial responsibility and restricted government by executive decree. Accordingly "the legality of governmental actions by the Emperor required the countersignature of a responsible minister." The *Reichsrat* was entitled to vote annually on the authorization of military conscripts, taxation and approval of the budget. The Parliament also received the right of supervision of governmental finances through the Office of Financial Controls. A law regulated the right of association and assembly.

On December 21 the Emperor approved five fundamental laws (*Staatsgrundgesetz*), referred to collectively as the December Constitution. The first, Act 141, modified the law on representation of the February Constitution. The second, Act 142, guaranteed basic civil and political rights to citizens. Act 143 established the *Reichsgericht*, the first European Constitutional Court. All citizens had the right to submit complaints to this court if the rights guaranteed in Act 142 were violated. Act 144 separated judicial from executive administration and declared the independence of judges. Act 145 regulated governmental and executive authority, the rights and responsibilities of the Crown and the government.

Following the approval of the bill on common affairs and their government (i.e. the Compromise) by the *Reichsrat*, and the endorsement of the December Constitution by the Emperor, the common ministers were appointed and the first Austrian government under the new constitutional system was formed by Prince Carlos Auersperg as prime minister.

Debate on the Compromise

The Compromise has been a subject of debate from the time of its birth to the present day. Ferenc Deák delivered a major address in the Hungarian Parliament in March 1867 presenting his justification of the Compromise. He contended that the April Laws of 1848 had laid down the principles of a transformed social-political system, but there was no opportunity to implement those principles at that time. The Compromise, however, provided such an opportunity. He emphasized the point that European public opinion "considers the continued existence of the Austrian Empire to be a political necessity," and therefore it was clear that the full independence of Hungary could not be achieved by force of arms and it was equally harmful to anticipate that unexpected events would offer such an opportunity. "We do not claim that our work is perfect. We know that it has deficiencies, but we could not produce a better one that could have been realized under the present circumstances." On the other hand, Gyula Andrássy, who had played a major role in the negotiations leading to the Compromise agreement, makes the following point: "Hungary has always had common affairs with the Monarchy as a whole. The difference is that prior to 1867 these affairs were governed by others without our participation and against our interests, while at present we participate in their direction in common with those who are affected by them as well."[9]

In exile, Lajos Kossuth wrote an open letter addressed to Deák in which he rejected the Compromise as a surrender of Hungarian independence and as an agreement that tied the future of Hungary to an empire in dissolution. He saw the major danger in the creation of hostility with neighboring peoples and making a satisfactory solution of the nationality question impossible. His supporters in Hungary, politicians and publicists of the Independence Party, repeated these arguments in the next half a century and claimed that the status of Hungary in the Monarchy "was a provincial and colonial existence instead of independence."[10] In contrast, Mihály Horváth, a one-time associate of Kossuth, a minister in the Hungarian revolutionary government in 1849 and one of the major historians of the nineteenth century, condemned to death after the War of Independence and hanged in effigy, evaluated the Compromise as follows, after his return from exile:

> For three and a half centuries our constitution was never based on a firmer foundation; our freedom never possessed so many guarantees. The laws of 1848 should have been expanded to include the present settlement in order to avoid the tragic civil war. As one who has studied our history for the past 30 years in depth, I believe that I am entitled to state that after the struggles of adversity of the last 350 years, our public laws have now been placed on secure foundations, which fully guarantee our constitution and national independence against attacks that have threatened us in the past.[11]

József Eötvös, minister of public instruction and acting prime minister in Andrássy's absence, expressed the following viewpoint:

> As a result of the Compromise, Hungary has attained such influence over the most essential branches of its state system as it has never exercised. It guarantees its economic welfare and an opportunity for its cultural development to an extent it was unable to achieve previously. We must now utilize the

> opportunity to build a modern Hungary. The Compromise has resolved the issue of public law and our self-government. The time has come to address the implementation of the 1848 legislation. Who does not feel and see the necessity of reform and progress in all areas? Our development has been violently retarded for centuries.[12]

Minister of Finance Menyhért Lónyay stated the following: "The age of creation and action and the possibility of cultural development and economic growth opened for us in 1867."[13]

The liberal political leaders who brought about the Compromise were therefore convinced that they could continue the modernization of the country that had been interrupted by war in 1848. In their view, 1867 was but the implementation of 1848. The overwhelming majority of twentieth-century Hungarian historians agree with this view.

Gyula Szekfű, one of the most prominent historians of the first half of the twentieth century, considered "the Compromise of Deák one of the most fortunate creations, the best solution of the age-old problem. 1867 is the climax of our four hundred years of public law. Since our union with Austria our independence was never as real and secure as it became in consequence of the Compromise law. We were unable to execute the 1848 legislation peacefully, but it was feasible to do so through Act 12 of 1867. 1867 is therefore equivalent to the potential, actually executed 1848 legislation."[13]

It is of interest that post-World War I Austrian historians evaluated the Compromise in the same way as Hungarian Independence Party publicists did, but with a diametrically opposite view of its benefits. According to Joseph Redlich, the Compromise meant the victory of Hungarians, since the more unified, purposeful Hungarians achieved predominance. Viktor Bibl expressed the theory of Hungary's predominance even more emphatically. In his view, mutual parity remained a modest wish, and in reality the will of the Hungarian government and Parliament prevailed throughout the Monarchy. After World War II Austrian historians expressed similar, but more restrained viewpoints. Hugo Hantsch stated that the more solid political structure of Hungary assured the country of greater influence, especially in foreign policy. Georg Franz referred to the double victory of Hungarians and the double defeat of the Austro-Germans. The French historian Jacques Droz referred to the predominance (*prepondérance*) of the Hungarians, the disparity in their favor and the "Hungarian guardianship" over Vienna. Robert Kann came to the conclusion *vis-à-vis* the Compromise, that that "tragic bargain subordinated the political leadership role of German Austria to Hungarian political leadership in Hungary and to a certain extent throughout the Empire."[14]

Contemporary Hungarian historians evaluate the Compromise as a "realistic compromise," which was the best achievable solution in the light of prevailing domestic and international conditions. It provided an opportunity for Hungary to participate in the following half a century in the rapidly expanding process of European modernization.

Notes

1 The census of 1850–1851 classified the Jews as a religious denomination and as a nationality. 82 percent of the Jewish population of the Empire identified itself also as being of Jewish nationality.

2 Ágnes Deák, ed., *Deák Ferenc: Válogatott politikai írások és beszédek. 2:1850–1873* [Ferenc Deák: Selected Political Writings and Speeches, vol. 2: 1850–1873] (Budapest, 2001), pp. 51–73.

3 Aurél Kecskeméthy, *Vázlatok egy év történetéből* [Sketches of the History of One Year] (Pest, 1862), p. 183.

4 Manó Kónyi, ed., *Deák Ferenc beszédei. 3: 1861–1866* [Speeches of Ferenc Deák, vol. 3: 1861–1866] (Budapest, 1889), p. 330.

5 Éva Somogyi, *Kormányzati rendszer a dualista Habsburg Monarchiában* [Governmental System in the Dualist Habsburg Monarchy] (Budapest, 1996), p. 17.

6 Éva Somogyi, *A birodalmi centralizációtól a dualizmusig. Az osztrák-német liberálisok útja a kiegyezéshez* [From Imperial Centralization to Dualism. The Road of the Austro-Germans to the Compromise] (Budapest, 1976), p. 181.

7 *Ibid.*, p. 184.
8 *Ibid.*, p. 193.
9 Béla Lederer, ed., *Gróf Andrássy Gyula beszédei* [Speeches of Count Gyula Andrássy], I (Budapest, 1893), p. 346.
10 Lajos Mocsáry, *A közösügyi rendszer zárszámadása* [The Accounting of the Common Affairs System] (Budapest, 1902), p. 39.
11 *Szegedi Híradó*, April 19, 1868.
12 József Eötvös, *Arcképek és programok* [Portraits and Programs] (Budapest, 1975), p. 729, 734.
13 Menyhért Lónyay, *Közügyeinkről. Nézetek Magyarország pénzügyi állapotáról* [Public Issues. Views on the Financial Condition of Hungary] (Budapest, 1873), p. 1.
14 Gyula Szekfű, *Három nemzedék és ami utána következik* [Three Generations and the Sequel] (Budapest, 1934), pp. 190–198.
15 The views of Austrian historians are quoted in Péter Hanák, *Magyarország a Monarchiában* [Hungary in the Monarchy] (Budapest, 1975), pp. 292–293.

2. THE STATE SYSTEM OF THE DUAL MONARCHY

According to the Compromise, the Habsburg Empire was transformed into two autonomous states joined together by the person of the ruler and the joint government of specific common affairs. Both states had bicameral legislatures and governments responsible to their Parliaments.

At the request of the Hungarian government, the designation "*Austro-Hungarian Monarchy*" was adopted, but *Austria* continued to be the designation used internationally. *Austria-Hungary* became the common designation at the turn of the century. The two autonomous states with equal rights were officially designated "The Countries of the Hungarian Crown" and "The Kingdoms and Countries Represented in the *Reichsrat*," but in practice the former was referred to as Hungary and the latter as Austria or Cisleithania, since the River Leitha was the dividing line between the two. In Hungary, Austria was the common designation for the latter. Subsequently we shall also use these short terms. Austria comprised 17 provinces (*Land*), while the countries of the Hungarian Crown consisted of Hungary, Croatia–Slavonia and the City of Fiume. The latter countries were preferably designated "Hungarian Empire" from the 1890s onwards even in official statistical publications. In Austria the ruler was called Emperor, in Hungary King, and therefore common institutions were designated "Imperial and Royal" (K. u. K. i.e. "kaiserlich und königlich").

The Austro-Hungarian Monarchy had a territorial extent of 625,000 square kilometers (Austria 300,000 and Hungary 325,000 square kilometers) and was the third-largest state of contemporary Europe, surpassed by Russia and the Swedish-Norwegian Union. According to the census of 1869 the population numbered 35.9 million persons, of which Austria had 20.4 million and Hungary 15.5 million. Hungary's territory was 52 percent of the Monarchy, while its population was only 43.2 percent. In terms of population too the Monarchy was the third-largest in Europe, surpassed by Russia and France. In subsequent years the Monarchy's population exceeded that of France, but the unified German Empire comprised a larger population than that of the Monarchy.

Even a cursory glance at the map confirms that Hungary was geographically a more unified and compact state than the other half of the Monarchy, which surrounded Hungary, protected by the Carpathian range, in a circular way. The nucleus and center of Austria were the hereditary provinces of Austria, Bohemia, Moravia and Silesia. To these were added in the late eighteenth century, as extensions in the northeast and south, Galicia, Bukovina, Dalmatia and Istria. The differentiation was valid not only in a geographical sense, but also in their political structure. Hungary was more unified. In the words of the prominent Austrian historian Hugo Hantsch, it was a state "with a more solid political structure," and the predominance of Hungarian political leadership was successfully asserted. The Austro-Germans envied the Hungarians and hoped to transform Austria into a similarly unified and solid state under German leadership following the Compromise.

The Common Affairs

The Act of Compromise states the following: "The relationship between the countries of the Hungarian Crown and the other countries and territories of His Majesty is based on the Pragmatic Sanction as specified in Acts I, II, III of 1723." This fundamental contract between the dynasty and Hungary guaranteed "on the one hand the joint and inseparable government of countries and territories included in the Imperial relationship and on the other the autonomous legislative and governmental independence of Hungary."

According to the Pragmatic Sanction the two countries had a common ruler. The Hungarian Act of Compromise (Act 12 of 1867) states the following concerning the common affairs between the two countries: “The defense and maintenance of common security by joint forces is a common mutual obligation based directly on the Pragmatic Sanction.”

“One of the instruments of common and joint defense based on the Pragmatic Sanction is the appropriate management of foreign affairs.” The common minister of foreign affairs was responsible for the diplomatic and commercial representation of the Monarchy, and the conclusion of international treaties. The minister of foreign affairs managed foreign affairs in agreement with, and with the consent of, the ministry of both countries. The other instrument of common defense was the armed forces, and therefore it was also a common responsibility. The Hungarian Parliament considered finances to be a common affair to the extent that they were to be utilized for the designated common affairs. The two countries were to determine expenditures for common affairs jointly.

According to the Pragmatic Sanction, therefore, the Hungarian Parliament recognized two common affairs: foreign affairs and the armed forces. This was a new position in comparison with that of 1848. At that time the Hungarian position had been that the relationship between the countries of the Hungarian Crown and the Austrian Empire was based on personal union, and it was therefore limited to the person of the common ruler. Accordingly, the Batthyány government made preparations for the issue of independent Hungarian banknotes, and initiated the organization of a Hungarian defense force and an independent foreign policy. At that time the Austrian government declared that these measures were contrary to the Pragmatic Sanction, which had affirmed the unity of the Empire, meaning that foreign, military and financial affairs were reserved to “a highest state authority,” and therefore these were common affairs of the Empire as a whole. In 1867 the Hungarians agreed that foreign and military affairs were common affairs, but they did not agree that a “highest state authority,” i.e. an Imperial government and Parliament, should govern these policies.

The Act of Compromise stated the following concerning the management of the common affairs: a common ministry is to be established for the purpose of managing these affairs, but that ministry may not exert any influence on the government of the two countries. The Act also stated that the basic condition of the new system was the ensuring of constitutional government in both countries. In the management of the common affairs there should be "full parity," meaning that "the countries of the Hungarian Crown on the one hand and all other countries and territories of His Majesty on the other hand should be considered as two separate and completely equal parties." Based on this parity, both Parliaments annually elected a committee equal in size, but with a maximum of 60 members, known as the *delegation*. The exclusive purpose of the two delegations was the legislative review of the common affairs and the common budget. Following the approval of the common budget both governments were to remit their approved share of the budget to the common minister of finance. The common ministers were to be responsible to the delegations.[1]

The two delegations were to hold their sessions on a rotating basis in the two capital cities, in Vienna and Budapest. Each delegation was to meet separately and was to communicate with the other in writing. If written communications failed to produce an agreement then they would hold a joint session, but they were not permitted oral exchanges. They were to vote on controversial issues.

The above statements indicate that the Hungarian political leaders proposing the Compromise attempted to ensure the parliamentary responsibility of the common ministers, but they wanted to exclude a common Imperial Parliament as the forum of responsibility. Therefore they invented the *delegation* and the related complicated procedures. Those Austro-German political leaders who supported the Compromise regarded the delegation as inappropriate, and they would have preferred a common Parliament for the management of common affairs. But since the Hungarians rejected it, they accepted the delegation for want of a better solution. They considered it to be the only bond that would unite the two separated parts of the Empire. The delegation embodied for them the idea of Imperial unity.

The sessions of the delegations held biannually in Budapest created the illusion for Hungarians that Budapest ranked as an equal with Vienna as a capital city of the Empire. On these occasions the Emperor-King, the common ministers and the officials of the common ministries came to Budapest for a visit. The sessions of the Common Council of Ministers were held here, as were diplomatic receptions whenever the Ministry of Foreign Affairs moved to Budapest.

According to the Pragmatic Sanction, therefore, foreign affairs and the armed forces were common affairs between the two countries. The ruler appointed the ministers responsible for these affairs. There was also a third common minister, the common minister of finance, who handled the funds provided by the two countries to finance the expenses of the common affairs. Each country was fully independent financially. The seat of the common ministers was in Vienna. A common practice in appointments was adopted: of the three common ministers one was always Hungarian, but Francis Joseph did not permit that two Hungarians hold office at the same time. Of the ten ministers of foreign affairs three were Hungarian. For more than three decades, from 1880 to 1912, the ministers of finance were all Hungarian. But the minister of the armed forces was always Austrian. When the Monarchy occupied Bosnia-Herzegovina in 1878, the common minister of finance was given responsibility for its administration, since it was a common acquisition. The common ministers were not allowed to intervene in the domestic affairs of the two countries. Nevertheless, this occurred several times. Two ministers of foreign affairs were forced from office for intervening in Hungarian domestic politics (Agenor Gołuchowski in 1906) or coming into conflict with the Hungarian prime minister (Gustav Kálnoky in 1895).

The common ministers discussed issues affecting the Monarchy as a whole in sessions of the Common Council of Ministers. Francis Joseph participated occasionally and the two prime ministers much more frequently. If necessary, ministers of the two countries also attended. The ruler chaired these sessions; in his absence the minister of foreign affairs took his place. The latter was considered to be the highest-ranking official of the Monarchy. Only the minister of foreign affairs was classified in Class 1 of the civil service ranks; the other two common ministers and prime ministers formed Class 2. As the minister of the Imperial house, the minister of foreign affairs had direct access to Francis Joseph. The ruler appointed the minister of foreign affairs, and he did not allow anyone to influence his decision. In the first ten years of Dualism Francis Joseph presided at one half of the sessions, but from the 1880s onwards he was present only at one third to one quarter. The prime ministers participated in only 60 percent of the sessions in the first ten years, but after 1880 they were invited to practically all sessions. In this period one of the other ministers of the two countries participated in 90 percent of the sessions. Between 1867 and 1915 there were some 600 sessions, annually 12 on average. But they were not distributed equally: in the first four years, between 1868 and 1871, there were 120 sessions. No law or regulation defined the jurisdiction of the Common Council of Ministers. Any common minister or prime minister could propose an issue for discussion.

The principal responsibility of the Common Council of Ministers was to resolve conflicts between the two countries or between the two governments and the Monarchy as a whole. It was not always easy to bring about a compromise between the three governmental bodies created by the 1867 settlement. It was more and more difficult to carry out this responsibility of the common government: to harmonize the interests and goals of the two states and the Empire. The commercial treaties with foreign countries gave rise to particularly serious difficulties, since the interests of the two countries were in conflict. The conflict arose as a result of differences between Hungarian agrarian interests and Austrian industrial interests. In resolving these differences the minister of foreign affairs or the Common Council of Ministers chaired by the ruler was called upon to resolve the conflict.

In the course of time it became customary to discuss important issues affecting the Monarchy as a whole not in the Common Council of Ministers, but in informal "confidential meetings" of the common ministers, the prime ministers and possibly the special ministers. If agreement was reached in these informal meetings, the issues were put on the agenda of the Common Council of Ministers, or the crown council chaired by the ruler. In such cases the Emperor was informed concerning the issues and the position of the ministers, and then he summarized the decision. There were also meetings of the crown council when the ministers were unable to agree and the ruler was expected to make a decision. This was primarily the case when the interests of the two countries were opposed, for example, concerning international commercial treaties or conflicts between national and Imperial issues.

The Act of Compromise stated that the common minister of foreign affairs had to conduct foreign policy in agreement with the two governments. The Austrian Act did not include this provision. Although the majority of ministers of foreign affairs were Austrian, Gyula Andrássy, who held that office from 1871 to 1879, established the basic principles of the Balkan foreign policy of the Monarchy and also formulated the Dual Alliance with Germany. Hungarian prime ministers such as Andrássy, Kálmán Tisza and István Tisza made a significant impact on the foreign policy of the Monarchy. The Ministry of Foreign Affairs was responsible for the preparation and conclusion of international commercial and customs treaties with third countries, naturally with the cooperation of special ministers of the two countries. The two Parliaments were required to approve these treaties and enact them in legislation.

The budget of the common ministries was first approved by the delegations, then incorporated into the budgets of the two countries, and finally voted by the Parliaments. Although the common ministries were accountable only to the delegations, the two Parliaments were able to control them indirectly through their legislative review of commercial treaties and the budget. Another means of control was the presence of the two prime ministers in the Common Council of Ministers, since they were responsible to their Parliaments for the management of common affairs. There was also a difference between the Hungarian and Austrian text of the Act of Compromise relating to the responsibility of the common ministers. The Hungarian text provided detailed regulations for judicial procedures in the case of violation. In fact, no such procedures were ever initiated. The Austrian text simply stated that the common ministers were responsible to the delegations, without mentioning judicial procedures, but indicated that details would be added subsequently.

The public view and interpretation of the dualist Monarchy in the two countries was quite different. Hungarians emphasized the autonomy and parity of the Hungarian state and denied the existence of a unified Empire standing above the two states. The Austrians, on the other hand, considered the Monarchy to be the continuation of the Empire. As a result, they referred to the common ministers as "Imperial" ministers, who were appointed as "*Reichsminister*" by Francis Joseph, to the end of the century. The Hungarians protested and insisted on the term "common": they were willing to accept only "common" affairs and "common" ministers, and they rejected "common" or especially "Imperial" government.

Can the three common ministers and the Common Council of Ministers be regarded as a common government? This question arose repeatedly in this period, but no one was able to provide an unequivocal response. The Hungarian Act of Compromise uses the term "common ministry or a member of this ministry." Contemporary usage understood "ministry" to refer not only to specific ministries, but to the entire government. The Austrian Act also uses the term "a common responsible ministry." The term "common government" is used in official documents in the early years. Prime Minister Andrássy did not object to it. But in 1876 he stated the following in the Common Council of Ministers: "It is doubtful whether the common ministers constitute a government in the corporate sense."[2] Subsequently Hungarians denied the existence of a common government; only common ministers were acknowledged. Their argument was that the ruler appointed and dismissed the common ministers independently of each other. It is a fact nevertheless that "the common ministers considered themselves to be an Imperial government, and not only ministers appointed to manage common affairs; they considered it to be their responsibility to address the issues of Imperial policies."[3]

In June 1867 Beust requested Francis Joseph to appoint him as Imperial chancellor (*Reichskanzler*). Actually, he wanted to play the role of an Imperial prime minister. Beust wrote the following to the Emperor: "The responsibilities of the Imperial Chancellery should include those issues that are not related either to the Ministry of Foreign Affairs or to the Cisleithanian territories and are political issues of the Empire as a whole." The appointment was duly made that month, but in the light of the protest of the Hungarians this office did not become permanent. With the consent of Andrássy, the Imperial Chancellery was merged with the Ministry of Foreign Affairs as its presidential department. This department in effect performed the role of an Imperial prime ministerial office. According to the Hungarian delegation the titles "Imperial Chancellery" and "Imperial minister" "are alien to our laws, they cannot be harmonized with the autonomy and independence of the Hungarian Crown."[4] Nevertheless, in accordance with the dualist system, two political department heads were appointed to the "Imperial Chancellery" (now the presidential department of the Ministry of Foreign Affairs): an Austrian and a Hungarian. After the retirement of Beust no one held the title of Imperial Chancellor. In 1880 Minister of Foreign Affairs Heinrich Haymerle dissolved the presidential department. But his successor Gustav Kálnoky, minister of foreign affairs from 1881 to 1895, expressed a view similar to Beust: "To conduct Great Power politics it is indispensable to have a consistent and unified top-level leadership, specifically as a permanent and constitutional organization. We need an Imperial chancellor." The presidential department was restored in 1895 by his successor, Agenor Gołuchowski, who thought it necessary to manage the affairs of the Empire as a whole, transcending the interests of the two countries. Aloys Lexa Aehrenthal, appointed as minister of foreign affairs in 1906, stated that the only appropriate office for the common minister of foreign affairs was the office of Imperial chancellor, so that he could perform the responsibilities of an Imperial prime minister. But since this was not possible legally, he should exercise that responsibility in practice. He attempted to transform the Common Council of Ministers into an organic government, with the two prime ministers as members. He regarded it as important that the two governments should receive more systematic information and that they should participate more actively in the management of the common affairs.[5]

> In the course of four decades of dualist politics the system of common institutions was organized and stabilized: the Common Council of Ministers and the delegation. This system proved to be functional up to the turn of the century in spite of problems and crises. The common ministers learned how to act within constitutional restrictions and the loopholes of the constitution. This was the art of common government and also that of the national ministers who secured a role for themselves in the maze of common affairs.[6]

The Compromise involved not only the common affairs and their management, but also appropriating the funds required for covering the expenses of common affairs management. One source was revenue from customs fees. At the time of the Compromise tariffs were rather low, and so this revenue was a modest amount, but subsequently tariffs were raised, resulting in the provision from that source of one third of common affairs funding. The balance was provided by the two countries. The proportion of funds to be provided by each country was negotiated for a ten-year period by two committees elected by the two Parliaments. Their proposal was reviewed and approved by the two Parliaments. The result was the proportion to be contributed by each country (*quota* as it was called). In the case of failure to come to an agreement, the ruler decided.

The first negotiations to determine the proportions of funding took place in August and September 1867. The two 15-member committees first determined the proportion of tax payments between the two countries in 1860–1865. The proportion was 30 percent for Hungary and 70 percent for Austria. This was the agreed-upon proportion to be contributed by the two countries for funding common affairs for the first ten-year period. Since Hungary's economic growth rate was higher than Austria's in subsequent years, the Hungarian proportion was increased periodically. The last determination was in 1907, at which time the Hungarian proportion was 36.4 percent.

The two committees also reviewed the issue of state debt incurred by the Habsburg Empire prior to 1867. The Act of Compromise stated that legally Hungary was not responsible for indebtedness incurred without its consent. But it also added that Hungary was willing to assume a part of the debt as a matter of equity and political cooperation. Therefore the Hungarian committee and the Parliament agreed to pay 29,188,000 florins (58.4 million crowns = £ 2.4 million or $ 11.68 million—according to the conversion rate of the time) annually to cover interest on the debt. With regard to the future, the Parliament declared that its prior agreement was necessary in the future assumption of joint loans by the two countries.

In the dualist Monarchy there existed in fact not two, but three centers of power. In addition to the Austrian and Hungarian Parliaments and governments, the common ruler exercised substantial political authority. Along with the possession of supreme command over the armed forces, he held legislative and executive authority and also important Church functions.

The ruler was entitled to convoke, adjourn and dissolve Parliaments. He usually opened Parliament with a throne address, outlining the principal legislative agenda. He had the right to dissolve or adjourn Parliament if there was sufficient time for the session to be convoked within three months in the current year to review the audit and the budget for the coming year. Acts were legally binding if the ruler approved them. But his most important prerogative was the right of pre-endorsement, approved by the council of ministers of both countries after the Compromise took effect. This prerogative meant that all legislative bills and government regulations had to be submitted to the Emperor for pre-endorsement.

The Emperor-King had the right to appoint the head of government from the majority party in Parliament. But if in his view this threatened the political system (dualism) then he appointed a government external to Parliament, as he did in Hungary in 1905. He appointed specific ministers nominated by the prime minister. He also appointed senior state officials and judges as recommended by the government. He appointed military officers on the advice of his Military Chancellery. The ruler exercised the right of supervision over autonomous Churches. The resolutions of Orthodox Church Congresses required his endorsement to be legally binding. The elected hierarchy required his confirmation. He exercised the right of patronage in the Catholic Church: he appointed bishops and archbishops; he was entitled to organize new archdioceses and to transform existing Church organization.

The civil list was not a common expense: it was included in the national budget of each country. The ruler spent several weeks or months in Hungary annually. He lived in the Buda Royal Castle, which was reconstructed and expanded at the turn of the century. In 1867 the Hungarian state purchased the Gödöllő estate and castle, built in the eighteenth century, 25 kilometers from Budapest, and presented it as a summer residence to the dynasty. Queen Elizabeth liked to reside there.

The common ruler of the Austro-Hungarian Monarchy in the dualist period, except for two years, was Francis Joseph, who ruled the Habsburg Empire from 1848 to 1916. He ruled for 68 years, longer than Queen Victoria. He was born in 1830, and therefore he was educated to rule by the grace of God over the peoples of the multinational Empire. He represented traditional supra-national dynastic patriotism: that was his basic conviction and government practice. He did not identify with any of the peoples and he did not sympathize with national movements. He considered Austro-Germans to be one of several "tribal peoples" (*Volksstämme*), as he did the Czechs, Poles, Croats and Hungarians. It was said that at a council of ministers he stated that he did not want to be a constitutional ruler, but a ruler who respected the laws that he had sanctioned. He kept his promise: after accepting the dualist system and the constitutional system of the two countries, he respected them. He was not an outstanding statesman, but an average, disciplined and conscientious bureaucrat. During his reign close to 600 common councils of ministers were held. "He was probably the only one who read all 600 minutes."[7]

The Common Armed Forces

The Compromise confirmed the supreme command of the ruler over the armed forces. This included the authority to direct the unified command, leadership and organization of the armed forces. Hungary, however, reserved certain prerogatives relating to military issues, including determination of manpower, the right to specify the number of recruits, periods of service, and the stationing and provision of troops. Therefore the agreement of the government and Parliament of both countries was necessary for the organization of the armed forces.

At first there were several conflicts of competence among military authorities: the common minister of the armed forces, the Military Chancellery of His Majesty, the chief controller of the armed forces Archduke Albrecht and the chief of staff. Each authority performed certain responsibilities. The Military Chancellery executed directives of Francis Joseph as supreme commander: its leader nominated officers, directed military diplomacy, defended military interests with the two governments, and served as mediator between them and military authorities. The chief of staff was responsible for the armed forces' development. The minister of the armed forces was involved with organizational and material issues.

Since the Compromise clarified the authority of the ruler and the rights of Parliaments, the first priority was the organization of a modernized military system, which was embodied in the Defense Force Act of 1868. Prime Minister Andrássy called it "the keystone of a reorganized Monarchy." Count Friedrich Beck, leader of the Military Chancellery, expressed a similar view: "The enactment of this law in Austria is one of the most important and timely issues... The Defense Act confirms the Compromise."[8]

The Prussian victory in 1866 was won with an army based on universal conscription. The lesson of Königgrätz was that the armed forces had to be modernized, and that universal conscription had to be introduced without substitution and redemption. The Austrian Ministry of the Armed Forces prepared the draft of the Defense Force Act and it was promulgated as a governmental directive in December 1866. However, since it gave rise to a general protest in Hungary, the Emperor was forced to withdraw it. The right to offer a specific number of recruits had been a traditional prerogative of the Hungarian Diet.

According to the Act of Compromise "the Hungarian defense force was a complementary part of the total armed forces." No one knew what this meant, and it gave rise to various interpretations. At the end of 1867 the leader of the Military Chancellery, Beck, held discussions with Prime Minister and Minister of Defense Andrássy. Andrássy was willing to accept universal conscription, but in return he wanted a Hungarian defense force and the appointment of Hungarian officers in Hungarian regiments. Beck did not object to these wishes. In January 1868 the Ministry of the Armed Forces appointed a committee of generals to prepare the professional elements of the Defense Force Act. Between April 18 and 26 a ministerial conference chaired by the Emperor reviewed the proposals of that committee. The common ministers, the two prime ministers and several other ministers participated in this review. The ministerial conference reached an agreement on the Defense Force Act, including the Austrian and Hungarian defense forces (in Austria *Landwehr*, in Hungary *Honvédség*). Franz Kuhn, common minister of the armed forces, wrote the following: "The two defense forces receive national colors, but the main armed force remains unified."[9] The two Parliaments reviewed and accepted the proposal and the Defense Force Act was approved (Act 40 of 1868 in Hungary, Act 151 of 1868 in Austria).

The Defense Force Act declared that all men who had reached the age of 20 were required to perform military service. The common army was to consist of a total strength of 800,000 for the next decade. Hungary was to provide 330,000. The period of service was three years for the common army and two years for the Hungarian defense force. Those who had completed secondary school were to serve for one year, and then after passing the officers' examination they would be transferred to the reserve officer corps. The Act stated rules for exemptions and standards of suitability. In the 1880s and 1890s 70 percent of those conscripted were unfit for active service. Hungarian conscripts were to be attached to Hungarian units of the common army.

The Hungarian defense force (*Honvédség*) was allowed only infantry and cavalry units, but no artillery or engineering units. The Act on the Hungarian defense force set the size of the force at 82 infantry battalions and 32 cavalry companies. Of these, four battalions and four cavalry companies were assigned to Croatia. In wartime the role of the defense force was to support the common armed forces and defense of the homeland; in peacetime it was the maintenance of order and security. The language of service and command was Hungarian, although in Croatia it was Croatian. The tricolor Hungarian flag and coat-of-arms were used. Parliamentary approval was necessary for using the defense force outside Hungary. The ruler was entitled to appoint officers both in the defense force and the common army. A similar military force, the *Landwehr*, was also organized in Austria to comply with the principles of Dualism. But the Austrians disliked it: they considered it to be an expensive and superfluous thing, which they were forced to accept on the basis of parity.

The common army was to receive 95,000 conscripts annually. The number provided by each country was set on the basis of the most recent census. In the 1870s and 1880s Hungary provided 39,000–41,000, 41 percent of the common army. After the requirements of the common army were met, the balance of recruits was assigned to the defense force.

The Defense Force Act of 1868 remained in effect for two decades. The revised Act of 1889 set the number of conscripts for the common army at 103,000. Of this Hungary provided 43,000–44,000. Conscripts for the Hungarian defense force numbered 12,500 and its organization was expanded. The revised Act remained effective for more than 20 years. The new Act of 1912 introduced essential changes, since the previous Act was no longer an effective basis for a modern army. Changes included a two-year period of service, increasing annual conscripts to 159,500, of which Hungary was to provide 68,000. The Hungarian defense force was to receive 25,000 annual conscripts, double the previous strength. Therefore Hungarian conscripts for the two armies were increased by 37,000. But population growth facilitated this increase. The population of Hungary increased between 1869 and 1910 from 15.5 million to 20.9 million, a growth rate of 35 percent. In previous years more than 30,000 conscripts were assigned to reserve status; they were not called up for active service, since they were a surplus. The Hungarian defense force was supplemented with artillery units, and units with machine guns were increased. The purpose was to raise the effectiveness of the defense force to the level of the common army.

By the end of the nineteenth century the total size of the common army ranged from 250,000 to 300,000. After the turn of the century it increased further and in 1912 it surpassed 400,000. In addition there were 1.3 million reservists who could be mobilized in the case of war. The size of the Hungarian defense force increased rapidly after the turn of the century, it reached 50,000 prior to World War I.

In 1869 the maintenance costs of the common armed forces were 171 million crowns.[10] Subsequently they increased gradually, so that at the turn of the century they amounted to 300 million. In the decade prior to World War I they increased sharply, so that by 1913 they had reached 910 million. In 1869 the costs of the Hungarian defense force were 12 million, and in 1913 they were 111 million. Hungarian state expenditures for the common armed forces and the Hungarian defense force combined averaged 64 million crowns in the years after the Compromise, but by the end of the century they were 100 million. The rate increased rapidly after 1905, in part due to inflation. In the three years preceding World War I they averaged 277 million. The rate of increase in military expenditures was nevertheless much lower than the growth rate of state revenues, and consequently they did not represent a significant expenditure. In fact, the proportion of military expenditures decreased between the Compromise and 1900 from 19 percent to 10 percent of the budget and increased only in the pre-war years to 14–15 percent. In 1913 military expenditures were 4.7 percent of GDP. International comparisons indicate that military expenditures per inhabitant in Hungary were the lowest in Europe. This was due to the fact that according to the Compromise, two thirds of the expenditures for the common armed forces necessary for the maintenance of the Great Power position of the Empire were covered by the other half of the Monarchy. This army also defended the autonomy and integrity of historic Hungary and the national supremacy of Magyars.

Of the common affairs the issue that gave rise to most conflicts in Hungarian politics was that of the armed forces. Hungarian public opinion had a hard time accepting the common armed forces with German as the language of command. It should be noted that at the time of the Compromise the soldiers of the Hungarian defense force of 1848–1849 were still alive and the memory of the fight for freedom was still very much present in Hungarian consciousness. The armed forces were in fact the most sensitive issue of the dualist system. They were a source of political conflicts and national sensitivity. Hungarians regarded the common armed forces with the German language and dynastic loyalty as an alien system, and nor did the other nations of the Monarchy identify with it. It is noteworthy, furthermore, that it was much more difficult to approve military requirements and budgets in the Austrian Parliament than it was in the Hungarian one. 4.5 percent of the corps of generals and the general staff were of Hungarian origin, 60 percent were German, and 18 percent were Slavic. Officers of the common armed forces frequently behaved arrogantly and were insensitive to national feelings.

While Hungarians were forced to give up an independent Hungarian army, their political leaders attempted to give the Hungarian units in the common armed forces a national identity. When the Parliament and the delegation were called upon to approve military expenditures, they demanded "national concessions." When this failed, opposition politicians used parliamentary obstruction to prevent the approval of defense bills. Francis Joseph, however, was strongly attached to the unity of the common armed forces and their supranational character. This was in his view the basis of their effectiveness and the guarantee of the Great Power position of the Monarchy. He wanted to keep rising national rivalries away from the armed forces. While it is true that the ruler had near absolute control of the armed forces, the Act of Compromise had given the two Parliaments substantial instruments of opposition. The two Parliaments were able to prevent for 14 years, from 1898 to 1912, the necessary modernization and development of the common armed forces by refusing to review or by rejecting new bills to replace the Defense Force Act expiring in 1898. This opposition had disastrous impacts in World War I, when the armed forces of the Monarchy proved to be deficient and unprepared.

The armed forces issue was also a suitable method for the opposition to use in order to overthrow the government. Agitation against defense force bills was very popular and proposals to force national symbols on the armed forces received a lot of popular support. This issue gave rise to major political crises in 1889, in 1903–1904 and in 1911–1912. The Balkan issue and the increasingly tense relationship with Russia focused attention on the unprepared condition and the inadequate size of the armed forces in the case of war. From the 1880s onwards major efforts were made to modernize the common armed forces. Reorganization was carried out under the supreme command authority of the Emperor, but increased manpower policy was subject to the approval of the two Parliaments.

Hungarian public opinion was dissatisfied with the common armed forces because the Hungarian language was never given sufficient prominence or emphasis in them and Hungarian state autonomy was not given expression. The Emperor and the military leadership on the other hand emphasized the supra-national character of the armed forces and wanted to preserve it. This character was represented primarily by the professional officer corps of 17,000–18,000 members, for whom loyalty to the Emperor and attachment to the armed forces were more important than national identity. In 1910 the total number of rank-and-file soldiers was close to 1.5 million, including active servicemen and reservists. Of these 25.2 percent were of German origin and 23.1 percent were Hungarian. Infantry troops were 24.6 percent Hungarian, cavalry and train service was 33 percent Hungarian, and artillery was 20.2 percent Hungarian. According to official statistics, 79 percent of professional officers were of German origin and only 9.3 percent were Hungarian in 1910. István Deák analyzed the personal data of officers and concluded that 55 percent were of German origin. The number of Hungarian officers increased slowly at the turn of the century. In the pre-war years 1911–1914 36 percent of students attending military academies and officer training schools were residents of Hungary, but only 18 percent were Magyar in terms of nationality. One third of future officers received Hungarian language instruction.

What was the meaning of the German language of command? It meant that 80 of the most important words of command were given in German. Officers and non-commissioned officers were required to use the native language of rank-and-file soldiers in communications. Each officer was required to pass an exam within three years in those languages that at least 20 percent of his unit used. If the exam was unsuccessful, he was not promoted until he passed the exam. In the autumn of 1914 142 major military units (regiments and independent battalions) were uni-lingual, but only 31 were German-speaking. In 162 units two languages were spoken, in 24 three, in some four. This meant that in more than 90 percent of the units officers had to know at least a second language in addition to German, but in many cases a third. In 1870 30 percent of the professional officers spoke German and Czech, 20 percent German and Hungarian, 18 percent German and Polish, 11 percent German and Croatian, 9 percent German and Romanian, 6 percent German and Serbian, and 5 percent German and Ruthenian or Slovenian. By 1904 the proportion of those speaking Hungarian was 34 percent. It was a typical event in the pre-war period that in one of the Viennese military installations the conscripts took the oath in ten languages in the presence of chaplains of seven religious denominations.

The Commercial and Customs Union

The Act of Compromise defined the common affairs and their management between the countries of the Hungarian Crown and the countries represented in the *Reichsrat*, then continued as follows: "There are other highly important public affairs, which are not defined as common in the Pragmatic Sanction, but which, in the light of their nature, and political considerations, and in the interest of the two parties, can be managed more effectively in common than separately."[11] These were referred to as affairs of common interest. They included the state debt of the Monarchy, which Hungary was legally not required to assume since it was incurred without its consent, although as a matter of equity Hungary assumed the payment of 29 million florins annually.

Another affair of common interest was commercial and customs policy. According to the Act of Compromise, Hungary was a sovereign and independent country and was free to act independently in these matters, but the Hungarian Parliament was prepared to negotiate a customs and commercial treaty between the Hungarian Crown and Austria, in the light of common economic interests and relationships. As a result, negotiations between the two governments produced a bill on a commercial and customs union, which was approved by the two Parliaments and took effect in late 1867. Accordingly, the territory of both countries formed a single customs and commercial area with a common customs boundary. The two countries established a common tariff system and negotiated commercial treaties with other countries jointly.

There were a number of economic issues that the two countries had to adjust on a uniform basis: railways, waterways, sea traffic, the post and telegraph system, measurements and copyright law. The Act stated the following: "Taxes on salt and tobacco, as well as indirect taxes having a direct effect on industrial production, and taxes on brandy, beer and sugar will be subject to uniform regulations in both countries for the duration of this treaty… patents will be equally valid in both countries… Residents of one country who wish to pursue trade or industry in the other country or seek employment shall be treated in the same way as native residents with regard to industrial activity and taxation, and they shall be accorded full equality of rights."[12] In order to harmonize economic policy regulations relating to these matters, joint consultations were held periodically between authorities of the two countries. The customs and commercial union treaties were negotiated for ten years, but after a five-year interval each party could initiate modifications and if unsuccessful, the union could be dissolved.

In November 1875, one month after his appointment as prime minister, Kálmán Tisza terminated the union for the purpose of renegotiating it with more benefits for Hungary. He made three proposals: excise duties should be paid not in the country of production, but in the country of consumption; tariffs should be raised for the import of products not produced in the Monarchy; the bank should be reorganized on the basis of parity. Austria was primarily interested in increasing industrial tariffs. Negotiations continued for over a year and agreement was reached at the end of February 1877, but only some of the proposals of Tisza were accepted. Tariffs were raised, but the proposal on excise duties was not accepted. In return for raising industrial tariffs, agricultural import tariffs were also increased. The new treaty of 1878 included an important new element: stock companies, insurance companies and industrial cooperatives established in one country could transfer their activities to the other country on the basis of full equality.

In 1887 the union was approved, but in 1897 the Austrian Parliament was unable to function, and therefore it was extended by one year. In 1898 a new treaty was negotiated between the Hungarian Bánffy and the Austrian Thun governments. This treaty introduced a favorable modification for Hungary: the proposal originally made by Prime Minister Tisza on payment of excise duties was accepted. Due to the inability of the Austrian Parliament to review the treaty, the union was extended to the end of 1903, the termination point of international commercial agreements. It was agreed that if no new agreement was reached at that time the current one would be extended.

Prime Minister Kálmán Széll, appointed in early 1899, announced a legal "formula" named after him: since the customs and commercial union was not in effect, "the countries of the Hungarian Crown were legally an autonomous customs area," according to the Act of Compromise. Nevertheless, he maintained the common economic system. In 1902 new negotiations were initiated by the two governments. The Hungarian government, under pressure from Hungarian agrarian interest groups, wished to raise agricultural tariffs, but in return it was forced to accept higher industrial tariffs. On New Year's Eve 1902 agreement was reached between the two governments on the commercial and customs union and on the principles of new tariffs (the Széll–Koerber pact). This agreement was based on the negotiations of 1898, and the opposition coalition acknowledged that it was the best agreement since the time of the Compromise. But it was necessary to delay its execution for several years, due to the Hungarian political crisis of 1903 and the inability of the Hungarian Parliament to review the agreement.

The coalition of the opposition parties won the elections of 1905. In an agreement concluded with the king in April 1906 the coalition gave up its demand for an independent customs area and agreed to support legislative confirmation of existing commercial treaties as well as the new tariffs. It also agreed to maintain a common customs union to the end of 1907, the termination of international commercial treaties, even if no agreement was reached with the Austrian government. The new agreement was concluded after lengthy negotiations in October 1907. Its new element was a difference of format: the two states did not conclude a treaty but a contract.

In summary, therefore, the position of Hungary with regard to its role in the economic system of the Empire changed substantially: it had assumed a position of equal rights and equal rank in place of its previous subordination. The customs boundaries between the two countries had been terminated in 1850–1851, so that the Austrian Empire was in fact a unified customs area, a "common market." But in 1867 the unified customs area of the centralized Empire had been transformed into the customs union of two economically independent and sovereign countries, which was negotiated freely for specific time periods. Naturally, there were difficulties and problems in the actual functioning of this economic community. It was not easy to harmonize the international commercial interests of two countries with divergent geographical and economic structures in setting tariffs and negotiating commercial agreements with third countries. There were also difficulties in harmonizing domestic economic policy issues.

The commercial committee of the Hungarian Parliament stated the following in 1878, following the most serious economic crisis of this era: "The customs union did not counteract the economic growth of our country; rather, it was one of its major contributing factors."[13] The believers in a common customs area emphasized the advantages of a large market area in the development of the economy and the application of modern technology. "The advantage of large market areas is that they facilitate the economic development of their countries in those sectors that are most viable and are based on the natural resources of those areas. The common and unified customs area of the Hungarian-Austrian Monarchy made an undeniably advantageous impact on the two divergent yet complementary parts."[14]

Historical development substantiated this argument. The common customs area with free competition and commerce provided an opportunity for both countries to develop those sectors of its economy that were of special advantage, to specialize in those products that were most suitable for development. The exchange of products between the two countries produced comparative advantages based on their divergent natural, historical and structural resources.

Common Currency and Bank

Another essential element of the economic relationships of the Austro-Hungarian Monarchy, in addition to the customs union, was the common currency and bank. The Act of Compromise states the following: "Closely connected with commerce is the monetary system. It is therefore not only desirable, but necessary, in the interest of both parties, to establish a unified monetary system in those countries participating in the customs union."[15] The treaty on the customs union stated that the Austrian silver florin would constitute a common currency.

At the time of the Compromise the monetary unit of the Monarchy was the silver-based Austrian silver florin, which replaced the conventional florin in 1857. Forty-five florins were minted from 500 grams of silver of 9/10 quality. Silver florins and silver and copper coins were used primarily in retail trade. In business transactions paper money was used, issued by the Austrian National Bank in 10-florin, 100-florin and 1000-florin banknotes, and state notes issued by the state in denominations of 1, 5 and 50 florins.

The Austrian National Bank, founded in 1816, was authorized to issue banknotes. The Bank was a private stock-based company, which issued banknotes and provided loans to the government and private individuals in various contemporary formats. In the spring of 1848 the ore supply of the Bank reached such a low level that it was forced to suspend payments by silver currency. It did not do so for the duration of the Monarchy, with the exception of several months in 1858–1859. The government took out loans of substantial amounts in 1848–1849 and at the time of the Crimean and 1859 Italian wars; this resulted in the issue of large amounts of banknotes without coverage.

In 1862 the *Reichsrat* clarified the relationship between the Bank and the state. The rights of the Bank were extended. The so-called *Bank Act* attempted to restore the stability of the currency. It prescribed that the Bank could circulate banknotes to the maximum value of 200 million florins without coverage, but even that amount had to be covered by bank loans or holdings. By 1866 this requirement was met: the government repaid its debts to the Bank, while the Bank reduced the circulation of banknotes and increased its ore holdings. Banknote circulation decreased between the end of 1860 and April 1866 from 475 million to 338 million. The ore holdings of the Bank increased from 89 million to 138 million, and therefore, starting from January 1, 1867, the Bank was scheduled to start covered payments. This strict deflationary policy involved significant economic sacrifices, since the constant reduction of monetary circulation and controlled credits limited economic investments, slowed economic growth and resulted in a period of economic depression for the Monarchy in the 1860s, unique at that time in Europe. But in spite of these sacrifices stabilization of the currency was not achieved, since the expenditures of the Prussian War of 1866 required further issues of paper money. In one year state notes to the value of more than 200 million were issued, resulting in the growth of paper money between April 1866 and the end of 1867 from 338 million to 575 million.

Nor did stabilization of the currency succeed after the Compromise, even though it was attempted several times. Both states made efforts to limit the circulation of paper money, with a certain measure of success. After 1867 neither Austria nor Hungary took out loans from the Bank, and neither used the money press. The Bank strictly observed the regulations of the *Bank Act*: circulation exceeded its reserves only by 200 million. The total value of state notes was maximized by law. But stabilization would have required the withdrawal of state notes and increasing the reserves of the Bank by that amount so that state notes without coverage could be replaced with banknotes with coverage. However, in the two decades following the Compromise neither the budgetary condition of the two states of the Monarchy nor international credit conditions facilitated such a major transaction.

The strict limitation of paper money circulation was successful in preventing the threat of inflation as a result of the large issue of state notes in 1866–1867. Although paper money circulation increased on the average by 5 percent annually from the end of 1866 to 1873, this covered the needs of the economy emerging from the depression and experiencing the most spectacular expansion of the half-century. Following the crisis of 1873 money circulation decreased for several years, then rose again to its former level in 1882 and then increased gradually.

The expanding economy of the 1880s needed a stable currency. Since paper money did not have silver coverage, it lost value in comparison with silver and gold currency. Therefore the practice developed between 1848 and 1878 of requiring a surcharge amount when exchanging paper money for silver currency. In 1867 100 silver florins required 124 florins in paper money, and thus 100 florins in paper money was worth 81 florins in silver currency. The amount of the surcharge varied from time to time, which created significant difficulties in business planning and management.

In the first two thirds of the nineteenth century the proportional value of gold and silver remained stable, but in the 1870s the value of silver declined in relation to that of gold. This led to the decline of the surcharge on silver currency and its disappearance in 1878. In fact, the value of silver currency fell below that of paper money. The ore value of silver money fell below its nominal value. Devalued silver from all over Europe streamed into the Monarchy, where it was minted into florins and then exchanged for the more valuable paper money. Therefore the minting of silver as well as the exchange of silver money for paper money was terminated in 1879. From then onwards the Monarchy's actual currency was paper money, with silver coins for everyday usage and gold coinage for international payments.

The measures of 1879 prevented the devaluation of the florin, and its exchange rate was detached from the global decline in value of silver. But the exchange rate of the paper florin continued to fluctuate between its nominal and ore value. The government and the Bank attempted to moderate the exchange rate fluctuations by strict limitations of future issues of paper money. This restrictive policy prevented the devaluation of the florin: its exchange rate between 1879 and 1887 declined, then rose again. But it also had a braking effect on economic growth, since monetary circulation was insufficient for a growing economy. The banking law of 1887 introduced a more flexible monetary policy by requiring that two fifths of banknotes in circulation had to be covered by ore value. The amount not covered could surpass 200 million, but only if the interest rate were to be raised above 5 percent, indicating the business need for such an amount. The Bank had to pay a 5 percent tax for surplus banknotes.

In the meantime the most important international partners of the Monarchy adopted the gold standard. With regard to such countries, the paper money of the Monarchy represented a currency with a fluctuating exchange rate. This created difficulties in commerce and capital transactions with these countries and limited the all-important capital investments in the Monarchy. Therefore the Monarchy became somewhat isolated in world trade and capital transactions, in the light of its monetary difficulties.

Several economic and financial developments created a situation favorable for a substantial reform of the currency: restoration of a balanced state budget, improvement of domestic and international credit systems, and economic growth in the Monarchy. The reform was the work of the Hungarian minister of finance, Sándor Wekerle. On the initiative of the Hungarian government, the law enacting the reform was approved in 1892. It provided for the introduction of a new currency, the gold-based *crown*. 3,280 crowns were minted from one kilogram of fine gold, or one crown contained 0.304878 grams of gold. One Austrian florin was worth two crowns. From January 1, 1900, the crown was the only legal tender. State notes without coverage were withdrawn gradually and the ore supplies of the Austro-Hungarian Bank were increased to such an extent that 60–70 percent of banknotes were covered, but there were no actual payments for currency.

The Act of Compromise did not make recommendations for a common bank, but stated that the financial system was one of the "affairs with common interest." Hungary was in principle entitled to establish an independent bank. The Hungarian government and Parliament did not accept the legal validity of the Austrian legislation of 1862, the *Bank Act*, but acknowledged current conditions. On September 12, 1867, the Austrian and Hungarian ministers of finance signed an agreement in Vöslau, according to which the latter accepted the obligation not to set up a separate bank in Hungary and to maintain the circulation of the banknotes of the Austrian National Bank until such time as a mutual agreement on the monetary system of the Monarchy would be concluded. At the same time the Hungarian minister of finance requested that the Austrian National Bank provide credit facilities for Hungary by establishing new branches and appropriate financial support for them.

The Austrian National Bank initially attempted to comply with the wishes of the Hungarian government. Although it did not establish new branches, it increased financial support from nine million florins to 36 million between 1867 and 1869. At the time of the crisis of 1869, however, it restricted credits significantly and from that time onwards Hungarian political and economic groups complained about the Bank. The opposition demanded an independent bank. In the spring of 1870 a national conference of financial experts discussed the issue at the request of the Hungarian Parliament and concluded that this would encounter significant difficulties at that time. It recommended that Hungary should accept the Austrian National Bank for the time being and attempt to negotiate with its directors. The Hungarian government accepted that advice and conducted negotiations with the Bank in 1872; this, however, failed to resolve the issue. The idea of a separate bank was revived, but dropped after the great crisis of 1873.

Prime Minister Kálmán Tisza terminated the commercial and customs union in 1875 because he wanted a reorganization of the Bank on the basis of parity. Negotiations continued for more than a year and resulted in an agreement, according to which the Austrian National Bank was reorganized as the Austro-Hungarian Bank, with two principal offices in Vienna and Budapest with equal rank. But the principle of parity was realized only in part. The Hungarian

Parliament recognized the continued status of the Austro-Hungarian Bank and its authorization to issue banknotes, and renewed this recognition whenever the Bank authorization expired. In subsequent years the Bank increased its branches in Hungary significantly and provided substantial financial support for them. The bank issue was dropped thereafter for a considerable period.

The "Croatian Compromise"

After the Compromise two other issues of public law related to the new political structure of the Monarchy had to be resolved: the public law status of Croatia and the Military Frontier.

Croatia had been a part of the Hungarian state system as an associated country since the end of the eleventh century. Croatia had preserved its territorial autonomy for centuries. It had its own Parliament, the *Sabor*, and the head of the autonomous government was the *ban*. In 1848, however, all political ties between Hungary and Croatia were terminated. Therefore at the time of the Compromise relationships between the two countries had to be placed on new foundations in accordance with the political structure established by the Act of Compromise.

The Croatian *Sabor* of 1861 declared that it was "prepared to enter into a closer state relationship with Hungary according to common interests and requirements," if Hungary recognized the independence and self-government of Croatia and its territorial demands (Fiume, the area between the River Mura and the River Drava (the Muraköz or Međumurje), Slavonia, the Croatian–Slavonian Military Frontier and Dalmatia). This relationship "should be limited to the common legislation of common affairs based on mutual agreement and an appropriate top-level governmental system." Croatia demanded full autonomy in the areas of public administration, judicial administration, education and religion. The representatives of the two Parliaments were to negotiate the restoration of the legal relationship, and the two Parliaments were to enact legislation confirming that relationship.[16]

Ferenc Deák, speaking for Hungary, emphasized the following in his article of March 1861 in *Pesti Napló*:

> The issue of union depends principally on Croatia. If Croatia wishes to unite with us, we shall be receptive to it. If Croatia wishes to set conditions relating to its nationality and self-government, if it wishes to expand the jurisdiction of its Parliament, if it wishes to participate with us in a common legislature in a different form and a different proportion, we shall not reject its conditions, we shall not oppose its modifications... If Croatia wishes to terminate all public law relationships that had existed between us and sever all ties, we shall not take steps to impede such secession and we shall not use violence even if we had the power to do so. Therefore union or secession principally depends on Croatia.[17]

In the autumn of 1865 the Croatian *Sabor* convened. The National Liberal Party possessed the absolute majority. Its leader was Josip Juraj Strossmayer, the bishop of Djakovo. In the spring of 1866 negotiations took place between representatives of the *Sabor* and the Hungarian Parliament, but they were unsuccessful, since there was no agreement on territorial issues. Both the Croats and Hungarians were attached to Fiume and the Muraköz. The latter was almost totally Croatian in population, but had been a part of Hungary since the Middle Ages.

Following the failure of negotiations, the Croatian Parliament advocated in an address to the Emperor of December 1866 the federalist reconstruction of the Monarchy, and declared that it wished to establish relations with the other countries of the Monarchy independently of Hungary, autonomously. Just prior to the conclusion of the Compromise, however, the Viennese government rejected the address of the *Sabor*. The Croatian issue was subordinated to the Compromise; it was a domestic Hungarian issue. The Emperor accepted the proposals of Andrássy on relationships with Croatia in the Common Council of Ministers of April 1, 1867.

Francis Joseph and the Hungarian Parliament invited representatives of the *Sabor* to the coronation and promised to grant Croatia the greatest possible self-government. But the *Sabor* submitted a new address demanding the autonomy of Croatia and recognition of its territorial demands as stated in Act 42 of 1861 and their confirmation in the Coronation Diploma. At the same time it refused to recognize the Austro-Hungarian Compromise as long as the *Sabor* did not accept it. In response, the Emperor dissolved the *Sabor* on May 25, 1867, and the coronation took place without the presence of the Croatian representatives.

On the proposal of Andrássy the Emperor appointed Baron Levin Rauch, a landowner and member of the Unionist Party, which favored close union with Hungary, as deputy ban in June 1867, with the mandate to break national resistance and create support for the acceptance of the Compromise. Rauch replaced officials of the National Liberal Party with Unionist officials and suppressed the National Liberal press. Using violence and bribery he assisted the Unionist Party, to win the elections of December 1867. The new *Sabor* sent its representatives to Pest for negotiations in the spring of 1868. The Croats submitted a detailed proposal. Ferenc Deák wished to grant the Croats a broader autonomy than the Croatian delegation was interested in, including financial affairs. Even the Croatian delegation refused to accept Deák's proposal. In the end, however, an agreement was reached. Both Parliaments accepted it and enacted it in law.

The Croatian–Hungarian settlement stated that Hungary and Croatia formed "one and the same state community" in relation to the other countries of the Monarchy and other foreign countries. Croatia recognized the Austro-Hungarian Compromise legislation after the fact, on condition that in the future comparable legislation had to be approved in advance by Croatia. Within the state community Croatia "is a nation with its separate territory and possesses its own legislation and government with regard to its domestic affairs." Self-government was to include domestic administration, religious and educational affairs, and the administration of justice. The *Sabor* of Zagreb was responsible for legislation concerning these affairs, while executive authority was exercised by "the autonomous national government," headed by the ban responsible to the *Sabor*. Nevertheless, the autonomous government was not a parliamentary government responsible to the *Sabor*. The ban was appointed by the king on the recommendation and countersignature of the Hungarian prime minister. The government consisted of the three heads of those departments that administered the three areas with autonomy. The Act stated that the official language of the autonomous government and the common governmental administration throughout Croatia was the Croatian language. In addition, the common ministry in Budapest was obligated to issue its regulations also in Croatian, to accept official documents in Croatian and to respond to them in Croatian.

Common affairs between Hungary and Croatia were military recruitment, the defense force, national financial affairs, economic affairs and the civil list. Common affairs were the legislative responsibility of the "common" Parliament in Budapest. Croatia was entitled to delegate 29, subsequently—with the integration of the Military Frontier—40, representatives to the Lower House, and two to the Upper House, who had the right to speak in Croatian. Four Croatian representatives and one member of the titled nobility were members of the delegation; they also had the right to speak Croatian.

The executive authority in common affairs was exercised by the central government in Budapest. One minister represented the interests of Croatia–Slavonia–Dalmatia in the central government. In common ministries with jurisdiction in Croatia, Croatian departments were to be established. Croatian "natives" were to be appointed in these ministries as well as in offices of these ministries in Croatia "to the extent possible."

Croatia was to contribute to expenditures supporting common affairs with Hungary according to its tax capacity. The proportion of contributions was set at 6.44 percent. But this proved to be unworkable. Croatia would have been deprived of all its income if that proportion had been paid. Therefore Croatia was able to retain first 45 percent, then 44 percent, of its income for covering the expenses of its autonomous government and contributed the balance to common expenditures.

The settlement recognized Croatian claims on the Croatian–Slavonian Military Frontier as well as on Dalmatia. Hungary gave up all its claims for the three Slavonian counties that it had claimed until 1848. No agreement was reached on the city of Fiume. Even the Unionists were unwilling to give it up. The Italian population of the city, however, was interested in retaining its traditional privileges, such as its linguistic and administrative autonomy, under Hungarian sovereignty. This was one of the arguments of the Hungarian government. Hungary hoped to develop Fiume as the port of Hungarian sea traffic. The Hungarian government dispatched a commissioner to the city in 1867. Negotiations continued in 1869 but no agreement was reached. Then a compromise solution, called the Fiume provisional system, was adopted in 1870, and lasted to the end of the Monarchy. The county of Fiume, including the city of Buccari, was annexed to Croatia, while the city of Fiume was given the status of "separate body attached to the Hungarian Crown" (*separatum sacrae regni coronae adnexum corpus*) and governed by a regent appointed on the recommendation of the Hungarian prime minister and subject to the authority of the Hungarian government. The Croatian areas of the Military Frontier were subsequently annexed to Croatia, while Dalmatia became a part of Austria. Croatia did not assert its claim to that territory. Nevertheless, the official designation of Croatia was *Croatia, Slavonia and Dalmatia.*

The Croatian–Hungarian Compromise of 1868 provided a broad autonomy to the Croats, one that was unrivalled in contemporary Europe. The autonomy included elements of a separate statehood, and facilitated the political role of the Croatian language, and the creation and free development of national, cultural and political institutions. But this autonomy did not satisfy the majority of the Croatian political elite. Ferenc Deák noted at the time of the Compromise negotiations that the Unionist majority of the Croatian delegation "appears not to represent the public opinion of Croats, it is not the accepted leadership."[18] Croatian developments following the Compromise justified Deák's remarks.

The national opposition excluded from the *Sabor* initiated a major agitation against the settlement, which gave up the program of Croatian national autonomy, and against the dominance of the Unionist landowner class led by Rauch. This led to a particularly forceful struggle in 1871, when political conflicts in the Monarchy appeared to favor forces aligned against the dualist system. The Croatian National Liberal Party had maintained close relations with the Slav federalists in Austria since the 1860s, and in 1871 it actively supported the struggle of the Czechs. In early 1871 they were able to defeat Rauch, who had been appointed as ban after he had managed to obtain parliamentary acceptance of the Compromise. He was replaced by another Unionist landowner, Koloman Bedeković, who, however, did not use violent methods. In the elections the National Liberals won a landslide victory, but the government had the king adjourn the session of the *Sabor* prior to its opening. In a proclamation of September 1871 the National Liberal Party declared the Croatian Compromise to be illegal and demanded a fully independent, responsible parliamentary government. It also demanded that the independent Croatia be connected with Hungary and the other parts of the Monarchy only through the person of the ruler, and that a Croatian delegation elected by the *Sabor* participate as an equivalent party with the Austrian and Hungarian delegations in the management of common affairs. Leaders of the Law Party, Eugen Kvaternik and Vjekoslav Bach, organized an armed uprising in the Ogulin Military Frontier district on October 8, 1871. The badly prepared uprising in Rakovica was violently suppressed two days later. Several days later the federalist Austrian Prime Minister Hohenwart was dismissed and the federalist movement was defeated. The conference of Slav political leaders of the Monarchy in Vienna on November 20, 1871, considered further common federalist initiatives to be unrealistic and advised national parties to negotiate with the Austrian and Hungarian governments.

The majority of the Croatian National Liberal Party also favored compromise solutions.

The possibility of a compromise was favored by the policy of the new Hungarian prime minister, Menyhért Lónyay, who attempted to strengthen his dwindling parliamentary majority by the support of nationality and especially Croatian representatives. Therefore he initiated negotiations with the Croatian National Liberal Party, which "represented to a large extent the Croatian public mood" and seemed to be willing to "remove the causes of dissatisfaction even at the price of concessions."[19] In negotiations during the winter of 1871–1872 Lónyay proposed the modification of the Croatian Compromise, expansion of the financial-economic autonomy of Croatia and facilitation of the opening of the *Sabor* if the National Liberal Party was willing to cooperate with the Unionists and send representatives supporting the government to the Hungarian Parliament. The negotiations did not prove successful, since the majority of the National Liberal Party refused to accept those concessions that the right wing of the party was ready to accept.

The result was that the *Sabor* was again dissolved, and the deputy ban, Antun Vakanović, replacing Beděković, utilized the methods of Rauch to defeat the opposition. The National Liberal Party was again victorious in the 1872 elections, but the government intervened by mobilizing aristocrats and the high clergy and utilizing pressure by the king to persuade the *Sabor* to send an equal number of Unionists and National Liberal Party members to negotiations on the revision of the Compromise. At these negotiations the Croats demanded an independent responsible parliamentary government and full financial independence, while the Hungarians offered only modest concessions.

The right wing of the National Liberal Party had favored a compromise since late 1871. This was strengthened to a great extent by the economic crisis of 1873, which forced foreign investors to restrict financial assistance in Croatia. Croats were unable to obtain credit in Vienna either, so they turned to the Hungarian government. In the new negotiations of that year Croats were forced to give up some of their national demands in return for financial assistance. In the spring of 1873 the right-wing group favoring compromise became dominant, and they gave up most of their essential national demands. The new agreement concluded in the summer of 1873 made only minor modifications in the Hungarian–Croatian Compromise.

The compromise of 1873 concluded the period of the Croatian national movement dominated by the intellectuals and the middle classes. The majority of the National Liberal Party accepted the dualist system, along with Croatian autonomy as set forth in the Hungarian–Croatian Compromise, and organized the new Croatian government party, the National Party, by uniting with the Unionist landowner class. Bishop Strossmayer retired from active politics, while the minority left wing of the former National Liberal Party fought in opposition against the Compromise. The office of ban was assumed by the leader of the former centralist group of the National Liberal Party, the Croatian chancellor of the 1860s, a prominent leader of the literary group of Illyrism: Ivan Mažuranić. Therefore the political system of the Austro-Hungarian Compromise was stabilized also in Croatia. The political stabilization of 1873 provided an opportunity to the Croatian autonomous government led by Mažuranić to develop autonomous institutions and ensure their efficient operations. As a result, this leadership established a modernized administration and judicial system, as well as a modern system of public education, including compulsory elementary schooling and the foundation of the University of Zagreb.

The Croatian territory at that time was less than 20,000 square kilometers in size, and its population was 980,000. The major part of Croatia was part of the Military Frontier and was administered directly by the Ministry of the Armed Forces in Vienna. For the realization of full autonomy in Croatia it was necessary to dismantle the Military Frontier structure, which was initiated in 1869 but was completed only in the 1880s.

Integration of the Military Frontier with Civilian Administration

The issue of the Military Frontier is especially appropriate for demonstrating the opposition between the common government, primarily the military leadership, on the one hand and the Hungarian and Croatian Parliaments and governments on the other. It also shows the resolution of that issue in the spirit of Dualism and the role of the Emperor in that process.

The origins of the Military Frontier can be traced back to the sixteenth and seventeenth centuries, when Hungary was a battlefield of the wars with the Ottoman Empire. One third of Hungary was under Ottoman occupation. This organization attained its final form after the expulsion of the Turks in the eighteenth century. The Military Frontier stretched along the southern boundary of Croatia and Hungary for a distance of 600 kilometers, on the northern shores of the River Danube and River Sava, from the Adriatic to the western border of Transylvania. At the time of the Compromise 1.2 million people lived in this area of 34,000 square kilometers, predominantly Serbs and Croats, but in the area of the Banat regiments there were Romanian and German border guards as well.

The Military Frontier belonged in the sense of public law to the Hungarian Crown, but in fact neither the Hungarian Parliament nor Hungarian government agencies played any role in their administration. Prior to 1848 it was under the supervision of the Court Military Council in Vienna, while subsequently it was transferred to the authority of the Ministry of the Armed Forces. By the middle of the nineteenth century it had lost its significance: its role as a border guard and public health cordon had become superfluous. It was also incompatible with universal military service enacted in the Act on the Defense Force of 1868, which was compulsory for the Monarchy as a whole.

The border guards were peasant soldiers, who received landed property in return for military service. There was a unique administrative system in the Military Frontier. It was based on the *zadruga*, officially called "house community" (*Hauskommunion*). The *zadruga* of the South Slavs was a form of the patriarchal joint family that united several related families and several family lines and generations in a common household and agricultural unit. The adult male members of the *zadruga* performed the border guard service in a specific sequence. The *zadruga* provided their clothing, equipment and food. In the case of war they were required to perform military service outside the country. The border guard *zadrugas* performed military service in return for their utilization of properties, consisting generally of plowing land and grassland. In addition, they owed personal service to their officers, who were generally their own people, and performed public works. They were free to utilize the vast forest areas for firewood, construction and grazing. The higher units of administration were military formations identified with specific areas: companies, battalions, regiments and their commands. General commands (*Generalkommando*) were the top authorities of regimental commands and of the free military cities, and they in turn were subject to the Ministry of the Armed Forces in Vienna.

The law on the Military Frontier of 1850 stated that the usufructuary rights of the border guards to their land were transformed into full property rights. In 1848, to win their allegiance and later as a reward for their services, the Austrian Ministry of the Armed Forces expanded the rights of the border guards to utilize forest lands in an extraordinary manner. All limitations and controls were terminated, and as a result the utilization of forests exceeded by far the needs of households, in fact, it was equivalent to the destruction of forests, as stated by a noted professor of forestry of Vienna in a report of 1868.

The Hungarian–Croatian Act of Compromise stated that the Croatian–Slavonian Military Frontier was a part of Croatia and promised that the Hungarian government would press for its unification. But no specific steps were taken. On the contrary, the Ministry of the Armed Forces emphasized the point that the Military Frontier was "a complementary part of the Imperial armed forces," and "is subject to the authority of the Imperial Ministry of the Armed Forces."

It should be noted in this connection that the top military leadership represented a special, informal center of power in the Monarchy. The Hungarian historian most familiar with the common institutions of the dualist system writes as follows: "In the dualist Monarchy there existed another 'common government,' which the legislation of 1867 did not mention, but which existed nevertheless. The minister of the armed forces, the two ministers of defense and the chief of staff formed a unique common military government. Occasionally the controller of the armed forces was invited to their meeting, the most important of which the Emperor chaired himself."[20] This military conference occasionally made decisions on very important Imperial political issues. It was a forum that did not need to consider the interests represented by the two governments and Parliaments, and it represented Imperial interests only. At times the two ministers of defense were requested to observe secrecy with regard to their respective governments.

In the summer of 1868 a proposal was made in the Common Council of Ministers to the effect that military expenditures exceeding the budget should be financed by the sale of forests in the Croatian–Slavonian Military Frontier. The Hungarian ministers, however, had reservations. Nevertheless, in October a decision was made in the Ministry of the Armed Forces to sell 47,000 acres of aged oak forests in the Slavonian Military Frontier to a Croatian lumber syndicate directed by a group of Viennese banks. The proceeds were to be used for improvements (railway and canals, river regulation and karst improvement) in the Military Frontier.

A general protest movement was initiated against the forest sale by border guards, who regarded the forests as their property. A delegation of border guards visited the ruler and submitted a petition. The petition requested the redemption of forest privileges prior to the sale. On February 23, 1869, Prime Minister Andrássy submitted a memorandum requesting the hearing of the Hungarian council of ministers on the issue. Andrássy saw an opportunity to press for the provincialization of the Military Frontier and its annexation to Hungary and Croatia. The Ministry of the Armed Forces, however, stated that the Hungarian and Croatian governments had no right to interfere in this matter. The Common Council of Ministers argued that since the Compromise left the Military Frontier under the authority of the Ministry of the Armed Forces and the income of the Frontier belonged to this ministry. This could be changed only in ten years, when the financial agreement providing for the contribution of the two countries to common expenditures was to expire. The contribution of Austria included the income of the Military Frontier. The Hungarian government emphasized the point that the Military Frontier was part of the Hungarian Crown. In addition, since the forest sale concerned the stock of forestry and had a future impact, the common Hungarian–Croatian Parliament and government were entitled to decide on the sale and the use of the proceeds. The Hungarian government also stated that prior to the sale the rights of border guards to use forests and grazing land should be clarified and only those forests could be sold that were actually the property of the Treasury. The government also proposed the provincialization of the Military Frontier and its annexation to Hungary and Croatia.

In the spring and summer of 1869 a major struggle was fought over this issue. In April the Croatian *Sabor* submitted a communiqué to the Hungarian Parliament requesting joint action concerning the forest sale. The Hungarian Parliament approved a resolution calling the attention of the government to the following proposals: 1. The forests should be sold only if it were necessary and advantageous from an economic point of view. 2. The rights of the border guards to utilize forests should be guaranteed prior to the sale. 3. Proceeds should be used only for improvements in the Military Frontier with the consent of the Hungarian and Croatian governments.

In the meeting of the Common Council of Ministers of May 26 Andrássy and Lónyay were able to obtain the support of Francis Joseph for the Hungarian position, as opposed to the position of Minister of the Armed Forces Franz Kuhn and common Minister of

Finance Franz Becke. They were successful in obtaining a resolution in support of the preparation of the transition to civilian government to be carried out by the military administration. Andrássy stated that the border guard system could no longer be maintained, since it was contrary to the dualist system and to the spirit of constitutional government in both countries. But influential military and court circles in Austria attempted to prevent the transition, justifying their position on the basis of military and foreign policy arguments. On August 12 and 13 Andrássy convinced the ruler of the necessity of placing the Military Frontier under civilian administration. It is of interest that Francis Joseph was the first to accept the "constitutional" arguments of Andrássy, in spite of the fact that he considered himself to be primarily a soldier, preferred to play the role of the supreme commander, and did not wish to become a constitutional ruler. At the same time, the common ministers (all three were Austrian at that time) wanted to retain the Military Frontier for ten more years under the authority of the Ministry of the Armed Forces. Following the consent of the ruler, the Common Council of Ministers also gave its approval and on August 19 a high-level ordinance authorizing the transition of the Military Frontier to civilian administration was published. The Emperor promised the transition of the two regiments of Varasd, and Companies 11 and 12 of the Sluin regiment, as well as that of the border guard communities of Zengg (Senj) and Sisek (Sisak), immediately and that of the others gradually.

At the meeting of the Common Council of Ministers of July 1, 1869, Hungarian Minister of Finance Lónyay was able to obtain agreement on the appointment of an Austrian–Hungarian committee to work out details of the proposed forest sale that had been suspended provisionally. The Hungarian members of the committee agreed that the sale of the aged forests along the River Sava was economically necessary within 30 years. There were differences of opinion, however, on the procedures: according to the Austrians the right to use the forests should not affect the sale. According to the Hungarians, it was necessary to separate the forests used by the border guards from those to be sold. The sale of the forests, in their view, would remove a significant element of the forestry stock, and therefore it could be undertaken only with the approval of the Hungarian–Croatian government, since it would definitely affect future development of the area.

The report of the Hungarian committee provides a detailed and objective review of the economic conditions prevailing in the Military Frontier and attempts to protect the rights of the border guards as against the Ministry of the Armed Forces. The report justifies the termination of the Military Frontier as follows:

> 1) It contradicts our constitutional principles to grant privileges in no small measure to the population of one section of the country, while its obligations, especially universal military service, are not greater or more burdensome than those of other citizens.
> 2) This region is situated on the border of territories populated by nationalities related to those of the Military Frontier. These people can be utilized against the security not only of Croatia and Hungary, but also of the Austrian Empire as a whole and the dynasty as well, in the struggle that will certainly take place in the near future. It is important to change the hostility of the people in the Military Frontier against Hungarians, to avert the danger of inciting them in the name of nationality and economic welfare against us and utilizing them as a military force.

The report also points out the serious difficulties of the transition to constitutional government: the border guard believed that he would be emancipated from the burdens of military discipline and subordination and would become a property owner with constitutional rights, but in fact the previous conditions would prevail. The border guard paid a comparatively small tax, he was exempt from all supplementary taxes, he received salt at a reduced price, he was free to grow tobacco for his needs, he was engaged in smuggling and he was the caretaker of vast forest areas. It was clear that he was not going to give up these benefits willingly "to attain happiness in the future." The report recommends a period of transition.

The most important and "most difficult and dangerous issue was the redemption of forest privileges. The redemption of the forests of the border guards of Brod would require the unimpaired transfer of all forests in the area of the Brod regiment to them." In addition, "the right of unlimited utilization of forests includes activities that lack all legal basis, for example illegal trade." There were two ways to redeem forest privileges: 1. The privileges of the border guards would be recognized as legal on the basis of the regulations of military government; in that case all forests would have to be turned over to the border guards and no forests would remain as state property. 2. Their privileges would be determined on the basis of their actual household requirements and an appropriate section of forest lands should be turned over to them. "Therefore, in our view it is necessary to reduce the forest privileges of border guards to the actual needs of their households. The privilege of unlimited use was motivated by political intentions directed against Hungary." The report states that "the Hungarian government cannot permit the transaction to take place prior to the settlement with the border guards." The current plans for the sale and clearance of the forests would fail to provide for legitimate household needs and would give rise to a serious crisis: "It would result in the complete and immediate transformation of the economic, employment and lifestyle practices of border guards to which they had become accustomed for a century and a half. Border guards make their living from the breeding of livestock and earn cash from transport services. If he is deprived of the forest, as the area where his cows are kept and are fed, and if he is deprived of wood required for sustenance, then his very existence is threatened."

The redemption of privileges should be executed on the basis of reduced entitlement by the military administration, "which had expanded the privileges of the border guards to a large extent since 1848." It should also moderate their dissatisfaction, to ensure that it should not be directed against Hungarian and Croatian civil administration. Therefore the Hungarian government should protest emphatically against the proposed sale as long as "an appropriate section of forest land is not provided for the redemption of the legitimate privileges of border guards."[21]

We considered it to be necessary to provide a detailed review of the Hungarian committee report for two reasons: it is the most thorough Hungarian account of the problems in the Military Frontier and it summarizes very well the economic, social and political difficulties of the transition to civilian administration. These difficulties were due to the contradiction between the artificially maintained border guard system and the requirements of a modernized society and political system. The transition could not be accomplished without a hitch. Some of the border guards would be dissatisfied: they would not readily accept the burdens of civil society along with its entitlements. But it was clearly not indifferent by whom and how the transition was executed. If the process took into account the social interests and conditions of the border guards, the conflicts could be minimized. The members of the Hungarian committee were certainly willing to make sure that this was so, but their recommendation was simply advisory, and the higher authorities did not always accept it. The Hungarian government was primarily interested in disclaiming responsibility for the difficulties and placing the blame on those who had given rise to them. The transition had to be coordinated by the military government. The latter was not motivated by the desire to protect the interests of the border guards. It suppressed the dissatisfaction of border guards forcibly, but at the same time attempted to place responsibility on the Hungarians. This was not difficult at all, if we are familiar with the precedents and the national and social conditions of the Military Frontier. These issues explain the border guard movements of the 1870s and the fact that the investigation of the uprising of 1883 concluded that its social causes were related to the grievances and the unresolved social problems of the transition to civil administration.

The Common Council of Ministers addressed this issue again on October 14, 1869, in accordance with the recommendations of the Austro-Hungarian committee, and instructed the Ministry of the Armed Forces to prepare the procedures of the forest sale and the plans for improvement and transition in agreement with the Hungarian government. Colonel Gustav König, the representative of the Ministry of the Armed Forces on the border guard issue, consulted with the Hungarian government, and their negotiations resulted in the acceptance of the Hungarian position, with some modifications. They accepted the sale of 43,000 acres of forest, but only after setting aside an appropriate section, and agreed on the gradual implementation of civil administration. They prepared an improvement plan in agreement with the wishes of the Hungarian government.

The agreement was summarized in several points, which served as the starting point of Military Frontier policies for several decades. The first point stated that the sale of 43,000 acres of aged forest land was an economic necessity and it had to be sold in a public competitive sale. But the redemption of forest privileges had first to be implemented in such a way that the forests were divided equally between the border guard communities and the State Treasury. The proceeds were to be used for railway and canal construction and regulation of the River Sava. According to the second point, the regiments of Varasd and the communities of Senj, Belovar, Ivanić and Sisak were to be placed under civil administration immediately. The third point stated that in preparation for the transition to civil administration specific reforms should be introduced in the Military Frontier. It was considered to be premature to authorize civil rights at that time. According to the Hungarian government, the authorization of the rights of assembly and association was still dangerous, and thus the unrest of the population should be moderated by appropriate measures.

The responsibility of preparing for the transition by appropriate reforms was assigned to Division 10 of the Ministry of the Armed Forces under the direction of Colonel König, who was required to prepare recommendations with the agreement of the Hungarian ministries. These preparations continued for a year and a half, while tensions and dissatisfaction increased in the Military Frontier.

The Serbian and Croatian opposition agitated actively. The "Court party" added to the dissatisfaction. Since it was unable to prevent the transition process, it attempted to place the blame for the difficulties on the Hungarian government. Anonymous pamphlets were circulated, "enlightening" the border guards as to the intentions of the Hungarians to confiscate their ancient rights, privileges and forests and treat them as disfranchised herds. When the newly appointed commander of the Military Frontier, Baron Antal Mollinary, toured the region in 1870 he encountered an extremely tense, indeed revolutionary, public mood, especially in the Ogulin and Lika area. The population protested against disarmament and demanded self-government and representation. The border guards of Belovar hoped that in return for their services over the past century they would be exempt from military service and taxation and their forests and public buildings would become their property. The simplified ideas of the border guards on civil society and the political system were productive soil for all kinds of agitation. This situation aggravated the position of the military authorities carrying out the transition and that of the Croatian and Hungarian civil authorities.

In the course of preparing the reforms those involved were not consulted; in fact, their requests and submissions, expressing simplified but legitimate requests, were generally rejected. The Croatian *Sabor* also protested that it was not consulted in the preparation of the reforms. In the course of the preparations there were repeated conflicts between the Ministry of the Armed Forces and the Hungarian government. Hungarian financial offices regarded the various forms of taxation, including the house tax, income tax, and the commercial, industrial, retail beverage and mill taxes, as being excessive. The very introduction of previously unknown taxes created turmoil. Thus, the Hungarian government attempted to consider the interests of the border guards. Mollinary recalls in his memoirs that Andrássy and Hungarian Minister of Finance Károly Kerkápoly addressed the problems of the border guards with understanding.

On June 8, 1871, the series of ordinances by the ruler comprising the reforms and procedures of transition to civil government was published. These ordinances implemented the transition of the regiments of Varasd and Körös and their annexation to Croatia. In other parts of the Military Frontier universal military service was introduced and thereby the previous military administration was terminated. For the period of the transition some of their privileges were retained: they were exempt from payments to redeem public works and supplements of the land tax. Tax, salt and tobacco privileges were retained for three more years. They redeemed forest utilization, wood and grazing privileges by transferring one half of their forest areas. Limitations of property ownership (inheritance and alienation) were terminated, and only limitations related to the *zadrugas* were retained. The minimum common property of the *zadruga* that remained inalienable and indivisible was set at 8.5 acres. This could be mortgaged or auctioned only with the permission of the local authority. Additional land could be divided among members of the house community or disposed of freely. Military communities were transformed into cities and organized in the manner of cities and communities of the civil territory. Border guard property communities were established to manage forests transferred to the property of border guards. Civilian judicial administration was introduced. The ordinance also included numerous educational and cultural reforms and listed the improvements to be implemented for the physical development of the Military Frontier.

In 1872–1873 the three Banat border guard regiments and the Titel boat battalion were placed under civil administration and integrated into the Hungarian county system.

Nine regiments of the Croatian–Slavonian Military Frontier remained for the time being under military jurisdiction. A newly organized Military Frontier governmental agency was responsible for the implementation of the reforms and the transition to civil government. The *Generalkommando* of Zagreb under Anton Mollinary received the same authority in the Military Frontier as was exercised by the autonomous government in the civil area. It prepared the budget in agreement with the Hungarian Ministry of Finance and submitted it through the Ministry of the Armed Forces to the ruler. Regimental commanders became directors of political, judicial and health administration, and the regiments were transformed into administrative units. In 1873 the political-administrative authority of the regimental commanders was terminated and six administrative districts replaced the regiments.

A total forest area of 1.76 million acres (714,000 ha) valued at 257 million florins was divided into two sections. Both the State Treasury and the border guards received a forest area of equal value, 128.5 million florins, but the size of the respective areas differed. The former received 700,000 acres, the latter 1,060,000. It is obvious that the Treasury received more valuable forests. The border guards received the aged, wet, distant forests. Their share was 60 percent of the forests, but even so their area of utilization decreased. This did not ensure their extensive livestock economy. As the report of the Hungarian committee had stated, their forest utilization as practiced after 1848 could be ensured by turning over to them the entire forest area. After the division of forests, a "Military Frontier improvement fund" was established, using the proceeds of the sale of aged trees of the section received by the Treasury. The Zagreb high command managed the fund in cooperation with a committee on improvements consisting of border guard representatives.

In the autumn of 1871 the competitive sale of the 43,000-acre oak forest took place. The "Croatian–Slavonian Lumber Syndicate" purchased the forest with the participation of Austrian bank capital and Croatian commercial capital as well as Hungarian capital. But as a result of the economic crisis of 1873 the syndicate was dissolved and the contract was terminated. Therefore the forest could not be sold as a unit, and it was sold piecemeal to French and Belgian lumber companies. Beginning in the 1880s demand increased and prices tripled. By 1910, when sales were completed, the income of the fund had reached 107.5 million crowns (54 million florins).

In the second half of the 1870s a lively controversy developed on the improvements between the border guards and the Croatian

Sabor on the one hand and the Hungarian Parliament and government on the other. The Hungarian Parliament enacted legislation on railway construction that was not in agreement with the wishes of the border guards and the railway construction plans of Mollinary, which reflected those wishes. In 1873–1874 Anton Mollinary, the high commander of the Military Frontier, prepared the railway construction plans to be financed by the Military Frontier improvement fund. Mollinary and his successor Field Marshal Franz Filipović pressed the start of construction in vain. The income of the fund increased slowly and by 1877 the balance was only 7.7 million florins in place of the projected 45 million. Nor was the Hungarian government in a position to provide a subsidy or state support. But in 1877 a law on "railways to be constructed in the Military Frontier" was enacted, to be financed in part by state support and the Military Frontier improvement fund. Thus the priority project of the Croats, the Military Frontier east–west railway connecting Semlin (Zemun) near Belgrade with Sisak and the sea coast, was completed in 1891.

The transition to civil government authorized in 1871 lasted for a decade, and this was due in part to international political events: the Bosnian crisis. In the period of transition, according to high commanders Mollinary and Filipović, there was serious revolutionary tension in the Military Frontier, which at times gave rise to a direct uprising (such as that in the autumn of 1871 in Rakovica). The Bosnian crisis contributed to increase the tension in the Military Frontier. A general movement to support the insurgents emerged among the border guards by raising funds, recruiting volunteers and smuggling arms.

On the initiative of the Croatian *Sabor*, Ban Ivan Mažuranić repeatedly spoke up for the unification of the Military Frontier with Croatia in the autumn of 1877. In his opinion, the process of the transition to civil government had made progress, and the situation had matured: the time was now ripe for the termination of the transition. At the meeting of the Common Council of Ministers of November 20, however, the king, Hungarian Prime Minister Tisza and the minister of the armed forces unanimously opposed unification at that time. Mažuranić requested without effect that if the immediate unification was not possible due to military and foreign policy reasons, at least a statement of principle should be issued and the date indicated. "If this is not done, the present majority will be dissolved." In the opinion of the king and Tisza, however, they were not in a position to project a future date. In February 1880 Mažuranić resigned, because his request relating to unification was not accepted. Shortly thereafter a significant part of the government party joined the opposition and established the "Independent National Party" (the *Obzor* Party).

Finally, after a decade-long transition, the highest ordinance proclaiming the unification of the Croatian–Slavonian Military Frontier with Croatia was published on July 15, 1881. Effective as of August 1, 1881, the ban assumed the governing role of the Zagreb chief commander, as the royal commissioner of the Croatian–Slavonian Military Frontier, while the Croatian government assumed the role of the Croatian–Slavonian Military Frontier's government office. The Hungarian government took over common affairs. The transition continued in some regards even after unification: tax allowances and lower prices for salt and tobacco remained in effect for three more years, as did the separate administrative system of six districts. The first elections took place in 1883. In 1886 the Croatian administrative system was reorganized: The area of the former Croatian–Slavonian Military Frontier was integrated into the counties and all distinctions between the areas of civil and military government were terminated. Nevertheless, the special economic and social development of the Military Frontier continued to have impacts for several decades and influenced the internal development, everyday life and economic-social structure of this region.

Attempt at Compromise with the Czechs

The reconstruction of the Habsburg Monarchy was not definitively concluded with the approval by the *Reichsrat* of the Act of Compromise and the coronation of Francis Joseph as King of

Hungary. Adherents of centralization and federalism were not satisfied with the dualist organization of the Monarchy. The supporters of both systems hoped that the settlement of 1867 would not succeed permanently. The military leadership and the so-called "Court party" wanted a restoration of the unitary Empire. This was not a real party, but it consisted of members of the dynasty, the Church hierarchy, the aristocracy, the armed forces and some groups of the bureaucracy. A conservative, supra-national, all-Austrian, dynastic state allegiance, free of national commitments, united them. The supporters of federalism were Slav politicians, especially Czechs, Croats and Slovenians. Between 1867 and 1918 there were many supporters of structural transformation of the Monarchy and numerous plans appeared, but there was only one serious political attempt to realize it, the attempt at compromise with the Czechs in 1871.

As mentioned, the representatives of the Croatian *Sabor* did not attend the coronation of Francis Joseph and did not accept the dualist structure, which placed them within the Kingdom of Hungary. The Poles wanted a greater autonomy for Galicia, one that was similar to or broader than the one that Croatia received. The Slovenians of Carniola desired a Slovenian state within the Monarchy with their own legislature and administration, and Slovenian as the language of administration and education. But the greatest danger threatening the new dualist structure was the demand of the Czechs for state rights. The Austrian government, however, granted concessions only to the Poles in Galicia.

The Czechs boycotted the *Reichsrat* convoked in May 1867, which was expected to approve the Act of Compromise without modification. They planned a joint opposition with the Poles of Galicia, but the Galician assembly (*Landtag*) voted with a large majority in favor of sending delegates to the *Reichsrat*. The Czech politicians decided, however, to continue their opposition, and refused to participate in the *Reichsrat* for several years. In mass meetings they protested against Dualism and the German centralization of Austria. Czech radical politicians, such as František

Rieger, attempted to seek support in Russian Pan-Slav circles and in France. The Russian connection not only alienated the Poles from the Czechs, but also created divisions among the Czechs themselves.

In August 1868 81 representatives of the Czech legislature (*Landtag*) publicized a declaration in which they called for a new political structure that recognized the historical rights of the "Czech crown." They demanded that the Lands of the Crown of St. Wenceslaus, Bohemia, Moravia and Silesia, should constitute a state equivalent to Austria and Hungary in the context of the Monarchy. This would mean "trialism" instead of Dualism. The Czech representatives of the Moravian legislature (*Landtag*) signed a similar declaration. But the assemblies of Moravia and Silesia with German majorities declared that they did not wish to enter into a closer relationship with Bohemia, and did not support the Czech wishes. According to the census of 1850 36 percent of the population of the three Czech lands was German. Germans formed a relative majority (48 percent) in Silesia, while 20 percent of the population was Czech and 32 percent was Polish. In 1868 a state of emergency was declared in Prague, lasting until April the following year, as a result of the series of Czech demonstrations.

A government crisis developed in Austria in the autumn of 1869 as a consequence of the Czech issue. Prime Minister Auersperg resigned; he was replaced by Eduard Taaffe, deputy prime minister, but he was equally unable to handle the Czech issue. A federal-autonomist minority consisting of German and Slav ministers seeking a settlement with the Slavs emerged in the Austrian government as opposed to the German centralists. This minority resigned from the government in 1869. As a protest against German centralization, Slovenian, Italian, Romanian and even Tyrolian clerical representatives left the sessions of the *Reichsrat*. In April 1870 Francis Joseph appointed the Polish Alfred Potocki as prime minister; the latter dissolved the *Reichsrat* and the provincial assemblies (*Landtage*) and called for new elections. In the summer elections the German liberals lost seats and the Czechs won a significant majority in the Czech provincial legislature (*Landtag*).

Since the Poles also refused to participate in the sessions of the *Reichsrat*, Potocki resigned at the end of November. The Emperor then looked about for a man who could settle with the Czechs.

Francis Joseph was concerned with the Czech opposition to Dualism. It was a special problem for him that in Bohemia the provincial aristocracy cooperated with the liberal national groups. The aristocratic families with close relations to the dynasty for several centuries, the families of Schwarzenberg, Thun and Clam-Martinic, played a leading role in the Czech national movement. Therefore he was increasingly inclined to recognize Czech historical state law, grant autonomy to the provinces of the Crown of St. Wenceslaus and have himself crowned as King of Bohemia. He did not really like the Austro-German liberals, and was more sympathetic to the conservatives and clerics who wanted to grant greater autonomy to the provinces and wished to restrict national movements to provincial structures. In early 1871 he told the Prussian ambassador that no nation could suppress another, and therefore from that time onwards they would govern "in a truly Austrian manner." On February 7, 1871, he appointed Count Karl Sigmund Hohenwart as Austrian prime minister, with the task of compromise with the Czechs. Hohenwart, an enemy of centralized German liberalism, formed a "government above parties" consisting of conservative Germans and Slav politicians of various persuasions. Albrecht Schäffle, a university professor, was the guiding spirit of the government. Two Czech ministers and one Polish minister were members.

In early March negotiations started between the government and Czech politicians. In May Schäffle traveled to Prague. His discussions with Czech politicians produced the Fundamental Articles of 18 Points approved by the provincial legislature (*Landtag*) of Bohemia and submitted to the Emperor on October 10, as the proposals of the Czechs. These were substantially more moderate than the demands three years earlier. They accepted the Compromise and the delegations, but expressed the view that the delegation of Austria should be elected not by the *Reichsrat*, but the provincial assemblies (*Landtage*). The common affairs would be the same as those between Austria and Hungary according to the Compromise. The common government was to consist of the Czech court chancellor, and the chancellors or ministers of other territories, who would govern the common affairs. The three Czech provinces were to receive an autonomy similar to that of Hungary and a common Parliament. Thus the basic demand was to transform Dualism into "trialism," which meant that in the long term the Monarchy or at least Austria was to be a federal state.

The government prepared well: the six provincial legislatures (*Landtage*) where liberal German centralists were in the majority were dissolved, and the new elections, assisted by manipulations and strong pressure, resulted in a significant majority for the government in the *Reichsrat*.

In his communication of September 12 to the Bohemian provincial assembly the Emperor recognized the rights of Bohemia and expressed his willingness to be crowned as King of Bohemia. In response the Bohemian *Landtag* submitted the Fundamental Articles. These developments had a major impact throughout the Monarchy. The Croats supported the Czech proposals immediately and declared the Croatian–Hungarian Compromise to be void. Galicia demanded a broader autonomy. The German population of the Czech provinces protested against the plans, with major mass demonstrations. The *Landtag* of Silesia also protested. The Austro-German liberal leaders traveled to Budapest to obtain the support of the Hungarians.

The issue also had an impact on foreign policy. The German Emperor William I, who visited Francis Joseph in Ischl in August, remarked that he would be happy if the legitimate rights of Germans in Austria were protected. Bismarck discussed the issue with Minister of Foreign Affairs Beust, stating that the dissatisfaction of Germans would involve much greater difficulties than the opposition of the Czechs. But Beust only listened for the time being; as a common minister he did not wish to interfere with the domestic affairs of Austria. He felt offended, since the Czech compromise had been prepared in secret without consulting him. But after the submission of the Czech declaration he prepared a memorandum to the Emperor on October 13. He attempted to convince the Emperor that a domestic policy favoring the Slavs was incompatible with a foreign policy orientation towards Germany, which the minister of foreign affairs had initiated that year with the approval of the Emperor. He pointed out that a federalist constitutional reform would make a unified and firm foreign policy impossible, and called the attention of the Emperor to the unfavorable impacts of the reform on domestic and foreign policies. On the following day Francis Joseph had a lengthy discussion with the minister of foreign affairs. Then he summoned the Hungarian prime minister to Vienna.

On October 16 the Common Council of Ministers, chaired by Beust, discussed the issue and stated that "a threatening situation has emerged for the common government, which endangers its policies."[22] On October 19 a new session of the Common Council of Ministers was held, to which the two prime ministers, Hohenwart and Andrássy were invited. The Hungarian prime minister at first was reluctant to express an opinion, stating that it would be contrary to the spirit of Dualism to intervene in the affairs of the Austrian government. But the present case concerned a transformation that would have a significant impact on Hungary, and therefore he considered it to be legitimate to express his views. He stated that the Czech proposals were unacceptable. The Compromise did not recognize independent Czech state rights. In the view of the Compromise, the countries represented in the *Reichsrat* constituted a unified state, as did the countries of the Hungarian Crown. "It is absolutely essential to maintain this demarcation separating Dualism from federalism."[23] The following day, on October 20, a crown council chaired by the Emperor discussed the Czech compromise. In addition to the common ministers, the entire Austrian government, the Hungarian prime minister and the personal minister of the king participated. Beust presented his arguments regarding domestic and foreign policies in opposition to the Czech proposals. The common ministers and the Hungarians agreed with Beust. The Austrian minister of finance stated that the Fundamental Articles were equivalent to state bankruptcy for the Monarchy.

Based on the text of the minutes it appears that Francis Joseph did not yet give up the possibility of a compromise. Following the arguments he closed the session without any explanation. After several days of reflection, on October 25, again without explanation, he dismissed Hohenwart and broke off negotiations with the Czechs. According to a majority of historians studying the issue, the viewpoint of Andrássy was of decisive influence on him.

A new session of the Common Council of Ministers drafted the Imperial response to the Czech declaration, calling on the Czechs to send their representatives to the *Reichsrat*, which would discuss their proposals. Hohenwart and his ministers departed in the last days of October. In early November their example was followed by Minister of Foreign Affairs Beust. He understood already early in the year, when the Hohenwart government was appointed without consulting him and negotiations with the Czechs were started without his knowledge, that his tenure was over. On November 14 the Emperor appointed Gyula Andrássy as common minister of foreign affairs.

Although Francis Joseph stated repeatedly that he did not want to appoint a liberal government, he had no choice but to do so at this time: on November 25 he appointed Adolf Auersperg, the brother of a former head of government, as prime minister. Thus the liberal course continued in Austria for several more years, until 1879.

That major change which we refer to as the dualist transformation of the Habsburg Monarchy in fact took place in two phases. The peace of Prague and the approval of the legislation of 1867 were the first steps. The external and internal conditions of the new system were stabilized in 1871, when the Monarchy made peace with Germany and in the smaller Austria the federalist attempts endangering German dominance were set aside. The governmental system became functional at this time, the national governments and Imperial authorities found their roles, and the government of common affairs became a routine procedure, a precedent, which could be referred to in subsequent years.[24]

Notes

1 Quotations are from Act 12 of 1867 legislation. *Magyar Törvénytár – Corpus Iuris Hungarici 1836–1868* [Hungarian Collection of Laws 1836–1868] (Budapest, 1896), pp. 327–344.

2 Éva Somogyi, *Kormányzati rendszer a dualista Habsburg Monarchiában* [Governmental System in the Dualist Habsburg Monarchy] (Budapest, 1996), p. 64.

3 *Ibid.*, p. 52.

4 Ibid., p. 25.

5 *Ibid.*, p. 178.

6 *Ibid.*, p. 177. Éva Somogyi is the contemporary Hungarian historian most familiar with the dualist state system, the common institutions, such as the Common Council of Ministers; she participates in the publication of the minutes of the Common Council of Ministers.

7 *Ibid.*, p. 99.

8 *Ibid.*, pp. 128–129.

9 Quoted in *ibid.*, p. 134.

10 The currency of the Austro-Hungarian Monarchy until 1892 was the silver florin. In 1892 it was replaced by the gold crown. One florin was worth two crowns. In the interest of clarity we indicate monetary values prior to 1892 in crowns, especially in the discussion of long-term economic and financial trends.

11 Act 12 of 1867, §52, cf. Appendix 1.

12 Act 16 of 1867. *Magyar Törvénytár – Corpus Iuris Hungarici 1836–1868*, pp. 346–354.

13 *A képviselőház vám- és kereskedelemügyi bizottságának jelentése a vám- és kereskedelmi szövetségről szóló törvényjavaslatról. 21* [Report of the Committee on Customs and Commerce of the House of Representatives on the Bill on the Customs and Commercial Union, vol. 21]. *Az 1875. évi augusztus hó 28-ra hirdetett országgyűlés képviselőházának irományai* [The Papers of the House of Representatives of the Parliament Convened on August 28, 1875] (Budapest, 1878), p. 342.

14 *Miniszteri előterjesztés a vám- és kereskedelmi szövetségről szóló törvényjavaslathoz* [Ministerial Statement on the Bill on the Customs and Commercial Union]; *Az 1875-ik évi augusztus*

hó 28-ára kihirdetett országgyűlés főrendi házának irományai. 8 [Papers of the House of Lords of the Parliament Convened on August 28, 1875, vol. 8] (Budapest, 1878), pp. 167, 171.

15 Act 12 of 1867, §66. cf. Appendix 1.

16 Stephan Pejakovic, "Die wichtigsten Akten des kroatisch-slavonischen Landtages vom Jahre 1861," in *Aktenstücke zur Geschichte des kroatisch–slavonischen Landtages und der nationalen Bewegung vom Jahre 1848* (Vienna, 1861), Anhang 3–27, pp. 42–43.

17 Ferenc Deák, "Zágráb megye körlevele és az egyesülés" [The Circular of Zagreb County and the Union], *Pesti Napló*, March 24, 1861.

18 Lóránt Csengery, ed., *Csengery Antal hátrahagyott iratai és feljegyzései* [The Papers and Notes of Antal Csengery's Legacy] (Budapest, 1928), p. 219.

19 *Az 1872. február 3-i minisztertanács jegyzőkönyve* [The Minutes of the Council of Ministers of February 3, 1872]; *Magyar Országos Levéltár* [Hungarian National Archives]; *Minisztertanácsi jegyzőkönyvek* [Minutes of the Council of Ministers], 1872-X/1.

20 Somogyi, *Kormányzati rendszer a dualista Habsburg Monarchiában*, p. 108.

21 *For the report of the Hungarian committee see Magyar Országos Levéltár*, *Miniszterelnökség Levéltára* [Hungarian National Archives, Archive of the Prime Minister] 1869-II–248 (1016, 1084)

22 Somogyi, *Kormányzati rendszer a dualista Habsburg Monarchiában*, p. 166.

23 *Ibid.*, p. 167.

24 Éva Somogyi, *Hagyomány és átalakulás. Állam és bürokrácia a dualista Habsburg Monarchiában* [Tradition and Transformation. State and Bureaucracy in the Dualist Habsburg Monarchy] (Budapest, 2006), p. 52.

3. THE NATIONALITIES QUESTION AND ATTEMPTS TO FIND SOLUTIONS

Both states of the Austro-Hungarian Monarchy were multinational. The dominant nations had only a relative majority. The census of 1850 and 1880 provided information on the ethnic composition of the population. The census of 1880 in Austria was based on the language commonly used (*Umgangssprache*) and in Hungary it was based on the native language. In Austria the percentage of Germans was 36.7 percent, while in Hungary the percentage of Hungarians was 41.2 percent, but even in Hungary proper, without Croatia, their percentage was less than an absolute majority: 46.6 percent. The other percentages in Hungary were as follows: Romanians 17.5 percent, Germans 13.6 percent, Slovaks 13.5 percent, Serbs and Croats together 4.5 percent, and Ruthenians 2.6 percent. Under these circumstances the protection of national rights, especially the language rights of citizens, was a major political issue in both countries. The nationalities question was a domestic issue of each country; therefore, immediately after the Compromise, both countries enacted legislation to protect the rights of national minorities and the utilization of their languages.

Austrian Constitutional Guarantees of National Equality

The Constitution of the Austrian Empire, dated April 25, 1848, guaranteed for each "ethnic group" (*Volksstamm*) the inviolability of nationality and language. The provincial assemblies generally supplemented this guarantee with the legal protection of national equality. The Imperial Constitution of March 7, 1849, issued in Olmütz stated that "each ethnic group has equal rights and each has the inalienable right to preserve and develop its language."

One of the main issues in Hungary and Austria in the 1860s was the nationalities question. The Austrian attempt to find a solution was different from that in Hungary. The different political structure of Austria, with 17 provinces and their self-government, suggested that national equality should be listed in the Imperial Constitution as a constitutional right and the several provinces should adopt detailed measures of protection.

The December Constitution of 1867 codified nationality rights following the adoption of the Compromise. Act 142 addressed the implementation of national equality in the context of the rights of citizens. Article 19 stated the following:

1. Each ethnic group of the state has equal rights and possesses the inalienable right to preserve and develop its nationality.
2. The state recognizes the equality of all languages used in the country in schools, administration and public life.
3. In those countries with several ethnic groups, public educational institutions should be organized in such a manner that each ethnic group would receive education in its own language without being forced to learn another language.

According to the report of the constitutional committee of the *Reichsrat*, the implementation of these principles was the responsibility on the one hand of the *Reichsrat* and the provincial assemblies (*Landtage*), and on the other of the government. The provinces expressed a diversity of views on the language issue, and therefore it was impossible to resolve it at the national level. In subsequent years the provinces adopted legal rules on language utilization. As in Hungary, one of the important laws adopted after the Compromise on the nationality issue was the Act on Public Education of 1869. According to Austrian law, provincial school authorities, after consultation with school management, were entitled to make decisions on the language of instruction and the instruction of a second national language.

The Austrian Constitution provided for two forums for submitting complaints relating to violations of national rights.

One was the Imperial Court (*Reichsgericht*), where each citizen whose constitutional rights were violated could lodge a complaint. In the case of violations by the authorities, citizens could contact the administrative courts (*Verwaltungsgerichthof*), which had the right to invalidate violations. Although the Imperial Court was entitled only to examine complaints and not to invalidate violations, its decisions and arguments in cases of complaints on nationality rights were highly important, since they served as a guideline for authorities. An example was its decision that communities and other legal persons, and even ethnic groups, could possess nationality rights, even though according to the Imperial Court the latter could not be regarded as legal persons. At the time of the Compromise Austrian liberals did not accept the idea that ethnic groups possessed nationality rights as legal persons. They thought that nationality rights were limited to the language rights of individual citizens.

In contrast to Hungary, in Austria neither the Constitution nor legislation recognized an official language of the state. The Germans attempted repeatedly to enact legislation to recognize German as the official language, but without success. But in fact German was the primary language in public administration. Nor was there any legislation on language use in the House of Representatives of the *Reichsrat*, but in the House of Lords German was the official language. After 1867 there were more and more instances of non-German language use, but these were not recorded in the minutes. The language use of the provincial assemblies was quite varied: by the early twentieth century two or more languages were used almost everywhere.

As for public administration, local languages became widespread in communications with the population, otherwise known as external services. The principle used was that citizens should be able to communicate with authorities, and therefore public officials were required to have a command of the local languages. The ruler and the central authorities generally asserted the interests of the minorities against oppressive tendencies of the majority in areas with mixed nationality. Public administration attempted to consider the use of all languages. In this regard, the situation of ethnic groups was more favorable in Austria than in Hungary. The major tendency was to expand language rights gradually.

Attempts in Hungary to Protect the Use of Languages

Beginning in 1848 the nationalities question was the most important political issue in Hungary, along with the issue of the relationship of Hungary and the Empire.

In contrast to Austria, the April Laws of 1848 establishing a new and modernized Hungary did not mention the nationalities question. They asserted that the official language of the Hungarian Parliament and of the county assemblies was exclusively the Hungarian language. This legal principle was an appropriate extension of the language laws prior to 1848, which created grave confrontation between Hungarian and national minority political leaders and intellectuals.

Between 1790 and 1844, primarily in the 1830s and 1840s, the Hungarian Parliament enacted a series of laws "on the use of the Hungarian language" and "on the Hungarian language and nationality," which declared that the official language of Parliament, legislation, public administration and the court system was the Hungarian language, in the place of Latin. Accordingly, only those with a command of the Hungarian language were qualified for public office or were able to take the bar examination or to be ordained as a minister in any religious denomination. The latter was required, since parish registers were to be recorded in Hungarian. Finally a law of 1844 required "that in schools within the country the language of instruction be Hungarian." Let us add that the counties, including those with a predominantly non-Hungarian population, ordered the exclusive use of the Hungarian language within their jurisdiction. It was clearly about time that Latin were replaced by a living language, but in Hungary, where the majority of the population was not Hungarian, it seemed excessive to make the Hungarian language the exclusive language of public life.

Hungarian political leaders failed to consider the legal protection of other languages used in Hungary. They allowed a few years as a period of tolerance for acquiring a command of the Hungarian language. They wanted to restrict the use of minority languages to private life. Representatives of the non-Hungarian peoples rightly protested against the excesses of these laws, and some Hungarian political leaders, such as István Széchenyi, defended the protection of minority languages in public life. This issue gave rise to an increasingly bitter and uncompromising "language battle" in political pamphlets and the press.

The Hungarian liberal political elite reasoned that the abolition of serfdom and the privileges of nobility, the introduction of legal equality and taxation of all classes, and a modernized political system would lead to the solution of the nationalities question. In March 1848 Lajos Kossuth stated in Parliament that common liberties would certainly resolve national differences and hostilities. In his lectures in England in the 1850s he stated with pride that the Parliament of 1847–1848 "had implemented the great principle of equal liberties, equal law and equal obligations for the entire Christian population of the Hungarian Crown without distinction of race, language and religion."[1]

The hope of the liberals, however, proved to be an illusion, a serious mistake. The non-Hungarian population of the multinational country greeted the achievements of the Revolution joyfully, but they were not willing to sacrifice their nationality in return for freedom. In addition to legal equality and freedom, they demanded the recognition and legal protection of their national existence and rights. Slovaks, Serbs and Romanians articulated their national demands in May 1848, calling for territorial self-government, recognition as a national community and establishment of their own political institutions. They stated their demands in the name of the Slovak, Serb and Romanian "nation." But Kossuth declared in Parliament that "I shall never, never recognize any other nation or nationality than the Hungarian under the Hungarian Holy Crown. I know that there are people and ethnic races who speak a different language, but there is only one nation."[2]

This confrontation can be understood if we recall that in nineteenth-century Hungary as well as in contemporary Europe there were two distinct concepts of the nation opposed to each other. One was the concept of the nation according to the French Enlightenment, which considered the nation to be a political concept, based on a definite territory, political system, and the state, identical with citizenship. In the *Encyclopaedia* of Diderot, language and ethnicity are not mentioned as criteria of the nation. According to this concept, only those people form a nation who possess a historically established independent state or at least political autonomy based on a territory. The modern state is therefore a nation state in which one nation exists, but all citizens regardless of language and ethnicity are its members. In his lectures in England in the 1850s Kossuth stated this principle: "Nationality is one thing, nation is another. The same nationality can be several nations and there may be several nationalities in one nation. Nation is the same as the state, it can be formed only by history."[3]

In contrast to this concept of the nation state, there was the second concept, ethnic-linguistic nationalism. It conceived of the nation as independent of the state, as prior to political organization, the product of natural development characterized by ethnicity, language, a common culture, native tradition, or, as stated by Johann Gottfried von Herder, German philosopher of history, the "folk spirit" (*Volksgeist*). All ethnic-linguistic communities with consciousness of their identity were said to have a natural right to national existence, to their own national political institutions and to national self-determination.

In the national ideology of most European peoples the elements of these two concepts were present, in proportion to their historical development. In the ideology of ethnic minorities without a state or territorial self-government and political institutions, ethnic-linguistic nationalism, arguing with natural law theories, played a decisive role. This was the argument of Slovaks, Serbs and Romanians for their recognition as a "nation." The Hungarian liberal reformers, on the contrary, professed the conception of the nation state, based on historical rights, or as it was called subsequently, the "political nation." This was the modern version of the "noble nation" concept, and it was identical with the multinational character of the Hungarian state. Prior to 1848 all noblemen were considered to be members of the noble "*natio Hungarica*" regardless of their ethnic identity or native language, even if they knew no word of Hungarian. The liberal reformers transferred this noble concept of the nation to all citizens of Hungary.

The committee commissioned to prepare the bill on nationality rights in the Hungarian Parliament of 1861 provided for the first time an unequivocal interpretation of the concept of the "Hungarian political nation," reflecting the understanding of the contemporary political elite: "Citizens of Hungary of all native languages constitute one nation in the political sense, the united and indivisible Hungarian nation of the historic concept of the Hungarian state. All peoples residing in the country, Magyars, Slavs, Romanians, Germans, Serbs and Russians, are considered to be nationalities with equal rights who can freely assert their nationality rights within the limits of the political unity of the country, based on individual freedom and the freedom of association, without any further restriction." Therefore the Hungarian political nation consisted of all citizens, while ethnic Hungarians (Magyars) were one of the nationalities with equal rights. With regard to the others it did not have any other privilege except as the nationality with a relative majority and as the historical supporter of the state. Its language was the official language of legislation, the government and state administration.

According to the Hungarian conception, the non-Hungarian peoples, with the exception of the Croats and Transylvanian Saxons possessing territorial autonomy, did not constitute a political nationality, and therefore they could not claim national political institutions or territorial autonomy. According to Kossuth, "to divide a country on the basis of language and to concede to all sections political nationality in separate territories means to dismember and destroy that country."[4] Another argument was that the several peoples were intermingled to such an extent that it was impossible to draw ethnic boundaries equitably. Kossuth and the Hungarian government therefore rejected on principle the recognition of ethnic minorities as "nations" as well as the authorization of territorial self-government.

Therefore the political and Church leaders of the larger ethnic communities, Croats, Serbs, Romanians and Slovaks, opposed the Hungarian struggle for freedom, while the Croat, Serb and Romanian border guards initiated an armed attack against Hungarians. But let us mention also the fact that about 40 percent of the Hungarian defense force were members of the national minorities. The Hungarian army included especially large numbers of Slovak, Romanian, Ruthenian and German soldiers.

In the course of negotiations with leaders of the nationalities, the Hungarian government authorized the use of languages of ethnic minorities in community administration, the school system and churches. An overall statement of principles was adopted only in the last days of the fight for freedom, in late July 1849. At its last session the Parliament accepted a resolution on the nationalities question: "We declare in this resolution, with regard to the different languages and the Greek Orthodox Church present in this country, for the purpose of satisfying our citizens of non-Hungarian languages and as a guideline to future governmental policies: The free national development of all peoples living in the Hungarian Empire is ensured as follows." The official language of the state was Hungarian, but "the other languages customary in this country" could be used in the following areas. Everyone was to be permitted to speak in his native language in community and county assemblies, and the language of the minutes was to be determined by the majority. Everyone could also use his native language in courts of the first instance. The language of instruction of schools and the language of parish registers and Church matters was to be the language of the community or of the Church parish. Counties were to correspond with the government and other authorities in Hungarian, but citizens were to have the right to address any authority in any language. Public appointments were to be made on the basis of merit and qualifications only, without regard for nationality or language. Prime Minister Bertalan Szemere, who submitted the proposed resolution, stated the following: "We not only provide freedom to citizens, but also provide their nationality to peoples." He expressed his view that these principles "will remove Hungarian politics from its prejudices."[5] In fact, this resolution served as a starting point, a guideline of principles for the bills of 1861 and 1867.

After the collapse of neo-absolutism (1860), the problem of the equality of nationalities became a primary issue again in the Habsburg Empire. In the meantime, under the impact of the events of 1848–1849, the ideas of the Hungarian political elite regarding this issue had changed significantly. This change of attitude and the emergence of a new conception of nationality policies could be traced clearly both in Hungary and among exiles. The major lesson of 1848–1849 for the Hungarian political elite was that it was unrealistic to fight with success against the Habsburgs for independence and against the nationalities for the maintenance of Hungarian domination simultaneously.

The constitutional plan of Lajos Kossuth, prepared in 1851, represented the official program of the Hungarian exiles in this regard. It proposed a democratic system of self-government, based on universal suffrage, and provided for the use of minority languages at each level of public life. It would also authorize national social and political institutions, not on the basis of territorial considerations, but rather on the basis of personal autonomy. The prominent representatives of the Hungarian political elite in Hungary emphasized the point that the policies of the language laws prior to 1848 had to be abandoned and the legitimate demands of the nationalities had to be accepted. Several liberal political leaders, notably József Eötvös, László Szalay, Zsigmond Kemény and Lajos Mocsáry, performed the task of formulating proposals and detailed programs. They viewed multinational Hungary as "the common homeland" of its peoples, where all citizens had equal rights and could use their native languages in all public forums and the free competition of individuals and peoples could take place in the context of liberal institutions and self-government of communities. They forcefully criticized the nationality policies of the reform age and the Revolution. They condemned the excesses of the language laws, the forced spread of the Hungarian language and other policies of that nature. Reviewing the experiences of the Revolution, they repudiated the liberal illusion that held that legal equality and civil liberties would resolve the nationalities question. They emphasized the point that the non-Hungarian peoples demanded not only individual freedom, but also national rights ensuring the free use of their languages in public life and education and facilitating the development of their nationality.

It was contrary to their liberal principles to accept the collective political rights and territorial autonomy of nationalities. In their view, individual citizens were entitled to exercise political and civil rights. But they emphasized the point that the Hungarian nationality would have to give up its exclusive domination as well as the major part of its historic rights and political supremacy. Its leadership would have to be based primarily on social, cultural and moral grounds. It could not receive special privileges, but rather should play the role of first among equals.

Lajos Mocsáry wrote as follows: "Our exclusive domination is no longer tenable… the full emancipation of the nationalities is inevitable."[6] Zsigmond Kemény had criticized the language laws of the reform age and the nationality policies of the Revolution in his political pamphlets of 1850–1851. He stated that "at this time Hungarians are not suspected of demanding sacrifices of nationality in return for freedom," as in 1848.[7]

József Eötvös expressed the Hungarian liberal conception on the nationality issue in the most comprehensive manner, first in his treatise on political thought entitled "The Influence of the Dominant Ideas of the Nineteenth Century on the State," and then in his book "The Nationalities Question," as well as in his diary notes and letters.[8]

As other Hungarian liberal political leaders did, Eötvös believed that the sustenance and unity of the common homeland was in the interest of all the small peoples living in the Carpathian basin, since this was the only way that they could preserve their freedom and national existence threatened by the aggressive policies of neighboring empires, such as Russia. But Hungary could not be organized like a Western European national state: in the light of the fact that the non-Hungarian peoples had achieved national consciousness, they could not be assimilated into one nation. Therefore he repudiated the organization of Hungary in any way "based exclusively on historical rights, while the demands of ethnic and language nationalities are not addressed." It was his conviction that "the nationalities question can be considered to have been resolved definitively if the solution satisfies the legitimate demands of both political and linguistic nationality equally." For that reason, "the peaceful solution of our nationality conflicts depends on resolving the conflict between the conditions of political unity and the demands of the several nationalities." It was not in the interest of the Hungarian nation to oppress the nationalities: "This state is sustained not by the dominance of one nationality, but by common freedom. It is the common interest of all nationalities to resolve the nationalities question, and the overall purpose is to satisfy the legitimate demands of all nationalities living in this homeland as far as possible. The only means of the resolution of the nationalities question in our homeland is the full guarantee of individual freedom. All nationalities of this country demand equal freedom and the organization of the country in such a manner that they can use that freedom." The new Hungarian state, therefore, should be so organized that the nationalities could identify their national existence with that of the country as a whole. The only way to achieve that would be to "secure a greater degree of welfare and freedom for them than they would enjoy in our neighboring countries." For that reason, centralization should be limited to the necessary minimum, and self-government should be expanded. The national demands of the non-Hungarian peoples could be satisfied in the structure of county, community and city self-governments and within the autonomous Church organizations.

Eötvös was also convinced that a permanent solution of the nationalities question would mean that "the Hungarian nationality can be given very few advantages." He forcefully opposed the conception that regarded the Compromise as an alliance of Germans and Hungarians, who "would oppose in a united manner the demands of other nationalities," which would thereby make it possible to enact legislation ensuring the superiority of Hungarians: "I am convinced that such a supremacy of our nationality is the greatest calamity for our nationality." For that reason he proposed that the Hungarian nation should give up its previous political supremacy. "Let us establish the Empire on the basis of freedom. Let us not strive to dominate other nations, but to achieve merits in the achievement of public purposes and thus be the first among equals." But he also realized that there were many "who give priority to the interests of nationality and not to freedom. Perhaps the majority in our homeland follow this conception." These people wanted to ensure the supremacy of the Hungarian nationality with privileges.

Ferenc Deák, the other prominent liberal politician of the age, professed similar views. He did not write major political treatises as Eötvös did. In one of his parliamentary comments advocating the establishment of secondary schools for minorities with instruction in their native language, he stated the following: "The proper way to win the cooperation of the nationalities is not to assimilate them, but to make Hungarian society acceptable to them. Both parties should strive to live together as neighbors with the greatest possible agreement."[9] He expressed his view on the role of the state in a multinational country in another parliamentary comment in November 1868. In the debate on the budget, the minister of the interior proposed state support for the Hungarian National Theater of Budapest. A Serb representative then spoke and stated that the Serb National Theater of Újvidék (Novi Sad) had requested state assistance, but the minister of finance had rejected the request on the basis of lack of funding. Several Hungarian representatives, including Deák, supported the request of the Serb representative. Deák said the following: "I cannot justify the principle that the state should provide support from public funds only and exclusively for the benefit of the people with one nationality and language. My belief is to support all of them or none. If we can support all of them, let us do so; if we do not, then let us not use public funds even for our own language."[10]

The above quotations indicate that in spite of differences of opinion the Hungarian liberal elite of the 1860s was in agreement that the only possible means of resolving the nationalities question was to ensure the fullest realization of civil and political rights, a system of public administration based on self-government and the ever-freer competition of individuals and peoples in the framework of the multinational liberal state. In their view, the state was not a Hungarian national state, but "a common homeland" standing above peoples and nations with the responsibility of ensuring and promoting the free national development of all citizens and peoples. But this liberal conception was not realized to the fullest extent in the legislative enactment on the nationalities question. This issue was taken up at first in the Parliament of 1861 and then in that of 1865.

One of the important responsibilities of the Parliament of 1861 was the creation of the nationality law. On the initiative of József Eötvös the House of Representatives commissioned a 27-member committee, including 12 non-Hungarian representatives, to prepare a bill on the nationalities question. According to the proposal of the committee the nationalities question was to be resolved by addressing two important issues: "satisfaction of the legitimate demands of individual citizens" and "assurance of the development of nationalities as corporations by free association." The committee proposed the resolution of these issues by the appropriate organization of community and county self-government on the one hand and the Church and educational autonomy of the several religious denominations on the other. The committee did not support territorial autonomy as proposed by the national meetings of Serbs and Slovaks, because "the several nationalities are intermingled and dispersed in Hungary" and the proposed autonomy would give rise to the possibility of the oppression of minorities. According to the proposal of the committee, individual citizens had the right to use their native languages in correspondence with their communities, counties and the state authorities, and to speak in their native languages in community and county assemblies. Communities were to choose their language of administration, but they were required to use the language of minorities as well. All Church parishes had the right to choose freely their language of administration, instruction and registers. The county assemblies were to choose their official language, which could be a non-Hungarian language. All minorities residing in the county could demand that their language also be used in the recording of the minutes. Several points of the proposal made it obligatory for community and county officials to communicate with individual residents and subordinate communities in the languages of the latter and use those languages in oral negotiations. The proposal also recognized the right of Church organizations and nationalities to establish secondary and higher educational institutions and the determination of the language of instruction and the instructional system. In the light of the dissolution of Parliament, the legislative review of the bill did not take place.

It was clear that there was opposition to this bill. There were those, and not a few of them, who wanted to continue the pre-1848 course concerning the nationality issue. János Török, editor of the most widely read conservative paper, the *Pesti Hírnök*, stated the following: "The Hungarian nation cannot do without the support of language laws. We do not agree with those who believe that freedom in public life and Hungarian nationality can be preserved without the political dominance of Hungarian nationality, on the basis of so-called national equality."[11] Many people in Hungary agreed with this point of view, especially among the provincial nobility, who wanted to preserve their dominant role at any cost, even in counties with large national minorities.

The Birth of the Nationalities Act

In its address to the Emperor the Hungarian Parliament convoked in December 1865 declared the following, as did the Parliament of 1861: "We shall not forget that the residents of Hungary of non-Hungarian languages are equally the citizens of Hungary, and we wish to guarantee by legislation both their interests and the public interest of the homeland. We shall observe the principles of justice and fraternity in the enactment of laws to protect the interests of the several nationalities."[12] In the debate on the address Serb and Romanian representatives protested against the exclusion of non-Hungarian representatives from the negotiations of the Compromise. In their view, there were several nations in Hungary, not only one, and all of them should be represented in negotiations with the Emperor and the Imperial government. Several nationality representatives and the press rejected the dualist system being prepared, and took a position favoring the federal reconstruction of the Monarchy.

On April 26, 1866, the House of Representatives chose a 40-member committee for the preparation of the nationalities bill, which included Serb, Romanian, Slovak and Saxon representatives. The committee delegated a sub-committee to draft the bill. Its work was delayed considerably, in part due to the Austro-Prussian War, but also because of the Compromise negotiations and the coronation festivities.

When the Hungarian government was organized, it rescinded the clause of Act 16 of 1848 that "directed that the official language of county committees was to be exclusively the Hungarian language" and authorized "that the county committees, town and district representative bodies may use in addition to the Hungarian language other languages customary in the country and prepare their minutes in languages other than Hungarian." But the government required that all these documents should be submitted to it in the Hungarian language.[13]

The nationality sub-committee prepared its proposal in June 1867. It had reviewed the submitted proposals of the nationality groups: the petition of the Slovak national meeting of 1861, the resolution of the Serb National Congress of 1861, the bill prepared by Romanian and Serb representatives, the request of a Greek Catholic dean concerning the national rights of Ruthenians, and a bill prepared by two Romanian representatives in 1861. In its report to the Parliament, the sub-committee stated that "it regarded as its primary principle the equality of the nationality of peoples living in the country and attempted to prepare a bill that, if accepted, would enable those peoples to assert their nationality demands freely, limited only by political unity, territorial integrity and the unity of the legislature and state government." The latter point meant that territorial autonomy beyond the county system was unacceptable. The concept of the "Hungarian political nation" was not included in the primary principle of the bill. The bill on the "equality of nationalities" prepared by the sub-committee discussed "nationality rights" in the areas of community, Church, county and state administration, association, judicial administration and legislation, in seven chapters and 35 paragraphs. In most cases it adopted the proposals of the bill of 1861 and developed them in more detail. So, for example, it provided more specific rules for the use of minority languages in communities and counties, requiring the preparation of minutes in the languages of all minorities with a proportion of 20 percent. The bill included a new chapter on the use of languages in the court system, which made it possible for anyone to participate in court hearings in the native language at the community, district and county levels. It proposed as the official language of higher court judges, appointed by the government, the Hungarian language, but the government would be required to "appoint judges of high-level courts from each nationality in sufficient numbers."

Community and county officials were to be required to use the language of citizens in their official communications. The proposal also stated that the government "is required to make appointments to the highest national and state offices, especially the county administrators, from nationalities in sufficient number. The persons appointed should be qualified to manage the concerns of counties, corporations, institutions, associations and individuals of non-Hungarian languages." Individuals, associations and Churches were to be entitled to establish schools at all levels and to determine freely the language of instruction. The state was required to establish elementary and secondary schools with non-Hungarian languages of instruction. In contrast to the 1861 bill, the sub-committee bill included the right of association for citizens of all nationalities.[14]

Along with the sub-committee bill of the majority sub-committee members, a minority bill was prepared by 26 nationality members, primarily Serbs and Romanians. While the majority bill gave primary emphasis to the rights of citizens in the use of languages, association and the establishment of schools, the minority bill expressed the demand that the five largest ethnic minorities be recognized as "country-wide nations" having rights equal to those of the Hungarian nation, and that these national communities, as legal persons, receive political rights. Thus according to one conception it was the individual citizen who was entitled to national rights, while according to the other it was the national community. The minority bill makes the following introductory statement: "In Hungary the following historical peoples, the Magyars, Romanians, Serbs, Slovaks, Russians and Germans, are recognized as country-wide nations with equal rights, for whom the political equality of nationality and language is guaranteed within the limits of the territorial integrity and political unity of the state." The six nations had the right to use their national flags and each "should be represented proportionally in the Upper House of Parliament, in central administration, in the higher courts, in the government of counties and districts and in all offices and honors dependent on appointments by the Crown and the government." The bill did not demand territorial autonomy, but requested that the counties and election districts be reorganized so that each would contain residents of only one nationality, or at least have a majority of one nationality. The official language in all communities, counties and towns was to be the language of the majority, "on condition that these majorities were one of the six country-wide nationalities." The language of the minorities was to be used everywhere as a second official language. Counties and towns could correspond with state authorities in their own official language, and they would receive correspondence from them in the same language. Another request was that members of Parliament could speak in other languages than Hungarian and that minority languages could be used in communications with central authorities. With regard to education, instruction should be given in the history of the country as well as in the history of their own nation. In universities and higher schools there should be lectures and examinations in minority languages. The following was proposed in the bill, in resemblance to the constitutional plan of Kossuth: "Each country-wide nation should be free to associate for the purpose of elementary education, national culture and enlightenment and to establish its expression of national unity in national assemblies or national congresses."[15]

The sub-committee bill met opposition not only in the nationality press, but also in some parts of the Hungarian political leadership, primarily in circles of the nobility in counties with mixed or large minority populations. Throughout the country alarm bells were ringing: "The dismemberment of our homeland is planned under the pretext of nationality." The county assemblies circulated their statements of protest, emphasizing their deep concern with the bill, which would destroy the Magyar national character of the counties. They protested primarily against the provision of choosing the language of administration by the majority, which made possible the choice of non-Hungarian languages. They demanded that the official language of all county administrations be Hungarian. The circular of Zemplén County wrote the following: "A law that would dismantle the Magyar national character of these great political corporations would create a multinational state, which could be free for a while, perhaps even flourishing, but it would not be Magyar and it would necessarily dissolve."[16] It was obvious that a widening difference of views was emerging at this time between the liberal political leadership and the provincial nobility, who represented a major element of the Hungarian leadership.

It took almost a year and a half for the nationality committee to prepare a new bill, based on the bill of the sub-committee and the protest movement of the counties. In the meantime the composition of the committee had changed since several members had joined the new government. This undoubtedly played a role in the transformation of the previous bill; this was especially true of the departure of József Eötvös from the committee.

The report of the committee dated October 28, 1868, stated that two questions were predominant in the drafting of the new bill. First, what interests of the residents of the country with a non-Hungarian language should be protected by law? Second, what is the interest of the common homeland? Responding to these questions, the report stated the following: "Citizens of non-Hungarian languages are free to exercise all political and social rights, since our laws do not discriminate between citizens and do not restrict political rights, property rights or the right to hold public office to any nationality. Citizens of non-Hungarian languages are subject to some limitation in one regard: the use of their native language." Therefore the committee addressed the issue of the use of the native language.

The new bill confirmed the equality of the rights of the individual in the use of his native language, with the following specific rights: "All citizens may use their native language in communications with the state, and in communications with their Church, school, county and community authorities, and they have a right to receive communications from these authorities in their native language. Communities, associations, private institutions and Churches may freely choose their language of administration and records. The counties may use along with the official language of the state any other language for their records. All citizens may speak in their native languages in community, county, Church and association meetings. Full legal equality is confirmed in the right of association, public education and Church administration, so that the residents of non-Hungarian languages may freely develop their nationality."[17]

The most important change in the new bill in comparison with the resolution of 1849 and the bill of 1861 was the stipulation that the minutes of the counties had to be prepared in Hungarian, while other languages could be used only secondarily if demanded by one fifth of the members. The bill also required that Hungarian remain the language of administration and allowed the use of other languages only exceptionally for officials for whom the use of Hungarian created difficulties. Correspondence among counties also had to be conducted in Hungarian, while the use of other languages was permitted secondarily. The committee therefore yielded to the pressure of the counties and cities and made the Hungarian language the official language of all counties. An introduction to the bill stated that "citizens of differing national origins have equal rights also with regard to the use of their native language" and the objective of the law was to regulate the exercise of these rights with regard to "the unity of the country, the practical requirements of government and administration and the prompt and equitable administration of justice."[18]

The central committee of Parliament, responsible for the review of legislative terminology, made several modifications in the bill, of which the most important was that county officials were not unequivocally required to use the language of residents, by inserting the clause "if possible."[19]

At the beginning of the debate on the bill Ferenc Deák submitted a new bill. This was substantially in agreement with the committee bill, but used a different structure and terminology. The Deák bill was unquestionably better organized and used unequivocal, clear language. A major difference was the fact that Deák drafted an introductory statement on the "constitutional conception" of the nation: "All citizens of Hungary constitute in the political sense one nation, the indivisible, unified, Hungarian nation, of which all citizens regardless of their nationality are members with equal rights. This equality of rights can receive legislative interpretation only with regard to the official use of various languages customary in the country and only as far as the unity of the country, the practical requirements of government and administration and the equitable administration of justice make it necessary."[20] Deák also considered it to be necessary to state that the state language of Hungary was the Hungarian language, which was required for Parliament and the central government. He stated the following: "At other levels of government, the counties, communities, the Church, I do not wish to restrict equal rights, but to let them develop freely."[21] His bill covered language rights at various levels of government and institutions, the counties, the court system, the Church, education and the communities, and agreed substantially with the committee proposals. He added two modifications. He required that county officials use the language of residents "if they so desire"; therefore he rejected the modification of the central committee providing an administrative loophole. He expressed his wish that "court procedures should be conducted in the language of the residents wherever they are not of Hungarian nationality, but given the current mood I do not think that we can get this approved."

In the general debate the Serb and Romanian representatives attacked the bill vehemently. They pointed out that individual liberties and individual use of language, however broad they were, would not satisfy the nationalities. They demanded collective national rights for their national communities as legal persons and recognition as political nations with corresponding political institutions. They also required that the counties be reorganized on an ethnic basis and these ethnic areas receive territorial autonomy. In these territories the language of the majority was to be the official language. The Serb, Romanian and Slovak press of Hungary also raised serious objections. A Slovak paper open to cooperation with the Magyars stated the following: "Whoever promises us personal equality of rights, does not appear to promise us anything."[22] It should be noted, however, that some representatives of non-Hungarian nationalities supported the Deák bill.

After the acceptance of the Deák bill by a substantial majority as a basis of discussion, the 26 Romanian and Serb representatives who had submitted the minority bill departed from the session in protest and refused to participate in the detailed debate. With some modification, both Houses of Parliament accepted the Deák bill, and the king signed it on December 6, 1868. It was designated Act 44 of 1868, "on the equality of nationality rights."

The Nationalities Act of 1868

The Act guaranteed above all the right of citizens to use their native language in all public forums. All citizens could speak in their native language in community, county and Church assemblies. They could submit written statements to all authorities in their native language and were entitled to receive responses in that language. Citizens could speak in court procedures of the first instance in their native language. The official language of higher courts was Hungarian, but they were required to translate non-Hungarian court documents into Hungarian at state expense. Citizens were entitled to receive court decisions affecting their cases in their native language.

Communities could choose their language of administration and record keeping. Community officials were required to use the native language of residents in communications. Communities used their language of administration in correspondence with the counties and the central government. Church parishes could also choose their language of administration and registers and their language of instruction in Church schools.

Counties and larger cities used the Hungarian language in record keeping, but also used other languages desired by one fifth of the membership of their assembly. The administrative language of counties was Hungarian, but in the case of difficulties "officials can also use any other language of their record keeping exceptionally."

"County officials will use the languages of communities, assemblies, institutes and individuals in official communications with them to the extent possible." Counties could use, along with Hungarian, any of the languages of their record keeping in correspondence with the government. The same principle applied to higher Church authorities, who would choose their own language of internal communication, administration and record keeping, but were required to submit their records in Hungarian translation to the government.

The official language of Parliament and the government was Hungarian, but all legislation had to be made public in all languages.

The government was required to respond to non-Hungarian language inquiries in that language. Churches and communities were to determine the language of instruction of schools maintained by them. The Act stated that "state schools are required to provide for opportunities for all nationalities to receive education in their native language in their areas of residence to the level of higher education." Universities were required to establish chairs of language and literature for nationalities.

The Act also confirmed the right of citizens of all nationalities to establish schools and associations: "Individual citizens have the right to establish associations or organizations for the purpose of supporting linguistic, artistic, scientific, economic, industrial and commercial activities, formulate their own regulations, undertake actions in accordance with government rules, and raise and administer funds according to their nationality aspirations." The founders were to determine the language of these associations and organizations.

The Act also stated the following: "In appointments to public offices the exclusive criterion is and will be in the future personal qualification. National origin is and will be no obstacle to being appointed to a public office or honor. In fact the government will pursue policies to appoint persons to national judicial and administrative offices, especially county administrators, who are members of nationalities, have a command of the appropriate languages and are qualified for such offices."

Several contemporary legislative acts complemented the provisions of the Nationalities Act in specific areas by reinforcing language rights in accordance with it. An example was the creation of József Eötvös, the Act on Elementary Education, Act 38, of 1868, guaranteeing the right of religious organizations, associations, communities and private citizens to establish and maintain schools. For national minorities the right of religious denominations to establish schools was highly important, as the Serbs, Romanians, Ruthenians and Transylvanian Saxons already had their own Church organizations with national characteristics. These denominations were free to elect their teachers, and to choose textbooks and teaching methods. The Act stated that in elementary schools all pupils were to receive instruction in their native language if that language was customary in the community. In communities with mixed languages a teacher was to be chosen who was able to teach in the customary languages. In communities with large populations and several languages assistant teachers with a command of several languages could be employed.[23] As mentioned, this provision was supplemented by the Nationalities Act, with the requirement that the state was obligated to establish elementary and secondary schools in which the language of instruction was one of the minority languages. In non-Hungarian elementary schools the Hungarian language was not a required subject of instruction to the beginning of the 1880s.

The Nationalities Act entitled all citizens to use their native language or any other language in court procedures of the first instance, to participate in their native language in all phases of the trial procedures and to receive all court documents in their native language. At the time of the Compromise the court procedures of the first instance were the responsibility of communities, districts and counties. In the succeeding years, however, the judicial system was radically transformed and modernized. Act 4 of 1869 separated judicial services from public administration, and the judicial system was placed under state control. The Act confirmed that only the higher courts, that is, the courts of appeal, were to use Hungarian as their official language, while the lower court system was subject to the provisions of the Nationalities Act. The same Act stated that "in appointments of judges to courts of the first instance consideration should be given to the residents of several nationalities of the court jurisdiction." Judges "must have qualifications in accordance with the provisions of Act 44 of 1868," since only the higher courts used Hungarian as their official language. Subsequent legislation relating to judicial officers and public notaries confirmed this principle. Appointments of county and community officials were also subject to the provisions of the Nationalities Act. The Act on public health required urban and community physicians to acquire facility in the language of the majority in their area.

This account refutes the frequently expressed statement of contemporary publicists and historical studies to the effect that the Nationalities Act was no more than a piece of paper and that Hungarian governments never took it seriously. The implementation of the Act was predominantly the responsibility of institutions of self-government, the counties, cities, communities and Church parishes, and therefore there was a great variety of conditions from county to county and from community to community. The increasing tendency, especially after 1880, was that the Hungarian language was used to a greater extent than its use was justified by the Nationalities Act. But even in the early twentieth century, at the time of the government of the opposition coalition, which pursued a less tolerant nationality policy than its liberal predecessors, we encounter a ministerial directive providing special emphasis to "the policy that county officials who maintain continuous and frequent contact with the population should have a command of the language of their district."[24] The minister of the interior stated in his justification of the bill on the franchise in 1913 that knowledge of the Hungarian language could not be a condition of the right to vote, in response to the proposals of several opposition representatives. He stated the following: "The tradition of the Hungarian state does not recognize privileges based on facility in the language of the state. Hungarian legislation never excluded anyone from the political nation because of ignorance of the Hungarian language."[25]

The Nationalities Act did not satisfy the most important political demand of the non-Hungarian peoples: it did not recognize their national existence, it did not accept collective nationality rights and political institutions, and it considerably limited the use of national languages in the county system. In addition, it recognized nationality rights to a lesser extent than did the promises of the liberal elite prior to 1867 and the original nationality bill of 1867. The advocates of a democratic and liberal policy on nationality rights remained in the minority, while the majority of the propertied nobility dominating the counties prevailed with the acceptance of the revised version of the Nationalities Act. The political objective of that majority was to maintain Hungarian national supremacy over the national minorities.

But even the compromise version of the Nationalities Act was an outstanding creation of Hungarian and East-Central European liberal policy. Although it accepted neither territorial autonomy nor collective national rights, it provided an important example to European states seeking to resolve similar problems, by codifying the right of all citizens to use their native language freely in all public forums and the right of nationalities to establish schools and organize associations freely. A leader of the opposition, Lajos Mocsáry, stated correctly that the basic principle of the Nationalities Act was that "the state must establish its public administration and judicial services in a manner that facilitates the seeking of justice by everyone in his/her own language."[26] It should be added that Mocsáry expressed a critical view of the Nationalities Act, stating that "it provides a restricted form of equal rights in public administration and legislation" and that it extended the sphere of the state language excessively. When in 1879 the government planned to introduce mandatory instruction in the Hungarian language in all elementary schools on the grounds that the knowledge of the state language was in the interest of all citizens, Mocsáry pointed out that if the Nationalities Act were implemented faithfully, then "there is no need for residents to learn the Hungarian language, since the Act provides opportunities for all citizens to participate in public life using their native languages."[27] By the turn of the century the representatives of nationalities acknowledged the liberal character of the Act and demanded its full implementation.

In conclusion let us quote a non-partisan and objective evaluation by the well-known American historian Arthur J. May, who considers the Act to have been "prudential and enlightened legislation": "All in all, the Nationalities Act of 1868 was one of the most enlightened measures of its kind ever adopted, even more liberal than the minority safeguards incorporated in the peace settlement of 1919–20, which, indeed, were very largely modeled on the Hungarian precedent of 1868."[28]

Notes

1 Ferenc Kossuth, ed., *Kossuth Lajos válogatott munkái* [The Selected Works of Lajos Kossuth] (Budapest, n.d.), pp. 57–58.

2 István Barta, ed., *Kossuth Lajos összes munkái XI. Kossuth Lajos 1848–49-ben I. Kossuth Lajos az utolsó rendi országgyűlésen 1847–48* [The Complete Works of Lajos Kossuth XI. Lajos Kossuth in 1848–1849. I. Lajos Kossuth in the Last Feudal Diet 1847–1848] (Budapest, 1951), p. 382.

3 Ferenc Kossuth, ed., *Kossuth Lajos válogatott munkái* [The Selected Works of Lajos Kossuth] (Budapest, n.d.), p. 59.

4 Quoted in Zoltán I. Tóth, *Magyarok és románok. Történelmi tanulmányok* [Hungarians and Romanians. Historical Studies] (Budapest, 1966), p. 244.

5 János Beér, ed., *Az 1848–49. évi népképviseleti országgyűlés* [The Representative Parliament of 1848–1849] (Budapest, 1954), pp. 868–869.

6 Lajos Mocsáry, *Programm a nemzetiség és a nemzetiségek tárgyában* [Program on the Subject of Nationality and the Nationalities] (Pest, 1860), p. 109.

7 *Pesti Napló*, January 1, 1861.

8 The subsequent quotations are taken from the following writings of József Eötvös, *A nemzetiségi kérdés* [The Nationalities Question] (Budapest, 1903); Miklós Bényei, ed., *Vallomások és gondolatok* [Confessions and Reflections] (Budapest, 1977); Ambrus Oltványi, ed., *Levelek* [Letters] (Budapest, 1976).

9 Ágnes Deák, ed., *Deák Ferenc, Válogatott politikai irások és beszédek II 1850–1873* [Ferenc Deák: Selected Political Writings and Speeches II 1850–1873] (Budapest, 2001), p. 599.

10 *Ibid.*, pp. 548–549.

11 *Pest Hirnök*, January 8, June 11 and June 23, 1861

12 *Az 1865-dik év december 10-dikére hirdetett országgyűlés képviselőházának irományai* [Papers of the House of Representatives of the Parliament Convoked on December 10, 1865], I, p. 27.

13 Gábor G. Kemény, *Iratok a nemzetiségi kérdés történetéhez Magyarországon a dualizmus korában. 1867–1892* [Documents on the History of the Nationalities Question in Hungary in the Age of Dualism] (Budapest, 1952), I, p. 21.

14 *Jelentése az 1865-dik évi magyar országgyűlés képviselőháza által kiküldött bizottság alválasztmányának* [Report of the Sub-Committee of the Committee of the House of Representatives of the Hungarian Parliament of 1865], in *Papers of the House of Representatives*, 1865–1868, II, pp. 251–276.

15 Kemény, *Iratok a nemzetiségi kérdés történetéhez Magyarországon*, I, pp. 5–9.

16 *Magyar Országos Levéltár, Miniszterelnökség Levéltára* [Hungarian National Archives, Archives of the Prime Minister] 1867 – Ib – 156.

17 *Jelentése a nemzetiségi kérdés tárgyában kiküldött bizottságnak* [Report of the Committee on the Nationalities Question], in *Papers of the House of Representatives*, 1865–1868, VI. p. 129.

18 *Ibid.*, VI. pp. 130–134.

19 *Ibid.*, VI. pp. 249–253.

20 *Ibid.*, VII. pp. 11–15.

21 Kemény, *Iratok a nemzetiségi kérdés történetéhez Magyarországon*, I, pp. 129–132.

22 *Slovenske Noviny*, 1868, No. 27.

23 1868: XXXVIII.tc. [Act 38 of 1868], *Magyar Törvénytár. 1836–1868. évi törvénycikkek* [Collection of Hungarian Laws. Acts of 1836–1868], p. 458.

24 *Rendeletek Tára* [Collection of Regulations], 41 (1907), 2108–2109.

25 *Az 1910. évi június hó 21-ére hirdetett országgyűlés képviselőházának irományai* [Papers of the House of Representatives of the Parliament Convoked on June 21, 1910], XXIII, p. 53.

26 *Mocsáry Lajos válogatott írásai* [Selected Writings of Lajos Mocsáry] (Budapest, 1958), p. 367; Kemény, *Iratok a nemzetiségi kérdés történetéhez Magyarországon*, I, p. 795.

27 Kemény, *Iratok a nemzetiségi kérdés történetéhez Magyarországon*, I, p. 603.

28 Arthur J. May, *The Hapsburg Monarchy 1867–1914* (New York, 1968), pp. 82–83.

4. THE POLITICAL STABILIZATION OF THE COMPROMISE

The people of Hungary welcomed the first major achievements of the Compromise: the restoration of a constitutional system, the appointment of a responsible government, the autonomy of the counties, and freedom of the press, association and assembly. In 1868 the agricultural crop was the highest in the decade, railway construction continued, and economic growth started a seven-year period of expansion (*Gründerzeit*). The response of the population to the political and economic consolidation of the Monarchy and its confidence in the future was indicated by demographic factors. The number of marriages increased by 44,000—that is, by 40 percent—in 1867–1870 as compared to the three years prior to the Compromise. The number of births grew by 41,000—that is, by 8 percent. Following the long period of absolutism, constitutional freedom generated a revival of social and political life. Social organizations, casinos and circles expanded, and there were frequent public meetings.

The Andrássy Government

In the summer of 1866 Francis Joseph had offered the leadership of the future Hungarian government to Ferenc Deák, but he had declined and recommended Gyula Andrássy in his place. The Andrássy government assumed office in February 1867. Andrássy not only served as prime minister, but at the request of Francis Joseph also accepted the post of minister of defense. It is noteworthy that there were two ministers in the government who after 1849 had been condemned to death and hanged in effigy and four who had spent years in exile or prison. But there was only one who had been a member of the Batthyány government in 1848: József Eötvös, who was then and in 1867 minister of education.[1]

The head of the government, Count Gyula Andrássy (1823–1890), was the most prominent Hungarian political leader next to Ferenc Deák in the years of the Compromise. The Andrássy family belonged to a special group of the Hungarian aristocracy. Their properties were located in eastern Hungary (today Slovakia), and therefore they were much less tied to Vienna and the Court than the western Hungarian aristocrats were. Opposition was a family tradition. Since their extensive properties included substantial iron ore deposits they had established foundries in the eighteenth century. The father and brother of Gyula Andrássy were among the most significant metallurgical entrepreneurs of Hungary, but he himself entered politics. He participated as an officer in the fight for freedom, and then in 1849 he accepted a diplomatic post. After the defeat he was condemned to death and hanged in effigy. He lived in exile for eight years, mostly in Paris, although he visited London frequently. With his conspicuous appearance and witty conversation, the young Hungarian aristocrat was a favorite guest of elegant salons in Paris and London. In Paris he was referred to as *beau pendu*. He returned to Hungary in 1857 and entered active politics in 1860. He belonged to the immediate following of Deák and played an important role in the Compromise negotiations. He presented Deák's ideas in a format acceptable to the Court. Francis Joseph confided in him without reservation, and Andrássy was able to get most of his objectives approved by the ruler. Against the resistance of the military leadership, he succeeded in establishing the Hungarian defense force and the termination of the Military Frontier. Deák thought of him as "the providential man donated by divine grace."

The most prominent member of his cabinet, who served as his deputy in his absence, József Eötvös, characterized Andrássy in this manner: "With the exception of Széchenyi I did not know anyone who, in my opinion, deserved the designation man of genius better than Count Andrássy. Others usually attain an understanding with a great deal of effort and exertion, but he attains the same by intuition. But he passionately hates routine official activity, in fact order as such."[2] Eötvös wrote to him in desperation at the time of one of his absences:

> We cannot do anything until you return, because all public issues are in your mind and we are uninformed about very important matters. Your personality alone maintains unity in our ministry and in your absence our ministry is paralyzed, since at such times the opposition is encouraged to weaken our unity. If the king believes that your absence results in instability, he is quite right. Circumstances and your individuality have combined to make you the only representative of the government.[3]

A prominent member of the Andrássy government was József Eötvös, minister of education and the president of the Hungarian Academy of Sciences, an outstanding author of political philosophy as well as a novelist of great merit. Another member was Boldizsár Horváth, the minister of justice, a prominent jurist and a good friend of Deák. He was responsible for the modernization of the judicial system. The economic and financial expert of the government was Menyhért Lónyay, who, like Eötvös, played an important role in the Compromise negotiations. In the spring of 1870 Lónyay was appointed as common minister of finance; his place was taken by the professor of economics Károly Kerkápoly.

After the Compromise *political parties* emerged in Hungary. As in other European countries of the age these parties were not based on a large membership, but they were organizations of elected parliamentary representatives, so-called club parties. Each party maintained a party club, to which only representatives belonged, but in time others, such as sympathizers, were admitted. There were provincial organizations as well, but these were active only at times of elections. The parties established in the 1890s, such as the Catholic People's Party, or the Social Democratic Party, were the first to establish national organizations.

Hungarian politics was not based on social classes or political programs, but on the position of the parties with regard to the

Compromise, meaning the relationship with Austria. The opposition party, which rejected the Compromise, was incapable of assuming the role of government. As a result, the traditional parliamentary practice of a change of government, based on political programs, did not develop in Hungary. At the turn of the century parties with ideological or social programs emerged, but the basic differentiation of politics remained the issue of the Compromise.

The parties of the Compromise period traced their origins to the two parties of the Parliament of 1861. At that time the question was whether members of Parliament should communicate officially with Francis Joseph, who was not the legitimate crowned King of Hungary. The majority of Parliament did not wish to present an address to the ruler, but intended to approve a resolution stating their position to public opinion and the international community. The leader of this *party of resolution* was Count László Teleki and after his death Kálmán Tisza. The minority did not want to reject the possibility of negotiations, even though they did not consider Francis Joseph to be the legitimate ruler, and therefore they decided to respond in an address. The leader of this *address party* was Ferenc Deák. Finally, the resolutionists did not assume the burden of cutting off negotiations and allowed the address party to receive a minimal majority.

In the parliamentary elections of 1865 the party representing Deák's position won by a large majority. Deák and his associates established the *Deák circle* in December 1865; this was the basis of the *Deák Party* or, as it was also called, the center-right. This party approved the Compromise and formed the basic parliamentary support of the Andrássy government. At that time Deák remained the leader of the parliamentary party. He did not join the government. According to Andrássy, he "was the almighty leader of the party." Lónyay wrote in his diary in February 1867 that "he [Deák] is the leader and the ministry will exist and proceed as long as he approves." According to one of the ministers, the minister of the interior "does not dare to make an important decision without Deák's agreement."[4] This situation at times created inconveniences for the government, since its policies not only had to be approved by the ruler, but also had to be cleared with Deák, as the viewpoint of the "old gentleman" was the guideline for representatives of the government party.[5]

The social basis of the Deák Party was primarily the Catholic and western Hungarian propertied nobility. Additional supporters were Magyar property owners of areas with national minority populations, especially in Transylvania and northern Hungary, highly educated intellectuals and the urban upper middle classes benefiting from rapid economic growth after the Compromise. Political leaders returning from exile and high-ranking military officers of 1848–1849 also joined the party. Finally the right wing of the party consisted of conservative aristocrats (Count György Apponyi, Baron Pál Sennyey and others) who played a significant role in the Compromise. The Deák Party represented the ideas of Western European liberalism, which were interpreted and publicized in Hungary by such outstanding associates of Deák as József Eötvös, Ágoston Trefort and Antal Csengery.

The members of the previous *party of resolution* did not accept the Compromise, and formed a club, and then a party led by Kálmán Tisza and Kálmán Ghyczy. They were known as the center-left, based on their parliamentary position. Originally the party defined itself as a loyal opposition and emphasized the point that if it obtained the majority it would modify the Compromise and "assert the principles of democracy that derive the freedom of the state from individual freedom." But its 1868 program, known as the "Bihar theses," reflected a more radical position. It rejected the delegation and common affairs, and demanded an independent Hungarian army, financial and commercial system and diplomacy: in summary it sought to transform the dualist system into one based on the personal union of the common ruler. The social basis of the party was the eastern Hungarian Protestant propertied nobility as well as the economically deprived provincial middle class, especially nobles.

At the end of 1865 a small radical group, the extreme left, seceded from this party. In 1868 it was organized as an independent party, known as the *1848 Party*, later the *National 48 Party*. Its program included an economically independent Hungary tied to Austria only by personal union, the implementation of the April Laws emphasizing democratic principles such as universal suffrage, a secret ballot and free public education, and it promised full equality of rights to the nationalities. They represented in Hungary the principles of the exiled Kossuth. Its representatives were noblemen with small and medium-sized properties and intellectuals, while its electoral supporters were lower-class Magyar social groups, such as peasants from market towns, provincial intellectuals with low incomes and craftsmen. Several prominent exiled politicians of the Kossuth circle (such as Dániel Irányi and Ernő Simonyi) returned to Hungary at the end of 1868 and joined its leadership.

All these parties differed from each other only on the issue of the relationship with Austria; from a programmatic point of view they were all *liberal parties*. The conservatives who joined the Deák Party and formed an independent party in the 1870s emphasized the point that their conservatism differed only in degree and not quality from the liberals: they simply wished to proceed gradually towards the realization of liberal ideals. Conservatism and liberalism at this time meant different approaches to identical political purposes. The common purpose was to eliminate Hungary's backwardness compared to Western Europe, and to adopt Western European political, economic and social institutions in Hungary. This was the predominant political program of the governments in the quarter of a century following the Compromise.

But this liberalism did not make political participation possible for the lower classes, or for three quarters of adult males, and nor did it allow the emergence of democratic self-government at the local level. The patriarchal relationships of the pre-1848 period were the primary forms of contact between the administrative system and the people. Liberal principles were not fully realized in the implementation of the nationalities question either. This was the issue that demonstrated most clearly that Hungarian political opinion deviated from the principles of Deák and Eötvös. For the Hungarian political elite the belief in the integrity and unity of historical Hungary and the Magyar character of the state was an unquestionable principle. Since they believed that the demands and movements of the nationalities endangered this principle, their policies towards the nationalities gradually moved away from liberal principles. One of the chief ideological exponents of the later Liberal Party, Gusztáv Beksics, who passionately defended liberalism against neo-conservatism, wrote as follows in the 1880s: "If liberalism and Hungarian interests were to come into conflict, then I would sacrifice the former without any doubt in the interest of the latter."[6]

In late 1865 180 representatives of Parliament supported Deák; in addition 21 conservatives joined them. The opposition center-left had 94 representatives and the extreme left had 20. After the union with Transylvania most of their representatives also supported the Deák Party, and thus a substantial majority supported the new government.

In the first two years the Andrássy government was faced with movements opposing the Compromise. It was evident that the majority of Magyars did not accept the Compromise, even though it was the achievement of the Magyar liberal elite. In May 1867 Kossuth, still in exile, published an open letter to Deák in which he protested against the Compromise. This was the signal to initiate political opposition. Kossuth was highly popular among the peasants of the Great Plains and the lower middle class and intelligentsia of provincial towns. He symbolized the ideas of the Revolution of 1848 and the fight for freedom. Several counties passed resolutions in his support and several electoral districts elected him to Parliament. The paper of the extreme left, *Magyar Újság*, published the open letters of Kossuth to Deák and his electors. The government initiated court procedures against the editor, László Böszörményi. In several counties with opposition support there was open agitation against the Compromise, taking advantage of the restored autonomy of the counties. The April Laws of 1848 had postponed the transformation of the counties to the subsequent Parliament, but this had not yet been done. Therefore the substantial autonomy of the pre-1848 period was still in force. The counties possessed not only administrative and judicial authority, but also political rights. They were entitled to protest against government directives and to refuse to execute them. Based on these prerogatives, Heves County made the implementation of government directives contingent on the permission of the county assembly and refused to implement a directive of the Ministry of the Interior. At that point the government suspended the autonomy of that county.

Kossuth was highly popular among members of the defense force of 1848–1849. The opposition groups utilized this to organize defense force (*honvéd*) associations and to demand state assistance for the widows and orphans of veterans as well as retirement pensions for the latter. The government, in consideration for the ruler, did not approve it, but the royal couple donated the coronation present of 100,000 gold florins, approved by Parliament, for the benefit of injured veterans and their widows and orphans. The king also ordered that all former professional officers who had been deprived of their entitlements due to their participation in the conflict should receive their pensions. Due to the continuing intervention of Kossuth, the defense force associations demanded an independent Hungarian army. The government prohibited a national demonstration planned for October 6, 1867. Former generals and officers of the revolutionary army (György Klapka, Mór Perczel and István Türr, a former general of Garibaldi) returned to Hungary, assumed leadership of the defense force associations and attempted to pacify the membership. The government prohibited the political activity of the associations, but they were allowed to function as relief associations.

Another political activity of the extreme left was the organization of *democratic circles*, which became very popular among the peasantry. The first circle was formed at the end of 1867 in Pest, and others were organized in early 1868. They sent letters of confidence to Kossuth and petitions protesting against the institution of common affairs to Parliament. The movement was popular primarily among poor peasants of market towns in the Great Plains who demanded "just" grazing land distribution and participation in local government. The government suppressed the movement with force. The center-left party also rejected it, and even the extreme left and Kossuth were concerned. This mass movement had a major impact on the future attitudes of the political leadership. From this time onwards politicians dissatisfied with the Compromise refrained from organizing popular support for agitation against it; they criticized the Compromise and the government only in Parliament.

After the Compromise the primary legislative activity of the government and Parliament was focused on the establishment of a modernized state structure and judicial system, as well as legal guarantees of civil, political and property rights. An equitable tax system was required and the surviving aspects of the old agrarian system needed to be eliminated. On all these issues legislation was enacted. Railway construction with state support was initiated and the urban development of Budapest expanded, also with state assistance. We shall consider the legislative and governmental activities following the Compromise in the next chapter.

According to Ferenc Deák, the Compromise established a favorable basis for the future development of Hungary. It was now Hungary's turn to strengthen its constitution as well as its material and cultural life. József Eötvös agreed that the Compromise had resolved the self-government of the country and the next step was the faithful implementation of the legislation of 1848. He expressed his dissatisfaction with Parliament, when two years after the Compromise there were still too many debates on that issue: "Is it not time to begin the task of reconstruction instead of sterile controversies? Do we see no other legislative task ahead than to argue about the common affairs? Who does not feel and see the urgent need for progress and reform in all areas? We are still engaged in legal debates ignoring the greatest danger threatening our country, which is unquestionably the fact that we have been forcibly retarded for centuries in our development."

Legislative activity to advance reforms was in many regards slowed on account of arguments on the legal issues of the Compromise initiated by the opposition. Even the government party was involved in this activity. According to Minister of Finance Károly Kerkápoly, "There are hardly 25 or 30 people who are doing their share of legislative activity and are committed to their vocation. The majority consider parliamentary activity to be a form of leisure."[7] Even Deák had difficulties with the majority of his party, and expressed dissatisfaction. His closest associate Antal Csengery wrote as follows in the summer of 1870: "Deák was shouted down in the Deák club as in an election battle. The old man realized what I have said repeatedly: that he no longer had a party, only 40–50 associates. This is a reactionary rabble and we cannot use them to pursue a genuine constitutional system or real reforms."[8]

At the end of 1868 the mandate of the Parliament establishing the Compromise expired. The elections of 1869 were the first in Hungary that involved real party conflicts. The Deák Party suffered some losses, but even so it won 59 percent of the parliamentary seats. The 48 Party made major gains with 52 seats and so did the center-left with 112 seats. These elections demonstrated clearly that the government majority was based on areas with nationality or mixed populations. In the Great Plains the government percentage was only 28 percent, while in western Hungary it was 50 percent, and thus in Magyar areas the government party failed to get the majority vote. This was a typical pattern for subsequent elections as well. In elections between 1869 and 1910 opposition candidates won 60 percent of the seats in Magyar areas.

The Dissolution of the Deák Party and Formation of the Liberal Party

In early 1871 József Eötvös died, in June Boldizsár Horváth resigned, and in November Andrássy was appointed as common minister of foreign affairs. The departure of three such prominent political leaders weakened the government party considerably. In addition, due to illness, Deák retired: at first gradually and then finally in the autumn of 1873.

Andrássy's successor as prime minister was Menyhért Lónyay. He was not popular, not even in the party. His qualifications were respected, but personally he inspired no affection. He was highly qualified as a financial expert and businessman, but the press and the opposition suspected him of corruption due to his increasing wealth. This was a period of reported cases of corruption throughout the country, especially related to railway construction. Therefore conflict of interest legislation was a frequent agenda item. In order to strengthen his party, Lónyay initiated negotiations with Croatian and nationality representatives, but it soon became evident that these proved to be unsuccessful, since the concessions offered were not satisfactory. In preparation for the elections of 1872 Lónyay introduced a new electoral law. It renewed the electoral law of 1848, but restricted voting rights by excluding those who had failed to pay their tax obligations. The 48 Party decided to prevent its enactment and organized continuous parliamentary debates (as a means of obstruction) against the bill, supported also by the center-left. This was a favorite technique of the opposition throughout this period. The Deák Party did not support the bill, since it did not wish to restrict freedom of speech in Parliament.

A new party emerged in the elections of 1872: the *Reform Party*, organized by members of the center-left who realized that continuous discussion of the Compromise issue was unproductive and decided to support the enactment of liberal reforms in Parliament. During the elections there were serious abuses and violent methods used by the two large parties. The Deák Party won the elections with 61 percent of the votes, but the support of the 48 Party declined sharply to 35 parliamentary seats. The Reform Party obtained three seats, and nine nationality candidates were also elected.

At the end of 1872 Lónyay resigned under pressure from his fellow ministers in the light of serious charges of corruption. His successor, supported by Deák, was József Szlávy, minister of agriculture, industry and commerce. During and after the elections the process of dissolution affected both large parties. In the Deák Party the conservatives under Pál Sennyey initiated a new party formation, while another group formed under Lónyay and his associates. It became evident that the center-left would not obtain the majority, and therefore one of their leaders, Kálmán Ghyczy, recommended support for the delegations and the institution of common affairs, along with union with the "better elements of the Deák Party." In 1873 the press reported the possibility of union or coalition between the two parties.

1873 was a year of disasters. Poor harvests in preceding years, drought and floods produced famine in some areas and a cholera epidemic nationally. In May the decline of the Vienna and Pest stock markets led to a major economic crisis, including the bankruptcy of numerous banks and industrial companies. The economic growth period following the Compromise was thus terminated for several years. In addition, the State Treasury neared financial bankruptcy.

The first independent Hungarian budget had a small surplus in 1868, but in the following years the deficit increased. Between 1868 and 1873 expenditures increased from 147.5 million to 251.2 million florins, by 104 million. In contrast with the 70 percent increase of expenditures, revenues increased only by 18 percent or 28 million florins (from 154.1 to 181.7 million). Loans were necessary. The reason for the rapid increase in expenditures was the necessity of expanding the administrative and economic infrastructure of the country. The financial committee of Parliament stated the following in its report of 1872: "The restoration of the constitution required major investments in all areas of state activity. There was a major need to initiate investments that would enable the country to replace the stagnation of past centuries with substantial material progress."[9] The expansion of a modernized state administration required significant expenditures. The number of state officials increased between 1868 and 1873 from 11,000 to 26,000. The organization of the defense force and the modernization of public education also required substantial funding. State expenditures for public administration, judicial services, the defense force and public instruction between 1868 and 1873 more than doubled, increasing from 23 million to 51 million florins. The annual average spent on investments was 27 million. Expenditures of state-owned enterprises increased from 25 million to 59 million florins in five years, while interest security for railway construction was 16 million in 1874. In addition there were comparatively stable but major expenditures for the common affairs (30 million annually), land redemption annuities (16 million) and Austrian state debt contributions (30–31 million).

Increased revenues could not keep up with the rapid growth of expenditures, since the major source was tax revenue, the growth of which was limited. Therefore investments were usually covered by long-term loans. Since neither of the two states of the Monarchy used the practice of the issue of paper money without coverage, the usual source of credit was state bond issue on the international market. Placement of the bonds was arranged by Austrian and Western European bank consortia. State loans of 30 million florins in 1871 and 54 million florins in 1872 were used to finance the deficit.

In the summer of 1873 the Treasury approached financial incapacity. It was impossible to collect taxes due to the cholera epidemic, the Treasury's reserves were depleted, the government was unable to honor contracts with construction companies, and at the end of July the minister of finance was unable to find funding to pay the salaries of state officials on August 1. In early August the Credit Bank and the Land Credit Institute, which survived the crisis without major losses, assisted the government. In subsequent months the Hungarian state was able to obtain short-term credit in Vienna, Berlin and London. At the end of the year a five-year loan to the value of 153 million florins (£ 13 million) was arranged. Almost all new investments after 1873 were cancelled, and proceeds from the loans were used to supplement the budget and to repay earlier loans. It was characteristic of the situation that after the resignation of Minister of Finance Kerkápoly in December 1873 no one was willing to accept the post. In the end Prime Minister Szlávy assumed its direction.

At this time members of the Deák Party and the center-left reconsidered their confrontation on the legal issues of the Compromise and proposed two alternatives: formation of a coalition government or fusion of the two parties. An additional factor that gave rise to this new attitude was the fact that the dualist system had been stabilized both internally and internationally, the common institutions proved to be functional, and therefore many did not see much sense in the confrontation. In addition, the center-left would be unable to form a government in the light of its program of opposition to the Compromise. In November 1873 one of the leaders of the center-left, Kálmán Ghyczy, and several associates resigned from the party and established a new center party for the purpose of preparing the fusion of the two large parties. At the same time, Kálmán Tisza was willing to consider participation in a coalition government, while retaining in principle the party program. Negotiations for a coalition started in early 1874, but failed. Prime Minister Szlávy resigned. His successor was István Bittó, chair of the Lower House Ghyczy joined the government. Bittó was successful in getting the new electoral law, which had failed two years earlier, approved.

In February 1875 Tisza made a significant statement in the course of the budget debate. He stated that the principal issue was the grave economic situation of the country, which had to be resolved, and so the issue of the Compromise had to be put aside. This meant that he postponed the confrontation for an indefinite period: as was said, "he put the Bihar program on the hanger." This removed the last impediment to the fusion of the Deák Party and the center-left on March 1, 1875. The new government party was called the *Liberal Party*. The fusion was rather smooth, since the social basis of both parties was identical: the provincial nobility that had medium-sized properties and held county offices. Deák approved the party and was the first to join. The Bittó government resigned. It was succeeded by the government of Béla Wenckheim, in which the center-left received three ministries.

Some members of the center-left refused to join the new party, and therefore they resigned one year prior to the fusion and formed a new party with the *48 Party* in 1874, headed by Lajos Mocsáry. Its name was the *Forty-Eight Independence Party*. Its program stated the following: "Hungary should be an independent Hungarian state, which should govern its affairs free of any alien intervention and should possess full independence along with public administration in military matters, financial matters, foreign relations and economic affairs." From that time up to World War I the Independence Party was the leading party of the left opposition. Its representatives were equally members of the propertied nobility, but before 1900 there were no aristocrats among them. This party was highly successful in Magyar election districts. Several representatives remained in the original 48 Party until 1884: at that time they too joined the Independence Party. The expanded party was renamed the *Independence and 48 Party* and its chairman was Dániel Irányi.

There was also a right-wing opposition party. This was the conservative aristocratic faction of the Deák Party, which did not want to join the center-left. It separated after the fusion and formed the *Right Opposition* under Pál Sennyey. Ferenc Deák approved this formation; he welcomed the formation of parties on the basis of ideological programs. Several representatives of the Liberal Party who disagreed with the new economic compromise joined the Right Opposition, renamed *United Opposition* in 1878, which accepted the Compromise and the institution of common affairs, but was interested in asserting the rights of Hungary in economic and military areas. Count Albert Apponyi replaced Sennyey after his retirement. The party was renamed again, first to be known as the *Moderate Opposition*, and then in 1892 as the *National Party*. The latter name indicated that the party wanted to move the Compromise in the direction of national interests: "We want national policies on the basis of the Compromise of 1867." Their program called for national symbols in common institutions, primarily the common army, such as the flag, the coat-of-arms and the Hungarian language.

As minister of the interior Tisza organized the elections of 1875, which resulted in a major victory for the Liberal Party, winning a majority of 80 percent. The Party elected 332 parliamentary representatives, while the Independence Party received only 36 and the Right Opposition 21. The Liberals were also victorious in the Magyar districts; this was the last time prior to the turn of the century that this happened. On October 20, 1875, the king appointed Tisza as prime minister. This event signaled the stabilization of the dualist system in Hungarian domestic politics. Stabilization is also indicated by the fact that while five governments replaced each other between 1867 and 1875, Kálmán Tisza held the office of prime minister for 15 years, the longest period for anyone in Hungarian history. The Liberal Party held governmental power for 30 years, until 1905.

The Government of Kálmán Tisza. The Stable Period of Dualism

The most urgent issue facing the new government was the solution of the catastrophic budget deficit. Kálmán Széll, the new minister of finance, managed to stabilize the financial situation using several credit, tax and austerity policies. He converted the previously assumed short-term state loans to more favorable annuity loans. Ministers of finance of the 1880s introduced economic management and new taxes (mainly indirect taxes), which measurably reduced the budget deficit. In the 1880s the budget situation gradually improved: by 1888–1889 the deficit was reduced to a minimum and in 1890 there was a surplus.

Another difficult issue concerned the commercial and customs union. One month following his appointment Tisza cancelled the union in order to renegotiate it with more favorable terms for Hungary on three points: payment of consumption taxes to be paid not in the country of production, but in that of consumption, raising tariffs on the import of products not produced in the Monarchy and reorganization of the Austrian National Bank on the basis of parity and dualism. Sugar and beer consumed in Hungary were produced mostly in Austria, and the consumption tax was paid to the Austrian government, incurring a loss of an estimated 6–13 million florins in tax revenue to Hungary. Raising the tariff would reduce the common expenditures for Hungary, since tariff revenue was used to finance common expenses. Since imported products for which tariffs were paid were primarily consumed in Austria, the Austrians opposed raising them; instead they supported higher industrial tariffs, which were in turn opposed by Hungary.

Negotiations continued for more than a year. At the end of February 1877 an agreement was reached, but it accepted only parts of Tisza's agenda. The National Bank was renamed and reorganized as the Austro-Hungarian Bank, but the principle of parity was realized only partially. Tariffs were raised, but the consumption tax modification was turned down. In return for higher industrial tariffs Austria agreed to raise agricultural tariffs. As a result of disappointments with the new commercial and customs union, several dozen representatives left the Liberal Party and joined the Right Opposition, renamed in April 1878 the United Opposition.

The insurrection in Bosnia-Herzegovina in 1875 and the corresponding "Eastern question" gave rise to new domestic political crises in both parts of the Monarchy. Hungarian public opinion had been concerned for several decades with the expansion of Russia in the Balkans, and in the Russo-Turkish war it supported Turkey. University students of Pest demonstrated in favor of Turkey and presented an honorary sword to the Turkish commander victorious in the Serbian–Turkish conflict. The opposition parties supported the continued integrity of the Ottoman Empire after the Russian victory and demanded that the Monarchy declare war on Russia. In Budapest and provincial cities pro-Turkish and anti-Russian demonstrations took place. When the Congress of Berlin authorized the Austro-Hungarian Monarchy to occupy Bosnia-Herzegovina,

Hungarian public opinion protested against the occupation, since it meant a substantial increase of Slavic populations in the Monarchy. But in Croatia demonstrations took place in favor of the integration and annexation to Croatia of the two provinces. The occupation of Bosnia-Herzegovina required a military operation and a significant loss of life in combat. Pacification lasted for several years. The occupation increased public expenditures significantly and threatened to undermine the consolidated budget achieved after years of effort.

Tisza survived the crisis generated by the new economic compromise and the Eastern question in spite of the fact that the government party lost numerous parliamentary seats in the elections of 1878. It lost nearly 100 seats and its majority was reduced from 80 percent to 58 percent. Both the left and right opposition won additional seats, increasing their representation to 76 and 75 respectively. In 1877 and 1878 Tisza resigned twice, but the ruler appointed him as prime minister again. On some issues his own party members voted against him, refrained from voting or were absent. In some instances he was sustained by just a few votes.

In the other half of the Monarchy events took a different course. In the elections of 1879 the German liberals who had been in power since the Compromise were voted out of office as a result of the domestic crisis generated by the occupation. The new government was a neo-conservative clerical coalition of German, Czech and Polish aristocrats and Czech middle-class representatives, led by Count Eduard Taaffe, known as the "iron ring." Taaffe governed for almost 15 years, as did Tisza, until 1893. By 1880 Tisza's position was stabilized as well.

In the 1880s both parts of the Monarchy experienced a period of stability, an age of economic and cultural development. The political viability of the dualist system was generally accepted. The only temporary disturbances were anti-Semitic demonstrations in both parts of the Monarchy in 1882–1883 and Croatian national movements in 1883 and an armed uprising in the Military Frontier. Under the impact of anti-Semitic movements in Europe, especially in Germany, similar movements took place in Hungary in 1882–1883. When a young girl disappeared in a village along the River Tisza in the spring of 1882 the rumor spread that she was the victim of Jewish ritual murder. The trial became a national event. Since her body was found and it came to light that she had drowned in the Tisza, the court dismissed the charges and acquitted the defendants. After the trial in 1883 Győző Istóczy founded the *National Anti-Semitic Party*, which had the declared purpose of "destroying Jewish power and the neutralization of Jewish influence." In the elections of 1884 the party gained 16, in 1887 11 parliamentary seats. The party divided into two groups and then disappeared. Apparently Hungarian liberal politics were not favorable soil for radical anti-Semitism at that time.

Kálmán Tisza (1830–1902) was the descendant of an eastern Hungarian Reformed noble family with large properties. His father was commissioned by the Habsburg government to break the reform opposition of his county in the 1840s, but the son supported the fight for freedom of 1848–1849. He played a prominent role in the political movements of 1859–1861, which established his popularity. For ten years he opposed the Compromise based on common affairs and was committed to personal union, but as he experienced the stability and viability of the dualist system he realized the futility of further opposition and assumed a leading role in the maintenance and reinforcement of the system. He recruited into the Liberal Party the aristocracy, the large and medium-sized property-owning nobility, and the emerging financial and business elite: basically the representatives of the upper and middle classes of Hungarian society who had an interest in maintaining and consolidating the dualist system.

Tisza was a natural parliamentary politician and party leader, a master political tactician. He was an excellent debater; no one could compete with him. His ideas were based on common sense and practical realities; he was not committed to principles. Personally he was not interested in material gain, but he overlooked the questionable practices of his associates and used material and political favors for strengthening his party following. Although his mother and wife were countesses, he refused to accept the title of count from the king. He remained committed to liberal principles, especially in economic life. He repudiated the anti-liberal programs of the right-wing opposition and neo-conservatism of the 1880s. He forcefully rejected anti-Semitism. He was less liberal in his approach to the nationalities question: he attempted to restrict the political activities of nationality politicians nationally and at the county level. The main purpose of his policies, in addition to the maintenance of dualism, was the expansion of the "Hungarian national state." In his conception this state was a Western European type of liberal state, where non-Magyars were free to develop their language and culture, but had to acknowledge the political supremacy of Magyars.

It was clear to him that he could achieve these purposes only with a strong parliamentary majority and a well-organized, disciplined government party. The governing party representatives carried out the directives of the "general" without reservation. The former were popularly known as "mameluks." In order to guarantee the parliamentary majority he was not at all reluctant to intervene in the electoral process using administrative methods. He increased the influence of the government in the county administration and limited the autonomy of counties and communities. During most of his tenure he directed the Ministry of the Interior, enabling him to exercise personal control over public administration, and to supervise county and local administration through his appointed administrators, the police system, to oversee associations and public demonstrations. He also controlled national elections. This office also controlled the newly (1881) established gendarmerie. According to Albert Apponyi, Tisza had developed in county and state administration "a discretionary governmental power not excessively limited by the guarantees of the rule of law."[10]

On the tenth anniversary of his tenure as prime minister, Tisza evaluated his activity as follows: There are ages when "the nation feels that its mission is not to progress rapidly, not to create spectacular things, but to construct the building of the state progressively from grain of sand to grain of sand, from brick to brick. Since my non-spectacular qualifications have enabled me to perform everyday, continuous, by no means brilliant, but beneficial activities, in my view that is the reason for the confidence of my king as well as of the majority of the nation."[11]

The legislative achievement of the Tisza government constitutes a very significant role in the history of modern Hungary. It is true that Tisza converted the government party into an obedient "voting machine," but he attempted to attract outstanding experts to the government and the ministries. With their contributions and the parliamentary majority, he coordinated the enactment of a great deal of legislation, which established a modernized economic system and the legal, institutional and educational foundations of civil society in Hungary. During his tenure of 15 years 650 laws were enacted. The Deák Party had defined the principles of the liberal state and the legal system; under Tisza these principles were elaborated in detail. To mention only the most important: legislation on commerce, public health, forestry, water development, veterinary health, secondary and higher education, railway construction and state support of industrial development. By the end of the 1880s the state budget was consolidated and balanced with a surplus. In the preparation and realization of these achievements Tisza's associates were his ministers of finance Kálmán Széll and Sándor Wekerle, subsequently both prime ministers, Gábor Baross the dynamic minister of transport, industry and commerce and his state secretary Sándor Matlekovits, the jurist Tivadar Pauler as minister of justice and Ágoston Trefort, who served for 16 years as minister of education.

The preparation of these laws followed an established process. Officials of the ministries prepared proposals on the basis of Western European precedents, and then coordinated roundtable discussions by outside experts and requested the opinions of chambers of commerce and interest groups regarding economic proposals. The prepared proposals were then reviewed by parliamentary committees, and then submitted to Parliament.

Tisza's position was undermined in 1889 on the occasion of the debate on the defense issue. The Balkan question and the tense relationship with Russia focused attention on the unsatisfactory quantity and unprepared condition of the armed forces in the case of war. Therefore the modernization of the common armed forces was initiated in the 1880s. While reorganization could be accomplished with the authority of the ruler, the expansion of the armed forces required the approval of the two Parliaments.

At the end of 1888 the Tisza government submitted a bill on the modernization of the armed forces, which led to a stormy parliamentary debate early in 1889. The opposition objected to the proposal, which would change the traditional prerogative of Parliament to approve increased military conscription at ten-year intervals by stating military requirements without any time limitation. The second objectionable point was the provision that those volunteer reservists who failed the German-language officers' test would have to serve one additional year. The opposition demanded "national concessions," and the use of the Hungarian language in the armed forces, in return for approval. The debate also involved stormy street demonstrations. University students protested in a national demonstration. They would be primarily affected by the German-language test. On the initiative of Tisza, Francis Joseph relented: the traditional practice of approving military requirements at ten-year intervals was restored and the officers' test could be taken in Hungarian and Croatian as well. Although the debate did not lead to the fall of the government, the obstruction that it caused, along with street demonstrations, undermined its position with the Emperor and the military leadership.

The debate on the defense issue demonstrated that Tisza was politically "depleted," as the saying went. The "general" realized that as well, but he wanted to retire as a "national hero" by using a proper occasion. Such an occasion arose in connection with another controversy, the question of the citizenship of Lajos Kossuth. According to the law on citizenship of 1879, each Hungarian citizen living abroad lost his/her citizenship unless the person requested its continuation by appearing at an Austro-Hungarian consular office. The Independence and 48 Parties requested modification of the act, since it was obvious that Kossuth would not appear at any consular office. Tisza promised the modification, but when Kossuth stated in an open letter that "I never considered myself nor will I consider myself in the future to be the subject of Francis Joseph, Austrian Emperor and King of Hungary." the Liberal Party and the ministers of the government reversed their decision, not wishing to provoke the ruler. But Tisza insisted on the modification against the unanimous opposition of his ministers and the parliamentary opposition. At the Council of Ministers on March 8, 1890, chaired by the ruler he was voted down by his ministers. On the following day he resigned.

His resignation signaled the beginning of a new age in the history of dualism, in spite of the fact that the Liberal Party remained in power for 15 more years. "With the resignation of the 'general' an age came to an end that witnessed the establishment of a liberal state and reforms of various dimensions were enacted with the consent of the majority of the ruling classes. The age of modernization when the government attempted to introduce contemporary European institutions now ended. From this time onwards continuation of modernization and further reforms would only be possible by dissolving the coalition of landowners and capitalists, by policies directed against the political and economic power of landowners."[12]

The Austrian liberals realized this clearly; they—possibly the only ones in the Monarchy—were sorry to see Tisza's departure. This is how they visualized the start of the new age: "Soon we shall see a change to the right, to agrarian oligarchy, to the destruction of liberal principles, and to feudal-aristocratic domination, which will appear in modern dress, occasionally mixed with a social drop of oil."[13]

Notes

1 Éva Somogyi states appropriately that the Austrians were envious, at the time of the Compromise, "that Hungarian political leaders were charismatic national leaders who enjoyed respect independent of Imperial favor or official position." She adds that the "Austro-German liberal leaders had a lesser reputation even in Austria than Deák or Andrássy." Éva Somogyi, "A dualizmus államrendszere" [The State System of Dualism], in András Gerő, ed., *A Monarchia kora – ma* [The Age of the Monarchy—Today] (Budapest, 2007), p. 115.

2 József Eötvös, *Levelek* [Letters] (Budapest, 1976), pp. 601–602.

3 *Ibid.*, pp. 612, 614.

4 From a section of the memoirs of Boldizsár Horváth: Manó Kónyi, ed., *Deák Ferenc beszédei. 5: 1867–1868* [Speeches of Ferenc Deák, volt 5: 1867–1868] (Budapest, 1898), p. 348.

5 Kálmán Mikszáth, the popular novelist and journalist of the age, wrote as follows: "In the time of Count Gyula Andrássy there were two courts in Hungary: one was the Vienna Burg, the other the hotel 'The Queen of England.' If the prime minister wanted to accomplish something, first he had to travel to Vienna and request approval and then he had to consult the old Ferenc Deák, the other center of power, in 'The Queen of England.' After that approval the fight could start in the ministerial council." Kálmán Mikszáth, *A tisztelt Ház* [The Honorable House] (Budapest, n.d.), p. 27.

6 [Gusztáv Beksics] Timoleon, *A legújabb politikai divat* [The Latest Political Fashion] (Budapest, 1884), p. 11.

7 Gusztáv Gratz, A *dualizmus kora. Magyarország története 1867–1918* [The Age of Dualism. The History of Hungary, 1867–1918], vol. 1 (Budapest, 1934), p. 31.

8 Lóránt Csengery, ed., *Csengery Antal hátrahagyott iratai és feljegyzései* [The Posthumous Papers and Notes of Antal Csengery] (Budapest, 1928), pp. 315–316.

9 *Az állandó pénzügyi bizottság általános jelentése az 1873-ik évi államköltségvetés tárgyában* [General Report of the Permanent Financial Committee on the State Budget of 1873] *Az 1872. évi szeptember hó 1-jére hirdetett országgyűlés képviselőházának*

irományai [The Papers of the House of Representatives of the Parliament Convoked on September 1, 1872] II (Buda, 1873), p. 275.

10 Albert Apponyi, *Emlékirataim. Ötven Év. Ifjúkorom – Huszonöt év az ellenzéken* [My Memoirs. Fifty Years. My Youth—Twenty-Five Years in Opposition] (Budapest, 1922), p. 138.

11 *Tisza Kálmán miniszterelnökségének tizedik évfordulója 1885. XI. 29.* [The Tenth Anniversary of the Prime Ministership of Kálmán Tisza, 29. 11. 1885] (Budapest, 1885).

12 Zoltán Szász, "A konzervatív liberalizmus kora. A dualista rendszer konszolidált időszaka (1875–1890)" [The Age of Conservative Liberalism. The Consolidated Period of the Dualist System (1875–1890)], in Endre Kovács and László Katus, eds., *Magyarország története 1848–1890* [The History of Hungary 1848–1890] (Budapest, 1987), p. 1331.

13 *Ibid.*

5. ESTABLISHMENT OF THE HUNGARIAN CONSTITUTIONAL AND POLITICAL SYSTEM

In the decades after the Compromise the Hungarian Parliament and government considered their primary purpose to be the establishment of a modern European state structure based on the rule of law. There was common agreement on this question. In his address from the throne opening the Parliament of 1869, as King of Hungary, Francis Joseph outlined the objectives and programs of this legislative activity, which was in fact the government program:

> Your responsibility is to focus the energy of the nation on the great task of internal transformation, to complete the process interrupted by the conflicts of 1848–1849, to break away from the traditions of the past, which obstruct modern progress, to transform national institutions according to the requirements of the present age, to develop the intellectual and material resources of the nation to enable it to fulfill its destiny as a guardian and instrument of Western culture as it takes its place among modern states.[1]

The Andrássy government had established the basic elements of the modern state, and the Tisza government continued the process during its 15-year tenure.

The Heritage of the "Constitution" of 1848

The April Laws of 1848 transformed the old, pre-1848 Hungarian state into a modern constitutional monarchy with a parliamentary system and a responsible government. This legislation was restored by the Compromise. The April Laws abolished serfdom, seigniorial services and the judicial authority of landlords. They enacted the principles of taxation of all classes, freedom of the press, and the equal status of recognized religious denominations. These laws were crunched out in three weeks, and therefore they stated only the principles, and failed to address important issues or did so only temporarily. The representative Parliament was to work out the detailed implementation, but in the light of the conflict with Austria there was no time for that during the Revolution.

As a result of these circumstances of revolution and conflict, the 1848 legislation failed to state the principle of the legal equality of citizens, in spite of the fact that this principle had been a basic premise of the 1847 reform program and the purpose of the 1848 legislation was "to unite all the Hungarian people in a common legal system and common interests." The latter principle and the declaration of the equality before the law were equally absent in the April Laws. In one of the laws of 1848, nevertheless, relating to the union with Transylvania, there is a statement to the effect that Hungary was prepared to accept those laws of Transylvania that "are favorable to legal equality." Contemporaries regarded it as evident that after the victory of "the legal revolution" all citizens had equal rights. Two months later the Transylvanian Parliament in its act on the union with Hungary confirmed this principle: "Since the legal equality of all residents is stated and implemented in Hungary, the same principle is hereby recognized for all residents of this homeland without regard for national, language and religious differences as an eternal and unchangeable principle, and all previous laws contrary to it are hereby abolished."[2] The Hungarian Parliament made a similar statement on the fiftieth anniversary of the April Laws in 1898: "The April Laws extended constitutional rights to all classes of the nation, and legal equality as well as the principles of political and civil liberties were implemented."[3] In the early twentieth century a Hungarian legal expert stated the following: "The principle of legal equality as a mandatory proposition is not stated in our country, but it is a consequence of the spirit of the 1848 legislation."[4]

The preceding statements characterize the Hungarian "constitution." In contrast to the written European constitutions, Hungarian legal principles were not codified in a unified constitution after the

Compromise, as was done in the December Constitution in Austria comprising five basic laws. Although contemporaries and historians frequently referred and refer to the April Laws as the constitution of 1848, these laws cannot be considered to be a real and complete constitution. The codification of the basic rights of citizens and the judicial principles of modern states are not included. This indicates that the Hungarian legal system had preserved the continuity of its historical development of several centuries. In his study on Hungarian constitutional law prior to the Compromise, Ferenc Deák wrote as follows: "Our constitution is a historical constitution: it has changed in relationship to national needs and the requirements of the age with regard to the rights of the nation and the rights of the king."[5] The Andrássy government also declared in 1868 that the Compromise was an integral part of the Hungarian constitution, as were the April Laws. The kings of Hungary, including Francis Joseph, took the oath to observe this conception of the constitution at their coronation: "We shall preserve the rights, privileges, liberty, entitlements, laws and ancient approved customs of the jurisdictions, and the ecclesiastical and secular residents of Hungary and its associated countries. We shall preserve unimpaired the rights, constitution, legal independence and territorial integrity of Hungary and its associated countries." The act on court jurisdiction of 1868 stated this as follows: "The judge is required to act and render judgments according to legally originated and declared regulations and according to customs with legal validity." Legal experts of the Compromise period preferred to compare the Hungarian "historical constitution," which included customary law, to the British constitution.

The April Laws specified the composition, jurisdiction and operation of the legislature and the government in detail. Law 3 of 1848 stated the following: "His Majesty shall exercise executive authority in all civil, ecclesiastical, budgetary and military affairs exclusively only through the Hungarian ministry."

Legislation and Government

The king was required to convoke the bicameral Parliament annually. Representatives to the Lower House were elected triannually; in 1886 this was changed to five years. The electoral laws of 1848 remained in force to the end of the Monarchy. There was a separate electoral law in Transylvania. In fact, there was a difference in the proportion of voters between Hungary and Transylvania. In 1910 6.3 percent of the population had the right to vote in Hungary, while in Transylvania the proportion was 3.1 percent. The electoral law of 1848 was based on qualifications of property and/or income; this was the general practice in all European countries. Those who had voting rights before 1848 retained those rights to their death, but they could not pass them on to their descendants. Intellectuals had voting rights independent of their property status. The electoral law of 1874 was based on the law of 1848, but specified property and income qualifications in greater detail and based them on direct taxes paid to the state. Those who owed tax payments were excluded from the vote, and thus the number of voters was reduced significantly. About one quarter of the male population over 20 had voting rights. In the dualist period there was an open ballot. Electoral districts were distributed inequitably. After the integration of the Military Frontier there were 413 electoral districts in Hungary proper, without Croatia. While voting rights were not expanded in Hungary between 1848 and 1913, in Austria suffrage was gradually expanded and in 1907 universal suffrage and the secret ballot were introduced.

In the dualist period in Hungary, at least to the turn of the century, politics was regarded as the special occupation of gentlemen, that is, of the urban and rural elite. At the same time in 1910 62 percent of the voters were peasants (30 percent were peasants owning less than 14 acres of land) and 16 percent were artisans or retail merchants. In political institutions, in Parliament and public administration, there were only aristocrats and propertied noblemen. Contemporary opinion held that the right to vote involved the ability to form an independent political opinion. This was the reason for the use of property and income qualifications, but no intellectual qualifications such as literacy were required, and thus in 1910 16 percent of the voters were illiterate. In 1904 57 percent of the voters stated that their native language was Hungarian. The new electoral law of 1913 increased voters by 50 percent and provided voting rights to more than 200,000 industrial workers and 150,000 agricultural workers. However, no elections were held on this basis, due to World War I. Voting in this period was done not on the basis of party, but directly for individual persons. Nevertheless, parties selected the candidates who propagated party programs.

The Upper House of Parliament preserved its traditional, aristocratic structure for some years after the Compromise: membership consisted of the adult male members of aristocratic families (princes, counts and barons) and the Catholic and Greek Orthodox bishops. The Upper House was reformed in 1885, as a result of which adult male aristocrats could retain their membership if they paid a minimum of 3,000 florins (£ 250) direct taxes. County administrators were excluded, and the representation of the Catholic Church was reduced, but the bishops of the Protestant Churches and their chief administrators were included. The king was entitled to appoint 50 members on the recommendation of the government. In this manner prominent persons of the economy and science became members. In 1890 out of the 369 members 278 were aristocrats, including some who had received their titles recently, and 49 were ecclesiastical leaders.

Laws of conflict of interest of 1875 and 1901 excluded from the Lower House state, county, city and community officials, entrepreneurs under contract to the state, and executives and officials of such enterprises.

The king set the time, convoked, dissolved or adjourned the sessions of Parliament and usually opened the new session with a speech from the throne. Dissolution or adjournment was subject to the availability of sufficient time for the next session to review the budget for the following year. Legislative bills proposed by the government had to be authorized by the king in advance of their submission. Bills approved by Parliament required the signature of the king to be certified as laws.

The government exercised executive authority at the highest level. It was responsible to Parliament. The king appointed the prime minister usually from the membership of the majority party. There was only one exception: in 1905. The prime minister proposed the members of the ministry, but the king appointed them. There were eight ministers: of the interior, justice, finance, education and religion, transport and public works, agriculture, industry and commerce (the latter three making up one ministry until 1889), defense, the minister of the ruler, and the minister for Croatia–Slavonia after the Croatian Compromise. In 1889 a reorganization took place: a separate Ministry of Agriculture was created, and transport, industry and commerce were combined. In 1870 the Office of Financial Control was established.

Modernization of Public Administration

The most important and most sensitive issue of reforming public administration was the transformation of local government and county government: essentially this concerned the relationship between the central government and the county government. In the period of the Compromise the debate on this issue was renewed. This had been an important controversy in the 1840s. Before 1848 the county had played an important political role: it had defended the Hungarian constitution against centralization and absolutism from Vienna. This was possible because it exercised not only administrative and judicial jurisdiction, but also political functions. It was entitled to disagree with government directives, protest against them and refuse to execute them. After the Compromise in the debate between municipalists and centralists the former insisted on retaining the traditional jurisdiction of the county, appropriately modernized, while the centralists contended that the county system was not compatible with the parliamentary system and responsible government. Since the Deák Party and the Liberal Party agreed with the centralist viewpoint, the reform of the county system was designed to reduce county prerogatives and increase the executive functions of the central government.

Shortly after taking office the Andrássy government proceeded to reform the county system. No new elections were held in the counties; the surviving members of the county committees elected in 1861 were convoked as the legitimate county assemblies. In cities and free districts elections were held for the representative assemblies on the basis of the electoral law of 1848. The modern tax system introduced in the 1850s and the separation of judicial and administrative functions had deprived the counties of some of their functions in the period before 1848. The new government assumed authority to collect taxes and in 1869 the judicial authority of the county was transferred to the newly organized state court system. The law of 1870 on "the organization of jurisdictions" was considered to be a "compromise between the state and the county." In this period there were two types of jurisdiction in Hungary: the county and the city with a special status, which meant that such cities were not subordinated to the county, but had equal rights with the county.

The self-government of the jurisdictions was retained, but the power of the government was expanded primarily by the increased authority of government-appointed county leaders, the high sheriffs. This was necessary, because the jurisdictions performed state administrative functions at the middle level. The political rights of the counties were retained, with limitations. They could still argue about public issues and submit their viewpoints to other counties, the government and Parliament in the form of petitions and statements. Their traditional right of resistance survived to some extent: they could submit protests against controversial government regulations to the competent ministry once, but they had to execute them if they were repeated. There was only one occasion of a nationwide protest: in 1905, when the majority of the counties refused to execute regulations of the caretaker government appointed by the king.

The autonomy of the jurisdictions was in the hands of the jurisdiction committees of 120–600 members, depending on the size of the population. These took the place of the former county assembly. The committee elected every six years the officials of the county or the city autonomy. The leader of the county autonomy was the deputy high sheriff (*alispán*) (while that of the city autonomy was the mayor). One half of the members of the committee were elected by adult males with the right to vote; the other half was made up of the top taxpayers of the county (virilists). Intellectuals were delegated by doubling their tax contributions. This system was utilized in cities and communities, but many members of the Deák Party opposed it, including Deák himself. However, Andrássy supported it.

Counties were entitled to issue statutes and to levy taxes for their expenditure. At first they had their own police system. The newly established administrative system upheld the practice of utilizing locally elected officials for local administration with the exception of tax management. The jurisdictions were also responsible for establishing election districts and for supervising the preparation and management of elections. In order to balance the substantial autonomy of jurisdictions the new system provided the government-appointed high sheriff (*főispán*) with extensive authority. He presided over the jurisdiction committee and also over the nominating committee designating officials for election. The high sheriff had the right to dismiss officials and initiate disciplinary action. Counties consisted of districts, each headed by a district administrator (*főszolgabíró*).

County administration became more professional in this period. New specialized offices were created, and their officials were appointed by the government. In 1876 the *administrative committee* was established to coordinate county autonomy and central administration. It consisted of 21 members, of which the county assembly elected ten, while five were tenured county officials and five were officials of the central administration. It was headed by the high sheriff. According to the relevant legislation, "all members of the central administration and the county and local officials in the area of the jurisdiction are required to carry out the directives of this committee." It supervised and controlled the entire administrative system at the county level. The exception was property management, which was reserved for county and local autonomies. However, in 1886 the Ministry of the Interior received authority of control and intervention in this area as well.

In 1876 the territorial reform of the counties was initiated. At the time of the Compromise the traditional medieval system still prevailed: besides the counties there were so-called privileged territories including the Jász-Kun (Jazygian-Cumanian) district, six towns in the Hajdú and 16 towns in the Szepes (Zips) district, in Transylvania five districts in the Szekler (Székely) area and the autonomy of the Saxons, nine districts and two special districts in Királyföld (Königsboden). These traditional autonomous areas were abolished and their territories absorbed into neighboring counties, or in some cases new counties were created. The territorial autonomy of the Transylvanian Saxons, dating back to the medieval period, was abolished. The organization known as Nationsuniversität lost its political and judicial authority; it was limited to educational and cultural functions. The territories of the counties had not changed much since the Middle Ages; as a result, there were significant differences in territory and population. There were counties with 1,000 square kilometers and a population of fewer than 100,000, and some with an area of more than 10,000 square kilometers and a population of one million. The former Croatian–Slavonian Military Frontier was integrated into Croatia in 1886. This completed the administrative organization of the Hungarian Crown, with 63 counties in Hungary and eight in Croatia, this remained unchanged up to 1918.

At the time of the Compromise the traditional urban network existed with 81 free royal cities, 88 towns with limited self-government and 719 market towns. In the 1870s the legal status of cities was reorganized. Only 23 of the free royal cities received the status of jurisdiction, while 50 received limited self-government status and seven lost their status as towns. Two market towns received the status of jurisdiction, and 56 the status of limited self-government, while the rest were classified as communities.

In 1873 the cities of Pest, Buda and Óbuda, situated on both banks of the Danube, were unified, creating the capital city of Budapest. Budapest had special status. Two hundred members of the legislative assembly (jurisdiction committee) of 400 members were elected by adult males with the right to vote, while the other half was elected from the list of the 1,200 citizens with the highest tax payments. The head of the city government was the lord mayor, elected by the jurisdiction committee from three persons nominated by the king for six years. The government had no authority to remove him. In Budapest there was a police force under the authority of the minister of the interior.

A law of 1871 provided for the administration of communities subject to the supervision and authority of counties. The law differentiated three types of communities: towns with limited self-government, headed by a mayor; large communities, which had a notary; small communities unable to provide for self-government, which united with other communities to form a notary district—however, these latter also had their own body of representatives. The community was entitled to issue statutes, to manage its property as a legal person, to levy a community tax, and to develop community infrastructure, educational and cultural institutions. The community assembly nominated, and citizens of the community elected, community officials and the village mayor (*bíró*), the top official, by open vote for three years. The community notary or the district notary in the case of several small communities was the head of administration, elected for life. The law of 1886 restricted community self-government by giving the district administrator the right to nominate the judge and the notary and giving the right of election to the community assembly, one half of which consisted of the highest taxpayers (virilists). The law increased the powers of the district administrator, representing the county, over the communities. In 1881 the police power was transferred from the counties to the nationwide constabulary.

By the end of the nineteenth century there had emerged in Hungary a governmental system characterized by parliamentary constitutional procedures, strongly controlled by royal authority, by the greater weight of the government over Parliament and by the discretionary authority of state administration over local self-government, civil organizations and citizens. This was the case even though Hungary adopted the institutions of Western Europe. The governing authorities, primarily Kálmán Tisza, considered this system to be necessary as a defense against those opposing the Compromise and as an assurance of Hungarian supremacy over national minorities.

Codification of Civil Liberties and Establishment of the Judicial System

After the Compromise one of the most urgent issues to be addressed was the foundation of a modern legal system and the establishment of the judicial organization. The first step was the enactment of the bill on the Code of Civil Procedure in 1868 prepared by the minister of justice, Boldizsár Horváth. The Act abolished all noble rights and established the legal equality of all citizens. Another Act on the prerogatives of judges enacted in 1869 separated public administration and judicial organization, thereby terminating the jurisdiction of counties in judicial administration. The Act also guaranteed the independence and irremovability of judges and prohibited their political activity. The minister of justice nominated, and the king appointed, judges for life tenure. The opposition argued in favor of the election of judges. Ferenc Deák proposed the establishment of a "*state court*," which would have a role in the appointment of judges. This would have been a kind of constitutional court comparable to the Austrian *Reichsgericht*. The government did not support this proposal, and allowed the opposition to vote against it; the majority of the government party was absent at the vote. In the following year, however, in the debate on the jurisdictions, the opposition demanded the establishment of the state court, which would review the constitutionality of government regulations.

In 1871 the courts of first instance were organized. 102 royal higher courts and 360 district courts were established. At the end of the period the district courts were increased to 381, while the higher courts were decreased to 67. The procedures of the latter used a three-member council for criminal and civil cases. The district courts handled minor property and criminal cases and consisted of a single judge. The press law of 1848 had provided for jury trials. After the Compromise jury courts were set up in five cities. In 1897 jury courts were added to the higher courts, which had jurisdiction over major political or criminal cases that could impose death sentences or a minimum of five years' imprisonment. Two appeal courts in Budapest and in Marosvásárhely (Tîrgu Mureş), in Transylvania were set up initially. They were increased to 11 in 1890. The highest court was the royal "*kúria*" (Supreme Court) in Budapest. In 1871 state prosecution was organized, consisting of the crown prosecutor attached to the royal "*kúria*," the high prosecutor attached to the appeal courts and the prosecutor attached to the higher courts. In 1896 the Administrative Court was set up to render decisions on disagreements between administrative authorities and on complaints submitted to them.

The Code of Civil Procedure of 1868 was regarded as temporary. In 1880 the preparation of a detailed civil code of procedures was initiated. After several drafts and revisions, the Act on the Code of Civil Procedure was enacted in 1911, but it became effective only in 1915. The Hungarian Code of Criminal Law, prepared by Professor of Law Károly Csemegi in 1878, became effective in 1880. Several acts on private law were enacted in the decades after the Compromise, but no unified code of private law was completed, in spite of the fact that in 1900 and 1913 plans and legislative bills were prepared.

To perform the preparation of public documents and the accreditation of private documents, public notaries were established in 1874. In the same year a law provided for procedures to be observed by attorneys and the association of attorneys.

As indicated, there was no constitution or unified law in Hungary for the codification of human and civil rights. From time to time ministerial statutes provided guidelines on the exercise of these rights. Personal liberties received extensive criminal law protection. Legislation guaranteed the freedom of free movement, residence, settlement and emigration. Similarly, the right of property and the freedom of learning and teaching were protected. With regard to rights of assembly and association no legislation was enacted throughout this period, in spite of the fact that the throne address of 1869 urged its enactment: "The resolution of the rights of assembly and association are urgently required in order to place one of the basic rights of constitutional government under legal protection and to define the borderline of the supervisory right and duty of the government."

The April 1848 statute of the Batthyány government defined the right of assembly. This was reaffirmed in 1868. The legality of assembly was determined by the head of jurisdictions, or in the case of cities by the chief of police. On the right of association the Nationalities Act provided "for the right of citizens to form associations or clubs under the legal supervision of the state" in the case of cultural and economic associations and societies. The legality of associations was dependent on the approval of their statutes by the government. The circular of the Ministry of the Interior under Kálmán Tisza stated that "nationality associations can be established only as literary and cultural associations." In spite of this rule, nationality parties of the Romanians, Serbs, Slovaks, Germans and Transylvanian Saxons existed throughout this period, and they made public statements and programs at times of elections. At the end of the nineteenth century about 3,600 associations existed.

An important step in the expansion of civic and political rights was the enactment of the resolution of the Parliament of 1849 on the civil and political equality of the Jews in 1867. The religious equality of Jews was enacted in a law of 1895.

In 1868 the equality of all accepted Christian denominations was confirmed by law, as enacted in 1848. This law provided that of children born in mixed marriages boys would follow their father's and girls their mother's religion. In his last parliamentary speech in 1873 Ferenc Deák proposed the legal settlement of Church and state relationships and the introduction of civil marriage. The time was not propitious for such a step, due to the opposition of the king and the Catholic Church. But in the 1880s controversies on mixed marriages surfaced again. Cases of "mistaken baptisms" were frequent: ministers baptized and placed in the register children who belonged to another denomination. Since it proved impossible to resolve the issue by statute, the Wekerle government decided to resolve it by legislation. In 1894–1895 Parliament enacted the "ecclesiastical legislation," which introduced civil marriage and registers under state direction, but as a compensation marriage partners were free to decide the religion of their children. The legislation also recognized the equality of the Jewish religion with Christian religions. The law on the free exercise of religion affirmed the freedom to change religions, and to join and leave a denomination freely, and permitted anyone not to belong to any denomination. It also made possible the recognition of additional denominations if they satisfied prescribed conditions. Contemporary Hungarian law recognized three types of denominations: accepted denominations, recognized denominations—the Jewish religion until 1895 and the Baptists and Muslims in the early twentieth century—and the tolerated religions, such as the Nazarenes, Methodists, Adventists and Jehovah's Witnesses. The latter were under police supervision and regulations: they were required to report their religious programs, and youth under 18 were not allowed to participate. They were also required to pay a church tax to the accepted denomination from which they had seceded.

After the Compromise an important requirement was the termination of the residues and problems of the traditional agricultural system that had not been terminated by the 1848 April Laws and the Urbarial Patent of 1853. Accordingly, in 1868 the compulsory redemption of vineyard payments was enacted and in 1871 the seignorial rights and monopolies of former landowners were terminated. The last issue was the redemption of the plots of serfs on landlord-owned properties (*allodia*) in 1896.

In the three decades after the Compromise a great deal was done to introduce a modern legal system in Hungary, but the Western institutions of the rule of law were not fully implemented. In this area Austria accomplished more than Hungary.

The State Financial System

After the Compromise Hungary was required to establish an independent fiscal system and financial administration. The beginning was not auspicious, since separation from Austria involved most of the practical difficulties. Minister of Finance Lónyay wrote as follows on these initial difficulties: "In early 1867 the treasuries were empty; nine tenths of the personnel of financial administration were persons of foreign origin who were ignorant of the official language. There were no native persons to take their place. Within the first weeks taxes were no longer received, since people were not accustomed to voluntary payments."[6]

After the Compromise the Hungarian state adopted the Austrian tax system of the 1850s, with minor modifications. Direct taxes included the real estate, housing and personal income tax; in addition, a supplementary real estate compensation tax was attached to each tax, and this was used to compensate former landlords. Indirect taxes included consumption taxes on salt, tobacco and the lottery; in addition, there were taxes on alcohol, wine, beer, sugar and meat, and also several dues and fees. Income from tariffs was used in both countries to finance common affairs.

This system was modified and expanded subsequently. A substantial reform took place in 1875: this introduced new types of direct taxes designed to tax incomes derived from capital investment activities and businesses. Examples of these taxes were the transport tax, mining tax, corporation tax, interest tax and annuities tax, as well as the general income surtax. Revenues from these new taxes increased rapidly, while the real estate tax remained unchanged.

A new land cadaster was completed in 1884, on the basis of which a combined real estate tax of 25.5 percent of net real estate income was assessed, with a maximum amount of 37 million florins (£ 3.1 million) payable.

While the 1875 reform concerned direct taxes, the reforms of the 1880s increased indirect taxes, especially consumption taxes. Between 1868 and 1890 revenues from consumption taxes quadrupled, and as a result of the structural transformation of the tax system the major tax revenue shifted from direct to indirect taxation. Tax policy attempted to tax primarily personal income and consumption and not so much real estate; as a result, tax revenues increased rapidly, from 1868 to 1890 from 116 million florins (£ 9.7 million) to 262 million (£ 21.8 million). One of the characteristics of the tax system, also confirmed by contemporary experts, was an "inequitable distribution of taxation. The current tax system places a larger burden on the lower classes than on the propertied class."[7]

In the course of economic growth and structural transformation, the tax base was expanded substantially. Between 1890 and 1913 the real estate tax remained unchanged, and income taxes increased moderately, but consumption taxes quadrupled. The corporation tax, the mining tax, the capital interest tax, the annuities tax, the transport tax and housing tax increased very rapidly. The tax reform derived the major part of revenues from the rapid growth of capital gains, purchases and consumption.

The consumption taxes, which represented the major element of tax revenues, were basically regressive, but even direct taxes were not progressive. The direct tax law of 1909 introduced a more progressive personal income tax, decreased the tax burdens of low-income persons, and established tax exemption for incomes of 800 crowns (£ 33).[8] It distributed tax burdens more equitably and would have introduced a more balanced tax system if it had been implemented. Its implementation was postponed, and it was partially implemented during World War I.

But local taxes increased even more rapidly than direct state taxes, and in some communities they constituted a larger burden than the latter. 80 percent of public expenditure was financed by the state budget, the balance of 20 percent by local governments. Available data enable us to examine the revenues and expenditure of the central government between the first budget year, 1868, and the last year of peace, 1913.

Tables 5.1 and 5.2 indicate the very rapid increase of state income and expenditure. Between 1868 and 1913 the population increased on a yearly average by 0.7 percent, and the GDP by 2.7 percent, while state income, calculated at current prices, increased annually by 3.3 percent and expenditure by 3.7 percent. Calculated at unchanged prices the growth rate of state income and expenditure was 0.1–0.2 percent less.

If we examine expenditure, its very substantial increase becomes evident and we can hardly find a comparison in contemporary Europe. Between 1868 and 1890 state expenditure increased in Austria by 72 percent and in Hungary by 142 percent. This rapid increase was the result of the establishment of the public administration system and investment support for economic development. In the first phase of the period, major expenditure financed the state debt and railway construction interest. The expenditure for public education also increased very rapidly from the modest initial outlay. Investments throughout the period made up 6.1 percent of total expenditure, but between 1868 and 1873 the proportion was 11 percent and in the post-1890 period it was close to 10 percent.

Contributions to the common affairs budget as a proportion of Hungarian state expenditure decreased from 16 percent to 11 percent in the period between 1868–1870 and 1906–1910. It increased in the years preceding World War I to 15 percent in support of expenditure for the common army and the navy. Since Austria covered two thirds of the costs of the common army, Hungarian military expenditure was much less than those of other European countries. This expenditure would have been much greater for an independent Hungary.

From the viewpoint of the relationships between state finances and economic development, it is important to consider the changes in the structure of state revenues and expenditure. The tax system adopted from Austria in 1867 was primarily based on the real estate tax and state monopolies: almost 60 percent of revenues came from these sources. In contrast, the tax reforms of the 1870s and 1880s derived an increasing tax revenue from capital incomes as well as from the complex system of consumption taxes. As a result, the proportion of state income from real estate taxes and monopolies decreased substantially, while those derived from personal and corporation income and consumption taxes increased. In addition, income from state enterprises also increased very substantially, from 16 percent to 40 percent.

State expenditure was also transformed similarly. The proportion of military and government expenditure and debt payments decreased, while the proportion of economic and social expenditure increased. The growth of expenditure for education and state enterprises was especially rapid. This indicates that the state attempted to support economic growth not only by legislative and regulatory policies, but directly as well by budgetary outlays.

If we examine the state and local government budgets from the point of view of expenditure, it is quite evident that the proportion of this public expenditure to the GDP was much higher in Hungary than in developed Western countries. In the years preceding World War I total public expenditure amounted to one quarter of the GDP, and if we add the expenses of government enterprises then the total amount was equal to one third of the GDP. Public expenditure without enterprise costs was approximately two billion crowns in 1913, of which one and a half billion was the state share, the balance the local government share. The breakdown of state expenditure by specific allocation was as follows: common army and defense force 19 percent, political, financial and judicial administration 16 percent, infrastructure and economic support 25 percent, health, education, culture and social support 19 percent, and debt payments 21 percent. The proportion of public expenditure to the GDP in Hungary was twice that of Great Britain. In 1913 the proportion was 24 percent, with the inclusion of public enterprises it was 37 percent. This unquestionably indicates underdevelopment including especially that of the private sector.

In the decades after the Compromise the Hungarian state carried a great measure of indebtedness. This was a necessary condition and also a normal and widespread European situation. The state was faced with expenditure, especially for investments, which it could not finance from current revenues; alternatively it could have financed them only by an unjustified tax burden imposed on taxpayers and the economy. Therefore to finance investments it was more advantageous to assume long-term credits at acceptable conditions. In the second half of the nineteenth century developing countries had access to long-term credits at favorable conditions in developed countries, and they took advantage of them.

In addition to the debt inherited from the previous age, a new debt of more than 1.7 billion florins was added in the period 1868 to 1890. In the 1880s and 1890s the state was required to pay 90–100 million florins annually for the principal, interest and annuities of the debt, and in addition an annual amount of 30 million for the Austrian debt prior to 1867. Of the state debt of nearly two billion florins in 1890 only 1.2 billion was derived from credits. More than 400 million was based on redemption obligations of the seigniorial system, and 350 million on the redemption of private railways by the state. One third of credits was used for economic investments, and income from these surpassed the repayment and interest expense of those credits.

The credit of the Hungarian state had improved by the end of the nineteenth century, and it obtained annuity credits at increasingly favorable conditions. Between 1888 and 1892 the unfavorable state debts were converted to annuity debts carrying 4.5 and 4 percent interest, and thereafter the growth of expenditure for indebtedness was terminated. In the 1890s the growth of total indebtedness slowed down and loans of large amounts were assumed only in the years preceding World War I. In contrast to the preceding decades, loans in the second phase of the period were assumed exclusively for long-term investments: regulation of the Danube basin, road construction and railway expansion. In the years preceding the War armed forces development and armaments also contributed to the growth of indebtedness.

As a result of the improvement of credit conditions, the expenditure for debt payments increased at a substantially slower pace than total indebtedness or state revenues. Not only was Hungary able to avoid state bankruptcy, which not all European states could manage, but it always paid its obligations on time and without difficulty. The state of indebtedness at the outbreak of World War I amounted to close to seven billion crowns, and to this must be added the one billion crown debt of local governments. The total debt of the public sector was approximately equal to the amount of an annual GDP.

According to our calculations, the investments of the central government between 1867 and 1913 constituted 20 percent of all investments. With the addition of the investments of local governments the public sector as a whole was responsible for 25 percent of all capital formation. This was an exceptionally large proportion in this age if compared with international trends.

In 1867 the Hungarian state inherited from previous centuries substantial productive resources: extensive landed properties and forests, ore and salt mines, metallurgical plants and tobacco plants. After the Compromise it was debated whether to keep these plants or sell them to private owners. It was decided to keep them, modernize them and develop them. State plants were especially important in the metallurgical and engineering industry, which played a strategic role in Hungarian industrialization. But in terms of scale and economic importance the most significant state enterprise of the period between 1867 and 1890 was the railway system. Hungarian state railways were established in 1867 on the occasion of the forced purchase of a private rail line, which had gone bankrupt. From that time onwards the state constructed the most important economic and strategic rail lines and in the 1880s it redeemed all private lines. 84 percent of the main rail lines were state-owned by the early 1890s and state railways operated 90 percent of local lines. The business surplus of the state railways substantially increased state revenues, and railway tariffs were an important instrument of state economic and industrial policies. In 1910 state railways and state industrial plants provided employment to 11 percent of all workers employed in the industrial and transport sectors, and produced 12 percent of industrial production.

Table 1: Revenues (annual averages in million crowns)

	1868–1870	1871–1875	1881–1885	1891–1895	1901–1905	1911–1913	*Index 1868–1870 = 100*
Tax for real estates	72	69	75	71	60	68	*94*
Tax for housing	13	16	18	23	25	46	*354*
Other direct taxes	33	43	93	117	121	199	*603*
Direct taxes together	*118*	*128*	*186*	*211*	*207*	*314*	*266*
Excises	26	27	56	155	181	290	*1,115*
State monopolies	81	90	116	143	157	228	*281*
Stamps, dues	25	39	49	70	88	166	*664*
Indirect taxes together	*132*	*156*	*221*	*368*	*425*	*683*	*517*
Other incomes	20	14	47	47	57	94	*470*
Total economic revenues	***270***	***298***	***455***	***626***	***689***	***1,092***	***404***
Revenues of the state industrial plants	49	74	145	345	390	713	*1,455*
Total	**319**	**372**	**600**	**971**	**1,079**	**1,807**	***566***
	As a percentage of revenues of the state economy						
Tax for real estates	26.7	23.2	16.5	11.3	8.7	6.2	
Tax for housing	4.8	5.4	4.0	3.7	3.6	4.2	
Other direct taxes	12.2	14.4	20.4	18.7	17.6	18.2	
Direct taxes together	*43.7*	*43.0*	*40.9*	*33.7*	*30.0*	*28.8*	
Excises	9.6	9.1	12.3	24.8	26.3	26.6	
State monopolies	30.0	30.2	25.5	22.8	22.8	20.9	
Stamps, dues	9.3	13.1	10.8	11.2	12.8	15.2	
Indirect taxes together	*48.9*	*52.3*	*48.6*	*58.8*	*61.7*	*62.5*	
Other incomes	7.4	4.7	10.3	7.5	8.3	8.6	
Total economic revenues of the state economy	***100.0***	***100.0***	***100.0***	***100.0***	***100.0***	***100.0***	
Incomes of the state industrial plants as a percentage of the incomes of state economy	18.1	24.8	31.9	55.1	56.6	65.3	

Table 2: Expenditures per main categories (annual averages in million crowns)

	1868–1870	1871–1875	1881–1885	1891–1895	1901–1905	1911–1913	*Index 1868–1870 = 100*
National defense	64	74	88	98	134	277	*433*
State debt	102	125	224	288	295	328	*322*
Administration, jurisdiction	57	98	124	155	243	386	*677*
Education	3	9	11	19	47	123	*4,100*
Economy, infrastructure	14	42	48	40	77	124	*886*
Produce and selling of tobacco	24	30	42	49	56	79	*329*
Total state expenditures	***264***	***378***	***537***	***649***	***852***	***1,316***	***498***
Expenditures of the state industrial plants	76	101	149	286	300	717	*943*
Total expenditures	**340**	**479**	**686**	**936**	**1,152**	**2,033**	***598***
Investments	38	45	51	50	73	200	*526*

As a percentage of the state expenditures

	1868–1870	1871–1875	1881–1885	1891–1895	1901–1905	1911–1913
National defense	24.2	19.6	16.4	15.1	15.7	21.0
State debt	38.6	33.1	41.7	44.4	34.6	24.9
Administration, jurisdiction	21.6	25.9	23.1	23.9	28.5	29.3
Education	1.1	2.4	2.0	2.9	5.5	9.3
Economy, infrastructure	5.3	11.1	8.9	6.2	9.0	9.4
Produce and selling of tobacco	9.1	7.9	7.8	7.6	6.6	6.0
Total state expenditures	***100.0***	***100.0***	***100.0***	***100.0***	***100.0***	***100.0***
Expenditures of state plants as a percentage of the expenditures of state economy	28.8	26.7	27.7	44.1	35.2	54.5
Total expenditures						
Investments as a percentage of the total expenditures	11.2	9.4	7.4	5.3	6.3	9.8

Notes

1 *Az 1869-dik évi április 20-dikára hirdetett országgyűlés képviselőházának irományai* [Documents of the House of Representatives of the Parliament Convoked on April 20, 1869], vol. 1 (Pest, 1870), p. 1.
2 Erdélyi 1848: 1.tc. [Act 1 of 1848 of the Parliament of Transylvania].
3 1898: 5. tc. [Act 5 of the Parliament of 1898].
4 Ernő Nagy, *Magyarország közjoga* [Public Law of Hungary] (Budapest, 1907), p. 129.
5 Ferenc Deák, *Adalék a magyar közjoghoz* [Contribution to Hungarian Public Law] (Pest, 1865), p. 88.
6 Menyhért Lónyay, *Közügyeinkről. Nézetek Magyarország pénzügyi állapotáról* [Public Issues. Views on the Financial Condition of Hungary] (Budapest, 1873), pp. 8–9.
7 Sándor Milhoffer, *Magyarország közgazdasága* [The Economy of Hungary], vol. 2 (Budapest, 1904), p. 224.
8 According to the currency reform of 1892, 2 crowns = 1 florin.

6. DEMOGRAPHIC AND ETHNIC CHANGES

Population Growth and Demographic Characteristics

Between 1869 and 1910 the population of the Lands of the Hungarian Crown increased from 15.5 million to 20.9 million. This was an increase of 35 percent in 41 years. A similar growth trend can be observed in the other half of the Empire. The population of Austria increased from 20.4 million to 28.6 million in the same period, that is, by 40 percent. In 1869 the Monarchy as a whole had a population of 35.9 million, and in 1910 a population of 49.5 million, and if Bosnia-Herzegovina is included then a total of 51.4 million. The larger rate of increase in Austria may be explained by the demographic disaster in Hungary in the decade following the Compromise. This resulted in a population increase of 1.5 percent in Hungary between 1869 and 1880, while in Austria the increase was 8.6 percent. Between 1880 and 1900 the rate of growth in Hungary was higher than that of Austria, but in the early twentieth century it slowed down again due to emigration.

In attempting to identify the cause of this growth rate we can point to the emergence in this period of a *demographic revolution*, more precisely a *demographic transition*, as demography refers to it. "Revolution" indicates the radical nature of the change and "transition" refers to the process itself. This was the beginning of the transition from the demographic model of pre-industrial agrarian societies to that of modern industrial-urban societies.

Table 1: Population Growth of Hungary and Croatia

	Hungary thousands	Croatia thousands	*Together thousands*
		Civilian population	
1850	11,618	1,574	*13,192*
1857	12,137	1,631	*13,769*
1869	13,579	1,838	*15,417*
	Total population (civilian population and soldiers)		
1869	13,664	1,849	*15,512*
1880	13,834	1,905	*15,739*
1890	15,262	2,202	*17,464*
1900	16,838	2,416	*19,255*
1910	18,265	2,622	*20,886*
	Average annual growth, per thousand		
1850–1857	6.2	4.8	*6.1*
1857–1869	9.4	10.0	*9.5*
1869–1880	1.1	2.6	*1.3*
1880–1890	9.8	14.8	*10.5*
1890–1900	9.8	9.6	*9.8*
1900–1910	8.1	8.4	*8.2*
1880–1910	9.3	10.7	*9.5*
1869–1910	7.1	8.6	*7.3*

Figure 1

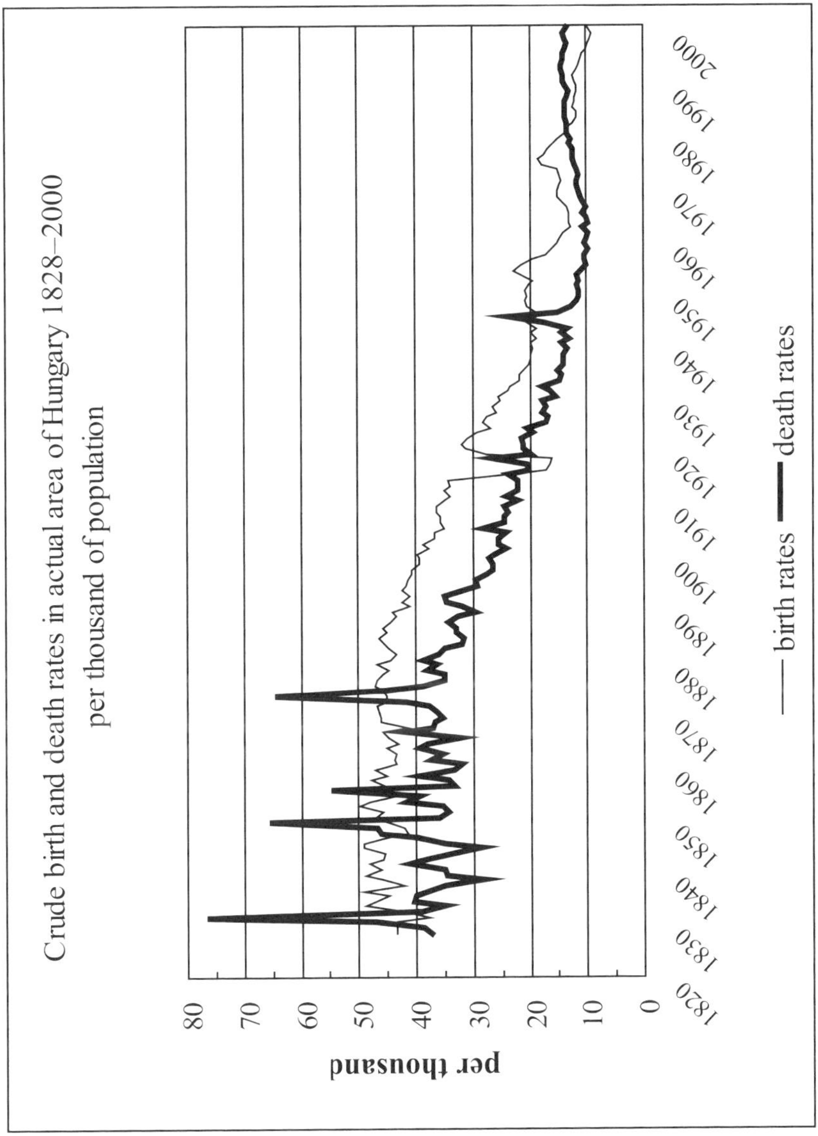
Crude birth and death rates in actual area of Hungary 1828–2000
per thousand of population
per thousand
0
10
20
30
40
50
60
70
80
1820
1830
1840
1850
1860
1870
1880
1890
1900
1910
1920
1930
1940
1950
1960
1970
1980
1990
2000
birth rates
death rates

In Hungary the dominance of the traditional demographic system continued from the 1850s to the end of the 1870s. Our chart indicates that both the birth rate and the death rate were very high. Calculated on the basis of the period 1828 to 1880, the birth rate averaged 45.3 per thousand, the death rate 39.5 per thousand, and natural increase 5.8 per thousand. In Hungary cholera epidemics caused periodic demographic disasters and high rates of mortality in 1831, 1849, 1855, 1866 and 1872–1874. There were also famines in the 1860s and the early 1870s.

The last traditional "medieval-type" demographic disaster took place in 1872–1874 in the form of the last great cholera epidemic, claiming 189,000 lives officially, but in fact many more. It was accompanied by failing harvests and even famine for several years. The mortality rate was 65 per thousand in 1873, and the number of deaths exceeded the number of births by 300,000. In 1872–1874 the number of deaths above the average of "normal" years was half a million; this was actually the number of victims of this last traditional demographic crisis. The population attained its 1871 state at the end of the 1870s, but the eastern and southeastern areas regained their traditional population only at the end of the 1880s. Between 1869 and 1880 15 of the 63 counties reported more deaths than births; all of these cases were centered in the eastern areas. According to the 1880 census, the population of 34 counties, all in the east and north, was less than it was in 1869. But between 1880 and 1890 there was no surplus of deaths over births in any county.

The average rate of annual population growth between 1857 and 1869 in Hungary was 9.5 per thousand. Between 1869 and 1880 the average rate of annual growth dropped to 1.3 per thousand. This minimal growth was concentrated in the first two years. After 1880 the average growth rate increased to 10.4 per thousand and remained at that level in spite of the losses due to much larger numbers of emigrants than in previous decades.

Table 2: Rough Population Rates in the Austro-Hungarian Monarchy, per Thousand

	Live births				Mortalities			
	Hungary (H)	Croatia (C)	Lands of the Hungarian Crown	Austria (A)	H	C	Lands of the Hungarian Crown	A
1865–1869	40.6			37.3	32.8			31.3
1870–1874*	42.1	41.8	42.1	39.0	44.2	49.2	47.3	32.3
1875–1879	44.1	45.5	44.3	39.0	36.8	37.5	36.9	30.3
1880–1884	43.9	44.0	44.0	38.0	34.7	32.1	34.4	29.9
1885–1889	44.1	45.4	44.3	37.9	32.2	29.8	31.9	29.0
1890–1894	41.5	41.6	41.5	37.0	32.3	34.1	32.5	28.1
1895–1899	39.7	41.5	39.9	37.2	28.2	29.6	28.3	25.9
1900–1904	37.6	39.8	37.9	36.2	25.9	26.9	26.0	24.2
1905–1909	35.9	39.8	36.3	33.8	25.4	27.0	25.6	23.1
1910–1914	34.9	36.8	35.2	31.4	23.5	25.3	23.8	21.1
1871–1913	40.5	41.9	40.7	36.7	31.6	32.2	31.7	27.2

	Natural increment			
	Hungary	Croatia	Lands of the Hungarian Crown	Austria
1865–1869	7.8			6.1
1870–1874*	– 2.1	– 7.4	–5.2	6.7
1875–1879	7.4	8.0	7.4	8.6
1880–1884	9.3	11.9	9.6	8.1
1885–1889	11.9	15.6	12.3	8.9
1890–1894	9.2	7.5	9.0	8.9
1895–1899	11.5	11.9	11.6	11.3
1900–1904	11.7	12.9	11.9	11.9
1905–1909	10.4	12.8	10.7	10.8
1910–1914	11.4	11.5	11.4	10.3
1871–1913	8.9	9.7	9.0	9.5

* In Croatia and in the Lands of the Hungarian Crown, 1871–1874.

The crisis of 1873 was also a turning point in the demographic history of Hungary. After 1874 until World War I there was no surplus of deaths over births; in fact, the rate of natural increase fell below 5 per thousand only in two years, 1878 and 1880. The termination of mass epidemics and famines introduced the first phase of "demographic transition", the emergence of modern "demographic revolution." After the mid-1870s the various phases of the transition emerged, some 120–130 years later than those in England, but crowded into a much shorter period.

In the 1880s the mortality of normal years began to decrease. Cholera was eradicated. Compulsory vaccination successfully eliminated smallpox. Childhood diseases, especially diphtheria, continued to claim victims, but these cases did not approach the number of earlier epidemics. After 1874 the mortality rate did not rise above 40 per thousand. In 1895 it declined to below 30 per thousand and after the turn of the century to below 25 per thousand. In the 1880s "demographic scissors" opened up and natural increase rose from the annual 5 per thousand persons to 11 in the period 1880 to 1914. These trends did not lead to the country's attaining the level of England (15–16 per thousand), since the number of births began to decline at the end of the 1880s. This phase of the transition lasted for a very short time, less than a decade, while in England it continued for almost a century. From the end of the 1880s to World War I the two graphs declined in parallel to each other. The birth rate of 45 per thousand prior to 1885 declined to below 40 per thousand in 1897 and to below 35 per thousand in 1910. After World War I the two graphs approached each other, and in about 1960 a new balance appeared with a natural increase of 3 per thousand, marking the end of the demographic transition.

Prior to 1848 the average life expectancy at birth, calculated from a variety of demographic samples, ranged from 24 to 28 years. There was no higher life expectancy in the 1860s, but the calculations of the Hungarian Statistical Office estimated a life expectancy at birth of 40 years in 1910. In Austria the newborn could expect to live one to two years longer, while in Western and Northern Europe life expectancy was more than 50 years.

Infant and child mortality was very high in Hungary to the end of the nineteenth century. In the 1850s 253 infants out of 1,000 died in their first year and an additional 159 children died between the ages of one and five. In the first half of the 1890s infant mortality was still 253 per thousand live births, but after 1895 it gradually decreased. In the pre-war years 198 infants did not survive their first birthday and 289 their fifth birthday. Infant and child mortality was especially high in the smallholder peasant and agricultural worker families of the Great Plains. Deaths due to tuberculosis in Hungary were the highest in contemporary Europe; this improved slowly in the early twentieth century.

Table 3:
Major Demographic Index Numbers According to Ethnic Groups

	Magyar	Germans	Slovaks	Romanians	Ruthenians	Croats	Serbs
Rough population rates per thousand, 1901–1910							
Live births	36.5	33.7	40.4	36.7	41.7	38.9	41.5
Mortalities	24.5	23.3	27.4	28.0	26.5	26.7	31.6
Natural increment	12.0	10.4	13.0	8.7	15.2	12.2	9.9
Marital fecundity* 1900–1901	223	198	241	193	236	244	217
Marital fecundity* 1910–1911	207	173	219	199	227	236	207
Neonatal mortalities** 1901–1910	209	207	200	210	198	200	232
Children's mortalities*** 1901–1910	116	101	127	144	148	135	162
Emigrants 1899–1913, in thousands	401	233	300	185	55	137	64
Emigrants per thousand inhabitants	2.8	7.5	10.1	4.2	8.1	4.7	

* Number of live births per thousand married women of 15–49 years of age
** Number of deceased under one year of age, per thousand live births
*** Number of deceased between 1 and 7 years of age, per thousand live births

The birth rate was high by European standards in the early twentieth century, due to early and rather widespread marriage. But marital fertility was the lowest in Europe, except for France, as early as the mid-nineteenth century. In 1900 there were 217 live births for every 1,000 married women of childbearing age (15–49 years of age) in Hungary, while in Austria there were 247. Among the ethnic groups of Hungary, marital fertility was above the national average among Croats, Slovaks and Ruthenians, essentially among those who were all or predominantly Catholic, while those with lower fertility were the Romanians and Germans. The fertility of Magyars coincided with the national average. Fertility was very low among Protestants and very high among Catholics, but there were also regional differences.

The explanation for the high birth rate was related to marriage customs. Along the western boundary of Hungary and Poland there was an important demographic demarcation. West of it people married late, between the ages of 25 and 30, and a significant part of the population, 15–20 percent, never married. To the east, however, early and standard marriage was the rule. These two models emerged at the end of the medieval period, but they were still observable in the marriage statistics of Hungary and Austria in the early twentieth century. In Austria in 1910 53 percent of women of childbearing age between 15 to 49 were married, while in Hungary 65 percent were.

Women in Hungary married very early in the early twentieth century: their average age at first marriage was 20–22. In 1911 40.3 percent of women preparing for marriage were below the age of 20. In Austria the percentage was 15.6 percent, but in the Austro-German provinces, in the area of contemporary Austria, it was only 6 percent. In 1910 61 percent of women aged 20–24 in Hungary were married, while in the other half of the Monarchy only 33 percent of that age group were, but in the Austro-German provinces (the Austria of today) the figure was 19 percent. In Hungary 5 percent of women over 50 (over childbearing age) never got married, while in the Austro-German provinces the figure was 19 percent.

Therefore, while a large proportion of women in Hungary were married in comparison with other European countries, the fertility of these marriages was exceedingly low by European standards. This indicates that in Hungary birth control within marriage was used much more frequently than the European average, not only in urban but also in village society. This type of birth control can be observed in Hungary as early as the end of the eighteenth century. Early twentieth-century demographers have paid a lot of attention to single-child families in southeastern counties of western Hungary (Transdanubia). There were similar practices in other regions. There was an area of low fertility in the southern and southeastern areas stretching from the Banat to southern Transylvania with predominantly German and Romanian populations. Another such area was the southern part of present-day Slovakia. Although low fertility was common predominantly in Protestant and Orthodox families, the primary cause of birth control was not religious, but related to the social problems of smallholder peasants. Early marriage resulted in high fertility rates, and therefore birth control was utilized to avoid the subdivision of peasant plots.

In this period there was a substantial and growing difference between natural and actual population growth. This was due to a major wave of emigration. The resulting population loss between 1869 and 1914 was close to 1.3 million. It reached the peak in the first decade of the twentieth century, with 600,000 emigrants. In the first phase of migration people in western Hungary migrated to neighboring Austrian provinces, while those living in Transylvania moved to Romania. Prior to World War I there were 80,000 Magyars in Romania. Their emigration became a much-discussed public issue, so much so that the government initiated economic improvements in that area. Overseas emigration commenced in the 1880s and reached a peak at the turn of the century. The first emigrants were Slovaks and Ruthenians. Magyars emigrated in greater numbers in the early twentieth century. According to US immigration statistics, 406,000 Magyar and 448,000 Slovak immigrants arrived in the 1898–1913 period.

Table 4:
Immigrants to the United States of America from the Austro-Hungarian Monarchy between 1899 and 1913

	Thousand people	Percentage of the immigrants	Percentage of the population in 1900
Poles	546	18.7	9.6
Croats, Serbs, Slovenians	493	16.9	10.7
Slovaks	448	15.4	4.4
Magyars	406	13.9	18.0
Germans	322	11.0	25.3
Jews	220	7.5	4.6*
Ruthenians	211	7.3	8.5
Czechs	126	4.3	13.5
Romanians	101	3.5	6.7
Italians	24	0.8	1.7
Other	19	0.6	0.4
Total	*2,915*	100	100

* Jews were registered as a religious denomination in 1900, while according to their language they were classified according to their different ethnic groups.

According to European port statistics, somewhat more than two million persons from the Kingdom of Hungary boarded ships to America between 1871 and 1913. One third of them returned to their homeland. In 1910 319,000 Magyars were identified in the United States, of whom 228,000 were born in Hungary. The Hungarian Statistical Office collected data on emigration from 1899 onwards. According to these, 1.4 million Hungarian citizens, including 401,000 Magyars, left Hungary between 1899 and 1913. The proportion of Magyars among all emigrants was 29 percent. Emigration from Hungary was considered to constitute an average range in comparison with other European countries. Two thirds

Figure 2

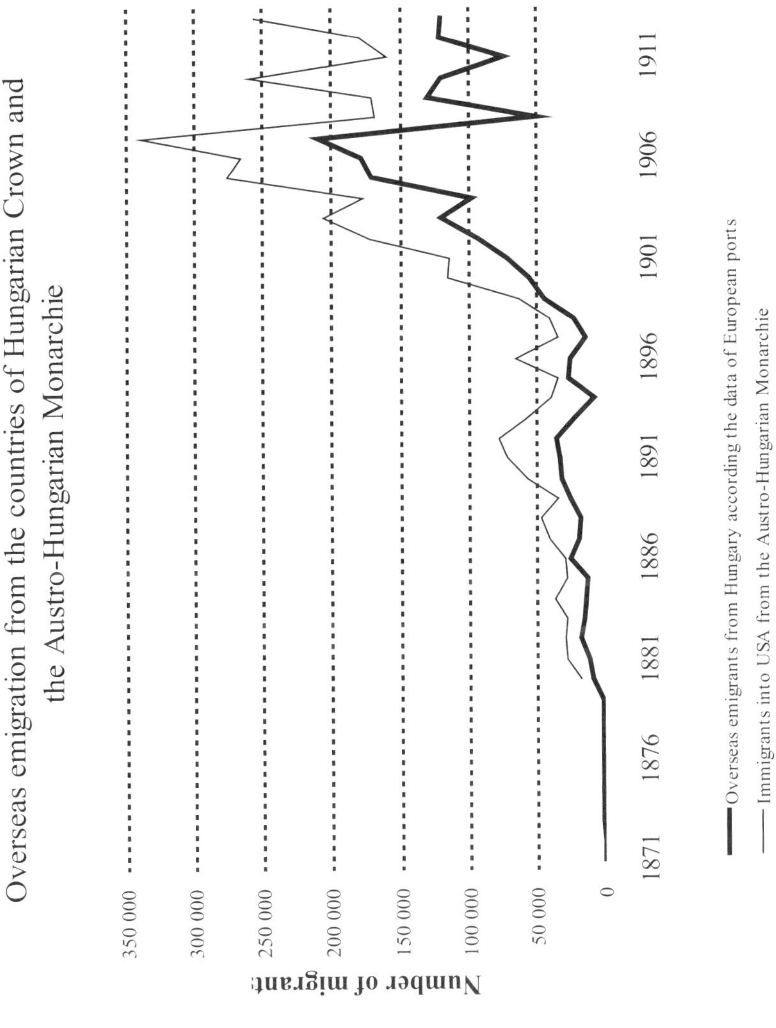
Overseas emigration from the countries of Hungarian Crown and the Austro-Hungarian Monarchie
Number of migrant
350 000
300 000
250 000
200 000
150 000
100 000
50 000
0
1871
1876
1881
1886
1891
1896
1901
1906
1911
Overseas emigrants from Hungary according the data of European ports
Immigrants into USA from the Austro-Hungarian Monarchie

of Magyar emigrants were agricultural workers without landed property, while many Slovaks and Ruthenians were peasants with small landholdings, who emigrated in order to save money for the purchase of additional properties in their homeland. In the early twentieth century emigrants saved and sent home more than 200 million crowns annually.

The age distribution of the population of Hungary was very "young." In 1910 35 percent of the population was less than 15 years old. Those over 60 made up 8 percent of the population, but as a result of a decreasing mortality rate this age group showed a growth trend.

The decrease of mortality trends was related to the establishment of a comprehensive public health policy, based on the Public Health Act of 1876. This law was a significant achievement, which unified the several branches of health policy and defined the role of the state, jurisdictions and local governments. It defined the responsibilities of physicians and midwives, and the requirements of the establishment and maintenance of hospitals, and provided for health standards in places of employment, schools, dwellings and public institutions, and preventive medical practices related to disease control. It required all cities and communities with over 6,000 inhabitants to support a physician who had to treat indigent patients without charge. Small communities were required to support a district physician. The law gave preventive medicine substantial priority, especially by setting health standards and requiring environmental improvements. These measures made the law internationally progressive.

The Public Health Act was not implemented everywhere in a uniform manner, since in many areas financial and professional resources were not available. Therefore its overall implementation took one and a half to two decades. Many communities lacked the financial basis to support physicians and in many cases physicians did not apply for poorly paid positions. In 1878 58 percent of 1,200 district positions were filled, but in 1895 16 percent of such positions remained unfilled. The medical services of urban areas were substantially better than those of rural areas

In 1869 there were 2,600 physicians and 900 surgeons in Hungary. In 1914 there were 6,100 professionally trained physicians. The number of midwives increased from 5,000 to 19,000. At the time of the Compromise hospitals were inadequate; there were only 44 hospitals or other health institutes, with 4,500 beds. In 1914 the number of hospitals was 461, with 50,000 beds, indicating a more than tenfold growth.

A substantial increase in agricultural crop production ensured abundant food requirements for the rapidly growing population. Károly Keleti, director of the Hungarian Statistical Office, evaluated food consumption in the first half of the 1880s and concluded that the dietary consumption of a large majority of the population was seriously out of balance. He noted that there was a deficient consumption of proteins. He also found that the Hungarian population consumed on average much more meat than those of most European countries did. A comparison of European data shows that the consumption of the Hungarian population was comparable to the average consumption pattern of other Central and Western European countries. According to the data collected by Keleti, the population of Hungary consumed 3,100–3,200 calories daily per person, while in Central and Western European countries the daily consumption was 2,800–3,200 calories. Annual meat consumption in Hungary was 34.5 kilograms, in Germany 37 and in France 35. In Hungary the average diet included much more fat (bacon or pork fat) and more baked goods, but fewer dairy products than was the case in Western Europe.

With regard to the quantity and quality of food consumption, there were numerous differences between urban and rural areas and between the central and peripheral areas. Annual food consumption per person on the national average was valued at 70 florins, but in urban areas it was valued at 94 florins. An urban resident consumed 64 kilograms of meat annually, but a rural resident only 28.8 kilograms. Urban residents consumed less bread, but that bread was of better quality, and they consumed many more dairy products than rural residents did. The value of food consumed in the central Danube–Tisza region was 81 florins, in western Hungary 70 florins, in Transylvania 60 florins and in northern and eastern Hungary only 61–62 florins. Residents of central Hungary—the Danube–Tisza region, along the River Tisza, the eastern part of Transdanubia—consumed the best-quality food, and they consumed the largest amount of meat and good-quality wheat bread, but ate less of it. Residents of southwestern Transdanubia, northern Hungary, Transylvania and northeast Hungary consumed less meat, more potatoes and more but lower-quality bread. Hungarian wheat and flour was valued globally. One third of wheat production was exported, but the population consumed surprisingly small amounts of wheat. Consumption per person of cereals was 200 kilograms, but only one third was wheat, whereas one quarter was rye and 40 percent was barley, oats and corn. White wheat bread was consumed in great quantities only in southern Hungary and along the middle of the River Tisza region. In western Hungary and central-northern Hungary rye bread was common, while in the northern Slovak counties the most common bread was rye, barley and oat, and in Transylvania and eastern Hungary corn bread was widespread. Consumption of brandy was very high if compared internationally: 23 liters per person. Consumption of coffee and sugar, however, was low: 0.52 and 2.76 kilograms respectively.

In 1863–1864 a major famine spread in the Hungarian Plain, but Hungarian agriculture quickly recovered and provided ample food supplies to the population in the following decades. In the early 1880s Károly Keleti complained about the low consumption of dairy products. But at that time the radical transformation of Hungarian cattle breeding was in progress and resulted in the substantial increase of dairy production. In 1870 82 percent of cattle stock consisted of the Hungarian "gray" breed, but by 1911 these were reduced to 28 percent and replaced by breeds producing large quantities of milk. The increasing consumer demand for dairy products brought about this change. Another change of the 1880s was the rapid growth of sugar beet cultivation, resulting in the tenfold increase of sugar production in the 30 years preceding World War I. Much of the produced sugar was exported, but domestic consumption increased as well: by 1913 it was 9.7 kilograms per person.

Ethnic and Linguistic Assimilation

In this period there were substantial changes in the nationality and native language distribution of the population. According to the 1850 census, the proportion of Magyars in the Lands of the Hungarian Crown was 36.5 percent. This proportion had increased to 48.1 percent by 1910. If we consider Hungary without Croatia the change was even more striking: from 42.3 percent to 54.6 percent. This is especially remarkable in the light of the fact that the proportion of ethnic Germans did not change during this period of 60 years in the other half of the Monarchy: it was 36 percent in 1850 and 1910. Between 1850 and 1910 the population of Hungary increased by 57 percent, but while the Magyar population more than doubled in 60 years (from 4.8 million to 10.1 million), the non-Magyar population increased only by 29 percent (from 8.4 million to 10.8 million). The Slovaks increased by 13 percent and the Ruthenians by 5 percent. The percentage of Magyars increased especially in the second half of the period, from 1880 to 1910.

Table 5:
Changes in the Number of Selected Ethnic Groups (1880–1910)

Mother Tongue	Hungary		Lands of the Hungarian Crown	
	1880 thousands	1910 thousands	1880 thousands	1910 thousands
Magyar	6,404	9,945	6,445	10,051
German	1,871	1,903	1,954	2,067
Slovak	1,855	1,946	1,865	1,968
Romanian	2,403	2,948	2,405	2,949
Ruthenian	353	464	356	473
Serbo-Croat	640	656	2,351	2,940
Other	223	401	265	469

Civilian population in 1880, total population in 1910

Table 6: Rate of Percentage of Selected Ethnic Groups

Mother Tongue (Nationality)	Hungary 1880 %	Hungary 1910 %	Lands of the Hungarian Crown 1850 %	Lands of the Hungarian Crown 1880 %	Lands of the Hungarian Crown 1910 %
Magyar	46.6	54.5	36.5	41.2	48.1
German	13.6	10.4	10.3	12.5	9.8
Slovak	13.5	10.7	13.2	11.9	9.4
Romanian	17.5	16.2	17.0	15.4	14.1
Ruthenian	2.6	2.5	3.4	2.3	2.3
Serbo-Croat	4.6	3.6	16.4	15.0	14.1
Other	1.6	2.2	3.3	1.7	2.2

There were passionate debates concerning the growth of the Magyar population, first among Magyar and national minority politicians and publicists in the dualist period, and then after 1918 between Hungarian historians and historians from successor states. According to the latter, this was the result of oppressive Magyarization, while the former contended that assimilation was a spontaneous and voluntary process brought about by multiple factors.

One of the factors was the fact that the natural increase of Magyars was higher than that of all other ethnic groups combined. Another element was emigration: three quarters of the emigration loss (of one and a half million people) reduced the population of national minorities. Between 1899 and 1913 there were only 2.8 Magyar emigrants per 1,000 Magyar residents, while for Slovaks the proportion was 10.1, for Ruthenians 8.1, for Germans 7.5, for Serbs and Croats 4.7 and for Romanians 4.2 per thousand. If we consider natural increase and migration balance, then we can conclude that from the growth of Magyars by 5.3 million in the period 1850 to 1910, two million of these people were gained due to the assimilation of other ethnic groups.

Which ethnic groups assimilated primarily? The largest assimilation was that of the Jewish population. In 1910 705,000 of the 932,000 Jewish residents gave Hungarian as their native language. The second-largest group was the Germans. In the 60-year period about 600,000 assimilated. The third group was the Slovaks, of whom 400,000 assimilated. The balance of 300,000 was made up of Catholic South Slavs, Croats, Slovenians, Bunjevci and Šokci, and of Ruthenians and other smaller groups such as Poles, Czechs and Italians. There was minimal assimilation among Serbs and Romanians. In Transylvania, with a Magyar minority, there were cases of Magyars merging into the Romanian majority.

A more detailed examination indicates that the urbanized, educated, geographically and socially mobile ethnic groups were most likely to assimilate. This process was facilitated by long-term contact with Magyars, membership of identical religious communities (Roman Catholic or Lutheran) and the great number of ethnically mixed marriages as well as bilingual practice. Assimilation was most likely in ethnic enclaves within Magyar-language areas, along language boundaries and in cities. It was much more restricted among traditional village societies of Serb and Romanian agrarian groups with the dominance of the Orthodox or Greek Catholic religions, lacking contact with Hungarian culture and historical traditions and preserving their Church and school autonomy. It was limited to small groups of intellectuals and urban residents.

Assimilation as a whole was a natural and spontaneous process facilitated by the geographic, economic and settlement conditions of the Carpathian basin, as well as the specific demographic, economic and social development of the nineteenth century. It is unquestionable that the contemporary Hungarian political leadership attempted to assist and accelerate this process. There was in fact only a single effective instrument for its promotion: the school system, the mandatory instruction of the Magyar language and the establishment of state schools with Magyar as the language of instruction. Facility in the Magyar language was of course not identical with assimilation, but it was a necessary condition for it. Prior to World War I the Romanian, Serb and Slovak political leaders of Hungary all spoke excellent Magyar, and several served as prominent political leaders in the successor states, such as Milan Hodža as Czechoslovak and Iuliu Maniu as Romanian prime minister. Between 1880 and 1910 the number of citizens whose native language was not Magyar but spoke Magyar increased by more than one million, and their proportion increased from 11 percent to 23 percent. But "magyarization" was successful only in those areas where long-term contacts between non-Magyars and Magyars took place: in other words, wherever economic, social and demographic factors were favorable for Magyars and consequently non-Magyars were inclined to assimilate.

Almost half of those who assimilated were nineteenth-century immigrants to Hungary. They were attracted to Hungary by economic opportunities as entrepreneurs and employees created by rapid economic growth, and they assimilated by following the example of Magyars who held key economic and political positions. Among nationalities born in Hungary, the nobility and German urban residents assimilated prior to 1848. In the second half of the nineteenth century modern economic growth, social and economic modernization, urbanization and disintegration of traditional lifestyles and communities facilitated the assimilation of ethnic enclaves within the central Magyar-language areas, especially of Germans, Slovaks and South Slavs, estimated as numbering several hundred thousands. Those who migrated from peripheral, overpopulated and economically underdeveloped and stagnant regions to urban and industrial centers of the Magyar-language area also assimilated in great numbers. Urban populations played a prominent role in assimilation. In 1880 64 percent of urban residents had Magyar as their native language, and that proportion had increased to 77 percent by 1910. In 1880 60 percent of residents of communities with more than 5,000 had Magyar as their native language, but only 40 percent of those with smaller populations. Overall, assimilation was successful within the major Magyar-language area and in cities or in larger communities with Magyar majorities.

Social mobility was one of the significant motivations of assimilation. An advanced level of education, a rise in the social hierarchy, and leaving traditional village society were accompanied by assimilation. The higher the social position the greater the proportion of those who considered themselves to be Magyars. Ferenc Herczeg, the popular author of German parentage from southern Hungary, wrote about this in his memoirs: "At that time it was a common belief in southern Hungary that you could remain a Serb or a German up to the possession of 700 acres, but beyond that you had to be Magyar to live an appropriate lifestyle."[1] Most of the assimilated merged into the emerging Hungarian social and economic groups of the age. The majority of the class of merchants, artisans and industrialists and of the class of intellectuals was made up of assimilated elements, and so was that of the class of the industrial workers. Assimilated individuals enriched Hungarian science, literature and the arts.

The usual form of assimilation was language change from generation to generation, especially in urban areas. We can refer to a reliable database from Budapest that indicates the profession of the native language by parents and children according to the censuses of 1880 and 1890. The data about 140,000 children in 56,000 families are based on the 1890 census. In originally German families 51 percent of the children retained the parental language, while 48.5 percent gave Magyar as their native language. 47.5 percent of children in Slovak families retained the parental language, while 42 percent changed to Magyar and 11 percent to German. In the Budapest district with the largest German majority, Óbuda, Magyars assimilated to the German language in larger proportions than did Germans to Magyar in 1880. In 17 percent of Magyar families the second generation professed German as their native language, while of those with the German language only 11 percent changed to Magyar. But in 1890 the proportions reversed: 17 percent of children born in German families professed Magyar as their native language, while only 10 percent of children in Magyar families changed to German. The comparison of data from the 1880 and 1890 census indicate that intergenerational assimilation expanded significantly.

It was clear, nevertheless, that in spite of significant assimilation it was unrealistic to expect the complete assimilation of all non-Magyar nationalities. It was not only the professional experts, statisticians, demographers and sociologists who realized this, but also realistic political leaders, who did not employ forcible assimilation, but expected that national minorities should acquire facility in the official language and remain loyal to the Hungarian state, while preserving their national traditions. The change of language and nationality was a complex, complicated and multigenerational process. The two million assimilated "new Magyars" underwent various phases of this process, but that process was by no means final or definitive.

We should address at this point the much-discussed question of whether the official census data were reliable. We can be certain that these data were not modified to flatter Hungarian national sentiment. Contemporary archival sources confirm this point. According to directors of the Central Bureau of Statistics, local officials gratuitously considered residents of multiethnic settlements who spoke both a minority language and Magyar as Magyar by native language. Therefore the government issued strict instructions in 1900 and 1910 on this issue, which ensured that the bilingual population was usually registered as non-Magyar.

It was no easy task to determine precisely and unambiguously the native language of residents, in part because various ethnic groups were intermingled within settlements. There were many bilingual or trilingual settlements and many ethnically mixed marriages. In 1910 23.4 percent of the population was fluent in two or more languages, speaking Magyar and additional minority languages.

In the early years of the twentieth century the Central Bureau of Statistics was commissioned by the Hungarian government to carry out complex investigations in several hundred villages situated on the Magyar–Slovak and Magyar–Romanian language boundary lines to compare census data on native language identification with the actual state of affairs. The final report of this survey characterizes the situation of these bilingual villages with mixed populations as follows: "It appears that these people live in an indefinite boundary line between the Magyar and Slovak languages, so that it is equally justified to regard them as Magyars and as Slovaks. They are fluent in and speak both languages in equal measure. It is usually up to the disposition of the census official whether to classify someone as Magyar or as Slovak. The 1890 census was more apt to increase the number of Magyars, while the 1900 census, as a result of strict central directions, classified those individuals as Slovak. It is nevertheless questionable which method was correct, since the national identification of these people was indefinite in both cases and it was just as arbitrary to consider them as Magyar in 1890 as to consider them as Slovaks in 1900. In many places it is disputable whether the optimism concerning the Slovaks gradually adopting Magyar ways was well founded, according to the 1890 census, which considered them as Magyar, or the stricter approach of the 1900 census, which added them to the Slovak population."[2]

The authenticity of the data on native languages in the Hungarian census is confirmed by contemporary Romanian sources in the case of Transylvania, a much-discussed territory with three nationalities. Professor Nicolae Mazere of Iaşi, using Romanian sources of the Orthodox and Greek Catholic Churches in Transylvania, investigated the number of Romanians in Transylvania settlement by settlement in the early twentieth century. In his study published in 1909 he stated that the total number of Romanians in Transylvania was 1,414,000, which was 3,000 fewer than the figure of the Hungarian census.[3]

On this issue it is worthwhile to quote the position of a British historian who had an exceptional understanding of the Habsburg Monarchy and Hungary: "It should be emphasized that, contrary to so much that has been written, practically all this increase in the Magyar element was real in almost every sense of the term. The censuses (which did not attempt to define the individual's 'national feeling' or 'nationality' but only his 'maternal language') were usually honestly compiled (if there were occasional abuses, they were very few) and in the overwhelming majority of cases, the man who put himself down as 'Magyar by mother tongue' regarded himself, or at least wished others to regard him, as a Magyar."[4]

Notes

1 Béla G. Németh, ed., *Herczeg Ferenc Emlékezései* [Memoirs of Ferenc Herczeg] (Budapest, 1985), p. 85.
2 Magyar Országos Levéltár (Hungarian National Archives), Archives of the Prime Minister 1909–XXV–181.
3 Nicolae Mazere, *Supliment la Harta etnografica a Transilvaniei* [Supplement to the Ethnographic Map of Transylvania] (Iaşi, 1909).
4 C. A. Macartney, *The Habsburg Empire 1790–1918* (London, 1971), p. 726.

7. TRANSFORMATION OF THE SETTLEMENT NETWORK AND URBANIZATION

An important indicator of modernization is the expansion of urbanization. The changes in the concentration of the population in urban areas and the analysis of the settlement network demonstrate that urbanization made significant progress in Hungary following the Compromise, but especially in the period after 1880.

Internal migration involved movement from small communities to larger centers. From 1869 to 1910 the population of communities with under 1,000 inhabitants decreased by 8 percent, while the population of those with between 1,000 and 5,000 increased by 29 percent and the population of settlements with over 5,000 doubled. The number of settlements with populations over 5,000 increased from 239 to 417 and their total population rose from 2.9 million to 6.2 million in four decades. In 1869 21.3 percent of the total population lived in these settlements, but in 1910 33.8 percent lived there. In Croatia the 1910 percentage was 12.3 percent and in Austria it was 26.2 percent.

Hungary had an unusual situation in Central Europe with regard to the density of settlements and their average population size. In 1910 there were 168 settlements per 1,000 square kilometers in Austria, but in Hungary there were only 44. The average population size per settlement in Austria was 583 residents, but in Hungary it was 1,456. There were historical reasons for these differences. In the sixteenth and seventeenth centuries, when the central area of the country was under Ottoman rule, the residents of the Great Plain moved to the market towns, which were protected by the Sultan. In this manner, agrarian settlements with large populations and territories covering 10–20 depopulated medieval villages were established. There were substantial differences regarding settlement density and their population size among the several regions of Hungary even at the end of the nineteenth century. In 1890 there were on average 12 settlements per 1,000 square kilometers in the Great Plain, while in western Transdanubia (Zala and Vas Counties) there were more than 100, in northern Hungary 70 and in Croatia 164. The average population size of settlements in the Great Plain was 5,300, while in hilly and mountain areas it was under 1,000. Several towns of the Great Plain—Szeged, Debrecen, Kecskemét and Szabadka (Subotica)—had areas close to 1,000 square kilometers.

In the agrarian settlements of the Great Plain with large areas and populations a unique agrarian settlement type became common, the detached farm, called the *tanya*. This was due to the transition from livestock farming to grain cultivation and flood control. Some of the people in these settlements established agrarian homesteads in the extensive agrarian territories outside populated areas, formerly used for grazing. They initiated grain cultivation in these territories. This process began in the eighteenth century, but it became widespread in the second half of the nineteenth century. Around 1850 the population of these new *tanya* settlements, attached to 65–70 towns, was 45,000–55,000, which represented about 2–3 percent of the area's population. But by 1870 the population of the new settlements was over 200,000 and in 1910 it was over 700,000. On the one hand this development was a consequence of economic growth and of the grain boom, but on the other it was an obstacle to the social and cultural development of the population. Most of the inhabitants and operators of the *tanya* farms were involved in extensive grain cultivation and lived isolated from urban settlements, transport routes, medical and educational facilities and community life. As a result, they subsisted under conditions of material, health and cultural deprivation, separated from traditional communities.

The transformation of manorial lordships into modernized large estates was based on a new class of agrarian laborers, the agricultural servants settled in special housing units, called *major*. Many hundreds of thousands of agrarian families were crowded into these ramshackle farm buildings, especially in the eastern and southern parts of western Hungary, separated from the outside world. They were subject to the absolute work discipline of estate administrators.

The second half of the nineteenth century introduced a qualitative change in urbanization, with extensive railway construction and industrial development. In addition, a modernized administrative and judicial system, as well as an expanded and progressive educational system, also had a substantial impact on urban development. As a result, the urban settlement network underwent significant changes.

At the time of the Compromise the traditional urban settlement network still prevailed in Hungary. In 1869 1.2 million people lived in the free royal cities, representing 8.9 percent of the total population. Only 27 of the 81 cities had populations over 10,000, while 30 cities had fewer than 5,000 residents. In the 1870s the legal status of cities was changed. As a result, 25 cities with rights of county jurisdiction and 106 cities with limited self-government (under the jurisdiction of counties) made up the new urban network. This system was a more appropriate basis for future urban development. In 1869 the population of these 131 cities was 1.9 million; in 1890 it was 2.4 million. Between 1869 and 1890 the total population increased by 11.7 percent, while the urban population expanded by 28 percent. In 1869 13.9 percent of the population and in 1890 16.1 percent lived in the 131 cities. In the early twentieth century seven additional settlements received urban status, so that in 1910 3.7 million residents lived in the 138 cities, which was 20.2 percent of the total population. The urbanization of Croatia was more modest: 237,000 residents, or 9 percent of the population, lived in 17 cities in 1910. The population of Fiume, the coastal city with a special status, trebled between 1869 and 1910 and increased to 50,000 prior to World War I. Nevertheless, it is clear that urban status and urban conditions were not always identical. Twenty-six of the 138 cities had populations under 5,000 and two had fewer than 2,000 inhabitants. At the same time the population of 62 other settlements (villages) exceeded 10,000, and nine of these surpassed 20,000.

Pál Beluszky reconstructed the urban network of the turn of the century on the basis of urban functions and organized it by urban hierarchies. Based on 75 urban functions he classified 245 settlements of the Hungarian Crown as cities in 1900. The population of these 245 cities was 3.9 million, which was 20.4 percent of the population. This analysis indicates that legal status and urban functions were not identical at all, since 26 cities with limited self-government were not classified as having urban functions, while 115 settlements with the status of communities were classified as cities.

Between 1867 and 1910 those cities expanded most rapidly that were located at central points of the new railway system or along the so-called market lines, the meeting points of grain-producing and mountain areas, at the edge of the Great Plain and the western plain (known as the *Kisalföld* or Lesser Plain (the plain in Northeastern Hungary) and the bank of rivers entering the Great Plain. The city of Szeged was the only provincial city that surpassed 100,000 residents before World War I. Ten cities had populations between 50,000 and 100,000: Szabadka (Subotica), Debrecen, Pozsony (Bratislava), Temesvár (Timişoara), Kecskemét, Nagyvárad (Oradea), Arad, Hódmezővásárhely, Kolozsvár (Cluj-Napoca) and Miskolc. In Croatia only Zagreb belonged to this group. Four of the 11 cities mentioned were extended settlements of the Great Plain—Szeged, Szabadka, Kecskemét and Hódmezővásárhely—where one third of the population, in Szabadka one half, did not reside in the city, but in the isolated farms (the *tanya*).

A characteristic feature of Hungarian urban development was the fact that a significant number of the largest cities had a low level of urbanization. There were 30 cities or settlements in the Great Plain with populations exceeding 10,000 in the mid-nineteenth century that differed physically, or in their employment and social structure, from traditional cities of Western and Central Europe and of western Hungary, northern Hungary and Transylvania. The agrarian cities of the Great Plain had extensive areas, and an increasing part of their population, about a third in the period after the Compromise, did not reside in the city, but in distant isolated farms, although some had residences in the city. Two thirds of the population, 40 percent in the largest and most urbanized town, Szeged, made their living from agriculture. But it is not justified to regard these settlements as giant villages. In the first place, residence and place of work were no longer identical, as they were in villages; secondly, they provided several typically urban functions such as regional markets, administrative and cultural centers, and in some cases railway junctions and early industrial development, in the 1880s. In the decades following the Compromise an urban core emerged, and in the larger centers, such as Szeged, Kecskemét and Szabadka, this had expanded significantly by the early twentieth century. The urban core was surrounded by a small town belt consisting of ground-floor residences, artisan shops and stores, while the outer circle was a broad village-type belt of traditional peasant houses and courtyards.

The physical image of a significant part of Hungarian cities was still traditional in the second half of the nineteenth century. Building statistics indicate that there were a small number of multi-storey buildings. In 1890 there was a total of 66,000 multi-storey buildings in the country as a whole, which represented a bare 2 percent of all dwellings. In 1910 12 percent of buildings in the largest cities were multi-storey, but even in Budapest ground-floor residences made up 59 percent of the total. At the end of the nineteenth century a modernized system of public utilities was initiated in the larger cities. In the early twentieth century electric lighting replaced gas lamps; earlier, in 1887, in transport electric tramways had replaced the omnibus in Budapest, an example followed by more than a dozen provincial cities prior to World War I. In 1896 the first underground railway line of the European continent was completed in Budapest. Housing construction accelerated at the turn of the century. In the early twentieth century—within the framework of actions taken on state and capital housing (building houses, building estates and building blocks of flats in towns)—9,000 new, comfortable and reduced-cost housing units were built in Greater Budapest, providing access to urban dwellings for larger groups of the population. In 1911 the majority of housing units in Budapest (55 percent) had a single room, 24 percent had two rooms, and 11 percent had three rooms.

Even in larger cities the majority of housing units (51 percent) were built of adobe or mud, and a minority (46 percent) of stone or brick. In the cities of the Great Plain the standard building material in the early twentieth century was adobe or mud. In large cities roofs were covered with fireproof materials, such as tile and slate, but even in these cities 20 percent of houses were covered with reed or thatch. In cities of the Great Plain 50 percent of houses were thatched or reed-covered.

There was a slow but gradual improvement of housing conditions as shown by the statistical information that in 1869 there were 3.8 residents per room and in 1910 there were 3.1 residents. Traditional building materials continued to be used in villages and in the outer belts of cities, but there was gradual improvement decade by decade. In 1890 15.3 percent and in 1910 22.1 percent of housing was built of bricks or stone, 46.4 percent of adobe or mud, and 31.5 percent of wood. In 1890 19 percent of housing used tile, slate or tin roofing, but by 1910 40 percent used fireproof materials for roofing. Stone and brick construction and tile roofing were common in the western counties of western Hungary (Transdanubia) and the central and western parts of northern Hungary, and well-to-do peasants in these areas used stone foundations for their adobe and mud houses. In the Great Plain and the eastern, southern and northern parts of western Hungary adobe and mud construction and reed or straw roofing were common. In northern Hungary and Transylvania wood construction was widespread.

The major change in the housing conditions of the peasantry was the introduction of a means of control of smoke in kitchens and rooms, although in some areas there were still houses without chimneys at the end of the nineteenth century. In the second half of the nineteenth century the porch became widespread in peasant houses and the pantry was integrated into the residence. The room looking out onto the street (the "clean room," as it was called) was set aside for visitors and not used for residence: this was decorated with traditional folk art. In one corner stood the oven heated from the kitchen, and in the opposite corner the table with benches. The furniture of peasant houses was renewed: chests were replaced by cupboards. This new furniture was made more and more frequently by village joiners. The prosperous peasantry of the Great Plains agrarian settlements adopted the furniture style of the nobility and urban middle class, especially the dark brown coloring of furniture sets. But in most regions, especially the less developed parts of the country, the custom of colorful painted furniture became widespread.

Budapest

There was only one city in Hungary that can be compared to European major cities: Budapest. The city became unified and the national capital in the decades after the Compromise, although its three constituent parts of Pest, Buda and Óbuda had already been closely related to each other and had already served as the transport, cultural and political center of the nation in the preceding decades. Since the three cities were subject to Ottoman rule in the sixteenth and seventeenth centuries, the political center of Hungary had been Pozsony (Bratislava). The Diet held its sessions there, and this was the seat of central government offices and the site of coronations. In 1848 Pest and Buda were designated as the seat of Parliament and the government. Francis Joseph was crowned here in 1867. In 1873 Buda with 54,000 residents and Óbuda with 16,000 residents were united with Pest with 200,000 residents. The unification was strengthened with several bridges connecting Pest and Buda: the Chain Bridge opened in 1848 and three additional bridges and two railway bridges were built after the Compromise. The population growth of the city in the second half of the nineteenth century was unique in Europe. In 1869 its population was 270,000, in 1880 371,000, in 1900 733,000, and in 1910 880,000. In 1870 it ranked seventeenth among major European cities and in 1900 it was eighth, preceded by London, Paris, Berlin, Vienna, St. Petersburg, Moscow and Hamburg.

The population of Pest increased much more rapidly than that of Buda prior to 1900, since economic growth was centered there. But after 1900 this changed: the development of Buda became more dynamic. The two new bridges built at the turn of the century integrated Buda into the process of growth, the role of the natural environment increased in importance and new residential development expanded to the Buda hills. The growth of Pest slowed down in the early twentieth century, and suburban areas as well as adjacent settlements became the centers of expansion.

The suburban settlements surrounding Budapest developed rapidly at the turn of the century. The 21 settlements annexed to Budapest in 1949 had 32,000 residents in 1869, 129,000 in 1900 and 229,000 in 1910. The designation Greater Budapest was used at the turn of the century for the present area of the city. The population of Greater Budapest surpassed 1.1 million residents in 1910.

Population growth in Budapest was due exclusively to immigration prior to 1880, since the number of deaths exceeded the number of births. After 1880, however, natural increase played a role in population growth, but additional immigration accounted for 72 percent of that growth between 1880 and 1910. The major part of the migrants came from the adjacent area of Pest County, the Slovak-populated areas of northern Hungary and the adjacent or nearby counties of northern Transdanubia. Migration from more distant areas, the south and east, increased at the turn of the century. Slovaks were employed primarily in construction and industrial plants. Since Budapest was the economic and cultural center of the country, it attracted Jewish migrants as well. In 1880 70,000 Jews lived in Budapest and by 1910 their number had increased to above 200,000. Their proportion of the population was 23 percent.

As a result of major immigration two thirds of the population (in 1910 64.7 percent) were born outside the city. Among contemporary European cities only St. Petersburg had a larger percentage of immigrants: 68 percent. London's proportion of immigrants in 1910 was 30.6 percent.

About a quarter of the immigrants were born outside Hungary, primarily in the Austrian half of the Monarchy, in Bohemia, Moravia, Galicia and Lower Austria. The number of foreign-born continued to rise, but their proportion decreased rapidly, from 11.1 percent in 1880 to 5.7 percent in 1910. In 1900 there were more than 50,000 foreign-born persons in Budapest, of whom 42,000 originated from the other half of the Monarchy. In the next decade the number of residents born in Austria decreased to fewer than 38,000. In contrast, the number of migrants from countries other than Austria rose: it exceeded 10,000 in 1910. Most came from Germany, followed by Italy, but at the turn of the century the number born in neighboring countries increased as well.

After the Compromise the Hungarian governments provided substantial financial and political support to the development of Budapest as a major European city, as the center of Hungarian economic and cultural life and as the second capital of the Monarchy along with Vienna. The Public Works Council of the Capital, established in 1870 and chaired by the prime minister in office, directed the city's development. The urban development programs were initiated in the 1870s. The grand avenue called Radial Boulevard (*Sugárút*), later designated Andrássy Boulevard, as it is still known today, opened in 1873. Other major developments included the Great Boulevard (*Nagykörút*), Heroes' Square and the City Park, completed in 1896. On both banks of the Danube wharves were built. The major sectors of modern economic development, wholesale trade, banking and industry, were all concentrated in the capital city. Budapest developed into the major industrial region of the country. One fifth of the industrial labor force and more than a quarter of factory workers were employed in its plants. The city was also the center of the national railway network. The important rail lines branched out from here in all directions.

Along with the growth of the city, the population assimilated to Magyar nationality and language. At the time of the census of 1850 it was not yet a Magyar city. At that time 38 percent of the population was Magyar, 40 percent was German, 15 percent was

Jewish and 5 percent was Slovak. In Buda and Óbuda Germans were in the absolute majority with 65 percent, while Magyars made up 18 percent, Jews 12 percent and Slovaks and Serbs 3 percent of the population. Jews were considered not only as a religious group, but also as a nationality. In 1880 Magyars had an absolute majority of 56.8 percent, but 34.2 percent of the population gave German as its native language and 6.2 percent gave Slovak. At this time Jews were considered only as a religious group. 59 percent of the Jewish population of 70,000 gave Magyar as its native language and 35 percent gave German. At this time Buda had a German majority (52.5 percent), while Magyars made up 42.1 percent and Slovaks 3 percent of the population. But in Pest Magyars had an absolute majority of 60.5 percent, while Germans made up 29.6 percent and Slovaks 7 percent. In the 21 suburban communities of Greater Budapest Germans were in the majority (48 percent), while Magyars made up 40 percent and Slovaks 10 percent of the population in 1880. Jews constituted 7 percent of the population in these communities. Therefore in 1880 Budapest continued to display German characteristics: it was a bilingual city, where more people spoke German (74.4 percent) than Magyar (72 percent).

In 1910 the population predominantly considered itself to be Magyar (86 percent), while 9 percent saw itself as German and 2.3 percent as Slovak. 90 percent of the Jewish population of 204,000 considered itself to be Magyar. In 1910 88 percent of the population of the suburbs gave Magyar as its native language, while 8 percent gave German and 2 percent Slovak. In addition to these three major ethnic language groups, there were several thousand people of other nationalities in the city, Poles, Czech-Moravians and Serbo-Croats, reflecting the multiethnic character of the Monarchy and of Hungary.

It is evident, therefore, that in this period a major process of assimilation took place in Budapest, one that primarily affected the German and Slovak population. It is clear that the immigration of Magyars, who settled in the city after the Compromise, played a major role in this process. Another important factor was the fact that the predominant majority of the Jewish population considered itself to be Magyar. We can conclude, therefore, that Budapest was a major ethnic and linguistic melting pot. At the turn of the century it was said that Budapest was the largest Slovak city, since it was the residence of the greatest number of Slovaks. It was estimated at the turn of the century that 50,000 to 80,000 Slovaks lived in the city, while the census of 1890 reported that those who gave their native language as Slovak did not exceed 27,000. This can be explained by the fact that a substantial number of Slovaks employed in Budapest were seasonal workers, who were not present in the city at the time of the census. But it also indicates Slovak linguistic assimilation. The population that considered itself to be Magyar but still spoke Slovak was three times as numerous as those who gave Slovak as their native language at the turn of the century. In 1880 the number of residents who spoke Slovak was 52,000 and in 1900 their number was 84,000, representing 15 and 12 percent of the total population respectively.

8. THE HUNGARIAN ECONOMY IN THE ERA OF DUALISM

At the time of the Austro-Hungarian Compromise in 1867, Hungary was still a backward agrarian country. More than three quarters of the population made a living from agriculture, while just 10 percent were employed in industry. Two thirds of Hungary's GDP stemmed from agriculture, while *per capita* national income was less than half that of Germany or France and less than a third of the figure for Great Britain. Still, national income or GDP estimates for this period are rather uncertain and not necessarily comparable. Perhaps the best indicator of economic development is the percentage of the population employed in non-agricultural sectors of the economy, such as mining, industry, commerce, transport and banking. In 1870, this share was 5.7 percent in Hungary and 2.6 percent in Croatia, but 17.6 percent in Austria and Bohemia, 15.6 percent in Germany and 28.5 percent in Great Britain. The Hungarian economy was backward not only in comparison with the countries of Western and Central Europe, but also in relation to Italy and the Scandinavian countries. Moreover, it had not yet reached the level of development from which the countries of Western Europe set out—in the late eighteenth and the early nineteenth century—on the path to modern economic growth and the industrial revolution.

This does not mean that Hungary was stagnating or immobilized by its traditional economy. On the contrary, the first half of the nineteenth century saw the beginnings of capitalist development and the modernization of the national economy. The 1848 Revolution brought an end to the country's traditional economic and social structure, enabling a decisive breakthrough in the process of modernization and removing the major obstacles to capitalist development. The post-revolutionary decades brought fundamental political, legal and institutional changes, which served to guarantee the application of the market laws of supply and demand and the mechanism of free competition. In the 1850s and 1860s, growth rates in production and sales significantly exceeded the population increase. The foundations of a capitalist economy were laid and the conditions for sustained economic growth put in place. Even so, the results were rather modest in international terms.

In the mid-nineteenth century, owing to backwardness in the agricultural and industrial sectors and low levels of capital accumulation, the impulse for economic growth came from outside the country—from the international economy. From the 1830s onwards, the industrialization of Western and Central Europe gave rise to a rapidly expanding market for Hungarian agricultural, timber and food industry products. Meanwhile, industrializing Europe contributed increasingly to the development of backward regions by making investments and by dispatching entrepreneurs, technical experts and skilled workers. In this manner, it supplemented the limited resources of such regions, compensating for the absence of certain production factors.

The economic growth of the decades leading up to the 1867 Compromise was largely the result of the country's increased participation in the European economy. Demand for agricultural produce and raw materials in the advanced industrial nations stimulated Hungary's agricultural sector; both agricultural production and the export of raw materials grew at accelerated rates. Progress in agriculture provided a stimulus to other branches of the economy: growth accelerated in areas such as transport, banking and the food industry. During this initial period of growth, industry played only a minor role. The conditions and factors necessary for a broader expansion were still absent. Accordingly, in the years following the Compromise, economic growth continued to be focused on the capitalist development of agriculture, an increase in agricultural production and exports, the establishment of modern transport and banking systems, the development of the production of industrial raw materials and fuels, and an improvement in the quality of labor. In broader terms, the industrial revolution had to wait until the turn of the 1890s, after a period of rapid growth in the agricultural and services sectors. Among other factors, government economic policy played an important role in this process.

Government Economic Policy

The Compromise was accompanied by a major change in economic policy. The aim of neo-absolutism had been to modernize the Empire. This had led the government in Vienna to subordinate the development of the Hungarian economy to Imperial interests. In 1867, the newly autonomous Hungarian legislature and government were required to define Hungarian economic policy. In the light of the trade and customs union, Austrian interests had to be taken into consideration, but Hungary's relationship with Austria was no longer one of subordination. Instead, the two countries were equal partners with mutual interests.

When drafting legislation and government policy measures in the economic field, government ministries always requested the written opinions of the various economic professional and lobbying bodies. The lobbying bodies included the chambers of commerce and industry, membership of which was compulsory. The chambers had been established in 1850 and were organized on a geographical basis. Their number had risen to 20 by the end of the century. In Hungary's major towns, retailers and wholesalers were grouped into separate associations. In 1878, there were 80 such commercial associations, and their total membership was 4,500. The largest associations, based in the capital city, were the Association of Pest Civil Retailers and Wholesalers and the Pester Lloyd Association (est. 1853). The early years of the twentieth century saw the establishment of the two largest and most influential employers' organizations: the Confederation of Hungarian Industrialists (GYOSZ, est. 1902) and the National Association of Hungarian Traders (OMKE, est. 1904).

In contrast to the large and medium-sized industrialists and commercial traders, the country's craftsmen were slow to organize. Although the Imperial decrees of 1851 and 1859 had introduced the principle of freedom to practice a trade of one's choice, the guilds continued to exist. They were abolished by the Industrial Act of 1872, when they were replaced by industrial associations. While the country had once had more than 3,000 guilds, in 1878 there were just 1,275 industrial organizations, with a total membership of 69,000. In the 1870s, craftsmen demanded the reintroduction of guilds. The Industrial Act of 1884 rendered the formation of industrial corporations compulsory in settlements where at least 100 craftsmen were working. After the Compromise of 1867, the National Industrial Association (*Országos Iparegyesület*), which had formed originally in the 1840s but had then dissolved in 1850, was reestablished. It actively contributed to the creation of the conditions for the country's industrialization and to the drafting of an effective industrial policy. The lobby organization of Hungary's large and medium-sized landowners was the National Hungarian Economic Association (OMGE), established in the 1830s. There was a rapid increase in the number of regional and county agricultural associations. In 1896, large landowners established a further organization, the Federation of Hungarian Farmers (*Magyar Gazdaszövetség*). This body also represented the interests of smaller farmers, and it even assisted in forming peasant cooperatives.

The economic associations and lobby organizations advised the government on economic matters, while also promoting economic development through their publications, periodicals, conferences and exhibitions. A national exhibition planned for 1871 had to be cancelled, but during the 1870s various agricultural and industrial fairs were held in towns throughout the country. The initial focus of such fairs was local agriculture and industry, but they were gradually transformed into events presenting national achievements. The first all-embracing national exhibition was held in Budapest in 1885. It was followed, in 1896, by the much larger Millennium Exhibition, which marked the thousandth anniversary of the Magyar conquest. More than five million people attended the Millennium Exhibition.

A series of economic policy debates were held in the country between 1873 and 1878; they were closely followed by both economic and political actors. One contemporary commentator described the result of the debates as follows: "Our country's economic policy, which has been molded by the principle of *laissez faire* and the primacy of agriculture, has taken a decisively new direction."[1] The debates focused upon the direction of economic development and the main principles and objectives of economic policy. Even after the Compromise, Hungary was still a predominantly agricultural country; indeed, its financial well-being and general economic status were dependent upon two factors: agricultural production and prices for agricultural products. The trade and customs policy of the Dual Monarchy tended to closely reflect Hungary's agricultural interests and Austria's industrial interests. Even so, as the first signs of a crisis in grain sales became apparent in the 1870s, more and more people took the view that "Hungary can no longer be an agricultural country… only through partly converting to industry will we be able to stand our ground in economic, political and cultural terms as a nation in Europe."[2] The country's economic and political elite agreed on the need for industrialization and agreed that Hungary could not remain a purely agrarian country. There were, however, differences of opinion on the desired nature and extent of industrialization and on the means of industrial development. A minority of participants in the debate—with advocates such as the leaders of the National Industrial Association and members of the opposition independence party—wanted industrial development to be the core principle of foreign trade and customs policy. They believed that the main obstacle to industrial development was the customs union and the lack of industrial protective tariffs. The other extreme was represented by large and medium-sized landowners, who wished to subordinate industrialization to agricultural interests. They desired a modest rate of industrial development, which would facilitate the processing of raw materials and produce, and would offer employment to agricultural laborers during the winter.

Most of the participants in the debate believed that a separate customs area and industrial protective tariffs were not sufficient guarantees of rapid and sustainable industrial development. They argued that the construction of a modern industrial economy was a drawn-out process that would encompass several stages of development and take decades to accomplish. In their view, several prerequisites had to be met before capitalist industry could take hold in Hungary, and the focus had to be on developing industries for which the country offered favorable conditions. "I am inclined to support industry where it can develop naturally, that is, in some parts of our country, development that reflects natural factors," said Prime Minister Kálmán Tisza.[3] According to the Parliamentary Trade Committee's spokesman, Gábor Baross, "The development of large-scale industry is an aim for which, even under normal circumstances, decades of untiring work and effort are necessary—even in places where the prerequisites are not lacking at all. In my humble opinion, Hungary's vocation is to support its agriculture and to develop and strengthen an industrial sector for which the prerequisites are already in place."[4] The Trade Committee defined the direction of economic policy as follows:

> The objective of Hungary's developing into a major industrial country lies far in the future, because the country is hardly likely to be successful in the struggle between the great industrial countries in the light of the lack of the major development factors of industry, such as capital and a suitable class of workers and artisans, and it would not be capable of achieving its goal. The Committee does not hesitate to state that in order to achieve this very distant and remarkably difficult objective, it would not dare to sacrifice or even risk the vocation of agriculture in its present advantageous and enormous development.[5]

Following the economic policy debates of the 1870s, it was generally acknowledged in economic and political circles that Hungary's economic development had been unbalanced and inadequate. The country's economic policy should strive therefore to make use of the resources available with a view to promoting a more balanced and even economic growth. The turn of the 1880s marked the beginning of a new phase in Hungarian economic policy; a feature of this new phase was increasingly diversified government support for private enterprise—above all manufacturing industry and agricultural sectors that had been ignored.

At the time of the 1867 Compromise, Hungary's leading political and economic actors were still supporters of capitalist free enterprise, or economic liberalism. However, the ensuing years of economic growth in Europe, the so-called *Gründerzeit* or founders' period, marked the end of a period lasting several decades that has come to be regarded as the classical era of capitalism and free enterprise. The crisis of 1873 and the subsequent economic depression led most European countries to change direction on economic policy. Anti-liberal social and political schools of thought sprang up; they demanded the regulation and restriction of capitalist enterprise—with a view to assisting those who were unable to compete. In Hungary, opposition to economic liberalism grew steadily in the 1870s. Many of the opponents were unable or unwilling to adjust to the conditions of capitalist enterprise, while others found that their competitive position had deteriorated. The country's artisans wished to limit occupational freedoms; they organized a national movement seeking a revision of the industrial law of 1872 and the reintroduction of guilds. The agrarian movement of the large and medium-sized landowners wished to impose restrictions on the sale of land, to introduce legal protections against the division of lands owned by noble medium-sized landowners and peasant smallholders, and to impose rules and regulations on the stock exchange. In 1882, a leading exponent of agrarian neo-conservatism, Count Albert Apponyi, stated the following during a parliamentary debate: "The unrestrained natural game of social and economic forces can only lead to a further strengthening of those who are already strong and to the suppression of the weak or even their complete destruction, and so the full weight of state institutions should be applied on behalf of society's weak and to sustain them." Moreover, "while maintaining the foundations of society's present form, one should improve on the deficiencies of those."[6]

In Austria the departure from a liberal economic policy came in 1879, when an anti-liberal coalition led by Count Eduard Taafe implemented an economic policy that reflected the values and principles of social conservatism. In Hungary, the rejection of liberalism was more gradual and less consequential. Indeed, supporters of a liberal economic policy continued to control the government, since their adversaries—the anti-liberal and neo-conservative mass movements and parties—proved incapable of establishing a broad front (as they had done in Austria). In Hungary the direction of economic policy was determined in a struggle between the so-called "mercantile" and "agrarian" wings of the ruling class and the governing Liberal Party. The government decisively rejected anti-liberal arguments. In his response to Apponyi, Kálmán Tisza turned away "from the theory of state absolutism with a social character. Who will measure the point in time when, with regard to one or another issue, the competition as regulator is insufficiently strong, and the state must take on the role of regulator?"[7]

Liberalism thus remained the fundamental principle of official economic policy. In the light of the economic difficulties, however, the state was required to intervene in a more direct manner. The need for such intervention was recognized even by the supporters of liberal economic policy. The state secretary for trade, Sándor Matlekovits, wrote as follows: "Under present economic circumstances, the state cannot adhere to the *laissez faire* system, and 'intervention' is clearly a justified and correct measure."[8] It is worth noting that the French economic liberals, in particular Michel Chevalier, who exerted considerable influence on leading Hungarian economic policy-makers at the time of the 1867 Compromise, also emphasized the importance of government initiative and cooperation to the development of several branches of the economy. "Our statesmen, who felt that we should make up for centuries of lagging behind and failure in a short time, were aware from the outset that society alone would not be capable of this, and that in our country the government would have a far greater role than in other states whose development had taken place under normal conditions. Thus the government not only sought to guarantee law and order and the free movement of social forces; it also actively interfered in economic affairs."[9] At the same time, the limits to government intervention were also set out: "The government should assist where private enterprise is unable to help, and it should also permit the free development of private enterprise. It is the state's duty to act in areas that go beyond the limits of private activity, but not to provide everything for everyone," wrote Menyhért Lónyay, the main economic policy-maker during the post-Compromise years.[10]

The government thus undertook large infrastructure investments that offered a long-term return (such as railway construction, river regulation, road and bridge building, and developing the Port of Fiume/Rijeka). All these projects exceeded the possibilities of private enterprise, particularly in a country with little internal capital formation. In these areas, private enterprise also received substantial public funding (such as railway interest rate guarantees and subsidies for shipping companies). The government also made efforts to develop vocational education and established a network of public technical services. The difficulties of industrialization and the growing agricultural crisis in Europe led to a reappraisal of policy in the late 1870s. It was concluded that the government should actively cooperate in developing manufacturing industry more quickly and in modernizing the agricultural sector and improving its competitiveness. "One should not just leave things alone. The *laissez faire* principle is justified only as long as natural development is a possibility. The obstacles faced by underdeveloped countries are so great that the removal of these obstacles can hardly be imagined in the absence of active government cooperation. Under normal circumstances, private enterprise in Hungary does not take the initiative, but if it is encouraged to do so and if we have defeated the initial difficulties of such an initiative, then enterprise will become active in our country, too."[11]

In response to pressure from various national actors, government support for industry was introduced in 1881. The industrial subsidies prescribed in the laws of 1881, 1890, 1899 and 1907 included 15-year exemptions on tax and duties for industrial plants as well as railway transport and customs concessions. Between 1881 and 1913, more than 1,700 companies benefited from these concessions. From the turn of the century, financial subsidies for new or expanded industrial plants and industrial workshops were favored. Between 1899 and 1914, almost 500 factories received a sum total of 55 million crowns in government subsidies. In return, these factories undertook to invest approximately 200 million crowns in fixed capital and create 48,000 new jobs. The actual levels of investment and the number of new jobs created exceeded the projected figures by 35–40 percent. Small industrial plants received 20 million crowns in government aid. As an important prerequisite for the receipt of such government aid, plants were required to have "up-to-date technology," and this was regularly monitored by government industrial supervisors. Contemporary European—mainly German—economists concluded that it was more beneficial to provide such government support than to employ protective tariffs against industrial competitors from Austria. In any case, such tariffs were no option for Hungary, in the light of the trade and customs union. Similar policies were also proposed for the Balkan countries, as they set out on the path towards industrialization.

In 1907, the new coalition government drew up a ten-year industrial development program, "which planned on achieving the industrial independence of the country by the expiry of the trading agreements" in 1917.[12] According to the plan, 100 million crowns of government aid would be used to establish 284 new plants, with fixed assets worth 360 million crowns and a combined workforce of 120,000, above all in the textiles and clothing industry. The plan was only partly realized, owing to the outbreak of war. By 1914, 121 new factories had been established using government aid.

Industrial subsidies promoted the development of rather backward light industries such as textiles, clothing and glassware, which accounted for just a small part of domestic consumption. The main beneficiary of the other type of government-assisted industrial development, a system of public contracts, was heavy industry. Public institutions, the railways, shipping companies, government-owned industry and industrial companies receiving state aid were obliged, under ministerial decrees, to obtain whatever they required in terms of industrial goods from domestic plants—if the latter were capable of supplying the necessary quantity and quality. The government also managed to ensure that Hungarian industry would benefit in proportion to the quota from orders submitted by the common army. The annual value of public contracts in the early 1890s was 50–60 million crowns, but by 1913 this amount had risen to 413 million crowns (£17 million). The Confederation of Hungarian Industrialists rightly concluded in 1908 that "in the countries of Western Europe, government orders as a proportion of total industrial production were nowhere as significant as they were in Hungary."[13]

A primary objective of government aid for industry was to encourage foreign capital and companies to establish industrial plants in Hungary and to ensure favorable conditions for such plants. In the early years of the twentieth century, large Austrian and Czech industrial enterprises founded dozens of plants and subsidiaries in Hungary. Their aim was to utilize government aid for industry so that they could retain the Hungarian market in the event of the introduction of a separate customs area. Most of the established plants were actually larger and more modern than those in the Austrian half of the Monarchy.

General demands for government agricultural subsidies were first made at the Farmers' Congress held in Székesfehérvár in 1879. Compared with the significant measures taken to develop manufacturing industry and industrial vocational education, the government initially spent little on agriculture. Since agriculture had been Hungary's leading sector for decades, this is perhaps understandable. In the 1880s and the first half of the 1890s, economic policy tended to reflect "mercantile" interests, but in the 1890s agricultural interests became an increasingly important factor, owing in part to the establishment of an independent Ministry of Agriculture in 1889. It was particularly during Ignác Darányi's two terms as minister of agriculture (1895–1903 and 1906–1910) that the Ministry contributed, in various ways, to the development of Hungarian agriculture and to the spread of modern production methods—especially among the country's peasant farmers. The government took the initiative and offered assistance in areas such as the replanting of vineyards that had been destroyed by philoxera, in livestock breeding, in modern animal health and veterinary services, in the provision of loans to farmers, in agricultural skills and knowledge, and in soil improvement. Hungary's leading economic sector was assisted by a whole series of academic research centers: a dozen or so "experimental stations" established by the government in the field of agricultural technology. At the turn of the century, the Ministry of Agriculture launched several programs to modernize agriculture—livestock breeding in particular—in the country's backward upland areas, where traditional farming methods still prevailed. These programs helped crisis-ridden areas such as the northern and northeastern parts of Upper Hungary and the Szekler (*Székely*) region of Transylvania. Government economic policy did not, however, interfere with land ownership, although at the turn of the century there was increasing pressure for action on peasant settlement and more equitable distribution of land. The government was unwilling to realize the ambitions of nationalist Hungarian social and political organizations concerning the need for restrictions on the activities of the banks of the minorities and the need to prevent the gradual break-up of lands owned by Hungarian medium-sized landowners in areas inhabited by minorities. Nor did it take land ownership policy measures to strengthen Hungarian dominance over the national minorities.

An important part of the government's economic and social policy was regulation of working conditions in agriculture and industry. Several major pieces of legislation were adopted in this field mainly after 1890. Laws were also passed (in 1891 and 1907) on health and accident insurance for industrial and commercial employees.

Thus, from the 1880s onwards, direct government action on the economy gradually increased in all areas, but this did not amount to the abandonment of economic liberalism. Government intervention in the domestic economy served to invigorate rather than limit private enterprise. Some government measures to develop the economy were designed to protect domestic entrepreneurs and help them to compete with more advanced foreign rivals. During the years prior to the outbreak of World War I, government intervention in the economy increased so much that a supporter of classical liberal economic policy could state the following, with some exaggeration: "Today in Hungary the government controls the major prerogatives relating to economic life and is able to completely influence competitive relations."[14]

The government became the largest economic actor and investor in the economy; it played a pivotal role in the development and maintenance of infrastructure. In 1913, government fixed property was worth 5.5 billion crowns (£230 million). This amounted to 11–12 percent of national wealth, representing a quarter of total fixed assets excluding land. Of this amount, 3.9 billion was accounted for by the transport and communication infrastructure, 1.1 billion by industrial, mining and agricultural plants, and 0.5 billion by public administrative and educational facilities. The government-owned industrial plants (coal, iron ore and salt mines, the iron foundries, engineering factories, money mint, printers and tobacco factories) accounted for 12 percent of industrial production. In 1913, government-owned plants employed 235,000 people, or 11 percent of all workers. The government funded 18–20 percent of all investments during the period.

The largest government-owned undertaking was Hungarian State Railways (MÁV), which was established in 1868 after the purchase of a bankrupt private railway. In the 1880s, railway policy became an important instrument of government economic policy. Gábor Baross was an influential figure in this development, serving initially as state secretary and then as minister. In previous periods, the government had rescued private railways in order to restructure bankrupt private companies. Now, in contrast, Baross undertook a planned nationalization policy in order to establish government control of a national network. He hoped to then use his influence to determine the transport policy of Hungarian railways and the system of charges. In 1890, he introduced a new system of fees for goods delivery; the new system benefited domestic rather than imported industrial goods. Regarding major Hungarian industrial articles, he introduced so-called "direction tariffs," which meant that the delivery of such goods from Budapest to Vienna was half as expensive as delivering from Vienna to Budapest. Understandably, a difference of view arose with the Austrian government, since Baross's policy seemed to violate the principles of the trade and customs union.

An important part of government economic policy was the foreign trade and customs policy, which the Monarchy's two governments and legislatures jointly oversaw.

In the mid-nineteenth century, reflecting the free trade ideas that held sway in European trade, the Habsburg Monarchy introduced general customs tariffs in 1852 and 1854, while repeated amendments to the latter piece of legislation reduced customs and abolished the import and export bans. In 1851, customs revenues amounted to 13 percent of the total value of imported goods, and this figure fell to 6.2 percent in 1860 and fluctuated between 3 and 4 percent during the 1870s.

Between 1865 and 1867, the Monarchy signed trade and customs agreements with other countries that were based on the principle of free trade and ensured most-favored status. Such agreements were signed with the German Customs Union, Great Britain, France and Italy. The Hungarian government contributed to a revision of the German customs treaty in 1868, and it signed supplementary treaties with Great Britain (1869), with Switzerland (1868), with the countries of East Asia (1869), with Spain (1870), with Portugal (1872) and with Sweden (1873). These agreements guaranteed the almost tariff-free export of all Hungarian agricultural produce to the countries of Central and Western Europe. Subsequently, trade agreements were signed with Romania (1875) and with Serbia (1881). Both agreements established customs-free zones for the most important export goods.

For Hungary, an agrarian country with significant exports of agricultural produce, the free trade policy had a beneficial effect. Austrian industrialists, however, protested against this policy; in the end, they managed to persuade the governments to retain modest industrial protective tariffs. At the time of the Depression that followed 1873 and during the corn sales crisis, protective tariffs began to be employed in Europe once again. In late 1876, Bismarck raised the prospect of the introduction of "warlike tariffs" against Hungarian agricultural exports. In the late 1870s, following the expiry of the trade agreements signed in the 1860s, the era of free trade drew to a close. In 1879, the Monarchy's main foreign trade partner, Germany, imposed a tariff on corn and livestock imports, and the scope of the tariff increased in the course of the 1880s. Other European countries experienced similar things, and for more than a decade protective tariffs were a feature of international trade, the rate of growth of which slowed considerably. There was no return, however, to the extremely high and prohibitive customs duties of the first half of the nineteenth century. Import bans were still a rarity; when they were imposed it was for reasons of animal health.

The new general customs tariff, which Austria-Hungary introduced in 1878, raised customs duties only on certain industrial goods. These were increased further by the customs tariff of 1882, which introduced moderate customs duties on agricultural imports. The customs tariff of 1887—which remained in force until the turn of the century—fully reflected the shift towards protective tariffs in Europe: customs duties on both industrial and agricultural goods were raised significantly. In comparison with those of other European countries, the protective tariffs of the Monarchy were rather moderate. They were far less onerous than those of France, Italy, Spain, Portugal and especially Russia. In the 1880s and 1890s, customs revenues increased to 8–9 percent of the value of imports (while in Russia they accounted for 28 percent of the value of imports). The trade agreement with Romania expired in 1886 and could not be renewed for three years. During the so-called customs war with Romania between 1886 and 1889, the Monarchy limited

Romanian livestock and corn imports, while Romania imposed high tariffs on Austrian and Hungarian industrial goods. Exports to Romania fell by half, while imports declined to just one tenth of their previous value.

In the early 1890s, a favorable shift took place in the foreign trade relations and customs policy of Austria-Hungary. The shift originated in Germany, whose stance exerted great influence on the trade and customs policy of the Monarchy, since more than 40 percent of its exports were destined for Germany. Bismarck's successor, Caprivi, abandoned the inflexible autonomous customs policy with its protective tariffs, and switched to a more moderate policy of agreements based on reciprocal concessions. In the 1890s, a broad trading zone, based on agreements, was formed in Central Europe, with reduced tariffs and enhanced transparency: Germany, Italy, Switzerland, Belgium and the Monarchy signed trade and customs agreements with each another. This led to a slight increase in trade with Germany and a significant increase with Italy. Even so, there was no real change in terms of the volume, structure and growth development of foreign trade. The most important result of the agreements was the fixing of tariffs: that is to say, the 12 signatory countries were not permitted to increase their tariffs against each other for a period of 12 years. This reduced uncertainty, which had been the greatest drawback of the era of autonomous tariff policies. In subsequent years, the Balkan countries joined the consensual tariff system.

The new trading agreements raised great hopes among Hungarian economic policy-makers. It soon became clear, however, that Hungarian agricultural exports would not be able to recoup their markets in the West. Under such circumstances, the main supporters of free trade, Hungary's agricultural producers, abandoned their former position and began pressing for higher protective tariffs for agriculture, in order to secure for themselves the Monarchy's market in opposition to growing Balkan imports. The German government also made concessions in response to pressure from the agrarian sector; in 1902, it raised agricultural tariffs once again. The

Monarchy did not fail to respond: the tariff of 1906 raised industrial customs duties as well as tariffs on agricultural goods. For a quintal of wheat, the import levy was 1.19 crowns in 1882, 3.57 crowns in 1887, and 6.30 crowns in 1906. The effect of the 1906 tariffs on price is shown by the increase in the average annual price of wheat between 1902–1906 and 1907–1911: the increase was 42 percent in Budapest and 39 percent in Vienna, but just 14 percent in London. Between the two periods, the price of flour rose in Budapest by 35 percent.

The customs tariff of 1906 had a contradictory effect on Hungary's economic development. For agriculture and the milling industry, it ensured a market of 50 million consumers within the Monarchy. Agricultural production grew, but so did sales. The milling industry attained a satisfactory capacity utilization rate. But the price of grain, flour and other foodstuffs rose more steeply than anywhere else in Europe.

Capital Accumulation and Employment

At the time of the Austro-Hungarian Compromise of 1867, the main obstacle to rapid and balanced economic growth was the inadequacy of domestic production factors. The lack of capital and experts became almost a cliché among contemporary Hungarian economic experts. The mechanization of agriculture, the development of a modern infrastructure, and the establishment of modern large-scale industry necessitated significant investments with slow rates of return. As a rather underdeveloped country, Hungary was in no position to realize such investments using domestic savings alone. For this reason—and similarly to other backward countries in Europe—Hungary was compelled to use foreign capital to develop the economy. All economic experts agreed with this strategy: "The nation is unable, by itself, to establish the major institutions that are necessary in all areas of the economy; all our railways and all our major banks are owned by foreign capitalists, and it is natural, furthermore, that the leading industrial companies have been established by foreigners."[15]

In the second half of the nineteenth century, underdeveloped countries could relatively easily make up for their lack of production factors. A developing country would attract capital, savings, entrepreneurs, technical experts and skilled workers. Hungary's import of capital was particularly significant in the years following the Compromise of 1867. In the first half of the period, most foreign capital entered the Hungarian financial system by means of government loans. From the 1880s onwards, a greater role in the mediation of capital import was played by fixed-interest-rate securities (bonds or mortgage bonds) issued by the largest domestic banks and placed on the international capital markets. A smaller amount of foreign capital arrived in the country through the purchase of shares in banks, railways and industrial companies. Securities issued in Hungary and placed on the international capital markets represented the main type of capital import. A secondary role was played by foreign entrepreneurs and companies when they founded new firms or subsidiaries in the country. One of the goals of government aid for industry was to encourage investment by foreign companies, by offering various benefits and concessions.

In 1892, two thirds of securities issued in Hungary were placed abroad, half of those in Austria. But the proportion was the reverse for securities issued between 1892 and 1912: two thirds were placed in Hungary and only one third abroad. This is evidence of a significant strengthening of domestic capital accumulation during the second half of the era. At the turn of the century, Austria's role in the provision of capital in Hungary declined. Its place was taken in part by domestic capital accumulation and in part by other foreign—above all German and French—capital. At the same time, there was a significant movement of Austrian capital investments from the government sector to private enterprise. Immediately prior to World War I, Hungary's principal creditor was Germany: its investments in the Hungarian economy exceeded two billion crowns in 1913 (14 percent). France was the second-largest investor, with one billion crowns (7 percent). Other major creditors were the Netherlands, Great Britain and Switzerland, each with around 200 million crowns.[16]

Table 1: Placement of Securities Issued in Hungary
(billions of crowns)

	Hungary	Austria	Abroad	Total
1892				
Government loans	1.3	2.4	0.7	4.4
Other securities*	0.7	0.6	0.2	1.5
Total	*2.0*	*3.0*	*0.9*	*5.9*
1912				
Government loans	2.1	1.4	2.3	5.8
Other securities	5.5	1.7	1.5	8.7
Total	*7.6*	*3.1*	*3.8*	*14.5*
	As a percentage			
1892				
Government loans	29.5	54.5	15.9	100
Other securities*	46.7	40.0	13.3	100
Total	*33.9*	*50.8*	*15.3*	*100*
1912				
Government loans	36.2	24.1	39.7	100
Other securities	63.2	19.5	17.2	100
Total	*52.4*	*21.4*	*26.2*	*100*

* Mortgage bonds, municipal bonds, banks, industrial and transport company shares and bonds

In 1914, 27 percent of Hungarian industrial shares, 11–12 percent of bank shares, and approximately 40 percent of transport company shares and priority bonds were placed abroad. In the years preceding World War I, however, the placement of Hungarian securities abroad sometimes encountered difficulties. The export of capital from Great Britain was directed primarily at the colonies and at the United States, while the French were investing billions in Russia and Latin America. Meanwhile, capital accumulation in Hungary's major creditors—Germany and Austria—was needed for domestic economic growth. Thus, in the early years of the century, the export of capital to Hungary decreased significantly. As a consequence "the inflow of foreign capital that streamed towards us in such abundance was prevented more than once during this period."[17]

The rate and in particular the structure of domestic capital accumulation did not meet in full the requirements of a modern industrial economy. There was a reluctance to invest domestic savings in modern capitalist enterprises and new industrial plants. Instead, money flowed into real estate and land holdings, townhouses and more modest but secure annuity bonds, government bonds in particular. "Local capitalists still like to walk along this widened road. There is not much capital for industrial enterprises, but a new bank never has a shortage of shareholders."[18] This preference of small and medium-sized investors is in part understandable: throughout the period, banks paid larger dividends than industrial joint stock companies did.

During the first half of the era, foreign capital played a decisive role in the accumulation of capital in Hungary. From the end of the nineteenth century, however, domestic accumulation accounted for an increasing proportion of total capital accumulation, and the ratio of foreign capital in investments gradually declined. More than 60 percent of investments were directed towards infrastructure. This high ratio reflected the undeveloped nature of Hungary's traditional infrastructure—particularly in comparison with countries in Western and Central Europe. The infrastructure needed to be developed to meet the requirements of a modern economy. In 1913, transport infrastructure accounted for 25 percent of national wealth, excluding land (the corresponding figures were 10 percent in Great Britain and 15 percent in Germany). Three major investment cycles can be discerned during the era: the post-1867 boom, the 1880s and 1890s, and the years preceding World War I. At the height of these three cycles, investments exceeded 10 percent of GDP. Between the Compromise and World War I, reproducible fixed capital increased from 5.3 to 23 billion crowns. This increase represented an annual growth rate of 3.3 percent.

Figure 1

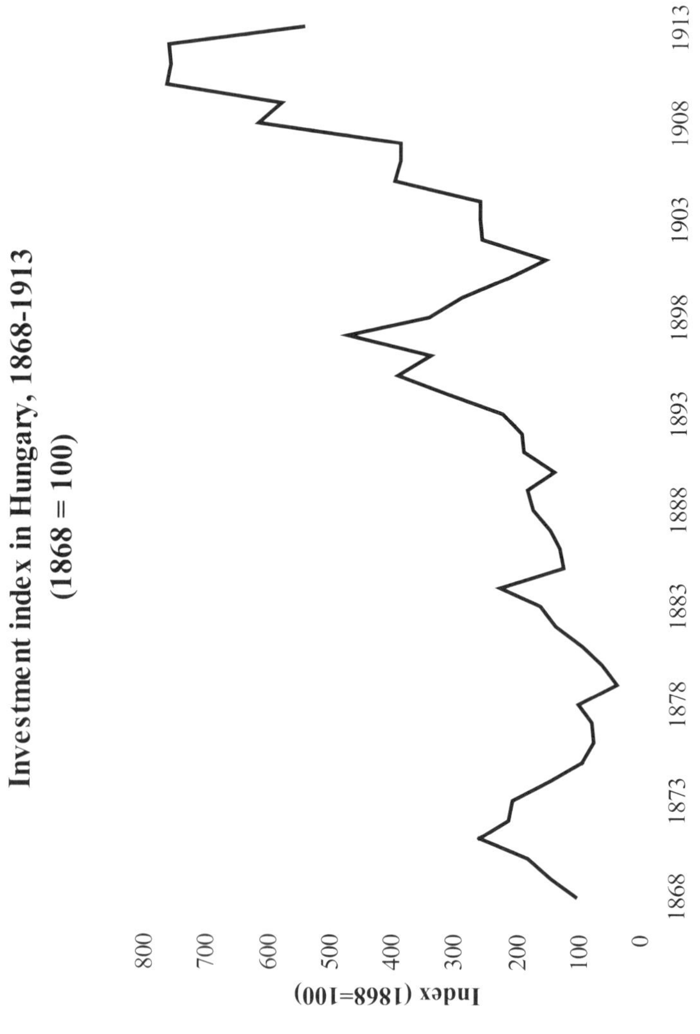
Investment index in Hungary, 1868-1913
(1868 = 100)
Index (1868=100)
800
700
600
500
400
300
200
100
0
1868
1873
1878
1883
1888
1893
1898
1903
1908
1913

Similarities with the accumulation of capital are exhibited by the human production factors, the labor force. Hungary had too few skilled and experienced experts; it could not ensure the adoption of modern technology and its successful application. Both quantitatively and qualitatively, the domestic labor supply failed to meet the requirements of sustained economic growth. Modern sectors of the economy suffered in particular from a persistent labor shortage; skilled job vacancies could not be filled. In 1869, only 40.8 percent of males aged over six years and 25 percent of women could read and write. In other words, approximately two thirds of the active population was illiterate. With such a labor force, it was difficult to adopt modern technology. "In all branches of the country's industry, a shortage of experienced and capable workers is the greatest obstacle to growth," wrote one commentator in 1868.[19] And similar complaints can be found in the 1898 statistics for manufacturing industry. Even in the northern part of Upper Hungary (now Slovakia), which had industrial traditions, the same difficulties were faced by a foreign businessman who established a cloth factory in Zsolna (Žilina): "The training of the workers has encountered the greatest difficulties, because their level of culture is very low; they find it difficult to learn how to use the machinery and are fully lacking the precision and orderliness that are so desirable at a well-managed industrial company; they often fail to turn up for work."[20]

The traditional value system of Hungarian society hindered the growth of a capitalist entrepreneurial class and the appearance of business and technical experts with higher or secondary educational qualifications. Minister of Education Ágoston Trefort rightly concluded that the country first had to "change its morals and customs, if we want to be transformed in an economic sense."[21] The Hungarian middle class tended to favor humanistic grammar schools (*gymnasia*) offering arts subjects, rather than technical and vocational secondary schools. Attendance rates at the latter lagged far behind those for similar schools in Germany and Austria. In 1913–1914, only 16 percent of secondary pupils attended technical secondary schools. In Austria and Italy, more than 30 percent of pupils chose to attend such schools, while in Germany the proportion was even higher, at 40–50 percent. A similar situation arose in higher education. In 1890–1891, 52 percent of Hungarian university and college students were either studying law or theology. As few as 15 percent of them attended technical and business colleges in Hungary or abroad. The number of Hungarian students attending technical universities and business colleges in Hungary or abroad increased from 1,800 in 1890 to 4,600 in 1914, but even in the latter year, law and theology students still accounted for 41 percent of college students, while just 23 percent of students were attending technical or business colleges (the corresponding figure in Austria was 33 percent). Thus, despite the nominal increase, secondary and higher education in Hungary continued to be dominated by the humanities, theology and law. This tendency reflected the prevailing value system in society, resulting in a shortage of young people trained for careers in business and technology.

Such factors explain why, in non-agricultural sectors of the economy, foreign entrepreneurs, engineers, technical and commercial clerks and skilled workers played such an important role in the development of the Hungarian economy after 1867. In the 1870s, one quarter of Budapest's industrial workers had been born outside Hungary. Over time, however, the proportion of foreign experts declined. Indeed, by the end of the nineteenth century, a stable pool of domestic engineers, technicians and skilled workers had developed, and they were quite capable of accomplishing the increasingly complex tasks. This advance was primarily a consequence of a large-scale expansion of primary and vocational education. Among the population aged over six, the share of those who could read and write rose from 31.3 percent in 1869 to 50.6 percent in 1890 and then to 66.7 percent in 1910. From the 1880s onwards, efforts were made to organize education and training for industrial apprentices as well as secondary industrial technical education. By the turn of the century, standards in both fields were broadly compatible with the European average. The number of three-year apprentice schools, which were made compulsory in 1884, had risen to 732 by 1913. Technical middle managers, supervisors and foremen were trained in various industrial vocational schools, of which there were 52 by the outbreak of World War I. Agrarian experts were trained at five agricultural academies. Between 1890 and 1914, more than 5,000 engineers graduated from the Technical University in Budapest, and approximately 2,000 Hungarian citizens obtained degrees from technical colleges outside Hungary.

The intersectoral mobility of labor was limited by the slow rate of agricultural modernization and mechanization, which also exhibited substantial regional differences. Agriculture tied up a disproportionately large share of labor, without making full use of it. Owing to the seasonal nature of agricultural work and discrepancies in the degree of mechanization of the various work phases, a significant proportion of agricultural labor was underutilized. Even so, such superfluous labor was only available to other sectors on a seasonal basis. Agriculture remained highly labor-intensive even at the turn of the century. Most workers coming from the agricultural into the industrial or service sectors were poorly educated and unskilled; many of them were day laborers commuting between village and town, agriculture and industry. A large number of people were transitional, vacillating between agriculture and industry and living in two places. During the agricultural off-season, hundreds of thousands of micro-landowners (also known as "dwarf" landowners) and rural day laborers undertook temporary work at industrial plants (sugar factories, sawmills, etc.) or on railway and river regulation projects and urban construction sites—without completely breaking their ties to agriculture. The modern industrial and transport sectors of the Hungarian economy suffered throughout the period from a shortage of permanent skilled workers and semi-skilled machine operators. At the same time, there was an abundance of temporary unskilled workers. The relatively large number of transitional, commuting workers was a major feature of the Hungarian labor supply during the last three decades of the nineteenth century. Even in the early years of the twentieth century, industrial managers

Table 2: Economically Active Population by Sector in Hungary (excl. Croatia)

	1869	1890	1910	1869	1890	1910	Average annual growth, %		
	1,000	1,000	1,000	%	%	%	1869–1890	1890–1910	1869–1910
Agriculture	5,002	4,499	4,656	75.8	67.5	60.1	– 0.5	0.2	– 0.2
Industry	657	862	1,418	10.0	12.9	18.3	1.3	2.5	1.9
Trade, banking, transport	126	242	467	1.9	3.6	6.0	3.2	3.3	3.2
Day laborers	177	289	203	2.7	4.3	2.6	2.4	– 1.8	0.3
Other	633	780	1,007	9.6	11.8	13.0	1.0	1.3	1.1
Total	*6,595*	*6,672*	*7,751*	*100*	*100*	*100*	*0.1*	*0.75*	*0.4*

in Budapest complained that the number of workers fell by a half during the summer months because they returned to their villages to assist in the harvest, threshing and other agricultural tasks.

Fluctuations between Prosperity and Depression in the Hungarian Economy

The timing of Hungary's integration into Europe's capitalist development was fortunate. The period between 1850 and 1873 saw an expansion of the world economy, with a rapid increase in production and trade. It was the golden age of enterprise; international trade volumes increased by 50–60 percent from decade to decade. Hungary was able to exploit, in a timely and intensive fashion, these years of economic growth, and grain imports from overseas were not the destructive force that they became subsequently. Between 1840 and 1890, crop production in Hungary increased threefold. From the 1840s until the 1870s, there was a 5 percent average annual increase in exports. In the 1840s, annual cereal exports amounted to 200,000–300,000 tonnes, but volumes increased to 1.2 million tonnes in 1867–1871 and to more than two million tonnes in the 1890s (with flour exports being included in total grain exports). After 1867, one third of Hungarian grain production was exported, with flour exports representing a growing share. At the turn of the century, Hungary was the world's second-largest flour exporter—after the United States. In the post-Compromise years, Hungarian exports reached 30 percent of GDP. This ratio was three times higher than the European average. Agricultural produce and food products accounted for 85 percent of exports. The spectacular growth in production and exports was accompanied, for several decades, by similar increases in price. Indeed, between 1823–1827 and 1872–1876, the price index for plant products rose by 260 percent, while animal products registered a 200 percent increase.

Figure 2

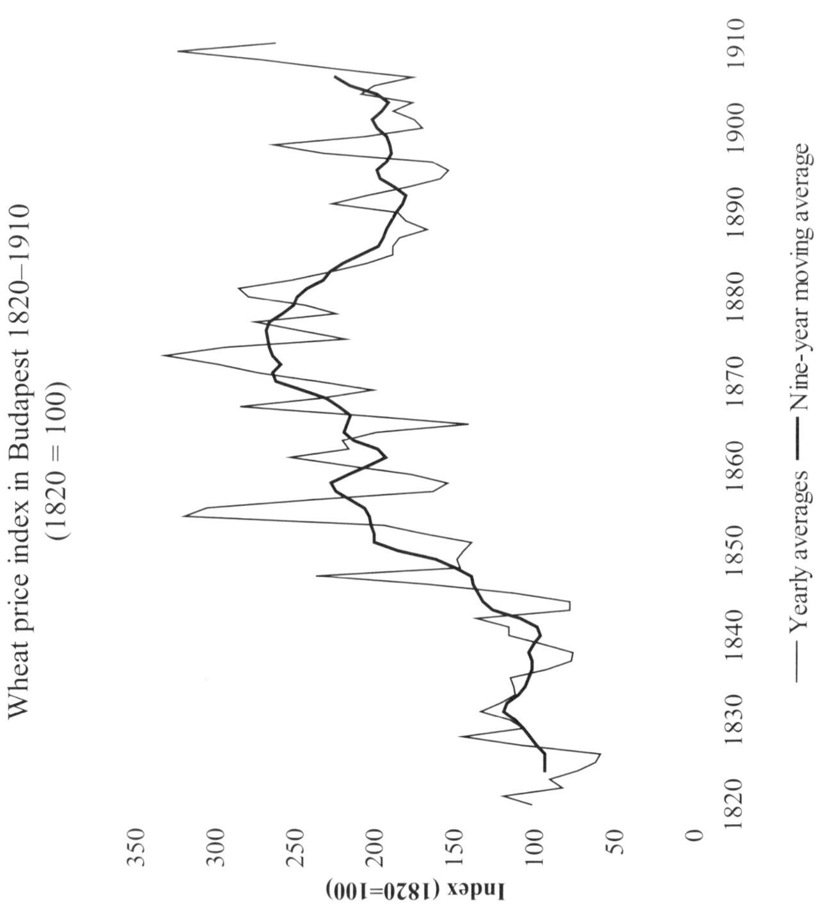
Wheat price index in Budapest 1820–1910
(1820 = 100)
Index (1820=100)
350
300
250
200
150
100
50
0
1820
1830
1840
1850
1860
1870
1880
1890
1900
1910
Yearly averages
Nine-year moving average

Capitalist expansion in the international economy reached its zenith during the years after the 1867 Compromise. It culminated in the founders' boom (*Gründerzeit*), a period of expansion unprecedented in the history of the nineteenth-century economy. The political consolidation of the Habsburg Monarchy—which followed the slow growth and stagnation of the first half of the 1860s—had a very beneficial effect on the development of capitalist enterprise. Economic growth soon spread to Hungary. Following the record production years of 1867 and 1868, grain exports increased exponentially. The money flowing into the country for grain sold at a good price, and the large-scale investments of foreign capitalists seeking opportunities in the backward country (such as railway construction and the establishment of large banks and industrial plants), as well as the increase in paper money following the Austro-Prussian War in 1866, gave rise to an impression of prosperity and wealth. Between 1867 and 1873, around 700 million florins (£57 million) were invested in the Hungarian economy, six times the amount invested in the previous seven years. More than 4,000 kilometers of railway were opened for traffic, and 170 new industrial joint stock companies were formed. During the seven-year period, 552 banks were established, with 88 million florins of registered equity capital.

Exaggerated hopes, however, were followed by disappointment and desperation, as the encouraging upswing of the early 1870s came to an abrupt end. In late 1873, Menyhért Lónyay, who had served both as minister of finance and as prime minister, concluded that "there is a great contradiction between our expectations of seven years ago and the present situation." More and more people were prepared to acknowledge that "we overestimated our own power" and "wanted everything at once." It became obvious that shortcomings going back centuries could not be compensated for in a few years, and that great efforts would be required over long decades in order to eradicate the country's backwardness, restructure the economy, and catch up with the advanced economies of Western Europe.

Many of the new enterprises lacked the conditions for successful operations in the long term, because only a fraction of their share capital had actually been paid in. Company start-ups had tended increasingly to be speculative. The stock market and credit crisis of 1869 was a foretaste of what was to come, but it did not stop the development of the broader economy and an increase in overall production. Nevertheless, several new companies collapsed, owing to the credit squeeze and despite government attempts to assist them through the provision of treasury funds. For a year or so, entrepreneurial spirits were dampened. Then, in 1871, the number of company foundations increased once again, reaching unprecedented levels in 1872 and early 1873.

All of this, however, was overshadowed by the coming crisis. A series of poor harvests in the early 1870s led grain exports to fall to a quarter of the previous level. The great cholera epidemic of 1872–1873 decimated the population. Purchasing power and consumption declined, while capital accumulation and investment slowed. Given the close relationship, panic on the Viennese Stock Exchange (May 9, 1873—"Black Friday") resulted inevitably in the collapse of a large proportion of businesses in Hungary. Foreign capital fled and banks withdrew lines of credit. A whole series of companies that had become embroiled in speculative deals became insolvent. As already noted, even the government faced bankruptcy in the summer of 1873. Fifty banks failed in the aftermath of the crisis, while the number of industrial joint stock companies fell from 174 to 110. Government investments declined significantly, as did also urban and railway construction. In the mining and metallurgy sectors, it was not until 1880 that production recovered and returned to 1873 levels.

The crisis of 1873 affected all European countries, but its effect on the economy of the Habsburg Monarchy was particularly severe. The situation was especially grave in Hungary, since the crisis weakened a modern industrial sector that was still in its infancy. Moreover, the effects of the first true cyclical crisis of Hungarian capitalism were reinforced by the last demographic and food crisis of the traditional society.

The crisis of 1873 was more than a simple cyclical crisis of overproduction. In its wake the whole climate of the capitalist economy changed. The golden age of economic expansion, with its rising prices and profits, and bold enterprises and start-ups, came to a close. The period between 1873 and 1896 has become known among economic historians as the "Great Depression." Growth in production and trade did not cease, but the rate of growth was lower than that of the preceding period. Prices fell, profit rates and volumes declined, and investment and entrepreneurial activity decreased. As prices fell, the cost of living decreased. In most countries, including Hungary, this meant a rise in the real wages and living standards of workers and employees. In Hungary, the depression following the crisis lasted until 1879. Economic growth did not come to a complete standstill, because the crisis barely affected milling, the country's main industry. From 1875, agriculture underwent a period of rapid and persistent growth, benefiting on this occasion from market demand within the Monarchy.

For less developed countries such as Hungary, the depression also had an upside. Since investments and the issuing of securities declined in the advanced countries, an abundance of funds arose on the international capital markets. Consequently, long-term loans could be obtained relatively cheaply and with favorable conditions. In the 1880s, foreign capital began to flow into Hungary.

On the other hand, Hungary was particularly affected by one aspect of the Great Depression. This was the agrarian crisis or, more precisely, the grain sales crisis. From the 1870s onwards, there was a long-term fall in the price of agricultural produce, and of grain in particular. Hungarian grain and flour were squeezed out of foreign markets, owing in part to competition from cheaper American and Russian grain and in part to the closure of Western markets. Relying mainly on markets within Austria-Hungary, Hungarian agriculture attempted to counter the effects of the price falls by rapidly increasing production. This policy was only partially successful, as producer incomes fell and production costs and public dues rose. The effects of the agrarian crisis were partly offset by the fact that industrial goods—consumer goods in particular—suffered even greater price falls. Consequently, an industrial price gap developed in the markets of the Monarchy, and the ratio of exchange (in terms of trade) in international trade developed favorably for Hungary.

The primary response of the Hungarian economy to the grain sales crisis was structural. In the crop structure, the proportion of cereals was reduced, while industrial crops (sugar beet) and fodder crops gained in significance. The area of land used for fodder crops grew more than fivefold, indicating a major shift in the agrarian sector away from crop production to livestock breeding. The advance of livestock breeding to the detriment of plant production was precipitated by a combination of factors. The most important of these was the price trend. Both on world markets and within the Monarchy, prices for animal products developed more favorably than prices for plant products did. Livestock breeding became relatively more important as a consequence; there was also a qualitative improvement above all in the species composition of cattle stocks.

For several years after the 1873 crisis, industrial production stagnated in most European countries. Growth resumed, however, in the 1880s. In Hungary, there was a renewed upturn from 1880. Investments increased and new banks were established. Industrial development was slower than before, but it was placed on firmer foundations than it had been prior to 1873. After 1887, the longest and most significant period of prosperity in the history of Hungary's capitalist economy began. The conditions were in place for sustained growth and increased industrialization. Investment volumes and total assets of the banks increased threefold over the course of a decade, while coal, iron ore and crude iron production doubled. More than 7,000 kilometers of railway were built, and the engineering industry achieved an annual growth rate of 7 percent. The number of industrial joint stock companies based in Budapest rose from 41 to 163, and their share capital increased from 83 million crowns in 1887 to 377 million crowns in 1900. The Millennium celebrations in 1896[22] set off a construction boom in the Hungarian capital. The Budapest Chamber of Commerce and Industry rightly referred to the

1890s as "a period of almost unprecedented economic development and growth." The height of the economic upturn came in 1896, the year of the Millennium celebrations. Meanwhile, the government had managed, by the end of the 1880s, to balance the budget. The government deficit, which had been a feature for 20 years, was transformed into a surplus in the year 1890.

At the turn of the century, construction and heavy industry suffered a crisis of overproduction, while railway construction ceased. In Hungary the economic crisis of the early twentieth century began earlier and lasted for longer than it did in the Western industrialized countries. Indeed, the recession continued in Hungary until 1904 or even 1905. The growing domestic political crisis was a contributing factor. Several years of good harvests made the situation less grave (1906 saw record production levels), and the crisis spared light industry—which underwent rapid development. According to Schulze's calculations and my own figures, the GDP growth rate fell between 1896 and 1913, doubtless as a consequence of the long recession between 1897 and 1905. The new upturn began in 1906, culminating in the years between 1909 and 1912. In addition to housing construction and investments in the railway and agricultural sectors, the period was characterized by large-scale industrial investments, which were undertaken in preparation for war.

For entrepreneurs and capitalists, this was the period of "happy peacetime" economic prosperity. Small-scale agricultural and industrial producers also benefited from the economic expansion—albeit to a lesser degree. For wage and salary earners, however, this was a period of inflation, particularly in urban areas. Wages and salaries could not keep abreast with the rising prices and with the increasing cost of living. Consequently, real incomes among wage and salary earners declined at an accelerating rate in the course of the 15-year period prior to the war. According to recent research, this trend only applied to the urban population; real wages in the agricultural sector were increasing during this period.

Modern Infrastructure and Banking

Traditional infrastructure in Hungary was extremely poor and did not meet the requirements of a modern developing economy. For this reason, most of the resources available, the funds invested in the economy, were spent in this area. The government played an important and direct role in infrastructure development. Moreover, most foreign capital flowed into this area of the economy. In the second half of the nineteenth century, there were two key fields of infrastructure development in Hungary: railway and water system projects. The latter included the regulation of rivers, flood protection and drainage projects. Work in both fields began in the 1840s, and radically altered—over a 50-year period—the country's landscapes and its natural and economic geography. The changes also had an effect on settlement patterns.

In the first half of the nineteenth century, approximately 13 percent of Hungary's territory, almost four million hectares (ten million acres), was subject to regular flooding as unregulated rivers burst their banks. More than half of the territory of the Great and Lesser Plains was subject to flooding, with enormous lakes forming in the wake of river floods. Even when flooding subsided, large amounts of land needed to be drained. Regulation of the River Tisza began in the 1840s. Most of the work had been undertaken in the 1850s and 1860s and had been completed after the Compromise by 1875. By cutting through the meanders, the River Tisza was shortened by 486 kilometers, reducing the number of enormous bends in the river, which had slowed the flow of water. Tributaries of the Tisza were regulated in a similar manner. Concurrently with the regulation of the rivers, flood protection of areas subject to occasional flooding was carried out in cooperation with flood protection associations established by landowners and local communities. The great Tisza floods of the 1870s and 1880s, including the flood of 1879 that destroyed Szeged, highlighted the fact that much work was still to be done. Following substantial government investments, the regulation of the river was recommenced: the riverbed was deepened and the protective dykes were reinforced.

The period after the 1867 Compromise saw the uniform regulation of the River Danube. In the 1870s the Budapest section of the Danube and the section of the river to the south of the capital were regulated. The year 1886 saw the regulation of the Upper Danube (from Győr to the Austrian border). Under an international commission, a large project to remove obstacles to shipping on the Lower Danube was begun in 1889. Owing to the success of river regulation, the distance navigable by steam ships had increased to 3,000 kilometers by 1910. This meant that for every thousand square kilometers, there were 11 kilometers of navigable waters—an unfavorable statistic in European terms.

Protective dykes—3,600 kilometers in length—were established alongside the River Tisza and its tributaries, while dykes running for 2,800 kilometers were placed alongside the Danube. In total 3.8 million hectares (9.4 million acres) of regularly or occasionally flooded land were protected from flooding and thus rendered fit for regular cultivation. In terms of their size and their effects on local community and economic life, these enormous river regulation and land drainage projects were unique in Europe at the time. A manager working on the projects, Jenő Kvassay, rightly referred to the great endeavor as "a second conquest." The drainage of waterlogged land led to the eradication of malaria, which had been endemic in the marshy areas. The large-scale earthworks accompanying the construction of railway and water systems offered employment opportunities to tens of thousands of rural workers on the Great Plain during the 1870s and 1880s. Still, the "second conquest" was only partly realized: river regulation and water drainage were not supplemented by the construction of irrigation systems on the Great Plain. Accordingly, the negative consequences of water regulation soon became apparent: salinization rendered an increasing amount of agricultural land useless in the region east of the River Tisza.

The spectacular increase in agricultural exports, which played such an important strategic role during the first stage of Hungary's economic growth, would not have been possible without the transport revolution. The Hungarian economy exported mainly rather large and heavy goods (such as grain, flour and livestock), which could not bear high transport costs. In the three years between 1867 and 1869, the average weight of Hungarian exports was two million tonnes, while the country's imports—worth roughly the same amount—weighed just 400,000 tonnes. Imports—mostly finished industrial goods—were worth 895 florins (1,790 crowns) per tonne, while exports were worth just 137 florins (274 crowns) per tonne. Rapid, cheap and regular transport alternatives for heavy goods became crucial to the ongoing success of Hungarian exports and the economy as a whole. Traditional transport methods, which were extremely backward in comparison with the countries of Western Europe, were no longer an option.

Before the railway era, Hungary's road network, river shipping and canals failed to meet the requirements of a modern economy. Grain and other products were transported by river. However, all of the country's navigable rivers flowed in an easterly or southerly direction, away from the export markets (which were situated to the west and north). Thus goods barges had to be drawn along by horses or men against the flow of water.

This explains why it was primarily agricultural interests that sought the construction of railways in the 1850s and 1860s. The country's 2,160 kilometers of railway at the time of the Compromise connected the grain-producing areas of the Great Plain to Vienna and the Port of Trieste—and through them to world markets. In northern and eastern parts of the country, there was still no railway. Between 1867 and 1872, the Hungarian Parliament authorized the construction of 20 railways, issuing guarantees in each case of a 5–6 percent profit on invested capital. Within seven years, more than 4,000 kilometers of railway had been opened to traffic. In the 1860s, grain and flour accounted for more than half of the total goods transported. In the years following the Compromise, exports accounted for between 50 and 60 percent of total transported goods. Passenger railway services were of minor significance; their share of total railway revenues never exceeded 30 percent. It was not until the 1890s that passenger services began to expand rapidly—after industrialization and urbanization had significantly increased people's mobility.

In the late nineteenth century, railway deliveries underwent a structural change. As a share of total goods transported, grain and flour had fallen to 18 percent by 1913, while wood and other construction materials, as well as industrial products, became more significant. In the early twentieth century, coal was the most significant transported good (21 percent). A similar change took place in the relative shares of export goods and domestic trade goods: the share of exports and imports decreased to 33 percent in 1891 and 21 percent in 1913, reflecting the development of the domestic market and internal trade.

Since 1855 Hungary's railways had been privately owned. However, after the 1867 Compromise, the system of private enterprise supported by government interest guarantees was transformed into a system of mixed ownership. The government had no choice but to take over several private railway companies that had gone bankrupt. Furthermore, in the case of a few lines of economic significance that had failed to attract private enterprise, the government itself stepped in. The year 1868 saw the establishment of Hungarian State Railways (MÁV), which still exists today. In the course of the subsequent two decades, this government-owned company extended its network to cover the whole country.

The 1873 crisis brought an end to the railway construction boom, which had begun in 1867. During the next eight years, only 954 kilometers of railway were opened to traffic. In the 1880s and 1890s, railway construction underwent a lasting recovery. Indeed, between 1882 and 1899, total investment in the sector amounted to almost 1.5 billion crowns, resulting in the construction of 10,000 kilometers of new railway. Also in the 1880s the Hungarian railway network was connected to cities in the Balkans such as Sarajevo and Bucharest. A connection with Thessalonica and Constantinople was made via Belgrade. A new chapter in Hungarian railway construction began at this time: after the 1880s, the construction of "railways of local interest" became the priority. Between 1890 and

Figure 3

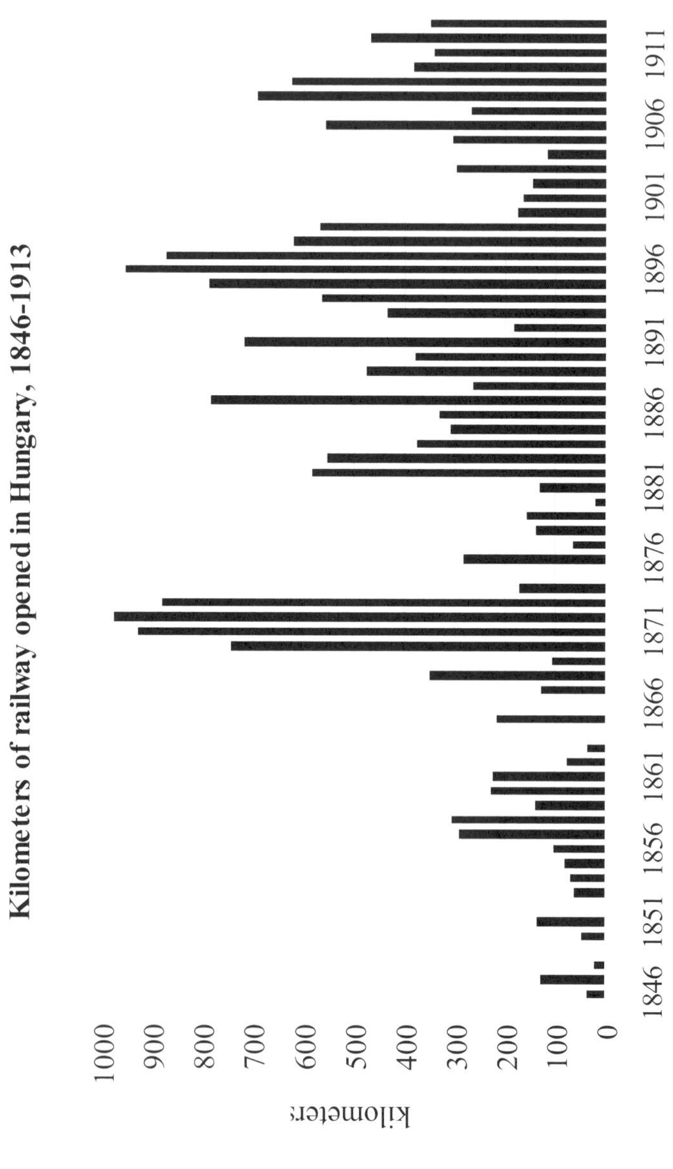
Kilometers of railway opened in Hungary, 1846-1913
kilometers
1000
900
800
700
600
500
400
300
200
100
0
1846
1851
1856
1861
1866
1871
1876
1881
1886
1891
1896
1901
1906
1911

1914, approximately 10,000 kilometers of local railway lines were opened to traffic. These lines, the substructure and performance of which were relatively weak, were consequently cheaper than the main lines. They were designed to meet the needs of local goods and passenger traffic. Whereas 94 percent of privately owned mainline railway lines and 56 percent of government-owned railway lines were built using foreign capital, most of the shares and bonds of the local railways—more than 70 percent—were located in Hungary.

The government-owned railway system was completed in the 1880s. Earlier on, the government had acquired railways in order to rescue them from bankruptcy or to extend the government-owned network. Now, however, the nationalization of the railways became an integral part of the government's comprehensive economic policy strategy. This planned strategy for the railways was implemented when Gábor Baross was serving as state secretary (1883–1886) and then as minister of transport (1886–1892). By means of internal reorganization, nationalization and the introduction of a new fare system, Baross transformed Hungarian State Railways into an enormous, uniform and profitable public utility. In the 1880s, a whole series of major private railways were nationalized. By 1891, 61.5 percent of the network and 84 percent of the main lines had fallen under public ownership, and the government-owned company also managed 88 percent of local railway lines. After 1891, government-owned railways accounted for 83 percent of passenger traffic and 89 percent of freight. Just 1,321 kilometers of railway continued to be owned and managed by three privately owned companies. Furthermore, the government could use its influence in drafting and managing railway policy. The nationalization of the railways brought greater efficiency and cost-effectiveness to railway traffic; it advanced the government's policy of economic development. Moreover, revenues from the government-owned railway helped to balance the budget. Through the acquisition of the private railways, the government took on a debt worth more than 300 million florins (600 million crowns); on the other hand, the railway's gross revenues exceeded by a significant amount the debts stemming from such burdens.

In 1890, new charges for freight traffic were introduced, which actually brought down the price of long-distance transport for Hungarian agricultural goods and granted significant price concessions in the case of major export goods and raw materials. Domestic industrial products were given preference (by means of concessions) over foreign industrial goods. A pioneer system of passenger fares was introduced by Baross; it became known as the zone fares. In 1889, passenger fares on Hungarian railways were among the most expensive in Europe, but passenger traffic was minimal; the trains were empty. The new policy on fares was supposed to assist in encouraging social mobility. Fares were reduced especially on local lines and on long-distance routes. These new fares were introduced so that even those of modest income could afford to travel. The result more than met Baross's calculations and expectations: growth in passenger traffic compensated for large reductions in fares. Indeed, during the initial years, the number of passengers traveling on a government-owned line increased sixfold.

During the Dualist era, the length of the railways in Hungary increased from 2,160 kilometers to 22,000 kilometers. More than four billion crowns were invested in the railways. In 1913, there were 67 kilometers of railway for every 1,000 square kilometers of land, and 102 kilometers for 100,000 people. By this time, Hungary's railway network density approached that of Western Europe and Central Europe, and it was higher than the figures for countries in southern and southeastern regions of Europe. As far as rolling stock, frequency of service and transport performance were concerned, Hungary still lagged behind the average for Western Europe. Double-track railway lines accounted for just 6 percent of the railway system.

Table 3: Railway Passenger and Freight Services in Hungary

Year	Railway	*Passenger traffic*		*Freight traffic*	
	Lines (km)	Passengers (million)	Passenger-kilometer (million)	Tonnes (million)	Tonne-kilometer (million)
1864	1,945	1.8	179	2.0	304
1876	6,682	9.2	510	9.0	1,096
1890	11,246	29.0	1,237	19.0	2,798
1900	17,108	64.0	2,318	40.0	4,648
1913	21,806	166.0	4,999	77.2	8,319

In the 1860s, more than 50 percent of total domestic trade was carried out by means of boat or ship. In the 1870s, most grain arrived in Budapest on horse-drawn barges (where it was processed at steam mills) or it was taken to Győr (whence it was transported to Vienna by rail). With the establishment of a railway network, however, the importance of water transport gradually diminished; its share in 1913 was just 14 percent, whereas in all Western European countries it exceeded 20 percent. Most of the steamship traffic on Hungary's rivers was undertaken by the Danube Steamship Company, established in 1830. Seventy-five percent of the company's passenger traffic and 50 percent of its freight traffic was performed in Hungary, but the management of the company was Austrian and the headquarters were in Vienna. For this reason, Gábor Baross took steps to establish an independent Hungarian river shipping company (while smaller companies meeting local needs had already formed after the Compromise). In 1895, the Hungarian River and Maritime Shipping Company was formed, and received regular government subsidies.

Until 1918, Hungary possessed a stretch of the Adriatic coast, including the major port of Fiume (Rijeka). Around the time of the 1867 Compromise, Fiume had been a traditional maritime shipping center: in 1871, 165 long-distance sailing ships were registered at the port, with a combined capacity of 79,000 tonnes. These large ships provided regular services, not only in the Adriatic but also in the Mediterranean and Black Seas. They sometimes even crossed the Atlantic Ocean. At the turn of the 1870s, sailboats were living their last heyday and the famous boatbuilding companies of Fiume were still operating at full capacity: between 1867 and 1869, 24 ocean-going sailing ships were built each year, each of them with a capacity of 500 tonnes. In the 1870s, however, the boatbuilding trade in Fiume went into recession, and the number of large ships also declined. The growing importance of steamships could not compensate for the decline of the sailboats. In the latter half of the 1870s, the Hungarian government signed an agreement with British shipping companies concerning the management of Fiume's shipping. Then, in 1882, the *Adria* Hungarian Maritime Shipping Company was founded as part of a cooperative venture between British, French and Austrian investors and the Budapest Commercial Bank. The company received significant financial support from the Hungarian government. In return, it agreed to establish regular services to ports in Western Europe. The Empire's maritime shipping towards the east was administered by an Austrian shipping company, Lloyd of Trieste, which until 1890 had also received a subsidy from the Hungarian government. The company *Adria* acquired numerous ships, but the Hungarian–Croatian commercial fleet of 134 steam ships (150,000 net registered tonnes) was rather insignificant in international terms even in 1913.

From the 1870s onwards, the Hungarian government made several large investments with a view to modernizing the Port of Fiume and thereby facilitating Hungarian exports. Fiume's trade volumes grew rapidly, particularly after the city was linked by rail with Budapest in 1873. The significance of maritime exports increased from the 1880s onwards, as German customs policy made it more difficult to transport Hungarian exports to the West by land. A new mole and warehouses were built in Fiume. In terms of shipping and trade volumes, Fiume had become Europe's tenth-largest port by 1913.

Communication underwent growth at an even faster rate than transport. Between 1868 and 1913, the number of post offices increased from 1,337 to 6,610, and the number of telegraph offices from 404 to 5,171. The length of the telegraph cables rose from 8,000 to 26,000 kilometers. In 1869, the world's first postcard was sold in the Austro-Hungarian Empire. Hungarian stamps were first sold in 1871. In 1881, the Budapest telephone service began operations, and subsequently several major provincial towns were integrated into the network. In the 1890s, telephone links were established with other European capitals. In 1887–1888, Gábor Baross merged the three communications sectors—post, telegraph and telephone—into one government-owned enterprise.

Owing to the backwardness of traditional means of transport in Hungary, the share of telecommunication and transport in the accumulation of capital was far greater than in the advanced industrial countries. For instance, the transport network absorbed approximately one third of total investments between 1867 and 1913. In 1913, the amount of capital invested in transport infrastructure was roughly equivalent to the capital stock of the agricultural sector, and significantly exceeded the amount of capital invested in industry. Transport infrastructure amounted to 25 percent of reproducible fixed capital (in Great Britain the corresponding figure was 10 percent, and in Germany it was 15 percent).

At the time of the 1867 Compromise, just 84 credit institutions were operating in the country: five banks, 57 savings banks and 22 mutual credit cooperatives. There were, in addition, six branches of the Austrian National Bank and the Budapest branch of the Viennese bank Creditanstalt. The total registered capital of all the Hungarian credit institutions was less than seven million florins, while the total value of assets was approximately 85 million florins. The period after the Compromise saw a great expansion of the money and credit markets: indeed, between 1867 and 1873, 564 new credit institutions were established within less than seven years. The registered capital of the credit institutions grew by 93 million florins, while deposits and debts increased by more than 150 million. In the Hungarian capital, foreign banks established branch offices that were perceived by local people as enormous. In 1867, the Viennese bank Creditanstalt (backed by the Austrian Rothschilds) founded, in cooperation with major Hungarian landowners and tycoons, the Hungarian General Credit Bank. The British-Austrian Bank founded the British-Hungarian Bank in 1868, while the Franco-Austrian Bank established the Franco-Hungarian Bank in 1869. With the foundation of these major banks, "alongside our old banks, which, having been squeezed into banking business in its stricter sense, were concerned only with the credit requirements of local commerce and industry, there arrived a new type of bank, unknown in our country, the *crédit mobilier* institutions."[23]

The establishment of major banks in Budapest was indicative of the large-scale penetration of foreign capital, while the growing number of provincial savings banks reflected the accelerating rate of domestic capital accumulation. However, in terms of their nature and function, Hungary's savings banks differed significantly from those of Germany and Austria. Rather than operating as business undertakings, the latter tended to be humanitarian institutions subject to government and community supervision. Their function was to serve as a deposit for ordinary people's savings and to promote various charitable goals. In contrast, Hungary's savings banks, having been freed from the restrictions of the pre-1867 period, developed into joint stock companies that sought to pay the largest possible dividend to shareholders. "In Hungary, the savings banks are actually deposit banks, where the savings of the lower social classes are far less important than the larger capital inflows, that is, business working capital available on a short-term basis."[24]

This rapid rate of development came to an abrupt halt at the time of the stock exchange crisis of 1873, which affected Vienna and then Budapest. In the first year of the crisis, 22 banks went bankrupt. In the following six years, 28 further banks collapsed. The Credit Bank (*Hitelbank*) was the only major bank to survive the crisis; the other banks were forced into liquidation after suffering great losses. The total registered capital of all banks fell from 56 million florins in 1873 to 27 million in 1879. It was only after 1880 that the banking sector finally recovered. The renewed upturn was closely related to an abundance of money on the international capital and money markets in the 1880s. This abundance became manifest in an increase in the amount of capital seeking placement, as well as a reduction in the interest rate and improved conditions for obtaining credit. Once again, large amounts of French capital flowed into the Austro-Hungarian economy, and German capital followed suit in the second half of the 1880s. During the two decades preceding World War I, the banking system continued to develop rapidly.

Hungary's leading major bank at this time was the Credit Bank (*Hitelbank*), a member of the Rothschild group, which had a market presence throughout Central Europe. Zsigmond Kornfeld was director of the bank. The Credit Bank served as banker for the Hungarian government: it administered the issuing, placement and conversion of government bonds. In the 1880s, a competitor emerged in the form of the Commercial Bank (*Kereskedelmi Bank*), which developed, under the direction of Leó Lánczy, into a modern large bank. The Commercial Bank became increasingly active in the Balkan countries.

Peasant farmers, craftsmen and retailers obtained credit from private bankers or the smaller regional savings banks. "The one was just as expensive as the other. The rapaciousness of the capitalists knew no bounds; many of the small regional savings institutions competed with the private financial capitalists in usury."[25] Thus, in the late 1880s efforts were made to organize local mutual credit cooperatives of the so-called Raiffeisen type, with a view to resolving the credit problems of ordinary people. The establishment of the Postal Savings Bank in 1886 had the same aim.

In 1913, 1,842 banks and savings banks and 3,191 mutual credit cooperatives were operating in the country. The branches of the Austro-Hungarian Bank and the Postal Savings Bank can be added to these. The total registered capital of the banks was 2.4 billion crowns, while the sum of total assets held by the banks was 15.2 billion crowns (£0.63 billion, $3 billion). One could observe an increase in the number of small regional saving institutions, as well as a greater concentration of bank capital in several major Budapest banks. In 1913, 62 percent of bank assets in Hungary were concentrated in banks in the capital city. More than 80 percent of the capital managed by the banks was so-called outside capital, that is, deposits, securities placed with the bank, and other borrowed funds. Whereas the banks attracted domestic savings by means of the deposits, most of their mortgage bonds and debenture bonds were placed abroad. In this way, they became major mediators of foreign capital, alongside the government bonds. The most important business for the banks—in addition to short-dated loans (credits against a bill of exchange)—was mortgage loans on land and homes. In the early twentieth century, current account loans issued to industrial and commercial enterprises became another significant area of business. As a result of rapid growth, at the turn of the century the Hungarian money and capital market reached the level of development required by a modern capitalist economy, gradually achieving independence. Rather than being dependent on the mediation of Viennese bankers for contact with the money and capital markets of Western Europe, the major Hungarian banks now established wide-ranging international relations and played an increasingly important role in the economies of the Balkan countries. Going beyond the narrow bounds of traditional banking, the banks gradually turned into the managers and leaders of the modern capitalist sector of the entire economy. They played an instrumental role in establishing new companies, in developing existing companies, and in organizing production and sales in whole industrial sectors.

An indicator of the rapid development of Hungary's modern capitalist sector, the economy's fastest-growing and most developed sector, was its banking sector. In 1913, the sum of capital collected and redistributed by the banks amounted to 170 percent of GDP. The rapid development of this modern credit system enabled the Hungarian economy—as it set out on the road to long-term growth—to overcome the difficulties stemming from inadequate capital accumulation in the domestic economy.

Development of the Agricultural Sector

In the early twentieth century, Hungary was still an agrarian country with a rapidly developing industrial sector; agriculture was the economy's largest sector. The importance of agriculture was still great in terms of both GDP and employment, although its relative significance in both areas rapidly diminished during the era of Dualism. However, even just prior to World War I, agriculture still accounted—according to different calculations—for 45–50 percent of GDP and employed 62 percent of the workforce. In Austria, the agricultural sector accounted for 23–28 percent of GDP and 52 percent of the workforce. Meanwhile, the share of agricultural labor was 38 percent in the Austrian and Czech provinces and 76 percent in Galicia and Bukovina.

According to the estimates of experts at the time, the net production value of Hungarian and Croatian agriculture (its contribution to GDP) was 4,572 million crowns in 1911–1913; plant production accounted for 51 percent of this value and livestock farming for 49 percent. According to recent detailed calculations, the average net agricultural production value in Hungary and Croatia was 3,129 million crowns between 1906 and 1910 (deducting seed grain and fodder consumed by livestock). Of this amount, arable production accounted for 1,527 million (48.8 percent), grape and wine production for 143 million (4.6 percent) and livestock for 1,459 million crowns (46.6 percent).

Table 4: Land Use in the Austro-Hungarian Monarchy (percentages)

	Arable	Market gardening	Vine-yards	Meadow and pasture	*Total agricult. land*	Forest	Reed	Non-produc-tive
Hungary 1914	45.38	1.35	1.07	21.07	*68.86*	25.82	0.19	5.12
Croatia 1914	33.48	1.32	0.74	24.04	*59.57*	34.89	0.06	5.48
Lands of the Hung. Crown 1895	41.43	1.33	1.21	23.39	*67.37*	27.80	0.26	4.76
Austria 1897	35.42	1.24	0.81	23.76	*61.22*	32.59	0.35	5.84

In the era of Dualism, agricultural production in Hungary exhibited an average growth rate of 2–2.1 percent per year. In addition to increased domestic consumption, foreign markets also played an important role in stimulating agricultural production. On average, between 1867 and 1871, unprocessed agricultural products accounted for 62 percent and foodstuffs for 15 percent of Hungarian exports. By the period 1909–1913, the share of unprocessed products had fallen to 51 percent, while that of foodstuffs had risen to 25 percent. Thus, the combined share was unchanged at around 76–77 percent. The great importance of the common customs area to Hungary's economic development becomes clear when we realize that three quarters of Hungarian exports were destined for Austria. For Hungarian agriculture and the food industry, the western half of the Empire represented a secure, long-term and expanding market—even during the European grain sales crisis at the turn of the century. In the period 1882–1886, foreign markets had been the destination for 22 percent of grain exports and 40 percent of flour exports. In contrast, by the period 1909–1913, 96 percent of grain exports and 98 percent of flour exports were destined for Austria or Bosnia.

Table 5: Average Annual Production of Principal Crops (1,000 tonnes)

	Wheat	Rye	Barley	Oats	Maize	Potato	Sugar beet
Hungary							
1871–1875	1,298	760	665	549	1,153	840	242
1891–1895	4,014	1,191	1,225	1,018	3,162	2,840	1,382
1911–1915	4,102	1,244	1,512	1,259	4,210	5,167	3,812
Average annual growth %	*2.92*	*1.24*	*2.07*	*2.10*	*3.29*	*4.65*	*7.14*
Croatia							
1891–1895	213	65	54	60	393	974	9
1911–1915	348	79	51	78	601	538	81

In the second half of the nineteenth century, there were ample opportunities for both extensive and intensive factors in the growth of agriculture. Between 1870 and 1914, the area of arable land increased by 30 percent, or three million hectares (from 9.9 million to 12.9 million hectares), and the sown area by 52 percent, or four million hectares (from 7.8 million to 11.8 million hectares). Most of the increase was due to the flood protection projects. The plowing up of pastureland was a further significant factor, made possible by the introduction of intensive farming methods. Finally, as a consequence of the switch to modern crop rotation from the traditional two-field or three-field system, the area of fallow land fell from 2.3 million hectares in 1871 to 1.1 million hectares in 1913. Thus, whereas fallow land had once accounted for 23 percent of arable land, it now represented just 9 percent. In other words, an increasing proportion of arable land was cultivated. In 1908, the traditional two-field or three-field system was practiced in just 26.4 percent of 13,000 rural communities; this indicates the growing popularity of modern cultivation practices. In Transdanubia and the Lesser Plain, the traditional field system was practiced in just 7–8 percent of rural communities, while in the eastern half of the country the figure was greater than 40 percent. Accordingly, regional differences are also manifest in the share of fallow land: only 4 percent in the Transdanubian counties, but as much as 22 percent in Transylvania.

Table 6: Arable Land, Fallow Land, Sown Area and Harvested Land in Hungary and Croatia

	Arable land 1,000 hectares	Fallow land 1,000 hectares	Sown area 1,000 hectares	Harvested land 1,000 hectares	Fallow land as a percentage of arable land %	Sown area as a percentage of arable land %	Harvested land as a percentage of arable land %
Hungary							
1871–75	10,464	2,290	8,174	8,126	21.88	78.12	77.66
1891–95	12,009	1,697	10,312	10,132	14.13	85.87	84.37
1911–15	12,969	1,149	11,820	11,535	8.86	91.14	88.94
Index	*124*	*50*	*145*	*142*			
Croatia							
1891–95	1,348	188	1,160	1,152	13.95	86.05	85.49
1911–15	1,447	111	1,335	1,328	7.70	92.30	91.82

Although the increase in the area of harvested land was an important factor, a greater role in production growth was played by intensive factors—improved average yields and product quality. Between 1867 and 1913, arable production values rose on average by 2.7 percent per year. While the increase in harvested land added just 1 percent, average yields added an additional 1.7 percent. In the four decades between 1871–1875 and 1911–1915, average per hectare yields for grain, maize and sugar beet doubled, while those for potato almost quadrupled. In the early years of the twentieth century, average yields for major crops in Hungary were exceeded only by those in Great Britain, Germany and the Benelux countries. They were similar to yields in other western, northern and southern European countries and significantly exceeded the averages for Russia and the Balkan countries. The exceptional product was maize: Hungary produced the largest amount of maize (one third of total European maize production) and its average yields for maize were the highest in Europe. For most crops, the improvement in average yields slowed down at the turn of the century. One explanation is the fact that fertilizers were slow to spread to Hungary and their use was less common than in Western Europe. For example, in 1908, just 4.1 kilograms of fertilizer (*superphosphat*) were used per hectare of arable land in Hungary—compared with 11.2 kilograms in Austria, 60 kilograms in Great Britain, 61 kilograms in Germany and 88 kilograms in Belgium.

Table 7: Average Yields for Major Crops
in the Countries of the Austro-Hungarian Empire

Quintals per hectare

	Wheat	Rye	Barley	Oats	Maize	Potato	Sugar beet
Hungary							
1871–75	6.1	6.1	7.4	5.4	7.4	23.0	123.5
1891–95	12.8	10.8	11.8	10.3	15.3	62.7	177.9
1911–15	12.4	11.5	13.6	11.7	17.2	83.4	246.5
Index	*202*	*188*	*185*	*217*	*231*	*363*	*200*
Croatia 1911–15	10.5	8.5	8.2	7.5	14.2	66.9	168.7
Austria 1903–15	13.3	13.0	14.0	11.5	12.1	103.7	253.7

The significant improvement in yields was also due to mechanization and the application of better and more effective soil cultivation and other practices. Mechanization was not undertaken in all areas, and nor was it applied to the same extent to all work processes. As far as the tilling of the soil was concerned, animal power (equine and bovine) was still the decisive factor, while steam plows and—from the early twentieth century onwards—tractors were used sparingly. It was largely due to market requirements that the mechanization of agriculture was most advanced in the field of threshing, although on the large estates other modern machinery (such as steam plows and harvesters) also appeared. The 1863 statistics for steam-driven machinery show that Hungary was already far ahead of the Austrian and Czech provinces in this field. At that time, 194 steam machines were in use in Hungarian agriculture, with a performance of 1,603 horsepower. In contrast, there were just 18 steam machines in use in Austrian agriculture (with 147 horsepower). The number of steam threshers in Hungary increased almost tenfold to 2,416 in 1870, and by 1895 there were 8,920 steam threshers in use. In 1915, in addition to 19,920 steam threshers, there were also 8,835 threshing machines with internal combustion engines; 86 percent of the country's grain was threshed using such machines. It was only in Transylvania, in the northern and northeastern parts of Upper Hungary (inhabited by Slovaks and Ruthenians) and in Croatia that the hand thresher continued to be widely used. The rapid spread and popularity of the threshing machine in Hungary was due to the fact that, for climatic reasons, grain harvests on the Great Plain took place several weeks earlier than they did in the countries of Western and Central Europe. It was important to reach foreign markets before local crops were harvested—in order to receive a higher price. Hungary's large landowners began to purchase steam threshers abroad as early as the 1850s. And in the 1860s, steam threshers began to be manufactured in Hungary.

The period between the 1850s and the 1880s was characterized by a rapid increase in plant production, particularly grain production. In the 1840s, grain and maize production had fluctuated between four and five million tonnes, but it reached six million in the 1870s, 11 million in the 1890s and 13 million prior to 1914. The 1890s saw a decrease in the rate of growth; the main feature at that time was a change in the structure of plant production. Wheat retained its leading position, while other grains exhibited a decline in terms of a percentage of the harvested area. In the case of maize, potato, sugar beet and the fodder crops, there were increases in both cultivated area and production levels. There was a more than eightfold increase in the harvested area of sugar beet, while that of the fodder crops exhibited a fivefold increase. Of particular importance was the rapid growth in sugar beet production (with an average annual growth of 7 percent), because this provided the raw product for the sugar industry, which was developing at the turn of the century.

Table 8: Harvested Area of Principal Arable Crops in Hungary and Croatia

	Hungary				*Croatia*	
	1871–75 1,000 ha	1891–95 1,000 ha	1911–15 1,000 ha	*Index*	1891–95 1,000 ha	1911–15 1,000 ha
Wheat	2,117	3,138	3,310	*156*	217	333
Rye	1,242	1,104	1,081	*87*	97	93
Barley	902	1,040	1,110	*123*	67	63
Oats	1,012	986	1,072	*106*	93	104
Maize	1,556	2,064	2,456	*157*	357	425
Potato	365	453	620	*170*	62	81
Sugar beet	20	78	155	*775*	1	5
Other	912	1,270	1,731	*170*	368	227
Harvested area	*8,126*	*10,132*	*11,535*	*142*	*1,262*	*1,329*
		As percentages				
Wheat	26.05	30.97	28.70		17.19	25.03
Rye	15.29	10.89	9.37		7.71	6.97
Barley	11.10	10.26	9.62		5.29	4.72
Oats	12.46	9.73	9.29		7.34	7.80
Maize	19.15	20.37	21.29		28.27	31.96
Potato	4.50	4.47	5.37		4.92	6.06
Sugar beet	0.24	0.77	1.34		0.09	0.35
Other	11.22	12.53	15.01		29.18	17.11

Grape and wine production became a less important segment of overall plant production. This was due to the destruction wrought by philoxera, which peaked in the 1890s. The area of land devoted to viniculture fell by a half, while wine production decreased to a quarter of the previous level. At the turn of the century, an important task of the Ministry of Agriculture, which had just become an independent ministry, was to promote the renewal of viniculture by offering effective support to vineyard reconstruction and the planting of new vineyards. The Ministry's action was successful: "The country's viniculture came out of the shock caused by philoxera at a higher level. The production of more noble species has spread, which, in turn, has required an improvement in production technology. With the planting of new vineyards, the significance of viniculture in areas with sandy soils increased—alongside the historical wine regions."[26]

Table 9: Relative Importance (in Terms of Value) of Crops Produced in Hungary and Croatia (1906–1910)

	%
Wheat	20.99
Other grains	14.52
Maize	13.49
Potato	5.07
Legumes, vegetables	3.68
Industrial crops	3.63
Fodder crops	8.32
Straw	11.71
Total arable	*81.41*
Grapes and wine	15.08
Meadow (hay)	3.51

The spread of viniculture in areas with sandy soils, above all the region between the River Danube and the River Tisza, was closely connected to fruit production. The turn of the century also saw an increase in market gardening to meet consumer demand among the rapidly growing urban population. Specialized regional cultivation also arose (such as peaches in the Kecskemét region, onions in the Makó region, and paprika in the Szeged and Kalocsa regions).

Figure 4

Price indices for agricultural and industrial goods
in the Austro-Hungarian Empire
(Index: 1867 = 100)

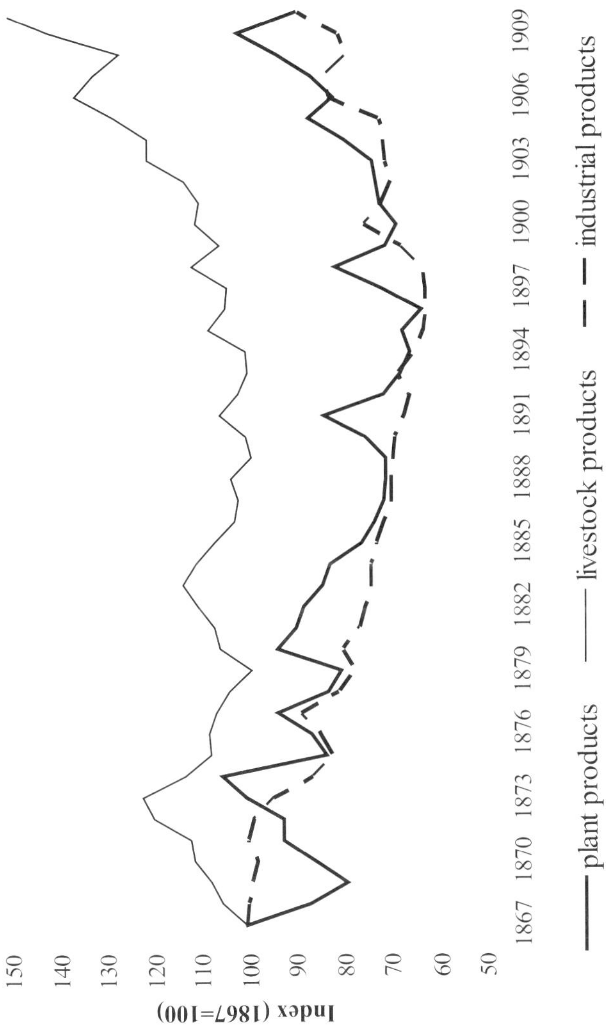

The more than fivefold increase in the cultivated area of fodder crops was indicative of the most important change in the structure of the agricultural sector, namely the increased relative importance of livestock farming as against plant production. The advance of livestock breeding was due to a combination of factors, including a change in the structure of food consumption as a result of modernization and urbanization. A second factor underlying the change was price development. In comparison with prices for plant products, the prices of livestock products developed more favorably in both world markets and the markets of the Monarchy. The change in consumer demand is also reflected in the changing structure of Hungarian agricultural exports. In the 1880s, plant products were predominant, accounting for 34 percent of total exports; livestock and livestock products accounted for 26 percent. By 1913, plant products' share had fallen to 26 percent, while the share of livestock and livestock products had remained unchanged. Thus, immediately prior to World War I, the two principal agricultural sectors were of equal importance in terms of Hungarian exports.

Table 10: Livestock in the Austro-Hungarian Empire
(thousand animals)

	Horses	Cattle	Pigs	Sheep
Hungary and Croatia				
1869	2,159	5,279	4,443	15,077
1884	1,997	5,593	5,554	11,181
1895	2,308	6,738	7,330	8,123
1911	2,351	7,319	7,580	8,548
Per 1,000 inhabitants (1911)	113	350	363	410
Austria 1910	1,803	9,160	6,432	2,428
Per 1,000 inhabitants	63	321	225	85

Cattle breeding was a particularly successful sector of Hungarian livestock farming in the era of Dualism. After a period of stagnation lasting several decades, the number of cattle began to grow in the 1880s, increasing from 5.6 million in 1884 to 7.3 million in 1911. This represented an increase of 31 percent. The growth in cattle exports was even more spectacular, increasing from an average annual figure of 50,000 animals in the period 1867–1874 to more than 300,000 animals at the beginning of the twentieth century. Even more important than such quantitative changes was the qualitative improvement: the switch from extensive and semi-extensive breeding to more intensive methods of breeding and the introduction of new breeds. In 1870, Hungarian Gray Cattle accounted for 82 percent of total stock, largely being bred extensively. By 1911, their share had fallen to 28 percent, while speckled cattle accounted for as much as 70 percent of total stocks. The change in breeds was principally a consequence of an increase in consumer demand for milk and milk products, since the milk yield of the new breeds was several times greater than that of Hungarian Gray Cattle. At the turn of the century, peasant farmers established a whole series of milk cooperatives in order to process and sell their milk.

The introduction of a new breed in pig farming was less successful; throughout the period the fattening pig was the principal breed, while the British porker accounted for just 15 percent of total pig stocks. The swine fever epidemic of 1890 also halted the quantitative growth. Before the epidemic, more than a million pigs had been exported in some years, but by 1896 exports had fallen to a quarter of previous levels; it was only a decade later that exports recovered to half a million.

The other rapidly developing sector at the turn of the century was poultry farming, which represented a significant source of supplementary income for small peasant farmers. Sheep farming, which had been the most successful sector in the first half of the nineteenth century, declined in significance, owing to a fall in demand for Hungarian wool. The number of sheep fell from 15 million in 1870 to almost half that number at the end of the century.

The important social consequences of changes in the relative importance of plant and livestock production should also be noted. In 1911, 80 percent of cattle and pig stocks and 86 percent of horses were owned by farms with less than 100 *hold* (58 ha, 142 acres) of land. This demonstrates that the principal beneficiaries of the restructuring of the agricultural sector at the turn of the century were small farming units, the peasant-owned farms. Eighty-three percent of income from livestock farming was made by peasant farms. The plantation of vineyards in the aftermath of the philoxera epidemic and the growth of the fruit and vegetable farming sector had similar social effects.

The increasing profitability of peasant-owned farms was particularly significant in the light of the absence of any real change in land ownership relations during the Dualist era. The ownership structure that had developed after the abolition of serfdom still existed. Two million peasant families, representing 99 percent of landowners, owned 46 percent of the country's land and used in common an additional 10–12 percent of the land. Still, when evaluating production relations in Hungarian agriculture, one should not ignore the fact that in 1914, 68 percent of land under intensive cultivation—arable land, market gardens, meadows and vineyards—was owned by small peasant farms with less than 100 *hold* (58 ha, 142 acres) of land. (Hungarian economic historians have tended to regard 100 *hold* (58 ha, 142 acres) as the dividing line between peasant farms and former noble estates.) Forest and pasture accounted for one half of the land belonging to large estates with more than 1,000 *hold* (1,420 acres, 575 ha) of land.

Forests covered 27 percent of the country and were an important arena of economic activity, particularly after the adoption of legislation on forests in 1879, which attempted to halt the wasteful exploitation of the country's forests. As a result of such efforts, planned sylviculture was operating in two thirds of forests in the Carpathian basin in 1914. Forests were planted in unwooded areas, such as the region between the River Danube and the River Tisza. Indeed, to bind the sandy soils of the region, 111,000 hectares of forest were planted, mainly acacia and poplar.

Table 11: Number of Farms by Size Category in 1895

Cultivated land (arable, market garden, meadow and vineyard)

*hold**	Number of farms	Area of farms in 1,000 *hold*	Number of farms (%)	Area of farms (%)
0–5	1,273,186	1,953	53.47	7.52
5–10	458,083	3,023	19.24	11.64
10–20	385,135	4,864	16.17	18.73
20–50	205,100	5,305	8.61	20.42
50–100	36,007	2,028	1.51	7.81
100–200	10,269	1,105	0.43	4.26
200–1,000	9,590	2,826	0.40	10.88
> 1,000 *hold*	3,769	4,867	0.16	18.74
Total	2,381,139	25,972	100.00	100.00

* 1 *hold* = 0.575 ha = 1.42 acre

The Development of Modern Industry

At the time of the 1867 Compromise, Hungary lacked the prerequisites for modern industrialization and the industrial revolution. The process of industrialization was founded on a rather underdeveloped base. The low level of development of urban and rural craftsmen's industry, the only modest development of the pre-industrial forms of capitalist industry (manufactories, rural industry) and the low ratio of participants in industry were all factors preventing the industrial productive force from meeting the qualitative and quantitative requirements of the large mechanized industrial plants. So-called "proto-industrialization" was very modest in Hungary. According to a census held in late 1869, only 9.5 percent of the active working population of Hungary and Croatia were employed in industry. The corresponding figure was 20 percent in Austria (26 percent in the western provinces) and 47 percent in Great Britain. As a percentage of the total population, the labor force of active persons employed in industry represented around 4.5 percent, whereas in Austria the figure was 11.7 percent. The difference between the two halves of the Monarchy is particularly apparent with regard to the textiles and clothing industry: 797,000 people were working in the sector in Austria (33 percent of the total industrial labor force), while in Hungary the figure was just 94,000 (13.4 percent).

In the countries of Western and Central Europe, the textiles industry was a leading and dynamic sector of the industrial revolution. In general, light industry producing mass consumer goods did not play a role in Hungary's industrialization until the end of the nineteenth century. In this area, competition from industrial companies in Western Europe and Austria had a paralyzing effect. With the construction of the railways, the Hungarian market was flooded with products from the Austrian and Czech textiles industry and other light industrial goods. In the early period of Hungary's industrialization, which began in the 1830s, two industrial sectors were particularly significant. The first was the food industry (particularly the milling, sugar and alcohol sectors) and the second was the iron and engineering industry. An additional important sector during this early period was the wood industry (timber, barrel staves and railway sleepers).

The milling industry was at the forefront of modern industrialization: the first steam mills were established in the second half of the 1830s, and their number rose to 147 in 1863, 910 in 1884, and 1,843 in 1895. In 1906, grain was milled in 2,200 steam mills and 562 motorized mills, as well as 16,600 water mills, 700 windmills, and 650 dry mills. In the 1860s, Hungary exported more flour than the rest of Europe together. Annual flour exports reached two million quintals in 1869–1871, increasing to 4–5 million quintals in the early 1890s and 6–8 million quintals in the early twentieth century. Great Britain was the second-largest consumer of Hungarian flour—after Austria. During the decades preceding World War I, Hungary was the world's second-largest flour exporter; its exports were exceeded only by those of the United States. Budapest developed into the world's largest milling center as early as the 1860s, retaining this position until the turn of the century, when it was overtaken by the American milling center of Minneapolis. The dozens of large mills in Budapest milled more than 600,000 tonnes of flour each year, even though they generally operated at just 60–70 percent of capacity.

The most dynamic sector of the food industry at the time of the Dual Monarchy was the sugar industry, the origins of which can be traced to the 1830s and 1840s. A true upturn in the sugar industry came only in the 1880s—due in part to effective government support. New larger factories were established and production levels increased rapidly. During the years preceding World War I, annual production reached half a million tonnes. All the sugar factories were backed by major capital and were equipped with the latest mechanical machinery. This kept them competitive on world markets. Seventy percent of production was exported to Western Europe, India, Egypt and Turkey.

A higher rate of urbanization led to more rapid growth in the brewing industry after 1890. Production gradually shifted from small family-owned breweries to large brewing plants. Four large breweries in Budapest accounted for roughly two thirds of production. In 1913, there were 19,000 people working in the tobacco industry; the majority were women.

The food industry was a major exporting sector throughout the period. In addition to meeting the demand for food in the domestic economy, it supplied the rest of the Monarchy and world markets with foodstuffs worth several hundred million crowns. In 1906, 30 percent of food industrial production was exported: 22 percent to Austria and 8 percent to world markets.

An abundant supply of raw materials served as the basis for development of the wood processing industry. Railways gradually improved access to the great forests of the Carpathians, thereby enabling the development of a lumber industry. House constructions and demand from countries with decreasing supplies of domestic timber guaranteed a broad and expanding market for semi-processed timber products (wooden planks, barrel staves and railway sleepers). Another factor was the growing use of timber in the chemical industry (for distillation of wood and for tanner abstracts). From the 1860s onwards, a whole series of steam sawmills were established, which diminished the role of the smaller sawmills that operated using water power. The number of steam sawmills in Hungary increased from 30 in 1873 to 114 in 1884, but at that time there were still 354 sawmills using water energy. In 1913, 347 sawmills produced goods worth 130 million crowns, mostly for export. In Croatia, oak forests were the principal source of raw timber. In the 1820s, international demand for Croatian oak steadily increased; French, Spanish and Italian wine producers were keen to purchase it. The Croatian economy's largest sector, the manufacture of wine barrels, was based on this growing demand. At the turn of the century, two out of three Croatia's industrial workers were working in timber-related sectors.

The importance of the food industry to an agrarian country is self-evident. In Hungary, there was an abundance of produce to be processed, and this also applied to the timber. More surprising was the growth of the heavy industrial sectors in the early phase of Hungarian industrialization. Growth took place not only in the iron ore mining and the metallurgy industry (which produced metals and semi-finished products) but also in the engineering industry. The latter sector underwent rapid development relatively early on. According to an assessment of the Ministry of Trade and Industry, the engineering industry was, in the 1880s, "one of the most advanced domestic industries. At the time, the turnover of the engineering factories in Budapest was greater than the combined output of all the Bohemian and Moravian plants."

In Hungary, the mining of non-ferrous metals and non-ferrous metallurgy had a past reaching back to the medieval period. At the end of the eighteenth century, Hungary had accounted for almost one fifth of world copper production. During the nineteenth century, however, the mines in Upper Hungary (now Slovakia) were gradually exhausted and the importance of non-ferrous metallurgy declined. At the same time, there was an upturn in iron ore and coal mining. There were significant reserves of iron ore in three regions of historical Hungary: Upper Hungary, the Banat region and southern Transylvania (now Romania). Since the sixteenth century, a major iron metallurgical sector had been developed, based on these reserves. Moreover, the sector had undergone a process of modernization since the second half of the eighteenth century. Unfortunately, coal suitable for coking was only available near just one of the three mining regions: in the Banat crown domain, which—together with the government-owned railways—was sold in 1855 to the Austrian State Railway Company, which had been established mostly by French capital. In 1882, it became the Austro-Hungarian State Railway Company. The company developed the country's most modern heavy industrial vertical structure: with coal and iron ore mines, blast furnaces, iron and steel works, an engineering factory and several chemical plants. An increasing number of coal mines were opened in the era of Dualism, but all of them produced only brown coal. At first, the enormous forests near the metal furnaces could be used as a source of fuel, but from the 1860s onwards, furnaces switched to the use of coke. The shortage of coal for coking was particularly acute in northern parts of Upper Hungary, and so Hungary had no choice but to import increasing amounts of coal and coke from Silesia.

In the second half of the nineteenth century, the technical innovations of the industrial revolution were applied in Hungarian ironworks (stirring furnaces, roller trains and steam hammers). The production of raw iron increased rapidly in the 1840s, and this growth continued in the 1850s and 1860s. Production levels rose from an annual 51,000 tonnes in the period 1851–1855 to 115,000 tonnes at the time of the 1867 Compromise, and then to 623,000 tonnes in 1913. After the Compromise, mass steel production began using the Bessemer converter (1868) and then the Martin furnace (1876). In both instances, the new procedure was applied within a decade of its being patented in Western Europe. By the outbreak of World War I, annual steel production had reached 800,000 tonnes. After the Compromise, the iron industry was concentrated in plants owned by three giant companies: the Austro-Hungarian Railway Company (Reşiţa and Anina), the Rimamurány-Salgótarján Ironworks Company (Likér/Hnúšťa, Ózd, Salgótarján and Borsodnádasd) and the State Ironworks (Vajdahunyad/Hunedoara, Diósgyőr and Zólyombrezó/Podbrezová). In 1913, these three companies accounted for 96 percent of iron and steel production in Hungary.

For the iron and engineering industry the mechanization of agriculture and the construction of railways guaranteed rapidly developing domestic markets. Accordingly, the industry's most advanced sectors were vehicle production (locomotives, carriages and boats) and the production of agricultural machinery. From the 1880s onwards, Hungary was self-sufficient in the production of vehicles and even became an exporter—mainly to the Balkan countries and to Russia. Central Europe's largest boatbuilding factories were located alongside the Danube in Budapest, producing boats for both domestic and foreign markets. In the years preceding World War I, the Ganz-Danubius boatbuilding company began building maritime ships at its plant in Fiume (now Rijeka). As a producer of torpedo destroyers, submarines and express cruisers, the company became involved in the Monarchy's program to develop the fleet. It was here that one of the Monarchy's four dreadnoughts was built—the 20,000-tonne *Szent István*. The steam locomotives that were designed and built at the turn of the century in the steel and engineering plant of Hungarian State Railways received international acclaim as well as the *grand prix* at the Paris World Exposition of 1900. By meeting the needs of the rapidly developing railway network, the modest foundry (est. 1844) of Ábrahám Ganz—who had come to Hungary from Switzerland—developed into an engineering factory with an international reputation. In the 1850s and 1860s, Ganz produced firm and durable chilled cast iron wheels for domestic and foreign railway companies. In the 1870s, the factory manager and chief engineer András Mechwart developed the chilled cast iron roller mill, which Ganz supplied to the world's modern mills. Even in international terms, the Hungarian engineering sector was effective in producing the various water turbines—particularly the Ganz factory. Donát Bánki was instrumental in this success; his turbines for lesser quantities of water and smaller waterfalls, were exported in the hundreds to France and Germany in particular.

Hungarian engineering established an international reputation in vehicle production and the manufacture of milling industrial and hydraulic machinery, but electro technology was the sector where it excelled for a period of two decades, competing with Germany and the United States. As far as the developing industries of the last third of the nineteenth century were concerned, the advanced countries lacked the advantages that they had with regard to the traditional industrial sectors. András Mechwart, the director of the Ganz company, was quick to appreciate the technological and business opportunities of electricity. In 1878, Mechwart established an electrical workshop in one of the Ganz factories; it was one of the world's first such workshops. He appointed the young engineer Károly Zipernowsky as manager of the workshop. At first, the workshop produced direct current dynamo machines and lighting systems. In the early 1880s, the workshop experimented with alternating current. Assisted by Miksa Déri, they managed to create an alternating current generator. Ganz's electrical machinery scored a great success at the international electrical technology exposition held in Vienna in 1883. Until the mid-1880s, the wider use of electricity was greatly hindered by the fact that electricity could only be supplied efficiently within a 1–1.5-kilometer radius of the site of production. Zipernowsky, Déri and Ottó Bláthy—who joined the group in 1883—developed the transformer system, which enabled electricity to be supplied efficiently over longer distances and resolved the problem of balanced distribution. Their system was presented for the first time at the National Exhibition, held in Budapest in 1885. It aroused international interest, and the company was subsequently swamped by orders from all European countries as well as America, Africa and Australia. In 1889, the company celebrated the production of the thousandth transformer system, and within ten years, 10,000 transformer systems had been produced. With these inventions, the Ganz company, which established a separate electrical technology factory in 1882, became an international trailblazer in the electricity industry, retaining its position—alongside the major American and German companies—until the early twentieth century. The company's success was due in large part to its engineers, who continued to innovate. They developed AC consumer equipment compatible with their system and undertook successful pioneering work in new fields of electro technology.

One innovation was the three-phase motor and generator series. It was designed by one of Ganz's young engineers, Kálmán Kandó. The system was put to practical use in 1897, when an Italian railway company commissioned Ganz to electrify a railway line in northern Italy. A team led by Kandó successfully accomplished the task. The Valtellina railway, Europe's first electrified railway line, opened in 1902. Thereafter, more than a thousand kilometers of railway line were electrified in Italy using Kandó's system.

The main area of business of the Ganz electricity factory was power current electrotechnics; in this area it was a world leader. The other main branch of the electricity sector, communication technology, was also introduced to Hungary in the early stages of its development. In the late 1870s and early 1880s, three factories were established, becoming major industrial plants by the early twentieth century. One of these, United Lightbulb (Tungsram), entered the market with a significant innovation: the wolfram electric bulb, developed by the company's engineers in the first years of the twentieth century.

Before the second half of the 1880s, modern machinery and factories were rare, being limited to a few industrial sectors such as the food industry, iron and engineering, and timber. According to industrial statistics compiled in 1884, these industrial sectors accounted for 92 percent of machinery used in the processing industry and for 79 percent of workers employed in plants using machinery. Additional sectors were the mining sectors supplying raw materials or fuel for modern industry, that is, the iron ore and coal mining sectors.

In other industrial sectors, traditional workshops and techniques continued to prevail for two decades after the Compromise. Domestic production in these sectors satisfied only a small part of demand,

and most of the market was held by foreign—Austrian and Czech—suppliers. In these sectors, with the exception of a few modern and mechanized plants, the sector was dominated by traditional plants and workshops. Until the late 1880s, craftsmen's workshops remained the typical form of industrial plant. As late as 1890, 73.7 percent of the labor force in the processing and construction industries worked in workshops with no workers or 1–5 workers. In Hungary, there were 126 employees and workers for every 100 independent craftsmen. The corresponding figure in Austria was 429.

The industrial statistics compiled during the period designated companies with more than 20 workers as major plants. In 1890, there were 1,129 major plants in the manufacturing and construction industries, in which 102,000 workers and employees were working (15 percent of all income earners in the manufacturing and construction industries). There were only 206 plants employing more than 100 workers, and these plants employed 66,000 workers (9.5 percent). The size of plant does not necessarily reflect the development of the mechanized industry in Hungary: in 1884, 46 percent of plants employing more than 20 workers used no machinery. Such plants were more like manufactories than modern factories. The 10–15-year period after the Compromise was characterized more by the temporary upturn in traditional pre-industrial forms such as manufactories, rather than by the appearance of modern mechanized large-scale industry. In this regard, Hungary resembled the Eastern European countries—such as Russia—where industrialization was also delayed.

In 1884, there were 1,802 industrial plants that used modern engines—with a combined output of 63,600 horsepower. In addition, industry also used water energy worth 59,000 horsepower. As much as 46,000 horsepower came from small water mills. In 1884—and ignoring the small water mills—Hungarian industry used 77,000 horsepower of energy, and plants using mechanical or water power employed 104,000 workers and employees. At the same time, Austria consumed 521,000 horsepower, and there were 790,000 people working in mechanical and water plants in Austria.

After the Compromise, the crisis and the dissolution of traditional craftsmen's industries deepened and the restructuring process, which had begun before 1867, continued. With the liquidation of the guild system, crafts became totally free (1872). Most of the craftsmen were slow to adjust to the change in circumstances. "The great transformation has found our craftsmen unprepared; they have no experience themselves of factory work and business. Craftsmen who had yet to free themselves from the patriarchal guild system suddenly faced free competition, but nothing happened to develop their competitiveness."[27] They had neither sufficient capital nor the required general and professional knowledge to adopt the modern techniques, develop their plants, and become competitive. The Budapest chamber characterized the situation of craftsmen as follows: "Production as a whole has declined to the extent that the craftsmen are concerned with the sale of goods related to their occupation that have been brought from abroad; they only undertake jobs and repairs, or they have completely abandoned industry and have moved into agriculture, or they have added to the numbers of the proletariat, which is growing at an accelerating rate in the towns."[28]

In certain industries, traditional craftsmanship completely disappeared, while in other industries it accommodated the quality and technological requirements of the new era. Changes in consumer needs led to the establishment of a whole series of new craftsmen's occupations. While some of the craftsmen, having rejected progress, sought protection from domestic and foreign competition behind their old privileges and obligations, an increasing number of them recognized that "the country's craftsmen would not defeat competition by fleeing from it, but by arming themselves with the weapons with which their competitors fight" and by modernizing "with intellectual and financial capital" investments, thereby raising their plants to an even higher level.[29]

In addition to the 750,000 full-time industrial workers recorded by the census in the early 1880s, there were also 760,000 women and 40,000 men who were active in household industries, in addition to their full-time jobs in agriculture. They spun, wove and sewed, above all for household needs. However, in Transdanubia and the Lesser and Great Plains, self-sufficient household industries only partially met the industrial needs of the rural population. In eastern and southeastern parts of the country, clothing produced in the home by Romanian, Serb, Ruthenian and Magyar peasants was reported by the Arad, Brassó and Debrecen chambers. In Transylvania, in the area covered by the Kolozsvár chamber, a survey of household industry noted the presence of 47,000 looms, in 204,000 rural homes, but according to other reports there may have been as many as 50,000–60,000 looms. "The clothing of nine tenths of the rural population is made up of cloth that they themselves make."[30] In the northeastern part of Upper Hungary (the Carpathian region), there were thousands of looms in rural homes, but they were rather uncommon in the Great Plain region.

After the depression that followed the crisis of 1873, the upturn of the 1880s marked a new stage in the process of industrialization—the industrial revolution. The changes in organization and technology affected all major industrial sectors. Following more than a decade of rapid growth, factory industry achieved predominance in industrial production at the turn of the century. Alongside many other factors, government support for industry contributed significantly to the accelerated rate of industrialization.

In Hungary and Croatia, the number of workers in the industrial and mining sectors rose from 698,000 in 1869 to 943,000 in 1890. It then increased to 1,533,000 in 1910. These numbers represent a 35 percent increase between 1869 and 1890 and a 62.5 percent increase between 1890 and 1910.

While the annual growth rate in employment was 2.5 percent, the output of machinery used in industry increased by an average of 7.4 percent between 1884 and 1913. In 1884, the total output of industrial machinery was 123,000 horsepower—and water accounted for almost half of this figure. By 1913, output used in industry had risen to a million horsepower, just 7 percent of which was provided by water wheels and turbines. The output of steam

Figure 5

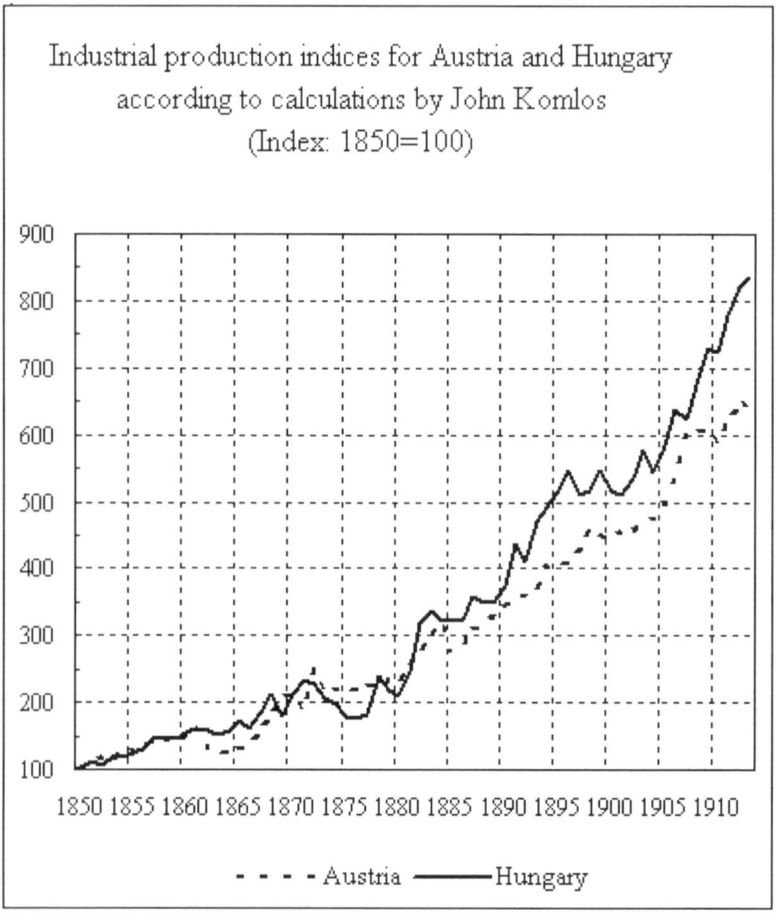
Industrial production indices for Austria and Hungary
according to calculations by John Komlos
(Index: 1850=100)
900
800
700
600
500
400
300
200
100
1850 1855 1860 1865 1870 1875 1880 1885 1890 1895 1900 1905 1910
Austria
Hungary

machines had increased tenfold in 30 years, rising from 64,000 to 638,000 horsepower. An increasing role was played by internal combustion and electrical motors. In 1910, there were 3,958 plants with more than 20 workers and 917 plants with more than a hundred workers. In total 465,000 workers were working in the former category and 339,000 in the latter, that is, 33 percent and 24 percent of industrial employees respectively. The number of larger plants increased rapidly, but it did not reach the level of the advanced industrial countries (In Austria, in 1902, 32 percent of industrial employees were working at plants with more than a hundred workers, while in Germany this was true of 35 percent of workers in 1907).

According to manufacturing industry statistics, there were 2,500 (factory-type) industrial plants at the end of the nineteenth century, but almost 5,000 of them in 1913. The number of people working in the manufacturing industry rose from 101,000 in 1884 to 244,000 in 1901, and to 475,000 in 1913. In the latter year, approximately 4,800 large industrial plants accounted for two thirds of manufacturing production, while several hundred thousand smaller industrial companies accounted for the remainder. Even so, the country's rapid industrialization was proceeding on a rather narrow base. As late as 1910, just 18.3 percent of the active population were employed in industry. The corresponding share was 23 percent in Austria and Italy, 38 percent in Germany and 46 percent in Great Britain. Hungary's *per capita* industrial production (according to my calculations) was about 55 percent of that of Austria—or 44 percent according to Schulze's most recent calculations. And it was just a quarter of *per capita* industrial production in Germany or Great Britain. According to various estimates, the average growth in Hungarian industrial production at the time of the Dual Monarchy was 3–4 percent. This rate was significantly higher than the figure for Austria.

Heavy industry was at the forefront of the industrial upturn in the 1880s. Indeed, heavy industry took up about 70 percent of new production resources of the manufacturing industry. This was because industrialization coincided with the railway construction boom, urban and public building programs, and the increasing significance of public utilities. The growth in heavy industry was halted by the crisis that began in 1900. Following a reduction in railway and other investments, production in the iron and engineering industry fell by 30–40 percent. It was only in 1907 that production in the sector returned to the levels of 1898–1899. The renewed upturn in heavy industry was in part the result of investments in the railway and construction sectors, but another important factor was government spending on the military and on armaments. The crisis in the early years of the century had little effect on light industry; it was at this time that the textiles, leather and clothing industries began to develop. Between 1906 and 1914, the sum of industrial investments exceeded one and a half billion crowns.

The manufacture of cellulose and paper became a substantial export industry. Semi-finished goods were produced for Austrian paper factories, while paper was sold abroad. The most advanced branch of the chemicals industry was starch production. During the 1880s, several fertilizer factories were established. It was at this time that petroleum refining, the most significant branch of the chemicals industry, began to develop. The smaller refineries processed Romanian oil in Transylvania. The first two major oil refineries were established in 1882–1884—one in Fiume and the other in Budapest. Most of the processed crude oil came from Galicia. At the turn of the century, refined oil became one of Hungary's important exports. For the building materials industry, the large-scale building projects underway in Budapest and the regional urban centers amounted to a dynamic market. Cement production became an industry of European significance with the modernization of the technological equipment and the application of innovations (such as firmer cement).

In this period, the most advanced sector in light industry was the printing industry, which "is excellently represented in our country in all regards. This industry is so well developed as a major industry in the capital city that one can find no equal in Europe," wrote a statistician during the 1880s (perhaps with some exaggeration).[31]

There were six large printing offices operating in Budapest; they were equipped with the latest foreign machinery. Newspapers were printed in tens of thousands of copies on the latest American rotation machines.

According to a statistician in the 1880s, there was one branch of industry—the textiles industry—"where conditions in this regard are the most disadvantageous... Domestic production covers only a few percent of the country's needs; the rest comes from abroad. It is no exaggeration to state that there is hardly anyone in Hungary who is dressed in urban clothes, whose clothing was produced domestically."[32] In 1877, the Budapest Chamber drew the following conclusion: "In the early sixties, Hungary's textiles industry found itself in a situation very different from that of today, when one can hardly speak of the existence of such an industry, since we encounter only scanty traces of it."[33] As already noted, there still existed a domestic industry in the more remote rural areas. Thus, in 1881, 293,000 hand looms and 24,000 spinning wheels were recorded in rural households—mostly in the eastern half of the country. The weakness of Hungary's textiles industry is reflected in the employment figures: in 1890, 31,000 persons were employed in the sector in Hungary, compared with 448,000 in Austria. The Saxon broadcloth industry of southern Transylvania (Brassó-Braşov, Nagyszeben-Sibiu, Nagydisznód-Cisnădie and Törcsvár-Bran) survived by switching to sales in Romania from sales in Transylvania and eastern Hungary. In 1883, a British investor established a textiles factory in Újpest, which began regular production in 1887. The arrival of the cotton industry in Újpest marked the beginning of the modern textiles industry in Hungary.

Having grown out of almost nothing, Hungary's large-scale textiles industry strengthened during the years preceding World War I. In 1885, as few as 5,000 workers were employed in textiles factories, above all in secondary branches of the textiles industry, such as calico printing, jute and hemp processing. The number of employees in the sector subsequently rose to 14,000 in 1898 and to 46,000 in 1913. Machinery output increased from 3,000 horsepower to 55,000 horsepower during the same period. Between 1896 and 1913, the number of spindles rose from 108,000 to 492,000, while the number of mechanical looms increased from 3,000 to 13,000. The cotton industry was at the forefront of developments; its rapid growth is indicated by an average annual increase in raw cotton imports of 10 percent. The Hungarian Textiles Industrial Company, established in 1895 (in Rózsahegy-Ružomberok, now in Slovakia), was the largest cotton weaver in the Dual Monarchy. The modern cloth factories tended to be established in the old wool-based industrial areas of Upper Hungary and southern Transylvania. After 1890, textiles became one of the most dynamic industries in Hungary, but it was still relatively small in domestic and international terms.

Table 12: Factory Production in Hungary (1898–1913)

Industrial sector	Output in millions of crowns			Value added** in millions of crowns			Value added**		
							%	%	%
	1898*	1906*	1913	1898*	1906*	1913	1898*	1906*	1913
Iron and metallurgy	194	305	502	85	128	177	16.1	13.9	14.8
Machinery, vehicles and instruments	141	209	263	78	115	134	14.8	12.6	11.2
Chemicals	84	158	231	32	66	95	6.1	7.2	7.9
Building materials	51	95	121	22	67	85	4.2	7.2	7.1
Timber	97	165	187	38	65	72	7.2	7.1	6.0
Textiles	54	153	194	16	45	59	3.0	4.9	4.9
Leather and clothing	51	117	111	15	34	35	2.8	3.7	2.9
Paper and printing	33	75	98	19	43	57	3.6	4.7	4.8
Food industry	646	931	1,236	205	343	456	38.9	37.3	38.1
Power stations	26	19	42	17	13	28	3.2	1.4	2.3
Total	*1,377*	*2,226*	*2,984*	*527*	*919*	*1,198*	*100.0*	*100.0*	*100.0*

* including Croatia.

** The value of fuels, raw materials and semi-finished products is precisely indicated only in the manufacturing industry statistics for 1906.

When calculating the annual value-added figures for the period 1898 and 1913, we used the value-added coefficients for 1906.

The development of factory industry was closely connected with the Hungarian investments of foreign entrepreneurs and the flow of commercial capital accumulated through trading in domestic agricultural products (cereals, tobacco, wine, leather, timber, etc.) towards industrial enterprises. Alongside these two forms of investment, there was also the classical route to the development of large-scale industry, whereby small industrial plants gradually developed into larger factories, by means of self-financing, specialization and technical innovation. This was most common in metallurgy, engineering and the timber industry. At the end of the nineteenth century, one in three factories had developed out of small plants, while two thirds had been established by foreign or domestic investors.

Joint stock companies were crucial to the foundation of new factories as well as the transformation of small workshops into large factories. The joint stock company was a means of bridging the difficulties caused by inadequate capital accumulation. Prior to the 1867 Compromise, there had been no more than around a dozen industrial joint stock companies. Between 1867 and 1873, 170 new industrial joint stock companies were formed, many of which proved to be economically unviable. There were 110 joint stock companies operating in Hungarian industry in 1876, and their number increased to 157 in 1890. Around half of these companies were completely new firms, while the other half had been formed through the restructuring or expansion of private firms. In 1913, there were more than a thousand industrial joint stock companies, with a total equity capital of 1.1 billion crowns. The largest industrial plants were owned by joint stock companies; in 1913, the 1,223 industrial plants owned by joint stock companies accounted for only one in four factories, but 59 percent of total wages paid to factory workers. The formation of industrial joint stock companies or the transformation of private enterprises into joint stock companies was accomplished in cooperation with banks. The banks also served to promote the merger of companies and the establishment of cartels. During the decades preceding World War I, the banks' important strategic role in the process of industrialization was a typical feature of Central Europe, one that could also be observed in Germany, Austria and Italy. Owing to the enormous capital requirements of modern industry, private entrepreneurs were rarely capable of establishing modern industrial plants at the turn of the century. Individual or family enterprises could no longer rely on their own resources, if they wished to keep abreast of developments.

The process and rate of industrialization in Hungary and the structure of major industrial sectors were determined in large part by free competition with the Austrian and Czech manufacturing industry within the customs union. After the 1867 Compromise, Hungary, seeking to promote its agricultural sector, renounced the implementation of protective tariffs against its nearest and strongest industrial rivals. In the case of competition from Germany, however, Hungarian industry was protected—by the protective tariffs of the common customs area. Competition within the common customs area had both advantages and disadvantages with regard to Hungary's industrialization. On the one hand, such competition was a cause of the structural imbalances and distortions of Hungarian industry, including the weakness of light industrial sectors, textiles in particular. On the other, the economic community of the Monarchy provided for the production factors that were necessary for Hungary's industrialization but were lacking in the domestic economy (such as capital, entrepreneurs and skilled workers). And this economic community also provided the necessary industrial background, including a network of collaborating industrial sectors and plants. Competition within the common customs area encouraged industrial plants in Hungary to innovate, to introduce new products and technologies, and to further concentrate productive resources. Meanwhile, the Dual Monarchy's 50 million people represented a sizeable market, enabling the efficient application of modern technology (thanks to economies of scale), mass production and specialization. Hungarian industry made good use of the opportunities presented by the Dual Monarchy's common market. Hungarian industry grew more quickly than Austrian industry did under the Dual Monarchy. And this also applies to the export of Hungarian finished goods to Austria: between 1882 and 1913, such exports grew at a faster rate than imports of Austrian industrial products did. This is true even with regard to textiles. The Austrian share of Hungarian industrial exports increased from 64 percent in the 1880s to around 71 percent in around 1910.

Hungary's rather unbalanced industrial sector of the 1880s became somewhat more balanced as the industrial revolution broadened. Despite this trend towards more balance, the structure of industry was still rather odd even just prior to World War I. Heavy industry and the food industry accounted for a relatively large proportion of production, while light industry—particularly textiles—was rather underrepresented.

Table 13: Percentage of Active Persons
Employed in Each Industrial Sector (1890–1910)

Industrial sector	Hungary 1890	Hungary 1910	Austria 1910	Germany 1910
Mining	6.0	5.5	4.3	7.4
Iron, metallurgy, engineering, vehicles, instruments	17.9	20.5	16.6	20.3
Timber	8.1	9.1	8.1	8.1
Building materials	4.5	5.0	6.4	6.9
Chemicals	0.6	1.5	1.4	2.2
Textiles	4.1	3.9	14.7	10.0
Leather and clothing	31.4	26.2	21.6	14.6
Paper and printing	1.7	2.8	3.2	4.2
Food industry	14.8	12.4	10.1	11.7
Gas, water and electricity	0.3	0.7	0.4	0.7
Construction	11.5	12.5	13.2	13.9

Another peculiar feature of the structure of Hungarian industry was the coexistence of a large number of small traditional plants alongside a small number of large plants with the most modern equipment. This polarization becomes particularly apparent if we compare the plant structure of Hungarian industry with that of the advanced industrial countries, such as Germany. The number of small plants was particularly high in Hungary—especially craftsmen working on their own. The relative significance of large plants was almost as great in Hungary as it was in the advanced countries, and it was actually greater than in Austria. But between the two, medium-sized plants were disproportionately few in number. Such structural imbalances become even more obvious when we examine the main industrial sectors. In Hungary's engineering sector, 60 percent of the labor force was concentrated in plants with more than 500 employees; the corresponding figure in Germany was just 35 percent. Mechanization and a high degree of concentration were typical features of the following industrial sectors: iron and steel, engineering, chemicals, textiles, paper and food (milling, sugar and brewing). In each of these sectors, more than 50 percent of the labor force was working in plants with more than 100 employees. In all sectors of Hungary's manufacturing industry, the number of factories was relatively small in comparison to the advanced countries. But for each factory, the number of workers and machines was higher, as was also the production value.

Figure 6

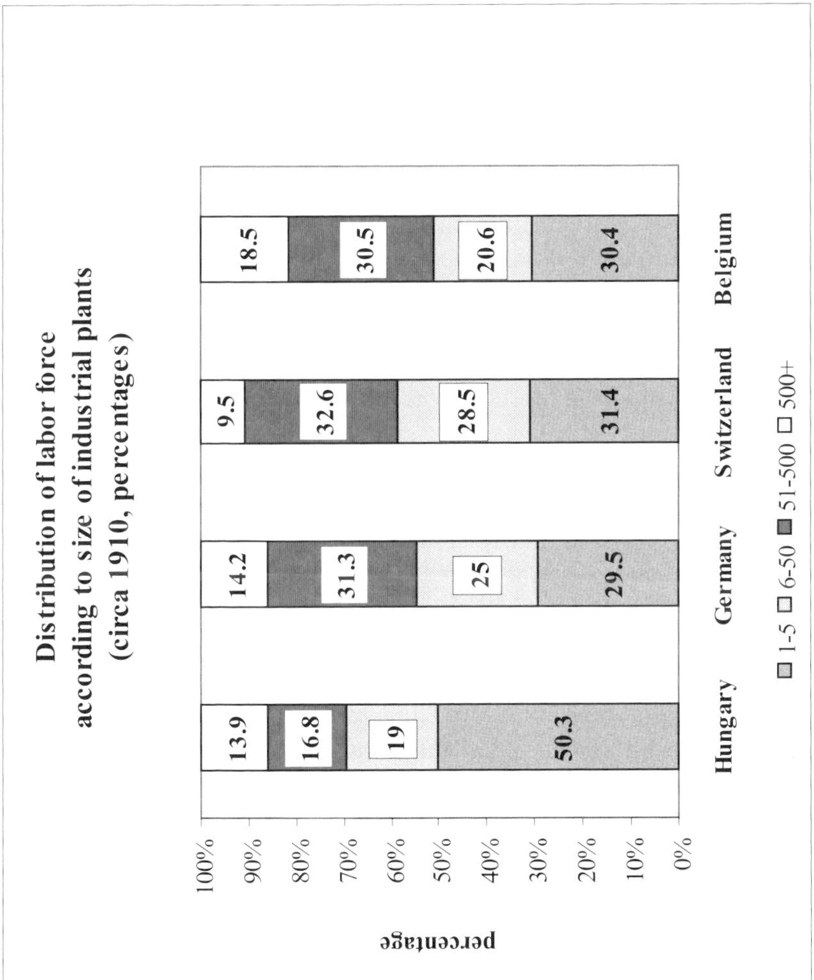
Distribution of labor force
according to size of industrial plants
(circa 1910, percentages)
percentage
100%
90%
80%
70%
60%
50%
40%
30%
20%
10%
0%
Hungary
Germany
Switzerland
Belgium
13.9
16.8
19
50.3
14.2
31.3
25
29.5
9.5
32.6
28.5
31.4
18.5
30.5
20.6
30.4
1-5
6-50
51-500
500+

In few countries was modern industry so concentrated in the capital city and its immediate environs as in Hungary. In 1910, 5.1 percent of the country's population resided in Greater Budapest, but 18 percent of industrial wage earners and 27.7 percent of factory workers were working in the city. Another major industrial region was in the central part of Upper Hungary. Access to fuel and other raw materials in the region, its industrial past and its relative agricultural overpopulation were all factors promoting industrialization. The central hill country—the Hernád, Garam, Sajó and Ipoly valleys—was the location of iron mining and smelting, while large iron and steel industrial plants were established on the southern fringe in a brown coal area (Diósgyőr, Ózd, Nádasd and Salgótarján). Textiles industrial centers came into being in the northern and northwestern margins of the region, based in part on the area's traditional broadcloth and linen industry. Heavy industry was established in southern Transylvania and the Banat region (Krassó-Szörény and Hunyad Counties). The region was the site of coal and iron mining, with iron and steel works and an engineering sector. Linked with this area were the towns of Temesvár (Timişoara) and Arad, which counted among the country's most industrialized provincial urban centers. In contrast to the heavy industry of these two regions, light industries—textiles and food—contributed to the development of the industrial region in western Hungary and the Lesser Plain, where there were strong traditions of craftsmanship. Engineering in Győr, Pozsony (Bratislava) and Magyaróvár was the only heavy industry in the region. Industrialization was a particularly slow process in the Great Plain region, central and eastern areas of Transdanubia, northeastern parts of Upper Hungary (Sub-Carpathia) and northern and central counties of Transylvania. In such areas, there tended to be isolated industrial centers: Pécs, Szeged, Debrecen, Nagyvárad (Oradea) and Kolozsvár (Cluj-Napoca).

Table 14: Average Annual Production of Major Raw Materials and Industrial Goods (1,000 tonnes)

	Coal	Iron ore	Crude iron	Steel	Sugar	Beer 1,000 hl	Raw cotton imports 1,000 q
1871–75	1,509	433	153	9	22	700	
1891–95	3,958	997	323	190	106	1,242	19.8
1910–13	9,585	1,977	574	734	477	2,930	170.0
Average annual increase (%)							
1871/75–1891/95	4.9	4.3	3.8	16.5	8.2	2.9	
1891/95–1910/13	4.8	3.7	3.1	7.4	8.2	4.6	12.0

Foreign and Domestic Trade

In the mid-nineteenth century, agricultural goods accounted for much of the growth in international trade; two thirds of exchanged goods were raw materials or foodstuffs. The proportion of raw products among the exports of the Habsburg Monarchy rose from 29 percent in 1854–1858 to 44 percent in 1864–1868. The share of food industrial products was as low as 3 percent in the 1850s, but it had risen to 17 percent by the end of the 1870s. In the meantime, textiles' share of exports fell from 36 to 11 percent. This trend was favorable to the Hungarian economy, which was a major exporter of agricultural goods and was rather dependent upon foreign markets. Between 1851 and 1855, the Monarchy's annual average grain and flour exports amounted to 64,000 tonnes, but between 1867 and 1870 the figure exceeded a million tonnes. Throughout the period, imports were almost equally divided between industrial products and raw materials—although the share of the latter increased a little in the long term. Half of the Monarchy's exports were destined for Germany, while other important trading partners included Great Britain, Italy and the Balkan countries. The latter, however, accounted for a decreasing share of the Monarchy's foreign trade.

Table 15: Foreign Trade of Austria-Hungary
(annual averages in millions of crowns)

Year	Exports	Imports	Export or import (–) surplus
1851–1855	442	412	30
1856–1860	477	517	– 40
1861–1865	612	499	112
1866–1870	800	700	100
1871–1875	933	1,166	– 233
1876–1880	1,311	1,125	186
1881–1885	1,451	1,237	214
1886–1890	1,455	1,136	319
1891–1895	1,541	1,331	209
1896–1900	1,700	1,573	127
1901–1905	2,052	1,889	163
1906–1910	2,366	2,568	– 202
1911–1913	2,636	3,385	– 749

Foreign trade greatly contributed to Hungary's economic development. According to our calculations for the period after the 1867 Compromise, the value of exports reached 30 percent of GDP. No other European country for which data are available had such a high export ratio. The ratio fell to 20–21 percent shortly before the outbreak of war in 1914, but it was still very high in European terms.

When discussing Hungary's exports, one should draw a distinction between trade with foreign countries and the exchange of goods with the other half of the Dual Monarchy. The latter more closely resembled domestic trade, in the light of the absence of customs borders and the presence of a common currency. This distinction, however, is only possible from 1882, because regular and more detailed foreign trade statistics began to be collected only in 1882. In these statistics, exports are divided up by country, thereby permitting a survey of the exchange of goods between the two parts of the common customs area.

If we compare data for the years around 1867 with data for the pre-1848 period, we find that the value of Hungarian exports more than quadrupled between 1845 and 1870. The rate of increase declined in the 1870s, but this decline was followed by a renewed upturn in the 1880s. The rapid rate of growth was accompanied by a restructuring of the composition of exports. In the 1840s, 89–90 percent of exports were accounted for by agricultural raw products, of which livestock and livestock products (wool) made up more than a half. In the post-Compromise years, the share of raw products decreased to 64 percent, with cereals in first place (29 percent). By that time, 36 percent of exports were industrial goods (of which food products accounted for 15 percent). Cereals and flour made up 38 percent of exports. In subsequent years, cereals' share fell, while that of flour rose. An increasing proportion of the country's wheat was exported—after processing—as flour. During the post-Compromise period, 40 percent of wheat production—a quarter of all grain production—was exported. In the 1880s, 33 percent of wheat and just 18 percent of other grain were exported. In addition to cereals and flour, Hungary's main exports were pork, wine, wool and timber. The late 1880s saw an increase in cattle exports, while sugar exports rose in the 1890s.

As far as imports were concerned, industrial goods accounted for about 80 percent of imports throughout the period. Three quarters of such imports were consumer goods, mainly textiles and clothing. In the years following the 1867 Compromise, investment goods' share of imports rose sharply for a time. In the 1880s, semi-finished goods requiring further industrial processing became more significant.

Table 16: Foreign Trade of Hungary and Croatia
(annual averages in millions of crowns)

Year	Exports	Imports	Exports or imports (–) surplus
1867–1870	643	680	– 38
1871–1874	630	935	– 305
1882–1885	843	920	– 77
1886–1890	902	897	5
1891–1895	1,059	1,050	8
1896–1900	1,161	1,142	19
1901–1905	1,339	1,243	96
1906–1910	1,644	1,686	– 42
1911–1913	1,899	2,123	– 224

According to the official statistics, the value of trade within the common customs area accounted for more than three quarters of Hungary's total foreign trade throughout the period. Until 1896, Austria's share of Hungarian imports was particularly significant—more than 80 percent. Subsequently, its share fell rapidly to 71–72 percent. No particular trend is observable in Hungarian exports: Austria's share fluctuated between 69 and 76 percent during the period 1882–1913. Some Hungarian exports were evidently delivered to foreign customers by way of Austrian middlemen; they do not feature in the foreign trade statistics. This happened even more often in the case of imports. In the light of this situation, we can say that at least two thirds of Hungary's foreign trade during the era of Dualism took place within the common customs area.

In terms of foreign trade, Austria's dependence on Hungary was far less acute than Hungary's dependence on Austria. Hungary's share of Austria's imports and exports was around 40 percent throughout the period. Raw products accounted for most of Austria's imports from Hungary, although their share of the total decreased from 90 percent in the 1840s to 65 percent in the 1880s.

This change reflects the significant increase in Hungarian industrial exports—particularly food industry exports—to Austria after the 1867 Compromise. Throughout the period, industrial goods—above all textiles, clothing and other consumer goods—accounted for 87–90 percent of Hungarian imports from Austria.

Hungary's principal foreign trade partner outside the common customs area was Germany, the destination for 11–12 percent of Hungarian exports and the source of 4–5 percent of imports. Great Britain, France and Switzerland each received about 2–3 percent of Hungarian exports, and a similar proportion went to the Balkan countries. Initially, the largest share of imports (approximately 8 percent) came from the Balkan countries—Romania and Serbia—but their significance declined at the time of the Romanian customs war in the late 1880s. In the early twentieth century, a further customs war led to a decrease in trade with Serbia. In 1906—primarily for foreign policy reasons—the borders of the Monarchy were closed to what had been Serbian livestock imports (cattle and pigs). In response, Serbia stopped purchasing industrial goods from Austria and Hungary. The Serbian customs war lasted for three years.

In terms of structure and development, significant differences may be observed between Hungary's trade with the common customs area and its trade with foreign countries. A division of labor between the agrarian and industrial sectors was reflected in trade within the common customs area. Agricultural and food industry products accounted for 80 percent of Hungary's exports, while 90 percent of imports were industrial goods—above all finished goods for domestic consumption. The industrialization of the Hungarian economy was more apparent in its trade with other foreign partners: half of exports—and as much as 60 percent immediately prior to World War I—were industrial goods (food industry goods in particular). Meanwhile, most imports were raw products (industrial raw materials and fuels in particular).

Table 17: Structure of Hungarian Exports (1867–1913)
(at market prices and as percentages)

Types of goods	Total exports			To the common customs area		To other foreign countries	
	1867–1871	1882–1886	1909–1913	1882–1886	1909–1913	1882–1886	1909–1913
Plant products	37.4	33.8	25.7	34.4	29.0	32.2	14.9
Livestock and livestock products	24.7	26.3	25.2	29.4	25.8	18.6	22.9
Agricultural products in total	*62.1*	*60.1*	*50.9*	*63.8*	*54.8*	*50.8*	*37.8*
Food products	15.4	17.8	24.5	16.3	25.0	21.5	23.1
Other industrial products	21.1	21.0	23.1	18.6	18.9	27.1	37.0
Other	1.4	1.1	1.5	1.3	1.3	0.6	2.1
Total	*100.0*	*100.0*	*100.0*	*100.0*	*100.0*	*100.0*	*100.0*
Of which							
Raw products and waste		61.2	52.4	65.1	56.1	51.4	39.8
Semi-finished goods		8.5	12.7	6.5	8.0	13.4	28.5
Finished goods		30.3	34.9	28.4	35.9	35.2	31.7

The changing structure of exports and imports reflects the structural transformation of the Hungarian economy and the country's gradual industrialization. The share of raw agricultural products in exports decreased, while industrial goods, including finished products, became more significant. Another clear trend is Austria's increasing appetite for Hungarian agricultural and food industry products. As far as imports are concerned, industrial raw materials, semi-finished products and investment goods increased their relative shares, while finished goods for domestic consumption became less significant. The latter's share declined from 63–64 to 52 percent, indicating the development of domestic industry and the increasing role of import substitution.

Table 18: Structure of Hungarian Imports 1867–1913
(at market prices and as percentages)

Types of goods	Total imports			From the common customs area		From other foreign countries	
	1867–1871	1882–1886	1909–1913	1882–1886	1909–1913	1882–1886	1909–1913
Raw food products, livestock		9.7	7.2	6.1	4.8	27.2	14.1
Industrial raw products, fuels		8.2	14.4	3.3	5.3	31.3	40.8
Total raw products	*16.0*	*17.8*	*21.6*	*9.4*	*10.1*	*58.5*	*54.9*
Semi-finished goods	4.4	12.9	18.3	12.6	18.7	14.6	17.0
Investment goods	16.6	5.0	8.1	4.8	7.2	6.1	10.8
Textiles, leather and clothing	36.5	44.4	32.9	51.4	41.8	10.7	6.6
Other consumer goods	26.5	19.9	19.1	21.8	22.2	10.1	10.7
Total finished products	*79.6*	*69.3*	*60.1*	*78.0*	*71.2*	*26.9*	*28.1*
Combined total	100.0	100.0	100.0	100.0	100.0	100.0	100.0

In the common customs area, the volume of Hungarian imports grew at a faster rate than the volume of exports did. This was possible due to a favorable change in the export and import price index, that is, in the terms of trade. In the period until 1896, prices for the main export goods—agricultural and food industry products—decreased to a lesser extent than prices for imported industrial goods did. Then, between 1896 and 1913, prices for the main export goods increased more rapidly than prices for imports did. According to calculations undertaken by Prof. Scott M. Eddie, the price index for Hungarian exports increased by 0.17 percent *per annum* between 1882–1886 and 1909–1913, while the price index for imports decreased by 1.02 percent *per annum*. As a consequence, Hungary's terms of trade in the common customs area improved by 26 percent. As far as trade with other foreign countries is concerned, however, the reverse was true: the price index for exports decreased twice as much as the price index for imports (by 0.97 percent *per annum* compared with

0.47 percent *per annum*). Thus, the terms of trade deteriorated by 13 percent.[34] Factors influencing such changes in the terms of trade included the economic division of labor within the common customs area, trade tariffs and developments in world markets.

Figure 7

Hungary's terms of trade 1882-1913 (1882=100)

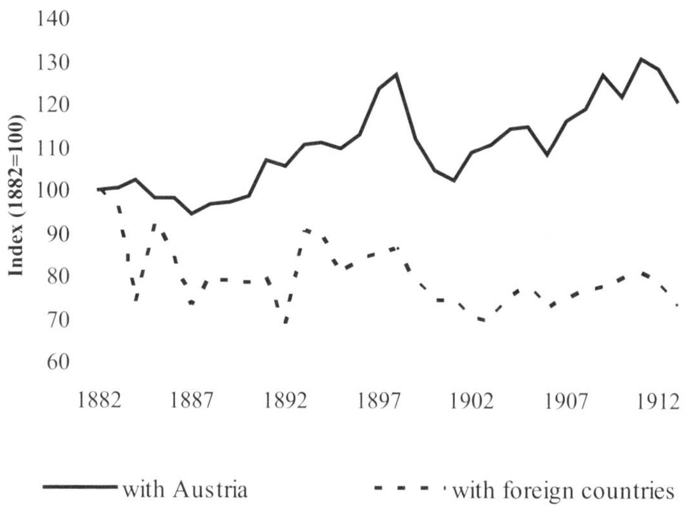

As far as domestic trade is concerned, the data available are less extensive than in the case of foreign trade. Even so, based on several indirect data, we may conclude that domestic trade grew at a similar rate to foreign trade.

The number of people employed in trade grew from 97,000 in 1869 to 255,000 in 1910 (an annual average increase of 2.4 percent). Another indicator of trade growth is the increase in transported goods: the volume of goods transported by railways and steamboats in Hungary increased from four million tonnes in 1866, to 26 million tonnes in 1890, and to 92 million tonnes in 1913.

In the second half of the nineteenth century, the unification of Hungary's domestic market—a process that had begun earlier on—was completed with the construction of the railway network. Diverse regional and local market environments gradually became part of a uniform national market. While retaining some of their features and functions, they lost their previous independence, and their function was transformed. Some of the former national and regional market centers became less important and were replaced by new centers. But even these new centers gradually became subordinated to Budapest. Benefiting from favorable geographical position and government policies, the Hungarian capital developed into the country's principal economic center in the years following the 1867 Compromise. The city soon became a major railway, banking and commercial center.

In the 1860s, Győr was the center of the grain trade; it was here that export grain was collected and stored. In the 1870s and 1880s, however, Budapest took the leading role, based on wholesalers' capital and benefiting from its superior railway links. The previously independent grain markets of southern Hungary—Szeged, Temesvár and Baja—also fell under the direction of the grain traders in Budapest. The latter not only bought, stored and exported grain from the Great Plain; they also processed it. Hungarian flour exports, which soon became a world leader, were based on production in large mills in Budapest. Most of these mills were established in the 1860s and 1870s. Budapest also became a national center for trade in other agricultural produce and livestock.

The previously independent traders of Hungary's provincial towns gradually became agents for wholesalers based in Budapest. Over a period of one or two decades, several hundred wholesale companies in Budapest managed to secure complete control of the country's wholesale trade. The concentration of trade in the capital city was also fostered by institutions such as the Budapest Commodity and Stock Exchange (est. 1864), which became the national center for trade in commodities and securities.

During these decades, trade was, in addition to agriculture, the main area of capital accumulation. Indeed, as far as the development of a capitalist sector was concerned, it was more important than agriculture, since capital accumulated in commerce could flow more rapidly and flexibly to other areas of the economy. Traders were instrumental in the development of a modern banking sector, manufacturing industry and the railway network. They also contributed to an upturn in urban construction, as well as the modernization of agriculture, as many of them purchased or rented agricultural land.

In the quarter of a century after the Compromise, Hungarian commerce exhibited a peculiar duality: traditional and modern capitalist forms coexisted and they both prospered. In international and national trade of mass consumer goods, modern capitalist types and techniques of wholesale prevailed. However, at the lower regional and local levels of the commercial sector, traditional forms of trade—fairs, markets and peddling—continued to exist and even expand.

By the second half of the nineteenth century, fairs had lost their international and national significance. Even so, they retained their local role and their number actually increased, as self-sufficiency in rural areas declined and non-agrarian and urban populations expanded. In 1895, 4,707 national fairs were held, in 1,477 towns and villages. At fairs and markets, goods tended to be sold by small producers. An increasing role was played by professional market traders, who traveled with their goods from market to market. In 1890, the country had 8,500 fair and market traders and 13,700 peddlers. Thus, 14 percent of those involved in trade and 26 percent of independent traders were involved in traditional trade. In domestic trade, however, the role of traditional forms of trade was actually much greater, as direct contact between small producers and consumers was still the norm, and many goods exchanged hands at fairs and markets without the mediation of traders.

Data from the 1890 census show that modern forms of the retail trade were fairly advanced. Of the 86,000 independent retailers,

58,000 (67 percent) had a permanent shop, above all in towns and larger villages. Of these, 27,000 were grocers and general dealers, selling diverse goods, while 31,000 ran specialist shops. Commerce thus became a constant and regular business. Permanent shops came into being throughout the country—and even the smaller villages had grocery stores. There was also an increasing specialization in the retailing network.

The expansion of the retail network is indicated by a 33 percent increase in the number of traders with their own shops between 1890 and 1910. The concentration of commercial activities in Budapest and the larger provincial centers was even more acute than in the case of industry. It was in the towns that the other main development trend of the era could be observed, namely specialization of the commercial network. In contrast to the slow increase in the number of shops trading in agricultural produce, livestock and food, there was a rapid increase in shops selling various industrial goods. Most of the latter were larger shops with several employees.

In addition to the expansion and specialization of the retail network and an increase in the size of shops, the modern institutions and techniques of commerce were introduced to Hungary. Six market halls were built in Budapest in the 1890s, and the year 1911 saw the opening of the city's first department store, the Parisian Department Store. In Budapest and other major towns, large companies with subsidiaries appeared. With their rational buying and distribution strategies, they were able to offer goods of standard quality to consumers at prices that were lower than those charged by small shop owners. The various consumer cooperatives also possessed extensive networks of shops. The Ant (*Hangya*) Cooperative, established in 1898, supplied goods to the country's peasant farmers; the members and purchasers of the General Consumer Cooperative, established in 1904, were drawn from urban workers and craftsmen in Budapest.

Economic Growth and Development

For supporters of the Austro-Hungarian Compromise, the most important task facing Hungary was to catch up with the leading European countries—or at least with the western half of the Monarchy. The country had to compensate for the lost opportunities of past centuries. "We accepted the theory of free trade and its consequences, such as free competition, and we believed that the nation would not rest until it caught up with its neighbors," said István Gorove, minister of agriculture, commerce and industry.[35]

The following decades fulfilled these expectations. The era of Dualism was the most dynamic period in the history of Hungary. This conclusion is underlined by the country's economic growth, the population increase, the rate of social change, the development of cultural institutions, and the improvement in everyday living standards. The most spectacular growth was achieved in the economic field.

It is worth identifying the areas of the economy where Hungary originally lagged behind Austria. To what extent was Hungary successful in "catching up" in these areas?

In the field of agriculture, Hungary was at roughly the same level as Austria at the time of the Compromise; indeed, it was somewhat more advanced in terms of mechanization. According to the latest calculations of Max-Stephan Schulze, in 1870 the value of agricultural goods *per capita* was 141 crowns in Hungary and 117 crowns in Austria. In the fields of industry, trade and transport, however, Hungary's GDP *per capita* was only one quarter of the figure for Austria.

The best indicators of the economic performance and dynamism of a country are *per capita* GDP and the average annual growth in GDP. The Hungarian economist Frigyes Fellner was the first to calculate these figures for the two halves of the Austro-Hungarian Monarchy in the period prior to World War I. According to Fellner's calculations, in 1911–1913, GDP *per capita* was 510 crowns in Austria and 406 crowns in Hungary–Croatia.[36]

Several subsequent attempts have been made to calculate GDP for the period going back to the 1867 Compromise. In the 1970s, I calculated Hungary's GDP for the period 1867–1913. According to my calculations, total GDP—at 1913 prices—rose, during the period, from 2.4 to 8.1 billion crowns, a more than threefold increase (the calculations excluded Croatia). During this time, *per capita* GDP increased from 176 to 435 crowns. The average annual growth was 2.7 percent for total GDP and 2 percent for GDP *per capita.* Also in the 1970s, Anton Kausel calculated Austria's GDP at the time of the Dual Monarchy. According to his calculations, Austrian GDP grew at an annual rate of 2.2 percent, while *per capita* GDP increased by 1.3 percent per year. According to my calculations, GDP *per capita* in 1913 was 435 crowns in Hungary and 304 crowns in Croatia. For the two countries together, it was 419 crowns. In Austria, it was 521 crowns (698 crowns in the Austrian and Czech provinces, 365 crowns in the southern Italian and South Slav provinces, and 255 crowns in Galicia and Bukovina).[37]

In recent years, there have been two attempts to reconstruct GDP figures in the Dual Monarchy. The first attempt was undertaken by the American historian David Good, and the second by Max-Stephan Schulze in London. David Good calculated *per capita* GDP in the countries, provinces and regions of the Monarchy between 1870 and 1910.[38] The table below contains the results of his calculations (since Good made his calculations in current dollars, the table contains indices for the various countries and provinces in relation to the average for Austria). As shown in the table, *per capita* GDP in Hungary and Croatia was about 59 percent of Austrian GDP in 1870, but increased to 75 percent by 1910. Evidently, the process of catching up with Austria was a fairly rapid one.

Table 19: Per Capita GDP Indices
according to David Good's calculations (Austria = 100)

	1870	1910	Average annual growth as a percentage
Austria	100	100	1.48
Hungary	62	78	2.05
Croatia	41	52	1.84
Countries of the Hungarian Crown	59	75	2.00
Monarchy	85	90	1.63

Max-Stephan Schulze undertook a radical recalculation of both Austrian and Hungarian GDP between 1870 and 1913. He concluded that both countries had a significantly higher level of GDP *per capita*, but the rate of growth was significantly lower (0.94 percent for Austria and 1.39 percent for Hungary).[39] Perhaps the essential point is that even according to Schulze's calculations, Hungarian economic growth was more dynamic; indeed, the difference between the two growth rates is almost identical to previous calculations (annual 0.4–0.5 percent). After almost a half a century, the difference in the two countries' growth rates had boosted the Hungarian economy; it had almost caught up. According to Schulze's calculations, Hungarian GDP *per capita* was 66 percent of Austria's in 1870, but 77 percent in 1910.

In Schulze's view, in terms of economic growth, Hungary was somewhere in the middle of the European league table during the half-century before World War I. As for the rate of economic growth, it was seventh among 15 countries, while Austria occupied thirteenth place. Countries achieving higher growth rates included Switzerland, Germany, Denmark, Sweden, Finland and France.

Table 20: Gross Domestic Product in Austria and Hungary according to Schulze's Calculations

	Per capita GDP At 1913 prices in crowns			
	1870		1910	
	Austria	Hungary	Austria	Hungary
Agriculture and forestry	117	141	145	245
Industry and mining	128	31	238	104
Trade, banking and transport	41	12	105	42
Services	150	104	146	99
Total GDP	*436*	*288*	*635*	*490*
	Distribution of GDP by sectors			
	1870		1910	
	Austria	Hungary	Austria	Hungary
	%	%	%	%
Agriculture	26.8	48.8	22.8	49.9
Industry and mining	29.5	10.8	37.4	21.2
Trade, banking and transport	9.3	4.2	16.5	8.7
Services	34.4	36.2	23.3	20.2
Total GDP	*100.0*	*100.0*	*100.0*	*100.0*
	Average annual growth %			
	Total GDP		*Per capita* GDP	
	Austria	Hungary	Austria	Hungary
	%	%	%	%
Agriculture	1.39	2.15	0.54	1.39
Industry and mining	2.40	3.82	1.54	3.05
Trade, banking and transport	3.27	3.95	2.40	3.18
Services	0.81	0.62	– 0.04	– 0.12
Total GDP	*1.80*	*2.09*	*0.94*	*1.34*

A different conclusion may be drawn from the latest edition of Angus Maddison's *Historical Statistics.* According to these statistics, Hungary—with an annual average growth rate of 1.53 percent—was at the forefront of European economic growth, since only three countries achieved a larger increase in GDP *per capita* between 1870 and 1913: Germany (1.61 percent), Denmark (1.57 percent) and Switzerland (1.55 percent). In 1870, the average *per capita* GDP for 12 Western European countries[40] was 91 percent higher than *per capita* GDP in Hungary. In 1910, it was only 76 percent higher. The average rate of growth (1.33 percent) for these countries was significantly less than Hungary's average growth rate. These figures show that Hungary was steadily—albeit rather slowly—catching up with both Austria and Western Europe. The indicators also suggest that Hungary was closer to the European average in 1913 than it is now. If Hungarian *per capita* GDP equals 100, then the average index for the 12 Western European countries was 176 in 1913, but 277 in 2000.[41]

Schulze also undertook calculations with regard to capital accumulation and productivity growth in the two halves of the Dual Monarchy. Between 1870 and 1910, capital assets used in the economy grew by 4.01 percent in Hungary and by 2.55 percent in Austria.[42] Schulze adopted my calculations for Hungary, according to which national wealth, or reproductive capital assets (the total combined value of all public and private buildings, production equipment, machinery and tools, roads, railways, transport facilities, bridges, hydro construction, urban and rural public utilities, and animal livestock), increased from 5.5 billion crowns in 1867 to 23 billion crowns (£960 million) in 1913—that is to say that it more than quadrupled.[43]

Labor productivity increased by 1.29 percent *per annum* in Austria and by 1.65 percent in Hungary. One of the main reasons for the rapid increase in labor productivity in Hungary was greater access to capital assets and an upsurge in the capital/output ratio (that is, the capital coefficient). Schulze emphasizes the fact that by 1913 Hungary had made up for its initial disadvantage in this

Figure 8

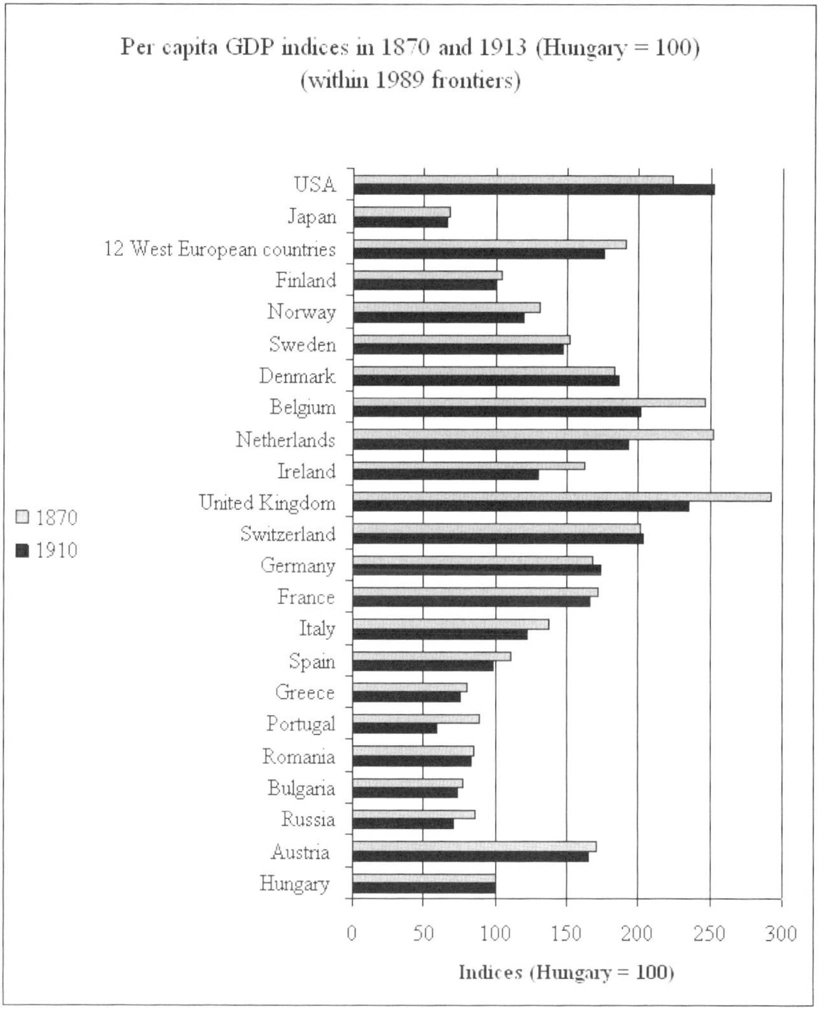
Per capita GDP indices in 1870 and 1913 (Hungary = 100)
(within 1989 frontiers)
USA
Japan
12 West European countries
Finland
Norway
Sweden
Denmark
Belgium
Netherlands
Ireland
United Kingdom
Switzerland
Germany
France
Italy
Spain
Greece
Portugal
Romania
Bulgaria
Russia
Austria
Hungary
1870
1910
0
50
100
150
200
250
300
Indices (Hungary = 100)

field, reaching 80–90 percent of the Austrian level with regard to the ratio of physical capital to unit of output. Thus, in this field too, Hungary managed to reduce its disadvantage, because the increase in productivity in Hungary was greater than it was in Austria in all sectors apart from mining.[44]

Table 21: Labor Productivity according to Schulze's Calculations

	Agri-culture	Mining	Industry and Mining	Trade, Banking and Transport	Other Services	Entire Economy
	Value added per worker at 1913 prices in crowns					
1870						
Austria	349	823	1,207	1,438	1,413	702
Hungary	338	648	822	784	934	455
1910						
Austria	544	2,122	1,855	1,899	2,039	1,171
Hungary	662	1,525	1,514	1,438	1,373	877
	Hungarian figures as a percentage of Austrian figures					
1870	97	79	69	55	66	65
1910	122	72	82	76	67	75
	Average annual increase 1870–1910, %					
Austria	1.12	2.40	1.08	0.70	0.94	1.29
Hungary	1.69	2.16	1.49	1.53	0.97	1.65

The rate of growth was not uniform throughout the economy: industry, commerce and transport grew twice as quickly as agriculture. Consequently, the economy was significantly restructured. According to my calculations, agriculture's share of GDP (at 1913 prices) decreased from 66 to 44 percent. At the same time, industry's share rose from 11 to 25 percent and the service sector's share increased from 23 to 31 percent. Schulze calculated that the contribution to the GDP of industry, commerce and transport increased from 15 percent in 1870 to 30 percent in 1910.

A similar change may also be observed in the employment structure. In Hungary and Croatia, the share of active persons employed in agriculture fell from 77 percent in 1869 to 62 percent in 1910, while the proportion working in industry rose from 9 to 17 percent and the proportion working in services increased from 14 to 21 percent. The absolute number of agricultural workers also declined, whereas the total number of industrial workers more than doubled, rising from 697,000 to 1,533,000. The number of workers in the services and transport sectors increased from 133,000 to 504,000.

Table 22: Distribution of Active Population among Principal Economic Sectors in 1910

	Austria %	Hungary %	Croatia %
Agriculture and forestry	51.6	60.1	78.4
Mining and industry	22.0	18.3	9.6
Services sector	26.4	21.6	12.0

The success of the Hungarian economy at the time of the Dual Monarchy was due in part to the common market of the Empire. It was largely thanks to this common market that the Hungarian economy's leading sector, agriculture, retained its dynamism even during the European grain sales crisis. Owing to competition from American, Russian and Romanian producers of grain and flour, as well as protective measures taken by countries in Western Europe, Hungarian grain and flour were deprived of markets abroad. Even so, the common customs area continued to absorb Hungarian agricultural and food industry products. The common market also played a significant role in the import of production factors, such as capital and skilled labor, which were necessary for the modernization of the Hungarian economy. This was especially true in the first half of the era.

The foundation of the common market was the division of labor between an agrarian country producing food and raw materials and a more industrialized country. This agrarian–industrial division of labor was retained throughout the period. As time passed, the division of labor reached a higher and more modern level between two industrializing national economies that were of a different structure and at a different level of development. Scott M. Eddie, an American historical researcher of the Hungarian economy at the time of the Dual Monarchy, concluded the following: "The regional specialization necessary for production in the unified market of the Monarchy had advanced significantly by 1882, compared with the situation in 1850. Hungary was not only the 'granary of the Empire' but also a significant exporter of certain manufactured goods, the manufacture of which was mostly based on the country's own production of raw materials."[45]

Between 1867 and 1914, economic growth and restructuring occurred more rapidly in Hungary than they did in Austria. This conclusion applies to total GDP, all main economic sectors, labor, productivity and capital assets—that is, to the principal macro-indicators of the national economy and its dynamism. This more rapid growth and Hungary's tendency to catch up with the more developed half of the Monarchy was acknowledged by contemporary observers. It was manifest in the quota that expressed the relative economic and monetary capacities of the two countries. This quota was used to calculate Hungary's contribution to the cost of common affairs; it increased from 30 percent in 1867 to 36.4 percent in 1907.

Despite the more rapid growth of the Hungarian economy, differences in the level of economic development could still be observed even immediately prior to World War I. Indeed, there were substantial differences between Austria's western provinces, Hungary and the eastern and southern peripheral regions (Galicia, Bukovina, Dalmatia and Croatia). The following question arises: did the integration of regions of different character, structure and development lead to the creation of a larger and more comprehensive economic community? This question is particularly poignant in the light of the disintegration that one can observe in the field of politics—leading ultimately to the dissolution of the Empire. The answer to the question is quite obvious, despite the political problems. Indeed, economic historical analysis indicates a clear increase in the interregional flow of goods, capital and labor in the late nineteenth century. Similarly, a trend towards a balancing out of regional differences in prices, wages and interest rates is also observable. All of this serves to indicate the advance of market integration. David Good, an American researcher of the economic history of the Habsburg Empire, undertook an analysis of the factors influencing economic integration, in which he came to this conclusion: "The quantitative evidence supports those who stress the more positive achievements of the Habsburg economic union. Judged in economic terms the Empire experienced substantial market integration in the decades before World War I."[46]

At the end of this economic review, we may conclude that in terms of the international factors influencing economic development in Hungary, a reversal of a long-term trend took place in the second half of the nineteenth century. Hungary's relative economic backwardness had steadily grown more acute between the sixteenth century and the mid-nineteenth century. This relative decline drew to a halt after 1848. Thereafter a reverse trend—a reduction in relative backwardness—could be perceived. To catch up with the advanced countries, Hungary was required to make a long-term effort. During the half-century prior to World War I, a higher rate of growth enabled Hungary to reduce its development lag with regard to the Western European countries and the other half of the Monarchy. Despite this success, Hungary proved unable to catch up completely. In terms of economic modernization and *per capita* income it drew ahead of the Balkan countries, Russia, Spain and Portugal, and came close to the other half of the Monarchy and to Italy; nevertheless, it still lagged far behind the Western European and Scandinavian countries. Still, it was during the years preceding World War I that Hungary lay closest, in terms of economic development, to the advanced Western European countries and to Austria—as is shown in the two diagrams on the next page.[47]

Figure 9

Per capita GDP indices
in Western Europe and Hungary
(12 West European countries = 100)

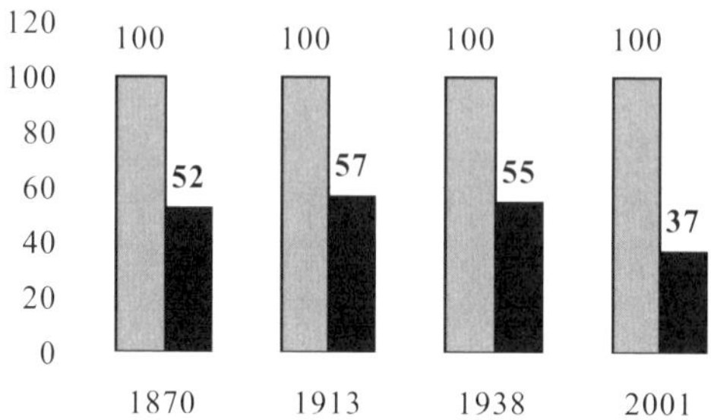

(Based on calculations by Angus Maddison.
Data refer to current national areas)

□ 12 West European countries ■ Hungary

Per capita GDP indices
in Austria and Hungary
(Austria = 100)

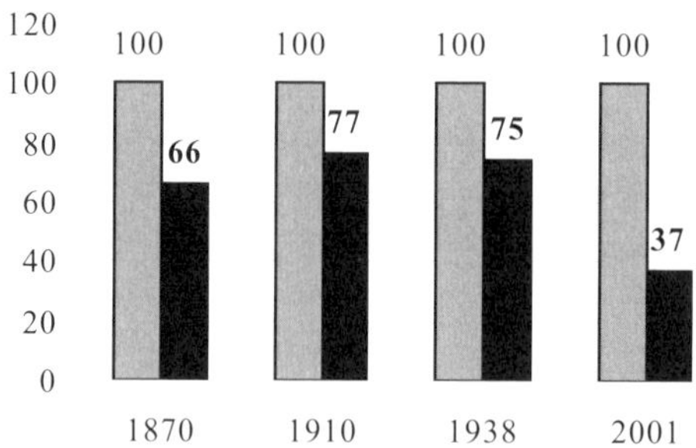

(Based on calculations by Schulze and Maddison.
Data refer to national area at the time)

□ Austria ■ Hungary

The data reflect relatively rapid growth as well as economic restructuring, but also significant backwardness in relation to the industrialized countries and to the western half of the Monarchy. This contradiction was a feature of the Hungarian economy not only in international terms but also in sectoral and regional regards. The capital sector was relatively well developed: the country had a highly concentrated and up-to-date large-scale industrial sector (some parts of which were at the forefront of world developments), an established banking sector and an extensive railway network. In leading areas of the economy, the capital sector quickly and effectively applied the technical, management and funding innovations of the advanced countries. Even so, this relatively well-developed and modern form of capitalism rested on rather narrow foundations; it proved unable to penetrate and mold in its own image the whole country or all branches of the economy. In significant areas of the country—particularly in the eastern and northeastern regions—pre-capitalistic structures or features of early capitalism continued to prevail in many economic fields. These included the residues of traditional production organization and techniques, partially self-sufficient and isolated households, and small agricultural and industrial producers. Such contradictions—the imbalances in sectoral and regional development—slowed down and distorted economic development. They were also a significant and growing source of tensions in the social and political structure, particularly because they largely coincided with the main fault lines of class status and ethnic origin.

Notes

1 Mór Gelléri, *Ötven év a magyar ipar történetéből. 1842–1892* [Fifty Years of Hungarian Industrial History 1842–1892] (Budapest, 1892), p. 434.

2 *Ibid.*, pp. 424, 432.

3 *Az 1875. évi augusztus 28-ára hirdetett országgyűlés képviselőházának naplója* [Journal of the Lower House of the Parliament Convoked for August 28, 1875], XIV (Budapest, 1877), p. 336.

4 *Ibid.*, p. 265.

5 *Az 1875. évi augusztus hó 28-ra hirdetett országgyűlés képviselőházának irományai* [Documents of the Lower House of the Parliament Convoked for August 28, 1875], XXI (Budapest, 1877), pp. 343–344.

6 *Az 1881. évi szeptember hó 24-ére hirdetett országgyűlés képviselőházának naplója* [Journal of the House of Representatives of the Parliament Convoked for September 24, 1881], VIII (Budapest, 1883), p. 168.

7 *Ibid.*, pp. 257–258.

8 Sándor Matlekovits, *Magyarország közgazdasági és közművelődési állapota ezeréves fennállásakor* [The Economic and Cultural State of Hungary a Thousand Years after Its Foundation], II (Budapest, 1898), pp. 1115–1116.

9 Gyula Vargha, *A magyar hitelügy és hitelintézetek története* [The History of Credit and Banking in Hungary] (Budapest, 1896), p. 345.

10 Menyhért Lónyay, *Közügyeinkről. Nézetek Magyarország pénzügyi állapotáról* [On Our Public Affairs. Views on Hungary's Financial Status] (Budapest, 1873), p. 16.

11 Jenő Zichy, *Emlékirat a magyar ipar fejlesztése érdekében* [Memorandum for Hungarian Industrial Development] (Budapest, 1880), pp. 15–16.

12 József Szterényi and Jenő Ladányi, *A magyar ipar a világháborúban* [Hungarian Industry in the World War] (Budapest, 1933), p. 16.

13 Magyar Gyáriparosok Országos Szövetsége. Közlemények [Confederation of Hungarian Industrialists. Announcements], May 30, 1908.

14 Pál Szende, *A magyar közgazdaság és az Országos Magyar Kereskedelmi Egyesülés tevékenysége* [The Hungarian Economy and the Work of the National Association of Hungarian Traders] (Budapest, 1914), p. 95.

15 "A falusi gazda" [The Village Farmer], *Nemzetgazdasági Közlemények,* November 5, 1871.

16 *Tabellen zur Währung-Statistik*. 2. Ausgabe. 2. Teil (Vienna, 1900–1904); Franz Bartsch, *Statistische Daten über die Zahlungsbilanz Österreich–Ungarns vor Ausbruch des Krieges. Mitteilungen des K. K. Finanzministeriums*. XXII (Vienna, 1917); Frigyes Fellner, *A nemzetközi fizetési mérleg és alakulása Magyarországon* [The International Balance of Payments in Hungary] (Budapest, 1908); idem, *Ausztria és Magyarország nemzeti jövedelme* [The National Income of Austria and Hungary] (Budapest, 1916).

17 Lóránt Hegedűs, *A Pesti Magyar Kereskedelmi Bank keletkezésének és fennállásának története* [The History of the Hungarian Commercial Bank of Budapest], II. *1892–1917* (Budapest, 1917), p. 39.

18 Vargha, *A magyar hitelügy és hitelintézetek története*, pp. 478–479.

19 Article in *Anyagi Érdekeink* [Our Financial Interests], November 21, 1868.

20 Hungarian National Archives. Budapest. *Kereskedelemügyi Minisztérium Levéltára* [Archive of the Ministry of Trade]. K 231. 1893–2–44384.

21 Ágoston Trefort, *Kisebb dolgozatok az irodalom, közgazdaság és politika köréből* [Minor Essays on the Subject of Literature, Economics and Politics] (Budapest, 1882), p. 332.

22 In 1896, Hungary celebrated the thousandth anniversary of the arrival in the Carpathian basin of the Magyar tribespeople.

23 Vargha, *A magyar hitelügy és hitelintézetek története*, p. 364.

24 Lajos Láng, ed., *Magyarország gazdasági statisztikája* [Hungary's Economic Statistics] (Budapest, 1887), p. 639.

25 Vargha, *A magyar hitelügy és hitelintézetek története*, p. 419.

26 Antal Vörös, in Péter Hanák and Ferenc Mucsi, eds., *Magyarország története 1890–1918* [History of Hungary 1890–1918], third edition (Budapest, 1988), p. 326.

27 *A Budapesti Kereskedelmi és Iparkamara jelentése a budapesti kamarai kerület kézmű- és gyáriparáról az 1870–75. években* [Report of the Budapest Chamber of Commerce and Industry on Artisanal and Factory Industry in the Chamber District of Budapest, in the Years 1870–1875] (Budapest, 1877), p. 117.

28 *Ibid.*, p. 119.

29 Imre Halász, "Kisebb iparosainkhoz" [To Our Artisans], *Anyagi Érdekeink* [Our Financial Interests], October 24, 1868.

30 *Jelentés az ipari szakoktatás és a háziipar jelen állásáról* [Report on the Current State of Vocational Education and Household Industry], published by the Ministry of Trade and Commerce (Budapest, 1881), p. 116.

31 Láng, ed., *Magyarország gazdasági statisztikája*, p. 345.

32 *Ibid.*, pp. 330, 333.

33 *A Budapesti Kereskedelmi és Iparkamara jelentése a budapesti kamarai kerület kézmű- és gyáriparáról az 1870–75. években*, p. 314.

34 Scott M. Eddie, "The Terms and Patterns of Hungarian Foreign Trade, 1882–1913," *Journal of Economic History* 37 (June 1977) 2: 329–358.

35 *Az 1865. évi december 10-ikére hirdetett országgyűlés képviselőházának naplója* [Journal of the Lower House of the Parliament Convoked for December 10, 1865], VI (Pest, 1868), p. 172.

36 Frigyes Fellner, *Ausztria és Magyarország nemzeti jövedelme* [The National Income of Austria and Hungary] (Budapest, 1916).

37 I take into account Waizner's calculations for Austrian GDP. See Ernst Waizner, "Das Volkseinkommen Alt-Österreichs und seine Verteilung auf die Nachfolgestaaten," *Metron* 7/4 (1928): 97–182.

38 David F. Good, "Revised Estimates of GDP *Per Capita* in Central and Eastern Europe, 1870–1910: Technical Notes and Tables," Working Paper (1998); David Good and Tongshu Ma, "The Economic Growth of Central and Eastern Europe in Comparative Perspective, 1870–1989," *European Review of Economic History* 3 (1999) 2: 103–137.

39 Max-Stephan Schulze, "Patterns of Growth and Stagnation in the Late Nineteenth Century Habsburg Economy," *European Review of Economic History* (December 2000): 311–340, and idem, "Origins of Catch-up Failure: Comparative Productivity Growth in the Hapsburg Empire, 1870–1910," London School of Economics. 2007, Working Papers No. 100/07. (This revises the previous information about

Austrian and Hungarian GDP. The table contains this revised data.) In my view, Schulze overestimated the contribution to GDP of the services sector in 1870.

40 Austria, Belgium, Denmark, Great Britain, Finland, France, Germany, Italy, the Netherlands, Norway, Switzerland and Sweden.

41 Angus Maddison, *The World Economy. 2. Historical Statistics* (Paris, 2006), pp. 438–445, 465, 478, 558. (GDP for all countries and all years, calculated in 1990 dollars.)

42 Max-Stephan Schulze, "An Estimate of Imperial Austria's Gross Domestic Fixed Capital Stock, 1870–1913: Methods, Sources and Results," London School of Economics, Working Papers No. 92/05 (December 2005).

43 László Katus, "Economic Growth in Hungary during the Age of Dualism (1867–1913). A Quantitative Analysis," in Ervin Pamlényi, ed., *Social-Economic Researches on the History of East-Central Europe* (Studia Historica Academiae Scientiarum Hungaricae, 62) (Budapest, 1970), pp. 109–111.

44 Schulze, "Origins of Catch-up Failure."

45 Scott Eddie, "Mit bizonyítanak az 1882–1913-as export-statisztikai adatok: Magyarország valóban csak a Monarchia 'éléskamrája' volt?" [What Do the Export Statistics for 1882–1913 Prove? Was Hungary Really the Granary of the Monarchy?], *Történelmi Szemle* 25 (1982) 3: 416–425.

46 David F. Good, *Economic Rise of the Habsburg Empire, 1750–1914* (Berkeley, CA, Los Angeles, CA, and London, 1984), p. 124.

47 See notes 40 and 41.

9. SOCIETY IN TRANSITION

The 1848 Revolution brought an end to the country's traditional society and the privileges of the nobility, while the adoption of legislation guaranteeing equality before the law facilitated the development of a modern civil society. To transform and modernize society, however, several decades of reforms would be required. Most of the privileges of the estates were abolished immediately, but the Catholic and Orthodox prelates as well as the aristocracy enjoyed residual privileges (for instance, seats in the Upper House of Parliament, and *fidei commissa*, that is, a form of entail). Noble titles continued to exist, but they offered no special rights, although the nobles and urban burghers of the pre-1848 period were permitted—in accordance with their previous rights—to vote in elections, even when they failed to meet the new criteria for voting (concerning property and income). In 1881, 92,000 voters—11.2 percent of those entitled to vote—fell into this category, but their number decreased to 21,000 (less than 2 percent of voters) in 1911. Noble titles continued to offer social prestige. Wealthy citizens, rich peasant farmers, upper-class Jewish families and highly qualified intellectuals often strove to acquire noble titles.

The speed of social change increased in the late nineteenth century. Economic progress and the capitalist development of several sectors gave rise to new social classes, while the position of existing groups within the social structure also changed. Industrialization and the creation of a modern transport network led to an increase in the mobility of the population: in 1910, 31 percent of the population—5.7 million people—were not residing in their place of birth. Less than half of the population of the major towns had been born locally, indicating that migration within the country was directed mostly at the urban and industrial centers. A change in residence—geographical mobility—was most often accompanied by a change in occupation and social class, that is, by social mobility. The main direction of migration within the country was southward, but at the turn of the century, migration from east to west increased; there was a flow of people from Transylvania and the northeastern periphery to the center of the country.

In the country's industrializing and modernizing regions, and especially in the major cities, the traditional social frameworks, based on community solidarity and close family and kinship ties, began to break down. They were replaced, to some extent, by the mass organizations and associations of modern civil society. In the country as a whole, the Western European type of nuclear family was characteristic, but among the rural agrarian populations of some regions, one could still encounter, even in the early twentieth century, the multiple family type, in which several married couples (parents, married sons or married younger brothers) lived together in shared households and farmed together. Such large families were a feature of southeastern Transdanubia (Baranya County) and the central part of Upper Hungary (among the *Palóc* ethnic group). In Croatia—particularly in the former Military Frontier—the patriarchal multiple family, or *zadruga*, proved remarkably resilient. Indeed, as late as 1900, one in four Croats lived in such families (one in two in the former Military Frontier). *Zadruga* households had on average 8.1 members, while the average size of other households was 4.2 persons.

Indicative of the modernization of society was the increasing economic activity of women. Between 1880 and 1910, the percentage of women among wage earners in modern sectors of the economy—that is, excluding agriculture and domestic service—increased from 10 to 17 percent. In 1880, 22 out of every 1,000 women aged over 15 were working in these sectors, but by 1910 the figure had risen to 59. The number of women working in industry doubled between 1890 and 1910. Women were particularly numerous in the clothing, textiles, food and catering industries. In 1880, there were just 400 female company officials working in the industrial, trade and transport sectors, but this number had

Table 1: Population of Hungary and Croatia by Social and Occupational Status in 1910 (including active and dependent population)

	Hungary		Croatia	
	1,000	%	1,000	%
Owners or leaseholders of more than 100 *hold* (142 acres)	71	0.39	4	0.14
Owners or leaseholders of 5–100 *hold* (7.1–142 acres)	4,581	25.08	1,234	47.02
Self-employed craftsmen, merchants or haulage contractors	1,923	10.53	165	6.28
Self-employed intellectuals	59	0.32	4	0.14
Other self-employed	283	1.55	15	0.56
Total self-employed persons	*6,917*	*37.87*	*1,421*	*54.14*
Private officials and farm managers	275	1.50	18	0.70
Public officials	379	2.08	37	1.40
Military officers	18	0.10	2	0.10
Private/public officials and military officer retirees	40	0.22	5	0.18
Total private and public officials	*712*	*3.90*	*62*	*2.37*
Public employees	192	1.05	16	0.59
Non-commissioned military officers (NCOs)	38	0.21	5	0.19
Public employees and NCO retirees	109	0.60	9	0.34
Total public employees and NCOs	*339*	*1.86*	*30*	*1.13*
Dwarf-holders, less than 5 hold (7.1 acres)	*2,437*	*13.34*	*640*	*24.38*
Agricultural and forestry workers	4,275	23.40	186	7.08
Industrial and haulage workers	2,458	13.46	176	6.71
Day laborers	453	2.48	48	1.83
Domestic servants	405	2.22	26	0.99
Total workers	*7,591*	*41.56*	*436*	*16.61*
Soldiers	88	0.48	18	0.69
Unknown or no occupation	179	0.98	18	0.69
Total	**18,265**	**100.00**	**2,625**	**100.00**

increased to 23,000 by 1910. The number of female public employees (working above all in education and health care) increased from 15,000 to 44,000 over a period of 30 years. Despite a substantial increase, the proportion of women employed in modern sectors of the economy was still relatively small in Hungary; it was far less than in Western and Central Europe. Indeed, in the early twentieth century, the proportion of women working in modern sectors of the economy was almost two times higher in Austria and Italy and at least three times higher in Western Europe.

The fact that 47 percent of the population in Hungary but only 20 percent of the population in Croatia made a living from wages or salaries is indicative of the differences between the two countries in terms of modernization. (If we include dwarf-holders, then the respective percentages are 61 percent and 44 percent.) Croatian society was more archaic than Hungarian society; the traditional agrarian structure was breaking down at a slower pace.

As elsewhere in Central and Eastern Europe, the traditional structure in Hungary was rather slow to dissolve in the second half of the nineteenth century. Although some parts of society adapted to the conditions of capitalism in terms of their economic activity, nevertheless they did not become—or they only partially became—middle-class citizens in the Western European sense. "A peculiar duality characterized social groups positioned at the same level in the social pyramid: there was a disharmonic coexistence of the old groups of feudal origin and the newly emerging classes. At the highest level, two groups shared in exercising power: the large landowners and the *grande bourgeoisie*."[1]

The landowning aristocracy controlled the political power positions and enjoyed the greatest social prestige. In Hungary, there were three aristocratic titles: (Imperial) dukes, counts and barons. New families were admitted into the aristocracy. Indeed, between 1848 and 1918, 204 aristocratic titles—mostly baronial—were granted to leading politicians and high-ranking military officers, senior public officials, and outstanding business or academic figures. Consequently, the composition of the aristocracy was significantly altered: initially the true historical aristocracy was dominant, but in later periods the new aristocracy had greater weight. At the end of the period, around 300 clans and 1,200 families constituted the aristocracy. Most of them were large landowning families, but a significant proportion owned less than 1,000 *hold* (1,420 acres). Almost a quarter of the country's territory was owned by these aristocratic families. Around 200 families possessed estates with more than 10,000 *hold* (14,200 acres) of land. A significant proportion of these estates, however, were *fidei commissa* (entailed estates). Some magnates made a living from their academic or official posts (for example, Baron József Eötvös).

The aristocracy was divided into various groups. The established Catholic aristocratic families of Transdanubia and the western counties of Upper Hungary (the Esterházy, Batthyány, Pálffy, Zichy, Erdődy, Széchenyi, Mailáth and Apponyi families) held the positions of the national feudal dignitaries prior to 1848, as well as fulfilling many of the various court functions. These families owned mansions or palaces in Vienna, where they spent much of the year in the vicinity of the Imperial court. They often intermarried with the aristocracy of the hereditary lands in Austria. Thus, in the course of the eighteenth and nineteenth centuries, there arose an Imperial aristocracy, whose members were interrelated. Some of these aristocratic families—those referred to at the time as the first-rate aristocratic families, such as the Esterházy, Festetich, Batthyány-Strattmann, Pálffy and Erdődy families—steered clear of politics. Others, however, such as the Apponyi, Batthyány, Szapáry and Zichy families, became actively involved in political life. Aristocratic families with lands in the eastern half of the country (the Andrássy and Károlyi families) had fewer links with Vienna; they tended to foster good relations with leading noble landowners in the counties. They tended to intermarry, and so foreign spouses were rare. A good number of these families were Protestant. The Transylvanian aristocracy comprised a larger number of families, but they were poorer than their counterparts in other parts of the country and they owned less land (the Bánffy, Bethlen, Jósika, Kemény, Teleki and Wesselényi families).

Under the 1885 reform of the Upper House of Parliament, aristocrats paying less than 3,000 florins in annual direct tax lost their membership. In this way, more than half of Hungary's aristocratic families, and two thirds of family members, were excluded from the legislature. Aristocrats still formed a majority in the Upper House of Parliament even after the 1885 reform, and there were also 50–60 aristocrats in the Lower House (11–16 percent of members); the number varied over time. Until the turn of the century, most of the aristocrats in Parliament were members of the historical families—particularly counts—but the situation altered in the early years of the twentieth century, when new barons, including commoners who had newly received the title of baron, formed the majority. During the period, nine out of 15 prime ministers were aristocrats, four were noble landowners, and two had middle-class backgrounds. We find, among the government ministers, more than 30 aristocrats (and this number excludes Francis Joseph's personal ministers, all of whom were magnates). The sons of aristocratic families often embarked on diplomatic careers, but fewer and fewer of them were to be found among the high-ranking soldiers and prelates. In addition to participating in politics, they were inclined to become executive and supervisory board members of banks or industrial and haulage companies. Besides political influence and social prestige, the power of the aristocracy was enhanced by the fact that several social groups were dependent upon them. Hundreds of thousands of laborers, sharecroppers and tenants on the estates, as well as peasant farmers in villages lying in the vicinity of such estates, were dependent upon the lords of the manor.

The families of the historical aristocracy lived rather isolated lives in their country houses and town mansions (in Budapest, such mansions were typically situated near the National Museum, in the Castle District, and along the outer part of Sugár—today Andrássy—Street); they rarely interacted with the lower social classes. They tended to intermarry, and some of them established close family ties with the aristocracy in the other half of the Monarchy, thereby forming a supranational "Imperial aristocracy." The aristocratic families were waited upon by a whole army of servants and other workers. To entertain themselves, they hunted, attended balls, and went traveling. Sports such as horse-riding were popular, and they were the first social group to purchase automobiles. Some aristocrats even went as explorers to distant places, including Count Béla Széchenyi, who traveled around Central Asia in 1877–1879, and Count Sámuel Teleki, who explored East Africa in 1886–1889.

The aristocracy was not equivalent to the large landowning class, since more than half of the large landowners did not bear aristocratic titles. Large landowners were those who paid at least 2,000 crowns in land tax per year and who owned more than 1,000 *hold* (1,420 acres) of land. At the turn of the century, there were around 2,000 such landowners, possessing 23 percent of the country's territory. More than half of this land, however, was forest, pasture, reed marsh or infertile. Almost half of the large landowners were noble landowners. Some of them held more than 10,000 *hold* (14,200 acres) of land, but most of them had just 1,000–2,000 *hold* (1,420–2,840 acres). The third group of large landowners—one fifth of the total—were commoner (non-aristocratic/noble) landowners, such as bank managers and industrial magnates, who had purchased a few thousand acres of land, often for reasons of prestige. Most of the large landowners did not farm their lands—which were managed instead by a skilled apparatus under the direction of stewards or simply let to tenants. The large leaseholders (half of whom were Jews), farming hundreds or even thousands of acres, were true capitalist entrepreneurs.

Unlike the aristocratic and noble landowners, who managed to rescue their leading positions from the old feudal world, the *grande bourgeoisie*—the class exercising economic power—was a product of the era. It was linked only by narrow threads with the patrician class of the era of estates before 1848. Most of the *grande bourgeoisie* accumulated capital initially by trading in grain, thereafter expanding it by lending money or constructing railways. From the 1860s onwards, people in this social class invested in business undertakings (mills, sugar and alcohol) and joint stock banks, and then, from the 1880s onwards, in all branches of industry. The large-scale construction projects of the era were excellent means of accumulating capital: timber merchants, builders and construction companies made up one part of the *grande bourgeoisie*. Several industrial entrepreneurs transformed small or medium-sized industrial plants into large-scale industrial companies. A characteristic group were those who used their expertise, acquired in the course of working as company officials and engineers, to move into bank management positions or company board membership. Some intellectuals also moved upwards to join the *grande bourgeoisie* as distinguished lawyers or newspaper editors.

At the beginning of the twentieth century, the *grande bourgeoisie* comprised 800–1,000 families. Among this number, there were 100–150 families bound by business and family ties that formed the supreme command of Hungary's capitalist economy—the financial bourgeoisie. Two thirds of the *grande bourgeoisie* resided in Budapest, being predominantly of Jewish descent. Most of the rest either had come from abroad or were Hungarians of German or Magyar descent. The country also had a wealthy middle bourgeoisie of 3,000–4,000 families.

The ethnic German and Magyar *grande bourgeoisie* readily fitted into noble society, establishing links with the aristocracy. The integration of the Jewish *grande bourgeoisie* was more fraught. The position in society of the *grande bourgeoisie*, who were often richer than the noble landowners, did not accord with their status in economic life. The social integration of the Jewish *grande bourgeoisie* during the period was facilitated by the granting of noble titles to 346 Jewish families and the granting of baronial titles to 28 families. The integration of the *grande bourgeoisie* into noble society tended to be rather superficial: although the upwardly mobile families had urban mansions built or purchased spacious residences in expensive condominiums, and even wore the *díszmagyar*[2] on certain public occasions, nevertheless they adhered to their bourgeois ethics and fostered middle-class virtues in their private lives. They were reluctant to adopt the lifestyle and leisure activities of the aristocracy and lesser nobles. In politics, they accepted the leading role of the aristocracy and the noble landowners, and supported—almost without exception—the governing Liberal Party.

The middle class in Hungary's nascent civil society was heterogeneous and diverse. It comprised three main groups: the so-called historical middle class, that is, the medium-sized noble landowners with 100–1,000 *hold* (142–1,420 acres) of land and their offspring, who were known at the time as gentry; the middle bourgeoisie; the public officials and intellectuals.

The historical middle class comprised the medium-sized noble landowners. After 1848, people in this class began to be called gentry, but as time passed, this term also came to mean descendants of landowners who had lost their land and been forced to accept jobs in order to earn a living. According to the estimates of Károly Keleti, the first director of the Hungarian Statistical Office, the number of noble landowners fell from 20,000–30,000 families in the 1840s, to about half that number in the early 1870s, and then to just 7,000 families prior to World War I. After the abolition of serfdom, some of the noble landowners, in particular those who still possessed relatively large landed properties even after the loss of tenements and services of their former serfs, could adapt to the changed conditions; they were able to modernize their landed properties and retain their political and social influence. The poorer landowners, having lost the free labor and services of their serfs as well as their tools and equipment, proved unable to modernize their farms and turn them into capitalist enterprises, as they lacked capital. It took years before they received compensation; in the meantime they became indebted and were forced to sell many or all of their lands. Sometime their lands were even auctioned off to settle unpaid debts. As Károly Keleti wrote, "There are few well-kept medium-sized farms in the country, but many nobles living off them… Since we came out of our patriarchal relations and survived the 'twenty wretched years' [1849–1867], the harmony between what we own and what we spend, between our work and our requirements, between the estimate of time and its use have been disturbed... Many landed properties have had to be auctioned, and many old families have been removed from the list of landowners."[3]

There were plenty of job opportunities for nobles who lost their lands or proved unable to make a living from their lands. They could work for the county administrations or for the central or local offices of the government apparatus, which expanded rapidly after the 1867 Compromise. Many of them tried their luck in the free intellectual professions. Few of them, however, chose careers in industry or trade. On this subject, Károly Keleti wrote the following: "The progeny of the so-called 'better families' do not have sufficient appetite for careers other than landowning... They do not dare to look fate in the eye, to consider what awaits them if, having left the class that is perceived as privileged, they should choose a decent middle-class career."[4] Most of the official county posts were still filled by nobles, while more than half of the officials working for central government and in some of the ministries were the sons of noble families, while in other ministries a quarter or a third of them were from such backgrounds. Their political influence was particularly great in the first quarter-century of the era of Dualism: almost two thirds of government ministers and members of Parliament were of gentry stock. Even so, from the end of the century, the proportion of government officials and politicians from a gentry background fell. Their prestige in society also declined. Until the turn of the century, gentry lifestyle, mentality and values were the model for Hungary's middle classes—which were largely made up of assimilated Germans and Jews. In the early twentieth century, however, these latter groups began to develop their own middle-class consciousness and way of life.

The bourgeois middle class—which was smaller and poorer than its counterpart in the Western industrial countries—comprised the owners of small industrial plants, trading companies and residential buildings, bank shareholders and medium-sized farm leaseholders. The strengthening of the bourgeois middle class at the turn of the century is indicated by a more than twofold increase in the number of medium-sized industrial plants employing 6–20 workers between 1890 and 1910, as well as a threefold increase in the number of plants employing 21–100 workers. To this group we should add the senior officials of industrial and commercial joint stock companies and banks, as well as better-off intellectuals working in the free professions, along with successful and popular artists. Assimilated or assimilating Germans constituted a large part of the bourgeois middle class, but other ethnic backgrounds were also represented; Jews were particularly numerous among certain groups (traders).

A peculiar feature of Hungary's social development was the relative dearth of wealthy middle-class people who were both economically and politically autonomous. The largest group of the middle class were the private and public officials, to whom we might add the freelance intellectuals. The nobility as well as all classes of non-noble society took part in the formation of this group: the middle class and *petite bourgeoisie*, peasant farmers and even some better-off skilled workers had sons who became officials or intellectuals. In numerical terms, public officials were more significant than the private officials employed in various sectors of the economy. The origins of the two groups and their social genesis differed significantly: men of noble descent were predominant among the public officials, while most private officials were recruited from non-noble backgrounds; they included many men of German or Jewish descent. Only 5 percent of public officials were of Jewish descent, but half of private company officials and more than 40 percent of freelance intellectuals were Jewish.

At the turn of the century, the middle classes liked to call themselves the "gentlemanly" (*úri*) middle class. Formerly, only noble landowners had been addressed as "gentlemen" (*urak*), but in the late nineteenth century, the criteria changed. (By this time, noble landowners constituted only a small part of the middle class.) Any male with a high school diploma or a similar qualification counted as a "gentleman" and was therefore entitled to become a reserve military officer, having successfully completed a year of voluntary military service. The rank of officer conferred the title of "gentleman" on the man; he became fit for partaking in a duel—a "gentleman" had to defend his honor in this way, even though duels were prohibited by law. A "gentleman" would use the informal "you" with his fellows and join them in discussing politics and playing cards. However, to be a "gentleman," one had to be Magyar. Thus non-Magyars and Jews were required to assimilate if they wished to join the "gentlemanly" middle class. The number of men meeting the criteria was not so great. Indeed, in 1910, there were only 180,000 men professing to be Magyars who were also high school graduates (3.7 percent of Hungary's male population aged over 20). In some rural areas, however, the category of "gentleman" was extended to include minor public officials, primary school teachers and notaries—even if they had completed only four or six grades of high school. In contrast, peasant farmers with hundreds of acres of land were not regarded as belonging to this class.

A contemporary sociologist summarized the main features of the middle-class way of life as follows: a city apartment with at least three rooms, a house with a garden in the country, at least one domestic employee, a three-course meal for lunch, second-class rail travel (at the time, there were three classes of travel) and summer holidays with relatives in the country or at one of the Monarchy's spas.

The *petite bourgeoisie* was larger than the middle class and just as diverse and heterogeneous. Around 13 percent of the population fell into this category. Craftsmen formed the largest sub-group—61–62 percent of them had no assistants, and they typically earned less than skilled factory workers. Even craftsmen with one assistant (18–19 percent) had similar standards of living. From the 1880s, the lives of craftsmen began to change: some of the traditional trades became less important or disappeared altogether—owing to modernization and urbanization. Even so, these latter processes also gave rise to new crafts and trades. At the turn of the century, the modernization of craftsmen's workshops was greatly facilitated by the advent of electric and combustion motors. The retailing sector offered the possibility of a slightly higher standard of living; shops were opened throughout the country. Jews accounted for more than half of retailers, and they were also numerous in the urban trades (butchers, bakers and tailors) and in the hotel and catering sector. Hauliers met transport demands, which were growing. Most historians include among the *petite bourgeoisie* junior officials in the various public institutions, members of the police force and the gendarmerie, junior railway and post officials, concierges and factory supervisors. Unlike ordinary workers, who received weekly wages, men in such posts tended to receive monthly salaries. Furthermore, most of them could expect to receive a modest retirement pension.

Even in the early twentieth century, Hungary was still an *agrarian society*. In 1910, 62 percent of the population made a living from agriculture, and the figure was even higher—79 percent—in Croatia. The division of land was crucial to the social structure. Before World War I, 72.7 percent of Hungary's land was privately owned, while 15.7 percent was under community or commonage ownership. In Transylvania, as much as a quarter of land was under community (municipal) ownership—mostly forest and pasture. Government-owned land accounted for 5.8 percent of all land, Church lands for 3.7 percent, and land owned by foundations and companies for 2 percent. The entailed land (*fidei commissa*) held by the aristocratic families constituted a significant portion of privately owned land: the 92 family *fidei commissa* covered 3.3 million acres of land, or 5 percent of all land. Still, cultivated land represented just 1,252,000 acres, with the rest being forest and pasture. Most of these *fidei commissa* were formed in the quarter-century after the Compromise of 1867.

Table 2: The Agrarian Population by Social Group in 1910
(active and dependent population)

	Hungary 1,000	Croatia 1,000	Hungary %	Croatia %
Owners and leaseholders				
0–5 *hold* (0–7.1 acres)	2,437	640	21.38	30.97
5–10 *hold* (7.1–14.2 acres)	1,930	582	16.93	28.17
10–20 *hold* (14.2–28.4 acres)	1,581	457	13.87	22.09
20–50 *hold* (28.4–71.1 acres)	823	175	7.22	8.45
50–100 *hold* (71–142 acres)	135	15.9	1.18	0.77
100–200 *hold* (142–284 acres)	32.7	2.6	0.29	0.12
200–1,000 *hold* (284–1,422 acres)	17.7	0.6	0.16	0.03
More than 1,000 *hold* (1,422 acres)	4.8	0.2	0.04	0.01
Leased more than 100 *hold* (142 acres)	16.2	248	0.14	0.01
Total owners and leaseholders	*6,977*	*1,873*	*61.21*	*90.63*
Other self-employed farmers	112	5.1	0.98	0.25
Officials	34.8	2.6	0.31	0.13
Farm laborers	1,265	76	11.10	3.68
Workers and day laborers	3,010	110	26.41	5.32
Total, agriculture	*11,399*	*2,066*	*100.00*	*100.00*
Self-employed	7,089	1,878	62.19	90.87
Official	34.8	2.6	0.31	0.13
Workers	4,275	186	37.50	9.00

Concerning the division of land ownership, detailed figures are available for 1895 (see Table 8.11). Almost 2.4 million farms with less than 100 *hold* (142 acres) of land accounted for 66 percent of the total area of cultivated land (59 percent in Transdanubia and the Lesser Plain region, 65 percent in the Great Plain region, 80 percent in northern and northeastern Upper Hungary and 83 percent in Transylvania). Croatia's division of land differed significantly from that of Hungary; in Croatia, farms with less than 100 *hold* (142 acres) of land accounted for 88 percent of cultivated land. Data from the 1910 census reveal similar differences between the two countries in terms of the structure of the agrarian population. In Hungary, 40.8 percent of the agrarian population were landholders, while 21.4 percent were dwarf-holders, 37.5 percent workers and 0.3 percent estate officials. Croatian agrarian society was characterized by small farms run by large joint peasant families (*zadruga*s); the share of wage-earning workers was just 9 percent.

In the early twentieth century, Hungarian agrarian society comprised two very distinct groups. On the one hand, there were the "gentlemanly" landowners—0.5 percent of the agrarian population—who owned around a quarter of the country's agricultural land. The second group was made up of the peasant farmers. In Western Europe, peasant farmers were men who cultivated their own land or leased land and who actually performed physical work. In Hungary and other parts of Eastern Europe, as a consequence of a specific process of social development, agricultural laborers were also regarded as peasants by contemporary commentators, and social and agrarian historians have also tended to classify them as peasants. Employing the statistical data, we struggle to distinguish between self-employed smallholders and agricultural laborers. First, many of the laborers owned or leased parcels of land, since one third of landowners and leaseholders possessed so little land that they were unable to secure livelihoods for their families and had no choice but to work as laborers. Second, the identical or similar way of life of dwarf-holders and agricultural laborers also bound them together. Meanwhile, historians and sociologists have tended to place the dividing line between the "gentlemanly" and peasant strata in agrarian society at the possession of 100 *hold* (142 acres) of land. Evidently, in some regions (in particular the Lesser

Plain region and the southern part of the Great Plain region), some peasants owned more than 100 *hold* (142 acres), while a good number of "gentlemanly" landowners had less than 100 *hold* (142 acres).

After 1848, more than eight million people were freed from the burdens of feudal tenancy, and almost a million frontiersmen (or *grenzer*s) acquired ownership of their plots. The number of peasants in Hungary and Croatia, together with the peasants who had been free before 1848 and the former peasant-nobles, lay between 10 and 10.5 million, or around 80 percent of the total population. By 1910 their number had risen to 13 million, but the relative percentage had fallen to 64 percent.

After the Compromise, there were still some residual feudal relationships that had to be dismantled. In 1868, a law was passed concerning the redemption of the grape tithe with the help of a government loan; in 1871, the issue of clearings was settled, and the monopolies of landowners were eliminated (duties on distilling of brandy, the running of taverns and butcher's shops). In the early 1870s, the socage court cases relating to the freeing of serfs came to an end. Finally, in 1896, a law was passed on the manor cotters: they also received opportunities to redeem their plots.

The landowning peasantry was usually divided into rich, middling and small peasants, as well as dwarf-holders. Rich peasants were those with between 50 and 100 *hold* (71 and 142 acres) of land, as well as larger landowners who were neither "gentlemanly" nor bourgeois landowners. Men with between 20 and 50 *hold* (28 and 71 acres) were regarded as middling peasants, while small peasants had between 5 and 20 *hold* (7 and 28 acres). In 1910, 2 percent of landowning peasants were rich peasants, 12 percent were middling peasants, and 51 percent were small peasants. The remaining 35 percent were dwarf-holders with less than seven acres of land or day laborers with small parcels of land. However, the size of a landholding did not necessarily correspond to the real level of income. There were, for instance, significant regional differences stemming from geographical conditions and soil quality. Productivity in agriculture is expressed in terms of "net cadastral income" (which is not identical to actual income). In 1914, the net cadastral income of 1 *hold* (1.42 acres) of cultivated land was 20 crowns in the Bácska region of the southern Great Plain, but only 1.5 crowns in Csík County in Transylvania. In the Great Plain and the Lesser Plain regions, net cadastral income was three times higher than it was in northern and northeastern parts of Upper Hungary or in Transylvania.

The dividing line between rich and middling peasants was 500 crowns of net cadastral income. This net cadastral income corresponded on a national average to 50 *hold* (71 acres) of cultivated land. But the dividing line was 42–50 acres in the Great Plain region, 57 acres in Transdanubia and more than 140 acres in Upper Hungary and Transylvania. The boundary between small and medium-sized peasants was 200 crowns of net cadastral income (50 crowns of land tax). On a national average, this required 20 *hold* (28 acres) of cultivated land (arable land, market gardens, meadows or vineyards)—15–17 acres in the southern part of the Great Plain region, 18–20 acres in the Lesser Plain region, 71–78 acres in Upper Hungary and 64 acres in Transylvania. The county averages varied between 14.2 acres (in Bácska County) and 182 acres (in Csík County). The medium-sized peasant level was reached by just 1–2 percent of landowning peasants in about 40 percent of the country (the northern and eastern countries), but by one quarter of peasants in the Great Plain region, and by one seventh of peasants in Transdanubia. The highest rates were in the counties of Bácska and Moson (46 percent) and the lowest rates in Csík County in Transylvania (0.3 percent) and Árva (Orava) County in Upper Hungary (0.2 percent); the national average was 11.4 percent.

There were, therefore, significant regional differences in the incomes and living standards of peasant landowners. In Transdanubia, the Lesser Plain region and the southern part and in the agrarian towns of the Great Plain region, a prosperous trade in peasants' produce arose in the 1880s; this furthered the modernization of the peasant way of life. In these areas, the annual income of a small peasant with 10–15 *hold* (14–21 acres) of land was roughly equivalent to the annual wages of an engineering or printing worker. On the other hand, in hilly or forested peripheral areas of the country, peasants were still poor even at the beginning of the twentieth century. Their situation led the government to take action to develop peasant agriculture (with programs for the Ruthenian counties, the *Székely* region and Upper Hungary). Land was a central element in the peasants' value system; their constant aim was to increase the amount of land held. There were, however, few opportunities for expansion and land acquisition. Occasionally, they were able to acquire the land of small peasants who had become indebted. In the early twentieth century, there were several plans and proposals (see, for example, Ignác Darányi's bills for settling peasants onto lands) aimed at resolving the land ownership issue, but few of them were realized.

The so-called dwarf-holders, who were referred to in the contemporary statistics as "smallholder day laborers," were those peasants with less than seven acres of land. The size of this social group grew rapidly after the abolition of serfdom: some of the cotters possessed small feudal plots, and all serfs had been entitled to smaller or larger amounts of pasture. However, the almost two and a half million people in this social group could not make a living from their land; some members of the family were required to undertake regular paid work. They were a transitional social group, falling somewhere between the peasant landowners and the agricultural, industrial and railway workers. Since they owned some land, they were reluctant to abandon the agricultural sector completely.

The agricultural workers can be divided into three groups. Agricultural laborers worked for a fixed wage and were tied to an estate, a medium-sized farm or a wealthy peasant landowner. Their contracts usually ran for a year, but a laborer working on an estate would often spend his whole life there. Indeed, it was common for families to remain on one estate for several generations; they were provided with housing and a small parcel of land there, and they were allowed to keep pigs and poultry. Most of the laborers' wages were received in kind, but they were also given a small sum in cash. Such laborers had limited mobility, and they were subject to the strict working discipline of the estate or the constant supervision of the peasant farmer. On the other hand, their work and livelihoods were guaranteed for a year or—as in the case of many laborers on the estates—for their whole lives. Their incomes and living standards were roughly comparable to those of small self-employed peasant farmers. The situation of the second group of agricultural workers, the day laborers—who were more than twice as numerous as the agricultural laborers—was not so favorable. Although they possessed greater personal freedom, nevertheless their employment was uncertain; they were forced to look for work on a daily—or at best weekly—basis. The third group of agricultural workers—less numerous than the previous two groups—were the migratory seasonal workers. They undertook work (hoeing, harvesting and threshing) on estates in well-organized gangs and for temporary periods. As a reward for their labor, they received a share of the crop, food or a cash sum. An agreement was signed between the landowner and the gang leader, who then distributed the reward among members of the gang. Many of the seasonal workers came from the overpopulated hill country lying to the north of the Lesser and Great Plains (today's Slovakia). Impoverished peasants from these regions came *en masse* to the Great Plain in order to undertake seasonal agricultural work there.

A social group that arose during this period was the industrial working class. The number of industrial workers increased rapidly in the 1850s and 1860s and then again after 1890. The census of 1910 recorded 923,000 industrial workers in Hungary and a further 52,000 in Croatia. Together with workers in the transport and trade sectors, the total number of workers was 1.2 million. Including family members, the country's working class numbered 2.6 million people.

In terms of its structure and situation, Hungary's industrial working class differed in many regards from the industrial working classes of the Western European countries, which had undergone industrialization earlier on. Such differences were related in part to the domestic peculiarities of early industrialization and in part to the supply of labor. The cradle of the industrial working class in Western Europe was the textiles industry and other branches of light industry producing consumer goods; these industrial sectors, however, played little part in the early period of industrialization in Hungary. Prior to 1890, the food industry and heavy industry, including the iron and engineering industries as well as mining, were at the forefront of Hungarian industrial development. In 1890, 70 percent of industrial workers were working in these branches of industry. The iron and engineering industries required relatively large numbers and various types of skilled workers, while the food industry required relatively few skilled workers and engineers. Both branches of industry were in need of a moderate number of unskilled workers and temporary seasonal workers. The absence of a textiles industry meant that Hungary did not have many semi-skilled workers—the group that formed the mass of workers in the advanced industrial countries. The lack of a textiles industry also explains the relatively small number of women and children employed in industry in Hungary.

The demand for labor associated with industrialization could not be met by the domestic labor supply—either quantitatively or qualitatively. For this reason, many of the qualified and skilled workers required by industry had to be brought into the country; many of them came from the other half of the Monarchy. With the development of industrial vocational education in Hungary, a supply of skilled workers was guaranteed by the turn of the century. Even so, as late as 1900, 10 percent of skilled workers were non-natives. An important domestic source of industrial workers was the northern part of Upper Hungary, a region with industrial traditions. Other industrial workers came from towns with a tradition of handicraft. All of this explains the high proportion of ethnic Germans and Slovaks among industrial workers born in Hungary. In 1875, Slovak was the native language of 22 percent of factory workers in Budapest. Unskilled workers formed an additional large group within the industrial working class; most of them were still part of the agrarian proletariat. They undertook temporary work in the factories, returning to their rural homes at times of seasonal agricultural work. There was a great discrepancy in terms of lifestyle, behavior and consciousness between the established body of skilled workers and the many unskilled transitory laborers. Even during the period immediately before World War I, the number of factory workers declined in the summer months, as workers from rural areas returned home to work on the fields.

As a consequence of these peculiarities, industrial development in Hungary was spared the acute social problems and mass impoverishment that were features of the industrial revolution in the Western countries. In Hungary, people were not marginalized when they became factory workers; on the contrary, their incomes and living standards improved. This was true for craftsmen, their assistants, and the agrarian proletariat. Skilled workers were always in short supply, and so wages were relatively high. In terms of housing, clothing and nutrition, factory workers enjoyed higher standards of living than did the many millions of rural poor. Housing estates—so-called colonies—were built for the workers of industrial companies in Budapest and other cities. In the early twentieth century, living standards among the industrial working class were roughly equivalent to those of the *petite bourgeoisie*, and workers were inclined to adopt the latter's tastes in furnishing, clothing and leisure. The average number of working hours was 10–12 in the factories and 12 in the mines.

Hungarian social historians with an interest in the era of Dualism have often noted the presence of many residual feudal elements in the political and social structures and in people's mentalities and value systems even in the early years of the twentieth century. Károly Keleti, the outstanding statistician whom I have already mentioned several times, noted despairingly "the wonderfully caste-like division that, alongside our haughtily voiced democratic principles, is such a fashion in this country." This was observable even among the lower strata, but "even more so among the landowning middle class and then upward as far as the aristocracy. Here what counts is not only the extent of ownership based on the number of acres, but a better-sounding name, and it may even be the extent of the noble background that determines the circles in which a person may move or even wishes to move. Here people are still inclined to ask whether a person comes from a 'good' family, and having a relative or an in-law still bears more weight than individual status does."[5] The fact that little had changed even by the turn of the century becomes apparent from the writings of middle-class radical sociologists and publicists. Other commentators also recognized the problem: one of the era's outstanding Catholic prelates, Ottokár Prohászka, a socially aware man from a lower middle-class background, wrote the following in an article published in 1899: "The spirit of feudalism still thrives in Hungary, with regard to the antagonism between noble and peasant. In this regard, the pre-1848 period lives on, not on paper or in legislative paragraphs, but in the sentiment of the social classes. The old dividing line between noble and peasant is still drawn today, but not with regard to the one wearing a coat and the other a traditional waistcoat [*lajbi*] or embroidered felt cloak [*szűr*] but with regard to the fact that the noble does not regard the peasant as a full person, still less as a brother, but rather, in the old constitutional manner, as a semi-idiot."[6] The same opinion was expressed in the first half of the twentieth century by the outstanding historian Gyula Szekfű: "The paper standards of the legislature of 1848 were not strong enough to destroy the old social framework and establish a new one: equality before the law among the aristocratic, noble and peasant classes in the social arena was realized only in a nominal sense; the feudal system no longer exists, but the magnate class, the gentry and the peasants, that is, the small farmers and the cotters, are still separate individuals, who are kept together by little more than a barely conscious feeling of a broader Hungarian community."[7]

Despite the continued existence of many residual feudal elements, the process of establishing a modern civil society based on equality before the law accelerated after the 1867 Compromise. This process was made more difficult by the country's substantial ethnic and religious divisions. And residual feudal divisions drove a wedge between the various groups and classes even among the

Magyar population. One should note that the feudal structure in Hungary had been very strong until 1848, and there had been little time for a change in the mentality, values and customs of the various groups and individuals. This explains why, even after the Compromise, a highly cultivated member of the political elite, the university professor and member of Parliament Gyula Schvarcz, noted in 1870 that "A Hungarian society does not yet exist in the manner that French, British, German and Italian society exists."[8] Two decades later, in 1889, he stated that while Hungarian society "is today a unified modern society of citizens, it is not yet so in the sense that the French, Italian, Danish, Dutch, Belgian and Norwegian ones are unified societies, and nor even to the degree that British society is such."[9] A similar opinion was expressed by one of the chief ideologists of the Liberal Party, Gusztáv Beksics: "Hungary has no uniform cultural development; it has no uniform national society."[10] The larger non-Magyar ethnic communities, together with intellectuals and citizens belonging to the national minorities, were increasingly unwilling to integrate into this Magyar national society; they endeavored to organize separate societies of their own peoples, in the hope that sooner or later these distinct national societies would gain territorial autonomy or even self-determination.

Capitalist development—which accelerated after the 1867 Compromise—and economic and social modernization did not begin simultaneously throughout the country; nor did these processes proceed at a uniform rate. Consequently, there were still significant differences, in terms of economic, social and cultural development, among the various regions, peoples and groups living in the country. Data concerning people's occupations and the social structure reflect such differences. The data in the table below show that, as far as Magyars and Germans are concerned, we can speak of a relatively developed and differentiated structure of civil society: only one in two people in these groups made a living from agriculture, while one in three was working in a modern sector (for instance, in industry, trade or transport). At the other end of the spectrum, we find the Ruthenians, Romanians, Serbs and Croats, among whom agriculture was a source of a livelihood for more than three quarters of the population (78–87 percent), while just 5–15 percent were working in modern sectors. These latter ethnic groups were largely peasant peoples, living in areas where two thirds of society comprised landowners with less than 100 *hold* (142 acres). Between these two extremes lay Slovak society, which had an agrarian majority as well as a sizeable *petite bourgeoisie* and an industrial working class. One should also note that, similarly to the Magyars and Germans, the ethnic Serb and Croat populations had significant intellectual and public administrative strata—evidently owing to Croatia's autonomous status.

Table 3: Breakdown of the Active Populations of the Ethnic Groups (Nationalities) by Main Occupation in Hungary and Croatia in 1910

	Hungarian (Magyar)	German	Slovak	Romanian	Ruthenian	Croat	Serb	Hungary and Croatia
Agriculture and forestry	51.79	47.21	69.13	84.32	87.10	78.33	81.54	62.5
Industry	21.23	27.60	16.00	6.41	4.18	9.98	7.84	17.1
Trade	4.71	5.40	1.26	0.64	0.18	1.75	2.17	3.4
Transport	3.60	1.56	1.18	0.64	0.49	1.16	0.67	2.3
Civil servants and intellectuals	4.73	2.46	0.88	1.18	0.48	2.00	1.89	3.1
Day laborers	2.49	2.90	3.50	1.93	3.14	1.55	2.08	2.5
Retirees and other beneficiaries	2.47	5.57	1.83	1.19	0.67	1.12	1.25	2.3
Domestic servants	5.99	4.24	4.60	2.22	2.86	2.23	0.82	4.3
Armed forces	1.72	2.18	1.15	1.20	0.73	1.50	1.42	1.6
Other and unknown	1.28	0.88	0.48	0.27	0.16	0.38	0.32	0.9
Total	100.00	100.00	100.00	100.00	100.00	100.00	100.00	100.0

Table 4: The Social Structure of the Various Ethnic Groups (Nationalities) in Hungary and Croatia in 1910

	Hungarian (Magyar)	German	Slovak	Romanian	Ruthenian	Croatian	Serb
Large landowners 1,000 + *hold* (1,420 + acres)	0.04	0.02	0.001	0.002	0.001	0.003	0.003
Medium-sized landowners 200–1,000 *hold* (284–1,420 acres)	0.14	0.09	0.02	0.02	0.01	0.01	0.07
Medium-sized landowners 100–200 *hold* (142–284 acres)	0.20	0.28	0.08	0.08	0.05	0.07	0.26
Large leaseholders 100 + *hold* (142 + acres)	0.13	0.09	0.01	0.02	0.00	0.00	0.01
Small landowners/lease-holders 50–100 *hold* (71–142 acres)	0.74	1.30	0.49	0.49	0.29	0.43	1.25
20–50 *hold* (28–71 acres)	3.86	6.61	4.49	4.94	4.21	5.06	10.00
5–20 *hold* (7–28 acres)	13.72	17.07	25.51	31.70	34.99	36.73	41.47
Less than 5 *hold* (seven acres)	9.57	10.39	17.61	22.87	27.01	30.24	14.00
Small landowners or leaseholders – less than 100 hold (142 acres)	*27.89*	*35.37*	*48.10*	*60.00*	*66.50*	*72.46*	*66.72*
Other self-employed agricultural producers	0.70	0.34	0.13	0.81	0.60	0.15	0.43
Self-employed craftsmen, merchants and hauliers	11.90	17.69	7.13	3.23	1.84	6.05	5.28
Total – self-employed persons	*41.01*	*53.88*	*55.47*	*64.16*	*69.00*	*78.75*	*72.77*
Private company officials	2.33	1.60	0.16	0.10	0.02	0.60	0.32
Public officials, intellectuals and military officers	3.63	2.00	0.37	1.13	0.30	1.59	1.47
Total – officials, intellectuals and military officers	*5.96*	*3.60*	*0.53*	*1.23*	*0.32*	*2.19*	*1.79*
Public employees and NCOs	1.67	1.34	0.68	0.40	0.25	0.80	0.86
Agricultural or forestry workers	25.29	12.98	22.19	24.19	21.75	5.98	15.95
Industrial workers	11.44	15.13	10.82	3.72	2.43	5.29	2.83
Workers in trade and haulage	4.79	2.56	1.95	0.68	0.61	1.84	1.11
Day laborers	2.34	2.91	3.28	1.85	2.87	1.50	1.98
Domestic servants	2.81	1.94	2.14	1.02	1.18	1.09	0.39
Total – workers	*46.67*	*35.52*	*40.38*	*31.46*	*28.84*	*15.70*	*22.26*
Retirees and other beneficiaries	1.93	3.60	1.19	0.79	0.34	0.94	0.90
Other and unknown	3.46	2.40	1.88	1.73	1.85	1.77	1.85
Total	100.00	100.00	100.00	100.00	100.00	100.00	100.00

Notes

1 Péter Hanák, "Magyarország társadalma a századforduló idején" [Hungary's Society at the Turn of the Century], in Péter Hanák and Ferenc Mucsi, eds., *Magyarország története 1890–1918* [History of Hungary 1890–1918] (Budapest, 1988), p. 435.

2 The *díszmagyar*, or Hungarian gala-dress, had arisen since the sixteenth century. It was a colorful ceremonial coat decorated with furs and precious stones, which was usually worn with an accompanying sword. During the era of Dualism and between the two world wars, members of the upper and middle classes—in particular prominent public figures—were expected or even required to wear it on festive occasions.

3 Károly Keleti, *Hazánk és népe* [Our Homeland and Its People] (Pest, 1871), pp. 151, 153.

4 *Ibid.*, p. 152.

5 *Ibid.*, p. 152.

6 Ottokár Prohászka, "Az ütött-kopott paraszt" [The Battered Peasant], in volume 21 of idem, *Összes Müvei* [His Collected Works] (Budapest, 1929), p. 129.

7 Gyula Szekfű, *Három nemzedék és ami utána következik* [Three Generations and What Comes after Them] (Budapest, 1934), p. 308.

8 Gyula Schvarcz, *Magyarország helyzete a reálunióban* [Hungary's Situation in the Real Union (i.e., the Austro-Hungarian Empire)] (Pest, 1870), p. 57.

9 Gyula Schvarcz, *Adalék a magyar állampolgári társadalom egységes természetének elméletéhez. Értekezések a társadalmi tudományok köréből* [Towards a Theory about the Uniform Nature of Hungarian Civil Society. Treatises from the Social Sciences] (Budapest, 1889), pp. 8, 28.

10 [Gusztáv Beksics], *Atticus: Új korszak és politikai programja* [Atticus: A New Era and Its Political Program] (Budapest, 1889), p. 36.

10. RELIGIOUS AFFILIATION AND THE CHURCHES

In the nineteenth century, Hungary exhibited the greatest religious diversity in Europe. Five Christian denominations had at least one million adherents each. In addition, the country had a rapidly growing Jewish denomination, with almost a million members in the early twentieth century. Religious diversity was a feature of the country as a whole, but Croatia was the exception: 72 percent of the Croatian population were Roman Catholics and 25 percent were Greek Orthodox. The other half of the Monarchy, Austria, was also far less religiously diverse: Roman Catholics accounted for 79 percent and Greek Catholics (Uniate) for 12 percent of the population there. The third largest denomination in Austria was the Jewish community, with more than a million members (4.6 percent), and the country also had smaller Protestant and Greek Orthodox communities (both around 2 percent). A majority of the world's Greek Catholics—more than five million at the turn of the century—lived in the Dual Monarchy. This was a consequence of the unification with Rome, in the seventeenth and eighteenth centuries, of the Orthodox Ruthenian and Romanian communities residing in Poland and Hungary, who became members of the Greek Catholic (or Uniate) denomination.

As the table on the next page shows, significant nominal and relative increases occurred only among the Roman Catholic and Jewish populations. Changes in the relative size of the denominations were influenced first and foremost by demographic factors (natural increase as well as emigration and immigration), while conversions were less significant. The increase in the Roman Catholic ratio was mainly due to a higher rate of natural increase, but the community also benefited from conversions. The significant growth in the Jewish ratio was the result of both natural increase and immigration. The decline in the Protestant ratio was rooted in a lower rate of natural increase, but emigration and conversion were also contributory factors. Natural increase was particularly weak among the Orthodox population. The number of adherents to other religious groups grew as a result of the spread of smaller religious communities. In 1910, 8,000 people said that they were Baptists, while 6,000 professed to be Nazarenes. There were no statistics for other minor religious groups, but Methodists, Seventh Day Adventists and Jehovah's Witnesses were already present in Hungary in the early twentieth century. Of these smaller religious groups, the Baptists were the only ones to be legally recognized by the government as a denomination in 1905.

Table 1:
Population of Hungary and Croatia by Religious Denomination

	1869	1910	1869	1910
	1,000	1,000	%	%
Roman Catholic	7,500	10,888	48.64	52.13
Greek Catholic (Uniate)	1,591	2,026	10.31	9.70
Greek Orthodox	2,579	2,987	16.73	14.30
Reformed (Calvinist)	2,024	2,621	13.13	12.55
Evangelical Lutheran	1,109	1,340	7.19	6.42
Unitarian	54	74	0.35	0.36
Judaism	553	932	3.59	4.46
Other	10	17	0.06	0.08
Total	15,420	20,886	100	100

Throughout this era, religion played an important role in the life and culture of the ethnic communities of the multinational country. For this reason, it is important to note the religious affiliations of the various ethnic groups. Most of the schools were run by the denominations. Moreover, clergymen and religious leaders could contribute greatly to the development of a national identity. Indeed, in the case of several national minorities, they became the leaders of the national political movements.

Table 2: Religious Affiliation by Native Language in 1910
(thousands of people)

	Catholic		Greek	Reformed	Evangelical	Unitarian	Judaism	Other	Total
	Roman	Greek	Orthodox	(Calvinist)	Lutheran				
Magyar	5,925	305	41	2,574	418	73	705	10	10,051
German	1,372	2	2	27	430		203	1	2,037
Slovak	1,406	79	1	11	464		6	1	1,968
Romanian	9	1,134	1,799	1	2	1		3	2,949
Ruthenian	5	464	1						473
Croatian	1,810	10	1	1	1				1,833
Serbian	4	2	1,099				1	1	1,106
Other	357	31	43	7	26		4	1	469
Total	10,888	2,026	2,987	2,621	1,340	74	932	17	20,886

Table 3: The Religious Affiliations of the Various Ethnic Groups (%)

	Catholic		Greek	Reformed	Evangelical	Unitarian	Judaism	Other	Total
	Roman	Greek	Orthodox	(Calvinist)	Lutheran				
Magyar	58.95	3.03	0.41	25.61	4.16	0.73	7.02	0.10	100.00
German	67.34	0.09	0.12	1.32	21.09	0.01	9.97	0.05	100.00
Slovak	71.45	4.03	0.04	0.54	23.57	0.00	0.30	0.06	100.00
Romanian	0.29	38.44	61.01	0.05	0.05	0.02	0.03	0.10	100.00
Ruthenian	1.08	98.10	0.22	0.01	0.01	0.00	0.57	0.01	100.00
Croat	98.75	0.52	0.05	0.06	0.04	0.00	0.57	0.02	100.00
Serb	0.35	0.17	99.36	0.00	0.01	0.00	0.01	0.09	100.00
Other	76.15	6.63	9.07	1.60	5.44	0.04	0.80	0.27	100.00
Total	52.13	9.70	14.30	12.55	6.42	0.36	4.46	0.08	100.00

Table 4: Native Language of Members of the Various Religious Denominations (%)

	Catholic		Greek	Reformed	Evangelical	Unitarian	Judaism	Other	Total
	Roman	Greek	Orthodox	(Calvinist)	Lutheran				
Magyar	54.41	15.04	1.37	98.18	31.22	98.61	75.66	55.02	48.12
German	12.60	0.09	0.08	1.03	32.06	0.23	21.80	5.75	9.75
Slovak	12.92	3.92	0.02	0.41	34.62	0.09	0.63	7.27	9.42
Romanian	0.08	55.97	60.23	0.05	0.12	0.75	0.11	17.31	14.12
Ruthenian	0.05	22.89	0.03	0.00	0.00	0.01	0.29	0.14	2.26
Croatian	16.63	0.47	0.03	0.04	0.06	0.01	1.11	1.58	8.78
Serbian	0.04	0.09	36.80	0.00	0.01	0.03	0.01	5.71	5.30
Other	3.28	1.54	1.43	0.29	1.90	0.28	0.40	7.23	2.25
Total	100.00	100.00	100.00	100.00	100.00	100.00	100.00	100.00	100.00

Roman Catholics formed an absolute majority of the population in the western half of Hungary—roughly in areas to the west of the River Tisza. Greek Catholics lived in the eastern and northeastern counties of Hungary and in Transylvania. Reformed Calvinists were in a majority among Hungarians living to the east of the River Tisza, in the northeastern counties and in Transylvania. They were relatively numerous in the central part of Hungary, on both sides of the River Danube. Evangelical Lutherans were to be found among the German and Slovak populations of the western counties and Upper Hungary. All the Transylvanian Saxons were Evangelical Lutherans; they had their own Church organization. Unitarians[1] were common among the Transylvanian Hungarian population (Szeklers). Orthodox Serbs lived in the southern counties, while Orthodox Romanians formed an absolute majority in the southern parts of Transylvania. Large numbers of Jews lived in the northeastern counties of the country bordering Galicia; in these areas they formed more than 10 percent of the population. In some towns and cities, such as Budapest, Miskolc, Nagyvárad (Oradea), Szatmárnémeti (Satu Mare), Ungvár (Užgorod) and Munkács (Mukačevo), their share of the population exceeded 20 percent.

After the 1867 Compromise, the equality of the received—that is, officially recognized—religious denominations (first proclaimed in 1848) was reenacted by Act 53 of 1868. Under the legislation, conversion from one denomination to another was permitted. In the case of a mixed marriage, sons were to adhere to the religion of their father and daughters to the religion of their mother. This legislative provision did little to resolve the disputes arising in mixed marriages. A common occurrence was the so-called "erroneous baptism," whereby a priest would christen a child who belonged, under the law, to another denomination. Such violations of the law took place among all the Christian denominations. The Catholic Church continued to consecrate mixed marriages only where the non-Catholic party to the marriage committed himself or herself to raising all the family's children in the Catholic faith. Where such a commitment was given, the baptized infant was registered as a Catholic. Under the government provisions, in such cases, the priest performing the baptism was required to inform the legally competent clergyman, so that the latter could then register the birth of the infant. In most instances, however, priests failed to inform their counterparts. The controversy became more acute in 1890, when Count Albin Csáky, minister of education and religion, announced that priests performing "erroneous baptisms" were to be fined a sum of money. Subsequently, the Wekerle government urged a radical solution to the issue.

In 1894–1895, the Parliament adopted the so-called "ecclesiastical policy laws," which introduced compulsory civil marriages and the government registration of all births, marriages and deaths. In return, however, married couples were allowed to decide for themselves the religion of their children. The Jewish denomination was "received" (granted official recognition) and declared to be equal in law to the Christian denominations. A law was then passed on free worship; it permitted conversions in all cases and freely allowed people to join and leave denominations or to have no religious affiliation. The legal provisions permitted the granting of recognition to other denominations subject to certain conditions (the operation of at least one Church community, and the submission and adoption of organizational rules and regulations).

Under the provisions of the statute book of 1848, the government was required to pay for denominations' Church- and school-related costs. Ever since the end of the eighteenth century, the Catholic ecclesiastical and educational institutions had received regular support from the Studies and Religious Fund, which had been established using the wealth of the dissolved religious orders. The other denominations, however, had to rely on their own resources. In 1898, legislation was adopted whereby the government supplemented the income of clergymen of the received denominations up to a level of 1,600 crowns and the income of assistant clergymen up to a level of 800 crowns. This initial legal provision did not apply to the Catholic denomination. A government supplement for Catholic clergymen was regulated by law only in 1909, when the annual income of clergymen (parish priests) was set at 1,600 crowns and the annual income of assistant clergymen at 1,000 crowns. This minimum level was not reached by one third of Roman Catholic priests and 97 percent of Greek Catholic priests; they therefore received the income supplement. The supplements were paid partly out of the government budget and partly out of the religious fund, and a contribution was also made by ecclesiastical figures with large incomes (bishops and so on).

Clergy incomes stemmed primarily from the compulsory contributions of congregants, which, if required, could be collected as public dues (this is the origin of the term "church tax"). Such contributions were made both in money and in kind. The church tax was significantly higher among Protestants and Jews than it was among Catholics, as the Catholic Church had extensive landed properties and wealthy foundations. According to the national agricultural statistical survey of 1895, the Catholic Church (including the Uniate Church) owned 2.84 million acres of land and forest, while the Greek Orthodox Church owned 176,000 acres, the Reformed (Calvinist) Church 234,000 acres, the Evangelical Lutheran Church 102,000 acres and the Unitarian Church 21,000 acres. The Jewish denomination owned just 1,420 acres of land. Thus, Hungary's "received" denominations owned in total 3.4 million acres of land, or just under 5 percent of the country's territory.

Church incomes from landholdings and other revenues were not just used to provide for the clergy and maintain religious institutions; they were also spent on funding social and educational institutions. Of these, the latter were the more significant, since primary and secondary education was largely under the control of the various denominations. In the final academic year before World War I (1913–1914), almost 12,000 out of 17,000 primary schools (69 percent) were denominational schools, attended by almost 63 percent of the country's two million primary school pupils. In secondary education, 127 of 195 grammar schools (65 percent) were denominational schools, attended by 64 percent of the country's 65,000 grammar school pupils.

Catholics

The organization of the Catholic Church in Hungary had already been established by the beginning of the period, and it did not change until 1918. Roman Catholics (including those in Croatia) lived in four ecclesiastical provinces comprising four archdioceses and 16 dioceses. Croatia had been a separate ecclesiastical province since 1853, when the Diocese of Zagreb was made into an archdiocese, with two subordinate dioceses. In addition, the Benedictine Abbey of Pannonhalma also had its own little diocese.

Among the Greek Catholics, the Romanians had been granted an ecclesiastical province in 1853, when the Pope—at Francis Joseph's request—made the Diocese of Gyulafehérvár–Fogaras (Alba Iulia–Făgăraş), with a seat in Balázsfalva (Blaj), into an archdiocese, with three subordinate dioceses: Szamosújvár (Gherla), Nagyvárad (Oradea) and Lugos (Lugoj). Hungarian Greek Catholics had to wait until 1912 for a diocese. At that time, the Greek Catholic Diocese of Hajdúdorog was formed, with a seat in Nyíregyháza. The liturgical language of the diocese was Greek, but baptism, marriage and funeral ceremonies were held in Hungarian.

In 1914, more than 6,000 ordained priests were working in 3,890 Roman Catholic parish churches. There were ample replacements, since there were as many as 1,500 novices. In addition, there were 2,000 monks, serving in 233 religious houses, and almost 8,000 nuns, in more than 500 religious houses. The Greek Catholics had 2,152 parish churches, with 2,300 priests caring for the faithful, while more than 400 novices were studying theology. The Greek Catholic religious orders were rather insignificant; there were only a few monks and no nuns.

Catholic bishops and archbishops were nominated by the minister of education and religion and appointed by the supreme patron of the Catholic Church, the King of Hungary (which is to say the Emperor). From the mid-1890s, the prior approval of the Holy See was requested, by way of the nuncio in Vienna. A nomination was made, and then the Pope's consent was requested. Parish priests were nominated by local patrons (landowners or municipalities) and then appointed by bishops.

János Scitovszky, Archbishop of Esztergom and Prince Primate of Hungary, headed the Catholic Church in Hungary from 1849. He died in the autumn of 1866, in the midst of discussions concerning the Compromise. As his successor, Francis Joseph appointed János Simor, Bishop of Győr. Simor was made a cardinal in 1873 and headed the Hungarian Church until his death in 1891. The same year saw the death of another great Hungarian churchman, Cardinal Lajos Haynald, Archbishop of Kalocsa, who, like Simor, had headed his archdiocese since 1867. Simor's successor as the Archbishop of Esztergom was Kolos Vaszary, Arch-abbot of Pannonhalma. This outstanding Benedictine teacher and scholar proved rather unsuited to the post, since political skills were required rather than priestly virtues. Having fallen sick, he almost completely withdrew from public life in the early years of the twentieth century, finally resigning in October 1912. A successor for Vaszary had already been spotted: János Csernoch, Archbishop of Kalocsa—who was transferred to Esztergom. As late as the eighteenth century, the seat of Esztergom—which was accompanied by the office of the Prince Primate—had been the preserve of aristocrats. Now, however, after a bootmaker's son (Simor) and a furrier's son (Vaszary), Csernoch, the son of a Slovak peasant, was appointed to head the Hungarian Church.

After the Compromise of 1867, the Hungarian government declared the 1855 Concordat between the Holy See and the Austrian Empire to be null and void with regard to Hungary. Even the Hungarian Bishops' Conference disapproved of its implementation, since it had been signed by the Austrian government during the suspension of the Hungarian constitution and contravened Hungarian constitutional law and legislation relating to the Church. In 1870, Francis Joseph informed the Holy See that he no longer considered the accord to be valid. Supreme patronage was reinstated, as was also the royal appointment of bishops. Even so, the ruler now exercised these rights in conjunction with the Hungarian government and the minister of education and religion—both of which were responsible to the Parliament. The government ministry managed the educational and religious funds, but Francis Joseph entrusted supervision of the funds to a 15-member committee with both clergy and lay members.

After the 1867 Compromise, the Church was criticized in the Parliament and the liberal press; the idea of secularizing Church lands and property was placed back on the agenda. At this point, however, the Andrássy government and the Bishops' Conference reached an implicit compromise – subsequently adhered to by the Liberal government after 1875. Under the deal, the Bishops' Conference offered political support to the government, which pledged in return to protect Church lands and property (Gyula Andrássy gave a personal assurance to this effect to the nuncio Falcinelli). The government also promised to uphold the constitutional status of the Church and the operation of its schools—subject to government overseeing.

The First Vatican Council increased tension between Church and state. Liberal politicians in both halves of the Dual Monarchy expressed opposition to the dogmatic constitution, *Pastor Aeternus*, adopted on July 18, 1870, which sought to impose the doctrine of papal infallibility. During the proceedings, the Hungarian bishops had sided with a group of mainly German and Austrian bishops who were opposed to the dogma of infallibility and who considered its pronouncement to be both unsuitable and untimely. During the discussions and at the time of a straw poll, these bishops registered their opposition to the dogma, subsequently leaving Rome on the eve of the final vote. At the behest of the Hungarian government, Francis Joseph responded to the Council's decision by reinstating the *placetum regium*,[2] abolished in 1850, and by outlawing the pronouncement of Council decisions.

As far as the quality of Catholic religious life was concerned, the second half of the nineteenth century saw little change to the situation that had arisen during the era of Josephinism. In 1869, the nuncio Falcinelli saw more signs of death than life in the

Hungarian Catholic Church. As the Catholic historian Gyula Szekfű wrote, "In the domestic Bishops' Conference, we encounter excellent, patriotic and generous men, who keep intact the customs of baroque representation, but who can hardly approach broad sections of the people through pastoral care."[3] Unsurprisingly, religious apathy prevailed, particularly among the upper and middle classes in society. According to the leading figure of Hungarian liberal Catholicism, József Eötvös, "Among our clerics, apathy and indifference have reached levels rarely seen in other countries, and a consequence of this is the highest degree of indifference among [ordinary] Catholics."[4]

The rural population and the urban lower middle class continued to foster the formal traditions and practices of religious life. Pilgrimages were especially popular. In contrast, among the middle and upper classes—particularly the nobles and intellectuals—religiosity declined. This is what the contemporary sources tell us, revealing a growing indifference towards religion. Some in these social classes continued to practice their religion, but they were the exceptions. In his memoirs, Ernő Szeghy, procurator-general of the Cistercian Order, wrote the following about middle-class Hungarian society in the 1870s: "Their religion was applied only in baptism and at funeral ceremonies. In the meantime, they had nothing to do with Church or priest… Religious fervor was unknown." As a young member of his religious order, he too had regarded himself "as a gentleman rather than a monk. This is how most members of the Order thought at the time, perhaps even some of the best of them. Yes, we were gentlemen. We wanted to be gentlemen."[5] In the way of thinking of the Hungarian social elite, there was an overemphasis on politics, suppressing all other philosophical and religious interests. Not even the Catholic prelates were an exception in this regard. It is no accident that it was said in Rome that "*Episcopi Hungarici sunt magis politici quam catholici*."

The Catholic renewal movements, which began to gain strength in France, Belgium, Germany and Italy in the first half of the nineteenth century, had largely been ineffectual in Hungary. Of the various Catholic movements in Europe, liberal Catholicism exerted the greatest influence in Hungary between the 1840s and 1870s. The manifestations of Hungarian liberal Catholicism were closely linked with the issue of so-called Catholic autonomy, whose major representative in Hungary was József Eötvös, a man who corresponded with one of the leaders of the liberal Catholic movement in France, Charles de Montalembert. The two men became good friends, and together they supported and promoted the principle of "a free Church in a free state": "It is my firm conviction"—Eötvös wrote to Montalembert—"that, in our century, the only thing that the state can do for the Church—the only thing required by the latter from the state—is to guarantee it the most complete freedom."[6]

The idea of autonomy arose in the spring of 1848. Under the April laws, the ruler could only practice his right of supreme patronage—as well as the other rights due to him in religious matters—in conjunction with the Hungarian government or the government minister responsible. The privileged position of Catholicism and its rank as state religion were abolished. In the new situation, the bishops were of the view that the Church should be completely autonomous, independent of the state. Since the Church had lost the patronage of the ruler, it should now "place itself under the protection of its own faithful." In the spring of 1848, the bishops held a conference, attended by members of the laity, at which the principles of Catholic autonomy were elaborated. It was declared that the laity should be given a role in the management of the Church. However, owing to events in 1848, autonomy was never realized.

The issue was placed back on the agenda after the 1867 Compromise. The bishops did not want Hungary's Liberal government to interfere in ecclesiastical appointments or to exert control over Catholic schools and funds. In the opinion of József Eötvös, minister of education and religion, one of the main reasons for the indifference of Catholics was the fact that "whereas the Protestant Churches enjoy the greatest degree of autonomy in their school and Church affairs, the Catholic Church has been made a ward of the state."[7] The other reason was the fact that Catholics, "having been denied any influence" over the Church and schools, "were accustomed to viewing matters concerning the Church and the schools as none of their business."[8] Consequently, in July 1867, Eötvös suggested to Archbishop Simor that the Bishops' Conference draw up a plan for Catholic autonomy. He also requested that "the laity should be given greater influence over schools and the non-religious affairs of the Church."[9] He suggested that two thirds of representatives in the autonomous bodies of the Church be laypersons, with the clergy making up the remaining third.

Liberal Catholicism—with a media presence from 1867—joined in the growing debate on the implementation of autonomy. The central element in the liberal program was "the theoretical and practical separation of matters that were divine and human, worldly and spiritual, religious and political, ecclesiastical and governmental, relating to the Church or to the state."[10] They called for certain liberal reforms in the Church and urged Catholicism's "reconciliation with contemporary society." "Our wish is that the spirit of the Gospel should reach beyond the walls of the Church and go beyond the clergy to touch upon all sections of society and all branches of public and cultural life. Our desire is that progress and development should recognize an ally in religion."[11] Correspondents, most of whom were junior clergymen from rural areas, sometimes voiced radical demands. They even demanded the following: civilian clothes, a Hungarian liturgy and the abolition of celibacy.

The bishops wished to make the Church independent of the state, but they were unwilling to grant the laity a greater role. For their part, however, liberal lay Catholics sought a two-thirds majority for themselves in the autonomous bodies of the Church. In the view of the practicing Catholic Ferenc Deák, a great figure of Hungarian liberalism, "The Roman Catholic Church is the sum of the clergy and the laity. This collectivity has a right to establish autonomy and to exercise the rights of autonomy… by way of representatives."[12]

At the Congress on Catholic autonomy in 1870–1871, the bishops finally accepted the liberals' proposals. Under the rules drafted at the Congress, the scope of autonomy would extend to all matters jointly affecting the clergy and the laity, with the exception of religious instruction, ecclesiastical government and discipline. Thus, autonomy was to apply to schools (with the exception of religious instruction and the training of priests), to Church and school property, and to the foundations. The autonomous bodies would be the parochial, deanery and diocesan assemblies and councils, as well as the national Catholic assembly and management board. In all of these bodies, laypersons would constitute two thirds of all representatives, with the clergy making up the remaining third. At the time, this degree of autonomy existed nowhere else in the world.

In the end, however, nothing came of the proposed autonomy. After the Vatican Council, it was obvious that the new rules would be rejected by Rome. Following the death of Eötvös, the Hungarian government lacked a keen supporter of autonomy. The government had no wish to lose control of the religious and educational funds or to give up its say in the appointment of bishops. Nor was the Bishops' Conference pressing for a decision; the bishops had been unsettled by the radicalism of Congress participants and regarded the role proposed for the laity as excessive.

The second Congress on Catholic autonomy, held between 1897 and 1902, was similarly unsuccessful. Even though the Congress reduced significantly both the scope of autonomy and the role of the laity, its proposals were rejected by the secretary of state of the Vatican, Cardinal Rampolla, who insisted that the bishops alone should represent the Church in the autonomous bodies. The government also proved unwilling to approve the new rules.

Interestingly, Catholic autonomy already existed in Transylvania. The roots of this autonomy went back to the seventeenth century, when Transylvania had been an independent principality. Between 1556 and 1713, Catholic bishops had not been allowed to operate in Protestant Transylvania, and so the affairs of the Catholic Church had been administered by a body known as the Roman Catholic Status, with members from both the clergy and the laity. After 1867, the Hungarian government authorized the operation of the

Transylvanian Roman Catholic Status—which was also tolerated by Rome. Lay Catholics formed a two-thirds majority in the annual assembly of the Status and on its board of directors. The lesser bodies of autonomy were the parochial assemblies and councils.

During the debates on autonomy, some commentators pointed out that a renewal of religious life was a prerequisite for institutional reform. Measures had already been taken to this end, but they had run into obstacles in the light of the prevailing Josephinist policies. In the 1880s, having returned from the Collegium Germanico-Hungaricum in Rome, Ottokár Prohászka—a leading figure in the subsequent Catholic "renaissance"—was surprised by the shallowness of the spiritual life of Hungary's Catholic clergy. In his view, "Hungarian ecclesiastical life lies in the throes of indifference and religious lethargy... What our powerless Church needs is to be attacked by someone similar to the German Görres."[13] In 1899, Prohászka even wrote a paper about the difficulties of Christian awakening and the reasons for such difficulties: "In our country, the process of creating an awareness of the Christian idea is slow and hesitant, indecisive and weak."[14]

The Catholic renewal began to flourish in Hungary in the 1890s, half a century later than it did in Western Europe.

Pope Leo XIII (1878–1903) "recognized the signs of the times." In a departure from his predecessor's rejectionist stance, he opened up a dialog with the modern world, attempting an adjustment to its economic, social and political realities. He urged Catholics in Hungary to abandon their passive role and form Catholic associations, establish a Catholic press, and become more active in social and public life. In spite of liberal laws on ecclesiastical policy, Catholics—acting at the Pope's behest—organized national protest movements. In 1895, a Catholic political party—the People's Party—was formed under the leadership of Count Nándor Zichy. The party fought to protect the rights of the Catholic Church and demanded an active social policy on behalf of peasants and craftsmen.

In 1887, at a meeting of the Fribourg Union, the Hungarian aristocrat Miklós Móric Esterházy complained that Hungary's

Catholic clergy were insensitive to social issues. Following the social encyclical of Pope Leo XIII, issued in 1891 and entitled *Rerum novarum*, social Catholicism began to make inroads in Hungary. As a theory it was promoted by Ottokár Prohászka, who wrote papers and articles on it. Another important personality was Sándor Giesswein, canon of Győr, who helped to found the Christian Socialist movement in Hungary. During these years, a whole series of Christian workers' associations and trade unions were formed—particularly in the provincial urban centers. The National Federation of Christian Social Associations was founded in 1905, and the year 1907 saw the formation of the Christian Socialist Party.

In Hungary, political Catholicism never became the successful mass movement that it was in Germany and in Austria. The main achievement of social Catholicism was to devise the various means and instruments of social care. In this area, one should note the contribution of the Social Mission Society, established by Edit Farkas in 1908 with Prohászka's help and encouragement. The sisters of the Social Mission Society, as well as lay external workers, undertook diverse tasks in many areas of social care.

One of the most important areas of Catholic renewal was social organization. Hundreds of cultural, social, charitable and devotional associations and organizations were formed, from the popular Catholic Clubs offering "noble entertainment" to the Congregations of Mary providing religious and spiritual instruction. Catholic credit cooperatives also appeared at this time. All parts of Catholic society established associations. By 1904, there were 1,400 Catholic associations in existence, and their number increased during the following decade. The Catholic League was founded in 1907; it had more than a thousand local branches and a membership of around 300,000. The Catholic Congresses held annually from 1900 onwards were national musters of Catholic society, at which topical issues were discussed by ordinary Catholics as well as experts. Similarly to the Catholic organizations, the Catholic press was also experiencing an upturn: by 1910, the Catholic printed media consisted of two Catholic daily newspapers, 14 weeklies, 26 literary or religious journals, 16 scientific or educational periodicals and four youth magazines. To promote and popularize these media, the Catholic Press Association was established in 1907.

All these facts demonstrate that at the turn of the century parts of Catholic society began to awaken after a century of apathy and indifference. Catholic men and women undertook not only to protect Catholic interests and rights but also to take part in social and public life as Catholics and representing the principles of the Gospel. This was only possible where social action and political action were accompanied by a rebirth of religious life. This spiritual renewal had to start with the training of priests; real spiritual pastors were needed, in place of "officials in cassocks." Ottokár Prohászka began the task of renewal at the Esztergom Seminary in the 1880s. The first fruits of his efforts became apparent at the turn of the century, when individual Catholic priests began to minister to sections of society that had eschewed religion, encouraging a return to religious life. A particular priority was the provision of religious instruction and spiritual care to secondary school pupils and university students. To further this aim, a group of clergy established the *Regnum Marianum* in 1903, and this was followed by the foundation of the Saint Emerich Student Hostels. The scouts were recognized as another potential area for action. The religious orders, which were experiencing a period of internal renewal, played a significant role in the education of young Catholics. It was during this period that the teacher-priest model was replaced by the youth pastor model, where the priest would devote his whole life to young people, serving as religious instructor, spiritual advisor and scout leader. Spiritual care gradually spread to sections of the country's youth that had been neglected, such as industrial apprentices and young female domestic servants. Efforts were made to activate women, with religious instruction and spiritual care being extended to women.

The evangelization of Budapest was an important achievement of Catholic renewal. In this rapidly growing city, the development of Church organization had failed to keep pace with the increase in population. Thus, by the early twentieth century, Budapest had some of the world's most populous parishes, with one priest serving tens of thousands of Catholics. Traditional forms of preaching and ministering to people were ineffective here; more modern methods were required. In this area too, the religious orders could play an important role: the Franciscans and Piarists were soon joined in the city by the Jesuits, Dominicans, Carmelites and Cistercians, whose churches and religious houses became important centers of pastoral and spiritual care.

A leading figure in the Catholic renewal movement at the turn of the century was Ottokár Prohászka, whom we have already mentioned. In place of a formal and superficial religiosity, Prohászka sought to embed religious belief in everyday life. In his writings, he summarized the program of Catholic renewal as follows: "Let us bind the natural with the supernatural world, earthly aims with the eternal goal... To stand on fully Christian foundations in matters of faith and morality, but to live in the cultural world of the twentieth century." Of course, the rebirth was not the achievement of one man acting alone; many others contributed to it.

Protestants

After the Compromise, the Protestant denominations faced the urgent task of establishing national Church organizations. After much debate and preparation, the national constitutional synod of the Calvinists convened in Debrecen on October 31, 1881. It was attended by representatives of the four church districts in Hungary, as well as the envoys of Transylvanian Calvinists. The synod established the national constitution of the Reformed (Calvinist) Church, which—with a number of additions and amendments—is still in force today. The basis of the constitution was the previously adopted "synod-presbytery" system, that is, a system of bottom-up corporate governance as well as parity between pastors and laypersons, with equal participation in the management and leadership of the Church. At every level of the Church organization, management was placed in the hands of an elected body headed by two chairmen: the pastor and the secular warden or chief warden. The basic unit of the organization was the congregation (mother church, *ecclesia*), which was led by the pastor and the congregational warden; the latter also chaired the presbytery elected by members of the congregation. Several congregations made up a deanery; deaneries were later also called dioceses. The deaneries, or dioceses, were headed by deans and the diocesan warden. Members of the diocesan assembly (*consistorium*) were elected by the presbyteries of the various congregations, as were also the members of the church district assemblies. Several dioceses together constituted a church district, led by a superintendent (bishop) and a chief warden. The diocesan and church district assemblies also served as Church justice forums. The Hungarian Reformed (Calvinist) Church comprised five archdioceses: Transdanubia (Pápa and Veszprém), Danube (Budapest), Cis-Tisza (Miskolc), Trans-Tisza (Debrecen) and Transylvania (Nagyenyed/Aiud and Kolozsvár/Cluj-Napoca). The highest level of the organization was the supreme legislative assembly convening every ten years, the 116-member *general synod*; there was also a 38-member *general convent* convening annually. The chairmen of both bodies were the highest-ranking bishop and the church district chief warden. The members of the synod and convent were elected by the church district assemblies. The first and second general synods, held in Budapest in 1891–1893 and 1904–1906, continued the elaboration of the constitution of the Church.

The organization of the Evangelical Lutheran Church was based on the same synod-presbytery principle and the parity of pastors and laypersons. The constitution of the Church was drafted by a general synod held in Budapest between 1891 and 1894 and subsequently amended by a second synod held in Budapest between 1913 and 1916. Here too, the mother congregation (*ecclesia*) was run by a presbytery elected by congregants and directed by the presbytery supervisor. The congregation elected and provided a stipend to the pastor. The congregation also maintained the school and paid the teacher. Several mother congregations formed a diocese, led by the dean and the secular supervisor. The situation was similar in the church district: in addition to the bishop (superintendent), there was also a church district supervisor. Both of them were elected by all mother congregations in the church district. The church district general assembly comprised delegates from the dioceses; it convened annually. The national organization was headed by the general Church and school supervisor; he was elected by the *ecclesias* from among the Lutheran members of the Upper House of Parliament. He chaired the general assembly that convened annually in Budapest and whose members were the bishops, the church district supervisors and the elected representatives of the church districts. The Evangelical Lutheran Church in Hungary consisted of four archdioceses: Bánya (mining towns in northern Hungary), Cisdanubia, Transdanubia and Tisza. The church districts did not have permanent seats; instead, the mother church of the pastor who had been elected as bishop served as the administrative center of the church district. The Evangelical Lutheran Church of the Transylvanian Saxons retained its separate organization.

Under the provisions of Act 7 of 1885 on an amendment to the organization of the Upper House of Parliament, in addition to the Roman Catholic and Orthodox prelates, Protestant leaders also became members of the Upper House: three bishops and three chief wardens from the Reformed (Calvinist) Church, three bishops and three supervisors from the Evangelical Lutheran Church, and a Unitarian bishop or chief warden. Thus, in addition to 32 Roman Catholic and ten Orthodox prelates, 13 Protestant leaders were also granted seats in the Upper House of Parliament.

In 1914, the Reformed (Calvinist) Church had 2,457 pastors and 358 trainee pastors, in 2,088 mother churches within a framework of 57 dioceses and five church districts. In the Evangelical Lutheran Church (together with the Transylvanian Saxons) the number of mother churches was 926 in 48 dioceses. There were 1,135 pastors as well as 364 trainees. The Unitarians had 115 mother churches in nine dioceses; most congregants lived in Transylvania, and there were 113 pastors.

It was József Eötvös who noted, several years before the Compromise, that "Protestants—even though they are outnumbered two to one by Catholics—have more influence than Catholics in all regards."[15] Such a view was supported by the statistics: a majority of members of Parliament were Protestant. Eötvös's claim is confirmed by current historians of the Protestant Churches: "Hungarian Protestantism was prepared to work together with the Liberal Party governments. This explains the high ratio of Protestants in the highest political offices of the state."[16] A crucial factor was a particular feature of Protestant Church organization, namely the equal participation of pastors and lay members in the direction of the Church. Among the Reformed chief wardens, we find the names of many leading politicians, government ministers and even prime ministers (Kálmán and István Tisza, Menyhért Lónyay, Dezső Szilágyi and Ignác Darányi). The Protestant leaders identified fully with the ideals of liberal nationalism. This explains why—unlike the Catholics, who were quick to take action to protect their schools—the Protestants, and especially the Calvinists, gave up some of their schools to the state. They considered state education to be a necessity for the nation. During the 20 years before World War I, the number of Reformed (Calvinist) primary schools fell by more than 500 (23 percent).

In the nineteenth century, rationalism and then liberalism exerted a great influence upon Protestant theology. The liberal theology that became dominant in mid-century applied the methodology of modern natural science and positivist historiography to issues of faith. Basic Christian dogmas were questioned, and faith was deprived of its supernatural aspects. The liberal theologians of the era interpreted religion first and foremost as reasoned faith and as a moral system, manifested in a person's ethical and intellectual conduct. Faith-based religions were considered to be unimportant; the principal task of the Church was to make people nobler in a moral sense. The liberal theologians held the view that if modern preachers were to remove the supernatural aspects from the person of Jesus—leaving the idea of inner spiritual freedom, the unconditional rule of morality, and a willingness to make sacrifices—then even modern intellectuals might choose to follow Jesus. Thus they denied the significance of scripture and religions of faith for modern religious belief. The liberal theologians of all three Protestant denominations supported an appeal for the establishment of a Hungarian Protestant Society in 1871. The society's aims were as follows: "A renewal of religious and moral life in the spirit of Jesus and in accordance with education in full." The society published periodicals and books; it held a series of lectures and became a center of the religious approach and conduct that became known as "cultural Protestantism." The society ceased functioning in 1890; its publishing work was continued by the Hungarian Protestant Literary Society, founded in 1889, which published the periodical *Protestáns Szemle* (Protestant Review).

Liberal theology naturally gave rise to a reaction: the 1860s saw the appearance of the so-called "new orthodoxy," which gave its support to a more scriptural approach as well as articles of faith based on such an approach. Its main promoters were Imre Révész of Debrecen and his disciple Ferenc Balogh. The latter's efforts went beyond promoting the "new orthodoxy," as he laid the foundations for the Protestant religious revival at the end of the century, becoming an instrumental figure in Debrecen of the so-called "awakening movement." The Protestant awakening came to Hungary from Western Europe via the Scottish Mission in Pest (est. 1841) and Hungarian theologians who returned to Hungary after studying at Protestant universities in Western Europe. Geneva's theologians considered Hungary's Protestants to have been "overcome by the wind of rationalism." By the end of the century, even in Hungary there was an awareness of the need for a "home mission" and a new wave of evangelization. Centers of the awakening movement in the Hungarian capital were the Scottish Mission and the German-speaking Reformed congregation. A leading figure in the Protestant awakening in Budapest at the end of the century was Aladár Szabó. He and his fellows called upon people to make radical changes to their lives, to undergo inner conversion, and to return to the living Gospel.

The Protestant awakening and home mission movement manifested results and achievements similar to those of the Catholic renewal: evangelizing talks, Sunday schools, Bible study groups, the publication of newspapers and periodicals, an upturn in community life, and the provision of spiritual care to young people. In 1883, Aladár Szabó and his co-workers established the Christian Youth Association. The turn of the century saw the foundation of several Protestant teachers' associations, women's groups, and various other mostly charitable bodies. All of this demonstrates that social and charitable work was an important part of the awakening. Hospitals, orphanages and old people's homes were established. To ensure a supply of workers for such social institutions, the training of deaconesses was begun in Hungary.

Greek Orthodox

Almost all Greek Orthodox believers in Hungary spoke either Serbian or Romanian—which explains the establishment of two separate Church organizations: likewise Serbian and Romanian. The separation took place shortly before the Compromise when, in 1864, Francis Joseph authorized the establishment of a Romanian Greek Orthodox archbishopric (metropolis), with its seat in Nagyszeben (Sibiu) and two subordinate bishoprics (Arad and Karánsebes/Caransebeş).

After 1864, six bishoprics were subordinated to the Serbian Orthodox metropolis of Karlóca (Sremski Karlovci): four of the bishoprics were in Hungary and two in Croatia. In 1914, the Serbian Orthodox Church included 657 mother churches, with 734 clergy, as well as 27 Basilian monasteries, with 128 monks. The Romanian Orthodox metropolitan had jurisdiction over 2,129 mother churches, with 2,392 clergy.

After the 1867 Compromise, the Hungarian legislature recognized, in 1868, the self-governing bodies of both the Serbian Orthodox Church and the Romanian Orthodox Church. In both Churches, the highest autonomous body was the national Church

Congress, comprising bishops as well as lay representatives elected by adult male congregation members; clergy made up a third of the Congress, while two thirds of its members were from the laity. The tasks of the Church Congress were to establish Church organization and the rules governing the operation of the Church, to manage Church properties and funds, and to provide overseeing to schools run by the Church. The Congress elected bishops and metropolitans, whose appointments were subject to the approval of the ruler. On several occasions, such approval was denied, at the government's behest. This was doubtless because the prospective appointee was considered to be unreliable in terms of nationalities policy.

The affairs of mother churches and the dioceses were administered by assemblies consisting of clergymen and elected representatives of the faithful, and the various committees established by the assemblies. The Serbian national Church Congresses held between 1869 and 1871 drafted organizational rules guaranteeing the laity a majority of places and a decisive voice in each of the forums and institutions of Church autonomy. The Church hierarchy was unhappy with this situation and campaigned for some decades to restore its hegemony. The clergy finally managed in 1912—with the government's support—to induce the king to repeal the rules and to order the Church Congress to draft a new constitution. Until the new constitution was adopted, however, the old pre-1871 rules applied—which benefited the hierarchy at the expense of the laity. In the government's view, this was an advantage, as the old constitution "suitably prevented, in the light of its clerical and conservative nature, ordinary nationalities policy from maneuvering behind the ramparts of autonomy." The drafting of a new constitution in accordance with Francis Joseph's instruction did not take place, owing to the outbreak of war.

The Jewish Denomination

During the era of Dualism, the Jewish denomination experienced the most rapid numerical growth, increasing to almost one million members by the outbreak of World War I—around 5 percent of Hungary's population (excluding Croatia). The largest Jewish community lived in Budapest—almost 200,000 people (23 percent). And there were also large Jewish communities (20 percent or more of the population) in cities such as Miskolc and Nagyvárad (Oradea).

Act 17 of 1867 established the legal equality of Jews as citizens. Even so, it was not until 1895 that Judaism became an officially recognized (or "received") religious denomination and was granted a status equal to that of the Christian denominations. A reason for this delay was the absence of a national denominational organization representing Jewish believers in dealings with the state. In April 1867, congregation leaders in Pest submitted a memorandum to the Parliament and to József Eötvös, minister of education and religion. In the memorandum, they suggested that the minister convene a national Jewish assembly, which would then draft a set of organizational rules for congregations and found a national central organization for the Jewish community. However, divisions began to appear within the community. In response to the memoranda submitted by the Neolog religious community, the Orthodox Jewish congregations drafted their own memorandum outlining the important differences between the two groups. In order to defend ancient beliefs, the Orthodox camp established an organization called the "Guardians of Religion" (*Shomrei Hadat*), which began publishing a magazine in Hungarian called *Magyar Zsidó* (Hungarian Jew).

In February 1868, Eötvös convened a preparatory conference with the task of drafting election rules for a Jewish Congress. The elections produced a narrow majority for the Neologs: 126 out of 220 members of the Congress were Neologs, while 94 belonged to the Orthodox camp. The general assembly of Hungarian and Transylvanian Jews, that is, the Jewish Congress, was opened by

József Eötvös on December 10, 1868. In the course of discussions at the Congress, which lasted until February 1869, several disputes arose between the Neolog majority and the Orthodox minority. In the end, the Orthodox Jews suspended their participation in the Congress. Thus, Neolog representatives voted alone on the organizational rules for the religious community. Under the adopted rules, rabbis' powers were limited to religious matters, ceremony and teaching. The rules stated that the religious community as a whole would be directed by a body of representatives and elected officials. Rabbis were then to be elected by the religious community. The country's religious communities comprised 26 districts, each with a general assembly in which there was one representative for every 100 members. These district representatives then elected the district officials. The 26 district chairmen formed a separate body, which convened annually, controlled the national school fund, and decided on whether to convene a general assembly. It annually elected the chairman of the National Office, which represented the Jewish community in its dealings with the Hungarian government. The Congress decided to establish a modern rabbis' training center in Budapest. The college was opened in 1877 and soon established a worldwide reputation and became a major center for the training of rabbis. It was the teaching staff of the National Rabbi Training Institute who began publishing a magazine called *Magyar Zsidó Szemle* (Hungarian Jewish Review) in 1884.

On June 14, 1869, Francis Joseph ratified the organizational rules adopted by the Congress. In this way the self-government of the Neolog (Congress) branch of the Jews in Hungary came into being. The Orthodox Jews, however, refused to accept the resolutions of the Congress, as they contravened the ancient laws of the Jewish religion. They appealed to the Lower House of Parliament and, having received its support, they convened the Orthodox Jewish Congress in August 1870—which also drafted organizational rules. The organizational rules stated that the basis of Jewish religious life should be a set of strict regulations laid down in the sixteenth century (the *Shulchan Aruch*); they also gave rabbis a greater say in directing congregations. Francis Joseph approved the Orthodox branch's organizational rules on October 22, 1871. Thereafter Hungarian Jewry was divided into three separate parts: the Congress (or Neolog) branch, the Orthodox branch, and the "*status quo ante*" congregations—that is, those who refused to join either of the other two branches and wished to uphold the situation prevailing before the Congress. As a consequence of this division, some towns had two or three Jewish religious communities, and Jewish believers were free to switch from one to the other. The problems arising as a result—including conflicts between the various branches—were mitigated to an extent by government intervention, following the adoption of ministerial decrees regulating the Jewish religious communities.

In 1914, there were 318 Orthodox congregations, 182 Neolog congregations and 60 "*status quo*" congregations. Orthodox rabbis numbered 260, Neolog rabbis 112 and "neutral" rabbis 34. Most of the Neolog communities were established in the major urban centers, while Orthodoxy prevailed in small towns and rural areas.

The official division accentuated the differences between the two camps. Discrepancies in lifestyle and conduct became more pronounced, and there was less chance of cooperation or unity. Moreover, the Orthodox branch was a fractured grouping; in some places, two Orthodox congregations arose. On this subject, the historian of Hungarian Jewry Nathaniel Katzburg wrote the following:

> Within Hungarian Jewish Orthodoxy, two types are distinguishable: 'western' Orthodoxy, which arose out of congregations in the western part of Hungary and some in the Danube-Tisza region, and the 'eastern' type in the northeastern counties. The western group includes migrants from Austria and Bohemia-Moravia. The eastern group was made up of people who were of Galician descent and mostly members of Hasidic communities… In Hungary, Hasidism established roots in areas where most of the population were poorly educated… In contrast to the Hasidic communities, which live in separation from the non-Jewish environment

> and are hostile to secular culture, the western Orthodox group never isolated itself from external influences. They can read and write in German; indeed, the western Orthodox groups are generally rather cultivated… Membership of one of the Orthodox congregations was conditional on strict adherence to the religious regulations. This was the main difference between the Neologs and the Orthodox; the wall dividing them was not only of a religious nature; it was also social in type.[17]

Hasidism was a Jewish religious school or approach with popularistic and mystical elements that developed in Galicia in the eighteenth century. It emphasized inner piety and prayer—often accompanied by ecstatic phenomena (dance)—rather than Talmudic traditions and narrowly interpreted rituals. It also underscored the emotional aspects of religion. The leader of the Hasidic community was the "tzadik," typically a charismatic man, noted less for his rabbinical knowledge than for his personality, his piety and his miraculous actions; his supporters regarded him as a "miracle rabbi." Hasidism spread to Hungary as Jews migrated from Galicia to the country; it was particularly strong in the eastern and northeastern counties among Jews living in rural areas and small towns. The Hasidic community gave rise to a rich heritage of literature, poetry, music, dance and humor.

In spite of their separate organizations, the Neolog and Orthodox communities joined forces to establish a number of institutions. Such cooperation led to the establishment of charitable organizations such as the *chevra kadishas* as well as women's groups, orphanages and care organizations. The year 1910 saw the establishment of a Jewish cultural organization—the National Hungarian Jewish Cultural Association.

Budapest was the birthplace of Theodor Herzl. In 1896, Herzl published *Der Judenstaat*, thereby launching the Zionism movement. He argued that Jewish people were first and foremost a nation, with the right to establish their own nation state. Zionism's first center in Hungary was Pozsony (now Bratislava). It was there that the first national Zionist Congress was held in 1903.

Notes

1 The Unitarians trace their origins to the anti-Trinitarians of the sixteenth century, who rejected Christ's divinity and the Holy Trinity.
2 The *placetum regium* was the right of the ruler to render the pronouncement of papal writings and edits subject to his prior approval. It was introduced in Hungary by King Sigismund in 1404. In the eighteenth century, it was applied by Maria Theresa on several occasions. Joseph II prescribed it for all documents coming from Rome.
3 Gyula Szekfű, *Magyar történet* [Hungarian History], vol. 5 (Budapest, 1943), p. 523.
4 József Eötvös, *Levelek* [Letters] (Budapest, 1976), p. 505.
5 Ernő Szeghy, *Emlékeim* [Memoirs] (Budapest, 1943), pp. 14–15, 122, 153.
6 Eötvös, *Levelek*, pp. 484–485.
7 *Ibid.*, p. 485.
8 *Ibid.*, p. 495.
9 *Ibid.*, p. 499.
10 *Autonómia*, March 7, 1869
11 *Független Lapok*, November 16, 1867.
12 Jenő Török, *A katolikus autonómia-mozgalom, 1848–1871. Adalékok a magyar liberális katolicizmus történetéhez* [The Catholic Autonomy Movement 1848–1871. The History of Hungarian Liberal Catholicism] (Budapest, 1941), p. 133.
13 Ottokár Prohászka, *Soliloquia* [Soliloquy], I (Budapest, 1929), pp. 94–95.
14 Ottokár Prohászka, *Korunk lelke* [The Spirit of Our Age] (Budapest, 1929), p. 66.
15 Eötvös, *Levelek*, p. 485.
16 Mihály Bucsay, *A protantizmus története Magyarországon 1521–1945* [The History of Protestantism in Hungary 1521–1945] (Budapest, 1985), p. 210.
17 Nathaniel Katzburg, *Fejezetek az újkori zsidó történelemből Magyarországon* [Excerpts in Modern Jewish History in Hungary] (Budapest, 1999), pp. 79, 100–102.

11. ESTABLISHING A MODERN CULTURE

In the Dualist era, cultural development and the advance of cultural institutions were some of the most important manifestations—alongside rapid economic growth—of the dynamism and success of Hungary's modernization. In addition to a modern economic infrastructure, the country acquired a cultural infrastructure that was vital to its proper development. This infrastructure included educational institutions, research facilities, museums, libraries, and academic, literary and artistic associations. Together they formed a cultural network that gradually spread to the whole country. The era also saw the appearance of a large number of academic journals and a good number of literary and cultural magazines. The process began during the decades before the 1867 Compromise, but it became far more dynamic with the establishment of a separate Hungarian state within the Dual Monarchy. A particularly important task during this initial period was to develop Hungarian culture; the government proved willing to devote significant budgetary resources towards furthering this aim.

The typical features of modern mass culture became apparent in Hungarian cultural life at the end of the nineteenth century. The scope of culture broadened and began to spread to all sections of society. Two characteristic features of modern culture—differentiation and specialization—strengthened; that is to say, the various cultural fields became separate or independent. A separation took place between fiction and science, and between natural sciences and human sciences; moreover, the various academic subjects were established. These developments resulted in the decline and subsequent disappearance of the "all-rounders" and polymaths. Stratification within culture also became more marked: the different modes of expressions reflected the demands and tastes of the various social classes and groups in society. Cultural development led to a significant expansion of the institutional, organizational and technological infrastructure in the course of the nineteenth century. Culture became a dense, structured network, capable of satisfying the scientific, literary and artistic needs of a modern society and an industrializing economy. The goal was to provide as many people as possible with access to cultural goods.

During the first decades of the Dualist era, large-scale financial and human investments took place in the cultural sphere. Based on these foundations, Hungarian culture—including its scientific, literary and artistic branches—was able to develop and expand during the two decades preceding World War I. Intellectual life underwent a general renaissance; the atmosphere was similar to that of the Reform period prior to the 1848 Revolution. There was, however, a difference: in the pre-1848 period, it was only in a few fields—such as literature, and political and social ideas—that Hungarian culture had been on a par with European culture. In contrast, by the early twentieth century, this was true of almost all branches of science, art, architecture and music. Like its predecessor, this cultural rebirth and development took place by means of a modern synthesis of Hungarian and European identities. In all branches of culture—in science, literature, art and the media—assimilated parts of Hungarian society (and especially Germans and Jews) played an important role.

Establishing a Modern Education System

An improvement in literacy rates represented the greatest contribution towards establishing conditions for cultural development. The government's literacy program was elaborated by József Eötvös, the minister of education in the Hungarian governments of 1848 and 1867: "I consider the future of the Hungarian nation to be a purely cultural question, and so I regard the issue of our children's education as the major national issue."[1] The scale of the task became apparent in the course of the 1869 census, which revealed that less than one third (32.8 percent) of the population aged six years or over could read and write. The male literacy rate was 41 percent and the female rate 25 percent (in Croatia, the corresponding rates were 28 percent and 15 percent respectively). Similar rates had been seen in Great Britain around 200 years earlier and in France around 100 years earlier. According to the 1869 survey, 14 percent of villages had no school—even though the Imperial government had placed great emphasis on developing and modernizing education between 1849 and 1867. Between 1851 and 1865, the number of elementary schools (*népiskolák*) increased by 3,000. The low literacy rate in 1869 reflected the fact that one in two children of compulsory school age did not attend school. Child school attendance rates varied considerably among Hungary's various ethnic groups: 68 percent among Germans, 54 percent among Magyars, 51 percent among Slovaks, 36 percent among Serbs and 30 percent among Romanians. Still, by the mid-1880s, the overall attendance rate had increased to 80 percent. And in 1905, child school attendance rates among the various ethnic groups were as follows: 89 percent among Germans, 84 percent among Slovaks, 81 percent among Magyars, 78 percent among Serbs, 64 percent among Romanians and 61 percent among Ruthenians. As the data indicate, the greatest advance in this area was achieved among Hungary's Serb community.

After the Compromise, elementary school education was regulated by Act 38 of 1868, which József Eötvös drafted. Elementary schools consisted of six grades, but pupils could transfer to high schools after four grades. On completion of six grades, pupils continued to attend school until they reached 15 years of age. Elementary school education was provided in the native language of students. It was only in 1879 that the Magyar language as a compulsory subject was introduced in all elementary schools (Act 18 of 1879). Between 1869 and 1914, the number of elementary schools increased from 13,798 to 16,929, and there was an even larger relative increase in the number of elementary school teachers (from 17,794 to 35,253). Accordingly, the teacher–pupil ratio fell from 1:128 in 1869 to 1:105 in 1905. Even immediately prior to World War I, 59 percent of schools still had just one teacher.

Improvements in elementary education led to higher literacy rates in the decades after the 1867 Compromise: by 1910, the literacy rate had doubled to 68.7 percent. Regional and ethnic differences continued to be significant. Thus, while the literacy rate was 82 percent in Transdanubia, it was as low as 53 percent in Croatia and 51 percent in Transylvania. In 1910, 79 percent of Magyars could write (82.8 percent of males and 75.5 percent of females). The rates among the other ethnic groups were as follows: 82 percent among Germans, 70 percent among Slovaks, 56 percent among Croats, 48 percent among Serbs, 33 percent among Romanians and 28 percent among Ruthenians. Due to the rapid increase in literacy, Hungary surpassed not only Russia and the Balkan countries in this area, but also Italy and other countries in southern Europe. In Austria, 81.3 percent of the population aged ten or over were literate. Here too, the literacy rate varied—from over 90 percent in the Austrian German and Czech provinces to just 36.5 percent in Dalmatia (59 percent in Istria, 54.2 percent in Galicia and 45.2 percent in Bukovina).

Pre-school education made its first appearance in Hungary in the 1820s. At the time of the Compromise, there were more than 100 kindergartens in the country, and the number increased to 700 in 1890. Legislation adopted in 1891 regulated the establishment and operation of kindergartens, as well as the training of kindergarten teachers. In 1914, 230,000 children aged 3–6 were attending more than 2,000 kindergartens.

After completing four grades of elementary school, pupils could continue their education at high school or at a transitional type of school called the higher elementary school (*polgári iskola*). This type of school was established by the Elementary Education Act of 1868 with a view to meeting the needs of the lower middle class as well as peasant farmers in rural communities. Under the legislation, each village with more than 5,000 inhabitants was required to have a higher elementary school. They had six grades, but most of the pupils completed only the first four grades. In 1914, 109,000 pupils were attending 526 higher elementary schools in Hungary; most of these schools were attended by girls. At these schools, pupils were taught modern languages rather than Latin. However, by successfully taking a Latin exam, students could transfer to the upper grades of a special high school (*reálgimnázium/Realgymnasium*).

After completing higher elementary school or four grades at high school, students could continue their studies at teacher training colleges for elementary school and kindergarten teachers or at commercial, industrial and economic vocational high schools. In 1914, there were 92 training colleges for elementary school teachers and nine training colleges for kindergarten teachers. Students who left elementary school after six grades and found employment in industry or commerce could still attend schools for industrial or commercial apprentices. The establishment of such schools was required wherever there were at least 50 apprentices. In 1914, there were more than 700 such schools for apprentices.

Eradicating illiteracy was just one of the conditions for the development of modern culture. Another requirement was a significant increase in the percentage of people participating in higher education. To further this goal, Hungary's high school system was radically reformed in the 1850s. As a result of these reforms, standards of tuition improved significantly. Under the reforms of the Imperial minister of education Leo Thun, initiated in late 1849, the high school (*gymnasium*) was transformed into an eight-grade school. The final examination, the high school diploma and the specialization of teachers were introduced at this time. To meet the demands of a modern society, a new type of school was established—the *reáliskola* (*Realschule*), or special high school for modern languages and sciences. After the 1867 Compromise, the minister of culture, Ágoston Trefort, regulated the operation of high schools through Act 30 of 1883. Under the reforms, the task of the ordinary and special high schools was to provide young people with an enhanced level of general education and prepare them for higher education. This was achieved at ordinary high schools (*gymnasia*) through the humanities and above all the study of Greek and Latin and at the special high schools (*Realgymnasium*) by providing tuition to them in modern languages, mathematics and natural sciences.

Both types of high school could consist of eight grades, but some only had four grades. In 1867, there were 143 ordinary high schools (*gymnasia*) and 21 special (or *reál*) high schools in Hungary, but by 1914 their numbers had increased to 195 and 34 respectively. Over the same period, the number of high school students increased from 36,000 to 78,000. Hungarian society continued to favor the old type of high school (*gymnasium*), which concentrated on the humanities; the special high schools (*Realgymnasium*) were less popular. Indeed, in the school year 1913–1914, as few as 16 percent of high school pupils were attending special high schools. In Austria and Italy, the corresponding percentage was above 30 percent, while in Germany 40–50 percent of pupils attended the *Realgymnasium*s. On completion of school, graduates of ordinary high schools could enroll in any university faculty, while those from special high schools had less choice; they could enroll in the technical university or in the natural sciences faculties of other universities.

For many years the higher elementary school offered the highest possible level of education for girls. The first high school for girls opened in 1869, but such schools were uncommon until 1895, when a ministerial decree rendered it possible for girls to take the high school diploma and then enroll in the humanities or medicine faculties of universities. By 1914, there were 35 girls' high schools, with almost 7,000 students.

Secondary vocational institutions included the commercial high schools and the various types of industrial vocational schools. In 1914, there were 47 commercial high schools for boys and seven for girls—with 10,000 pupils. In addition, there were 52 industrial vocational schools, including 11 such schools for young women. Five agricultural schools also existed; they were gradually transformed into academies. The veterinary school of Budapest also became a college of higher education at this time.

In the initial period, the University of Budapest was Hungary's only university, with faculties of theology, philosophy, law and medicine. In 1872, the country's second university was established at Kolozsvár (Cluj) in Transylvania. The University of Kolozsvár had no theological faculty, but it succeeded in establishing Hungary's first natural sciences faculty. In 1874, a third university was established in Zagreb, with Croatian as the language of tuition. By the turn of the century, the two Hungarian universities had become inadequate for the task. Legislation was thus adopted in 1912 concerning the establishment of universities in Debrecen and Pozsony (Bratislava). The two universities opened during World War I. (In the early 1920s, the Hungarian university in Pozsony/Bratislava was relocated to Pécs in southwestern Hungary, while the Hungarian university in Kolozsvár/Cluj was relocated to Szeged in southern Hungary.) The Royal Joseph Technical University was established during the 1871–1872 academic year; its predecessor was the Joseph Industrial College, which had been founded in 1846 and had become a polytechnic in 1857. The Royal Joseph Technical University became one of the largest and most accomplished technical universities in the world. Students of law could enroll in one of ten law academies, but doctorates in law could only be obtained at the universities. Trainee clergymen and monks could study theology at university or at one of 44 seminaries and theological colleges.

University facilities and infrastructure were expanded after the Compromise and particularly during Ágoston Trefort's term as minister of education in the 1880s, when major investments were undertaken: new departments, seminars and laboratories were established at the universities, while the various faculties received buildings suited to the task. In both Budapest and Kolozsvár, clinics necessary for the training of medical students were established. In the 1913–1914 academic year, there were almost 17,000 students studying at university or at one of the law academies or theology colleges. A significant proportion of students were studying law (38 percent) or medicine (22 percent). Smaller but sizeable numbers of students were attending technical university (16 percent) or studying theology (12 percent). Nine percent of students were enrolled in the faculty of humanities and 3 percent in the faculty of pharmacology. One in two college and university students came from families where the father was a private/public official or an intellectual,

21 percent had lower middle-class backgrounds, and 11 percent were from peasant backgrounds. About 5 percent of students had fathers working in the industrial and transport sectors, and a similar percentage had fathers who were large or medium-sized landowners. The *grande bourgeoisie*'s share was about 7 percent. At universities and colleges, Jewish students accounted for as many as 29 percent of the total number of students. (At boys' high schools, 21 percent of pupils were Jewish, while at girls' high schools the percentage was higher at 34 percent). Austrian university students were far more likely than Hungarian students to choose technical subjects or the humanities. Hungarian students were more likely than Austrian students to choose law, medicine or theology. In 1914, more than 1,600 Hungarian students were studying at foreign universities, mostly in Austria or Germany.

The training of experts—who were required in the dynamically growing economy—was undertaken at the commercial academies. There were two such academies in Budapest, one in Kolozsvár and one in Fiume (Rijeka). Experts for the mining and forestry sectors were trained at a special academy in Selmecbánya (Banská Štiavnica). Musicians were taught at the Academy of Music, established in 1875. (The Academy was headed first by Franz Liszt and then by Ferenc Erkel, the most important Hungarian composer in the nineteenth century.) Artists could attend the Art Teacher Training College, established in 1871. After the addition of painting and sculpture departments, this institution developed—at the end of the century—into the Art College. Actors were trained at the National Theater Studies Academy. Finally, in 1872, the Military Office College, the Ludovika Academy, was opened. Officers and NCOs were also taught at the Monarchy's eight cadet schools and at the naval academy in Fiume.

At the time of the Compromise, most of Hungary's educational institutions were run by the religious denominations or local authorities. Later on, however, the government—no longer satisfied with its mere supervisory role—became actively involved in developing a network of schools. During the era of Dualism, government funds were used to found more than 3,000 new primary and secondary schools, and the government was also instrumental in the establishment of vocational schools, colleges and new universities. Education became the fastest-growing area of public expenditure. In the years prior to World War I, average annual expenditure on education amounted to 123 million crowns, or 9 percent of total government spending. In addition to such expenditure, ever-larger sums were spent on science institutes, central and local museums, libraries and archives, and subsidies for art.

Cultural Institutions and Associations

After the Compromise, the network of public libraries, archives and museums, which had started to develop in the late eighteenth century, was expanded. New major central libraries and museums were opened. The second half of the nineteenth century saw the establishment of a great number of specialized libraries—often linked with a scientific or professional association or institution. It was during this period that public libraries became true academic workshops. Museums underwent a similar development, leading to greater specialization and differentiation. It was in the second half of the nineteenth century that the new type of museum, the specialized museum, appeared in Hungary. The Hungarian National Museum, which had been established in 1802 as a universal museum, was gradually transformed into a series of specialized museums. The museum, originally consisting of two departments, was divided into three departments in 1814 and then into eight departments in 1870. In subsequent decades, some of these departments developed into independent museums. The National Educational Equipment Museum was founded in 1877, the Technological Industrial Museum in 1879, the Applied Arts Museum in 1881, the Historical Portrait Hall in 1885 and the Museum of Fine Arts in 1903. At the time of the millennium celebrations in 1896, two new specialized museums were opened: the Museum of Agriculture and the Museum of Transport. All these national museums were situated in Budapest; most of them acquired modern premises at the turn of the century.

From the late nineteenth century, Hungarian towns and counties established a series of mostly public libraries—the municipal and county libraries. Some of the museums and libraries—founded by associations, counties or municipalities—were eventually taken over by the state. The numerical increase was so great that professional supervision by the state became a necessity. Accordingly, in 1897, the National Council and Supervisory Board of Museums and Libraries was established. An important research workshop for historians was the National Archives, established after the Compromise. The archives preserved the correspondence and documents of central government institutions.

In 1910, Budapest had 12 museums, and there were 45 additional museums in other parts of the country. Hungary also had 132 public libraries with more than 10,000 volumes.

Throughout the period, universities and colleges were the main academic workshops. High schools also played a role in academic life: some of the corresponding members of the Hungarian Academy of Sciences were high school teachers, who devoted some of their time to earnest academic and scientific scholarship.

In the second half of the nineteenth century, there already existed several institutions whose priority was scientific research, experimentation and observation. "Instead of being the product of a planned scientific policy program, such [institutions] tended to have arisen, owing to economic interests or through action taken by ministers… There is only one example of a large number of institutions being established, and this one example is related to agricultural methods: the agricultural experimental institutions founded by Ignác Darányi."[2] Such research institutions were established exclusively in the field of applied and natural sciences, while research work in the social sciences was undertaken primarily at universities and in archives, libraries and museums.

Several astronomical observatories were established in the first half of the nineteenth century, including the famous university observatory in Pest. Another observatory with an international reputation was a private one founded by Miklós Konkoly Thege in 1871. It was taken over by the state in 1899. The world-famous astronomer Gyula Fényi, a Jesuit, worked at the observatory established in Kalocsa by Archbishop Lajos Haynald in 1878. The Viennese meteorological institute established its own weather stations in Hungary from 1851. After the Compromise, the Royal Hungarian Magnetic and Meteorological Institute was brought into being in 1870; it began to develop particularly after 1890. The number of observatory stations had increased to 765 by 1900. It was out of this institute that the Seismic Observatory developed; it was established in 1905. Immediately after the Compromise, in 1869, the Institute of Geology was founded; in 1899, it moved to new premises, an *art nouveau* building designed by the architect Ödön Lechner. The year 1907 saw the establishment, at Lóránd Eötvös's initiative, of the Institute of Geophysics, the last of the natural sciences institutes.

A special group among the government-owned science institutes comprised the 11 agricultural research institutes, which were established by the Ministry of Agriculture at the behest of agricultural science teachers. Most of the institutes were situated in Budapest, but several were located in Mosonmagyaróvár. These central research institutes were linked with chemical and seed improvement laboratories in other parts of Hungary. In this way, a whole series of scientific research institutes provided support to agriculture, Hungary's principal economic sector.

In addition to the science institutes established and funded by the government, an important role in science was also played by academic and scientific associations and societies established by scientists themselves. Such organizations represented the interests and views of the profession on various issues and at various forums; they also held readings and debates around the country. The associations and societies published scientific journals and educational works, and they awarded grants to experts in the various professions. The most important organizations were the national professional bodies, whose membership included top scientists, practicing scientists and other people who were simply interested in science. An important function of such bodies was to involve experts living outside the country's major urban centers in scientific life.

It was during this period that Hungary's central academic and scientific body, the Hungarian Academy of Sciences (est. 1825), was transformed from a linguistic and literary institute into a fully professional academic and scientific forum, coordinating and supervising scholarly work in Hungary. In the 1860s, under the direction of the chairman, József Eötvös, and the general secretaries, László Szalay and János Arany, the Academy became a center of modern scientific excellence. In earlier periods, the emphasis had been on the Hungarian language and Hungarian literature. Now the focus was on natural sciences and technology. The realist school of the social sciences flourished, and in all areas of scholarly study scientists were expected to apply the standards of more advanced countries in Europe.

In 1869, Francis Joseph approved new rules governing the scope of tasks and the requirements of modern academic scholarship. With minor amendments, these rules governed the operation of the Academy until 1945. The composition of the membership also changed. In 1890, Eötvös Lóránd, the Academy's chairman, reminded members that the Academy's tasks before 1848 had been different. At that time, the Magyar national identity had required protection, but now "since our existence is assured, we must endeavor—in addition to strengthening our existence—to take the most distinguished place possible among the more cultivated peoples." He continued as follows: "With the new era come new people; sons follow fathers; statesmen and poets are replaced by scientific workers."[3] On the outbreak of World War I, the Academy had 224 full or corresponding members. Specialized committees coordinated and directed scholarly endeavor. Between the 1850s and the outbreak of World War I, a dozen or so committees were formed, subsequently coordinating various projects. The Academy's publication of books and journals contributed greatly to the development of scholarship in Hungary.

A second major scientific body in Hungary was the Royal Hungarian Society for Natural Sciences (est. 1841). Its main purpose was to increase people's knowledge of the natural sciences, to which end it published journals as well as a large number of books by both Hungarian and foreign authors. Its membership was under 600 in 1868, but had increased to more than 5,000 by 1878. In 1912, it had over 10,000 members.

In addition to the two major scientific associations, there were several other specialized associations and societies. Among the first to be established were the Royal Budapest Association of Physicians (est. 1837) and the Hungarian Geological Association (est. 1851). Such organizations became far more numerous after the 1867 Compromise: the Hungarian Historical Society (with its journal *Századok* (Centuries)) and the Hungarian Association of Engineers and Architects were both established in 1867. The latter organization established 16 branches in Hungary's provincial urban centers. Subsequently, each branch of science established its own professional association or society, which then published a journal. In addition to the national scientific associations, there were also many regional and local associations. Among the various regional associations, the Transylvanian Museum Association was the most important; it began work in 1860.

Associations were established not only by scientists, but also by literary professionals and enthusiasts as well as artists working in various fields; these associations and societies then received premises and exhibition halls. The first major literary society, the Kisfaludy Society, was founded in 1837 by ten friends of Károly Kisfaludy in commemoration of this excellent writer. The Society held readings and offered grants, with awards for excellent literary and artistic pieces. The Society undertook important publishing tasks: in addition to the publication of works by Hungarian authors, it also arranged for the translation into Hungarian of major works by foreign authors and supported the collection of folk poetry. In 1876, the Petőfi Society, chaired by Mór Jókai, undertook similar work—albeit in more modest circumstances. Among the various literary groups outside Budapest, one should mention the Csokonai Circle in Debrecen as well as the Vörösmarty Society in Székesfehérvár. Writers and poets such as Endre Ady and his fellows joined together in the Society for Tomorrow (*Holnap*), established in Nagyvárad (Oradea) in 1908.

In the second half of the nineteenth century, the representative body of Hungarian art was the National Hungarian Society of Fine Art (est. 1861), which held exhibitions and funded artists. In the 1870s and 1880s, the Society had 800–900 members, and by 1914 membership had risen to almost 4,000. It was at the Society's initiative that the Art Hall was built in Budapest in 1877 and then replaced in 1896. The Society tended to reject modern art, and so the 1890s saw the establishment of several new institutions and associations that were more sympathetic to novel tastes and modern schools in art. These included the National Salon, founded in 1894. The Salon had a dual profile, serving as a bridge between conservative and progressive ideas about art. The associations formed in the early years of the twentieth century more adamantly represented modern art; these included the Kéve Art Association (est. 1907) and the Artists' House (est. 1909). Fans of a new form of art, the cinema, joined together in the National Hungarian Association of Cinematographers (est. 1909). One should also note the artists' colonies, where artists could work for extended periods of time or even reside permanently. Such colonies became important artistic workshops. Most of the colonies were set up by artists themselves, but over time local municipalities also came to support them, even by providing grants. The government attempted to promote but also to control the development of art by offering artistic awards, grants and study scholarships, and by commissioning works. The National Hungarian Arts Council, whose members were renowned artists, contributed greatly to the drafting of government policy towards art.

In the second half of the nineteenth century, theatrical art also saw a differentiation according to both genre and the demands of the various audiences. Opera received a suitable home in the form of Miklós Ybl's grand neo-renaissance building, the Hungarian

State Opera House, which opened in Budapest in 1884. Gustav Mahler was director of the State Opera between 1888 and 1891. The People's Theater, which opened in 1875, specialized in folk plays, attracting mainly middle-class audiences. Those with an interest in more modern pieces could see performances at the Comedy Theater (est. 1896), while fans of the new musical genre, the operetta, could attend the *Király* (King or Royal) Theater (est. 1903). The turn of the century also saw the construction and inauguration of modern theaters in Hungary's provincial cities. The country's symphonic orchestras, performing regularly, were established in the second half of the nineteenth century. Ferenc Erkel founded the Budapest Philharmonic Society as early as 1853, and permanent orchestras were formed in Pozsony, Sopron, Pécs, Kassa (Košice) and Kolozsvár in subsequent decades.

Cultural associations and organizations differed not just in terms of their specialization but also in terms of their ideological and religious affiliations. The Catholic Saint Stephen Society began its work primarily as a publisher of books in the 1840s. Under the auspices of the Society, the Scientific and Literary Department was formed in 1886; this became the Saint Stephen Academy in 1915. In 1888, an organization with a similar purpose was established by Protestants: the Hungarian Protestant Literary Society. In 1910, Hungary's Jewish community established its own cultural organization, the National Hungarian Jewish Cultural Association. The Jewish Museum opened in 1916.

Written culture had to be brought to the widest possible audience. The success of Hungary's printing industry—it became the most developed branch of light industry in the second half of the nineteenth century—is indicative of progress in this area. By 1913, 1,208 printing houses were in operation in the country, including 251 (the largest ones) in Budapest.

In the Dualist era, Hungary, like other countries, was experiencing a media revolution. The number of newspapers and journals increased from 603 in the first half of the 1880s, to 999 in 1896, and to 1,892 in 1914. Within a 30-year period, the number of political newspapers grew from 82 to 366 and the number of local newspapers from 196 to 386. The number of specialist magazines and periodicals increased from 242 to 1,017. Literary journals and magazines were far more modest in number: 63 in the early 1880s, rising to 102 in 1914. The expansion of the printed media was accompanied by an increase in circulation. Before the 1867 Compromise, the most popular political newspapers had been printed in 3,000–5,000 copies, but by the 1880s some were printed in tens of thousands of copies. The introduction of rotation printing presses in the early years of the twentieth century enabled the sale of hundreds of thousands of copies. Each political persuasion's group and party had its own daily newspaper. The publication of newspapers and magazines developed into a profitable business undertaking. The 1880s saw the arrival of cheap newspapers with no affiliation to political parties. In the early twentieth century, tabloid newspapers (the so-called "penny press") addressed to the masses and focusing on scandal and sensation appeared on the market. Magazines aimed at the various social classes were very popular, as were the pictorial family publications. There was a similar increase in literary readership. At the turn of the century, fiction books (above all novels) were published in hundreds of thousands of copies. A Hungarian specialty was an invention by Tivadar Puskás, the so-called "telediffusion" (*telefonhírmondó*) service, which began regular broadcasts in 1893. Initially, broadcasts were limited to news items and language lessons, but soon musical, opera and theater performances were also offered. In 1900, the service had more than 6,000 subscribers. The "telediffusion" service ceased broadcasting in 1943.

Catching Up with European Standards in Science

In the first half of the period, Hungarian natural and applied scientists were increasingly able to become acquainted with the findings and methods of the international scientific community. The conditions that made this possible—university facilities, modern laboratories and research workshops—were established during the 1870s and 1880s. Generally speaking, most branches of the natural and technical sciences had reached the average European level of development by the end of the century. Indeed, Hungary's second generation of scientists actively contributed to the international development of various scientific fields. The achievements of Hungarian scientists received international recognition, particularly in the fields of mathematics (Gyula Kőnig, József Kürschák, Lipót Fejér and Frigyes Riesz), physics and technical science. Lóránd Eötvös and his student Győző Zemplén, who died as a young man in World War I, are regarded as the last great exponents of classical physics. In chemistry, significant advances were made by Károly Than and Vince Wartha. In the technical sciences, several outstanding inventions and developments were made by Hungarian experts, including Károly Zipernowsky, Miksa Déri, Ottó Bláthy, Kálmán Kandó and Sándor Just (electrotechnology), Tivadar Puskás (communications), Donát Bánki (hydraulics) and Antal Kerpely (metallurgy). Among the natural sciences, medicine was particularly well developed in Hungary. Hungarian medicine had traditions going back centuries. The second third of the nineteenth century saw the establishment of a school of medicine in Pest, and this school proved capable of securing its professional independence from Vienna's school of medicine. Outstanding medics in Hungary included Ignác Semmelweis, János Balassa, Kálmán Balogh, József Lenhossék, Endre Hőgyes, Frigyes Korányi, and the founder of Hungarian public health, József Fodor. Hungarian agricultural science also achieved an international reputation; it had ready access to various research institutes and experimental facilities.

In the 1860s, the most important perceived task was the scientific investigation of the natural features of the Carpathian basin. This task had been largely accomplished by the beginning of the twentieth century, owing to the cooperation and input of various branches of science, such as geography, geology, botany and zoology.

Noteworthy are two scientific expeditions undertaken by Hungarians. The first was an expedition by Béla Széchenyi, who—

accompanied by Hungarian scientists such as the geographer and geologist Lajos Lóczy—traveled in east Asia between 1877 and 1880. The second was Sámuel Teleki's expedition to Africa between 1886 and 1888, in the course of which he explored unknown regions in the east of the continent.

In the field of the social sciences, the so-called "national sciences"—history and literary history—gradually freed themselves from romanticism and dilettantism and developed into modern academic subjects. Even so, it was only in the early years of the twentieth century that standards caught up with those prevailing elsewhere in Europe. As far as history is concerned, the second half of the nineteenth century saw the publication of a great number of archival sources—under the auspices of the Academy and the Historical Society. Hungarian histories were published by László Szalay and by Mihály Horváth. At the end of the century, a ten-volume Hungarian history was published to mark the thousandth anniversary of the Magyar conquest; the work was edited by Sándor Szilágyi and had several authors. Partial research—in the spirit of positivism—served first and foremost to clarify the basic issues of political history, based on a large number of newly published sources. Such research also sought to reveal the background to events and to resolve chronological issues. A new generation of historians arose, young men who became acquainted with modern methods of source criticism at seminars held by Henrik Marczali at the University of Pest, as scholarship students at foreign universities, or under the guidance of Árpád Károlyi in the research group established at the *Staatsarchiv* in Vienna. Some of these historians went on to publish important works in the interwar period (Sándor Domanovszky, Gyula Szekfű, Bálint Hóman and Ferenc Eckhart).

In linguistics, the century-old controversy surrounding the origins of the Magyar language was finally resolved—in favor of the Finno-Ugric relationship—thanks to the work of Antal Reguly, Pál Hunfalvy, József Budenz, Bernát Munkácsy and József Szinnyei. Ármin Vámbéry, who believed in the Turkish origins of the Magyar people, is regarded internationally as one of the founders of modern

Turkology. Another orientalist who achieved international renown was Ignác Goldzieher, an expert on Semitic philology and the history of Islam. For anthropologists, the Millennium Exhibition was an opportunity to present changes in folk architecture and material culture; significant results were also achieved by folklore researchers such as Gyula Sebestyén and Lajos Katona. In the field of art history, Imre Henszlmann's work achieved international recognition.

In the study of law, the historicizing approach of the common law prevailed initially (Imre Hajnik and Ákos Timon). At the turn of the century, however, the new positivist legal philosophy gathered strength (Ágost Pulszky, Gyula Pikler and Bódog Somló). Pulszky and Somló were also some of Hungary's first sociologists. In the field of psychoanalysis, an international reputation was achieved by Freud's Hungarian disciple Sándor Ferenczi. Among the philosophers, one should mention Károly Böhm and Bernát Alexander, both of whom were followers of German idealism and adhered to the ideas of Kant and Fichte. New paths were explored at the beginning of the twentieth century by the young philosophers György Lukács and Károly Mannheim, but Lukács, who worked in the field of aesthetics, was still wavering between neo-conservatism and leftist ideals. In applied science, Hungarian statistics was fairly well developed in international terms (Károly Keleti, József Körösi and Lajos Láng).

Zoltán Magyary, the outstanding cultural political figure of the first half of the twentieth century, evaluated scientific development in the Dualist era as follows:

> In the last fifty years, a large number of cultural and scientific institutes were established in Hungary, and the cultivation of science produced significant results externally and—in many regards—substantial results internally. With the rise and development of the cities, Hungary's educated middle class became stronger, and they can now provide a supply of people for scientific careers, while sufficiently strong financial backing is provided for the publication of

> works containing the results of science and the movements promoting science... The cultivation of science tended to be extensive rather than intensive. Scientific inquiry and scientific research in the narrow sense were the consequence of certain people's individual efforts, rather than the effect of a school of science or a scientific plant... The international relations of science became well established prior to the war. Hungary frequently took part in and contributed to international scientific societies and congresses.[4]

The first great Hungarian encyclopedias, the results of cooperation between academics, scientists and experts, appeared: they included the Pallas and Révai encyclopedias. Similar collective endeavors were two series entitled *Osztrák-Magyar Monarchia írásban és képben* (The Austro-Hungarian Monarchy in Words and Pictures) and *Magyarország vármegyéi és városai* (The Counties and Cities of Hungary).

Literature and the Arts

The artistic and literary styles and schools of the era—historicism, realism, naturalism, impressionism, symbolism, surrealism, expressionism and *art* nouveau—were rather slow to appear in Hungary. It was only in the early twentieth century that Hungary fell into synch with literary and artistic developments in Western Europe. In Hungarian literature, "national classicism" (otherwise known as the popular-national style), which had prevailed earlier on, became less significant after the Compromise; it degenerated into academicism and epigonism. Leaving aside Petőfi, the old high standards could be seen only in the poetry of János Arany, a major poet of the school, who was now of advanced age. Even so, "official" literature continued to represent the aesthetic and moral norms of the popular-national style—once formulated by the strict critic Pál Gyulai—and to demand that they be applied by new writers. These transitional decades were a time of searching and questing. In poetry, János Vajda, Gyula Reviczky, Jenő Komjáthy and László Arany turned against the "official" style. In the last quarter of the century, novels and short stories became the dominant genre and aroused the interest of readers. Between the Compromise and the end of the century, more than 500 Hungarian novels were published; most of them were concerned with the problems of Hungarian society. Two of the period's most popular writers were novelists (whereas in the previous period, poets had tended to be at the forefront of literary development). The grand old writer and storyteller Mór Jókai continued to be the most widely read and popular novelist. In the 1880s, a similar popularity was achieved by Kálmán Mikszáth, who portrayed, in an original written style, the tragicomic decline of the world of the noble middle class. However, perhaps his novels portraying the lives of peasant farmers represented the zenith of his work.

The new modern literature grew in strength in the 1890s. The literary shift is usually dated to the launch of the magazine *A Hét* (The Week), edited by József Kiss (1890). The poets publishing in the magazine turned away from the aesthetic principles of "official" literature and adopted the norms of contemporary Western, primarily French, literature. The real breakthrough in modern Hungarian literature, the literary revolution, came a decade and a half later with the publication of a poetry volume by Endre Ady entitled *Új versek* (New Verses) (1906) and the launch of the journal *Nyugat* (West) (est. 1908). This was first and foremost a revolution of the poets (Endre Ady and Mihály Babits, Dezső Kosztolányi, Gyula Juhász and Árpád Tóth) and of poetic language and expression. Still, the poets were soon joined by the country's prose writers (Zsigmond Móricz, Géza Csáth, Frigyes Karinthy and Margit Kaffka). The magazine *Nyugat* was related less to contemporary Western European literature than it was to the literary schools and developments (mostly French) of the 1880s and 1890s, which were already passing away in France. In the world of theater, the foundation, in 1904, of the Thália Society under Sándor Hevesi (1904) meant the realization of new ideas. In the first years of the twentieth century, conservative literature—which rejected the revolutionary ideas of *Nyugat*'s writers—had several representatives of quality, such as Géza Gárdonyi and Ferenc Herczeg.

In architecture, the second half of the nineteenth century was dominated, in Hungary too, by historicism, an offshoot of romanticism. Various historical styles were copied. Frequently, elements from several styles were combined in a building. Historicizing eclecticism thus molded the external appearance of dynamically growing Budapest as well as that of the provincial towns. After the Compromise, in the course of city planning, impressive mansions and condominiums were built in the historicizing style, particularly on Sugár Street (later Andrássy Street) and the Grand Boulevard. Outstanding architects associated with this style include Frigyes Feszl (Vigadó Concert Hall, Budapest), Miklós Ybl (the Opera House), Frigyes Schulek (Matthias Church and the Fisherman's Bastion) and Imre Steindl (the Parliament building). The 1890s saw the development of the first modern architectural style: Hungarian *art nouveau*, or secessionism. Ödön Lechner and his pupils sought to develop a peculiarly Hungarian national style, combining *art nouveau* forms with decorative motifs originating in Hungarian folk art. The colored ceramics manufactured by the Zsolnay factory in Pécs were used in several buildings (such as the Applied Arts Museum and the Postal Savings Bank in Budapest). In the early twentieth century, several young architects (such as Károly Kós and Dezső Zrumeczky) drew inspiration from Transylvanian Hungarian folk architecture as they designed their buildings. Among Lechner's pupils, Béla Lajta began to apply the characteristic forms of modern functionalist architecture.

In the art of painting, historical and mythological themes prevailed during the first decades of the Dualist era (Viktor Madarász, Bertalan Székely, Gyula Benczúr and Károly Lotz). An important painter and graphic artist in the second half of the nineteenth century was Mihály Zichy, who spent much of his life in Russia as the court painter to the Russian Tsars. From the 1870s, realist tendencies began to appear in painting in Hungary. The best realist painter artist was Mihály Munkácsy, who received wide acclaim in Paris; even so, his latter paintings show signs of academicism. The other great Hungarian painter living in

France was László Paál, a late exponent of the Barbizon school. Munkácsy's realism lived on at the turn of the century in the works of the "Great Plain" painters. Pál Szinnyey-Merse, the pioneer of modern Hungarian art, produced an impressionist *plein air* painting (*May Picnic*) as early as the 1870s—that is, at roughly the same time as the French impressionist painters. Discouraged by rejection, he soon abandoned such experiments. The styles (mainly French) of earlier decades only became a part of Hungarian artistic life in the second half of the 1890s. The Nagybánya artists' colony was founded in 1896; it soon became a center of Hungarian impressionist and *plein air* painting (Simon Hollósy, Károly Ferenczy, Béla Iványi Grünwald, István Réti and János Thorma). The main workshop of Hungarian *art nouveau* and applied art was the artists' colony founded in Gödöllő in 1901 (Aladár Körösfői-Kriesch). The works of the artists at the colony in Kecskemét were also in the *art nouveau* style—with avant-garde elements. The artists' colony in Szolnok was a center of artistic realism, but it also attracted *plein air* painters and sculptors. József Rippl-Rónai became a leading exponent of the Hungarian *art nouveau* painting. In his younger years he had lived in Paris, where he belonged to the *Nabis* group. The post-impressionist and avant-garde schools were established by young artists who had separated off from the artists' colony in Nagybánya. The modern art revolution was represented by several rather short-lived artistic associations, such as the Hungarian Impressionists and Naturalists Circle (MIÉNK, est. 1907), as well as the Group of Eight (*Nyolcak*, est. 1909), whose members were supporters of avant-garde art. One particular and important artist did not belong to any of these groups: this was Tivadar Kosztka Csontváry, who maintained his independence throughout the period. Other artists resembling Csontváry in terms of their independence were László Mednyánszky and Lajos Gulácsy.

The upturn in sculpture art reflected in part the projects undertaken in the course of urban development—with orders for statues and sculpture. Leading Hungarian sculptors included Alajos Stróbl, György Zala, János Fadrusz, Miklós Ligeti and Ede Telcs.

In this field of art, the modern approach was represented by Márk Vedres and Füöp Ö. Beck.

An important gain for Hungarian musical life was the fact that Franz Liszt—who always considered himself to be Hungarian, even though he could not speak the language—spent several weeks or months in every year in Hungary from the mid-1860s onwards. In 1875, he became chairman of the Music Academy. The most important domestic composer until the turn of the century was Ferenc Erkel, who drew material for his operas from Hungarian history. In his works, the motifs of the popular "Hungarian" music of the late eighteenth century and the first half of the nineteenth century are welded to the contemporary style of European opera. At the beginning of the twentieth century, a revolution resembling that seen in literature and the fine arts took place in Hungarian music. Two young composers, Béla Bartók and Zoltán Kodály, began to collect and elaborate Hungarian folk music. Using this source, they established the modern Hungarian music style.

In the first two decades of the twentieth century, cinema and film became a part of art. In 1908, there were several dozen movie theaters in the country—mostly in Budapest. At first, short films lasting several minutes were produced, but as film technology developed, so feature films could be made. The production of feature films began in 1912. Annual film production increased from 18 in 1914 to more than 100 in 1918. Present during the infancy of Hungarian filmmaking were figures such as Mihály Kertész and Sándor Korda, who subsequently received international recognition (the latter under his Anglicized name of Alexander). The best actors and actresses of the era appeared in these early films.

Leisure Culture

With the development of modern society, culture became increasingly layered and diverse. Such diversity reflected the different expectations of the various social classes. So-called high culture was at the top; it comprised quality literature, art theater, fine art, classical music, the opera and exhibitions. High culture was favored by a very narrow section of the society: intellectuals, parts of the middle class and the aristocracy. For the rest of society, culture's entertainment value took precedence. Still, entertainment had its quality and popular versions. In literature, the entertainment genre, so-called popular fiction, meant novels and short stories that were easy to read and required little mental effort on the part of the reader. Such works were written even by such esteemed authors as Ferenc Herczeg and by the great storyteller Mór Jókai. Even Mikszáth's novels and short stories were widely read and considered to be popular. At the lower end of the market, we find the so-called pulp (or trash) literature, which sold in great quantities to several social groups: urban, lower middle class and rural. Workers and peasants generally read this type of literature. At the theater, entertainment meant comedies and light middle-class drama. Folk plays were very popular, especially among the lower middle class both in Budapest and elsewhere. Such plays portrayed a kind of idyllic pseudo-peasant world. At the end of the century, however, a rival to the folk plays appeared in the form of the operetta (which spread to Hungary from Vienna). In terms of action and script, the operetta was on a level similar to the folk play. Its strength, however, lay in the music, which, in the case of some operetta composers, could be of similar quality to opera music (and today operettas by Johann Strauss and Ferenc Lehár are performed at opera houses). In the early twentieth century, the Hungarian operetta matured and even became an exportable commodity (Jenő Huszka, Imre Kálmán, Viktor Jacobi and Albert Szirmai). Music hall (*café chantant,* in Budapest: *Orpheum*) was the lightest form of musical entertainment, but it was only for the wealthy, as one had to consume food and drink. Another form of entertainment favored by the urban middle class was cabaret. Gypsy music (*magyar nóta*), a type of Hungarian song in the folk style, reached its zenith in the second half of the nineteenth century and the early twentieth century. It was, first and foremost, a form of musical expression popular among the rural middle class, but it was sung and listened to by the whole of Hungarian society. Indeed, prior to the discovery of real Hungarian folk song, it was considered to be the true Hungarian music.

On Sunday afternoons, workers and domestic servants as well as lower middle-class families liked to visit the circus or the funfair (in Budapest it was called *English Park*). One third of Hungarian society lived exclusively within oral culture. In isolated rural communities, the traditional customs of folk culture still prevailed: people recited folk tales and sang folk songs. The nineteenth century saw the appearance of a "new style" of Hungarian folk song, greatly influenced by the music of the middle class.

During the era of Dualism—and particularly in its second half—sport became a popular aspect of leisure culture among various sections of Hungarian society. In earlier periods, the aristocracy had pursued sports such as horse riding, hunting and fencing. The latter sport was important to them, given that duels were still a part of aristocratic and gentlemanlike life. At the turn of the century, the upper and middle classes took to spending summer vacations at Lake Balaton or at one of the Adriatic resorts; Abbazia (Opatija) was a favorite destination. They also traveled to the Tatra Mountains. Cycling and skating became increasingly popular pastimes. Two gold medals were won by Hungary at the first modern Olympics, held in Athens in 1896. At each of the Olympics in the pre-war period, Hungarian sportsmen won several silver and gold medals in fencing, swimming, athletics and competitive shooting. The champions were still amateurs during this period. Budapest's first soccer match was played in 1896; soccer soon became a very popular sport. The year 1901 saw the establishment of the Hungarian Football Association and the holding of the first championship.

Notes

1 Cited in László Felkai, *Eötvös József közoktatásügyi tevékenysége* [József Eötvös's Work in Public Education] (Budapest, 1979), p. 216.

2 Zoltán Magyary, ed., *A magyar tudománypolitika alapvetése* [The Establishment of Hungarian Policy on Science] (Budapest, 1927), p. 369.

3 *A Magyar Tudományos Akadémia másfél évszázada 1825–1975* [150 Years of the Hungarian Academy of Sciences, 1825–1975] (Budapest, 1975), p. 158.

4 Zoltán Magyary, ed., *A magyar tudománypolitika alapvetése* [The Establishment of Hungarian Policy on Science] (Budapest, 1927), p. 369.

12. DOMESTIC POLITICS IN THE SECOND HALF OF THE DUALIST ERA

The resignation of Kálmán Tisza signaled the beginning of a new historical period in the Dualist Era. Indeed, at the turn of the 1890s, Hungary experienced change in all aspects of national life. In economic and social terms, this was the period in which the process of establishing a modern capitalist economy and a civil society was concluded. A fundamentally capitalist economic and a modern social structure emerged—albeit with many residual elements of the old, pre-1848, regime and other features of backwardness. It was also at this time that the effects of the industrial revolution were felt throughout the economy and that the country embarked upon a period of sustained economic growth. In the political sphere, Tisza's resignation not only marked the end of a government that had prevailed for a decade and a half, but also signaled the conclusion of a relatively stable period in the history of the Dualist system. The domestic political balance that had arisen after the 1867 Compromise was disrupted in both halves of the Dual Monarchy—first in Austria and then in Hungary (after the turn of the century). Over time, the contradictions and crisis features of the Dualist system were exposed. At the Ministerial Council held after the elections of February 1892, Francis Joseph anxiously noted that the Dualist system was in jeopardy, since opposition to the system was steadily growing on the extreme left of politics and among the general public. In his view, if this process continued, the forces opposed to the 1867 Compromise would become predominant, thereby ruling out the possibility of a peaceful and constitutional solution. In 1892, this was still not a direct threat, but 13 years later such a situation did indeed arise.

The 1890s saw the appearance of new overt tensions in Hungarian politics; by the end of the decade, the functioning of the Dualist system itself had begun to falter. After two decades of relative calm, the nationalities issue resurfaced (the following chapter discusses this issue in detail). The advent of large-scale industry led to a strengthening of the workers' movement, while the peace in the countryside was disturbed by the agrarian socialist movement and the harvesters' strikes. The Hungarian "culture war"—the liberal reform of ecclesiastical policy—led to mass demonstrations, protests and counter-protests throughout the country. New actors and party colors appeared on the parliamentary benches. Outside the legislature, new political parties and interest and pressure groups were formed.

The most important new phenomenon was the political stand taken by organized labor and by the associated agrarian socialist movement. Both groups posed a (theoretical) threat to the country's economic and social system.

The Socialist Workers' Movement

The pioneer advocates of socialist organization in Hungary were knowledgeable workers with a broad perspective, who—like many apprentices in the period—had traveled to and worked in other parts of Europe. In the mid-1860s, the ideas of Ferdinand Lassalle had been in the ascendant in Germany and Austria. It was his views that were heard by migrant workers from Hungary, who then imparted the ideas to fellow workers after their return home. In 1868, two workers' unions were formed in Pest-Buda: the Buda-Pest Workers' Union, which was a self-help organization, and the General Workers' Union, whose members supported Lassalle. Both these organizations were established by print workers, the best-organized group of skilled workers at the time. In subsequent years, a good number of workers' associations offering assistance and education were formed both in Budapest and in other urban centers. The associations providing assistance were grouped in a central body, the General Workers' Sickness Assistance and Disability Fund (est. 1870). Membership of this insurance fund was to rise to 52,000 by

1889. The year 1872 saw the organization of trade unions for workers employed in the same industrial branches; these unions then also fought for political rights and improved working conditions. The first coordinated strike in Hungary took place in 1871. Following a protest expressing sympathy with the Paris Commune, the leaders of the workers' unions in Budapest were arrested and then put on trial for "disloyalty." Although these men were acquitted by a court, the workers' movement organizations were thrown into disorder for several years; the General Workers' Union was even disbanded.

The workers' movement recovered a little when Leó Frankel, one of the leaders of the Paris Commune, returned to Hungary in 1876. In 1878, two political parties were formed: the Non-Voters' Party (at the time, workers were not entitled to vote) and the Hungarian Workers' Party. In 1880, the two parties merged to form the Hungarian General Workers' Party. In terms of its aims and principles, this new formation was a social democratic party, but the government did not permit it to call itself such. The party was weakened by internal power struggles, and Frankel left the country, having been found guilty in a libel case. The most stable workers' organization, forming the backbone of the movement and its financial base, was the sickness insurance fund. The party leadership drew support from the fund and had close personal links to it. The main group within the workers' party and sickness fund favored peaceful and lawful means—such as public talks, meetings and petitions—of promoting reforms of the electoral and factory laws as well as social policy. The party's moderate leadership faced criticism from various opposing factions. The leaders of the radical group were detained by the authorities in 1884.

In 1888, the Austrian Social Democratic Party was established through the merger of various workers' movements at the Hainfeld congress. The party's leader, Victor Adler, undertook to assist the organization of the Hungarian Social Democratic Party, having been inspired to do so by the leaders of the Second International. In 1890, 60,000 workers took part in a demonstration in Budapest to mark May 1. In December 1890, the founder congress of the Hungarian

Social Democratic Party was held. The "declaration of principle" published at the time repeated almost word for word the Hainfeld program of the sister party in Austria. Accordingly, the party's aim was to end the private ownership of the means of production, transferring them to common ownership. The declaration also demanded the introduction of general, direct and secret elections as well as civil rights—particularly the right of assembly and association. The first chairman of the party was Pál Engelmann, who belonged to its radical branch. In opposition to Engelmann there soon arose a more moderate grouping, for whom socialism's realistic path was organizing and educating the working class and implementing reforms within the framework of parliamentary democracy. This opposition group managed to defeat Engelmann, who was then expelled from the party. In response, the more radical group established the Hungarian Social Democratic Workers' Party. Later on, however, the two parties reunited (1894). The party merger congress addressed the agrarian issue, arguing that all land should be taken into public ownership and that large estates should be run collectively. However, landless agricultural workers and peasants with just 1–3 acres of land were keen to receive land and hoped for a land redistribution program in the event of a socialist victory. In 1897, the agrarian socialists left the party; under István Várkonyi's leadership, they established the Hungarian Independent Socialist Party, which undertook a successful agitation among the agrarian proletariat and poor peasant farmers of the Great Plain and Transdanubia.

In 1896–1897, a wave of strikes took place—more significant than before in terms of the number of strikers and their persistence. In 1897 and 1898, in the Great Plain and in Transdanubia, socialist-type agricultural workers' movements and poor peasants' movements sprang up. The Bánffy government attempted to subdue these movements, even resorting to unprecedented violence. A few dozen workers were shot dead by the gendarmerie or army. Several social democratic leaders were banished from Budapest. In the early twentieth century, the wave of strikes resumed. The largest disruption was the national rail strike of 1904, with the wave of strikes by industrial and agricultural workers peaking in 1905. In that year, the mass movements received an impulse from two sources. The first was the deteriorating financial situation due to the economic crisis, while the second was the example of Russia. "The whole country underwent a fundamental shift. In trade after trade, the workers of workshops, factories and buildings are putting down their tools… there is perhaps no other country—with the exception of Russia—in which the earth began to move to this extent," wrote the social democratic daily newspaper *Népszava* (People's Word).[1]

In the 1890s, trade unions were successfully organized. Indeed, the decade saw the establishment of a network of trade unions at the major industrial plants and the creation of national organizations representing the principal trades. The first trade union congress was held in 1899. By that time, the country had 126 trade unions with a total membership of more than 23,000. By 1904, membership had risen to 50,000. In the early twentieth century, the Social Democratic Party became welded to the trade unions.

The workers' movement in Hungary made significant progress by the end of the nineteenth century. It managed to popularize the ideas of socialism among the industrial and agricultural proletariat in the course of a long struggle against the government authorities. At the turn of the century, the leadership of the Social Democratic Party began to accommodate the conditions set by the government. Exploiting the legal framework, it successfully organized the urban and rural proletariat, serving as a beacon in the political and economic struggle. Although the party—as a legal mass party—became a significant factor in national politics, nevertheless it did not receive parliamentary representation for the duration of the Dualist Era.

The new program adopted at the party congress in 1903 defined "the liberation of the working class" as the movement's ultimate goal. This aim could only be achieved "through a systematic and resolute class war," "by conquering political power," and by ensuring "public ownership of the means of production." Among the immediate goals of the party, the first priority was universal and equal suffrage and a secret ballot—with voting rights for women too. The party proved unable to draft appropriate programs and develop successful policies on the agrarian issue and the national issue. In neither area did its position correspond to the admittedly odd and complex conditions prevailing in the country. Instead, it relied on generalities and was doctrinaire. In the twentieth century, the workers' movement began to organize along ethnic lines in multinational Hungary. Most workers belonging to the nationalities were kept within the party due to the establishment, from 1904, of special committees for the nationalities, which were under the auspices of the party. In Croatia, the Croatian Social Democratic Party was formed in 1894. A greater stir was caused by the establishment of an independent Slovak party in Pozsony (Bratislava) in 1905. The founders of the new party claimed that the Hungarian Social Democratic Party had fallen under the influence of Hungarian nationalism and was failing to acknowledge non-Hungarian workers. In their view, the party had become an instrument of the policy of Magyarization. A year later the Slovaks also returned to the united national party.

Agrarian Socialist Movements

At the turn of the 1890s, socialism began to penetrate the country's villages. This development marked the start of a revival of the agrarian movement among agricultural workers and poorer peasant farmers. To understand this process, one has to examine the situation in the middle of the century.

In 1848, 60 percent of serfs in Hungary were cotters possessing 1–3 acres of land or they were landless. After the abolition of serfdom, when the common pastures and forests were divided up among the landowners and peasant communities, the cotters also received a small amount of land. In this way, 60 percent of Hungary's agrarian population comprised landless laborers or poorer peasants, the so-called "dwarf-holders" who had some land but could not make a living from it and who were therefore required to undertake paid employment. According to the 1895 national agricultural survey, 53 percent of farms had less than seven acres of cultivated land. In the 1850s and 1860s, landowners who had lost the free labor (*robot* service) of their serfs, let their land to their former serfs, who generally became sharecroppers. The agrarian proletariat and poorer peasant farmers found abundant work on the railway and dyke construction projects. In the late 1860s and 1870s, as international demand for Hungarian grain increased, the landowners took control of their wheat-growing land and let only their maize-growing land to sharecroppers—who received one half and then one third of the crop. Poor peasant farmers had fewer and fewer opportunities to rent land. Maize sharecropping opportunities became increasingly scarce, while the number of applicants grew. It thus became customary for the chosen sharecropper—the peasant or worker winning the lease—to give presents in money and in kind to the landowner (this was called "usury" or "the tithe") and to work for free on his estate or in his household (the *robot* service). Agricultural paid work also became scarcer, as horse-drawn equipment and hand-threshing were replaced by machine-threshing, and tasks such as seed-sowing and hoeing became mechanized. The length of the harvest time was reduced by a half. Thus share-harvesters could take less and less grain home. Due to the grain sales crisis, the price of grain fell dramatically. This in turn meant that employers could pay lower and lower wages. In the meantime, the population underwent rapid growth, and the rate of natural increase was highest on the Great Plain. In the course of the 1880s, the large-scale railway and dyke construction projects were gradually concluded. In railway construction, local railways became the priority—and their construction required fewer workers. Indeed, opportunities for waged work on such projects decreased dramatically. Despite its rapid growth, factory industry was still modest in size; it was unable to provide employment to large numbers of workers. It was towards the end of the 1880s that socialist agitators appeared in the country's towns and villages. This doubtless explains why the increasingly impoverished agrarian population of the Great Plain was attracted to the movements in the early 1890s. After the turn of the century, they were joined by the agrarian poor of Transdanubia.

The movement first appeared in the southeastern part of the Great Plain, in the counties of Békés, Csanád and Csongrád. It was here that the ratio of agricultural workers and dwarf-holders was the highest. The first two actions were connected with the May 1 celebrations in 1891, thus indicating that socialist ideas, as well as local factors, were a contributory factor. In May and June 1891, in Orosháza, Békéscsaba and Battonya, thousands of workers clashed with the gendarmerie and with soldiers deployed in order to restore order. Three years later, in April 1894, protesting workers clashed with soldiers in Hódmezővásárhely. The organizer of the demonstration, János Szántó Kovács, chairman of the General Workers' Union in Hódmezővásárhely, and his associates were arrested and received prison sentences of several years. In January 1895, thousands of agricultural laborers held a protest in Szeged. The government announced a state of emergency in the region and dispatched military reinforcements.

The immediate aims of the movement were to improve working conditions, to raise wages, to increase the share received by share-harvesters, to ensure the abolition of the *robot* service and tithe, and to secure protection for workers against abuses of power on the part of landowners and rich peasants. As far as long-term goals were concerned, there were two factions. One faction adhered to the social democratic program: achieving public ownership of the large estates and then cultivating such land collectively. The other group sought land redistribution; it wanted the land taken from large landowners to be divided up equally. The agrarian movements of the early 1890s clearly succeeded in drawing the attention of the political elite to the agrarian issue and to the poverty suffered by poor peasant farmers.

The agrarian movement of the rural proletariat remained true to its socialist roots throughout the period, but the Social Democratic Party soon lost control of the movement. In 1897, the Hungarian Independent Socialist Party was formed under the leadership of

István Várkonyi as the party of poor peasants and agricultural workers. The party demanded that Church-owned lands be taken into public ownership. Under its plans, these lands—together with government-owned lands—would then be leased in seven-acre lots to peasants. It wished to see the same procedure applied to privately owned land in excess of 100 *hold* (142 acres).

In 1897 and 1898, further large-scale agrarian actions took place. In the summer of 1897, 15,000 agricultural workers in 14 counties (the Great Plain and Transdanubia) went on strike at the time of the harvest. This harvest strike soon spread to the northeastern areas of the Great Plain. In February 1898, a series of land-squatting actions took place in Szabolcs County.

The Bánffy government attempted to put a stop to the agrarian actions by deploying unprecedented force and by calling in the army. (It had employed similar tactics against urban industrial workers earlier on.) At the time of the Bánffy terror, hundreds of workers were arrested and convicted, including István Várkonyi, the leader of the Independent Socialist Party. The agrarian socialist movement led by Várkonyi—which had successfully agitated among poor peasant farmers in eastern Hungary in the final years of the nineteenth century—fell into decline in the early years of the twentieth century. In its place the organization and direction of the peasants' movement in the Great Plain region and to the east of the River Tisza fell to another formation that had broken away from the Social Democratic Party, the Reorganized Social Democratic Party, founded by Vilmos Mezőfi in 1900. This group even managed to organize a thitherto neglected group, poor peasants belonging to one of the nationalities. In 1906, Mezőfi was elected as a representative in one of the constituencies to the east of the River Tisza. He thus became the first avowedly socialist member of the Hungarian Parliament. Mezőfi and his group rejected internationalism and supported the idea of the Hungarian state. Gradually, they fell under the influence of the pro-independence opposition.

The agrarian actions became less vigorous for several years after 1898. In the summer of 1905, harvest workers and agricultural estate workers in southern Transdanubia held a series of strikes. Five thousand soldiers and gendarmes were deployed to deal with the 20,000–25,000 striking day laborers and agricultural estate workers. Furthermore, 6,000 "reserve workers" were brought in (legislation governing work contracts in the agricultural sector did not recognize the right to strike; on the contrary, participating in a strike was a punishable offense).

The strikes of agricultural workers tended to be successful. The harvesting of the crop was of vital importance to landowners. This task was still performed by hand even in the early twentieth century (as mechanized harvesters were still rather scarce in Hungary), and so partial concessions were often made to the workers. One of the fiercest strikes of the era took place in 1905. It was concluded by the end of the harvest with better wages and conditions for workers.

The agrarian socialist movements were manifestations of a peculiar rural form of the socialist idea. In earlier periods, religious beliefs and respect for traditions had defined the mentality of Hungarian peasant farmers. According to Péter Hanák, who studied in depth the ideas of Hungary's agrarian socialist movement in the late nineteenth century, "Socialism caught the imagination of poor peasants and agricultural laborers languishing in impoverished conditions: they adopted many of its demands, slogans, fighting methods, forms and symbols, subsequently integrating them into their own traditional and religious mentality." The movement "developed the forms characterizing the peasant-farmer interpretation of socialism (its reinterpretation as a religion) and characterizing the socialistic secularization of traditional religions."[2]

Old and New Political Parties

Hungary's first modern mass political party was the Hungarian Social Democratic Party, which formed local branches and levied a membership fee (the "party tax"). In the light of limited suffrage, the party could not gain seats in Parliament, but it was capable of taking a hundred thousand people onto the streets. It could also organize strikes, paralyzing the whole country or a particular industrial sector.

In the 1890s, a new type of party appeared in the Parliament—the Catholic People's Party. This party was founded in 1895 at the time of the "culture war" surrounding the ecclesiastical policy laws. The party's chairman was Count Nándor Zichy, who shared leadership of the party with Count Miklós Móric Esterházy as well as the parish priest of Komárom, János Molnár. The party was founded on Christian ideals; its stated goal was a revision of the ecclesiastical policy laws and the realization of Catholic autonomy. Its program contained demands for social policy measures on behalf of smallholder peasant farmers, industrial artisans and workers. The party emphasized the importance of fair and equitable procedures with regard to the nationalities. It did so because it wished to win over Catholic peasant farmers and lower middle-class people among the German, Slovak and Ruthenian populations. It was the first parliamentary party to establish a national organization, reliant principally upon a broad network of Catholic associations, on Catholic Circles, and on the Catholic League. In the early years of the twentieth century, the Catholic People's Party drifted towards support for the constitutional opposition and it neglected its social program. This program was then taken up by the Christian Socialist movement, which, in 1907, became organized in the National Christian Socialist Party (Sándor Giesswein was its only representative in the Parliament). In early 1918, the People's Party and the Christian Socialist Party merged to form the Christian Social People's Party, adopting the principal parts of the Christian Socialist program.

In 1900, Vilmos Vázsonyi founded the Bourgeois Democratic Party. Both the Bourgeois Democrats and the Christian Socialists demanded the introduction of universal suffrage, the abolition of parliamentary seats awarded on the basis of wealth, legal guarantees for civil rights, free public education, government social policy provisions offering protection to small agricultural and industrial producers, the regulation and government control of worker–

employer relations, compulsory accident, sickness disability and pension insurance for workers, the legal protection of the family home, small farms, workshops and shops, a system of progressive taxation, the abolition of consumption taxes, and a tax exemption for the minimum wage. The Christian Socialist program proposed changes to "unhealthy" land ownership relations, the division of land into plots, and the settlement of lands owned by the government or by local municipalities and public foundations. The non-constitutional parties emphasized the need to resolve social problems and stressed the importance of greater democracy in the political system.

Vázsonyi's party received most of its support from the lower and middle echelons of the urban middle class. Indicative of the search for political independence among peasant landowners was the foundation of a whole series of peasant parties in the early twentieth century, including the Hungarian Independent Socialist Peasant Party, established in 1906 by L. András Áchim, a rich farmer from Békéscsaba. Its members were mostly peasants from the region to the east of the River Tisza. Meanwhile, in 1908, in Balmazújváros, the National Agricultural Workers' Party was founded. In 1909, smallholders in Transdanubia formed the National Forty-Eighter and Independent Smallholders' Party under the leadership of István Nagyatádi Szabó. In addition to their democratic and social policy demands, all three of these parties emphasized the need to resolve the land issue and the need for a government plan to divide the large estates into peasants' plots. Finally, in 1914, progressive intellectuals established their own party, the Civic Radical Party.

These new political parties—all of which were unconstitutional parties—were unable to bring radical change to parliamentary politics. The Catholic People's Party was the only one to obtain 20–30 seats at the elections; the others sent the occasional one or two representatives to the Parliament, where the traditional constitutional parties and their various splinter groups continued their bickering.

In early 1892, the conservative Moderate Opposition led by Albert Apponyi renamed itself the National Party. The party's program included the following explanation for the change in name:

> We want a national politics based on the Compromise of 1867: we adhere to the policies of Ferenc Deák, and we are supporters of the Compromise, which in fact merely gave substance to the Pragmatic Sanction's Dualist principle, to joint defense and to Hungary's national and state independence. The government and its party said the same thing about themselves. But their policy has turned the Compromise into a slope, which they will slip down until they renounce the idea of an existence of an independent nation and state.[3]

The basic position of the National Party continued to be defined by its agrarian ideas, to the extent that when in 1899 Kálmán Széll, who belonged to the agrarian wing of the government party, became the head of the government, Apponyi and his fellow parliamentarians joined the Liberal Party. In the 1890s, the conservative agrarian wing of the governing Liberal Party grew stronger in relation to the mercantile group (which had been dominant until then). Agrarian views were also put forward vociferously by a group of 17 men—the Forty-Eighters—who had left the Independence Party in 1890. This group was headed by Gábor Ugron and promoted a moderate pro-independence program in constitutional matters. In its election manifesto published in late 1891, the Independence and Forty-Eighter Party restated its belief in Hungary's full independence within a purely personal union. In 1895, the party elected as its chairman Ferenc Kossuth, who had returned to Hungary from Italy. The son of Lajos Kossuth, Ferenc Kossuth was a railway, bridge and tunnel engineer of European repute, but he had inherited little of his father's talent for politics.

In addition to the parties, an ever-greater role in politics was played by various lobby or pressure groups, whose representatives were present in several political parties, where they tried to influence the policies of these parties for the benefit of a particular organization or social group. The lobby groups tended to reflect the opposing agrarian and mercantile interests. Agrarian interests were represented initially by the Hungarian National Economic

Association, which had been established during the Reform Era, in the 1830s. In 1896, the Hungarian Farmers' Association was established; it lobbied principally on behalf of large and medium-sized landowners, but it also represented the interests of smallholders and even assisted in organizing peasant cooperatives. The chairman of the Farmers' Association and the founder of the cooperative movement was Count Sándor Károlyi. The National Federation of Industrialists (GyOSz, est. 1902) and the Hungarian National Commercial Association (OMKE, est. 1904) were organizations representing "mercantile" big capital and the entrepreneurial *grande bourgeoisie*. In the early twentieth century, the Society of Szekler Parliamentary Representatives and the Alliance of Szekler Societies were formed to represent the interests of a particular region (in Transylvania).

Political Ideologies and Social Ideas

Liberalism was the leading ideology in the Dualist Era. Most politicians subscribed to it—both government and opposition politicians. Indeed, liberal ideology was the cornerstone of the country's legal system and government apparatus. However, the liberalism of the Dualist Era became ever more detached from the liberalism of the middle third of the nineteenth century; rather than continue the process of modernizing the country, it wished to conclude it. Moreover, it sought to conserve rather than continue to develop prior achievements and progress. For this reason, it is often referred to as conservative liberalism. The system failed to continue developing the system in a democratic manner, because an expansion of political rights (including the right to vote) would have threatened the Dualist system as well as Magyar hegemony. As in other parts of Europe, liberalism forged ever closer links with nationalism. Thus, in order to maintain Magyar hegemony, limits could be imposed on liberalism. The chief ideologue of the Liberal Party, Gusztáv Beksics, frankly admitted that "if liberalism and Magyar interests were to clash, then I would, without any consideration, sacrifice the former on the altar of the latter."[4] The gradual replacement of classical liberalism with a new kind of revisionist liberalism was a general European phenomenon at this time. The primary manifestation of neo-liberalism was government intervention. From the 1880s onwards, such intervention took place even in the most advanced countries. In Hungary it was particularly justified in the light of the challenges faced by the country as it tried to catch up with Western Europe.

A peculiar version of liberalism fused with nationalism was the Great Power nationalism at the turn of the century. The essence of this development was that the Magyar people should take on the leading role within the Dual Monarchy, and that Magyars should be ready to run the Monarchy's Great Power politics—particularly with regard to the Balkans. The arguments and goals of Great Power nationalism were formulated by Count Gyula Andrássy, Jr.:

> Rather than negate our joint institutions, we should try to achieve a position on the matter of joint institutions in which our influence is decisive... The Monarchy's relations render it natural and its interests desirable that we should take the leading role within it in a political sense. We constitute a united country with a great past. Austria, meanwhile, is a mosaic of nationalities and provinces without domestic unity. In addition, the Hungarian race far exceeds in political and statehood matters the peoples who are allied to us.[5]

Dezső Bánffy and István Tisza also agreed that "the Magyar nation was the one destined to take charge of the political leadership of this Monarchy."[6] The special "state-constituent capacity" of the Magyar people—which in the eyes of contemporary public opinion legitimized Magyar "supremacy" over the nationalities and the idea that the multinational country should be regarded as the "Magyar national state"—received historical "verification" from the contemporary legal historical school.

Some nationalist publicists and journalists became rather detached from reality; for instance, they wrote of the complete assimilation of the nationalities, 30 million Magyars, Greater Hungary, and even a Hungarian empire, Hungarian imperialism, and expansionism in the Balkans. Such ideas were without foundation, but in the nationalist atmosphere of the era they certainly had an effect on Magyar public opinion.

At the turn of the century, as a further development of liberalism, the progressive ideology of the Hungarian left wing—civic radicalism—was elaborated. Its supporters were middle-class intellectuals with a European cultural perspective. From 1900, this group published the journal *Huszadik Század* (Twentieth Century). The group held debates on Hungarian society and politics under the auspices of the Society of Social Sciences and of the Galilei Circle (a university students' group). They sought the consequential conclusion of Hungary's modernization, the eradication of the residual elements of the old aristocratic-feudal system, and the realization of a democratic Hungary. The group was particularly influenced by the ideas of Herbert Spencer; its main supporters were positivist philosophers of law as well as sociologists such as Ágost Pulszky and his students Bódog Somló and Gyula Pikler. Oszkár Jászi gradually became the most important representative of middle-class radicalism.

The late 1870s and early 1880s saw the appearance—as demands were made for greater government intervention—of a second major ideological current: neo-conservatism. There were two major versions of it. It was initially supported by an agrarian group of large and medium-sized landowners. Then, in the 1890s, Catholic neo-conservatism appeared. Neo-conservatism was in effect a response to economic liberalism and to the negative consequences of free capitalist competition. Unlike liberalism, it called for social solidarity and government policies and legislation to protect ordinary citizens and workers as well as those harmed by capitalist competition. It also sought to reorganize society on a more representative basis. The neo-conservatives did not call into question the achievements of political liberalism and the establishment of civil rights; indeed, Catholic neo-conservatism desired an extension of political rights (universal suffrage). Supporters of neo-conservatism considered it to be more a modern option than liberalism and a more effective response to the problems of a modern society. There can be no doubt that neo-conservatism introduced to Hungary new methods in the field of societal organization and mobilization as well as new organizational frameworks.

The agrarian group demanding government subsidies for agriculture never transformed itself into an independent political party; members of the group were thus to be found in both the government party and the opposition. They attempted to realize their goals by means of the Hungarian Farmers' Association (est. 1896), which was in effect their lobbying organization. Major supporters of the group were Count Albert Apponyi, Count Sándor Károlyi and the ministers of agriculture of several governments, including Ignác Darányi.

The social program of Catholic neo-conservatism was more radical; its main aim was to address the problems faced by peasant farmers, the lower middle class and workers. It did so in the spirit of Pope Leo XIII's social encyclical, *Rerum Novarum* (1891). Catholic neo-conservatism also gave rise to political parties (the People's Party and the Christian Socialist Party), but these parties usually maintained contact with the masses by way of the associations, cooperatives and labor organizations. As many of Hungary's capitalists were Jewish, the neo-conservative groups became increasingly affected by moderate or more radical anti-Semitism.

The Szapáry Government

After the resignation of Kálmán Tisza, Francis Joseph appointed Count Gyula Szapáry—who had been serving as minister of agriculture—as prime minister. Szapáry was a typical aristocratic politician of the era; he brought with him his good name and connections rather than skills and talent. During the previous 17 years, he had held various ministerial posts, which had allowed him to become acquainted with the governmental and parliamentary routine. In none of these posts, however, had he managed to score successes. Similarly, most of the lasting achievements of his government were connected to the names of excellent government ministers—principally Sándor Wekerle and Gábor Baross. Wekerle's great achievement was a deficit-free budget and the reform of the taxation system, with the introduction of alcohol tax and sugar tax to stimulate production, as well as the foundation of new factories, the successful conversion of all government debt, and, finally but importantly, a reform of hard currency, the realization of the conversion to gold currency (the crown). Meanwhile Baross broadened government industrial subsidies and introduced a system of rail freight tariffs that gave preference to domestic industrial products over imported industrial articles, thereby stimulating Hungarian industrial exports. He also offered tax allowances to banks providing support to domestic industry. In 1890, at Baross's initiative and with the cooperation of the Wiener Bankverein, the Hungarian Commercial and Industrial Bank was formed with the purpose of supporting the formation and development of industrial companies. In 1891, in order to benefit the milling industry, the government introduced the so-called "milling traffic" mechanism. Under the mechanism, major exporting mills could import cheaper foreign wheat without having to pay customs duties, as long as they undertook to export the flour produced from the wheat to foreign markets within a year. Baross also played a key role in launching government social policy: he submitted a bill concerning compulsory sickness insurance for industrial workers.

In contrast to its rather effective economic and social policy, the Szapáry government's principal aim—public administrative reform and its control by central government—was a failure. The government sought the reform because the middle and lower levels of the system of public administration were controlled by the elected representatives of the county governments. Szapáry and liberal politicians in the government party believed that the counties were guilty of pursuing a politically active role in national affairs rather than focusing upon local government concerns. It urged for a clear distinction between political administration, which it regarded as the task of central government, and the tasks of local government, such as looking after local interests. The bill for a change in the legal status of the counties was supported even by the moderate opposition. The pro-independence opposition, however, obstructed passage of the bill, leaving Szapáry with no choice but to withdraw it. In its place a shorter piece of legislation was adopted, which laid down the stipulation that "public administration in the counties is a task of the state [central government], which is to be performed by appointed agents of the state" and which instructed the minister of the interior to submit a bill on the practical realization of this principle. Such a bill was never drawn up.

The pro-independence opposition, which formed a sizeable minority, managed to force the government to withdraw its public administrative reform. It was at this time that a possible revision of the house rules (*cloture*) was raised, but the liberal politicians of the government party were reluctant to limit freedom of speech in this manner. In subsequent years, the opposition used the weapon of obstructionism with increasing frequency. At the elections in February 1892, the government party lost 20 seats, while both the constitutional opposition parties strengthened their position. Thus 243 government party representatives faced 101 pro-independence representatives and 61 moderate opposition representatives, as well as eight representatives with no party affiliation.

Hungary's "Culture War": The Reform of Ecclesiastical Policy

After the failure of the public administrative reform, an opportunity to continue the liberal reforms arose in the field of ecclesiastical policy. Five different marital laws were in force in Hungary, and each of the officially recognized religious denominations had its own jurisdiction in marital disputes. This gave rise to problems, especially in the case of mixed marriages. Most of the problems surrounded the religious affiliation of children in mixed marriages. In this regard, the provisions of the Catholic Church clashed with the law of the land (1868), whereby sons were to adhere to the religion of their father and daughters to the religion of their mother, and which also disqualified agreements between parents concerning the religion of their children. A common occurrence was the so-called "erroneous baptism," whereby a Catholic priest would christen a child who belonged, under the law, to another denomination. This, however, counted as a petty offense under the Criminal Code. In 1884, Minister of Education and Religion Ágoston Trefort decreed that in such cases, the priest performing the baptism was required to inform the legally competent clergyman, so that the latter could then register the birth of the infant. Priests did not always adhere to this.

Trefort had no desire for a conflict with the Catholic Church, and turned a blind eye to "erroneous baptisms." His successor Count Albin Csáky, however, wished to restore order in this area. In February 1890, he repeated Trefort's previous decree concerning illegal baptisms, now holding out the possibility of punitive sanctions. Most of the Catholic priests were still not obedient to the ministerial decree, citing Rome's protests. Pope Leo XIII even sent a letter to Francis Joseph, in which he emphasized the point that the decree and the 1868 law "trample underfoot the rights of the Church" and the rights of parents with regard to the choice of religion of their child.[7] The Pope asked for an amendment of the 1868 law and the revoking of Csáky's decree. A whole series of court actions was initiated against "baptizing" Catholic priests accused of minor offenses. In the autumn of 1890, the government—with the consent of Francis Joseph—decided that, if necessary, it would submit a bill on the introduction of civil registration. For the time being, however, it wished to settle the matter through negotiations with the Bishops' Conference and with Rome. The possibility of a *modus vivendi* was explored in Rome, but it was emphasized that the Church was not prepared to give up its principles concerning marriage. Much of the Catholic priesthood as well as believers joined together to form a movement opposed to liberal ecclesiastical policies.

In the spring of 1892, Kolos Vaszary, who had been appointed as the new Prince Primate in 1891, traveled to Rome to mediate on this sensitive matter. To his astonishment, he was told the following by the Pope:

> These secular institutions (the civil registration of births and deaths and civil marriages) exist almost everywhere... In spite of these institutions, our Church and our religion remain firm; indeed, in many places they are growing and strengthening. You should resist, for as long as you can, the introduction of these secular institutions in Hungary, because it would be better if they did not come into being. If, however, they are introduced, you will cope somehow, as others have done elsewhere, and the Church will not be destroyed in Hungary because of them.[8]

These words show that Rome had effectively come to accept the civil registration of births and deaths as well as civil marriages, but that it wished to use the struggle against the introduction of liberal ecclesiastical policy laws to shake up Hungary's rather passive and apathetic Catholics and encourage them to become more active in public life and in politics.

The former Benedictine teacher and abbot Vaszary, who had little political experience, misinterpreted the Pope's words. He told Szapáry that there was no objection to the partial introduction of the civil registration of births and deaths and compulsory civil marriages, and that even the Holy See had come to terms with this idea. "Without doubt, Vaszary made a grave tactical mistake by telling Szapáry these things. One might say that he even encouraged the government to make the ecclesiastical policy reforms, reassuring them that Rome would be unlikely to raise objections even if civil marriages were introduced," wrote a Catholic historian of the "culture war" in Hungary.[9]

Having heard Vaszary's position, the government decided to introduce the partial civil registration of births for children born in mixed marriages. For its part, however, the Lower House adopted a more radical resolution, which served as the foundation for bills elaborated by Albin Csáky, the minister of education and religion, and Dezső Szilágyi, the minister of justice, with regard to compulsory civil marriages, the general introduction of the civil registration of births and deaths, free worship, and the "reception" of the Jewish religion (that is, its official recognition by the state). In September and October 1892, the proposals were discussed in the course of several Ministerial Councils. Government ministers could not reach an agreement. Prime Minister Szapáry wished to introduce the partial civil registration of births and deaths but not compulsory civil marriages. A majority of ministers, however, insisted upon the more radical original proposals. For his part, Francis Joseph considered it to be unnecessary to regulate all ecclesiastical policy matters. Since he was opposed to compulsory civil marriages, he refused to authorize the government to announce their introduction. In response, Csáky resigned, and this action was followed by the resignation of the whole government. Szapáry's position in the government party suffered a blow, as a majority of representatives made clear that they would only support a government that was in favor of compulsory civil marriages.

Francis Joseph found himself in a difficult and awkward situation. His Catholic conscience—which led him to agree with the position of the Church—conflicted with his perceived responsibility as the head of state with the primary task of upholding the Dualist system. In this latter regard, his sole support came from the Liberal Party, which, however, was one of the main advocates of radical ecclesiastical policy reforms. As a result, Francis Joseph became increasingly resentful of the liberal government and the government party; he felt that they were forcing him to take measures that conflicted with his Catholic conscience. Indeed, he was told that a failure to take these measures might result in the collapse of the government party's majority—with grave consequences for the Dualist system. In the light of the government crisis, Francis Joseph inclined towards a conservative shift, based on a fusion of the government party's right wing and the National Party. Still, he was alarmed by the national program of Apponyi and his supporters, a program that theoretically accepted the Compromise but attacked its very foundations by calling for the common army to be organized on a "national" basis. Such a measure would have been unacceptable to Francis Joseph. He thus had no choice but to entrust Wekerle with the formation of a new government. Wekerle made no substantial changes to the composition of the government. On appointing Wekerle, Francis Joseph gave his consent to the announcement of the introduction of compulsory civil marriages—and the new prime minister did include this in his program speech. But Wekerle also pledged that the law on marriage rights would repeal the provision of the act of 1868 concerning the religion of children in mixed marriages. That is to say, parents would be able to freely choose the religion of their children.

Sándor Wekerle was Hungary's first prime minister of a non-noble background. In some ways his appointment marked the beginning of a new era in Hungarian public life: aristocratic or noble descent and the ownership of land were still important accessories of a political career, but they were no longer indispensable to it. A man could compensate for their absence through his talent, knowledge and expertise. Wekerle's career is a good example of this: he began working for the Ministry of Finance at the age of 22, gradually ascending through the ranks until his appointment as a government minister 19 years later. Between 1892 and 1918, he was appointed three times as prime minister and also served as minister of finance for 12 years. He was the most successful minister of finance in Hungary's history, and he also headed each of the other government ministries for shorter and longer periods. A contemporary politician and historian, Gusztáv Gratz, who knew Wekerle well, described him in the following terms: "The country had not had such an excellent politician since 1867; he was one of the best on domestic issues. His great knowledge and resourcefulness and his unparalleled experience in managing political issues enabled him to conceive of new solutions in the most difficult of situations. He was one of a rare breed of Hungarian statesmen whose world of ideas was made more fertile and enriched by economic knowledge and ideas. He made a creative contribution to all types of matters. There was no one who was better informed about issues affecting Hungarian political life, government administration and economic necessities. In these issues he demonstrated great creative power; he played a constructive role in everything that he undertook."[10] Wekerle was certainly an excellent speaker, who avoided vacuous speech and presented what he had to say in a professional manner; his clear and logical arguments usually convinced even the opposition. Contemporary observers compared him to Gladstone.

The ecclesiastical policy issues caused divisions within the constitutional parties. There were both supporters and opponents of radical ecclesiastical policy reform in the government party, the National Party and the Independence Party. Since supporters of reforms were in a majority in each of the parties, the new government could expect a higher level of parliamentary support for its reform program. The greatest problem was distrust and hesitation on the part of Francis Joseph. Through his patience and clever tactics, Wekerle managed to secure the ruler's consent to the submission of a bill. Thus, in the spring of 1893, Albin Csáky submitted the legislative proposals concerning the civil registration of births and deaths, the legal equality of the Jewish religion, and free worship. Francis Joseph still refused to give his consent to a proposal for civil marriage.

In 1893–1894, the country and the media became an arena for the Hungarian "culture war." Those protesting against the ecclesiastical policy reforms included not only the Catholics but also the Romanian and Serbian Orthodox Churches as well as the Lutheran Slovak and Transylvanian Saxon communities. The Reformed (Calvinist) dioceses, however, supported the government. Both sides in the debate organized mass meetings and other demonstrations. In May 1893, the Upper House adopted a resolution condemning the government's ecclesiastical policy. Tensions were raised further when the Pope addressed an encyclical to the Hungarian bishops beginning with the words *Constanti Hungarorum*. In the encyclical the Pope called upon the bishops to defend the rights of the Church firmly and to hold annual meetings promoting an awakening of the Catholic spirit. "It is time to begin something bigger," wrote the Pope, targeting in particular the press, the religious education of young people and the training of priests. The effect of the papal encyclical was counterbalanced by the pronouncements of Lajos Kossuth, who had not returned to Hungary but enjoyed great popularity in the country. Kossuth gave his clear support to the ecclesiastical policy reforms: "I do not consider it to be liberalism, but quite simply a sensible and elementary postulate." He wished to leave the issue of the religion of children in mixed marriages to parents because this was the natural right of parents. Addressing a delegation from the Independence Party, Kossuth stated the following:

> I am very pleased that the Wekerle government has included the resolution of ecclesiastical policy issues in its program. I would be very sorry if the government should fail because of the ecclesiastical policy issues. The power of the Independence Party will never be complete unless it takes a definitive position in the field of 'liberal' progress and in the resolution of ecclesiastical issues.[11]

The government wanted to submit to the Parliament legislative proposals concerning compulsory civil marriages and an amendment to the act of 1868. Faced with the ruler's opposition and hesitation, Wekerle twice offered his resignation. Finally, at the Ministerial Council of November 6, 1893, Francis Joseph declared the following:

> I consider the marriage legislation to be a danger to the peaceful development of the country. Under normal conditions, I would consider it to be a duty of conscience to deny my consent. However, under these circumstances, I recognize the political necessity of strengthening the government in its energetic defense of its existing constitutional basis, and so I shall consent to the introduction of the act.[12]

When Kossuth heard that some of the Independence Party's representatives were planning to vote against the reform in order to bring down the government, he dissuaded them from doing so in his last letter, written a month before his death: "Whatever corresponds to the liberal position of the constitutional opposition must be accepted—even if this comes from the devil himself."[13] In the light of Kossuth's position, the overwhelming majority of the Independence Party's representatives voted in favor of the proposals. Even half of the members of the National Party supported the reforms, despite the fact that Apponyi, the party's leader, declared his opposition to compulsory civil marriages. Thus, in April 1894, the Lower House voted by a large majority for the introduction of compulsory civil marriages, having also given its support to the three other proposals. In May, however, the proposal was rejected in the Upper House by 20 votes. The proposal was sent back to the Lower House, where, however, it once again received the support of a large majority of representatives.

In the meantime, Imperial Court circles as well as the two common ministers—Minister of Foreign Affairs Count Gustav Kálnoky and Minister of Finance Benjamin Kállay—voiced their opposition to the liberal reforms, advising Francis Joseph to express a lack of confidence in the Wekerle government. For his part, Wekerle was quite aware that he had failed to secure Francis Joseph's trust. He thus decided to bring the issue to a head, demanding that Francis Joseph express clear support for the proposed reforms and overrule opposition to the reforms in the Upper House by appointing new members to that house. When Francis Joseph refused to meet these demands, Wekerle submitted his government's resignation. Francis Joseph accepted it and entrusted an old confidant, Károly Khuen-Héderváry, with the formation of a government. When, however, ministers from the Wekerle government returned home from Vienna, they were greeted by a cheering crowd, and the Liberal Party also gave them a vote of confidence. Under such circumstances, Khuen-Héderváry could not even begin to form a government. Thus Francis Joseph had no choice but to appoint Wekerle once again. Csáky retired voluntarily, and his place was taken by Lóránd Eötvös, the internationally renowned physicist. In this way, the crisis of May 1894 ended with the victory of the Wekerle government.

In the end, Francis Joseph caved in, considering the enactment of the proposals to be a political necessity. He personally requested several opposition members of the Upper House to be absent at the time of the second vote. The Upper House then approved the new marriage law by a majority of four votes. It also gave its approval to legislation governing the registration of births and deaths, as well as the religion of children. On the other hand, it sent the two other legislative proposals—free worship and the "reception" (or official recognition) of the Jewish religion—back to the Lower House. The ruler then delayed ratifying the civil marriage legislation. By doing so, he expressed his ill feeling towards the government and its liberal reforms. In late November, a rather dispirited Wekerle offered his government's resignation in return for ratification of the laws. Francis Joseph accepted this and proceeded to ratify the three ecclesiastical laws: the civil marriage legislation; legislation concerning the religion of children—enabling prospective marriage partners to agree, prior to their marriage, upon the religion of children born into the marriage; the civil registration of births and deaths. At the end of the year, Wekerle duly submitted his government's resignation. Under the Bánffy government, the other two legislative proposals were subsequently adopted by the Upper House—after the appointment of five further new members by the ruler. Thus, in the autumn of 1895, Francis Joseph ratified legislation granting recognition to the Jewish religion and guaranteeing freedom of worship.

These developments marked the end of the Hungarian "culture war," a process that saw the strengthening of the government party's position. The struggle also had positive consequences for the Catholic Church. As a Catholic historian concluded, "The recent culture war purified and strengthened the Catholic Church and led to a renaissance of Hungarian Catholicism."[14] Rome's expectation was fulfilled: in the course of the ecclesiastical policy struggles, Catholics became more active in public life, while political Catholicism extended its influence, even organizing itself into a political party (the People's Party was formed in early 1895). The number of Catholic associations and journals increased substantially.

At a critical stage in the struggle over ecclesiastical rights, the government also had to address a very different problem. In Turin, on March 20, 1894, Lajos Kossuth, the political leader of the Hungarian War of Independence of 1848–1849, died at the age of 92. In 1849, Kossuth had been made Hungary's regent-president; at his behest, the National Assembly had declared the dethronement of the House of Habsburg. Francis Joseph prohibited public mourning for Kossuth and forbade the "Crown's" ministers, senior public officials, and military officers from attending the funeral. Wekerle covertly assisted the administration of the funeral ceremonies. At his behest, the City of Budapest undertook to bury Kossuth as an honorary citizen. Tens of thousands of people from near and afar made a pilgrimage to Kossuth's bier. His burial in Budapest on April 2 was an expression of national remorse. Members of the government were not the only ones absent from the funeral; also not attending were members of the Upper House, senior churchmen (with the exception of two bishops) and the high sheriffs (*főispán*).

The Bánffy and Széll Governments

Francis Joseph tried once again to exploit the resignation of the Wekerle government to realize his favorite plan for a merger of the right-wing parties and the establishment of a conservative political force. He was encouraged by the fact that at the time of the ecclesiastical policy debates, several representatives had left the Liberal Party temporarily, while the conservative National Party was also a supporter of the Compromise. Francis Joseph himself held negotiations on this subject for almost two weeks in Budapest. In order to be included in the government, however, the National Party would have had to renounce its military-related demands (for instance, that a Hungarian Magyar national feature be applied in the common army), because such demands were unacceptable to Francis Joseph. Apponyi—the leader of the National Party—was not prepared to do this. Still, as he later wrote in his memoirs, there were some within the party who implicitly blamed him for failing to seize this opportunity to join the government and for his refusal to countenance a merger—at the cost of renouncing some of the National Party's demands.

After the failure of talks aimed at securing a conservative party fusion and the formation of a government, Francis Joseph was forced to turn once more to the Liberal Party, appointing the chairman of the Lower House, Baron Dezső Bánffy, to the post of prime minister. Since everyone considered Bánffy to be a rather insignificant figure and unsuited to the post, his appointment was accepted merely as a temporary solution. The ruler himself was less than impressed with the man, it seems, as he wrote the following to Minister of Foreign Affairs Kálnoky: "Regrettably, no other choice remained but Bánffy, who enjoys the support of the party. However unsatisfactory this solution may be, there is no alternative at the moment."[15]

Dezső Bánffy was a Transylvanian aristocrat—but one of the poorest. According to his biographer, as the high sheriff (*főispán*) of two Transylvanian counties, "he relentlessly pursued the interests of the Hungarian state, as the most determined representative of Magyar chauvinism."[16] He may not have been a statesman, but Bánffy certainly had substantial routine knowledge of public administration, in the light of his long career in the counties. Contemporaries said that even when he became head of the government, he was still a high sheriff, treating the whole country as a large county. In Bánffy a great national awareness was combined with a rather narrow perspective and a parochial way of thinking. His government did not include the big names, but was composed of "second-rate" politicians. Even so, the greatly mocked "gray cabinet" turned out to be a strong and functional body. An outstanding member of the government was the minister of agriculture, Ignác Darányi, who initiated an active social policy with the aim of regulating working relationships in agriculture. Darányi also drafted legislation concerning the reconstruction with government assistance of vineyards destroyed by philoxera. To reduce poverty among Ruthenian peasants in the Carpathian region and to develop their economy, he set in motion the so-called "hill-country action plan."

At the time of Bánffy's appointment, the ruler himself established the "main thrust" of the government's program: the ecclesiastical policy laws should be implemented with moderation and by taking into account the sensitivities of the Churches; there was a need for suppression of the "increasingly dangerous workers' movement, in particular the agrarian movement of the Great Plain"; also to be suppressed was any agitation on the part of the nationalities that was "unlawful and disruptive, endangering the idea of the Hungarian state," but at the same time there was an appreciation of the rightful wishes of the nationalities.[17]

Bánffy considered his primary task to be the suppression of the growing socialist workers' movement and the agrarian movement and bringing to a halt agitation by the nationalities (for he ignored Francis Joseph's instruction to satisfy the rightful demands of the nationalities). To facilitate the task, he set up, within the prime minister's office, a "department for nationalities and socialistic affairs." He tried to slow down the advance of the workers' and agrarian movements by means of increased administrative controls, legal actions, and sometimes brutality—with the assistance of the police and the military. The nationalities protested at the adoption of legislation governing the names of villages and other places (1898), which declared that a village could have no more than one official name and that decisions in this field would be taken by the minister of the interior or a national committee on villages. The law did not state that the official name should be in Hungarian, but in subsequent years a growing number of villages that were not inhabited by Magyars received official Magyar names.

In 1896, the whole country celebrated the thousandth anniversary of the Magyar conquest. There were spectacular processions and colorful celebrations. In addition to the Millennium Exhibition in Budapest, other projects were finished at this time, including more than 900 kilometers of new railway. In Budapest itself an underground railway, the Grand Boulevard, two bridges over the Danube, two new museums and a new theater were opened. The Parliament ordered the construction of 400 new government-run elementary schools and the establishment of the Fine Arts Museum. In the same year, the economic boom of the 1890s reached its zenith. Francis Joseph, the Imperial Court, and a large part of the Viennese diplomatic corps spent most of the year in Budapest, and it was at this time that the Interparliamentary Union held its conference in the city. Budapest seemed almost to have become the Monarchy's capital, and this greatly enhanced the national consciousness of the Hungarian political elite. The rather heated debates in the Parliament ceased for a time, owing to the *Treuga Dei* between the political parties—an agreement proposed by Albert Apponyi. On the other hand, the leaders of the nationalities boycotted the country's Millennium celebrations.

At the time of the parliamentary elections in 1896, Bánffy's administrative apparatus tried to prevent the election of opposition candidates—particularly those of the People's Party. This action, which included unscrupulous measures, was successful: only 18 of 98 People's Party candidates received seats in the Parliament. Meanwhile the government party managed to strengthen its position, receiving 70 percent of seats.

In order to soothe the feelings of an opposition annoyed by such electoral abuses, the government made an extension of the modern civil justice system the focus of its legislative activity. In 1896–1897, the Court of Public Administration was established, and this measure was followed by the enactment of Hungary's first code of criminal procedure, which supplemented in a fitting manner the Criminal Code of 1878. Another innovation was the establishment of juries at all criminal sentencing courts. Of no lesser importance was the introduction of detailed legal regulations governing public finance. Bánffy also managed to persuade the ruler to agree to several measures that had long been urged by the opposition. Thus, in 1897, legislation was adopted concerning the establishment of three Hungarian military colleges, while the Ludovika Academy, where military officers for the Hungarian defense force (*honvédség*) were trained, received a higher academic status and was made equal in status to the academies of the common army. On the fiftieth anniversary of the 1848 Revolution, a memorial day was instituted in law. However, the date selected as the national holiday was not March 15, the day of the Revolution in Pest-Buda, but April 11—the day on which the 1848 laws were ratified.

The opposition could not be pacified by liberal legislation, military-related concessions or the "rehabilitation" of 1848. Underlying the various government crises were grave conflicts festering among the ruling classes: an economic conflict of interests between the agrarian and mercantile lobbies, as well as the anti-liberalism of the gentry middle class. Behind the scenes, agrarian interest groups were stoking antipathy towards the government. At the end of the century, their main demand was an increase in agrarian tariffs. They campaigned against grain speculation on the exchange and for an end to customs exemptions on grain imported for milling purposes. They also disapproved of government subsidies for industry. Overall, they demanded a radical modification of the liberal economic policy.

In 1897, a renewal of the economic aspects of the Compromise (the Commercial and Customs Union) became due. Austrian and Hungarian agrarian interests exerted substantial pressure on their respective governments with the aim of ensuring that the new agreement provided for increased agrarian tariffs. Industrial and commercial interests within the Monarchy opposed substantial agrarian tariff increases. Austria's middle class, which watched jealously as Hungary made progress in the field of industrial development, sought limits to subsidies for industry and an increase in the quota, or contribution ratio, payable by Hungary. Meanwhile, Hungarian industrialists and artisans once again demanded the introduction of a separate customs area. The two governments actually managed to agree upon the necessary changes. Nevertheless, the draft legislation could not be brought before the Austrian Parliament, because the *Reichsrat* had become incapacitated due to the opposing national interests, while the government suffered repeated crises. Accordingly, the Parliament extended the existing Compromise for one year—until the end of 1898. In 1898, the two governments agreed upon the fundamental principles of the new agreement. The agreement was advantageous to Hungary with regard to the bank of issue and the accounting of consumption taxes. Such taxes were now to be due to the country in which the goods had been consumed. This had been Tisza's plan 20 years earlier. Meanwhile, agrarian tariffs were raised. Since the *Reichsrat* once again proved unable to discuss the issue, the two governments agreed that the existing Compromise would be extended until 1903. At the behest of the Austrian government, this was subject to the proviso that if a new economic compromise was not established by the end of 1903, then the old agreement would remain in force indefinitely.

The opposition interpreted this clause as the government's renunciation of a right due to the country, namely its economic independence. It began to obstruct the government's budgetary legislation as well as its four-month indemnity proposal. In early 1899, the country had no approved budget; for the first time in its history the country found itself in an unconstitutional situation, or *ex lex*. There was no doubt that Bánffy's government had fallen, but the identity of his successor was unknown. In the Liberal Party, Kálmán Széll seemed to be the most suitable candidate. In the 1870s, Széll had excelled as minister of finance. Since quitting the government, he had worked in banking. He had good relations with both the agrarian lobby and finance capital. At Francis Joseph's request, he held negotiations with the opposition, which, in return for Bánffy's dismissal, was prepared to agree to a compromise. After the pact had been established, Francis Joseph appointed Kálmán Széll as prime minister. In effect, the party merger urged by the ruler at the time of earlier government crises was finally made: the National Party merged with the government party "without any reservations." As a result of the fusion, the government had its largest-ever majority.

Széll's government brought several years of calm to domestic politics. Beneath the surface, however, the old political antagonisms remained. The government party broke into three parts: the "old guard" liberals led by Kálmán Tisza and his son István, Apponyi's group, supported by most of the agrarians in the government party, and a group of aristocrats centered around Count Gyula Andrássy, Jr. The advance of the agrarian group became manifest in the elections of 1901. Although the Liberal Party maintained its large majority, nevertheless the opposition strengthened significantly. The leader of the agrarian group, Count Sándor Károlyi, announced an antiliberal and neo-conservative program that was radically opposed to the principles of the government party.

At the behest of the opposition, a law was passed concerning the supervision of elections to the Parliament, which made the Royal Curia responsible for the fairness of elections. A law of incompatibility was adopted as well. The rules introduced in 1875 were tightened up: an entrepreneur in a business relationship with the government could not be elected to the Parliament, and nor could members of the executive or supervisory board of a company in such a business relationship. Minister of Agriculture Ignác Darányi proceeded with his social policy legislation. He established a national assistance fund for agricultural workers and laborers. At the behest of agrarian interests, he abolished the customs exemption on grain imports that were to be milled and then re-exported. Széll managed to reach an agreement with the Austrian government concerning economic aspects of the Compromise. The Austrian government accepted the so-called Széll formula, according to which if a new compromise could not be reached Hungary could theoretically become "a separate customs area." At the same time, the old economic compromise agreement (signed in 1887) was declared valid until the end of 1907. Széll consented to an increase in Hungary's quota (its contribution ratio) from 31.2 to 34.6 percent. On the last day of 1902, Széll and the Austrian prime minister Koerber agreed on the principles of the new economic compromise, which increased both industrial and agricultural tariffs significantly. However, neither the Hungarian Parliament nor the Austrian Parliament could confirm the new agreement.

The Crisis

The modernization of the army necessitated an increase its size. Thus, in January 1903, the Széll government submitted a bill concerning an increase in the size of the common army and the Hungarian army. The opposition wanted to ensure the use of the Hungarian language in the common army. Since Francis Joseph rejected such a change and insisted upon the unity of the army and its supranational character, the opposition adopted a policy of obstructionism. In June Széll resigned and Francis Joseph requested Count István Tisza (the son of the former prime minister Kálmán Tisza) to form a government. Tisza declared that he would even resort to armed force to reestablish order in the Parliament. Consequently, no one from the government party was prepared to join his government. Károly Khuen-Hédervįry then formed a government, but he too was unable to resolve the parliamentary crisis. Finally, in November 1903, Francis Joseph once again appointed István Tisza as prime minister, who tried to bring an end to the obstructionism—to which he referred as "a policy of killing the nation"—by changing the house rules. In his view, "Hungary's complete national existence is linked with the order of the Parliament and the functioning of the constitution."[18] Apponyi and his supporters consequently left the government party, soon reorganizing the National Party. In the spring of 1904, the opposition retreated, and there was a short period of peace in the Parliament. Even so, Tisza continued to insist upon a revision of the house rules. On November 15, he submitted a legislative proposal to this effect, and three days later, government party representatives accepted the proposal—by means of a parliamentary coup and amid scandalous and unprecedented scenes in the Parliament. (Tisza's new regulations included measures that had been implemented decades earlier in the parliaments of Western Europe.) Tisza wanted to end the "obstructionism" game, which he believed would result in disaster for the country—but in fact it brought about the end of 30 years of rule by the Liberal Party. The following day a coalition of the two opposition parties—which had been bickering among themselves until this point—was formed; it included the various Independence Party factions as well as the National Party, the People's Party, the Bourgeois Democratic Party, and the New Party formed by Dezső Bánffy. The coalition was joined by politicians from the government party who disapproved of Tisza's policy, a group led by Count Gyula Andrássy, Jr. In response to the government's coup, opposition representatives destroyed the fixtures in the Lower House (in the impressive neo-Gothic building, which had just been inaugurated). The Parliament was dissolved and in the elections held in early 1905 the Liberal Party suffered a defeat. The leading party in the opposition coalition, the Independence Party (which had merged with Apponyi's National Party shortly before the elections) received, on its own, more seats than the government party. After the elections, the Tisza government resigned; however, at Francis Joseph's behest, ministers remained at their posts until mid-June.

Thus, in early 1905, a situation arose that had not been seen since 1867. According to parliamentary practice, the ruler should have chosen someone from the opposition coalition—which had received an absolute majority in the elections and enjoyed widespread public support—to form a government. However, the program of the main party in the coalition—the Independence Party—rejected the Dualist system, including the common army and the customs union. And even the smaller parties in the coalition—those that accepted the Dual Monarchy—insisted on Hungarian as a language of command in the common army. The coalition's program promised political, economic and social policy reforms in rather generalized terms, including an extension of the right to vote, the economic separation of the two halves of the Monarchy and preparations for independence, as well as "an emphasis on the national character of the Hungarian army both linguistically and symbolically."[19] Such demands were unacceptable to Francis Joseph, who firmly insisted upon the army's unity and its supranational character, which he saw as the supreme guarantee of the Monarchy's Great Power status. He was supported in this by the Gautsch government in Austria and the

Parliament in Vienna, as well as by Archduke Francis Ferdinand, who considered Magyars to be natural rebels and who had an antipathy towards "the Magyar rabble, to which every Magyar belongs, whether he be a government minister, a prince, a cardinal, a burgher or a peasant."[20]

Among the coalition leaders, Francis Joseph tried initially to win Gyula Andrássy over, but he too was insistent that the opposition's military demands be met. As discussions concerning the formation of a government continued, the crisis became increasingly grave; strikes by industrial and agricultural workers spread throughout the country. As discussions were fruitless, the only solution was the appointment—in 1905—of a government of extra-parliamentary officials, led by the former minister of defense, Baron Géza Fejérváry. The government faced an atmosphere of general distrust and hostility; even Tisza and the Liberal Party refused to support it. After the Lower House and the Upper House held a vote of no confidence in the government, a call was made by the coalition to "national resistance." Most of the counties refused to fulfill the decrees of the government, to collect taxes, and to dispatch new recruits. At Minister of the Interior József Kristóffy's behest, the promise of universal suffrage was made in order to win the Social Democratic Party's support as well as the support of progressive radical intellectuals such as Oszkár Jászi and Endre Ady and progressive bodies such as the Society for Social Science, and the journal *Huszadik Század.* In July, Kristóffy and the leaders of the Social Democratic Party signed an agreement: the minister of the interior revoked police supervision of the party and authorized greater freedom to action, while the party began organizing workers' meetings and demonstrations in support of the government—which had promised universal suffrage—and against the coalition's national and military demands.

Meanwhile in Vienna, other options were considered, in addition to the political solution: the office of the General Staff drafted war plans "for an armed solution to a crisis in Hungary" and a possible "war against Hungary" (*Kriegsfall U*).

Possible solutions to the Hungarian crisis were discussed at a meeting of the Crown Council, held at Francis Joseph's summer residence in Ischl on August 22. Three options were considered. The first was an agreement with the coalition—which was subject to the ruler's conceding to Hungarian military-related demands. Prime Minister Fejérváry was in favor of the second option: the government should try to win the support of the people at a renewed election by announcing a reform program (universal suffrage, social reforms, a homestead law, and a revision of economic relations, including the establishment of a separate customs area and an independent Hungarian bank of issue). The third option was the introduction of overt absolutism and a military response, which was regarded as likely if the Hungarian Parliament were to embark on a revolutionary path at the beginning of the autumn session on September 15. Austrian Prime Minister Gautsch recommended the revision of the Compromise; he considered the division of the Monarchy into two parts to be a lesser evil than the introduction of universal suffrage—which, in his view, would lead to great disruption and destroy even the foundations of the system. The minister of foreign affairs, Gołuchowski, also opposed a reform of the electoral law. In the end, Francis Joseph was more inclined to allow preparations for a reform of the rules on suffrage than to make concessions concerning the Hungarian military-related demands.

Still, on September 15, 1905, there was no repeat of the events of March 15, 1848. Despite the expectations of the military commanders in Vienna, the day did not turn into the start of a new Hungarian revolution. In late August, some of the coalition's leaders—Dezső Bánffy, Gyula Andrássy and Ferenc Kossuth—had initiated secret talks with Vienna, primarily with Gołuchowski, who wrote the following about them to the ruler: "They are no longer so certain of success, the possibility of violent measures is a great problem for them, and the radical socialist program of the Fejérváry cabinet has frightened them."[21] Since everything pointed to a softening position on the part of the coalition, as a sign of his willingness to hold discussions, Francis Joseph accepted the government's resignation on September 12; he then showed a willingness to receive the opposition leaders.

The Social Democratic Party planned to hold its largest demonstration to date on September 15—the day of the opening of the Parliament's autumn session. Throughout the country workers spoke of revolution. The protests in Budapest took place on September 15, or "Red Friday," and they were linked with a general strike. In the Parliament, party leaders submitted a petition demanding the introduction of universal suffrage. Thereafter the crowd quietly dispersed. Francis Joseph received the leaders of the coalition on September 23. In a short statement he ruled out military-related changes and emphasized the continuance of common affairs. He demanded from the coalition leaders—in return for their being entrusted to form a government—an immediate response to the budgetary problem and an urgent vote on bonuses for new recruits.

After this "five-minute audience" the coalition leaders negotiated among themselves but could not reach an agreement: the moderate more conciliatory leaders were opposed by a more hostile element, mostly from rural areas. The "national resistance" regained strength, In Budapest there were clashes between supporters of the coalition and workers. At a meeting in Fiume (Rijeka) the Croatian opposition parties decided to support the Hungarian coalition (the "Fiume Resolution") and the Serbs soon followed suit. The Croat–Serb coalition became an important ally to the Hungarian coalition. In early October the situation became very tense. On October 8, couriers dispersed orders relating to "*Kriegsfall U*" to the army's command centers in Hungary. However, at what was expected to be a critical session of the Parliament on October 10, nothing happened; members of the coalition simply acknowledged the adjournment of the Parliament. Several days later, couriers took the secret commands back to the Ministry of Defense in Vienna, where they were burnt. On October 16, Francis Joseph once again requested Fejérváry to form a government. Since the ruler had now given his consent, universal suffrage and certain social reforms were included in the government program. The struggle for voting rights in Hungary was supported by social democrats and liberals in Austria and even by the neo-conservative Christian Social Party on the right of the Austrian political spectrum. In Austria too, a great suffrage movement was appearing, which questioned how the Emperor could deny to Austria what he had conceded to Hungary (i.e., universal suffrage). The demonstrations and protests in Vienna and Prague were larger and more violent than those in Budapest and other Hungarian cities. On November 3, Francis Joseph informed the Austrian premier Gautsch that he intended to consent to universal suffrage in both halves of the Monarchy. (This concession was indeed granted in Austria in 1907, but it was never implemented in Hungary prior to 1918.)

The Fejérváry government published its political and social reform program in late October 1905 and began to organize its own party. Both these endeavors ended in failure. Even the Liberal Party unanimously rejected the government's program. Francis Joseph had no choice but to repeatedly adjourn the Parliament. The Budapest government was no longer in control of public administration; indeed, most county and municipal authorities took no heed of central government orders. By the end of the year, the national resistance had spread to 45 of the country's 63 counties. On the other hand, organized labor in Budapest and several other major cities supported the government—whose situation, however, was hopeless in the absence of the support of the Parliament and the public administration apparatus. On several occasions Fejérváry signaled a desire to resign, but Francis Joseph would not accept his resignation. In January 1906, Fejérváry wrote the following to the ruler: "It is quite impossible here in the heart of Europe, among cultivated states, to continue to tolerate such unbridled rampaging, which is bringing the country to moral, political and economic ruin and is also severely jeopardizing its Great Power status and thereby monarchical and dynastical interests." He suggested the proclamation of a state of emergency, a dictatorship with a program of radical political and social reforms. The proposal was rejected by Francis Joseph and his advisors, but the ruler did consent to

Kristóffy's submitting his electoral reform bill—which foresaw the granting of voter rights to all men aged over 24.

In early 1906, a will to compromise was felt by a growing number of members of the coalition's steering committee, and public officials in an increasing number of counties grew tired of the stand-off. Thus secret negotiations between Francis Joseph and the coalition leaders were recommenced in December 1905. The latter surrendered an increasing number of their demands in early 1906. In February, Francis Joseph dissolved the Parliament—whose building was then occupied by the military. These actions did not lead to national protests. By March, opposition in the country was limited to just ten counties. A majority on the coalition's "steering committee" was prepared to make a "fair deal." Ferenc Kossuth played a leading role in brokering a settlement (and thus, in 1906, Lajos Kossuth's son assumed the role played by Ferenc Deák in 1867). Francis Joseph was also prepared to make a deal, and so a pact was arrived at in early April 1906. The coalition agreed to drop its military-related demands, to vote in favor of the budget and the bonus for new recruits, to maintain the customs union, to enact the foreign trade agreements and the autonomous customs tariff, and to implement electoral reform. The "new compromise" thus led to the abandonment of the coalition's complete program, a fact that it sought to conceal from the public. The coalition thus portrayed the pact as a sacrifice made in order to restore the constitution and as the victory of the national idea. This was an expression of the circumstance that in Hungary the politics of 1848 could only be pursued on the basis of the Compromise of 1867. One of Tisza's supporters noted: "The coalition was in the saddle, but it soon transpired that it could not ride."[22]

Another factor inducing a compromise was fear of the social and political movements of the workers. In the country's cities, industrial workers held meetings and protests where they demanded universal suffrage and a secret ballot. In early 1906, it was reported from the counties of the Great Plain that agricultural workers were planning to strike at harvest time. According to the minister of agriculture, "A more extensive strike during the harvest would be a fatal blow to the country in the current situation... and it would also mark the start of economic and social chaos, which the government authorities would not be able to cope with in today's disheveled conditions."[23] The Ministerial Council also believed that the country "faced a social threat that might become fatal."[24]

The government was prepared to accept a continuation of the conditions set by the 1867 Compromise, but a majority in the Parliament was in favor of independence. Most of the representatives and ordinary members of the Independence Party were completely unaware of the commitments made by their leaders prior to the formation of the government. These leaders had portrayed the pact as a victory, whereas in effect it had been a capitulation. They claimed that they had undertaken to form a government while upholding their principles. Except for members of the government, no one knew that Francis Joseph had completely ruled out acquiescing to the demands of the Independence Party. When the expected successes—the "national achievements"—failed to materialize, the Independence Party became wracked by disaffection and discord, which led ultimately to the development of an internal opposition and the break-up of the party.

The Coalition Government

Sándor Wekerle became the head of the coalition government. He was a convinced supporter of the 1867 Compromise, who had not belonged to either of the coalition parties but was acceptable to both the coalition and Francis Joseph in the light of his earlier success as a statesman. Wekerle also became minister of finance. In 1906, he joined the Constitution Party, led by Gyula Andrássy. The leaders of the coalition parties became government ministers: Ferenc Kossuth (trade and transport), Gyula Andrássy (the interior), and Albert Apponyi (education and religion). Ignác Darányi, who had been a successful minister in previous governments, became the minister of agriculture.

At the behest of István Tisza, the Liberal Party declared its dissolution in April. Thus the coalition parties faced no rivals in the elections of May. The Independence Party secured more than 60 percent (253 seats). The Constitution Party, comprising representatives who had left the Liberal Party in 1904, had 84 seats. The Catholic People's Party secured 33 seats. Meanwhile the parties of the nationalities received 25 seats in the Parliament. After long and difficult negotiations with the other side, the government finally upheld the customs union with Austria (subject to minor amendments). It was renamed: instead of being referred to as a Commercial and Customs Union, it was called a Commercial and Customs Contract, and this change was subsequently presented to the public as a great advance. Hungary's contribution to joint costs, its quota, was increased from 34.6 to 36.4 percent. A significant increase in agricultural tariffs favored the interests of rural landowners—who were well represented in the coalition.

In its pact with the ruler, the coalition agreed to an extension of voting rights. Minister of the Interior Andrássy drafted an electoral rights bill, which was based on a very complicated pluralistic electoral system, but the bill was opposed by the coalition partners and the legislation was never adopted. Organized labor continued, however, to demand universal suffrage and a secret ballot. In October 1907, this movement held a general strike to press its demands; almost 100,000 workers demonstrated in Budapest and the country's regional urban centers.

The coalition government's principal achievements were in the field of social policy: for instance, in 1907 it passed a law on the provision of compulsory accident and sickness insurance to industrial and commercial employees. This legislation significantly increased the number of insured persons; it also increased the amounts of assistance provided and placed the whole insurance scheme under government control. The government provided funds for the construction of housing for workers and initiated the construction of modern residential estates near Budapest. Steps were taken to resolve the working conditions of agricultural laborers—including the provision of compulsory accident insurance. Government aid for industry was greatly increased, while livestock breeding received additional support and incentives with a view to improving the quality of herds. The taxation system was reformed and modernized in order to meet the new social conditions.

The government's policies with regard to the nationalities were far less successful. The year 1907 saw the adoption of two legislative provisions that were greatly criticized by the nationalities. The Railway Service Act prescribed that all railway employees—even those in Croatia—be able to speak Hungarian. This provision turned the Croat–Serb coalition against the Hungarian coalition. The heroes of the obstructionist "comedies" of earlier years were shocked to see their former allies, representatives from Croatia, employ the same tactics against them: for several weeks the Croats made never-ending speeches (in Croatian) in the Parliament (for the Croats were allowed to make speeches in Croatian in the Lower House in Budapest), thereby testing the patience of representatives from other parts of the country. The legislation introduced by Albert Apponyi, the minister of education and religion, provided for a satisfactory settlement of the supplementary salary paid by the government to teachers in non-government (municipal or denominational) schools, but by repeating a provision of an earlier piece of legislation (the Education Act of 1879) it prescribed the following: "In elementary schools where Hungarian is not the language of instruction, the Hungarian language is to be taught in all classes of ordinary courses to that the extent that children whose native language is not Hungarian are able, on completion of the fourth grade, to express their thoughts in Hungarian, both in writing and orally." What became known as the "*lex Apponyi*" also prescribed the following:

"All schools and all teachers should develop and strengthen in the children a spirit of devotion to the Hungarian *patria* and a sense of belonging to the Hungarian nation. This aspect must be applied to all teaching; moreover, as an external expression, the Hungarian coat-of-arms should be placed above the main entrance in all schools and in appropriate places in classrooms; wall-charts relating to Hungarian history should be displayed in classrooms, and the Hungarian flag with the ensigns should be raised on the building on national holidays."

If a school taught a curriculum that had not been established by the minister, or if it used unauthorized textbooks, then teachers at the school were not to receive the government-funded salary supplements. The coalition government continued its tough policy against the nationalities: with increasing frequency, disciplinary proceedings were launched against teachers in schools where Hungarian was not the language of tuition; furthermore, an increasing number of lawsuits were initiated against nationality politicians and journalists, often leading to prison sentences of one or two years.

The coalition made little progress in terms of securing "national achievements"—and yet this was the public's main expectation of the new government. A successful action was the negotiated return to Hungary of the ashes of Prince Ferenc Rákóczi II and his fellow émigrés, who had died in Turkey, and the holding of a ceremonious reburial in Kassa (Košice) Cathedral in October 1906. But even this was not really an achievement of the coalition, because István Tisza had already obtained Francis Joseph's consent to the action in 1904. Meanwhile no progress was made on the military issue, even though the government significantly reduced its demands. Francis Joseph was unwilling to make any concessions in this area and Francis Ferdinand, the heir to the throne, was even more adamantly opposed. The Austrian government supported Francis Joseph in his stance. At the time of the Hungarian crisis and during the period of the coalition government in Hungary, there arose in Austrian politics a movement that sought a detachment from Hungary. For supporters of the "*Los von Ungarn*" movement, the best option was the complete separation of the two countries—which would remain linked by a joint ruler. In their view, this would be better than conceding to the Hungarian demands of 1848 in relation to the army and other joint institutions.

The final collapse of the coalition was caused by the central bank issue. The issue had not been addressed during negotiations concerning the economic compromise. The coalition parties, including the Independence Party, could not reach an agreement. In late 1908, there developed within the party a banking group led by Gyula Justh. This group sought an independent central bank for Hungary. In subsequent months, it managed to win the support of a majority of Independence Party representatives. However, Wekerle, Kossuth and Apponyi did not agree with them. As a compromise solution, the so-called “cartel bank” plan was drafted: two independent banks would form a cartel, so that the advantages of a common currency could remain and “Hungarian” demands could also be satisfied. However, after lengthy hesitation, Francis Joseph rejected the plan. In response, the Wekerle government resigned in late April 1909. The government crisis then lasted for more than two months. When negotiations aimed at establishing a new coalition government were unsuccessful, Wekerle’s old government returned to office in July. During the summer, the ruler and Francis Ferdinand tried to involve former Liberal Party politicians in the coalition government, by means of the former minister of finance, László Lukács, but their efforts were in vain. In late September, the Wekerle government resigned once more. In November, owing to differences of opinion on the central bank issue, the Independence Party broke into two parts: the Independence and 1848 Party led by Gyula Justh—which sought an independent Hungarian central bank as well as universal suffrage—and the Forty-Eighter Independence Kossuth Party, led by Ferenc Kossuth. This development marked the final breakdown of the coalition of the opposition parties established in 1904.

It was at this point that the old supporters of the 1867 Compromise resurfaced. In late November, Francis Joseph asked Tisza to establish a coalition government, but Tisza refused to even try to do so. A month later, the ruler turned to László Lukács, but Lukács was unable to form a government. Finally, in mid-January 1910, the king appointed his old confidant Károly Khuen-Héderváry as prime minister, who then managed to form a government consisting exclusively of members of the former Liberal Party. Neither in Vienna nor in Budapest did people think that the government would succeed. It was decisively opposed in the Parliament, and so Francis Joseph dissolved the Parliament and ordered new elections. The failure of the coalition government to achieve progress in the field of "national achievements" led voters to reject the constitutional opposition parties. Voters' support and sympathy switched to politicians that supported the 1867 Compromise. The Constitution Party was dissolved and most of its representatives became a part of the National Work Party, which was the new name for the old government party that had been reorganized by István Tisza. At the elections in June, the National Work Party scored a resounding victory, winning 255 seats (62 percent) as against 95 seats won by the two pro-independence parties. The People's Party and the Christian Socialists won 13 seats, while the parties of the nationalities received eight seats. Small parties with just one or two seats were now far more numerous, as were also independent representatives. After the elections, Francis Joseph announced, with satisfaction, "It was my old desire that the liberal politics of 1867 should receive retribution. I am pleased that this has now happened. I trust that the Hungarian nation will adhere to Deák's construction in the future too."[25]

The National Work Party Government

The government then placed the long-needed reform of the armed forces on the agenda, including an increase in the number of new recruits and the overall military budget. The largest items in the military budget were large-scale investments related to the construction of a fleet and strengthening the artillery. The opposition once again made its support for such expenditure conditional upon "national achievements" and language concessions. Furthermore, a part of the opposition—the Justh party—made electoral reform one of its requirements. When these conditions were not met, the opposition resorted once more to obstructionism, thereby preventing the adoption of the legislation. In the spring of 1912, the minister of finance, László Lukács, took control of the government, while István Tisza became chairman (speaker) of the Lower House. Tisza was convinced that the Dual Monarchy was the only framework in which the existence of historical Hungary could be guaranteed. He rightly foresaw the coming war in Europe and was anxious about the Monarchy's failure to prepare militarily for such a war. He was determined, therefore, to secure the passage of the defense forces legislation, with a view to enabling—at the last minute—the development and modernization of the army. However, the election of Tisza as chairman of the Lower House led to a general political strike in Budapest. Severe clashes between protesting workers and the police then followed, with several fatalities. Despite the protests, Tisza managed to push through his legislation proposal concerning a reform of the armed forces: he refused to grant representatives of the opposition the chance to speak and then had them removed by force from the chamber. In the same year, legislation was adopted concerning the extraordinary measures that would be necessary in time of war.

In 1911, social democrats, civil radicals, and members of the Independence Party led by Gyula Justh joined forces to demand universal suffrage. The labor movement had been demonstrating in favor of voting rights ever since 1905, and so the National Work Party government could not circumvent the issue of electoral reform. In 1913, the Parliament adopted the new electoral law—which combined intellectual and wealth/income criteria and also raised the age at which a man became entitled to vote (to 24 years for high school graduates and to 30 years for everyone else). According to the data of the Hungarian Central Statistical Office, the new law increased the number of people entitled to vote by 60 percent (from 1.16 to 1.8–1.9 million), while granting more than 300,000 industrial and agricultural workers the right to vote. Even after the changes, however, only 44–45 percent of males aged over 24 were entitled to vote (while, in the other half of the Monarchy, universal suffrage had been in operation since 1907). Magyar was not the native language of 40 percent of people entitled to vote. Elections were never held on the basis of this law, owing to the outbreak of war. The electoral reform did not meet the demands of workers, left-wing political parties and intellectuals for universal suffrage—which was feared by Hungarian liberal politicians because, in István Tisza's words, "The political leadership would slip out of the hands of the intelligent Magyar middle class. Universal suffrage would cut off the vitality of the nation and would bring about the destruction of the nation."[26]

In the summer of 1913, Lukács was forced to resign as prime minister and was replaced by István Tisza. The Tisza government's program foresaw a reform of workers' insurance, the regulation of the right to strike, the "nationalization" of county and municipal authorities (that is, the appointment by central government of public officials working for such authorities), the drafting of a new civil code, the revision of the criminal code, and the amendment of the press law. Owing to the outbreak of war, only one of these goals was realized: the adoption of a new press law, with severe restrictions on press freedom.

For Tisza an important task was to achieve peace with the nationalities. He recognized that peace was threatened not only by Romanian nationalist "agitators" but also by impatient Magyar chauvinists. The estates owned by the Tisza family were in Bihar County, which had a large Romanian population. As early as the 1890s, Tisza had spoken out, in the local county assembly, for the rights of Romanians, condemning the anti-Romanian sentiments of the Magyar nationalists. His favorite concept was that of the mutual dependence of the Magyar and Romanian peoples, faced with the threat from north and south of being caught in the Slavic pincer. "The Romanian and Magyar races are dependent upon each other, faced with pressure from the Slavic sea that threatens them both," were Tisza's words to the Romanian Orthodox bishop of Arad.[27] In 1912, he began talks with leaders of the Romanian National Party, having raised the possibility of various concessions. These discussions, however, had led to no specific results by the outbreak of war.

Tisza's policy towards the Croats was more fruitful: he abrogated the language provisions in the Railway Service Act (which had been opposed by the Croats) and then reinstated the Croatian constitution, which had been suspended in 1912. He arranged for Francis Joseph to appoint a new ban of Croatia, and he also signed an agreement with the Croat–Serb coalition.

In 1913, the various pro-independence factions in the Parliament merged to form the United Independence and Forty-Eighter Party. The party's program contained demands for universal suffrage, legal regulations governing the right of assembly and association, enhanced autonomy for counties and municipalities, and a separate customs area and bank of issue. Count Mihály Károlyi played an increasingly important role in the party's leadership.

In the early twentieth century, domestic political tensions and parliamentary crises in the Monarchy's two halves were indicative of the growing dysfunction, or indeed crisis, of the Dualist system. An economic compromise could not be secured even after ten years of negotiations. Owing to obstructionism in both the Austrian and the Hungarian Parliament, it took more than two decades to achieve an increase in the size of the army and the military budget. Meanwhile, other European countries increased the size of their armies and equipped them with modern armaments. In Austria, the Dualist system was increasingly unpopular, while federalism gained strength. Francis Joseph's nephew, Francis Ferdinand, who became heir to the throne after the tragic death, in 1889, of Rudolf, the ruler's only son, became increasingly active in politics from 1905 onwards. He made no secret of his wish to limit—after his accession to the throne—Hungary's independence through a revision of the 1867 Compromise. His stated desire was a strengthening of the Monarchy's cohesion. At the Belvedere Palace in Vienna, plans were drawn up in Francis Ferdinand's military office regarding the future transformation of the Monarchy. The archduke could count on the support of Croatian, Romanian and Slovak nationality politicians for his plans; indeed, some of these politicians were in contact with his military office. One of them, Aurel C. Popovici, published a book (in 1906) entitled *Die Vereinigten Staaten von Groß-Österreich*, in which he elaborated a plan for transforming the Monarchy into a federation consisting of 15 ethnically defined states. Czech politicians also drafted plans for a federal transformation of the Monarchy. Among Croats and Slovenians, "trialism"—a framework that foresaw a Southern Slav state alongside Hungary and Austria—gained popularity. Hungarian politicians rejected all such trialist and federalist ideas, insisting upon the continuation of the Dualist system established in 1867 or its transformation into a simple personal union.

This was Austria-Hungary's situation at the outbreak of war in the summer of 1914.

Notes

1 *Népszava*, April 5–7, 1905.

2 Péter Hanák, "Az agrárszocialista mozgalom mentalitása és szimbólumai" [The Mentality and Symbols of the Agrarian Socialist Movement], in idem, *A Kert és a Műhely* [The Garden and the Workshop] (Budapest, 1988), p. 204.

3 Gyula Mérei and Ferenc Pölöskei, eds., *Magyarországi pártprogramok 1867–1919* [Hungarian Party Programs 1867–1919] (Budapest, 2003), p. 155.

4 Timoleon (Gusztáv Beksics), *A legújabb politikai divat* [The Latest Political Fashion] (Budapest, 1884), p. 11.

5 Gyula Andrássy, *Az 1867-iki kiegyezésről* [The Compromise of 1867] (Budapest, 1896), pp. 416–417.

6 József Barabási Kun, ed., *Gróf Tisza István képviselőházi beszédei* [The Speeches of Count István Tisza in the Lower House], vol. 2 (Budapest, 1930), pp. 313–314.

7 Gábor Salacz, *A magyar kultúrharc története, 1890–1895* [The History of the Hungarian Culture War, 1890–1895] (Vienna, 1938), p. 385.

8 Moritz Csáky, *Der Kulturkampf in Ungarn* (Graz, Vienna and Cologne, 1967), p. 77.

9 Salacz, *A magyar kultúrharc története*, p. 161.

10 Gusztáv Gratz, *A dualizmus kora* [The Dualist Era], vol. 2 (Budapest, 1934), pp. 124–126.

11 Lajos Kossuth, *Kossuth Lajos iratai* [Writings of Lajos Kossuth], vol. 10 (Budapest, 1904), pp. 401, 405.

12 Salacz, *A magyar kultúrharc története*, p. 392.

13 Kossuth, *Kossuth Lajos iratai*, vol. 10, p. 410.

14 Salacz, *A magyar kultúrharc története*, p. 380.

15 Cited in Péter Hanák, "A dualizmus válságának kezdetei a 19. század végén" [The Beginnings of the Crisis of Dualism in the Late Nineteenth Century], in Péter Hanák and Ferenc Mucsi, eds., *Magyarország története 1890–1918* [The History of Hungary 1890–1918] (Budapest, 1988), p. 149.

16 D. Kálmán Gyulai, *Losonczy Bánffy Dezső élete* [The Life of Dezső Losonczy Bánffy] (Marosvásárhely, 1913), p. 16.

17 Hanák, "A dualizmus válságának kezdetei a 19. század végén," p. 150.

18 Kun, ed., *Gróf Tisza István képviselőházi beszédei*, vol. 2, p. 131.

19 Hanák, "A dualizmus válságának kezdetei a 19. század végén," p. 569.

20 Francis Ferdinand's letter to Baron Max Wladimir Beck, the Austrian prime minister. Cited in Robert A. Kann, *Erzherzog Franz Ferdinand Studien* (Vienna, 1976), p. 114.

21 Hanák, "A dualizmus válságának kezdetei a 19. század végén," p. 587.

22 Cited in Gábor Vermes, *Tisza István* [István Tisza] (Budapest, 1994), p. 142.

23 *MOL Földművelésügyi Minisztérium iratai, elnöki iratok* [Hungarian National Archives, Papers of the Ministry of Agriculture, Chairman's Papers], pp. 1127–1906.

24 *MOL Minisztertanácsi jegyzőkönyvek, 1906. február 16* [Hungarian National Archives, Ministerial Council Records, February 16, 1906].

25 Hanák and Mucsi, eds., *Magyarország története 1890–1918*, p. 788.

26 Kun, ed., *Gróf Tisza István képviselőházi beszédei*, vol. 2 (Budapest, 1930), pp. 765–766.

27 Vermes, *Tisza István*, p. 83.

13. THE NATIONALITIES ISSUE

In the late fifteenth century, Magyars accounted for 75–80 percent of the country's population, but this share fell to 45 percent at the beginning of the eighteenth century and to less than 40 percent in the early nineteenth century. Magyars became a minority in their own land, and the ethnic shift seemed to be irreversible. Moreover, in the course of the nineteenth century, the country's non-Magyar population groups became modern nations seeking self-determination. In the light of the strength of nationalism among the various ethnic groups, the disintegration of both Hungary and the other half of the Dual Monarchy (Austria) appeared to be inevitable. The same process of disintegration was also affecting Europe's other multinational states.

Despite the increase in the Magyar share of the population of Hungary and Croatia from 36.5 percent in 1850 to 48.1 percent in 1910, Magyars still constituted only a minority of the total population. Even so, in Hungary proper—that is, without Croatia—the Magyar population formed an absolute majority in 1900 (51.4 percent). Similarly to the land issue and the democratization of the country's socio-political structure, the nationalities issue remained unresolved throughout the period. However, whereas the ruling classes were directly responsible for the failure to resolve the other two issues, in the case of the nationalities issue a solution guaranteeing the integrity of historical Hungary probably did not exist. A timely reorganization of the Monarchy along federalist lines might have saved it, but this would have resulted in the carving up of Hungary and the creation of several ethnically defined entities.

The Situation of the Non-Magyar Peoples

The status of the national minorities (who together formed a majority of the total population) and the rights of citizens whose native language was not Magyar were governed by the Nationalities Act of 1868. (This act was examined in detail in Chapter Three.) Complaints concerning the non-implementation of the provisions of the Nationalities Act gradually became more frequent, both in the press of the nationalities and in the statements made by nationality politicians. In the middle echelons of public administration and in the courts, practices that infringed upon the language rights of minority citizens were widespread. In 1883, Prime Minister Kálmán Tisza stated in the Parliament that the government had not adopted provisions prohibiting the use of an individual's native tongue, but he recognized that "overzealousness with regard to the Magyar race had resulted in the introduction of such procedures in some municipalities; whenever I heard of such a case, even if it was a decree of a public official or authority, I destroyed it."[1] Still, the government generally did little to prevent or hinder the nationalist excesses of local authorities or even to verify compliance with the language provisions of the Nationalities Act.

At the time of the 1867 Compromise and subsequently, members of the minorities frequently occupied official positions in central government, in the county administrations and in the higher courts. However, employment in such areas was conditional upon "political assimilation" and sometimes even required ethnic and linguistic assimilation—the latter perhaps entailing a perfect knowledge of Hungarian. Political assimilation was understood as the process whereby an individual identifies with "idea of the Hungarian state," making it his own. At this time, many public officials who had been active in the nationalities movements prior to the Compromise were dismissed from their posts or pensioned off. The public administrative and judicial apparatus thus became dominated by Magyars. Although as few as 54.5 percent of the inhabitants of Hungary (excluding Croatia) identified themselves as native Magyar-speakers in 1910, nevertheless in that year Magyars accounted for 95.6 percent of public officials, 92.9 percent of county officials, 87.5 percent of municipal office workers and 96.8 percent of judges and public prosecutors. Similarly, even though a majority of the rural population was not Magyar (51 percent), nevertheless 87.1 percent of local notaries identified themselves as Magyar. Magyars also accounted for 79.1 percent of workers in education, 74.7 percent of health workers and 63.7 percent of clergymen and ecclesiastical staff.

Most violations of the provisions relating to the nationalities occurred in the field of education. In this area the right of the nationalities—contained in the Nationalities Act—to receive primary and secondary education in their native languages was increasingly disregarded. In 1880, among the country's 15,681 elementary schools, the language of tuition was Magyar in 46.8 percent of schools and a nationality language in 38.6 percent. The language of tuition was both Magyar and a nationality language (mixed) in 14.6 percent of schools. Thus, in 53.2 percent of schools, nationality children could receive tuition in their native language. By 1905, this ratio had declined to 29.4 percent, while in a further 13 percent of schools nationality languages were used as "auxiliary languages" alongside Magyar as the language of tuition. During the following ten years, the number of schools providing tuition in a nationality language declined at an even faster rate. In 1905, 40 percent of minority German pupils were attending schools in which Magyar was the language of tuition and their own language was not even used as an auxiliary language; this was also true of 35 percent of Croat pupils (in Hungary) and 30 percent of Slovak pupils. Most of these children lived in ethnically mixed areas; they were frequently bilingual, having learned to speak Magyar in their own homes. In contrast, as few as 8 percent of minority Serb pupils and 12 percent of minority Romanian pupils attended such schools.

Table 1: Language of Tuition at Elementary Schools in Hungary (Excluding Croatia)

	Magyar	German	Slovak	Romanian	Ruthenian	Croatian, Slovenian	Serbian	Other	*Total non-Magyar*
Unilingual schools									
1869*	5,818	1,232	1,822	2,569	473	93	159	7	*6,355*
1880	7,342	867	1,716	2,756	393	68	245	7	*6,052*
1905	11,664	272	326	2,433	45	1	155	14	*3,246*
Bilingual or multilingual schools where pupils were taught in the above languages									
1869*	1,455	856	333	204	119	27	65	180	*1,784*
1880	2,287	919	597	394	246	52	79	150	*2,437*
1905	1,598	331	599	413	113	41	113	10	*1,620*
Total schools where pupils were taught in the above languages									
1869*	7,273	2,088	2,155	2,773	592	120	224	187	*8,139*
1880	9,629	1,786	2,313	3,150	639	120	324	157	*8,489*
1905	13,262	603	925	2,846	158	42	268	24	*4,866*
Auxiliary language in schools where pupils were taught in Magyar									
1905		653	944	111	320	136	3	51	*2,218*
Index (1880–1905)	138	34	40	90	25	35	83	15	*57*

* Excluding around 300 schools in the Banat Military Frontier district, where pupils were taught in German, Serbian and Romanian.

As the table indicates, the reduction in schools offering tuition in the native language particularly affected the country's German, Slovak and Ruthenian communities, as well as the Croat and Slovenian communities in western Hungary. In contrast, the Romanian and Serb communities—largely due to the efforts of their ecclesiastical autonomous bodies—managed to keep their schools. Who could decide to change the language of tuition in a school? Even at the turn of the century, around 80 percent of elementary schools were still being run by religious denominations, while 10 percent of schools were maintained by municipalities. This fact limited the extent of the government's influence. Decisions concerning the language of tuition were taken by the maintainers of schools—the municipal or Church school boards. We know also of cases where Hungarian was the official language of tuition, but pupils were actually taught in one of the minority languages. Evidently, this was only possible in bilingual areas where a majority of pupils also spoke Magyar. Hungarian was the exclusive language of tuition in just 800 government-owned schools (5 percent) in 1890, but by 1914 this number had increased to 3,500 (21 percent). In such schools, minority languages were, at best, auxiliary languages.

The nationalities had even fewer opportunities to study in their own languages at the three types of high school (*Gymnasium*, *Realschule*, and commercial high school). The Transylvanian Saxons had nine high schools, the Romanians seven high schools, and the Serbs one high school. The Ruthenians, the Croats and Slovenians (in Hungary), and the Germans had no high schools, while the three Slovak high schools in Upper Hungary were closed by the government in 1874. In many areas inhabited by minorities, pupils could use their own languages in the first grade of Magyar-language high schools but not thereafter. Still, around 40 percent of Romanian and Serb high school students completed their studies in their native languages. All of this was reflected in the statistics concerning the native language of high school students: in 1910, the native language was Magyar for 80.7 percent of students, German for 8.6 percent, Romanian for 6.0 percent, Slovak for 2.3 percent,

Serbo-Croat for 1.9 percent, Ruthenian for 0.1 percent, and another language for 0.5 percent of high school students.

In higher education, the language of tuition was always Magyar—with the exception of the theological colleges. At the country's universities, the major nationalities had their own language and literature departments. Even so, when the Romanians urged that Romanian become—in addition to Magyar—a language of tuition at the University of Kolozsvár (Cluj) (est. 1872), their request was rejected.

Even after the 1867 Compromise, the teaching of Magyar as the state language was not compulsory either in elementary schools or in high schools. It was only in 1879 that the teaching of Magyar was prescribed in elementary schools, becoming a compulsory subject in all schools only in 1883 (the delay was to allow time for elementary school teachers to learn the language). The ecclesiastical and political leaders of the nationalities protested against the legislation, perceiving it as an infringement of the rights contained in the Nationalities Act and as the first step in an aggressive program of Magyarization. Of course, teaching pupils the state language was not in itself an aggressive attempt at Magyarization. Indeed, in the justification for the bill, it was emphasized that there was no wish to force anybody to learn Magyar; instead, the aim was to provide everyone with the opportunity to learn the language, since every citizen had an interest in knowing the state language. In the end, it proved difficult to implement the legislative provisions. As late as 1890, there were around 2,000 elementary schoolteachers who could not teach the Magyar language, and the teaching of the state language failed in approximately 2,400 nationality schools. In 1907, a new law, the so-called "*lex Apponyi*," prescribed once again the compulsory teaching of the Hungarian language, introducing measures to make such teaching more effective. In 1883, Hungarian language and literature became compulsory subjects in high schools. High school students also had to pass examinations in these subjects in order to receive their high school diploma. The Kindergarten Act of 1891 ensured that kindergarten tuition be used to introduce children to the state language, Magyar.

The nationalities were free to establish economic, literary and other cultural associations and groups. Even so, an 1875 decree of the Ministry of the Interior prohibited such cultural associations from using the word "national" (*nemzeti*) in their official names. During the decades after the Compromise, hundreds of minority associations (reading circles, choral societies, literary and drama societies, academic and social associations, and women's groups), as well as book and magazine companies, industrial enterprises, banks and savings institutes, were formed. Most of these were locally based, but each major national minority established its own national cultural body prior to the 1867 Compromise (*Matica Srpska*, *Matica Slovenská*, Astra—a Romanian organization in Transylvania—and the Saint Basil Society—a Ruthenian organization). All these organizations continued to function after the Compromise; only the *Matica Slovenská* was banned in 1875. Many of the minority cultural associations also published books and periodicals. In 1913, in addition to the 1,500 Magyar newspapers and journals published in Hungary, there were also 236 German, 39 Romanian, 33 Serbo-Croat, 35 Slovak and two Ruthenian publications. Editors and journalists working for the political newspapers were often summoned to appear before the Press Jury, having been accused of "propaganda against the state" or "inciting hatred among the nationalities." Sometimes they were sentenced to several months or—in the more serious cases—several years in a state prison (as those convicted of political or press offenses were placed in a state prison (*államfogház*) rather than a penitentiary).

In contrast to Austria, where economic, demographic, political and cultural relations between the various nationalities became more balanced after the Compromise, inter-ethnic relations deteriorated in Hungary. The predominance of the Magyar nation was felt in all social, political and cultural arenas. The Magyar share of the population grew steadily throughout the Dualist Era, and there was a corresponding increase in the relative influence of Magyars in the modern sectors of the economy and society. The hegemony of the Magyar ruling class in areas traditionally inhabited by other ethnic groups drew its strength from land ownership. Sixty percent of the country's land was Magyar-owned; even in counties where minorities formed a majority of the population, 40 percent of land was owned by Magyars. However, the position of medium-sized Magyar landowners in Transylvania and in northern Hungary weakened during the post-Compromise decades; the ownership of a great deal of land passed to peasant farmers and middle-class landowners belonging to other ethnic groups.

In 1900, Hungarians accounted for 89.7 percent of landowners with more than 1,000 *hold* (1,422 acres) of land and 71.7 percent of landowners with between 100 and 1,000 *hold* (142 and 1,422 acres). In contrast, just 37.7 percent of small peasant farmers with fewer than 50 *hold* (71 acres), while 44 percent of all agricultural earners were Magyar. The percentage of industrial workers whose native language was Magyar increased from 48.6 percent in 1880 to 57.9 percent in 1900, while the corresponding increase in the commercial sector was from 54 percent to 67 percent. At the turn of the century, Magyars accounted for 81.2 percent of officials working in various sectors and 77.1 percent of professionals working as public officials.

The statistics collected by the Statistical Office in 1904 and 1910—which relate to the taxation of male adults and were drawn up in the course of preparations for electoral reform—provide a rough picture of the relative wealth of the various ethnic groups. These statistics show that Magyars were not the most prosperous group: in 1904, Magyar males aged over 24 paid on average 32 crowns in direct tax, whereas ethnic German males paid 37 crowns and ethnic Serbs 33 crowns. The poorer groups were the Ruthenians, Romanians and Slovaks, among whom the average tax paid was just 10–14 crowns. A similar picture is shown by the data for 1910: 25 percent of male Magyars paid more than 20 crowns in tax, while this was true of 32 percent of Germans and 30 percent of Serbs. Just 3 percent of Ruthenians, 10 percent of Romanians and 15 percent of Slovaks belonged in this relatively prosperous group. Magyars were particularly likely to fall into the poorest category: 36 percent of adult male Hungarians paid no direct tax, while the corresponding figures were 35 percent among Serbs, 34 percent among Croats, 33 percent among Slovaks, 29 percent among Romanians, and only 22 percent among Ruthenians. The explanation for the Serbs' relative prosperity is that most of them were living in Hungary's most productive region in the southern part of the Great Plain region; the proportion of wealthy peasant farmers with 20–100 *hold* (28–142 acres) of land was the greatest among the Serb population.

By the time of the Compromise in 1867, the Serbs, Romanians, Slovaks and Transylvanian Saxons had already formed political movements and political parties—although the Magyar political parties still contained many politicians from non-Magyar backgrounds. The national (minority) movements were directed by smaller and larger groups of intellectuals—1,000–2,000 people—who were sometimes joined by small numbers of middle-class people (some of whom were rather wealthy). In the Slovak, Romanian and Ruthenian national movements, a leading role was played by clergymen and lawyers. Catholic priests were also instrumental in the launch, in the 1870s and 1880s, of the cultural movements of the *Bunjevci* minority in the Bácska (Bačka) region and of the Croats and Slovenians of western Transdanubia. The Serbs' movement was the only one with an almost exclusively secular leadership—the priests having been kept out.

For several years after the disappointment that followed the Nationalities Act, the Romanian and Serb politicians continued to fight for an acceptable settlement. In the Parliament, representatives of the nationalities fought, in cooperation with the Hungarian Magyar opposition (in particular the extreme left), against the government's centralizing efforts. During a debate of the electoral reform bill, they urged the introduction of universal suffrage. They repeatedly called for legal guarantees of democratic civil rights and the decentralization of government. They wanted the Nationalities Act to be amended and supplemented. As the Serb leader Mihajlo Polit-Desančić emphasized, "The question is not whether or not one can submit a petition to the authorities in Serbian, Slovak, Romanian or German. No, it is whether villages, towns and counties reflect—based on self-government—the type of the various nationalities."[2]

In the 1870s, the Dualist system became more consolidated in both the domestic policy and the foreign policy field. Opposition to the system weakened and retreated. Under the Liberal government, there was a growing emphasis on manifesting the Magyar nature of the state. More than once the government employed harsh measures to limit or even destroy the nationality movements. The government's policy on the nationalities was supported—and sometimes even "outdone"—by the pro-independence opposition. The nationality politicians no longer found allies among the Magyar opposition or support in Vienna. They could not even count on assistance from the kin-states, since both Serbia and Romania were allies of the Monarchy.

As already noted, it was during this period that minority intellectuals were gradually removed from the central institutions of the state. Even at the local or county levels of government, there were few suitable opportunities for them. The first Parliament elected in 1865 included 25 Romanian and Serb representatives. The Slovaks had no representatives promoting their national program. In subsequent years, the number of Romanian and Serb representatives actually decreased, owing to the narrow scope of voting rights, as well as pressure from the administration at the time of elections. The decline in the number of minority representatives was also due to the fact that only a small percentage of the hundreds of thousands of non-Magyar voters possessed national consciousness. Accordingly, most of the constituencies inhabited by minority groups elected government party politicians to the Parliament. Under such circumstances, the nationality parties retreated into passivity, failing even to field candidates at elections.

During these years of passivity, the leadership and middle ranks of the nationality organizations attempted to adapt to the new circumstances. They sought ways to make progress even within the increasingly consolidated Dualist framework. Although they resisted Magyarization, they nevertheless learned Magyar and became more or less involved in the increasingly Magyarized public life of the country. In addition to those who attempted to fit in, there were, among all the nationality groups, a small number of non-Magyar intellectual and middle-class people who had a strong sense of national awareness and consciously steered clear of the Magyarized public life and Magyar political and social institutions. Their goal was to establish their own national societies.

The 1890s were a time of cooperation between politicians of the various nationalities. The first Nationalities Congress in Hungary was held in Budapest in 1895. Those attending made public a whole range of grievances on the part of the national minorities.

"They [i.e. the Magyars] consider Hungary to be something that belongs to a single people; the authorities are trying to impose the stamp of the representation of a national state on the Hungarian Parliament… A people in a minority seeks to possess the attributes of statehood and they wish to subjugate all the other peoples—who together form a majority—with the help of this misappropriated state power… The nature of the Hungarian state, which stems from its ethnic composition and historical development, precludes a single people—one that does not even constitute the majority of the population—from demanding for itself the attributes of statehood. Only the various peoples of Hungary in their totality have the right to identify themselves with the state."[3]

The Growing Vigor of the Nationalities Movements from the 1890s

Until the 1880s, the waves of modernization that were passing from west to east—manifested in economic growth, industrialization and improved living standards—affected first and foremost the western, central and southern parts of the country. The major manifestations of economic growth were limited to Transdanubia, the Great and Lesser Plains, and the hill country lying to the north of the Great Plain. Among the various areas inhabited by minorities, the only areas to integrate successfully into this economic growth were the western and northern parts of the Lesser Plain, the wheat-producing areas of Bácska and the Banat with their mixed populations, the middle part of Upper Hungary (Gömör, Zólyom and Szepes Counties) and the heavy industrial districts of Krassó-Szörény County, which were rich in metals and coal.

With the exception of the heavy industrial regions mentioned above, the Carpathian regions in the north and east of Hungary missed out on capitalist development. Still dependent upon the traditional economy, these regions became increasingly crisis-ridden. Faced by the twin challenges of relative overpopulation and growing poverty, hundreds of thousands of people migrated from these regions; some of them moved to the developing industrial regions of central Hungary, while others sought out new lives overseas or in Austria and Romania.

The initial period of modern economic growth thus saw an increase in economic disparity: the country's western and central regions were relatively prosperous, while the upland areas in the north and east tended to stagnate. One should emphasize the fact that these differences reflected regional factors rather than ethnicity. Even so, it is true that the population of the more dynamic western and central regions was predominantly Magyar. Indeed, Hungarians accounted for more than two thirds of the population in such areas—although there were also German, Croat, Serb and Slovak minorities. Meanwhile, the population of the backward regions consisted mainly of groups such as Slovaks, Ruthenians and Romanians. In Transylvania it also included a group of Magyars known as the Szeklers.

The 1890s saw a change in the regional patterns of economic development. The wave of modernization and industrialization finally reached the country's peripheries in the north and east. Consequently, the economic discrepancies between the western and eastern parts of the country abated. The trend was one of reversal: economic differences began a gradual but steady decline. Marginal areas stagnating under the old, traditional economy began to experience capitalist development, launching themselves on the path to modernization. By the outbreak of war in 1914, the level of economic development of these regions had surpassed that of neighboring regions in other Eastern European and Balkan countries.

The industrialization of regions inhabited by minorities was encouraged by government aid for industry: most of the subsidies for factory production were spent in these regions. Government assistance was also used to develop and modernize the backward agricultural sector of these marginalized regions. The "hill-country action"—the provision of assistance to Ruthenians with the aim of advancing their economy—was extended to Transylvania and the Slovak-inhabited areas of Upper Hungary in the early twentieth century.

The accelerated rate of capitalist development and industrialization in minority-inhabited regions was primarily the result of the advance of Austro-Hungarian and Western European big capital; local minority entrepreneurs played only a secondary role in this process. Although there existed Slovak entrepreneurs in Upper Hungary and Saxon and Romanian business owners in Transylvania, most of these entrepreneurs owned small or medium-sized plants. A notable industrial bourgeoisie appeared only among the Transylvanian Saxon population and the Slovaks.

The nationality bourgeoisie was far stronger in the banking sector. At the turn of the century, the development of Slovak, Romanian and Serb banks speeded up. Their number grew from 30 in 1890 to 222 in 1915; over a period of 25 years, their equity capital increased from 5 million to 58 million crowns. Most of these institutions were relatively small local banks or savings institutes, but there were also a number of larger banks with higher levels of equity capital, such as the Albina (Nagyszeben–Sibiu), a Romanian institution, and the Tatra-Bank, a Slovak one, of Turócszentmárton (Martin). Including the wealthy institutions of the Transylvanian Saxons, the total assets of all 317 nationality-run banks rose to 800 crowns in 1915, but this still represented only 6 percent of the total capital of banks in Hungary. Despite the relative insignificance of the nationality-run banks, their rapid growth is a sign of the accelerating rate of capital accumulation and the development of a nationality bourgeoisie.

The economic strength of minority peasant farmers is demonstrated by the advance of various forms of cooperatives. At the outbreak of war, their number exceeded 400. After the turn of the century, the country saw a significant increase in the amount of land owned by minority peasant farmers and medium-sized landowners. This development took place largely at the expense of Transylvanian and Upper Hungarian medium-sized noble landowners who were unable to make the switch to modern production methods. The purchase of land by minority peasant farmers was assisted by payments coming from family members who had emigrated abroad and by the parceling out of Magyar-owned land bought up by the nationality-run banks. Between 1905 and 1917, approximately 310,000 *hold* (442,000 acres) of Magyar land were divided up into plots and placed under the ownership of nationality small farmers. In Transylvania, during the decade preceding 1913, as many as 700 Magyar-owned estates, each comprising more than 50 *hold* (71 acres) of land, were taken into the ownership of Transylvanian Romanians or Saxons. The total land area of these estates amounted to 157,000 *hold* (223,000 acres).

The social consequences of economic development in areas inhabited by minorities—such as the growth of a minority middle class and the development of a minority industrial working class—added significantly to the social foundations of the nationality political movements.

The structure of Romanian and Ruthenian society was still traditional at the outbreak of war: more than 85 percent of the population made a living in agriculture, and fewer than 8 percent or even 5 percent were employed in industry, trade or transport. As few as 4.5 percent of Romanians and 1 percent of Ruthenians lived in towns. As in other peasant societies in eastern and southeastern Europe, smallholder peasants accounted for 60–70 percent. There were only a small number of artisans, merchants, *petite bourgeoisie*, and industrial workers. Agricultural workers made up between a quarter and a fifth of the population. Apart from several hundred priests, the Ruthenians had basically no intellectual class. Among the Romanians, the situation was different: under the protective wings of their autonomous Church school system, a significant intellectual class had arisen. At the turn of the century, the Romanian intellectual class included more than 7,000 priests and teachers, 1,000 public officials, and 300 lawyers. If we add to this class landowners with more than 100 *hold* (142 acres) of land, artisans, and merchants, we arrive at a figure of 12,000–13,000 families composing the Romanian middle class—with intellectuals forming the largest group within this number. In contrast, among the Ruthenians, the middle class seems to have consisted of fewer than 500 families.

The social structure of the Slovak, Croat and Serb populations was rather different. The agrarian population accounted for just 70–71 percent of the total population among the Slovaks and the Croats and for 77 percent among the Serbs. Between 15 and 20 percent of the population made a living from industry, commerce or transport, while the urban share of the population was far larger among these groups than it was among the Romanians and Ruthenians. Landowning peasants accounted for half of the population among the Slovaks, Croats and Serbs, but the breakdown of the traditional peasant way of life had advanced further. All three peoples had relatively significant artisan and merchant classes. Industrial workers were an additional significant group among the Slovak and Croat populations. In contrast, the industrial proletariat was rather insignificant among the Serbs. In 1910, more than 60,000 Slovaks were working in large-scale industry; this represented 13 percent of all large-scale industrial workers. The number of ethnic German workers was only slightly greater (65,000). Both groups were larger than the sum of industrial workers from all other ethnic groups (45,000).

The Serbs had a sizeable large and medium-sized landowner class with a strong merchant bourgeoisie. Meanwhile, a noteworthy industrial middle-bourgeoisie arose among the Slovak population.

After the Germans, the Serbs had the strongest intellectual class in relation to the size of their community; in this group, intellectuals could realize their ambitions as clergymen and teachers and in the free professions or as public officials. The Slovak intellectual class was rather weak; it comprised almost exclusively priests and elementary school teachers. Few public or private officials were prepared to identify Slovak as their native language—even though some of them must evidently have been of Slovak origin. Relatively small numbers of Slovaks were working in the free professions. In the Slovaks' case, this reflects a significant degree of Magyarization.

Among the country's peoples (including Magyars), the social structure of the German-speaking population was the most developed and "modern." In the upper and middle strata of society in Hungary—among large and medium-sized landowners, independent artisans and merchants—the number of German-speakers exceeded the number of Magyar-speakers, while industrial workers also included a higher number of German workers (they were more numerous than other groups).

In terms of their origins, composition and social positioning, the leading groups among the nationality populations differed substantially from the Hungarian middle class: they were more homogeneous in terms of their origins, lifestyle, mentality and approach to problems. Their links with the lower parts of their own ethnic group, especially with the peasants and *petite bourgeoisie*, were closer than was customary among the Magyar "gentlemanly middle class." Among the various ethnic groups, the divisions between the various classes were less rigid, the differences in consciousness and prestige were smaller, and the middle class was far more open downwards towards the lower classes. In contrast, it firmly rejected forming a relationship with the Hungarian "gentlemanly" class—despite the fact that most of the non-Magyar middle classes had in the meantime assimilated into the Magyar middle class, principally in terms of lifestyle and values, and even linguistically. These latter groups became separated from their own national societies, even when they still spoke the minority language.

As capitalist development accelerated at the turn of the century, there was a structural change in the middle classes of the nationalities. The old type of intellectual class, which had played a leading role in local life (clergymen, teachers and lawyers), was joined by middle-class elements with direct links to the capitalist economy, particularly the banking sector. These new elements soon took control of the economic and political leadership of their own national societies. With the help of banks, cooperatives and other business organizations, they brought most of the intellectuals, artisans, merchants and peasants into their sphere of influence. These two social classes—the middle class and peasants—clearly formed the backbone of the nationality movements. All the nationality populations were essentially lower middle-class and peasant societies. Whereas the nationalities accounted for just 27 percent of medium-sized and large landowners (with more than 100 *hold* or 142 acres of land) and 41 percent of agricultural workers, they composed as much as 60 percent of the peasant population.

With the exception of the Ruthenians, the nationalities and their social and political movements began to reflect the changing structure of society after the turn of the century. In the light of the economic and social factors, an objective interest of the middle class, which led the various nationality populations as well as their national movements, was the democratic transformation of the country's social and political system. This circumstance meant that the growing nationalism of the nationality movements could be linked with democratic ambitions. Accordingly, the programs of the nationality movements included democratic demands—alongside nationalist aims.

In the first half of the 1890s, the nationalities issue reappeared at the level of national politics; passions ran high in a manner not seen for two decades. The various political actions of the nationalities during these years—such as the Romanian Memorandum (acclaimed throughout Europe), the Budapest Nationalities Congress of 1895, and the Catholic People's Party agitation at election time among the Slovak, German, South Slav and Ruthenian populations—did not, however, bring direct results. As a consequence of the obvious bankruptcy of the tactics of passivity, important changes in the political movements of the minority peoples took place at the turn of the century. The parties and their organizations were revamped, and changes were also made to the forms and means of the political struggle, its program and tactics. The old leaderships, which had become rather conservative and increasingly isolated from broad sections of the minority population, were replaced by new progressive elements—whose policies were more radical than those of their predecessors. The focus among the various nationality movements gradually switched to organizations and institutions of an economic type, such as banks, savings institutes, cooperatives and business associations. In general, such entities had greater potential for action than the old cultural and ecclesiastical bodies did.

The most manifest changes occurred in the programs and tactics of the minority parties. In the early years of the twentieth century, these minority programs reflected, on the one hand, the democratic endeavors of the middle-class elements that now led the movements. On the other hand, they also reflected the demands of the lower middle class, the peasantry and workers—all of whom were beginning to become involved in the nationality movements.

Demands for universal and secret voting as well as other civil rights were included in the programs of the nationalities. Other social demands included a progressive taxation system and an amount of land for peasants that could not be divided up or sold off (homestead), a division into plots of government-owned land, government economic development program, social legislation promoting safety at work, and mandatory social security.

With the advance of a democratic and social program, national claims became more moderate than they had been in the past. They acknowledged the political realities, including the stability of the Dualist system and the strengthening of the Hungarian state. The programs no longer included plans for regional autonomy and a federalist transformation of the country. The political parties of the nationalities, which had earlier condemned the 1868 Nationalities

Act, now demanded the realization of the rights guaranteed in the legislation. After 1900, the Slovak, Romanian and Serb nationality parties abandoned their traditionally passive tactics and attempted to exploit the opportunities provided by the parliamentary struggle. They emphasized their loyalty and were prepared at all times to negotiate with the Hungarian government and reach compromise agreements by making partial concessions. At the same time, they kept in contact with the Hungarian progressives, who were fighting for the country's democratization, as well as maintaining ties with the kin-states and the political forces of those nations.

Little progress was made, however, by this type of political activity and participation. Although 40–45 percent of those entitled to vote were not native Magyar-speakers, the constituencies were formed in such a manner that non-Magyar voters represented a majority in fewer than one in four of the country's 413 constituencies. The situation of the Romanian minority was particularly unfavorable in the light of the Transylvanian electoral law—which prescribed a higher quota than was the case in other parts of Hungary.

Throughout the period, the Transylvanian Saxons retained control of the dozen or so constituencies with a Saxon majority. Political activity on the part of minority politicians seemed worthwhile in the hundred or so constituencies with Romanian, Slovak and Serb majorities. In reality, however, minority politicians faced a grave disappointment. Many minority voters chose not to vote for the nationality candidates even when they were not subject to official pressure. The nationality parties achieved their greatest successes in the elections of 1906. They fielded candidates in 79 constituencies, receiving in total 65,000 votes. Twenty-five of their candidates were thus elected to the Parliament.

In 1905 and 1906, nationality representatives formed a joint club in the Parliament, and they jointly submitted their demands—which were essentially a summary of the programs of the nationality parties. The response of the majority of Magyar representatives to all nationality contributions to the parliamentary debate (even when they were made in a spirit of loyalty and moderation) was

Table 2: The Native Language of Males Aged over 24 and Entitled to Vote in Elections (in 1910)

	Magyar	German	Slovak	Romanian	Ruthenian	Croatian	Serbian	Other	*Total non-Magyar*
Hungary (without Transylvania)									
Breakdown of total voters (%)	*59.85*	11.44	10.69	9.13	3.06	1.16	2.89	1.77	*40.15*
Breakdown of males aged over 24 (%)	*58.81*	10.67	11.23	10.48	2.39	1.26	3.25	1.92	*41.19*
Voters as a percentage of males aged over 24	*27.93*	29.41	26.14	23.92	35.11	25.29	24.41	25.30	*26.74*
Transylvania									
Breakdown of total voters (%)	*56.24*	15.32	0.08	28.16	0.01	0.01	0.03	0.16	*43.76*
Breakdown of males aged over 24 (%)	*33.98*	8.60	0.11	55.66	0.09	0.03	0.02	1.53	*66.02*
Voters as a percentage of males aged over 24	*20.90*	22.50	9.12	6.39	1.73	4.78	19.44	1.33	*8.37*

one of chauvinistic impatience. Negotiations and deals with the government were equally unfruitful.

Under such circumstances, the nationality politicians keenly watched the growing crisis affecting the Dualist system. They maintained contacts with forces opposed to Dualism in the other half of the Monarchy, forces that sought the reorganization of the multinational Empire and its transformation into a federation with autonomous national areas. Such forces included the Czech and South Slav national movements, with whom the South Slavs and Slovaks in Hungary had increasingly close links. They also forged links with Austria's Christian Social Party and Archduke Francis Ferdinand, whose advisors included a good number of distinguished leaders of the Romanian, Slovak, Croat and German national movements in Hungary.

In the early years of the twentieth century, Hungary's nationalities began to place greater emphasis on relations with their kin-states in the field of culture, politics and economics. The advance of the Czechoslovak, South Slav, and Romanian unification movements, and the increasing popularity of Pan-Germanism among the Transylvanian Saxons and the country's other ethnic German groups, signaled the growing significance of national consciousness and unity in nationality politics. Still, these unification movements only gradually transformed themselves into secessionist endeavors. Both the Czechs and the South Slavs envisioned achieving national unity within the framework of a democratic and federalist Habsburg Empire. The dissolution of the Monarchy, the development of independent nation states, and political unification with the kin-states were not specific and explicit goals of the political parties and leadership of the nationalities. At the time such goals were unachievable. And they remained so until the path to independence and unification was laid open by changes in the international political system at the time of the 1912–1913 Balkan wars and World War I.

The 1890s saw the outbreak of class conflicts between the country's industrial and agrarian workers. In the industrial areas of Upper Hungary, the Banat region, Transylvania, and the southern and eastern extremities of the Great Plain region, Slovak, Romanian, Serb and German industrial and agricultural workers fought alongside Magyars against capitalist exploitation and to safeguard their economic and democratic rights. In terms of their political aims and their organization, these groups differed greatly from the middle-class national movements. Moreover, their actions were internationalist. The leaders of the nationalities tried once again to win the support of working-class people for their own national goals. Still, throughout the period, the Hungarian Social Democratic Party maintained control of the process of organizing minority workers. In Croatia the independent Social Democratic Party retained control.

Hungarian Nationalities Policy

The 1867 Compromise gave a free hand to the Hungarian ruling classes in dealing with the country's domestic affairs, including the nationalities issue. For all groups and factions among the Magyar political elite—which included liberals and conservatives as well as supporters and opponents of the Compromise—the need to uphold the integrity of historical Hungary was axiomatic; none of them wished to jeopardize the territorial and political unity of the country. "In our country, we consider the principle of unity to be of priority public interest, and all other demands must be subservient to it," emphasized a petition of Szepes County in 1867.[4] In 1890, the government's leading ideologist wrote the following: "A united and indivisible state, a united and indivisible nation: this is the point of departure, the goal of our endeavors, and the regulator of our deeds. All reforms are subject to this categorical imperative."[5]

The ideal of the Magyar liberal political elite was a unified nation state of the Western European type; they wanted the new Hungary to be established in this vein. However, Hungary had a multinational population, which could no longer be welded into a unified nation. During the decades prior to the Compromise, the leaders of Hungary's nationalities had demanded collective national rights, political institutions and regional autonomy within the Habsburg Monarchy and the borders of historical Hungary. For the Magyar political elite, however, the fulfillment of such demands was incompatible with the principle of the territorial integrity and governmental unity of the country. According to the Hungarian approach, which was codified in the Nationalities Act, the non-Hungarian peoples living in the country did not constitute political nations and thus could not demand autonomy. (The Croats were the only exception to this, as they had always been recognized as a separate political entity.) As citizens, however, members of the nationalities enjoyed full individual freedoms and equality. They had the theoretical opportunity to "freely develop their nationality in all directions."[6] The extent to which they were able to exploit this opportunity depended upon the workings of the state, the administrative structure, the legislature, governments, and the position taken by the executive bodies of middling and lower rank—that is to say, it depended upon the sum of nationality policy.

Supporters of a consistently liberal nationality policy formed only a minority of the Magyar political elite—even at the time of the Compromise. And in the 1870s and 1880s, liberal voices fell silent. Lajos Mocsáry, for instance, became almost totally isolated. Like a "white crow," he spoke out in favor of the principles of the men who had been in the vanguard of Hungarian liberalism in the 1860s, such as Ferenc Deák, József Eötvös, Zsigmond Kemény and László Szalay. A majority among the Magyar ruling classes supported an interpretation of the Compromise that had been condemned by Eötvös: namely, it wished to transform the "shared homeland" into a Magyar national state and use any power that it received to uphold its economic, social and political hegemony throughout the country and concerning all its national groups.

According to Gusztáv Beksics, a leading publicist of the government party, the main aim of Magyar politics could only be the establishment of "a unified and national state." By the 1890s, nationalist public opinion and a majority of pro-independence politicians were demanding that the liberal provisions of the

Nationalities Act be ignored or even revised. In their view, the provisions governing language rights were too generous and thus hindered the construction of a Magyar national state. By this time all factions and groups within the Magyar political elite supported the "idea of the Hungarian state," which meant that Hungary was to be considered as a nation state even though it was ethnically and linguistically divided and could not be rendered a unified state. Their goal was to ensure that the state served primarily Magyar national interests (or exclusively Magyar interests, according to some) and that Magyar national development be promoted. A further aim was to guarantee the political supremacy of the Magyar ruling classes over all other national groups in the country.

The Hungarian political elite did not interpret the formation of a single Hungarian political nation in the spirit of the liberal concepts put forward by Eötvös and by Deák. Instead, they were inclined to identify the Hungarian political nation with the genetic national group, the ethnic "Magyars." Such an interpretation was facilitated by the fact that the Hungarian language makes no distinction between "Hungarian" (*Ungar*, *ugarski*, or *uhorský* in various other languages, meaning a citizen of Hungary) and "Magyar," using the word *magyar* to refer to both. After the Compromise, this nationalist interpretation of the Hungarian political nation became increasingly dominant in Magyar political thought.

The Hungarian political elite sought to uphold its hegemony not only in the legislature and the central bodies of government, but also in the middle and lower echelons of public administration. This explains the further narrowing of the rights and competences of county and local authorities—accompanied by an expansion of the powers of the government-appointed high sheriffs (*főispán*) and the administrative committees. The apparent aim was a strengthening of central government. "It is said that we need a strong center and a strong government against the nationalities, which can put a brake on all centrifugal endeavors—by keeping a tight rein on public administration and the judiciary."[7]

In debates concerning the electoral legislation of 1874, both the government and the center-left opposition ruled out an extension of voting rights. Mór Jókai, whose position on the nationalities issue was otherwise conciliatory, wrote that universal suffrage was right in theory, but that in practice its introduction in Hungary would raise the following question: "Should there even be a Magyar state in Europe? The answer: nine million non-Magyars against six million Magyars, with universal suffrage?" This "removes even the possibility that Hungary as a unified state will ever *exist* based on constitutional representation... It removes the basis of our state constitution... And it opens up the way to disintegrative passions."[8]

Most Magyar politicians regarded the movements of the nationalities as being under the influence of outsiders. They thought that the issue could be settled through force and through action taken by the authorities and the police. During the post-Compromise years, the toughest measures were directed against the Serbian and Slovak national movements, owing to a fear of Pan-Slavism and the possibility of a Russian intervention. Leading minority politicians were convicted for ethnic incitement. The Serb *Omladina* and Slovak *Matica* were dissolved and the Slovak high schools were closed. A royal commissioner was dispatched to Újvidék (Novi Sad), and public officials and judges involved in the nationality movements were suspended or pensioned off. Initially, an attempt was made to force nationality politicians to leave national political forums. Subsequently, the government attempted to exert control over the Churches, schools and cultural institutions of the nationalities. In the 1890s, the focus of Magyar nationalities policy switched to the Romanian minority.

In the 1860s, the country's liberal politicians considered it to be impossible to Magyarize and assimilate the nationalities—who were in the process of developing their own national consciousness. They condemned attempts to force the nationalities to assimilate. As late as the 1880s, the "idea of the Hungarian state" did not mean forcible linguistic and ethnic assimilation. Prime Minister

Kálmán Tisza stressed repeatedly the point that "I have never been and will never be a supporter of forcible Magyarization, because I am convinced that it is impossible to spread a nationality or a language by force."[9] In the light of the spontaneous Magyarization of parts of the non-Magyar population and the overestimation of its size, some publicists argued that the complete Magyarization of the country's population was imminent. They blinded Magyar public opinion with illusory predictions of 20–30 million Magyars. At the same time, even the most chauvinistic politicians were quite aware that "the mass Magyarization of the non-Magyar population was impossible… but this was no obstacle to national and cultural unity."[10] They tried, wherever possible, to promote and accelerate the process of spontaneous Magyarization. A priority was the idea that the non-Magyar intelligentsia and middle class should learn Hungarian, develop a sense of national cohesion and patriotism, and become involved in Magyar public life, culture and literature. In the words of Gusztáv Beksics, "political assimilation" was desired of the nationalities, rather than their "grammatical assimilation." Intellectuals and middle-class people among the nationalities should "feel themselves to be Hungarians, share in the emotions, goals and ambitions of the Magyar nation, and refrain from looking beyond the country's borders."[11]

The moderate constitutional opposition party, the National Party, noted the following in its program of 1892:

> When we speak of Hungarian national unity, we do not mean forcible Magyarization in linguistic terms, but rather the political unity of the nation, which makes no distinctions—in terms of rights or duties—between citizens speaking various languages, and which cannot accept nationalities as recognized constitutional groups. The spread of the Magyar language, however, we consider to be necessary, so that the non-Magyar intelligentsia can take part in public service… but above all as a means of welding together society, without which political unity remains an empty form.[12]

In their efforts to Magyarize minority intellectuals, the ruling Magyar classes assigned an important role to schools, particularly those secondary schools where Hungarian was predominantly the language of tuition. “The secondary school resembles a great machine; hundreds of Slovak boys are fed in at one end, coming out as Magyars at the other end.”[13] Such expectations regarding the influence of secondary school were not completely without foundation, as some nationality intellectuals and middle-class people did become Magyarized at these schools. This trend was particularly strong among those national groups that lacked their own native-language secondary schools.

In the 1880s, the Hungarian elite of minority-inhabited regions inhabited launched a campaign to speed up the process of Magyarization. A series of associations were formed with this goal in mind, including the Hungarian Cultural Association of Upper Hungary (FEMKE, est. 1882) and the Hungarian Cultural Association of Transylvania (EMKE, est. 1885). The purpose of such bodies was “to strive for a Magyar reconquest, employing all permitted legal means but excluding brutality and immorality.”[14] The supposed aim of the associations was not to attack the nationalities but to assume the national defense of the Magyar nation, because many Magyars had been Romanized or Slovakized in Transylvania and Upper Hungary. In fact, however, the work of the cultural associations was directed at propagating the Magyar language and Magyar culture in regions inhabited by nationalities. The counties provided funds in support of these so-called cultural associations, even levying supplementary taxes in order to do so. All of this constituted a social initiative, but the government tolerated such endeavors. “The government sees a great force in the chauvinist current and therefore does not dare to oppose it. It thinks that it will gain in popularity through its actions.” Increasingly, the general view was that “anything is permitted when it comes to spreading Magyarization; the end justifies the means, so that through such corrupt practices one and all can obtain merits in the eyes of the government.”[15] Although Kálmán Tisza claimed to be no friend of chauvinism (even when it furthered the interests of his nation), nevertheless his nationalities policy in effect opened up the way to the spread of intolerant nationalism in various areas of Magyar public life.

National chauvinism was expressed in Hungarian public opinion with increasing vociferousness at the end of the century. However, there were also (quieter) voices of sober moderation, as well as attempts to understand the demands made by the nationalities. Although several representatives of the Independence Party even managed to outdo the government in terms of national impetuousness, nevertheless several distinguished figures within the party and most of the ordinary membership continued to foster the party's traditionally liberal policy towards the nationalities. Lajos Mocsáry, who led the party between 1874 and 1884, fought particularly hard for the rights of the non- Magyar peoples. "It is an outcome of legal equality that the citizens of the country should not be attacked either by the Hungarian state or by Magyar society, as they seek to retain and foster their language and nationality, and that they should not be hindered in keeping to the letter and the spirit of the laws that guarantee the equal rights of the nationalities, that is, the Nationalities Act of 1868."[16]

Mocsáry was not alone in his views. "I can say that many serious people have stated to me in private that they share my views and regard the prevailing current as erroneous and damaging."[17] In 1887, the Serb Liberal Party requested Mocsáry to stand as the party's candidate in Újvidék (Novi Sad). After losing that election, he was elected, in 1888, by supporters of the Romanian National Party as their representative in the seat of Karánsebes (Caransebeş).

Some Hungarian heads of government (including Dezső Bánffy) proudly stated that they were "Magyar chauvinists," but there were some who condemned the manifestations of extreme nationalism. In 1894, at the time of the Memorandum libel case, which received international attention, Prime Minister Wekerle made it clear in an interview with the French magazine *Figaro* that he held the Magyar gentry in Transylvania just as responsible as the nationalist Romanian press and the Romanian National Party for the deterioration in relations between the two communities: "A big step forward could have been taken, if the arrogant and silly Transylvanian gentry with their seven cherry trees and empty pockets had abandoned their pretensions to being noble lords and had not held the Romanian peasants in contempt."[18] Another prime minister, István Tisza, made a similar statement: "I have never hesitated to oppose the immature chauvinists who, with their violent attempts at Magyarization and their insulting and mistrustful conduct, alienate the Romanian people from the Hungarian state and the Magyar nation."[19]

In the late nineteenth century, the attention of Western Europe's press was drawn to the nationalities issue in Hungary by the libel case involving the leaders of the Romanian National Party, the so-called Memorandum libel case. The main French, Italian and British newspapers reported on the trial. Students expressed sympathy with their oppressed Latin fellows in the east at demonstrations and protests held at universities in France and Italy. In the international arena, the Memorandum case undermined people's generally favorable opinions of Hungary and Hungarian liberalism; instead, people felt sympathy for the country's minorities as they struggled for their rights. In the 1890s, the nationalities issue received coverage in the French and Italian press in particular, while in the early years of the twentieth century the aggressive nationalities policy of the coalition government was condemned in no uncertain terms by the British press. Hungary's domestic politics were followed closely by H. W. Steed, *The Times*'s correspondent in Vienna, and by *The Spectator*'s columnist R. W. Seton-Watson (Scotus Viator), both of whom showed particular interest in the nationalities issue. Seton-Watson even authored several books on the subject, in which he sharply criticized the nationalities policies of successive Hungarian governments as well as the chauvinism of the Magyar ruling classes. In the wake of these articles and books, the British public's favorable opinion of the Hungarian people—who were valued for their love of freedom and their liberalism—dissipated. Respected international figures such as Tolstoy and the Nobel prizewinning Norwegian author Björnson also criticized the coalition government's policy of "oppression" with regard to the nationalities.

International condemnation peaked at the time of the "bloodbath" in Černova in 1907, when 15 Slovak peasants were killed. In this particular case, however, the government was not to blame.

A church was built in Černova, the native village of Andrej Hlinka, the parish priest of Rózsahegy (Ružomberok) and head of the Slovak People's Party. Catholics in Černova wanted Hlinka to consecrate the church. Hlinka's bishop had suspended him as a punishment for his involvement in political acts, and so he was not able to take part in the consecration ceremony. Local Catholics, however, insisted upon his presence and launched a protest against the consecrating priest who had been selected by the bishop. After a series of delays, the consecration of the church by the bishop was scheduled for October 27. By that time, Hlinka was on a speaker's tour in the Czech lands. Since the local community was preparing to prevent the consecration and following a request by the administrator of the parish church in Rózsahegy, the head of the district ordered the deployment of gendarmes to Černova and attempted on the Sunday morning to dissuade the district dean and other priests from going to the village. They, however, were determined to go ahead with the consecration, and set off for the village in two carriages. On the outskirts of the village, on a road in a narrow valley (Černova lies in northern Slovakia at high altitude) they encountered 300–400 men. The seven gendarmes tried in vain to clear the road towards the church, as there was no possibility of turning back. When the mass of people began to throw stones at the clergymen and the gendarmes, the sergeant ordered his men to fire. The result was 15 fatalities and almost 50 casualties. The leaders of this "rebellion" were put on trial and convicted. Not only were the villagers Slovaks, but so too were the priests calling impatiently for a consecration, as were the gendarmes and the sergeant. The church was finally consecrated by Hlinka three years later. Černova's becoming a symbol of Hungary's nationalities policy was unjustified.[20]

The Status and Movements of the Various Nationalities

Most of the country's one million or so Serbs lived in Croatia, particularly in the former Military Frontier region. Among all the peoples in Hungary, the Serbs had the highest proportion of rich peasants. They also had a relatively large commercial and intellectual middle class, which had managed to remove the prelates from the leadership of the national movement and even from the leadership of the ecclesiastical community. At the National Church Congress and in the leading bodies of the ecclesiastical autonomous body, secular members were always more numerous than priests. From mid-century, Újvidék (Novi Sad) rose to become the cultural center of Serbian nationality life. In 1864, *Matica Srbska*—which had been founded in Pest in 1826—moved to Újvidék, and it was followed there by the Serb literary and political newspapers. It was also in Újvidék that *Omladina* (a Serb youth organization) was founded; it promoted Serbian youth and student unions in Austria, Hungary and Serbia—officially for cultural purposes, but secretly in order to liberate the Serbs and advance their political unification. At Belgrade's request, the government dissolved *Omladina* in 1871.

Serb nationality politics were controlled at the time of the 1867 Compromise by the Serb National Liberal Party, which had been founded by the mayor of Újvidék, Svetozar Miletić. In 1870, Miletić was sentenced to one year's imprisonment, and then in 1876 he was accused of recruiting Serb volunteers to serve with the Bosnian rebels: he received a five-year prison sentence, but was freed in an act of clemency in 1879. In the 1880s, the party broke into two parts. Then, at the turn of the century, leading positions in the Serb national ecclesiastical autonomous body and in nationality politics were taken by the Radical Party under Jaša Tomić's direction. This party wished to broaden the liberal program to incorporate social democratic ideas; it also wished to respond to the needs of the *petite bourgeoisie* and wealthier peasants. The Radical Party fostered good relations with the Magyar coalition; the party was encouraged to do so by Belgrade. The good relationship came to an abrupt end when Bosnia was annexed. As relations deteriorated, the Work Party government ordered the suspension of the ecclesiastical autonomous body in 1912 and appointed a government commissioner to manage the Serbian Church's funds.

National political movements did not arise among Hungary's smaller South Slav groups—the *Bunjevci* of the Bačka region, the *Šokci* of the Baranya region, and the Croats and Slovenians of southern and western Transdanubia. Most of these communities' intellectuals were Magyarized, while the peasants—many of whom were bilingual—had no South Slav national consciousness. Several conscientious Catholic priests and teachers attempted to fashion a literary language out of the local dialects: calendars, newspapers and religious books were published for *Bunjevci*, Croat and Slovenian peasants. The Hungarian authorities tolerated and occasionally supported the development of local dialects into literary languages that could be used in tuition, seeking to detach these groups from the main South Slav bloc and thereby hinder the advance of Serbo-Croat and Slovenian as the principal literary languages.

After the Germans and the Hungarians, the Slovaks were the most economically advanced national group in the Carpathian basin. But they experienced the greatest ethnic and social losses. Although natural population growth among the Slovaks was higher than the national average, their population increased by just 5 percent between 1880 and 1910. The Slovak population then fell by 52,000 between 1900 and 1910, despite a natural increase of 260,000. Two factors explain the decrease: emigration and Magyarization. The Scottish publicist Seton-Watson, who carried out research in the field, noted that Slovaks were in the process of becoming fully assimilated. In addition to the counties of Upper Hungary, significant numbers of Slovaks lived in the Great Plain region, while several tens of thousands of Slovak workers were employed in factories and on construction sites in Budapest.

In 1861, at the national assembly of Slovaks held in Turócszentmárton (Martin), the establishment of an autonomous Slovak national region was mooted. During the post-Compromise decades, one representative of the Slovak National Party managed to gain a seat in the Parliament (in 1869), but thereafter Slovak representatives remained absent from the Parliament for three decades—despite the existence of several hundreds of thousands of male Slovaks with voting rights. The year 1874 saw the closure of Slovakia's three Slovak high schools, which had been established in the mid-1860s. The authorities' justification for closing the schools was that they promoted "the spread of Pan-Slavism." The Slovak cultural association—*Matica Slovenská* (est. 1864)—was wound up. Such measures also sealed the fate of a group of Slovaks living in Budapest who were known as the "New Slovak School" and who cooperated with Magyar liberals, seeking to become involved in national public life and to identify opportunities for Slovak national development. The seat of Slovak national politics after the 1867 Compromise was Turócszentmárton (Martin), a small town in Upper Hungary. In the 1870s, the Slovak national movement withdrew completely from national politics, becoming a passive force.

The stand taken by two new political forces resulted in a revival of Slovak national politics at the end of the nineteenth century. The first of these new forces developed under the framework of the Catholic People's Party. It spun off to form the Slovak People's Party under the leadership of the Catholic parish priest Andrej Hlinka. The other was a radical middle-class group—"Hlasist"—that favored cooperation and close unity with the Czechs. Taking their name from their newspaper *Hlas* (Voice), published in Szakolca (Skalica), the "Hlasists" were students of Tomaš G. Masarýk at the University of Prague. They were joined by Slovak university students and young intellectuals living in Budapest, who were led by Milan Hodža. Both groups sought to promote national consciousness and cooperation among Slovak peasants and the lower middle class, but they also attracted supporters from among the industrial working class. Attempts to achieve unity among Czechs and Slovaks were directed by an organization called Czechoslovak Unity (*Československá Jednota*), which was established in Prague in 1896. In the early twentieth century, several Slovak national politicians won seats in the Lower House.

The Romanians constituted the largest national minority in historical Hungary. Roughly half of them lived in Transylvania, and the remainder lived in the Banat region and in eastern Hungary. After the Compromise, two parties, each one calling itself the Romanian National Party, were formed—one in Transylvania and one in Hungary. In 1881, these two parties merged. The Romanian authorities protested against the union between Hungary and Transylvania, since they wished to restore the autonomy of Transylvania. In political terms, the Romanians in Hungary were in a more favorable position than those in Transylvania, where as few as 6 percent of adult male Romanians were entitled to vote, owing to the strict voting conditions. The total number of Romanian voters in Transylvania was thus as few as 20,000, while there were 90,000 Romanian voters in eastern Hungary and the Banat region, where 24 percent of adult male Romanians were entitled to vote. For this reason, the Romanian National Party in Transylvania pursued a policy of passiveness, while the Romanians in Hungary were more active. In the 1880s, leadership of Romanian national politics switched to the young intellectuals grouped around the newspaper *Tribuna* of Nagyszeben (Sibiu), led by Ion Slavici. It was under their influence that the central committee of the Romanian National Party decided to submit to Francis Joseph a memorandum containing the Romanians' grievances and demands. In 1892, the memorandum was taken by a delegation of 300 to Vienna, but Francis Joseph refused to receive the delegation and arranged for the unopened petition to be forwarded to the Hungarian government in Budapest. The Hungarian government then returned the petition—still unopened—to the chairman of the Romanian National Party. The Romanians, however, published the text of the Memorandum in the press and distributed translated copies of it abroad. This led the Public Prosecutor's Office to launch a libel case against the leaders of the party. Many foreign journalists came to Kolozsvár to follow the Memorandum trial. The Romanians used the trial to draw international attention to the nationalities issue in Hungary and to the grievances of the country's minorities.

During most of the nineteenth century, the economic, cultural and political centers of the Romanians were in southern Transylvania (Brassó-Braşov, Nagyszeben-Sibiu and Balázsfalva-Blaj). At the turn of the century, however, the focus of Romanian politics switched to southern Hungary (Arad, Temesvár-Timişoara and Lugos-Lugoj) and to Budapest. In 1905, the Romanian National Party entered the political stage, fielding its leading politicians as candidates in the elections. After neighboring Romania became an independent kingdom, there was a strengthening of the Romanian irredentist movement, which strove for the cultural and political unity of Romanians living on both sides of the Carpathians. Since Romania was an ally of the Monarchy, it was always the opposition party in Bucharest that offered financial and political support to the Romanians of Transylvania. The main propagandist for Romanian national unity was the *Liga Culturală*, an organization established in Bucharest in 1891 with the task of promoting Romanian cultural unity. During the period preceding the outbreak of war in 1914, István Tisza held negotiations with the Romanian political leaders, but they considered his concessionary proposals to be insufficient. The negotiations were fruitless; they were broken off after an intervention by Archduke Francis Ferdinand.

No political movements or national political parties arose among the Ruthenian population of the Carpathian region. The national movement was limited to attempts to preserve and develop the minority's language and culture. Greek Catholic priests were practically the only bearers and cultivators of national culture. In the mid-nineteenth century, a Russophile position had emerged, leading to the spread of the Russian language among the few literate Ruthenians. Initially, a Russophile position was taken by the Ruthenians' cultural institution, the Saint Basil Association. In the 1870s, however, the association's position changed, and it began to promote the transformation of the local dialect into a literary language.

In the late nineteenth century, the "Ruthenian question" manifested itself as a social problem. Mass emigration, the underdevelopment of agriculture, and the poverty of the Ruthenian peasants forced the government to intervene. In 1897, the minister of agriculture, Ignác Darányi, launched the so-called "Hill-Country Action" under the leadership of Ede Egán, a man of Scottish extraction. The aim was to develop livestock breeding and milk production in harmony with local environmental features. The early twentieth century saw the appearance among the Ruthenian peasants of the so-called Schismatic Movement, whereby Greek Catholic peasants returned to the Orthodox faith that their forebears had abandoned in the seventeenth century. Migrants returning from the United States brought the schismatic ideology to Hungary, while Russia also offered encouragement and support to the movement. In 1913, the government launched a grandiose political trial of the schismatic peasants of the Máramaros region, who were accused of treason and anti-government incitement.

Of the two million Hungarian citizens who spoke German as their native language, the Transylvanian Saxons were the only group with a national consciousness and a well-organized political movement. There were approximately 200,000 Transylvanian Saxons; they were regarded as historical Hungary's most developed national group in economic and cultural terms. The Saxons enjoyed substantial autonomy in the so-called *Királyföld* or *Königsboden*, and within the framework of their institution of self-government, the *Nationsuniversität*. They had considerable national wealth, an independent Lutheran Church and a highly developed education system. In 1876, however, the Hungarian government abolished the Saxons' territorial autonomy and incorporated the *Königsboden* into the newly established counties. It also removed the political and administrative powers of the *Nationsuniversität*, reducing its activities to the management of national wealth and schools. After a decade of sulking, the Saxons became reconciled to the new situation in 1890. The Saxon representatives joined the government party, while the Saxon youth increasingly found employment in the government bureaucracy.

The Saxons, who had resided in Transylvania for almost 800 years and had their own national institutions, were reluctant to build ties with ethnic Germans in other parts of Hungary—who numbered 1.5 million. These Germans were descendants of people who had come to the country at different points in time; they lived in various parts of the country, forming smaller and larger ethnic pockets. There was little interaction between the various groups; most of them had mixed with other ethnic groups. There was no contact between the German burghers of urban areas, whose forebears had come to the country in the medieval period, and the so-called "Swabian" peasantry of rural areas, whose forebears had arrived in the eighteenth century. The rapid Magyarization of the German communities began as early as the first half of the nineteenth century. In the 1870s, the efforts of Edmund Steinacker to develop a modern German national consciousness among the country's German urban burghers were in vain. It was only in the early twentieth century that a modern national movement arose among the Swabians of the southern Great Plain and Banat regions and that the German People's Party of Hungary was established on Steinacker's initiative in 1907.

Croatia during the Dualist Era

In 1873, a consolidation of the Compromise-based system took place in Croatia. Political consolidation did not mean, however, the resolution of Croatia's grave social problems. It seemed that sooner or later the political balance would be upset.

During the two decades following the Compromise, Croatian society was in a state of transition and crisis; there were many unresolved economic and social problems. Railway construction and the banking sector experienced an upturn in the 1880s, while industrialization accelerated in the 1890s. In 1890, 85 percent of the population was making a living from agriculture or forestry. The agrarian population's share decreased only to 79 percent in the course of the subsequent 20 years. In the latter third of the nineteenth century, the Croatian peasantry struggled with two great social problems. The end of self-sufficiency in economic management and the gradual advance of a modern market economy led to the gradual disintegration of the *zadruga*—a patriarchal complex family living in a shared household. The *zadruga* had been very common among the South Slav peasant farmers of the region. The break-up of the *zadrugas* was closely connected with another great social problem, namely, efforts to bring an end to the Military Frontier system, which had been the subject of squabbles for decades. (This issue has been covered in depth in a previous chapter.) The knock-on effects of these social problems continued to be felt in the twentieth century. In 1900, more than one in four Croatian peasants lived in *zadruga*s, and the proportion was even higher—40 percent—in the former Military Frontier.

The relative peace of the Mažuranić era lasted no more than five years. When Austria-Hungary occupied Bosnia and Herzegovina in 1878, the Croatian *Sabor* requested in a petition to Francis Joseph that the occupied territory—whose population included Catholic South Slavs, who were regarded at the time as Croats—be attached to Croatia. This plan—the implementation of which would have upset the balance of the Dualist system—was rejected by the ruler. At the time of the renewal of the financial agreement, the Croats failed to secure an extension of the right of their autonomous government to manage financial affairs and certain economic issues. Moreover, Mažuranić argued in vain for the final incorporation into Croatia of the Military Frontier. Consequently, the ban resigned in 1880, and some of the representatives of the National Party left the government party and formed the Independent National Party, which was also referred to as the Obzor Party—after the newspaper *Obzor*. The new party wished to place Croatian–Hungarian relations on a new foundation within the Dualist framework, with full political and financial independence and a responsible parliamentary government.

Those who became dissatisfied with the rule of the Croatian National Party—which had become welded to the Compromise system—from 1878 offered their support to the Law Party led by Ante Starčević. The disaffected included in particular the urban and rural lesser bourgeoisie, intellectuals and the lower clergy. The new program of the Croatian constitutional opposition reflected the realities of international relations and the domestic and foreign consolidation of the Monarchy. It foresaw a kingdom in which all South Slavs would be united under Croatian leadership and the Habsburg scepter. Between 1878 and 1883, the party pursued a successful policy of agitation among the peasants as well as the border guards, a group that was particularly dissatisfied with the process of winding up the Military Frontier. By skillfully drawing a connection between social and national problems, the party was able to mobilize large groups in both urban and rural areas.

The Croatian opposition movement was thus in the midst of a process of revival and reorganization when the Tisza government launched an attack on the autonomy of Croatia as well as Croatian language rights. The arena for this attack was the joint government institutions in Croatia, particularly the bodies of financial administration. In 1879, the Hungarian minister of finance, Gyula Szapáry, appointed a Magyar by the name of Antal Dávid as finance director in Zagreb. Szapáry's express wish was that Dávid, as the Hungarian government's confidant in Croatia, should represent the interests of the Hungarian state—and not just in a financial sense but also politically. He was expected to gradually enforce the "requirements of the idea of the Hungarian state." Croatian finance officials were required to study Hungarian, the correspondence of Croatia with the Ministry of Finance in Budapest was carried out in Hungarian, and serious efforts were made to ensure that large amounts of tax arrears were paid. All of this not only increased social discontent among the taxpaying public, but also led to protests from the Croatian government party and the aristocracy, since the actions of both the minister of finance and the finance director were in violation of the provisions of the Compromise Act—according to which the Croatian language was the official language of the joint government and official communications in Croatia.

When, in August 1883, signs in the Hungarian language and bearing the Hungarian coat-of-arms appeared on taxation offices in rural areas and then on the financial directorate building in Zagreb, Croatian public opinion—including the opposition and the Croatian government party—voiced its opposition. Workers and students in Zagreb held street protests and tore down the Hungarian signs. In late August and early September, the protests intensified and spread to areas outside the capital. In the villages of Varaždin and Zagreb Counties, the peasants attacked public offices and the tax offices. In the Military Frontier, an armed uprising was mooted. Neither the ban, Count Ladislav Pejačević, nor the autonomous government and public administration were prepared to take action to disperse the crowd. Claiming that action was needed to uphold the reputation of the Hungarian state and the Monarchy's security, Tisza persuaded Francis Joseph, who was initially inclined to accept the Croats' position, to suspend the Croatian constitution. A royal commissioner was appointed in the person of General Ramberg, the military commander in Zagreb. By deploying significant military force, Ramberg was able to put down the Zagorje peasant movements and the growing armed rebellion in the Military Frontier.

In the face of such mass demonstrations, the Hungarian government and the Croatian ruling classes came to an agreement once more. Tisza abandoned the Magyar language policy in Croatia, while the National Party, which had been weakened by the crisis surrounding the coat-of-arms, continued to act as the governing party. The Compromise system was only really consolidated in Croatia after 1883. This political consolidation was closely connected to the growth in capitalist development, industrialization, and the economic upturn of the 1880s and 1890s. The Croatian crisis abated, and for two decades the situation was relatively calm.

The consolidation of the Compromise system in Croatia took place under Károly Khuen-Héderváry, who was appointed as Ban of Croatia in late 1883 and who remained in that post until 1903. Although he was a large landowner in Slavonia, Khuen-Héderváry had no direct links with the Croatian political elite; he clearly represented the interests of the Hungarian government in Zagreb. He managed to stabilize the government's position by exerting his power and employing clever tactics. He reorganized the Croatian National Party, offering membership to any politician with an interest in sustaining the Compromise system. At the same time, he took steps to ensure that the Hungarian side did not violate the provisions of the Compromise Act or extend the use of the Magyar language in official matters.

Efforts to exploit the conflicts between Croats and Serbs became an important part of Khuen-Héderváry's policy of counteracting Croatian national ambitions. In the 1870s, the use of the Serbian flag and Cyrillic alphabet was prohibited in Croatia. Attempts were also made to limit the autonomy of the Serbs in the field of education. Several of the leaders of the Law Party even denied the existence of a separate Serb nation, considering Serbs to be degenerate Croats. Under such circumstances, the Croatian Serbs chose not to support the Croatian opposition but rather to organize themselves independently. The ban made economic and other concessions in order to win the support of middle-class Serbs in Croatia; he often employed Serbs in various positions within the Croatian government. One in four of Croatia's people were Serbs, but they accounted for almost 40 percent of the Croatian government party representatives. The ban's situation was made easier by the opposition's gradual retreat and the extremely limited voting rights. As late as 1910, just 8 percent of male adult Croats were entitled to vote. This may be compared with a figure of 25 percent in Hungary. Thus, in Croatia, fewer than 50,000 people were entitled to vote.

The Law Party drafted its new program in 1894—and this served as the joint program of the constitutional opposition until 1918. According to the program, the party was to "use all legal means to ensure that the Croatian people, who reside in Croatia, Slavonia, Dalmatia, Fiume and the surrounding area, the Mura region, Bosnia and Herzegovina, and Istria, unite in an independent state entity within the Habsburg monarchy; the Croatian people will assist fellow Slovenians in their endeavor to achieve the attachment of the Slovenian territory to this state entity. The Kingdom of Croatia shall—in equality with the Kingdom of Hungary—administer matters shared by the whole Empire with the other countries of His Highness."[21] The program stood, therefore, somewhere in the middle between "trialism" and Dualism, and it was formulated in such a manner that it could be interpreted in both ways.

Hungary's prime minister, Dezső Bánffy, tried once again to increase the Hungarian government's direct control and influence over matters addressed by the Croatian government. Bánffy was dissatisfied with Khuen-Héderváry's performance; in his view, Khuen-Héderváry had made too many concessions on the question of Croatian sovereignty. There is no doubt that on some issues—above all those concerning the official language of the joint institutions—Khuen-Héderváry supported the Croatian standpoint. In his submission to Francis Joseph, however, Bánffy chose to emphasize the point that he could not recognize "Croatia's national government as the government of a state under a separate political leadership and thus as independent," and he proposed a revision of the Croatian Compromise. Francis Joseph, however, refused to agree to any changes; he insisted on retaining Khuen-Héderváry as ban.[22]

In the early twentieth century, the opposition parties and groups of various persuasions were united under the slogan of economic and financial independence, with the aim of taking political action. Such action reached its zenith in the popular movements of 1903. There was a repeat of events that took place 20 years earlier. Spokesmen and mass protestors chanted the slogans of financial independence, universal suffrage, and Croatian as a language of command in the army. Protestors vented their anger by tearing down Hungarian signs and flags displayed on public buildings. It was only by introducing martial law that the authorities were able to maintain order; this marked the beginning of a series of protests lasting several months. In 1903, Khuen-Héderváry resigned from his post in order to become Hungary's prime minister. He left to his successor, Count Teodor Pejačević, a country in turmoil with its prisons full.

At the turn of the century, the nationalist conflicts between the Croat and Serb middle classes intensified. In August 1902, anti-Serb demonstrations, which sometimes descended into violence, were held in Zagreb and several other Croatian cities. These demonstrations, however, turned out to be the last such manifestations. In 1904 and 1905, the most important development was a rapprochement between the Croat and Serb parties.

The new line in South Slav politics—at the time referred to as the "new course"—developed in Dalmatia rather than Croatia in the autumn of 1903. Its instigators were Ante Trumbić, the mayor of Split and leader of the Law Party in Dalmatia, and Frano Supilo, the editor of the Fiume newspaper *Novi List*. Dalmatia's South Slav politicians regarded the Croat and Serb peoples as members of the same nation. In their view, the main threat to the South Slavs came from the "*Drang nach Osten*"—that is, German and Austrian expansionism in the Balkans. To counteract this threat, it was necessary to join forces with all other political forces, in particular the Hungarian opposition. The ultimate goal was the establishment of an independent South Slav state. However, this was regarded as something that could only be achieved gradually.

At a conference of Dalmatian and Croatian Croat representatives, held in Rijeka on October 3, 1905, the "new course" was adopted as the official policy of the Croat opposition. The Fiume Resolution emphasized the mutual dependence of the Croat and Hungarian national movements; it supported the Hungarian opposition's struggle for Hungary's independence. The hope was that if the Hungarians were successful, they might share the rights gained with the Croats, thereby fulfilling their national demands: the unification of Dalmatia and Croatia, the upholding and further development of the autonomy guaranteed in the Compromise, electoral reform, and the general democratization of political life. In Zadar, on October 17, a conference of Serb representatives gave its support to the Fiume Resolution. The Croat–Serb coalition's election summons, published in December 1905, outlined the new national program of the Croat and Serb middle classes. Alongside the demands made in the Fiume Resolution, emphasis was laid on the public's democratic demands and the enactment of social legislation protecting peasants, the lower middle class and industrial workers.

In 1906, the Croat–Serb coalition won a majority in the elections and assumed leadership of the country. Cooperation with the Hungarian coalition soon ended, owing to tensions caused by legislation prescribing knowledge of Hungarian for railway workers. In the summer of 1907, the Ban of Croatia, Count Teodor Pejačević, and the whole of his autonomous government resigned. The Croat–Serb coalition went into opposition; anti-Hungarian protests flared up throughout the country.

Bosnia's annexation and other policies aimed at consolidating the Monarchy's position in the Balkans increased the importance of the Croatian issue to the Monarchy's foreign and domestic politics. The ruling circles in Vienna tried to arrange for an appropriate solution to the Croatian issue: these circles comprised the "Greater Austria" faction associated with Archduke Francis Ferdinand, the Christian Social Party, which cooperated closely with the former, and the minister of foreign affairs, Aehrenthal, who was working on preparations for the annexation. The minister of foreign affairs tried to justify the annexation by revealing the existence of a Greater Serbian conspiracy against the Monarchy. In the summer of 1908, 53 members of the Serb National Independence Party in Croatia were arrested and accused of treason and of plotting against the Monarchy. In the course of the treason trial, held in Zagreb in 1909, it transpired that some of the documents serving as evidence were forgeries. In the meantime, the crisis in Bosnia had been resolved, and so the Zagreb trial became somewhat of an inconvenience for Austro-Hungarian diplomacy. The accused were convicted, but then pardoned two years later.

After Bosnia's annexation, emphasis was laid on a "trialist" solution to the South Slav question: that is, the merger into one state of the Monarchy's South Slav countries and the transformation of the Monarchy into a tripolar state. In South Slav politics, this development was accompanied by a shift in the center of gravity to the Law Party and associated groups in Croatia, Dalmatia, Istria and Bosnia. In Croatia, the original Law Party broke up into different factions, which subsequently became independent parties; by 1908 there were three of them. These parties were oriented towards Vienna, as all the Hungarian political parties firmly rejected "trialism." Statements made by conservative leaders in Vienna raised hopes among Croat and Slovenian supporters of the Law Party that they could be persuaded to support a "trialist" reorganization of the Monarchy.

In reality, however, the Croats' "trialist" ideas differed significantly from the "Greater Austria" blueprint of Francis Ferdinand and the plans of the Christian Social Party in Austria. Based on the historical law of nations, the Croats wished to merge regions inhabited by South Slavs into a third sovereign state within the framework of the Monarchy; this third state would share with Austria and Hungary the same status and rights. For their part, however, the politicians in Vienna sought a unified and centralized "Greater Austria" with provincial autonomy for a unified South Slav administrative unit. Francis Ferdinand and the Christian Social Party were so successful in making vague "trialist" promises that they managed to influence the policies of the Croats and Slovenians for several years.

The year 1911 saw the formation of a united bloc comprising the law parties of Croatia, Dalmatia, Istria and Bosnia. This bloc was in close contact with the Slovenian People's Party, which also sought a "trialist" solution. In 1912, a joint Croat–Slovenian political organization was formed. In early 1912, the assembly of the various law parties—which the press referred to at the time as the "trialist Parliament"—submitted a memorandum, signed by 55 representatives, to Francis Joseph and Archduke Francis Ferdinand. Since the response was negative, the law parties announced at a conference in March 1913 that they could not count on any external support and would not allow the Croat people to be used for some anti-national political purpose. "We shall continue to move forward based on the existing constitutional and national program, and we shall place our trust in nobody but God and Croats."[23] The "trialist" memorandum submitted by the Slovenian People's Party to Archduke Francis Ferdinand in the spring of 1913, urged a prompt decision, since "we are the last representatives of the generation that sought guarantees of its national existence within the framework of the Monarchy."[24] Hungary's leaders exhibited grave political shortsightedness when they rejected "trialism." They effectively prevented the Catholic South Slav populations (the Croats and Slovenians), who were opposed to Serb hegemony, from satisfying their desires for national self-determination within the framework of the Monarchy.

From 1907 onwards, Croatia was beset by permanent crisis: the *Sabor*, which was dominated by the opposition, was repeatedly adjourned or dissolved. The Croat–Serb coalition fought with the law parties—and both these groups were opposed to the governments in Budapest and the bans appointed by them. Apart from a period of several months in 1910, the *Sabor* did not convene for years. During a short period in 1910, it voted in favor of a new electoral law, which did not introduce universal suffrage but did broaden the electorate to a greater extent than in Hungary. The approximate number of men entitled to vote increased from 50,000 to 200,000; 32 percent of adult males could vote. In 1912, however, the domestic political situation in Croatia deteriorated to such an extent that Francis Joseph suspended the Croatian constitution, appointing a royal commissioner to run the country.

A return to normality was achieved during István Tisza's term as prime minister. In 1913, he reached an accord with the Croat–Serb coalition, which had an absolute majority in the *Sabor*. As part of the accord, the language provisions relating to the railway were abrogated. Once the compromise had been made, Tisza appointed his former secretary, Ivan Skerlecz, as ban. At the subsequent elections, the Croat–Serb coalition achieved an absolute majority. The agreement between the government and the coalition was sealed by Tisza's visit to Zagreb in January 1914. Although the coalition held a majority in the *Sabor*, it could not form a government. The

Hungarian position was that the Croatian autonomous government was not a parliamentary government, and so members of the coalition could not be appointed to the position of ban or become heads of department (making up the autonomous government) or high sheriffs.

Prior to 1914, the concept of the national unity of the South Slav peoples was promoted by radical groups within the youth movement. In 1913–1914, the nationalist youth movement became stronger; it mostly represented the idea of Yugoslav national unity, although there was still no uniform position among the various youth groups concerning the form, route and methods of realization. The ideas and plans varied; sometimes they foresaw a Yugoslav nation and state comprising three equal peoples, while at other times it was suggested that the two weaker peoples should assimilate into the strongest, the Serb nation and its state. The idea of a Greater Serbia was strongly promoted by Serb students. Among Croat nationalist youths, the most popular idea was the free and equal merger of the three nations into one nation—under the auspices of a nation state. They wished to achieve this through "revolutionary" means: that is, terrorist acts.

The South Slav socialists also proclaimed unity—but on an internationalist basis. They wanted to establish the unity of the Balkan Slav nations through a federation of states with equal rights and status. They too proved unable to develop a uniform position on the specific features of this federation. In November 1909, delegates of the Monarchy's South Slav social democratic parties attended a conference in Ljubljana, where they announced the national goal of the South Slavs in Austria-Hungary: the unification of the South Slavs as an integral nation within the framework of a democratic and federal Austria-Hungary. The first conference of Balkan socialists, held in Belgrade in January 1910, came out in favor of establishing a federation of Balkan countries—which would be transformed into republics. The proposal was reiterated at subsequent conferences. At these conferences, however, there were sharp differences in opinion between Croat and Slovenian delegates, seeking South Slav unity in a democratic and federal Austria-Hungary, and Serb and Bulgarian delegates, who sought a free and independent federation of Balkan republics.

Notes

1 Gábor Kemény, *Iratok a nemzetiségi kérdés történetéhez Magyarországon a dualizmus korában. I. 1867–1892* [Documents Relating to the History of the Nationalities Issue in Hungary in the Era of Dualism. Vol. 1, 1867–1892] (Budapest, 1952), p. 679.

2 *Ibid.*, p. 602.

3 Gábor Kemény, *Iratok a nemzetiségi kérdés történetéhez Magyarországon a dualizmus korában. II. 1892–1900* [Documents Relating to the History of the Nationalities Issue in Hungary in the Era of Dualism. Vol. 2, 1892–1900] (Budapest, 1956), p. 379.

4 *Magyar Országos Levéltár, Budapest. Miniszterelnökség levéltára* [Hungarian National Archives, Budapest. Prime Ministers' Archive], 1867–Ib–156/1877.

5 Gusztáv Beksics, *Közigazgatásunk reformja és nemzeti politikánk* [Hungarian Public Administrative Reform and National Policy] (Budapest, 1890), p. 156.

6 *Jelentése a nemzetiségi kérdés tárgyában kiküldött bizottságnak. Az 1865-dik évi december 10-dikére hirdetett országgyűlés képviselőházának irományai. VI.* [Report of the Committee on the Subject of the Nationalities Issue. Papers of the Lower House of the Parliament Announced for December 10, 1865] (Pest, 1868), p. 129.

7 Gábor Kemény, ed., *Mocsáry Lajos válogatott írásai* [Selected Writings of Lajos Mocsáry] (Budapest, 1958), p. 371.

8 Cited in Viktória M. Kondor, *Az 1875-ös pártfúzió* [The 1875 Party Merger] (Budapest, 1959), pp. 130–131.

9 Gábor Kemény, *Iratok a nemzetiségi kérdés történetéhez Magyarországon a dualizmus korában. I. 1867–1892* (Budapest, 1952), p. 679.

10 *Ibid.*, pp. 670–671.

11 Gusztáv Beksics, *A magyar faj terjeszkedése és nemzeti konszolidációnk* [The Spread of the Hungarian Race and Our National Consolidation] (Budapest, 1896), p. 17.

12 Gyula Mérei and Ferenc Pölöskei, eds., *Magyarországi pártprogramok 1867–1998* [Hungarian Party Programs, 1867–1998] (Budapest, 2003), p. 158.
13 Béla Grünwald, *A Felvidék. Politikai tanulmány* [Upper Hungary. A Political Study] (Budapest, 1878), p. 140.
14 Cited in Zoltán I. Tóth, *Magyarok és románok. Történelmi tanulmányok* [Hungarians and Romanians. Historical Studies] (Budapest, 1964), p. 437.
15 "Mocsáry Lajos 1887. február 15-i beszéde a képviselőházban" [Lajos Mocsáry's Speech to the Lower House on February 15, 1887], in Kemény, *Iratok a nemzetiségi kérdés történetéhez Magyarországon a dualizmus korában. I. 1867–1892*, p. 732.
16 *Ibid.*, p. 725.
17 Lajos Mocsáry, *Néhány szó a nemzetiségi kérdésről* [A Few Words on the Nationalities Issue] (Budapest, 1886), p. 12.
18 Gábor Kemény, *Iratok a nemzetiségi kérdés történetéhez Magyarországon a dualizmus korában. II. 1892–1900* (Budapest, 1956), p. 289.
19 Gábor Vermes, *Tisza István* [István Tisza] (Budapest, 1994), p. 83.
20 This account of the events in Černova is based on the documents of the contemporary inquiry and a publication by the Slovak historian Roman Holec entitled "Tragédia v Černovej a slovenská spoločnosť" [The Tragedy of Černova and Slovak Society], *Matica Slovenská* (1997).
21 Kemény, *Iratok a nemzetiségi kérdés történetéhez Magyarországon a dualizmus korában. II. 1892–1900*, p. 288.
22 *Bánffy Dezső 1898. március 5-i felterjesztése az uralkodóhoz. Magyar Országos Levéltár, Budapest. Miniszterelnökség levéltára* [Dezső Bánffy's Submission to the Ruler Dated March 5, 1898. Hungarian National Archives, Budapest. Prime Ministers' Archive], 1898–XVII–1685.
23 Mirjana Gross, "Hrvatska politika velikoaustrijskog kruga oko prijestolonasljednika Franje Ferdinanda" [The Croatian Policy of the "Greater Austria" Faction Associated with Archduke Francis Ferdinand], *Časopis za suvremenu povijest* 2 (1970): 58.
24 "Inhalt des trialistischen Memorandums an den Thronfolger," *Grazer Tagblatt*, April 5, 1913.

14. THE FOREIGN POLICY OF THE MONARCHY

In the mid-nineteenth century, the Habsburg Empire was still regarded as a major European power in terms of the size of its population and territory. However, it lagged behind the Western European powers and Germany in terms of economic development and military strength. By the end of the century, it had become a second-rate power, unable to participate in the scramble for colonies or to sway world politics. Nevertheless, throughout the period, until the beginning of 1918, the Western powers regarded the Monarchy's survival as vital to the stability of southeastern and east-central Europe and as a key factor in countering Russian and German power ambitions.

In the Dual Monarchy, foreign affairs were an area of common policy. In accordance with the Compromise of 1867, foreign affairs were administered by a joint minister of foreign affairs and a joint Ministry of Foreign Affairs "in agreement with both governments and with their consent." Hungarian governments exerted considerable influence upon the Monarchy's foreign policy, particularly under the Hungarian prime ministerships of Gyula Andrássy, Kálmán Tisza and István Tisza. At the time of the annual discussions on the foreign affairs budget, there were often heated debates about the principles and direction of foreign policy. The Hungarian Parliament also frequently addressed foreign policy issues. As an Austro-Hungarian minister wrote, "In Berlin and Vienna the complaint is made that the Lower House in Hungary is excessively concerned with foreign policy issues; indeed, Bismarck's blunt question is whether it will be possible to remain in a lasting alliance with Austria-Hungary, when the parliamentary majorities here have such far-reaching influence upon foreign policy."[1] Nevertheless, under the political framework of the Dual Monarchy, the monarch, Francis Joseph, could enforce his will in many aspects of foreign policy decision-making.

The multinational character of the Austro-Hungarian Empire and the absence of national unity imposed limitations upon the Monarchy's foreign policy. The two halves of the Empire and various national groups had different foreign policy interests; it proved difficult to reconcile and coordinate their foreign policy ideas and preferences. For the German Austrians, the German question was the main foreign policy issue; they were rather indifferent to other issues, including policy towards the Balkans. Meanwhile, the Magyars were opposed to a Western-oriented foreign policy; they regarded the Balkan peninsula as the Monarchy's principal sphere of operation. They sought a pro-active stand against Russia and they carefully monitored the changing national relations in the Balkans. The Czechs, for their part, tended to be anti-German and pro-Russian, while the Poles were hostile to both Germans and Russians.

Between 1848 and 1871, the question of German unity lay at the center of the Empire's foreign policy. The dynasty's desire was to establish German unity with the participation of Austria and under Habsburg leadership. Hungary's liberal politicians also attached great hopes to such ideas. They believed that the attachment of the Hereditary Lands (Austria and Bohemia) to Germany would allow the Kingdom of Hungary to become independent. (Links with the Habsburg countries would be maintained at most in a personal union.) The question of German unity was decided in Prussia's favor by the Austro-Prussian War of 1866. In the Peace of Prague, Austria recognized the dissolution of the German Confederation and accepted that it would have no part in Germany's reorganization. Even so, Habsburg diplomacy hoped that France would be victorious in its unfolding conflict with Prussia.

In the late 1860s, Beust, the minister of foreign affairs of Austria-Hungary, limited his efforts to halting Prussian expansionism in an attempt to protect the independence of the southern German states. When Francis Joseph and Napoleon III met in Salzburg in the summer of 1867, the French emperor offered a defensive alliance to counter the Prussians. Beust, however, regarded such an alliance as unacceptable, in the light of the Monarchy's sizeable German population. Francis Joseph accepted his minister of foreign affairs' argument, even though he and his Court supported a policy of revenge.

When the Franco-Prussian War broke out in the summer of 1870, Austria's political elite would have liked to join forces with France. The Monarchy's position in this European conflict was discussed at the joint Ministerial Council on July 18, 1870. Potocki, the Austrian prime minister, noted that the Empire's German-speaking population sympathized with Germany, while he personally—and his Slav federalist backers—supported France. The "Court Party" (*Hofpartei*) represented by Archduke Albrecht was similarly supportive of the French. Beust argued for neutrality, explaining that the Monarchy could not pursue a foreign policy that offended the Austrian Germans. Andrássy, the Hungarian prime minister, supported Beust's position, although he too expected a French victory. In the end, the Ministerial Council decided upon a "wait-and-see approach"; it pursued a policy of "armed neutrality" but deemed it to be necessary to prepare the Monarchy to exploit the advantages of the anticipated French victory militarily.

Prussia's victory and the proclamation of the German Empire in 1871 resolved the question of German unity once and for all. This led inevitably to a reversal of the Monarchy's foreign policy. The anti-Prussian stance was no longer an option, and Beust drew the inevitable consequences. In December 1870, Bismarck offered the Monarchy a timely rapprochement. On May 18, 1871, Beust submitted to Francis Joseph his new foreign policy strategy, which envisaged the Monarchy's future at the side of the newly founded German Empire. Francis Joseph "acknowledged his consent" to the strategy. Germany's cordial relationship with Russia presented an opportunity for a normalization of relations between Austria-Hungary and the Russian Empire. There was clearly a need for this, because with the conclusion of the question of German unity, the focus of Austro-Hungarian foreign policy now switched to the Balkans—where, however, it clashed with Russian interests.

Concerning policy in the Balkan peninsula, Beust took his cue from the Russophile traditions of Austrian foreign policy; he had no wish to upset existing relations. However, in November 1871, Beust was forced to resign for domestic political reasons. He was succeeded by Gyula Andrássy, who had been Hungarian prime minister.

Andrássy's views contrasted starkly with the dynastic conservative traditions of Austrian foreign policy. His ideas were nurtured by European liberalism and Hungarian nationalism. He had no intention of placing hurdles in front of the natural process of reorganization in the Balkan peninsula, reckoning on the formation of nation states at some point in time. He believed that the Monarchy could become guarantor of the process of national reorganization in the Balkans, and he was willing to take under his wing the peoples emerging from under Ottoman rule. In return, the small countries of southeastern Europe would be expected to accommodate the interests of the Monarchy. This foreign policy led inevitably to a clash with Russia. Although Russia supported the liberation movements of the Balkan Slavs against Ottoman rule, nevertheless its desire was to bring these peoples under its own influence. Meanwhile, the Monarchy sought to prevent the formation on its southern borders of a large South Slav state under Russian influence. To this end, it tried to uphold Turkey's integrity for as long as possible. Andrássy's view—which was shared by Hungarian political public opinion—was that Russia's power ambitions represented the greater threat to the Monarchy and to Hungary. Accordingly, having been appointed as minister of foreign affairs, he tried to establish an anti-Russian European alliance. His efforts were in vain, and so he had no choice but to accept Bismarck's Three Emperors' League, an agreement between the Russian, German and Austrian emperors that was signed in 1873. The agreement prescribed "consultations" in the event of a European conflict; it was thus a "consultative pact" rather than a formal alliance. Still, as far as Balkan policy was concerned, the agreement of Russia, as a cosignatory to the agreement, had to be reckoned with.

In the summer of 1875, a rebellion broke out in Herzegovina, which lay under Ottoman rule. The following year the rebellion spread to Bulgaria in the eastern Balkans. Neither Russian diplomacy nor Austria-Hungary welcomed these developments. Both powers thus attempted to persuade Turkey to implement reforms benefiting the Christian populations in the Balkans. Their joint action proved fruitless. The Turks ruthlessly suppressed the Bulgarian rebellion; this action led Serbia and Montenegro to declare war on the Porte. The Turks were victorious in the conflict, and so the Russians determined upon military intervention. Prior to this, however, the Austro-Hungarian and Russian ministers of foreign affairs signed a secret agreement in Budapest stipulating the maximum extent of any Russian conquests in the Balkans and prohibiting any Russian military action in the western Balkans. For the Monarchy the agreement held out the prospect of an annexation of Bosnia-Herzegovina. In the ensuing conflict, the Russians overcame Turkish resistance but refrained from seizing Constantinople in reaction to diplomatic pressure from both Great Britain and Austria-Hungary and the arrival in the Bosphorus of the British fleet. In February 1878, Great Britain stood prepared for war against Russia. Andrássy also argued the case for war, at the joint Ministerial Council on February 24. In his view, the situation that had arisen was unlikely to be repeated: with Europe's assistance, the Monarchy could settle its differences with the Slavs. The only support for Andrássy's proposal came from Kálman Tisza, the Hungarian prime minister. Claiming the support of Hungarian public opinion, Tisza urged action against Russia. Austria's national groups—with the exception of the Poles—opposed the war, and the Ministerial Council rejected Andrássy's proposal. In the Peace of San Stefano, signed on March 3, 1878, Russia ignored existing agreements and reorganized the Balkans in line with its own interests. Greater Bulgaria was created in the eastern Balkans. Austria-Hungary found itself almost completely excluded from the Balkan arena. The "Three Emperors" policy had failed. On receiving news of the treaty, Andrássy sent notes to the Great Powers, proposing—with reference to the provisions of the

Treaty of Paris of 1856—an international congress to resolve the Balkan question and a revision of the San Stefano peace treaty. Great Britain gave its support to the proposal. Several days after the signing of the peace treaty, the emphatically worded British and Austro-Hungarian notes were dispatched. The two countries called upon Russia to submit the peace treaty to examination by an international congress of the guarantor powers. They held out the prospect of military action by the Great Powers, if Russia chose to reject this proposal. Since the Russians were fearful of a war with the Western powers, they accepted the proposal. At the Congress of Berlin in the summer of 1878, representatives of the seven powers signed a treaty that returned Macedonia to Turkey and proclaimed the full independence of Romania, Serbia and Montenegro. Austria-Hungary received authorization to occupy Bosnia-Herzegovina and the Sanjak of Novibazar.

Andrássy's greatest diplomatic success was the convening of the Congress of Berlin in 1878, where relations in the Balkans were effectively settled for a period of three decades. His success was due in no small part to cooperation between British and Austro-Hungarian diplomats and their determined stand against Russia. On his return from Berlin, however, Andrássy was given a cool reception in both Vienna and Budapest. The occupation of Bosnia was not popular in any of the Monarchy's countries. In Austria it even caused a domestic political crisis, leading ultimately to the collapse of the government and the governing party, the Liberal Party. Under Taaffe's leadership, a conservative-clerical Slavophile coalition government was formed. The effects of the domestic political changes were also felt in foreign policy: there too the influence of supporters of the conservative-dynastic policy grew. This meant first and foremost a Russian orientation. Andrássy, who was anti-Russian and liberal, had no choice but to leave his post.

In the summer of 1879, Bismarck offered an alliance to Andrássy, who accepted the offer. In this way, a secret treaty was established between Austria-Hungary and Germany. Under the treaty, if either party were attacked by Russia, the other party would offer full military assistance. When, on the first renewal of the Dual Alliance, the German side indicated a desire to extend the alliance to cover all attacks against one of the two parties, the idea was rejected by the Austro-Hungarian minister of foreign affairs, Kálnoky, who claimed that such an amendment would lead the Hungarian government to oppose the renewal of the treaty: "The idea that Austria-Hungary would be threatened by France is not something that a Hungarian person can fathom."[2] The Dual Alliance became the Triple Alliance with the inclusion of Italy in 1882; Romania joined in 1883. Italy needed the support of Germany and Austria-Hungary against France; it renounced its irredentist territorial claims against Austria (south Tyrol, Trieste and Istria). Romania, which needed support against Russia, did the same with regard to Transylvania and Bukovina. The signing of the Dual Alliance was Andrássy's last diplomatic act. On the following day Francis Joseph relieved him of his duties and appointed Heinrich Heymerle as the new minister of foreign affairs. Thereafter the Monarchy's ministers of foreign affairs were—in contrast to Andrássy—career diplomats; they were chosen from among the senior officials at the Ministry of Foreign Affairs.

The Three Emperors' League was renewed in 1881 at Bismarck's behest. It prescribed reciprocal neutrality in the event of a war with a fourth party. Russia gave its consent to the Monarchy's occupation of Bosnia-Herzegovina becoming a formal annexation at the appropriate time. The Three Emperors' League marked out the various spheres of influence in the Balkans. Russia was given a free hand in Bulgaria, while the Monarchy was to control the western Balkans, in particular Bosnia. The Serbian prince, Milan Obrenović, received the title of king, but his country became dependent on Austria-Hungary in all regards.

Heymerle, who died in 1881, was replaced by Count Gustav Kálnoky, an Austrian of distant Hungarian descent. He was a convinced supporter of the traditional dynastic policy of spheres of influence, and he made great efforts to uphold the cordial relationship with Russia. The Three Emperors' League was renewed once more in 1884, but in 1887 an agreement could not be reached. Instead, war almost broke out between the Monarchy and Russia. In 1885, the three powers took a joint stand against the unification of Bulgaria and eastern Rumelia. Bulgaria, however, protested against the Russian protectorate; it wished to become a truly independent country. In response, the Russians threatened a military occupation of the country. Bismarck and Kálnoky supported this measure, but the Hungarian Parliament and Prime Minister Tisza opposed it. In the light of the prime minister's protests, Kálnoky was compelled, in the autumn of 1886, to voice his support for Bulgaria's independence. He thus broke with the Monarchy's policy of spheres of influence in the Balkans, but he wished to maintain good relations with Russia. In practice, there was no possibility of this, however. When the Bulgarian Parliament elected, as prince, Ferdinand of Coburg—whom the Russians regarded as Austria's man—the Russian government, acting under pressure from Pan-Slavic circles, threatened the Monarchy with war. On Galicia's borders, large Russian troop concentrations were undertaken.

Among Austro-Hungarian circles, many regarded war with Russia as inevitable. At the joint Ministerial Council in January 1888, Kálmán Tisza spoke out in favor of war. Hungarian public opinion uniformly supported him on this issue. Even the military were in favor of a preventive war against Russia. However, Taaffe, the Austrian prime minister, and Kálnoky, the Austro-Hungarian minister of foreign affairs, were against war; Kálnoky warned that if the Monarchy became the aggressor, then it could not count on Germany's assistance. In early 1888, in an attempt to silence the war party, the secret provisions of the Dual Alliance were made public. Since Russia did not actually want a war, the great tensions of 1887–1888 were dispelled without further escalation.

In late 1887, Great Britain, Italy and Austria-Hungary came to an agreement on maintaining the status quo in the Balkan peninsula. This treaty—known as the Eastern Triple Alliance—was also directed against Russia, as it called for joint action in the event of a unilateral attempt by a fourth power to alter the status quo in the Balkans. Joint action was never taken, however, as Russia also sought to maintain the status quo. In the 1890s, its attention switched to the Far East.

The Monarchy's foreign policy tended to be anti-Russian even after the crisis of 1887–1888. Still, neither from Berlin nor from London did Kálnoky receive the anticipated support for an active anti-Russian policy in the Balkans. Kálnoky was forced to resign in 1895, following a conflict with the Bánffy government in Budapest. His successor Agenor Gołuchowski was no more successful in this area. Great Britain was unwilling to renew the Eastern Triple Alliance of 1887. Its reticence signaled a change in direction of British policy towards the region. In the light of these circumstances, Austria-Hungary also had to revise its Balkan policy, basing it once more on cooperation with Russia. In 1897, after reciprocal visits by the two monarchs, an agreement was signed on maintaining the Balkan status quo. "After the accord had been signed, the Russian minister of foreign affairs stated with satisfaction that Russia and Austria-Hungary would no longer squabble over the Balkan peoples. For the time being the peoples under the Turkish yoke could not hope for anything from the two Great Powers, as they reinstated the conservative negotiating policy."[3] The accord, signed at the Mürzsteg hunting lodge during Nicholas II's visit to Austria in 1903, as well as a further treaty signed in St. Petersburg in October 1904, enhanced relations between the two powers and their cooperation in the Balkan peninsula.

In 1902, the Triple Alliance was renewed, but there were already signs of a growing detachment on the part of Italy, which found the alliance increasingly burdensome. Because of its irredentism and its ambitions in the western Balkans, Italy increasingly found itself at odds with the Monarchy.

At the turn of the century, other alliances were formed in opposition to the Triple Alliance. In the 1890s, relations between Italy and France became increasingly cordial. In 1904 Great Britain and France established the *Entente Cordiale*. And in 1907, an Anglo-Russian agreement was signed.

It was at this time that a change unfavorable to the Monarchy took place in the Balkans. In 1903, a band of military officers murdered Alexander I of Serbia and his wife. The Karadjordjević dynasty acceded to the Serbian throne. The new regime cast an eye on Bosnia and made approaches to the Entente Powers. It wished to free itself from the Monarchy's economic and political guardianship. In 1904, Bulgaria and Serbia signed a treaty under the slogan "The Balkans for the Balkan peoples." This indicated that they wished to liberate the peninsula themselves and encourage solidarity among the Balkan peoples. In 1906, in an attempt to exert pressure on Serbia, the Monarchy banned the import of Serbian livestock, thereby launching the customs war between the two countries (the "pig war"). Russia's ability to take action in the Balkans was limited at this time, in the light of the revolution and its recent grave defeat in the war against Japan. Besides other factors, this explains why war did not break out at the time of the Bosnian crisis in 1908.

After Gołuchowski's resignation, Alois Lexa von Aehrenthal took over the direction of the Monarchy's foreign affairs. "The diplomat, who revived the dynastic policy of dividing [into spheres of influence], was willing to consent to Russian rule of the straits and Constantinople in return for Austro-Hungarian possession of the western Balkans."[4] In 1908, the Young Turks' Revolution was victorious in the Ottoman Empire; Austria-Hungary believed that the time was ripe for its annexation of Bosnia and Herzegovina, that is, the legal incorporation of the provinces into the Monarchy (as until then Bosnia and Herzegovina had been part of the Ottoman Empire under international law, and Austria-Hungary had occupied them only temporarily). Russia, however, was required to consent to the annexation. At a meeting in Buchlau (Moravia), Izvolsky, the Russian minister of foreign affairs, consented to Bosnia's planned annexation, while Aehrenthal promised diplomatic assistance towards a revision of the status of the straits (permitting Russian ships of war to pass through the Bosphorus and the Dardanelles). However, Francis Joseph proclaimed the annexation prematurely. In response, the Russian minister of foreign affairs sent notes to the signatories of the Berlin Treaty (1878); he proposed the holding of an international conference to discuss the Balkan difficulties, including, as a matter of priority, the issue of annexation. Great Britain, France and Italy supported the proposal, but Germany backed the Austro-Hungarian position. Serbia vehemently protested against the incorporation of South Slav provinces into Austria-Hungary. The Monarchy ordered a partial mobilization, deploying its troops to the Serbian border. Faced by threats of war from Austria-Hungary and Germany, Russia recoiled; it withdrew its proposal for a conference.

The annexation represented the final blow to relations between the Monarchy and Serbia. Serbia wanted to obtain a port on the Adriatic, and the Monarchy was preventing it from doing so. Secret organizations were formed in Serbia with the aim of carrying out attacks against leading politicians in Bosnia and Croatia.

By 1910, preparations for war were underway throughout Europe. At the time of the annexation crisis, the Monarchy's military leadership proposed a preventive war against both Serbia and Italy, but the political leadership rejected this proposal. Aehrenthal and—after his death in 1912—his successor Leopold Berchtold tried to maintain normal relations with Russia. The first overt conflict occurred in the Balkans: in the autumn of 1912, Montenegro, Serbia, Bulgaria and Greece declared war on Turkey. The belligerents seized what remained of Turkey's domains in Europe, apart from the Edirne (Adrianople) region. They divided up these territories among themselves, but soon squabbled over the booty. In the summer of 1913, the Second Balkan War took place. Bulgaria was defeated and dismembered by the other three states. In terms of territory and self-confidence, Serbia and Romania were considered to be the biggest winners of the two Balkan wars. This had a significant effect on the Romanians and Serbs living in Hungary.

In response to the collapse of Ottoman rule in the Balkan peninsula, Austro-Hungarian diplomacy made efforts to secure the formation of an independent Albania. Such efforts were designed to cut Serbia off from the Adriatic Sea and prevent Italy from gaining a foothold in the western coastal strip of the Balkans. However, in November 1912, Serbian troops reached the Adriatic coast. Once again war threatened between the Monarchy and Serbia—as well as Russia, which now backed Serbia. In this critical situation, relief came from traditional dynastic solidarity. Direct contact between Francis Joseph and Tsar Nicholas II led to an agreement. However, when in 1913 Montenegrin troops laid siege to and then occupied the city of Scutari, the Austro-Hungarian fleet blockaded the Albanian coast, while the Monarchy's army massed on the Montenegrin border. In response, the Montenegrins withdrew from Scutari. On receipt of the Austro-Hungarian ultimatum, Serbia withdrew its troops from the Albanian coast, and so an independent Albania could be established. By the end of 1913, matters had settled down in the Balkans. Even so, Vienna now realized that the Monarchy was in grave danger, since it was threatened from the south by Serbia and from the east by Russia. Thus, from late 1913, war was regarded as inevitable even in Vienna. No one knew, however, what the spark to ignite the fire would be.

On June 28, 1914, students belonging to one of the secret Serb organizations mentioned above—the "Young Bosnia"—assassinated Archduke Francis Ferdinand and his wife in Sarajevo. The assassins were supported by the secret Serb organization "Unification or Death" (also known as the Black Hand), which was also in conflict with the Serbian government.

The General Staff and the minister of foreign affairs were in favor of declaring war on Serbia immediately. However, István Tisza, the Hungarian prime minister, had reservations; he considered it to be inopportune to start a war and was unconvinced of Serbia's guilt. Moreover, he feared a Romanian attack on Transylvania. At the joint Ministerial Council on July 7, Tisza argued that a war was to be avoided on this occasion, because more favorable conditions would surely arise in the future. He suggested that tough but not unacceptable demands be made upon Serbia; an ultimatum would only be delivered if Serbia rejected these demands. Tisza was alone in this position, as all other participants were in favor of war, and it was known that the Kaiser and government of Germany also supported military action by the Monarchy. The next day, in a memorandum to Francis Joseph, Tisza made his objections known. However, the German leadership considered the opportunity to be a favorable one and urged Vienna to embark on war. Berchtold thus attempted to convince Tisza to change his position. His efforts appear to have borne fruit, because on July 14, Tisza also consented to the dispatch of an ultimatum to Serbia. He did so despite the fact that a day earlier Berchtold had been informed by telegraph that the investigation in Sarajevo had not found any evidence of the Serbian government's involvement; on the contrary, there were several indications that this possibility could be excluded.[5] By mid-July, Tisza was convinced that the time for a reckoning with Serbia had come. Even so, he trusted that the conflict could be contained, as did other leaders in Austria-Hungary and Germany. He also made it clear that the Monarchy had "no intention of annexing the Kingdom of Serbia."

The note delivered to the Serbian government included several unacceptable demands and required their "acceptance without reservation." Although the Serbian government wished to avoid war and took a concessionary position, it did not accept the ultimatum without reservation. The Monarchy thus declared war on Serbia on July 28, a month after the Sarajevo assassination. On July 29, Sir Edward Grey, the British foreign secretary, proposed the holding of a conference to be attended by the Great Powers, at which the dispute could be settled. However, his overtures were rejected by the governments in both Berlin and Vienna. On August 1, Germany declared war on Russia. Over the next few days France, Belgium and Great Britain also entered the war. Thus began World War I, which led to the dissolution of the Austro-Hungarian Empire and the dismemberment of historical Hungary. On one of those days in the summer of 1914, Lajos Thallóczy, a senior Austro-Hungarian official, wrote the following in his diary: "Everyone suspects deep down that the survival of the Monarchy is at stake."[6]

Notes

1 Gusztáv Gratz, *A dualizmus kora. Magyarország története 1867–1918* [The Era of Dualism. Hungarian History 1867–1918], vol. 1 (Budapest, 1934), p. 237.
2 *Ibid.*, p. 235.
3 István Diószegi, *A hatalmi politika másfél évszázada* [One and a Half Centuries of Power Politics] (Budapest, 1994), p. 206.
4 *Ibid.*, p. 220.
5 Gábor Vermes, *Tisza István* [István Tisza] (Budapest, 1994), p. 256.
6 *Ibid.*, p. 259.

CHRONOLOGY

1867	
Jan. 9–11	Gyula Andrássy, József Eötvös and Menyhért Lónyay held talks in Vienna on the Compromise (*Ausgleich*).
Feb. 7	Richard Belcredi was dismissed as Austria's minister-president in favor of Friedrich Ferdinand von Beust.
Feb. 17	Emperor Francis Joseph appointed Gyula Andrássy as Hungarian prime minister.
Feb. 20–Nov. 14, 1871	The Gyula Andrássy administration.
May 29	Legislation on the Austro-Hungarian Compromise was passed by Hungary's Lower House of Parliament.
June 8	Emperor Francis Joseph was crowned as King of Hungary.
July 28	The king gave royal assent to legislation governing the new constitutional conditions (Acts I–XII of 1867).
Nov. 21	The Lower House of the Austrian Imperial Council approved the proposed Compromise legislation.
Nov. 26	The Austrian and Hungarian governments agreed to form a trade and customs union.
Dec. 21	The monarch gave assent to the Austrian constitution.
Dec. 27	Legislation granted equal civil and political rights to Jews.
1868	
April 28–July 24	Delegations of the Croatian and Hungarian National Assemblies negotiated on constitutional relations between the two countries.
Nov. 17	The king gave assent to the law on the Hungarian–Croatian Compromise (Act XXX of 1868).
Dec. 5	Act XXXVIII of 1868 on education in peoples' schools.
Dec. 6	Act XLIV of 1868 on equal rights for national minorities.
	Hungarian State Railways (MÁV) was formed.

1869	
July 14	Legislation was introduced to separate the judicial system from the apparatus of state.
Aug. 19	A royal decree was passed placing the Military Frontier districts under civilian administration.
1870	
July 28	The *provisorium* placed Fiume under the Hungarian Crown.
Oct. 26–Nov. 3 and March 11–29, 1871	Congress of Catholic Autonomy.
1871	
Nov. 14–Oct. 8, 1879	Gyula Andrássy served as joint Austro-Hungarian minister of foreign affairs.
Nov. 14–Dec. 4, 1872	The Menyhért Lónyay administration.
	Foundation of the National Statistical Office.
1872	
Oct. 12	Act on the Foundation of Kolozsvár University.
Dec. 5–March 21, 1874	The József Szlávy administration.
1873	
May 9	"Black Friday" on the Vienna stock exchange marked the beginning of the economic slump of 1873.
June 27	The Banat Military Frontier district and the Titel Battalion area were demilitarized and annexed to Hungary.
Oct. 22	The Three Emperors' League was formed by Austria-Hungary, Germany and Russia.
Nov. 17	Official union of Buda, Pest and Óbuda as Budapest.
	Hungary suffered its last big outbreak of cholera.
1874	
March 21–March 2, 1875	The István Bittó administration.
May 17	The '48 Independence Party was formed.
Nov. 26	Suffrage legislation (Act XXXIII of 1874).

1875	
March 1	The Deák Party and center-left merged to form the Liberal Party.
March 2–Oct. 20	The Béla Wenckheim administration.
July 9	There was an anti-Ottoman uprising in Herzegovina.
Oct. 20–March 15, 1890	The Kálmán Tisza administration.
Nov. 12	The minister of the interior dissolved the Slovak national organization *Matica Slovenská.*
1876	
June 19	The privileged areas of the *Székely* and Saxon communities were abolished and subsumed into the county system.
1877	
April 24–March 3, 1878	The Russo-Turkish War.
1878	
April 13	Formation of the United Opposition.
June 13–July 13	The Congress of Berlin of the Great Powers.
June 27	The trade and customs union was renewed. The Austro-Hungarian Bank was founded.
July 29–Oct. 20	Austro-Hungarian forces occupied Bosnia and Herzegovina.
1879	
March 12	Szeged was left in ruins by flooding of the River Tisza.
Oct. 7	Austria-Hungary and Germany made a Dual Alliance.
1880	
May 16–17	The General Workers' Party of Hungary held its inaugural congress.
1881	
Feb. 14	The Hungarian gendarmerie was established.
May 30	Legislation on state preferences for domestic industry.

1882	
May 20	The Triple Alliance was formed by Austria-Hungary, Germany and Italy.
1883	
August 14–Sept. 12	There were anti-Hungarian demonstrations in Croatia and an armed uprising in the Croatian border territory.
Oct. 30	Romania joined the Triple Alliance.
1884	
Sept. 27	The Royal Opera House in Budapest opened.
Sept. 29	The Independence and '48 Party was formed.
1885	
April 25	Legislation reforming the Upper House was passed.
1887–1888	Sámuel Teleki traveled in east Africa.
1889	
Jan. 30	The death of the heir apparent, Prince Rudolf.
June 16	Ministries of Agriculture and Commerce were founded under a reorganization of ministries responsible for the economy.
1890	
March 15–Nov. 17, 1892	The Gyula Szapáry administration.
Dec. 7–8	The Social Democratic Party of Hungary held its inaugural congress.
1892	
May 28	The Romanian Memorandum was taken to Vienna by a 300-strong delegation.
Aug. 2	Currency reform introduced the gold crown.
Nov. 17–Jan. 14, 1895	The Sándor Wekerle administration.
1894	
March 20	Lajos Kossuth died in Turin and was buried in Budapest (April 2).
May 17–25	The Memorandum Trial took place in Kolozsvár.

Dec. 9	Church-related legislation on civil marriage, religion of offspring, and state registration of births, etc., was passed.
1895	
Jan. 14–Feb. 26, 1899	The Dezső Bánffy administration.
Jan. 28–29	The Catholic People's Party held its inaugural conference.
Aug. 10	A congress of national minorities was held in Budapest.
Oct. 16	The Jewish religion became legally acknowledged.
1896	
Jan. 19	The Hungarian Farmers' Union was formed.
May 2	Francis Joseph opened the Budapest Millennium Exhibition.
1898	
Sept. 10	Queen Elizabeth was murdered in Geneva by an anarchist.
1899	
Feb. 26–June 27, 1903	The Kálmán Széll administration.
1900	
Jan. 1	The first number of the review *Huszadik Század* appeared.
1901	
Jan. 23	The Social Scientific Society was founded.
1902	
May 29	The National Association of Hungarian Industrialists (GyOSz) was founded.
Oct. 8	The new Parliament building was inaugurated.
1903	
June 27–Nov. 3	The Károly Khuen-Héderváry administration.
Nov. 3–June 18, 1905	The István Tisza administration.

1904	
Nov. 19	The opposition parties formed a coalition.
1905	
Jan. 26–Feb. 4	Parliamentary elections brought defeat for the Liberal Party after thirty years in power.
June 18–April 8, 1906	The Géza Fejérváry administration.
Dec. 19	Minister of the Interior József Kristóffy presented a bill on franchise reform.
1906	
April 4	The coalition leaders reached agreement with the monarch.
April 8–Jan. 17, 1910	The Sándor Wekerle administration.
1907	
April 6	Legislation on sickness and accident insurance for industrial and commercial employees.
Oct. 8	The Lower House approved the new Austro-Hungarian economic agreement on trade and tariffs.
1908	
Jan. 1	The first issue of the literary journal *Nyugat* appeared.
Oct. 6	Bosnia-Herzegovina was annexed to the Monarchy.
1909	
April 11	Wekerle's tax reform simplified the fiscal system.
Sept. 28	Wekerle and his administration resigned.
1910	
Jan. 17–April 22, 1912	The Károly Khuen-Héderváry administration.
Feb. 19	The National Workers' Party was founded.
1912	
March 31	Francis Joseph suspended the Croatian constitution.
April 22–June 10, 1913	The László Lukács administration.
May 23	"Bloody Thursday": a mass socialist demonstration in Budapest.

June 4	Speaker István Tisza pushed the armed forces act through the Lower House.
June 8	The Greek Catholic see of Hajdúdorog was founded by a papal bull.
July 7	Legislation established the universities of Debrecen and Pozsony.
Oct. 9–May 30, 1913	The First Balkan War.
1913	
April 30	New franchise legislation.
June 10–June 15, 1917	The István Tisza administration.
June 29–Aug. 10	The Second Balkan War.
Nov. 26	The Croatian constitution was reinstated.
1914	
June 28	The heir apparent, Francis Ferdinand, and his consort were murdered in Sarajevo.

BIOGRAPHIES OF KEY PERSONALITIES

Ady, Endre (1877–1919)
Poet and journalist. A revolutionary innovator, his influential volume *New Verses* marks the beginning of modern Hungarian lyric poetry.

Albrecht Friedrich Rudolf, Archduke (1817–1895)
Habsburg Archduke. Military and civilian governor of Hungary (1851–1860), commander-in-chief (1866), then chief controller of the armed forces (from 1869).

Andrássy Gyula, Count (1823–1890)
The Hungarian government's representative in Turkey in 1849, prime minister of Hungary (1867–1871), foreign minister of the Austro-Hungarian Monarchy (1871–1879).

Apponyi, Albert, Count (1846–1933)
Hungarian politician. Member of Parliament and speaker of the Parliament (1901-1903). He headed the Hungarian delegation to the Paris peace talks after World War I. He represented Hungary at the League of Nations (1924-1925).

Apponyi, György, Count (1808–1899)
Hungarian court chancellor (1846–1848), lord chief justice (1860–1863).

Arany, János (1817–1882)
He and Sándor Petőfi were the most prominent nineteenth-century Hungarian poets. In 1865 he became secretary (later secretary-general) of the Hungarian Academy of Sciences.

Auersperg, Adolf Carl Daniel, Prince (1821–1885)
A liberal politician who served as Austrian prime minister from 1871 to 1879.

Auersperg, Carlos Wilhelm, Prince (1814–1890)
A liberal politician who was Austria's first post-*Ausgleich* prime minister in 1867–1868.

Babits, Mihály (1883–1941)
Hungarian poet, writer and translator. Editor-in-chief of *Nyugat* from 1929 until his death.

Bach, Alexander, Baron (1813–1893)
Before 1848 a lawyer, a member of the Austrian liberal opposition, minister of justice (1848–1849), then interior minister (1849–1859), ambassador of the Austrian Empire to the Holy See (1859–1867).

Bánffy, Dezső, Baron (1843–1911)
A Hungarian liberal politician from Transylvania, he served as prime minister in 1895–1899.

Baross, Gábor (1848–1892)
One of the outstanding economic politicians of the Dualist Era, he was made secretary of state for transport in 1883, then minister of transport and later minister of commerce from 1886 until his death.

Bartók, Béla (1881–1945)
Hungarian composer, pianist and collector of Eastern European and Middle Eastern folk music. He is considered one of the greatest composers of the twentieth century.

Batthyány, Lajos, Count (1807–1849)
Hungarian reform politician. Prime minister of the first independent Hungarian government in 1848. He was executed by the Habsburg tyrants on October 6, 1849.

Beck-Rzikowsky, Friedrich von, Count (1830–1920)
Austrian military officer of German origin. Chief of the General Staff between 1881 and 1906.

Becke, Franz Karl von, Baron (1818–1870)
Austrian minister of finance until the *Ausgleich*, then common minister of finance in 1867–1870.

Beck-Rzikowsky, Friedrich, Count (1830–1920)
General. He was made head of Francis Joseph's military chancellery in 1867 and served as chief of staff of the Monarchy's armed forces in 1881–1906.

Belcredi, Richard, Count (1823–1902).
Lord lieutenant of Bohemia (1864–1865), minister of state (1865–1867).

Berchtold, Leopold, Count (1863–1942)
An Austro-Hungarian diplomat who served as minister in St. Petersburg in 1907–1912 and common minister of foreign affairs in 1912–1915.

Bethlen, István, Count (1874–1946)
Great estate owner from Transylvania. A significant political figure of the twentieth-century Hungarian political scene. Prime minister (1921–1931), he consolidated the Horthy regime. He was deported to the Soviet Union by the Red Army.

Beust, Friedrich Ferdinand, Count (1809–1886)
Prime minister of Saxony, from 1866 foreign minister of the Austrian Empire, prime minister of Austria from 1867, then imperial chancellor and common foreign mininister until 1871.

Bittó, István (1822–1903)
A Hungarian liberal politician who was minister of justice in 1871–1872 and prime minister in 1874–1875.

Burián, István, Count (1851–1922)
Hungarian diplomat and politician. Common minister of finance (1903–1912, 1916–1918) and foreign minister (1915–1916, 1918).

Charles IV (1887–1922)
King of Hungary and Emperor of Austria as Charles I in 1916–1918.

Csáky, Albin, Count (1841–1912)
A Hungarian liberal politician who served as minister of religion and education in 1888–1894.

Csernoch, János (1852–1927)
Consecrated as Roman Catholic Bishop of Csanád in 1908, he became Archbishop of Kalocsa in 1911 and Archbishop of Esztergom and Cardinal Prince-Primate of Hungary in 1913.

Darányi, Ignác (1849–1927)
The most important agrarian politician of the Dualist Era, who served as minister of agriculture in 1895–1903 and 1906–1910.

Deák, Ferenc (1803–1876)
Hungarian statesman, liberal politician, one of the leaders of the Opposition Party before 1848. Minister of justice (1848). In 1861 leader of the so-called Rescript Party, then from 1865 the Deák Party. He played a major role in negotiations leading to the Compromise of 1867.

Eötvös, József, Baron (1813–1871)
Minister of cults and public education in the Hungarian government in 1848, and in the Andrássy government (1867–1871).

Fejérváry, Géza, Baron (1833–1914)
An army general who served as minister of defense in 1884–1893 and prime minister of the so-called *darabont* (guardsman) government of Hungary in 1905–1906.

Francis Ferdinand, Archduke (1863–1914)
Archduke of Austria-Este, Prince Imperial of Austria, Prince Royal of Hungary and Bohemia, and heir to the Austro-Hungarian throne from 1896. His assassination in Sarajevo precipitated the Austrian declaration of war that triggered World War I.

Francis Joseph I (1830–1916)
Emperor of Austria (1848–1916) and King of Hungary (1867–1916).

Gautsch von Frankenthurn, Paul, Baron (1851–1918)
An Austrian politician who was prime minister and minister of defense in 1897–1898, prime minister again in 1905–1906, and prime minister for a third time for a few months in 1911.

Garami, Ernő (1876–1935)
Hungarian mechanic and socialist politician. Leader of the Socialdemocratic Party of Hungary (1898–1919) and minister of trade (1918–1919).

Gołuchowski, Agenor Maria Adam, Count (1849–1921)
An Austro-Hungarian diplomat of Polish origin, who was common minister of foreign affairs in 1895–1906.

Gorove, István (1819–1881)
A liberal Hungarian economic politician who was minister of agriculture, industry and trade in 1867–1870 and minister of transport until 1871.

Haymerle, Heinrich, Baron (1828–1881)
An Austro-Hungarian diplomat who was common minister of foreign affairs in 1879–1881.

Herczeg, Ferenc (1863–1954)
Hungarian writer, journalist, editor, M.P. (1896).

Hlinka, Andrej (1864–1938)
A Slovak politician and Roman Catholic parish priest of Rózsahegy (Ružomberok). He became the founding president of the Slovak People's Party in 1905 and the leading advocate of Slovak autonomy after 1919.

Hodža, Milan (1878–1944)
A Slovak politician, lawyer and journalist, who until 1918 edited Slovak papers in Budapest and was deputy president of the Slovak People's Party. He served as Czechoslovak minister of agriculture in the 1920s and 1930s and prime minister in 1935–1938.

Hohenwart, Karl Sigmund von, Count (1824–1899)
An Austrian conservative and federalist politician who attempted as prime minister and minister of the interior in 1871 to achieve an Austro-Bohemian *Ausgleich* and the coronation of Francis Joseph as King of Bohemia.

Jászi, Oszkár (1875–1957)
Hungarian social scientist, publicist and politician. Ideological leader and practical director of Hungarian bourgeois radicalism. Editor of *Huszadik Század.*

John, Franz von, Baron (1815–1876)
A lieutenant general who served in 1866–1868 as Austrian minister of defense, then as common minister of defense, and from 1874 until his death as chief of staff.

Jókai, Mór (1825–1904)
Hungary's most popular nineteenth-century novelist and foremost writer of romantic prose. He was active in the

March 1848 Revolution in Pest. He edited several papers and periodicals. After the *Ausgleich*, he was in Parliament for three decades, first for the center-left, then from 1875 with the Liberal Party.

Kállay, Benjámin (1839–1903)

A diplomat, historian and politician under the Dual Monarchy who was consul-general in Belgrade in 1867–1875, common deputy minister of foreign affairs in 1879, then common minister of finance from 1883 until his death. He was largely in charge of the affairs of occupied Bosnia-Herzegovina.

Kálnoky, Gustav Sigismond, Count (1832–1898)

An Austro-Hungarian diplomat who served as common minister of foreign affairs in 1881–1895.

Kandó, Kálmán (1869–1931)

Hungarian engineer, who developed high-voltage three-phase alternating current motors and generators for electric locomotives, and is known as the "father of the electric train".

Károlyi, Mihály, Count (1875–1955)

Hungarian aristocrat and politician of controversial reputation. Prime minister (1918–1919) and temporary president of the First Hungarian Republic. He lived in exile after 1919.

Kerkápoly, Károly (1824–1891)

A Hungarian economic politician, economist and university professor. He was common minister of finance in 1870–1873.

Khuen-Hédervár, Károly, Count (1849–1918)

A great landowner in Hungary and Croatia, he was Ban of Croatia in 1883–1903 and Hungarian prime minister in 1903 and in 1910–1912.

Kodály, Zoltán (1882–1967)

Hungarian composer, ethnomusicologist, educator and linguist.

Koerber, Ernest von (1850–1919)

A politician, he was Austrian prime minister in 1900–1904, then common minister of finance in 1915–1916 and briefly prime minister again at the end of 1916.

Kossuth, Ferenc (1841–1914)
The son of Lajos Kossuth, he spent most of his life in exile as an engineer of European repute. He repatriated in 1894 and became president of the Independence Party. In 1906–1910 he was minister of trade, industry and transport in the coalition government.

Kossuth, Lajos (1802–1894)
Hungarian lawyer and politician. Regent-president of the of Kingdom of Hungary in 1849. After 1849 he lived in emigration. He was widely honored during his lifetime as a freedom fighter.

Kuhn von Kuhnenfeld, Franz, Baron (1817–1896)
A general who served as common minister of defense in 1868–1874.

Liszt, Ferenc (*Franz*) (1811–1886)
A world-famous composer and pianist of German-Hungarian descent, he spent a few days in Hungary each year after the *Ausgleich*. In 1875, he agreed to become president of the Budapest Academy of Music.

Lónyay, Menyhért, Count (1822–1884)
Hungarian minister of finance (1867–1870), minister of finance of the Austro-Hungarian Monarchy (1870–1871), prime minister of Hungary (1871–1872).

Lukács, László (1850–1932)
A liberal Hungarian politician and financier, he served as minister of finance in 1895–1905 and in 1910, and then as prime minister and minister of the interior in 1912–1913.

Majláth György (1818–1883)
Before 1848 one of the leaders of the Conservative Party, lord high treasurer in 1860–1861, head of the Lieutenancy Council, Hungarian court chancellor (1865–1867), president of the Table of Magnates and the King's Bench (*királyi tábla*) (1867–1883).

Masaryk, Tomáš Garrigue (1850–1937)
Czech statesman, philosopher and liberal politician. He favored national independence for the peoples of Austria-Hungary. First president of Czechoslovakia (1918–1935).

Mažuranić, Ivan (1814–1890)
A Croatian poet and politician, he was the Croatian Court chancellor in 1861–1865, and, after the 1873 revision of the Croatian Settlement, Ban of Croatia until 1880.

Mikszáth, Kálmán (1847–1910)
A writer and journalist, and the great master of Hungarian realist prose. Since the 1880s, he and Mór Jókai have been the most popular and widely read Hungarian authors. He was elected to Parliament in 1887.

Miletić, Svetozar (1826–1901)
A lawyer and leader of the Serbian National Liberal Party. He was mayor of Újvidék (Novi Sad) in the 1860s and elected to the Hungarian Parliament in 1865, but sentenced in political trials to one year's imprisonment in 1870 and five years in 1876.

Mocsáry, Lajos (1826–1916)
A Liberal Independence politician and commentator, and a prominent representative of the opposition to the Dualist system. He chaired the Independence Party for a time. He fought throughout his life for fully equal rights and free development for the national minorities.

Mollinary, Anton, Baron (1820–1904)
A general. As commander of the Zagreb army corps, he directed the elimination and return to civilian rule of the Croatian–Slavonian Military Frontier region.

Molnár, Ferenc (*Ferenc Neumann*) (1878–1952): One of the greatest Hungarian dramatists and novelists of the twentieth century, known also as Franz Molnar. He emigrated to the USA in the 1930's.

Nagyatádi Szabó, István (1863–1924)
Founder of the Hungarian Smallholders' and Peasant Party (1909). Minister on several occasions (1919–1924). His name has become a symbol of the democratic Smallholders' movement.

Prohászka, Ottokár (1858–1927)
Hungarian Catholic writer, bishop of Székesfehérvár, representative of Christian Socialism and leader of the Catholic renewal.

Rudolf, Archduke (1858–1889)
Austrian archduke, Hungarian and Bohemian royal prince, heir apparent to the thrones of Austria and Hungary. His liberal outlook led to several clashes with his father, Francis Joseph. He and his lover committed suicide at the Mayerling hunting lodge in 1889.

Schmerling, Anton, Ritter von (1805–1893)
Imperial minister elected by the Frankfurt German Parliament in 1848, Austrian minister of justice (1849–1851), minister of state (1860–1865), president of the Austrian Supreme Court (1865–1891).

Schwarzenberg, Felix zu, Prince (1800–1852)
Diplomat, lieutenant general, prime minister (1849–1852).

Scitovszky, János (1785–1866)
Bishop of Rozsnyó (1827–1838) and of Pécs (1838–1849), archbishop of Esztergom and prince-primate (1849–1866), from 1853 cardinal.

Sennyey, Pál, Baron (1824–1888)
Leader of the Conservative Party after 1875, lord high treasurer and head of the Lieutenancy Council (1865–1867), president of the Table of Magnates (1884–1888), lord chief justice (1884–1888).

Simor, János (1813–1891)
Roman Catholic prelate. He was consecrated as Bishop of Győr and appointed as Prince-Primate and Archbishop of Esztergom in 1867. He was created a cardinal in 1873.

Starčević, Ante (1823–1896)
A Croatian national opposition politician who founded and headed the Party of Law (*Stranka prava*, 1861). He opposed the Dualist system and sought a threefold structure for the Monarchy.

Strossmayer, Josip Juraj (1815–1905)
Roman Catholic Bishop of Diakovár (Đakovo) and a Croatian national politician. He headed the Croatian National Liberal Party in 1861–1873 and founded the Zagreb Academy of Science

and Arts. He played an important role at the First Vatican Council of 1870 as leader and spokesman of the opposition.

Szapáry, Gyula, Count (1832–1905)

A liberal Hungarian politician. He served as minister of the interior in 1873–1875, minister of finance in 1878–1887, minister of agriculture in 1889 and prime minister in 1890–1892.

Széll, Kálmán (1843–1915)

A liberal Hungarian politician and expert on economics and finance, he was minister of finance in 1875 and 1878 and prime minister in 1899–1904.

Szilágyi, Dezső (1840–1901)

A jurist, university professor and liberal politician. As minister of justice in 1889–1895 he undertook important work of codification.

Taaffe, Eduard von, Count (1833–1895)

A neo-conservative Austrian politician, he served as prime minister in 1869–1870 and 1879–1893. His second term of office saw important reforms in social policy.

Teleki, László, Count (1811–1861)

One of the leaders of the Opposition Party before 1848, the Hungarian government's representative in Paris in 1848–1849, leader of the so-called Resolution Party in 1861.

Thun und Hohenstein, Leo Leopold,Count (1811–1888)

Deputy governor of Galicia (1847–1848), minister of cults and public education (1849–1860).

Tisza, Kálmán (1830–1902)

Leader of the so-called Resolution Party in 1861, leader of the Left-Center (1865--1875), leader of the Liberal Party and prime minister (1875–1890).

Tisza, István, Count (1861–1918)

Hungarian great estate owner and lawyer. Prime minister (1903–1905, 1913–1917). He was murdered in his home (1918).

Trefort, Ágoston (1817–1888)

A liberal cultural politician and commentator. He served as minister of education and religion from 1872 until his death.

From 1885 he was also president of the Hungarian Academy of Sciences.

Vázsonyi, Vilmos (1868–1926)

Hungarian lawyer and politician. Founder of the Democratic Party (1900), M.P. (1901) and minister of justice (1917–1918).

Wekerle, Sándor (1848–1921)

A liberal politician and superb financier who served as minister of finance in 1889–1895. He was three times Hungarian prime minister (in 1892–1895, 1906–1909 and 1917–1918), in each case taking also the finance portfolio.

Zichy, Nándor, Count (1829–1911)

A neo-conservative politician and economic policy-maker. He founded and led the Catholic People's Party in 1895.

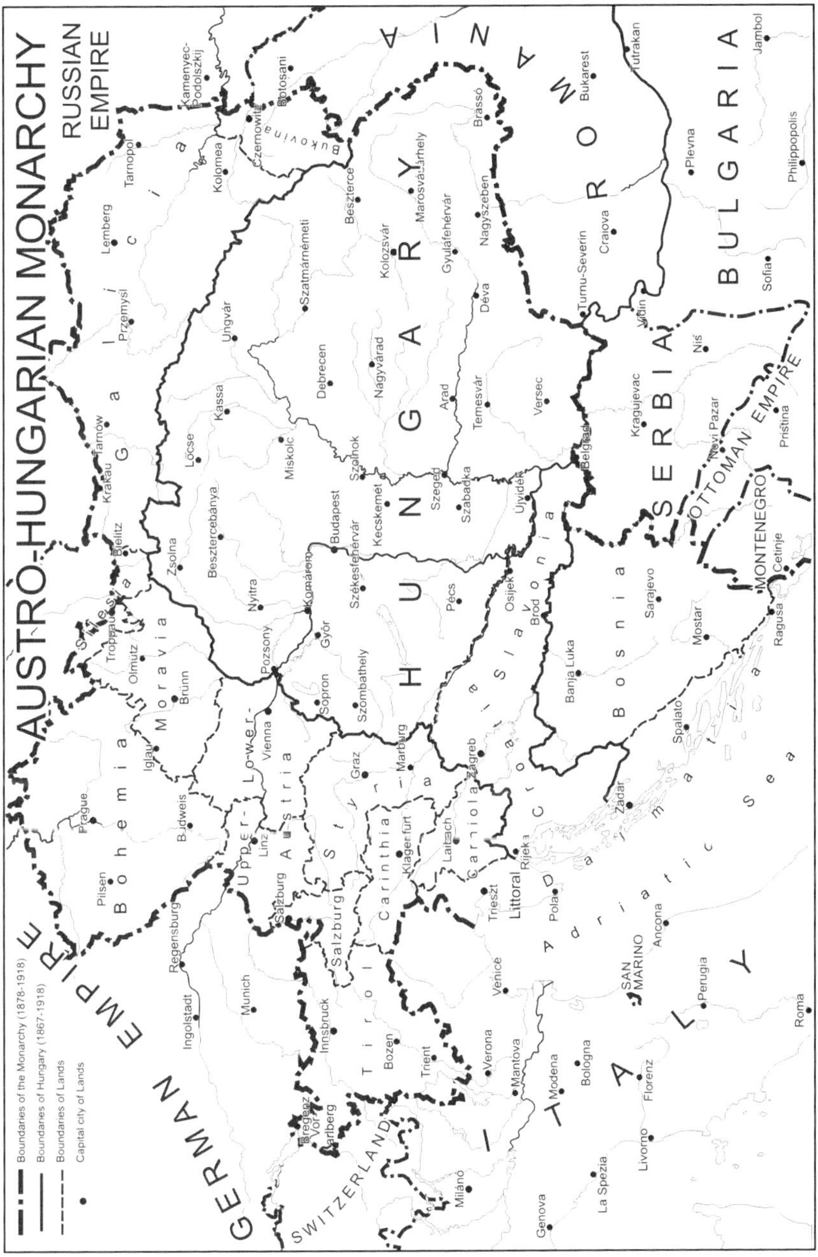
AUSTRO-HUNGARIAN MONARCHY
Boundaries of the Monarchy (1878-1918)
Boundaries of Hungary (1867-1918)
Boundaries of Lands
Capital city of Lands
RUSSIAN EMPIRE
GERMAN EMPIRE
SWITZERLAND
ITALY
BULGARIA
SERBIA
OTTOMAN EMPIRE
MONTENEGRO
SAN MARINO
HUNGARY
Bohemia
Moravia
Silesia
Lower Austria
Upper Austria
Salzburg
Styria
Carinthia
Carniola
Tirol
Vorarlberg
Littoral
Bukovina
Bosnia
Adriatic Sea
Prague
Pilsen
Budweis
Iglau
Brünn
Olmütz
Troppau
Bielitz
Krakau
Tarnów
Przemysl
Lemberg
Tarnopol
Kamenyec-Podolszkij
Kolomea
Czernowitz
Botosani
Regensburg
Ingolstadt
Munich
Salzburg
Linz
Vienna
Pozsony
Sopron
Szombathely
Győr
Komárom
Nyitra
Zsolna
Besztercebánya
Lőcse
Kassa
Miskolc
Ungvár
Szatmárnémeti
Debrecen
Nagyvárad
Budapest
Székesfehérvár
Kecskemét
Szolnok
Szeged
Szabadka
Arad
Temesvár
Versec
Pécs
Osijek
Brod
Újvidék
Belgrad
Kolozsvár
Beszterce
Marosvásárhely
Gyulafehérvár
Nagyszeben
Déva
Brassó
Bukarest
Craiova
Turnu-Severin
Vidin
Tutrakan
Plevna
Philippopolis
Sofia
Jambol
Niš
Kragujevac
Novi Pazar
Priština
Sarajevo
Mostar
Banja Luka
Ragusa
Cetinje
Spalato
Zadar
Rijeka
Laibach
Klagenfurt
Zagreb
Marburg
Graz
Trieszt
Pola
Innsbruck
Bozen
Trient
Bregenz
Venice
Verona
Mantova
Milano
Modena
Bologna
Florenz
Livorno
La Spezia
Genova
Ancona
Perugia
Roma

HUNGARY IN 1900

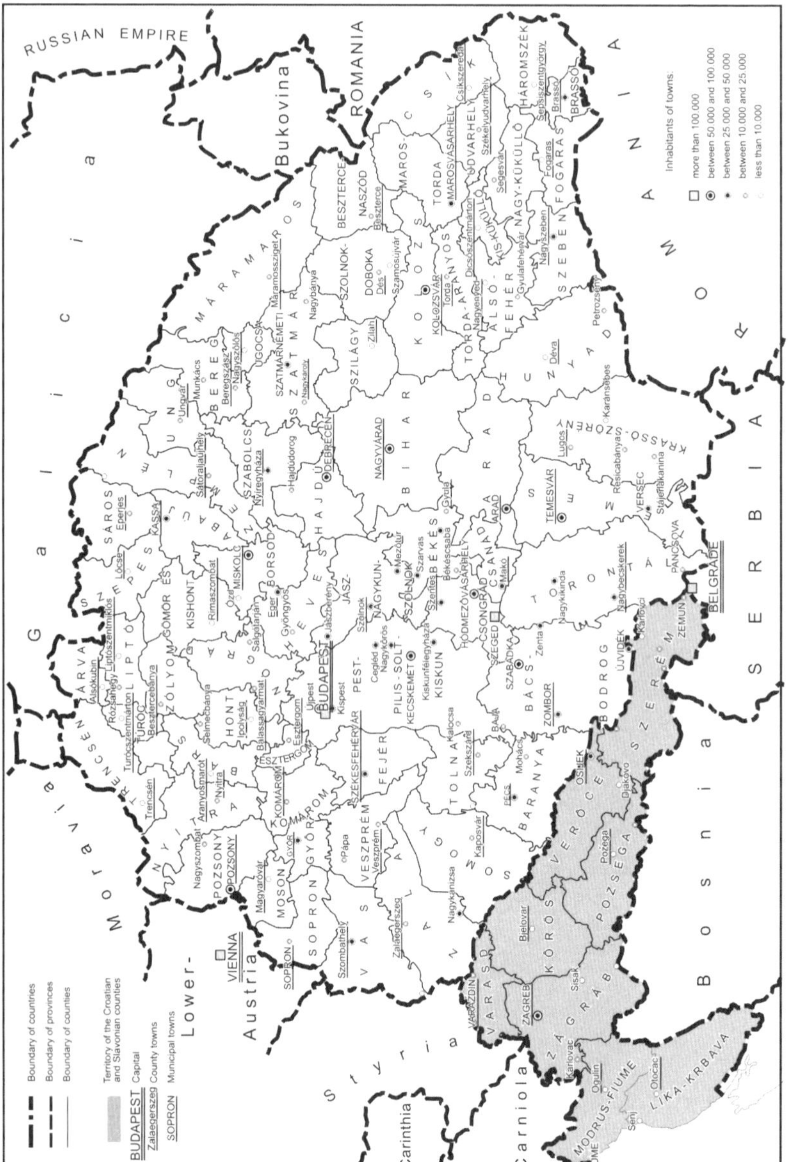

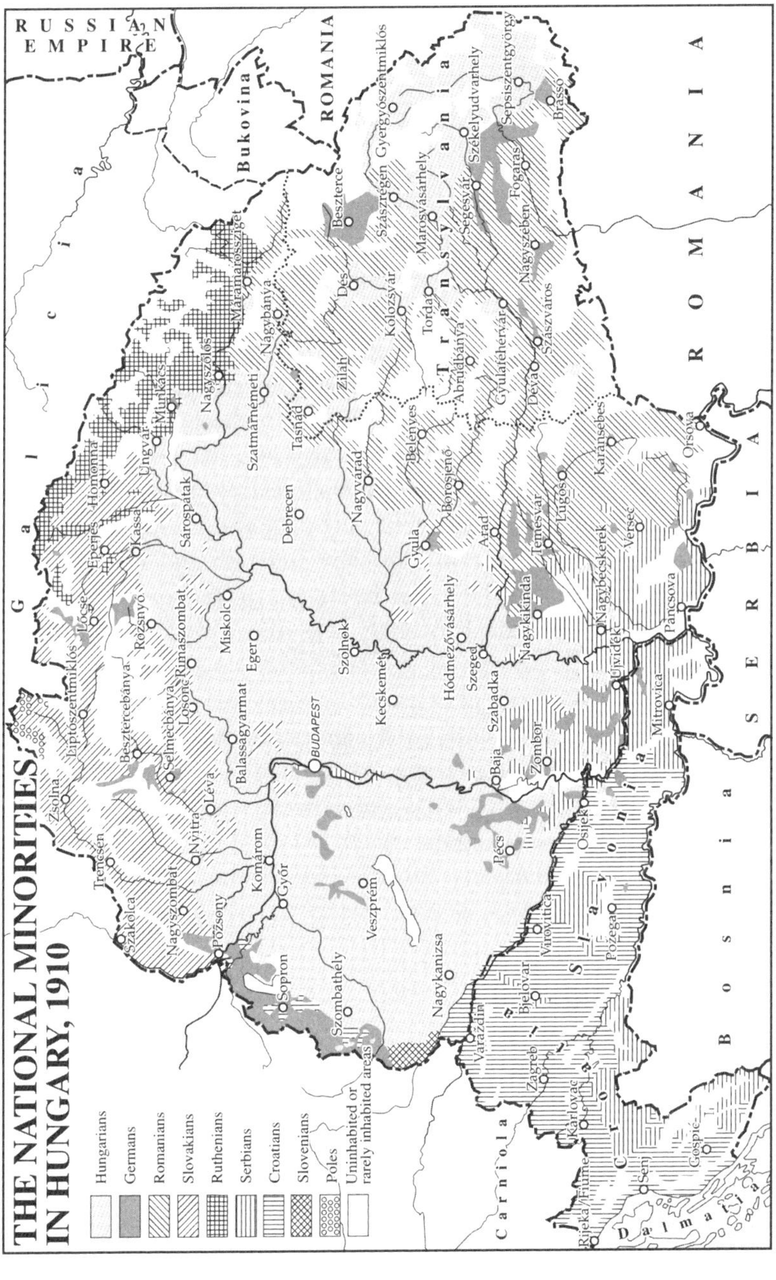
THE NATIONAL MINORITIES IN HUNGARY, 1910
Hungarians
Germans
Romanians
Slovakians
Ruthenians
Serbians
Croatians
Slovenians
Poles
Uninhabited or rarely inhabited areas
RUSSIAN EMPIRE
G a l i c i a
Bukovina
ROMANIA
T r a n s y l v a n i a
R O M A N I A
S E R B I A
B o s n i a
S l a v o n i a
C r o a t i a
C a r n i o l a
D a l m a t i a
BUDAPEST
Pozsony
Szakolca
Nagyszombat
Trencsén
Zsolna
Nyitra
Komárom
Győr
Sopron
Szombathely
Veszprém
Nagykanizsa
Léva
Selmecbánya
Besztercebánya
Liptószentmiklós
Lőcse
Rozsnyó
Losonc
Rimaszombat
Balassagyarmat
Eger
Miskolc
Eperjes
Kassa
Homonna
Ungvár
Sárospatak
Munkács
Nagyszőlős
Máramarossziget
Szatmárnémeti
Nagybánya
Debrecen
Szolnok
Kecskemét
Hódmezővásárhely
Szeged
Szabadka
Baja
Zombor
Pécs
Újvidék
Nagybecskerek
Nagykikinda
Versec
Pancsova
Mitrovica
Osijek
Virovitica
Pozega
Bjelovar
Varaždin
Zagreb
Karlovac
Rijeka (Fiume)
Senj
Gospić
Gyula
Arad
Temesvár
Lugos
Karánsebes
Orsova
Nagyvárad
Belényes
Borosjenő
Tasnád
Zilah
Dés
Beszterce
Kolozsvár
Torda
Abrudbánya
Gyulafehérvár
Déva
Szászváros
Nagyszeben
Segesvár
Marosvásárhely
Szászrégen
Gyergyószentmiklós
Székelyudvarhely
Fogaras
Sepsiszentgyörgy
Brassó

THE AUTHOR

LÁSZLÓ KATUS (b. 1927)
Graduated from the Loránd Eötvös University in Budapest in 1950. He worked at the National Széchényi Library until 1957, when he joined the staff of the Hungarian Academy of Sciences' Institute of History, where he dealt with the history of the Habsburg Monarchy in the 19th century and up to 1918, concentrating initially on the minority question, especially the history of the South Slavs, and later on the economic and social history and the demography of the Monarchy. In 1963, he defended his doctoral thesis. In 1984, he also became involved in university education, teaching courses at Pécs University on medieval European and 18th and 19th century Hungarian history. In 1992, he became a professor of the new Péter Pázmány Catholic University and director of its Historical Institute. Since his retirement in 1997, he has continued to work at the Hungarian Academy of Sciences' Institute of History and at the Habsburg Historical Institute in Budapest, as well as lecturing at Pécs University and contributing to the doctoral program there.
He has authored and edited several books including *Economic Growth in Hungary during the Age of Dualism (1867–1914)* (1970), *Hauptzüge der kapitalistischen Entwicklung der Landwirtschaft in den südslawischen Gebieten der Österreichisch-Ungarischen Monarchie* (1961).

SELECTED BIBLIOGRAPHY

Primary Sources

Apponyi, Albert. *Emlékirataim. Ötven Év. Ifjúkorom – Huszonöt év az ellenzéken* [My Memoirs. Fifty Years. My Youth – Twenty-Five Years in Opposition]. Budapest: Pantheon Irodalmi Intézet R.T., 1922.

Balogh, Sándor, and Levente Sipos, eds. *A magyar állam és a nemzetiségek. A magyarországi nemzetiségi kérdés történetének jogforrásai 1848–1993* [The Hungarian State and the Nationalities. Legal Sources of the History of the Nationalities Issue in Hungary 1848–1993]. Budapest: Napvilág Kiadó, 2002.

Bernatzik, Edmund. *Die österreichischen Verfassungsgesetze*. 2nd ed. Vienna: Manz, 1911.

Beust, Ferdinand. *Aus drei Vierteljahrhunderten*. Vols. 1–3. Stuttgart: Verlag Cotta, 1887–1889.

Csengery, Lóránt, ed. *Csengery Antal hátrahagyott iratai és feljegyzései* [The Papers and Notes of Antal Csengery's Legacy]. Budapest: Magyar Történelmi Társulat, 1928.

Deák Ferenc. *Válogatott politikai írások és beszédek* [Selected Political Writings and Speeches]. 1850–1873. Ed. Ágnes Deák. Budapest: Osiris Kiadó, 2001.

Diószegi, István, ed. *Die Protokolle des gemeinsamen Ministerrates der österreichisch–ungarischen Monarchie*. Vol. 4. 1883–1895. Budapest: Akadémiai Kiadó, 1993.

Eötvös, József. *Eötvös József művei* [Works of József Eötvös]. Ed. István Fenyő *et. al.* Vols. 1–12. Budapest: Szépirodalmi Kiadó, 1973–1981.

Erényi, Tibor, *et. al.*, eds. *A magyar munkásmozgalom történetének válogatott dokumentumai* [Selected Documents on the History of the Hungarian Labor Movement]. Vols. 1–4. Budapest: Szikra Kiadó, 1951–1966.

Kemény, G. Gábor, ed. *Iratok a nemzetiségi kérdés történetéhez Magyarországon a dualizmus korában. I. 1867–1892* [Documents Relating to the History of the Nationalities Issue in Hungary in the Era of Dualism]. Vols. 1–6. Budapest: Tankönyvkiadó, 1952–1985.

Kemény, G. Gábor, ed. *Mocsáry Lajos válogatott írásai* [Selected Writings of Lajos Mocsáry]. Budapest: Bibliotheca, 1958.

Kónyi, Manó, ed. *Deák Ferenc beszédei* [Speeches of Ferenc Deák]. Vols. 4–6. 2nd ed. Budapest: Franklin Társulat, 1903.

Kossuth, Lajos. *Kossuth Lajos iratai* [Writings of Lajos Kossuth]. Ed. Ignác Helfy and Ferenc Kossuth. Vols. 1–13. Budapest: Athenaum, 1880–1911.

Lakos, János, ed. *A Szapáry- és a Wekerle-kormány minisztertanácsi jegyzőkönyvei* [Minutes of the Council of Ministers in the Time of the Szapáry and Wekerle Governments]. Vols. 1–2. Budapest: MOL, 1999.

Léderer, Béla, ed. *Gróf Andrássy Gyula beszédei* [Speeches of Count Gyula Andrássy]. Budapest: Franklin Társulat, 1893.

Litván, György, and László Szűcs, eds. *A szociológia első magyar műhelye. A Huszadik Század köre* [The First Hungarian Workshop of Sociology. The Circle of the *Huszadik Század*]. Vols. 1–2. Budapest: Gondolat Kiadó, 1973.

Márkus, Dezső, and Gyula Térfi, eds. *Magyar Törvénytár. Corpus Juris Hungarici*. Budapest: Franklin Társulat, 1896–1915.

Mérei, Gyula, and Ferenc Pölöskei, eds. *Magyarországi pártprogramok 1867–1998* [Hungarian Party Programs 1867–1998]. Budapest: Akadémiai Kiadó, 2003.

Pajkossy, Gábor, ed. *Magyarország története a 19. században. Szöveggyűjtemény* [History of Hungary in the 19th Century. A Chrestomathy]. Budapest: Osiris, 2003.

Pribram, Alfred Franzis, ed. *Die politischen Geheimvertrage Osterreich-Ungarns 1879–1914. Nach den Akten des Wiener Staatsarchivs*. Vienna, 1920.

Somogyi, Éva, ed. *Die Protokolle des gemeinsamen Ministerrates der österreichisch–ungarischen Monarchie*. Vol. 1/1. 1867–1870. Budapest: Akadémiai Kiadó, 1999.

Somogyi, Éva, ed. *Die Protokolle des gemeinsamen Ministerrates der österreichisch–ungarischen Monarchie*. Vol. 5. 1896–1907. Budapest: Akadémiai Kiadó, 1991.

Steinacker, Edmund. *Lebenserinnerungen*. Munich: M. Schick, 1937.

Tisza, István. *Gróf Tisza István Összes Munkái* [The Complete Works of Count István Tisza]. Vols. 1–6. Budapest: Magyar Tudományos Akadémia, 1923–1937.

Tisza, István. *Válogatott politikai írások és beszédek* [Selected Political Writings and Speeches]. Ed. László Tőkéczki. Budapest: Osiris, 2003.

Tőkéczki, László, ed. *Magyar liberalizmus* [Hungarian Liberalism]. Budapest: Századvég, 1993.

Vezér, Erzsébet, ed. *Ady Endre publicisztikai írásai* [Political Writings of Endre Ady]. Vols. 1–3. Budapest: Szépirodalmi Könyvkiadó, 1987.

Comprehensive Works

Balogh, Margit, and Jenő Gergely. *Egyházak az újkori Magyarországon 1790–1992* [Churches in Modern Hungary 1790–1992]. Vols. 1–2. Budapest: MTA Történettudományi Intézete, 1993–1996.

Bölöny, József. *Magyarország kormányai, 1848–2004* [Governments of Hungary 1848–2004]. 5th ed. Budapest: Akadémiai Kiadó, 2004.

Bucsay, Mihály. *A protestantizmus története Magyarországon 1521–1945* [The History of Protestantism in Hungary 1521–1945]. Budapest: Gondolat Kiadó, 1985.

Diószegi, István. *A hatalmi politika másfél évszázada* [One and a Half Centuries of Power Politics]. Budapest: História – MTA Történettudományi Intézete, 1994.

Estók, János. *Magyarország története, 1849–1914* [History of Hungary, 1849–1914]. 2nd ed. Budapest: Nemzeti Tankönyvkiadó Zrt., 2004.

Fehér, Katalin, ed. *Magyar ipar- és technikatörténet* [History of Hungarian Industry and Technical Studies]. Budapest: Kertek 2000 Kiadó, 2000.

Gergely, András, ed. *Magyarország története a 19. században* [History of Hungary in the 19th Century]. Budapest: Osiris, 2003.

Hanák, Péter, ed. *The Corvina History of Hungary*. Budapest: Corvina Books, 1991.
Hanák, Péter, and Ferenc Mucsi, eds. *Magyarország története 1890–1918* [History of Hungary 1890–1918]. 3rd ed. Budapest: Akadémiai Kiadó, 1988.
Hantsch, Hugo. *Die Geschichte Österreichs*. Vols. 1–2. 2nd ed. Graz, Vienna and Cologne: Styria-Verlag, 1962.
Hermann, Egyed. *A katolikus egyház története Magyarországon 1914-ig* [History of the Catholic Church in Hungary until 1914]. Munich: Aurora Könyvek, 1974.
Honvári, János, ed. *Magyarország gazdaságtörténete Trianontól a rendszerváltásig* [Economic History of Hungary from Trianon to the Change of System]. Budapest: Aula, 2005.
Kósa, László, ed. *Magyar művelődéstörténet* [History of Hungarian Culture]. Budapest: Osiris, 1998. 3rd ed. Budapest: Osiris, 2006.
Kovács, Endre, and László Katus, eds. *Magyarország története 1848–1890* [The History of Hungary 1848–1890]. 2nd ed. Budapest: Akadémiai Kiadó, 1987.
Liptai, Ervin, ed. *Magyarország hadtörténete* [Military History of Hungary]. Vol. 2. Budapest: Zrínyi, 1985.
Mezey, Barna, ed. *Magyar alkotmánytörténet* [Hungarian Constitutional History]. 5th ed. Budapest: Osiris, 2004.
Mezey, Barna, ed. *Magyar jogtörténet* [Hungarian Legal History]. Budapest: Osiris, 2003.
Romsics, Ignác. *Magyarország története a XX. században* [History of Hungary in the 20th Century]. Budapest: Osiris, 1999.
Sőtér, István, ed. *A magyar irodalom története* [The History of Hungarian Literature]. Vols. 4–5. Budapest: Akadémiai Kiadó, 1965.
Steindorff, Ludwig. *Kroatien. Vom Mittelalter bis zur Gegenwart*. Regensburg: Friedrich Pustet Verlag, 2001.
Sugar, Peter F., ed. *A History of Hungary*. Bloomington, IN: Indiana University Press, 1990.
Szász, Zoltán, and Béla Köpeczi, eds. *A History of Transylvania from the Beginning to 1919. Vol. III. From 1830 to 1919*. New York: Atlantic Research and Publications, 2002.
Szekfű, Gyula. *Három nemzedék és ami utána következik* [Three Generations and What Comes Afterwards]. Budapest: Királyi

Magyar Egyetemi Nyomda, 1934. Reprint: Budapest: ÁKV-Maecenas, 1989.
Szekfű, Gyula. *Magyar történet* [Hungarian History]. Vol. 5. Budapest: Egyetemi Nyomda, 1943.
Veszprémy, László, and Béla K. Király, eds. *A Millennium of Hungarian Military History*. New York: Atlantic Research and Publications, 2002.

Studies on Subjects Referred to in This Book

Andrássy, Count Gyula, Jr. *Az 1867-iki kiegyezésről* [The Compromise of 1867]. Budapest: Franklin Társulat, 1896.
Apponyi, Albert. *Die rechtliche Natur der Beziehungen zwischen Österreich und Ungarn*. Vienna and Leipzig: K.u.k Hof-Buchdruckerei, 1911.
Beer, Adolf. *Die österreichische Handelspolitik im XIX. Jahrhundert*. Vienna: Manz, 1891.
Behschnitt, Wolf Dietrich. *Nationalismus bei Serben und Kroaten 1830–1914. Analyse und Typologie der nationalen Ideologie*. Munich: R. Oldenbourg, 1980.
Bencze, László. *The Occupation of Bosnia and Herzegovina in 1878*. New York: Atlantic Research and Publications, 2005.
Benedikt, Heinrich. *Monarchie der Gegensätze. Österreichs Weg durch die Neuzeit*. Vienna: Ullstein Verlag, 1947.
Benedikt, Heinrich. *Die wirtschaftliche Entwicklung in der Franz-Joseph Zeit*. Vienna and Munich: Herold, 1958.
Berend, Iván T., and Tamás Csató. *Evolution of the Hungarian Economy, 1848–1998*. Vol. I. *One-and-a-Half Centuries of Semi-Successful Modernization, 1848–1989*. New York: Atlantic Research and Publications, 2001.
Berend, Iván T., and György Ránki. *Economic Development of East-Central Europe in the 19th and 20th Centuries*. New York: Columbia University Press, 1974.
Berend, Iván T., and György Ránki. *The European Periphery and Industrialization 1780–1914*. Cambridge: Cambridge University Press, 1982.
Berend, Iván T., and György Ránki. *Hungary – A Century of Economic Development*. Newton Abbot: David & Charles, 1974.

Berend, Iván T., and György Ránki. *Underdevelopment and Economic Growth*. Budapest: Akadémiai Kiadó, 1979.

Berend, Iván T., and Miklós Szuhay. *A tőkés gazdaság története Magyarországon 1848–1944* [History of the Capitalist Economy in Hungary 1848–1944]. Budapest: Kossuth Kiadó, 1973.

Berger, Peter, ed. *Der österreichisch-ungarische Ausgleich von 1867. Vorgeschichte und Wirkungen*. Vienna and Munich: Herold, 1967.

Biró, Sándor. *The Nationalities Problem in Transylvania, 1867–1940*. New York: Atlantic Research and Publications, 1992.

Bödy, Paul. *Joseph Eötvös and the Modernization of Hungary, 1840–1870. A Study of Ideas of Individuality and Social Pluralism in Modern Politics*. Philadelphia, PA: American Philosophical Society, 1972.

Bödy, Paul, ed. *Hungarian Statesmen of Destiny: 1860–1960*. New York: Atlantic Research and Publications, 1989.

Boros, Zsuzsanna, and Dániel Szabó. *Parlamentarizmus Magyarországon (1867–1944)* [Parliamentarianism in Hungary (1867–1944)]. Budapest: ELTE Eötvös Kiadó, 1999.

Bridge, F. R. *From Sadowa to Sarajevo. The Foreign Policy of Austria-Hungary 1866–1914*. London: Routledge, 1972.

Cieger, András, ed. *A kiegyezés* [The Compromise]. Budapest: Osiris, 2004.

Csáky, Moritz. *Der Kulturkampf in Ungarn*. Graz, Vienna and Cologne: Böhlau Verlag, 1967.

Csizmadia, Andor, ed. *Die Freiheitsrechte und die Staatstheorien im Zeitalter des Dualismus*. (Studia iuridica auctoritate Universitatis Pécs publicata 48.) Budapest: Tankönyvkiadó, 1966.

Csizmadia, Andor, and Kálmán Kovács, eds. *Die Entwicklung des Zivilrechts in Mitteleuropa (1848–1944)*. Budapest: Akadémiai Kiadó, 1970.

Czedik, Alois. *Zur Geschichte der k. k. österreichischen Ministerien 1861–1916*. Vol. 1. 1861–1893. Teschen, Vienna and Leipzig: Karl Prochaska k. u. k. Hofbuchdruckerei, 1917.

Deák, Ágnes, and András Molnár. *Deák Ferenc* [Ferenc Deák]. Budapest: Vince Kiadó, 2003.

Decsy, Janos. *Prime Minister Gyula Andrassy's Influence on Habsburg Foreign Policy*. New York: Atlantic Research and Publications, 1979.

Diószegi, István. *Bismarck und Andrássy: Ungarn in der deutschen Machtpolitik in der 2. Hälfte des 19. Jahrhunderts.* Vienna: Oldenbourg, 1999.

Džaja, Srećko M. *Bosnien-Herzegowina in der österreichisch-ungarischen Epoche (1878–1918).* Munich: Oldenbourg, 1994.

Eder, Karl. *Der Liberalismus in Alt-Österreich.* Vienna and Munich: Herold, 1955.

Eisenmann, Louis. *Le compromis austro-hongrois de 1867.* Paris: G. Bellais, 1904.

Engel-Janosi, Friedrich, and Helmut Rumpler, eds. *Probleme der Francisko-Josephinischen Zeit 1848–1916.* Vienna: Verlag für Geschichte und Politik, 1967.

Estók, János, ed. *History of Hungarian Agriculture and Rural Life 1848–2004.* Budapest: Argumentum – Magyar Mezőgazdasági Múzeum, 2004.

Fejtő, François. *Requiem pour un empire defunt: histoire de la destruction de l'Autriche-Hongrie.* Paris: Lieu Commun, 1988.

Fellner, Frigyes. *Ausztria és Magyarország nemzeti jövedelme* [The National Income of Austria and Hungary]. Budapest: Verlag von Gustav Fischer, 1916.

Fellner, Frigyes. *A nemzetközi fizetési mérleg és alakulása Magyarországon* [The International Balance of Payments in Hungary]. Budapest: Politzer-féle Könyvkiadóvállalat, 1908.

Fink, Krisztina Maria. *Die österreichisch-ungarische Monarchie als Wirtschaftsgemeinschaft.* Munich: Rudolf Trofenik, 1968.

Flachbart, Ernest. *Histoire des minorités nationales en Hongrie.* Paris and Clermont-Ferrand: Les Presses Universitaires de France, 1944.

Flachbart, Ernest. *A History of Hungary's Nationalities.* Budapest, 1944.

Franz, Georg. *Liberalismus. Die deutschliberale Bewegung in der Habsburgermonarchie.* Munich: Verlag Georg DW Callwey, 1955.

Gergely, Jenő. *A kereszténysszocializmus Magyarországon 1903–1923* [Christian Socialism in Hungary 1903–1923]. Budapest: Akadémiai Kiadó, 1977.

Gergely, Jenő. *Being Hungarian – Christian – European.* Budapest: L'Harmattan – ELTE BTK TDI, 2006.

Gergely, Jenő, ed. *Autonomien in Ungarn 1848–2000*. Budapest: ELTE TDI, 2006.
Gerő, András. *The Hungarian Parliament, 1867–1918: A Mirage of Power*. New York: Atlantic Research and Publications, 1997.
Gerő, András. *A magyar polgárosodás* [Hungarian Embourgeoisement]. Budapest: Atlantisz, 1993.
Gerő, András, ed. *A Monarchia kora – ma* [The Age of the Monarchy – Today]. Budapest: Új Mandátum, 2007.
Geyr, Géza Andreas von. *Sándor Wekerle 1848–1921. Die politische Biographie eines ungarischen Staatsmannes der Donaumonarchie*. Munich: Oldenbourg, 1993.
Glatz, Ferenc, ed. *Ethnicity and Society in Hungary*. Budapest: MTA Történettudományi Intézete, 1990.
Glatz, Ferenc, ed. *Hungarians and Their Neighbors in Modern Times, 1867–1950*. New York: Atlantic Research and Publications, 1995.
Glettler, Monika. *Pittsburg – Wien – Budapest. Programm und Praxis der Nationalitätenpolitik bei der Auswanderung der ungarischen Slowaken nach Amerika um 1900*. Vienna: Verlag der OEAW, 1980.
Gogolák, Ludwig. *Beiträge zur Geschichte des slowakischen Volkes. Vol. III. Zwischen zwei Revolutionen [1848–1919]*. Munich: Oldenbourg, 1972.
Gonda, László. *A zsidóság Magyarországon 1526–1945* [The Jews in Hungary 1526–1945]. Budapest: Századvég Kiadó, 1992.
Good, David F. *Economic Rise of the Habsburg Empire, 1750–1914*. Los Angeles, CA, and London: University of California Press, 1984.
Gottas, Friedrich. *Ungarn im Zeitalter des Hochliberalismus. Studien zur Tisza-Ära 1875–1890*. Vienna: Verlag der Österreichischen Akademie der Wissenschaften, 1976.
Gratz, Gusztáv. A *dualizmus kora. Magyarország története 1867–1918* [The Age of Dualism. The History of Hungary 1867–1918]. Budapest: Magyar Szemle Társaság, 1934.
Gross, Mirjana. *Die Anfänge des modernen Kroatien. Gesellschaft, Politik und Kultur in Zivil-Kroatien und -Slawonien in den ersten dreissig Jahren nach 1848*. Vienna, Cologne and Weimar: Böhlau, 1993.

Grunzel, Joseph. *Handelspolitik und Ausgleich in Österreich-Ungarn.* Vienna and Leipzig: Hölder, 1912.

Gumplowitz, Ludwig. *Das Recht der Nationalitäten und Sprachen in Oesterreich-Ungarn.* Innsbruck: Verlag der Wagner'schen Universitäts-Buchhandlung, 1879.

Gunst, Péter, ed. *Hungarian Agrarian Society from the Emancipation of Serfs (1848) to Re-privatization of Land (1998).* New York: Atlantic Research and Publications, 1999.

Gyáni, Gábor, György Kövér and Tibor Valuch. *Social History of Hungary from the Reform Era to the End of the Twentieth Century.* New York: Atlantic Research and Publications, 2003.

Gyurgyák, János. *Ezzé lett magyar hazátok. A magyar nemzeteszme és nacionalizmus története* [History of the Hungarian Idea of Nation and Nationalism]. Budapest: Osiris, 2007.

Gyurgyák, János. *A zsidókérdés Magyarországon. Politikai eszmetörténet* [The Jewish Question in Hungary. A History of Political Ideas]. Budapest: Osiris, 2001.

Hambuch, Wendelin, ed. *Deutsche in Budapest.* Budapest: Deutscher Kulturverein, 1999.

Hanák, Péter. *1867 – európai térben és időben* [1867 – In European Space and Time]. Ed. Éva Somogyi. Budapest: MTA Történettudományi Intézete, 2001.

Hanák, Peter. *The Garden and the Workshop: Essays on the Cultural History of Vienna and Budapest.* Princeton, NJ: Princeton University Press, 1998.

Hanák, Péter. *Der Garten und die Werkstatt.* Vienna, Cologne and Weimar: Böhlau, 1992.

Hanák, Péter. *Magyarország a Monarchiában* [Hungary in the Monarchy]. Budapest: Gondolat, 1975.

Hanák, Péter, ed. *Bürgerliche Wohnkultur des Fin de Siècle in Ungarn.* Vienna, Cologne and Weimar: Böhlau Verlag, 1994.

Hanák, Péter, ed. *Nationale Frage in der Österreichisch-Ungarischen Monarchie 1900–1918.* Budapest: Akadémiai Kiadó, 1966.

Hanák, Péter, ed. *Zsidókérdés, asszimiláció, antiszemitizmus. Tanulmányok a zsidókérdésről a huszadik századi Magyarországon* [Jewish Question, Assimilation, Anti-Semitism. Studies on the Jewish Question in Twentieth-Century Hungary]. Budapest: Gondolat Kiadó, 1984.

Hanák, Péter, *et al.*, eds. *Kultur und Politik in Österreich und Ungarn.* Vienna, Cologne and Weimar: Böhlau, 1994.

Hantsch, Hugo. *Die Nationalitätenfrage im alten Österreich.* Vienna: Herold, 1953.

Haselsteiner, Horst. *Bosnien-Hercegovina. Orientkrise und Südslavische Frage.* Vienna, Cologne and Weimar: Böhlau, 1996.

Haselsteiner, Horst. *Die Serben und der Ausgleich. Zur politischen und staatsrechtlichen Stellung dér Serben Südungarns in den Jahren 1860–1867.* Vienna, Cologne and Graz: Böhlau. 1976.

Hauszmann, Janos. *Bürgerlicher Radikalismus und demokratisches Denken im Ungarn des 20. Jahrhunderts. Der Jászi-Kreis um "Huszadik Század" 1900–1919.* Frankfurt am Main: Lang, 1988.

Hickmann, Anton Leo. *Die österreichische Reichsrat. Seine Parteien und Wahl Verhältnisse 1873–1901.* Vienna, 1901.

Historisches Geschehen im Spiegel der Gegenwart. Österreich-Ungarn 1867–1967. Vienna: Institut für Österreichskunde, 1970.

Hitchins, Keith. *Studien zur modernen Geschichte Transsilvaniens.* Klausenburg: Dacia Verlag, 1971.

Horváth, Zoltán. *Magyar századforduló. A második reformnemzedék története 1896–1914* [Hungarian Turn of the Century. History of the Second Reform Generation 1896–1914]. Budapest: Gondolat, 1961.

Ihrig, Dénes, ed. *A magyar vízszabályozás története* [The History of Regulation of Waters in Hungary]. Budapest: Országos Vízügyi Hivatal, 1973.

Izsák, Lajos, ed. *Magyarország miniszterelnökei 1848–1990* [Hungary's Prime Ministers 1848–1990]. Budapest: Cégér Könyvkiadó, 1993.

Janos, Andrew C. *The Politics of Backwardness in Hungary 1825–1945.* Princeton, NJ: Princeton University Press, 1982.

Jászi, Oscar. *The Dissolution of the Habsburg Monarchy.* Chicago, IL: The University of Chicago Press, 1929.

Jelavich, Barbara. *The Habsburg Empire in European Affairs, 1814–1918.* Chicago, IL: Rand McNally & Company, 1969.

Jelavich, Barbara. *History of the Balkans.* Vols. 1–2. Cambridge: Cambridge University Press, 1983.

Jeszenszky, Géza. *Az elveszett presztízs* [Lost Prestige]. Budapest: Magvető, 1994.
Kann, Robert A. *The Habsburg Empire: A Study in Integration and Disintegration*. 2nd ed. New York: Octagon Books, 1973.
Kann, Robert A. *The Multinational Empire*. Vols. 1–2. New York: Columbia University Press, 1950.
Kann, Robert A. *Das Nationalitatenproblem der Habsburgmonarchie. Geschichte und Ideengehalt der nationalen Bestrebungen vöm Vormärz bis zur Auflösung des Reiches im Jahre 1918*. Vols. 1–2. 2nd ed. Graz and Cologne: Hermann Böhlaus Nachf., 1964.
Katzburg, Nathaniel. *Fejezetek az újkori zsidó történelemből Magyarországon* [Excerpts in Modern Jewish History in Hungary]. Budapest: MTA Judaisztikai Kutatócsoport – Osiris, 1999.
Keleti, Károly. *Hazánk és népe* [Our Homeland and Its People]. Pest: Athenaeum, 1871.
Kerpely, Anton. *Das Eisenhüttenwesen in Ungarn, sein Zustand und seine Zukunft*. Schemnitz, 1872.
Király, Béla K., ed. *The Crucial Decade: East Central European Society and National Defense, 1859–1870*. New York: Atlantic Research and Publications, 1984.
Király, Béla K., and Walter Scott Dillard, eds. *Selections, Social Origins, Education and Training of East Central European Officers Corps*. New York: Atlantic Research and Publications, 1988.
Király, Béla K., and Dimitrije Djordjević, eds. *East Central European Society and the Balkan Wars, 1912–1913*. New York: Atlantic Research and Publications, 1986.
Komlos, John. *The Habsburg Monarchy as a Customs Union. Economic Development in Austria-Hungary in the Nineteenth Century*. Princeton, NJ: Princeton University Press, 1983.
Komlos, John, ed. *Economic Development in the Habsburg Monarchy*. New York: Columbia University Press, 1983.
Komoróczy, Géza, ed. *Jewish Budapest*. New York: Atlantic Research and Publications, 1999.
Kondor, Viktória M. *Az 1875-ös pártfúzió* [The 1875 Party Merger]. Budapest: Akadémiai Kiadó, 1959.
Kosáry, Domokos, and Béla G. Németh, eds. *A magyar sajtó története* [History of the Hungarian Press]. Vol. 2. 1848–1892. Budapest: Akadémiai Kiadó, 1985.

Kubinszky, Judit. *Politikai antiszemitizmus Magyarországon* [Political Anti-Semitism in Hungary]. Budapest: Kossuth Könyvkiadó, 1976.

Lakatos, Ernő. *A magyar politikai vezetőréteg 1848–1918* [The Hungarian Political Leading Class 1848–1918]. Budapest: privately printed, 1942.

Lang, Ludwig. *Hundertjahre Zellpolitik.* Vienna and Leipzig: Carl Fromme, 1906.

Lukács, Lajos. *The Vatican and Hungary 1846–1878. Reports and Correspondence on Hungary of the Apostolic Nuncios in Vienna.* Budapest: Akadémiai Kiadó, 1981.

Macartney, Carlile Aylmer. *The Habsburg Empire 1790–1918.* London: Weidenfeld and Nicolson, 1971.

Magocsi, Paul Robert. *The Shaping of a National Identity: Subcarpathian Rus', 1848–1948.* Cambridge, MA: Harvard University Press, 1978.

Magyary, Zoltán, ed. *A magyar tudománypolitika alapvetése* [The Establishment of Hungarian Policy on Science]. Budapest: Egyetemi Nyomda, 1927.

Matis, Herbert. *Österreichs Wirtschaft 1848–1913. Konjunkturelle Dynamik und gesellschaftlicher Wandel im Zeitalter Franz Josephs I.* Berlin: Duncker und Humblot, 1972.

Matlekovits, Sándor, ed. *Magyarország közgazdasági és közművelődési állapota ezeréves fennállásakor* [The Economic and Cultural State of Hungary a Thousand Years after Its Foundation]. Vols. 1–9. Budapest: Pesti Könyvnyomda, 1897–1898.

May, Arthur J. *The Hapsburg Monarchy 1867–1914.* New York: W. W. Norton, 1968.

Mazsu, János. *The Social History of the Hungarian Intelligentsia in the "Long Nineteenth Century," 1825–1914.* New York: Atlantic Research and Publications, 1997.

McCagg, William O., Jr. *A History of Habsburg Jews, 1670–1918.* Bloomington, IN: Indiana University Press, 1989.

McCagg, William O., Jr. *Jewish Nobles and Geniuses in Modern Hungary.* New York: East European Monographs, 1972.

Melville, Ralph, and Hans-Jurgen Schröder, eds. *Der Berliner Kongress von 1878. Die Politik der Grossmächte und die Probleme der Modernisierung in Südosteuropa in der zweiten*

Hälfte des 19. Jahrhunderts. Wiesbaden: Franz Steiner Verlag, 1982.
Mikó, Imre. *Nemzetiségi jog és nemzetiségi politika* [Nationalities Law and Nationalities Policy]. Kolozsvár [Cluj]: Minerva, 1944.
Miskolczy, Julius. *Ungarn in der Habsburger-Monarchie*. Vienna and Munich: Herold, 1959.
The Nationality Problem in the Habsburg Monarchy in the Nineteenth Century: A Critical Appraisal. Austrian History Yearbook. Vol. 3. Parts 1–3. Houston, TX: Rice University, 1968.
Novotny, Alexander. *Franz Joseph I. An der Wende vom alten zum neuen Europa*. Göttingen, Frankfurt and Zürich: Musterschmidt-Verlag, 1968.
Offergeld, Wilhelm. *Grundlagen und Ursachen der industriellen Entwicklung Ungarns*. Jena: Verlag von Gustav Fischer, 1914.
Offerman, Alfred von. *Das Verhältnis Ungarns zu Österreich*. Vienna and Leipzig, 1902.
Ormos, Mária, and Béla K. Király, eds. *Hungary: Governments and Politics, 1848–2000*. New York: Atlantic Research and Publications, 2001.
Der österreichisch-ungarische Ausgleich von 1867. Seine Grundlagen und Auswirkungen. Munich: Oldenbourg, 1968.
Pach, Pál Zsigmond, ed. *A Magyar Tudományos Akadémia másfél évszázada 1825–1975* [150 Years of the Hungarian Academy of Sciences, 1825–1975]. Budapest: Akadémiai Kiadó, 1975.
Pamlényi, Ervin, ed. *Social-Economic Researches on the History of East-Central Europe*. (Studia Historica Academiae Scientiarum Hungaricae, 62.) Budapest: Akadémiai Kiadó, 1970.
Pölöskei, Ferenc. *István Tisza. Ein ungarischer Staatsmann in Krisenzeiten*. Budapest: Akadémiai Kiadó, 1994.
Potthoff, Heinrich. *Die deutsche Politik Beusts*. Bonn, 1968.
Pressburger, Siegfried. *Österreichische Notenbank 1816–1966. Geschichte des österreichischen Noteninstitutes*. Vienna: Verlag der Oesterreichischen Nationalbank, 1966.
Puskás, Julianna. *Kivándorló magyarok az Egyesült Államokban 1880–1940* [Emigrant Hungarians in the United States, 1880–1940]. Budapest: Akadémiai Kiadó, 1982.
Redlich, Joseph. *Das österreichische Staats- und Reichs-problem*. Vols. 1–2. Leipzig: Verlag Dr. Peter Reinhold, 1920–1926.

Redlich, Joseph. *Kaiser Franz Joseph von Österreich.* Berlin: Verlag für Kulturpolitik, 1928.

Romsics, Ignác. *István Bethlen: A Great Conservative Statesman of Hungary, 1874–1946.* New York: Atlantic Research and Publications, 1995.

Romsics, Ignác, and Béla K. Király, eds. *Geopolitics in the Danube Region. Hungarian Reconciliation Efforts, 1848–1998.* Budapest: CEU – Atlantic Research and Publications, 1999.

Rothenberg, Gunther E. *The Military Border in Croatia 1740–1881. A Study of an Imperial Institution.* Chicago, IL: University of Chicago Press, 1966.

Rumpler, Helmut, and Peter Urbanitsch, eds. *Die Habsburgermonarchie 1848–1918.* Vol. 7: *Verfassung und Parlamentarismus.* Vienna: Verlag der Österreichischen Akademie der Wissenschaften, 2000.

Rumpler, Helmut, and Peter Urbanitsch, eds. *Die Habsburgermonarchie 1848–1918.* Vol. 8: *Politische Öffentlichkeit und Zivilgesellschaft.* Vienna: Verlag der Österreichischen Akademie der Wissenschaften, 2006.

Salacz, Gábor. *A magyar kultúrharc története, 1890–1895* [The History of the Hungarian Culture War, 1890–1895]. Vienna: privately printed, 1938.

Sándor, Vilmos, and P. Hanák, eds. *Studien zur Geschichte der Österreichisch-Ungarischen Monarchie.* Budapest: Akadémiai Kiadó, 1961.

Schmidt, Isolde. *Beiträge zur Geschichte des südostdeutschen Parteiwesens 1848–1914.* Munich: Schick, 1939.

Seton-Watson, R. W. *The Southern Slav Question and the Habsburg Monarchy.* London: Constable and Co., 1911.

Sieghart, Rudolf. *Zolltrennung und Zolleinheit. Die Geschichte der österreichisch-ungarischen Zwischenzoll-Linie.* Vienna: Manz, 1915.

Silber, Michael K., ed. *Jews in the Hungarian Economy 1760–1945.* Jerusalem: The Magnes Press, 1992.

Somlyódy, László, and Nóra Somlyódy, eds. *Hungarian Arts and Sciences, 1848–2000.* New York: Atlantic Research and Publications, 2003.

Somogyi, Éva. *A birodalmi centralizációtól a dualizmusig. Az osztrák-német liberálisok útja a kiegyezéshez* [From Imperial

Centralization to Dualism. The Road of the Austro-Germans to the Compromise]. Budapest: Akadémiai Kiadó, 1976.

Somogyi, Éva. *Hagyomány és átalakulás. Állam és bürokrácia a dualista Habsburg Monarchiában* [Tradition and Transformation. State and Bureaucracy in the Dualist Habsburg Monarchy]. Budapest: L'Harmattan, 2006.

Somogyi, Éva. *Kormányzati rendszer a dualista Habsburg Monarchiában* [Governmental System in the Dualist Habsburg Monarchy]. Budapest: MTA Történettudományi Intézete, 1996.

Srbik, Heinrich. *Franz Joseph I. Charakter und Regierungsgrundsätze.* Vienna, 1949.

Steinacker, Harold. *Austro-Hungarica. Ausgewählte Aufsätze und Vorträge zur Geschichte Ungarns und der österreichisch-ungarischen Monarchie.* Munich: Oldenbourg, 1963.

Strach, Hermann, ed. *Geschichte der Eisenbahnen der Österreichisch-Ungarischen Monarchie.* Vols. 1–3. Vienna, Teschen and Leipzig: Cotta, 1898–1908.

Sugar, Peter F., and Ivo J. Lederer, eds. *Nationalism in Eastern Europe.* Seattle, WA, and London: University of Washington Press, 1969.

Süle, Tibor. *Sozialdemokratie in Ungarn. Zur Rolle der Intelligenz in der Arbeiterbewegung 1899–1910.* Cologne and Graz: Böhlau Verlag, 1967.

Szabó, István, ed. *A parasztság Magyarországon a kapitalizmus korában 1848–1914* [The Peasants in Hungary in the Era of Capitalism 1848–1914]. Vols. 1–2. Budapest: Akadémiai Kiadó, 1965.

Szabó, Miklós. *Politikai kultúra Magyarországon 1896–1986* [Political Culture in Hungary 1896–1986]. Budapest: Atlantisz, 1989.

Szabó, Miklós. *Az újkonzervativizmus és a jobboldali radikalizmus története (1867–1918)* [History of Neoconservatism and Right-Wing Radicalism (1867–1918)]. Budapest: Új Mandátum, 2003.

Szentpéteri, József, ed. *Magyar Kódex 5. Az Osztrák-Magyar Monarchia (1867–1918). Magyarország művelődéstörténete 1867–1918* [Hungarian Codex, Vol. 5. The Austro-Hungarian Monarchy. A Cultural History of Hungary (1867–1918)]. Budapest: Kossuth Kiadó, 2001.

Szita, Szabolcs. *A Magyar Gyáriparosok Országos Szövetsége. A GyOSz kiépítése és tevékenysége 1902-től 1948-ig* [Hungarian National Federation of Industrialists. Structure and Activity 1902–1948]. Budapest: MGyOSz, 1997.
Szterényi, József, and Jenő Ladányi. *A magyar ipar a világháborúban* [Hungarian Industry in the World War]. Budapest: Franklin Társulat, 1933.
Taylor, A. J. P. *The Habsburg Monarchy 1809 –1916*. London: Hamish Hamilton, 1951.
Teutsch, Friedrich. *Die Siebenbürger Sachsen in den letzten fünfzig Jahren 1868–1919.* Hermannstadt: Verlag W. Krafft, 1926.
Tezner, Friedrich. *Ausgleichsrecht und Ausgleichspolitik*. Vienna: Manz, 1907.
Tezner, Friedrich. *Die Wandlungen der österreichisch-ungarischen Reichsidee*. Vienna: Manz, 1905.
Török, Jenő. *A katolikus autonómia-mozgalom, 1848–1871. Adalékok a magyar liberális katolicizmus történetéhez* [The Catholic Autonomy Movement 1848–1871. The History of Hungarian Liberal Catholicism]. Budapest: Stephaneum Nyomda, 1941.
Toth, Adalbert. *Parteien und Reichstagwahlen in Ungarn 1848–1892*. Munich: Oldenbourg, 1973.
Tunstall, Graydon, Jr. A. *Planning for War against Russia and Serbia. Austro-Hungarian and German Military Strategies, 1871–1914.* New York: Atlantic Research and Publications, 1993.
Vantuch, Anton, ed. *Der österreichisch-ungarische Ausgleich von 1867. Materialen (Referate und Diskussion) der internationalen Konferenz in Bratislava 28. 8.–1. 9. 1967.* Bratislava: Vyd. SAV, 1971.
Varga, Lajos. *Garami Ernő* [Ernő Garami]. Budapest: Napvilág Kiadó, 1996.
Vargha, Gyula. *A magyar hitelügy és hitelintézetek története* [The History of Credit and Banking in Hungary]. Budapest: Pesti Könyvnyomda Részvénytársaság, 1896.
Vermes, Gábor. *Tisza István* [István Tisza]. Budapest: Századvég, 1994.
Wagner, Walter. *Geschichte des k. u. k. Kriegsministeriums.* Vol. 2. 1866–1888. Vienna: Hermann Böhlaus Nachfolger, 1971.
Wandruszka, Adam, and Peter Urbanitsch, eds. *Die Habsburgermonarchie 1848–1918.* Vol. 1: *Die wirtschaftliche Entwicklung.*

Vienna: Verlag der Österreichischen Akademie der Wissenschaften, 1973.
Wandruszka, Adam, and Peter Urbanitsch, eds. *Die Habsburgermonarchie 1848–1918*. Vol. 2: *Verwaltung und Rechtswesen*. Vienna: Verlag der Österreichischen Akademie der Wissenschaften, 1975.
Wandruszka, Adam, and Peter Urbanitsch, eds. *Die Habsburgermonarchie 1848–1918*. Vol. 3: *Die Völker des Reichs*. Vienna: Verlag der Österreichischen Akademie der Wissenschaften, 1980.
Wandruszka, Adam, and Peter Urbanitsch, eds. *Die Habsburgermonarchie 1848–1918*. Vol. 4: *Die Konfessionen*. Vienna: Verlag der Österreichischen Akademie der Wissenschaften, 1985.
Wandruszka, Adam, and Peter Urbanitsch, eds. *Die Habsburgermonarchie 1848–1918*. Vol. 5: *Die bewaffnete Macht*. Vienna: Verlag der Österreichischen Akademie der Wissenschaften, 1987.
Wandruszka, Adam, and Peter Urbanitsch, eds. *Die Habsburgermonarchie 1848–1918*. Vol. 6: *Die Habsburgermonarchie im System der internationalen Beziehungen*. Vienna: Verlag der Österreichischen Akademie der Wissenschaften, 1989.
Weber, Johann. *Eötvös und die Nationalitätenfrage*. Munich: Oldenbourg, 1966.
Wertheimer, Ede. *Gróf Andrássy Gyula élete és kora* [The Life and Times of Count Gyula Andrássy]. Vol. 3. Budapest: Magyar Tudományos Akadémia, 1913.
Žeguc, Ivan. *Die nationalpolitischen Bestrebungen der Karpato-Ruthenen 1848–1914*. Wiesbaden: Harrassowitz, 1965.
Žolger, Ivan. *Der staatsrechtliche Ausgleich zwischen Österreich und Ungarn*. Leipzig: Duncker & Humblot, 1911.
Zwitter, Fran, Jaroslav Šidak and Vaso Bogdanov. *Les problèmes nationaux dans la monarchie des Habsbourg*. Belgrade: Comité national yougoslave des sciences historiques, 1960.

Name Index

Place Index

A – Austria, BH – Bosnia-Herzegovina, C – Croatia, CR – Czech Republic, F – France, G – Germany, GB – Great Britain, GR – Greece. I – Italy, R – Romania, RU – Russia, S – Serbia, SK – Slovakia, SL – Slovenia, SW– Switzerland, T – Turkey, U – Ukraine, USA – United States of America

Volumes Published in "Atlantic Studies on Society in Change"

No. 1* T 1 — *Tolerance and Movements of Religious Dissent in Eastern Europe.* Edited by Béla K. Király. 1977.

No. 2 — *The Habsburg Empire in World War I.* Edited by R. A. Kann. 1978.

No. 3 T 2 — *The Mutual Effects of the Islamic and Judeo-Christian Worlds: The East European Pattern.* Edited by A. Ascher, T. Halasi-Kun, B. K. Király. 1979.

No. 4 — *Before Watergate: Problems of Corruption in American Society.* Edited by A. S. Eisenstadt, A. Hoogenboom, H. L. Trefousse. 1979.

No. 5 — *East Central European Perceptions of Early America.* Edited by B. K. Király and G. Barány. 1977.

No. 6 — *The Hungarian Revolution of 1956 in Retrospect.* Edited by B. K. Király and Paul Jonas. 1978.

No. 7 — *Brooklyn U.S.A.: Fourth Largest City in America.* Edited by Rita S. Miller. 1979.

No. 8 — *Prime Minister Gyula Andrássy's Influence on Habsburg Foreign Policy.* János Decsy. 1979.

No. 9 — *The Great Impeacher: A Political Biography of James M. Ashley.* Robert F. Horowitz. 1979.

No. 10 W I** — *Special Topics and Generalizations on the Eighteenth and Nineteenth Century.* Edited by Béla K. Király and Gunther E. Rothenberg. 1979.

No. 11 W II — *East Central European Society and War in the Pre-Revolutionary 18th Century.* Edited by Gunther E. Rothenberg, Béla K. Király, and Peter F. Sugar. 1982.

No. 12 W III — *From Hunyadi to Rákóczi: War and Society in Late Medieval and Early Modern Hungary.* Edited by János M. Bak and Béla K. Király. 1982.

* Vols. T 1 through 17 refer to the series *Tolerance and Discrimination in the Danubian Region*

** Vols. W I through XLI refer to the series *War and Society in East Central Europe*

No. 29 *The Beginning of Cyrillic Printing—Cracow, 1491. From the Orthodox Past in Poland. Szczepan K. Zimmer.* Edited by Ludwik Krzyżanowski and Irene Nagurski. 1983.

No. 29a *A Grand Ecole for the Grand Corps: The Recruitment and Training of the French Administration.* Thomas R. Osborne. 1983.

No. 30 W XI *The First War between Socialist States: The Hungarian Revolution of 1956 and Its Impact.* Edited by Béla K. Király, Barbara Lotze, Nandor Dreisziger. 1984.

No. 31 W XII *The Effects of World War I, The Uprooted: Hungarian Refugees and Their Impact on Hungary's Domestic Politics.* István Mócsy. 1983.

No. 32 W XIII *The Effects of World War I: The Class War after the Great War: The Rise of Communist Parties in East Central Europe, 1918-1921.* Edited by Ivo Banac. 1983.

No. 33 W XIV *The Crucial Decade: East Central European Society and National Defense, 1859-1870.* Edited by Béla K. Király. 1984.

No. 35 W XVI *Effects of World War I: War Communism in Hungary, 1919.* György Péteri. 1984.

No. 36 W XVII *Insurrections, Wars, and the Eastern Crisis in the 1870s.* Edited by B. K. Király and Gale Stokes. 1985.

No. 37 W XVIII *East Central European Society and the Balkan Wars, 1912-1913.* Edited by B. K. Király and Dimitrije Djordjevic. 1986.

No. 38 W XIX *East Central European Society in World War I.* Edited by B. K. Király and N. F. Dreisziger, Assistant Editor Albert A. Nofi. 1985.

No. 39 W XX *Revolutions and Interventions in Hungary and Its Neighbor States, 1918-1919.* Edited by Peter Pastor. 1988.

No. 41 W XXII *Essays on East Central European Society and War, 1740-1920.* Edited by Stephen Fischer-Galati and Béla K. Király. 1988.

No. 42 W XXIII *East Central European Maritime Commerce and Naval Policies, 1789-1913.* Edited by Apostolos E. Vacalopoulos, Constantinos D. Svolopoulos, and Béla K. Király. 1988.

No. 43 W XXIV *Selections, Social Origins, Education and Training of East Central European Officers Corps.* Edited by Béla K. Király and Walter Scott Dillard. 1988.

No. 44 W XXV	*East Central European War Leaders: Civilian and Military.* Edited by Béla K. Király and Albert Nofi. 1988.
No. 46	*Germany's International Monetary Policy and the European Monetary System.* Hugo Kaufmann. 1985.
No. 47	*Iran Since the Revolution—Internal Dynamics, Regional Conflicts and the Superpowers.* Edited by Barry M. Rosen. 1985.
No. 48 W XXVII	*The Press During the Hungarian Revolution of 1848-1849.* Domokos Kosáry. 1986.
No. 49	*The Spanish Inquisition and the Inquisitional Mind.* Edited by Angel Alcala. 1987.
No. 50	*Catholics, the State and the European Radical Right, 1919-1945.* Edited by Richard Wolff and Jorg K. Hoensch. 1987.
No. 51 W XXVIII	*The Boer War and Military Reforms.* Jay Stone and Erwin A. Schmidl. 1987.
No. 52	*Baron Joseph Eötvös, A Literary Biography.* Steven B. Várdy. 1987.
No. 53	*Towards the Renaissance of Puerto Rican Studies: Ethnic and Area Studies in University Education.* Maria Sanchez and Antonio M. Stevens. 1987.
No. 54	*The Brazilian Diamonds in Contracts, Contraband and Capital.* Harry Bernstein. 1987.
No. 55 T 5	*Christians, Jews and Other Worlds: Patterns of Conflict and Accommodation.* Edited by Philip F. Gallagher. 1988.
No. 56 W XXVI	*The Fall of the Medieval Kingdom of Hungary: Mohács 1526, Buda 1541.* Géza Perjés. 1989.
No. 57	*The Lord Mayor of Lisbon: The Portuguese Tribune of the People and His 24 Guilds.* Harry Bernstein. 1989.
No. 58	*Hungarian Statesmen of Destiny: 1860-1960.* Edited by Paul Bödy. 1989.
No. 59	*For China: The Memoirs of T. G. Li, Former Major General in the Chinese Nationalist Army.* T. G. Li. Written in collaboration with Roman Rome. 1989.
No. 60	*Politics in Hungary: For A Democratic Alternative.* János Kis, with an Introduction by Timothy Garton Ash. 1989.
No. 61	*Hungarian Worker's Councils in 1956.* Edited by Bill Lomax. 1990.

No. 62 *Essays on the Structure and Reform of Centrally Planned Economic Systems*. Paul Jonas. A joint publication with Corvina Kiadó, Budapest. 1990.

No. 63 *Kossuth as a Journalist in England*. Éva H. Haraszti. A joint publication with Akadémiai Kiadó, Budapest. 1990.

No. 64 *From Padua to the Trianon, 1918-1920*. Mária Ormos. A joint publication with Akadémiai Kiadó, Budapest. 1990.

No. 65 *Towns in Medieval Hungary*. Edited by László Gerevich. A joint publication with Akadémiai Kiadó, Budapest. 1990.

No. 66 T 6 *The Nationalities Problem in Transylvania, 1867-1940*. Sándor Bíró. 1992.

No. 67 T 7 *Hungarian Exiles and the Romanian National Movement, 1849-1867*. Béla Borsi-Kálmán. 1991.

No. 68 T 8 *The Hungarian Minority's Situation in Ceausescu's Romania*. Edited by Rudolf Joó and Andrew Ludanyi. 1994.

No. 69 *Democracy, Revolution, Self-Determination. Selected Writings*. István Bibó. Edited by Károly Nagy. 1991.

No. 70 T 9 *Trianon and the Protection of Minorities*. József Galántai. A joint publication with Corvina Kiadó, Budapest. 1991.

No. 71 *King Saint Stephen of Hungary*. György Györffy. 1994.

No. 72 *Dynasty, Politics and Culture. Selected Essays*. Robert A. Kann. Edited by Stanley B. Winters. 1991.

No. 73 *Jadwiga of Anjou and the Rise of East Central Europe*. Oscar Halecki. Edited by Thaddeus V. Gromada. A joint publication with the Polish Institute of Arts and Sciences of America, New York. 1991.

No. 74 W XXIX *Hungarian Economy and Society during World War Two*. Edited by György Lengyel. 1993.

No. 75 *The Life of a Communist Revolutionary, Béla Kun*. György Borsányi. 1993.

No. 76 *Yugoslavia: The Process of Disintegration*. Laslo Sekelj. 1993.

No. 77 W XXX *Wartime American Plans for a New Hungary. Documents from the U.S. Department of State, 1942-1944*. Edited by Ignác Romsics. 1992.

No. 78 W XXXI *Planning for War against Russia and Serbia. Austro-Hungarian and German Military Strategies, 1871-1914*. Graydon A. Tunstall, Jr. 1993.

No. 95 W XXXVI *Through the Prism of the Habsburg Monarchy: Hungary in American Diplomacy and Public Opinion during World War I.* Tibor Glant. 1998.

No. 96 *Appeal of Sovereignty in Hungary, Austria and Russia.* Edited by Csaba Gombár, Elemér Hankiss, László Lengyel and Györgyi Várnai. 1997.

No. 97 T 11 *Geopolitics in the Danube Region. Hungarian Reconciliation Efforts, 1848-1998.* Edited by Ignác Romsics and Béla K. Király. 1998.

No. 98 *Hungarian Agrarian Society from the Emancipation of Serfs (1848) to Re-privatization of Land (1998).* Edited by Péter Gunst. 1999.

No. 99 T 12 *"The Jewish Question" in Europe. The Case of Hungary.* Tamás Ungvári. 2000.

No. 100 *Soviet Military Intervention in Hungary, 1956.* Edited by Jenő Györkei and Miklós Horváth. 1999.

No. 101, T 13 *Jewish Budapest.* Edited by Géza Komoróczy. 1999.

No. 102 *Evolution of Hungarian Economy, 1848-1998. Vol. I. One and a Half Centuries of Semi-Successful Modernization, 1848-1989.* Edited by Iván T. Berend and Tamás Csató. 2001.

No. 103 *Evolution of Hungarian Economy, 1848-1998. Vol. II. Paying the Bill for Goulash-Communism.* János Kornai. 2000.

No. 104 *Evolution of Hungarian Economy, 1848-2000. Vol. III. Hungary: from Transition to Integration.* Edited by György Csáki and Gábor Karsai. 2002.

No. 105 *From Habsburg Agent to Victorian Scholar: G. G. Zerffi (1820-1892).* Tibor Frank. 2000.

No. 106 *A History of Transylvania from the Beginning to 1919. Vol. I.* Edited by Zoltán Szász and Béla Köpeczi. 2000.

No. 107 *A History of Transylvania from the Beginning to 1919. Vol. II.* Edited by Zoltán Szász and Béla Köpeczi. 2002.

No. 108 *A History of Transylvania from the Beginning to 1919. Vol. III.* Edited by Zoltán Szász and Béla Köpeczi. 2002.

No. 109 *Hungary: Governments and Politics, 1848–2000.* Edited by Mária Ormos and Béla K. Király. 2001.

No. 110 T 14 *Hungarians in the Voivodina, 1918–1947.* Enikő A. Sajti. 2003.

No. 111 *Hungarian Arts and Sciences, 1848–2000.* (Hungarian Nobel prize winners, innovators, film makers, Olympic champions, etc.) Edited by László Somlyódy and Nóra Somlyódy. 2003.

No. 112 *Hungary and International Politics in 1848–1849.* Domokos Kosáry. 2003.

No. 113 *Social History of Hungary from the Reform Era to the End of the Twentieth Century.* Edited by Gábor Gyáni, György Kövér and Tibor Valuch. 2004.

No. 114 W XXXVII *A Millennium of Hungarian Military History.* Edited by László Veszprémy and Béla K. Király. 2002.

No. 115 *Hungarian Relics. A History of the War Banners of the Hungarian Revolution and War of Independence, 1848-49.* Jenő Györkei and Györgyi Cs. Kottra. 2000.

No. 116 *From Totalitarian to Democratic Hungary. Evolution and Transformation, 1990-2000.* Edited by Mária Schmidt and László Gy. Tóth. 2001.

No. 117 *A History of Eastern Europe since the Middle Ages.* Emil Niederhauser. 2003.

No. 118 *The Ideas of the Hungarian Revolution, Suppressed and Victorious, 1956–1999.* Edited by Lee W. Congdon and Béla K. Király. 2002.

No. 119 *The Emancipation of the Serfs in East and East-Central Europe*. Emil Niederhauser. 2004.

No. 120 *Béla K. Király: Art of Survival. Hungarian National Defense and Society in Modern Times.* Edited by Piroska Balogh and Tamás Vitek. 2003.

No. 121 W XXXVIII *Army and Politics in Hungary, 1938–1944.* Lóránd Dombrády. Edited by Gyula Rázsó. 2005.

No. 122 T 15 *Hungary and the Hungarian Minorities (Trends in the Past and in Our Time).* Edited by László Szarka. 2004.

No. 123, T 16 *Roma of Hungary.* Edited by István Kemény. 2005.

No. 124 T 17 *National and Ethnic Minorities in Hungary, 1920–2001.* Edited by Ágnes Tóth. 2005.

No. 126 W XXXIX *The Occupation of Bosnia and Herzegovina in 1878.* László Bencze. 2005.

No. 127	*Wars, Revolutions and Regime Changes in Hungary, 1912–2004. Reminiscences of an Eyewitness.* Béla K. Király. Edited by Piroska Balogh, Andrea T. Kulcsár and Tamás Vitek. 2005.
No. 128 W XL	*1956: The Hungarian Revolution and War for Independence.* Edited by Lee W. Congdon, Béla K. Király and Károly Nagy. 2006.
No. 129 W XLI	*The History of the Hungarian Military Higher Education, 1947–1956.* Miklós M. Szabó. 2006.
No. 130	*Reform and Revolution, 1825–1848.* András Gergely. 2009.
No. 131	*From Habsburg Neo-Absolutism to the Compromise, 1849–1867.* Ágnes Deák. 2008.
No. 132	*Hungary in the Dual Monarchy, 1867–1914.* László Katus. 2008.
No. 133	*Hungary in the Age of the Two World Wars, 1914–1945.* Mária Ormos. 2007.
No. 135	*From Dictatorship to Democracy. The Birth of the Third Hungarian Republic, 1988–2001.* Ignác Romsics. 2007.